SUCCESS IN
PSYCHOLOGY

To Wendy and John – with love and grateful thanks.

Success Studybooks

Advertising and Promotion

Book-keeping and Accounts

Business Calculations

Chemistry

Commerce

Commerce: West African Edition

Communication

Economic Geography

Economics: West African Edition

Electronics

Elements of Banking

European History 1815–1941

Information Processing

Insurance

Investment

Law

Managing People

Marketing

Office Practice

Politics

Principles of Accounting

Principles of Accounting: Answer Book

Principles of Catering

Psychology

Sociology

Statistics

Twentieth Century World Affairs

World History since 1945

© Keith Twining 1998
First published in 1998
by John Murray (Publishers) Ltd
50 Albemarle Street
London W1X 4BD

Layouts by Eric Drewery
Illustrations by Art Construction
Cartoons by Andrew Reid

Typeset in 10.5/12 pt Sabon by Wearset, Boldon, Tyne and Wear

Printed in Great Britain by The Bath Press, Bath

A CIP catalogue record for this book is available from the British Library

ISBN 0 7195 7204 5

SUCCESS IN
PSYCHOLOGY

KEITH TWINING

JOHN MURRAY

Acknowledgements

The publishers would like to thank the following sources for permission to reproduce material.

pp.19-20 written by Graham Davies for the Association for the Teaching of Psychology, c/o The British Psychological Society, St Andrews House, 48 Princess Road East, Leicester, LE1 7DR; **pp.25-6** AEB; **p.67** from *The Antecedent of Self-Esteem* by Stanley Coopersmith. © 1967 by W.H. Freeman and Company. Used with permission; **p.68** from *Culture and Social Behaviour* by H. Triandis © 1994 The McGraw-Hill Companies; **p.73** from 'Perceiving the causes of success and failure' by Weiner, Friese, Kukla, Reed and Rosenbaum in *Perceiving the Causes of Behaviour* edited by Jones, Kanuouse, Kelley, Nisbett, Vlains and Weiten, 1972. Permission granted by Dr Bernard Weiner; **p.75** from *Psychology: Themes and Variations* by Wayne Weiten, 1994. Copyright © 1998, 1995, 1992, 1989 Brooks/Cole Publishing Company, Pacific Grove, CA 93950, a division of International Thompson Publishing Inc. By permission of the publisher; **pp.90 and 94** David G. Myers, *Exploring Psychology*, third edition. Worth Publishers, New York, 1996; **p.102** from *Social Psychology: An Introduction* by M.A. Hogg and G.M. Vaughan © Prentice Hall Europe, 1995; **p.107** from 'Bystander intervention in emergencies: diffusion of responsibility', *Journal of Personality and Social Psychology*, Volume 8, 1968; **p.171** adapted from 'Working Memory' by A.D. Baddeley and G. Hitch in *Recent Advances in Learning and Motivation*, Volume 8, Academic Press, New York, 1974; **p.224 and 227** adapted from *Psychology: Themes and Variations* by Wayne Weiten. Copyright © 1998, 1995, 1992, 1989 Brooks/Cole Publishing Company, Pacific Grove, CA 93950, a division of International Thompson Publishing Inc. By permission of the publisher; **p.236** from *The Telegraph Magazine*, 6 September 1997 © Telegraph Group Limited; **p.239** Dr Baddeley, Service for People with Learning Disabilities, East Gloucestershire NHS Trust; **p.241** adapted from *Psychology: Themes and Variations* by Wayne Weiten. Copyright © 1998, 1995, 1992, 1989 Brooks/Cole Publishing Company, Pacific Grove, CA 93950, a division of International Thompson Publishing Inc. By permission of the publisher; **p.254** © Keith Twining; **p.262** © The Stock Market Photo Agency Inc.; **p.273** © Keith Twining; **pp.274 and 275** from 'The Social Readjustment Rating Scale' by T.H. Holmes and R.H. Rahe, *Journal of Psychosomatic Research*, Volume 8, 1967, with permission from Elsevier Science; **pp.280, 293 and 312** © Keith Twining; **p.361** from 'The Social Readjustment Rating Scale' by T.H. Holmes and R.H. Rahe, *Journal of Psychosomatic Research*, Volume 8, 1967, with permission from Elsevier Science; **p.417** adapted from *Abnormal Psychology*, 2nd edn, by R. Comer © 1995 by W.H. Freeman and Company. Used with permission; **p.447** extract taken from 'Psychology and Advertising' by P. Banyard, *Psychology Review*, Volume 3, 1996, with permission from Philip Allan Publishers.

While every effort has been made to contact copyright holders, the publishers apologise for any omissions, which they will be pleased to rectify at the earliest opportunity.

Examination questions are reproduced by kind permission of The Associated Examining Board (**pp.55–9, 61, 119–21, 208–11, 281–2, 321, 323–4, 377–80, 434–5, 437–8**) and The Northern Examinations and Assessment Board (**pp.58, 61, 122, 211, 282, 380, 437–8, 451**).

Any answers or hints on answers are the sole responsibility of the author and have not been provided or approved by the Board. They may not necessarily constitute the only solutions or approaches.

Contents

Preface

I have attempted, in the presentation and style of this textbook, to make a large amount of material, principles, theories and so on, as accessible as possible. I have also attempted to provide as much help as possible to enable you – the reader – to learn the material in the most efficient way possible. I have a bit of a 'thing' about both of these! Let me explain.

I had a rather undistinguished time as a student – perhaps I was more interested in sport of all kinds, old motor bikes and so on, and rather less interested in passing exams – despite the best efforts of my teachers. I then spent nearly twenty very happy years in the aerospace industry as a flight-test engineer working on aircraft flight control and automatic landing systems. Following this, I went back to school for postgraduate work in the USA, and became very enthusiastic about teaching and learning. I rapidly came to the – perhaps blindingly obvious – conclusion that learning *how* to learn is a vital part of the process of learning, no matter what the content of the learning. I also concluded that teachers often do the latter rather better than the former, and as a consequence many students do not reach their potential. I have tried to balance both in the book. If you work conscientiously at the study skills section – the 'how to' of learning – and apply these skills to your own learning, I am confident that you will do well and, of course, these skills will work for any subject content.

Finally, but by no means least, there are many to whom I wish to record my most sincere thanks. To the editorial staff at John Murray's, particularly Carolyn Burch, for guidance and valuable advice at all stages of the project – and that has to be the understatement of the year! To Andy Reid, friend, past student and now a teacher, for the cartoons. To my students who have provided many helpful comments – 'that bit's rubbish, sir!' – and on whom, and it has to be said, I have 'piloted' various sections of the book; and to Diane Hewitt, who typed the whole manuscript with diagrams more than once, for her never-failing commitment and enthusiasm – I am most grateful.

Keith Twining
Cheltenham, 1998

1 'Doing psychology': skills for study and research

The purpose of this unit is to develop your study skills. This will help you to obtain the best possible results from your course – not only in terms of your final grade but also in finding your studies of psychology as meaningful and enjoyable as possible.

Examinations in psychology usually have two main requirements:

- the research and presentation of one or more written projects (variously called coursework, project work, research studies, etc.); and
- the written examination.

This unit aims to develop the skills you will need to do well in both of these. It is divided into three sections:

- The first section offers advice on how to develop **general study skills**.
- The second section sets out some guidelines on how to go about doing **research** and on using and interpreting **statistics**. It includes advice on planning and writing coursework and essays.
- The last section deals with preparation and revision for the **written examination**.

General study skills

> ### *Think about it*
>
> - Think of your experience so far of studying and learning.
> - Make a list, in order of usefulness, of the skills or habits that have worked for you.

This unit offers several suggestions on how to develop your study skills, but all of them are linked to one key principle:

- Be organised! Use your time efficiently.

While that sounds obvious, the reality is that very few of us use our time as efficiently as we could.

> ### *Think about it*
>
> - Look at your notes. How organised are they?
> - How organised has your use of time been for, say, the past week?

You have more time than you think

In the section on memory (Unit 4, pages 159–86), you will learn that an early psychologist, Hermann Ebbinghaus, proposed a law based on his research, which says that the more time we spend learning something the better we remember it. If your goal is to learn and remember something, then you need to spend time on it. You can make this time by becoming better organised.

Think about it

- How did you spend your time yesterday when you either were or could have been studying?
- Jot down the hours and minutes that you spent studying, waiting for the bus, riding on the bus, standing around chatting, 'free' time and so on.

The average 'free' or discretionary time in a typical school day is about five hours, as you can see in the summary below:

07.30–22.30	15 hours 'available'
Time spent in class	5 hours
Time spent on meals	3 hours
Time spent on travel	1 hour
Time spent on misc. activities	1 hour
Total hours accounted for	10 hours = 5 hours free time

It is obviously not practical to spend *all* your spare time studying, even in the final run-up to an examination. The point is that you have a lot more time than you think. You need to identify your total 'free' time and then decide how much and which bits of that time you are going to use for study.

As you approach the exams or a deadline for coursework, it is worth making the effort to get up early (rather than staying up late). This is not as difficult as it might sound, but it will require motivation and self discipline. If you get up about an hour and a half earlier than you usually do, make yourself a hot drink and start work, you will find that you will have at least a full hour of quality time with no interruptions, no telephone, no television, no friends dropping in.

Use the syllabus

Try to get hold of a copy of your syllabus. There are a number of ways that you can use it to your advantage.

- Most syllabuses make a statement in general terms and then expand that statement into precise areas of study on which you can be examined. Use the titles of the relevant areas as a contents list for your notes. See the diagram below.

Contents list for notes

5.3 MEMORY (with reference to the AEB 1998 syllabus)	Page Nos.	
	Textbook	Notes

A Theories and research findings relating to the **nature** of memory
  i) Structure
  ii) Processes
  iii) Types		

B Explanations of the **organisation** of information in memory		
C Explanations of **forgetting**		

D Practical **applications** of research into memory and forgetting
  e.g. i) Eye witness testimony
    ii) Memory for medical information		

- Remember you will only be asked questions from the syllabus content, so *know* the content. Then, for your own practice and revision, try rephrasing syllabus content statements as questions.
- Read carefully the section of the syllabus on 'Objectives'. This tells you what skills you will be expected to show in your work – for example, 'describe', 'analyse', 'evaluate'. Some guidance on what the examiner expects of you under these various headings is given on pages 8 and 25–6.
- You can also use the syllabus to help you prepare your revision (see page 26).

Improve your reading skills

When you are working at advanced level, you need a method which enables you to read widely and efficiently; you need to be able to analyse as well as remember what you read. There are various ways to organise your reading, but one simple and effective method is called SQR4. This works as shown on page 4.

Use a range of sources

Your textbook and class notes will not provide you with all you need to know. It is always worth doing specific additional 'parallel' reading, in other words reading more than one book on a particular theme. As well as books, the professional journals are useful for parallel reading, at least skim-reading. *The Psychologist* is the journal of the British Psychological Society, and there are others that your library may stock – either on the shelf or in electronic form. You should also consider subscribing to the student magazine *Psychology Review*, which is widely available – perhaps a group could take out a joint subscription to spread the costs. Finally, train yourself to notice when psychological issues are raised by items on television and radio or in the newspapers.

Another source that you ought to use are 'electronic' resources – the Internet and CD-ROMs. Check what is available through your library. One extremely useful CD-ROM is PSYCHLIT. It holds literally thousands of abstracts of studies and cross refers to their sources. Web sites are constantly changing and being up-dated, so this too is a valuable resource.

- To make good use of this material, write brief notes and integrate them into your main notes at the appropriate point.

Use selective highlighting

Highlighting is probably something that you do already. The key to effective use of highlighting is being *selective*. Indiscriminate, almost total, use of a highlight pen will not help. The point of selective highlighting (this is the **von Restorff effect** – see Unit 4, page 184), is to pick out a key word or phrase in some clearly visible way so that it can be remembered easily. If you want a general rule: *highlight less, not more*.

Something to do

- Look at the section of text on social representation, on pages 69–70. Decide what you would highlight in this passage, then compare it to what is recommended below (page 5).
- If you think that you have highlighted too much in your notes, photocopy them. The highlighting will not show, and you can now rehighlight more appropriately.

Using the SQR4 method of reading

The letters SQR4 stand for:
S = Survey
Q = Question
R = Read
R = Restate
R = Record
R = Review

The following is an example of how to apply SQR4 to a 28-page section of this book, pages 159–86.

S = Survey

Read the introductory paragraphs on page 159 to get an idea of the scope of the section. Then go through pages 159–86 from start to finish, simply noting the main section headings. Read these a couple more times until you are fairly confident of them. This should take about five minutes. Now do the same for secondary or minor headings – another five or ten minutes.

MEMORY

The study of memory
- The Ancient Greeks
- Hermann Ebbinghaus
- Frederick Bartlett
- The 1960s onwards

Three kinds of memory
- Episodic memory
- Semantic memory
- Procedural memory

Three processes of memory
- Encoding
- Storing
- Recalling

Three stages of memory
- Sensory memory
- Short-term memory
- Long-term memory
etc.

You have now given yourself a framework or basic understanding onto which you can add detail that 'fits'.

Q = Question

Now turn each heading into a question. Do this for all the headings in the 28-page section. In our example on 'memory', the questions to ask are: 'What are the three kinds of memory?', 'What is episodic memory?', and so on. Having a question in mind results in spontaneous attempts to answer it, and frustration until it is answered.

R = Read

Read the passage to find the answer to the question(s). It is important to move quickly, sort out ideas and evaluate them. If the content does not relate to the question, give it only a passing glance. The key is to read selectively.

R = Restate

Put the answer to the question briefly in your own words, not the author's.

R = Record

Now you need to make notes. Do this briefly, section by section, noting the main points, key ideas, dates, people and theories. Use only what is needed to record the main ideas.

R = Review

Read your written questions, and try to remember the answers without reference to your notes. If you can't, then look for the answer(s) immediately in your notes.

Repeat this process about a week later and thereafter at less frequent intervals.

This method really does work, but you must stick at it until it becomes an automatic part of your study habits.

Social representation

Recommended use of selective highlighting

This topic is related to the above discussion in that **social representation** is concerned with the way in which society has certain beliefs and views that are common to the majority of that society or major groupings within it. A key theorist in this field is Moscovici who, with others, has written extensively (see Moscovici, 1984, in the bibliography).

Taking it as given that you are an ordinary member of your society, where have you got your understanding of your society's values, norms, customs and behaviours from? Social representation theory would answer this question by saying from consensual understanding acquired by informal everyday experiences. It is the social interaction that is occurring most of the time as we go about our daily routines – working, playing, reading the papers, watching television, 'socialising' – that forms our ideas, opinions and understanding. We may have our own opinions and understanding of specific issues, but we have also formed certain reactions that are common to the society of which we are a part. For example, in the UK, people greet each other with the phrase, 'Good morning, how are you?' and may respond, 'Fine, thank you' when in fact they feel terrible.

This is an example of the split or difference between European and American social psychology. The European idea of the influence of society on the shaping of the individual comes initially from the French sociologist Emile Durkheim. The American emphasis is on the derivation of principles from the study of the individual. This is partly historical and stems from the great variety of people and races who came to America seeking their fortune; and is also partly due to a lack of social class structures and, perhaps as a consequence, the American idea of the worth of the individual.

Make notes that work

Efficient notes are vital. You must develop the skill to write accurate, precise, short notes. Here are some tips for how to make good quality notes which will be clear and useful when you come back to them for revision.

- Write a table of contents based on the syllabus section.
- Number the pages of your notes.
- Keep an index. Ideally, your notes should be in a ringbinder with an index at the back; alternatively, use file-dividers.
- Check your notes soon after class and top them up from library books and textbooks. Do this by turning syllabus statements into questions, and then making sure that your notes fully answer each question.
- Add textbook page numbers in the margin of your notes to indicate where you will find the text relevant to that topic. Transfer these page numbers to the main section index or contents.

Know the key people

To write successful essays and coursework you need to quote key people and key studies. At the back of your folder of notes, start a biography section with thumbnail sketches of key people and studies. Update this frequently. This should be cross-referenced to the relevant page numbers in your textbook. For example:

EBBINGHAUS, Hermann (1850–1909)   German

An early experimenter in the study of memory. Used himself to experiment on. Developed learning and forgetting curves mainly by the use of nonsense syllables.
Success in Psychology, pages 31–2, 159–60, 180.

Know the key terms

Like any subject, psychology has its own terminology, and you need to become familiar with the key terms. Include a list of the key terms for each topic in your notes. For example:

Memory

Short-term memory (STM)   The mental function of retaining (for 15–20 seconds) information about stimuli, events, images, etc., after the stimulus is no longer present.

Long-term memory (LTM)   Information that has been processed and stored. LTM is thought to have unlimited capacity and duration.

It is a good idea to put meanings into your own words rather than simply copying definitions from a reference source.

Something to do

• Use the glossary in this book to test yourself on the meanings of key words.

Use note cards

As you have probably discovered, you often mean to remember something that you have just read, seen on television or heard in a conversation; but later, when you try to recall it, it has gone. Get hold of a set of small note cards or file index cards (that are small enough to fit into clothing pockets but big enough to hold a moderately lengthy note) and use them to make instant notes (see page 22). You can then transfer them into your main psychology file next time you use it.

Note cards are also useful when you are engaged in any kind of research, particularly at the early stages when you are gathering material. For example, imagine you are researching for an essay or a piece of coursework, and you are sitting in the library with a pile of books in front of you. Note down key points (names of theories and theorists, references to key psychological experiments or studies, dates, evaluation, application, implications and so on) onto your cards, together with the (vitally important) book title and page numbers. Later, with all your initial ideas on cards, you can simply shuffle the cards into the order that you feel is best to meet the set assignment.

If you keep your cards filed by topic, you can use them later as a helpful examination revision aid.

Record your sources

As stated above, you should write details of the source of your notes on your note cards. This can save you hours when it comes to writing up the bibliography (list of sources) for your coursework.

• Write the note on the front of the card and the source on the back.
• Write the source in correct bibliographic style, for example:

Twining, K., *Success in Psychology* (John Murray, 1998)

Now all you have to do is to put the cards for the sources you have used into alphabetical order by author's surname – and type up your bibliography card by card.

Use diagrams

Using diagrams is a valuable technique for reinforcing your learning, and is particularly useful for revision. As with reading, you start with a general framework and progressively add more detail. These diagrams are variously known as spider diagrams, spidergrams, schematics, etc., but with all of them the principle is the same. Taking the 28-page section that we used earlier, the first part of the framework would be as follows:

Spider diagram (Memory, pages 159–86)

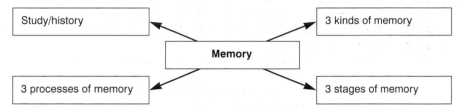

You would further develop this by adding more information:

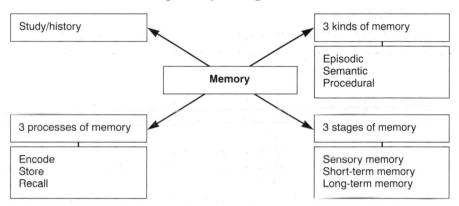

You go on adding more detail as your reading and understanding increase, until it looks like this:

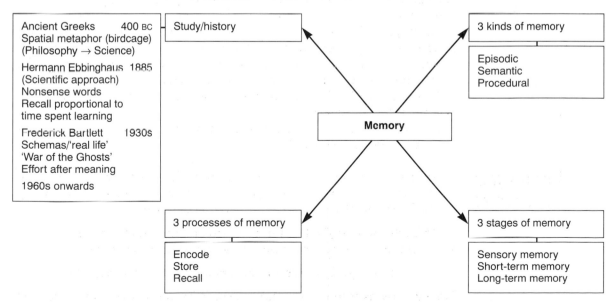

You can now add this diagram to your notes and continue to add more detailed information.

Use mnemonics Mnemonics are mental 'tricks' to help us remember. You probably use lots of mnemonics already. Does R O Y G B I V seem familiar? (If not, these are the initial letters of the colours of the rainbow.) Or how about '*i* before *e* except after *c*'? These are everyday examples of mnemonics. There are of course many others and we discuss the topic and give examples in Unit 4 in the section on memory.

Something to do

• Turn to the section on mnemonics (pages 184 and 185) and skim-read it.

Use topic summaries Make a summary of your notes – about one page maximum for each topic. The purpose of this is to provide you with a short, quick reminder of key issues, theories, people and studies. Use these summaries frequently. They are your first line of revision and will stay with you throughout your whole course.

Use tapes Get together a small group of fellow students, decide who will prepare which topic and then each of you record your topic summary (see above). For the most efficient use of this technique, build the tapes up, topic by topic, as the course proceeds, so that by the end – or by examination time – you have the material 'taped'. Then make enough copies of each tape so that each person in the group has a complete set. The rest is easy! Just play the tape to yourself whenever you can: walking to school or college, on the bus, in the common-room, and so on. In addition to having a valuable revision resource, preparing and dictating the notes is in itself valuable revision.

Something to do

• Make a very short tape of one topic and use it to experiment with content and presentation.

Know the syllabus skill areas The two skill areas of knowledge and analysis are crucial to your success in psychology. You will need to apply them frequently to examination questions.

These skill areas carry more than 80 per cent of the marks in an advanced psychology exam. (Research skills and quality of language account for the rest.) For example, you may be asked to:

• **Describe:** You need to show your knowledge of the stipulated topic area.
• **Analyse** (or **critically analyse**): You need to show your understanding by being able to refer to, and recognise the relationship between, different aspects of a topic.
• **Evaluate** (or **critically evaluate**): You need to be able to make an informed judgement regarding the value of psychological work in a particular topic area, based on systematic analysis and examination.

The full list of injunctions is given on pages 25–6.

Make the connections

Although the way textbooks are written makes psychology look like a number of separate topics, there are always connections that exist between the topics. Looking for and making these cross-topic connections is a valuable study skill. You must deliberately train yourself to do this as you study psychology. Look at the following diagram, 'Showing connections across syllabus areas'. To make these connections yourself, choose a topic or a term and then see how many times, and in what areas of the syllabus, it appears. Then write a brief sentence defining each use of the term.

Showing connections across syllabus areas

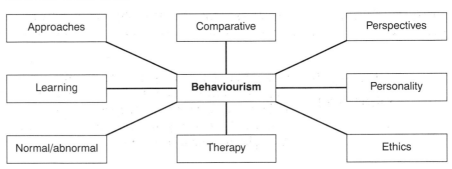

Research – how do we 'do' psychology?

At the most basic level, 'doing' psychology – or any subject area for that matter – is finding out what we do not know and then applying it. This means research.

Research can be very simple, for example finding out the date an important psychologist completed a study; or very involved, for example designing and conducting the research for a major project. Whatever the nature of the research, however, the basic principles remain the same.

In the remainder of this section, we work through some typical and specific examples, ranging from the simple to the complex.

Checking a simple fact

Referring to the diagram on page 10, consider Example 1. You need to know the date that Gregory defined 'perception'. Perhaps you are preparing your revision notes for a test and now realise that you must have nodded off in the lecture when this was discussed. You now need to 'research' for this fact. You could look for the answer by looking up the entry for 'Gregory' in a dictionary of psychology. What if the entry is two pages long but does not include what you are searching for? Try again. You now go to a major text, but there is no entry in the index for 'Gregory'. Try the index for 'perception' – and there you have it!

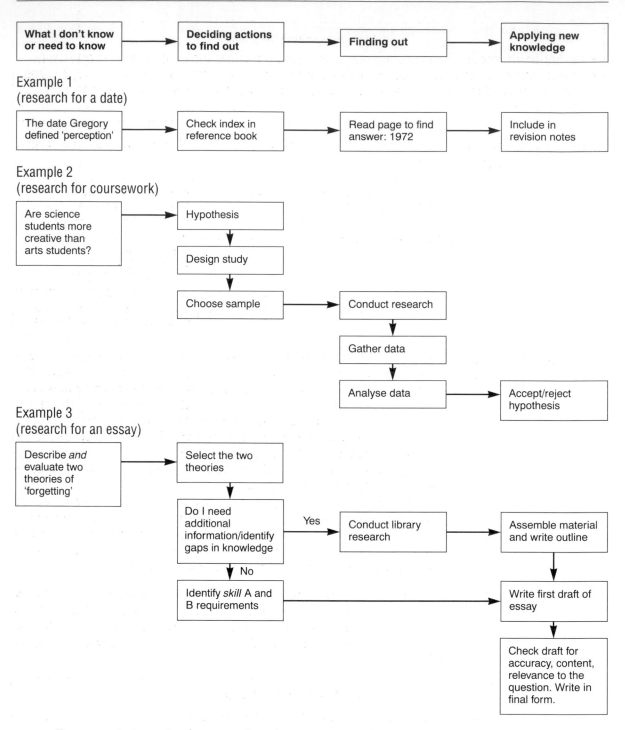

| What I don't know or need to know | → | Deciding actions to find out | → | Finding out | → | Applying new knowledge |

Example 1
(research for a date)

| The date Gregory defined 'perception' | → | Check index in reference book | → | Read page to find answer: 1972 | → | Include in revision notes |

Example 2
(research for coursework)

Are science students more creative than arts students? → Hypothesis → Design study → Choose sample → Conduct research → Gather data → Analyse data → Accept/reject hypothesis

Example 3
(research for an essay)

Describe *and* evaluate two theories of 'forgetting' → Select the two theories → Do I need additional information/identify gaps in knowledge — Yes → Conduct library research → Assemble material and write outline → Write first draft of essay → Check draft for accuracy, content, relevance to the question. Write in final form.

No → Identify *skill* A and B requirements → Write first draft of essay

Research for coursework

In the second, rather more complex example in the above diagram, we are looking at research for coursework. The 'what I don't know' in this case is the result of the coursework. The 'actions to find out' now require a number of different actions, all of which are necessary and which need 'finding out' in the right order (each provides an answer to be used for the next step). You cannot 'find out' until you have completed all the steps in the correct order.

A note on research methods

- Library-based research is called using secondary sources as it involves re-using other people's data.
- Primary research – collecting your own data – can be carried out in various ways: survey, experiment, questionnaire and observation. These are explained in the section on research methods in Unit 2 (pages 41–6).

Research for an essay

In Example 3 in the diagram on page 10, the research needs to be organised as follows:

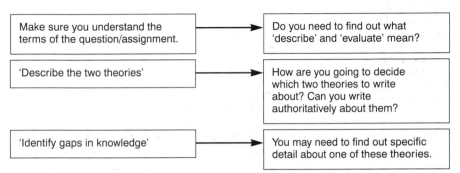

| Make sure you understand the terms of the question/assignment. | → | Do you need to find out what 'describe' and 'evaluate' mean? |

| 'Describe the two theories' | → | How are you going to decide which two theories to write about? Can you write authoritatively about them? |

| 'Identify gaps in knowledge' | → | You may need to find out specific detail about one of these theories. |

Working with statistics

To carry out successful research in psychology, and to produce successful coursework, you need a basic knowledge of how statistics operate. You will have to understand their significance in order to answer questions in the examination, and you will have to use them yourself to prepare and present your findings in your coursework. (See Coolican, 1994.)

Statistics does not involve difficult maths. All you need to be able to do is add, subtract, multiply, divide, square and find the square root – you are allowed to use a calculator. You will not have to do calculations in the exam, but you will for your coursework.

In the exam, you are likely to be presented with the results of a completed study (or possibly two studies) and asked to answer a number of short-answer questions based on the study or studies. It is therefore essential that you can make sense of the statistics used to present the data to you and the method the psychologist has used.

Descriptive statistics

The term 'descriptive statistics' means just that: we use these statistics to summarise, describe or illustrate graphically the data collected for a study. Descriptive statistics simply present data in a clear way; they do not manipulate the data, nor do they present conclusions, trends or deductions.

Methods of presenting statistics

There are a number of methods you can use. Some of these are listed below.

- tables;
- graphs, including: histograms, bar charts, line graphs, frequency charts, polygons and scattergraphs;
- summaries (of raw data);
- measures of central tendency (mean, median, mode);
- measures of dispersion (range, standard deviation).

Refer to a statistics text such as Coolican (1994) if you are unfamiliar with these terms.

The purpose of descriptive statistics is to give the reader a more-or-less instant visual impression of the data, so the method you choose should be one that does this as clearly as possible.

It is of course vital that whatever statistics you use you remember to:

- identify graphs and figures with a suitable number and title;
- label fully all graph axes;
- clearly indicate all units (to show what you are talking about: periods of time, number of people, within which age group, which gender, etc.).

Always be clear about what you wish to describe and why. Do not try to force your data if they do not suit a particular method. Some studies produce **quantitative data,** for example results in seconds, number of words remembered, or data in other standard units. This form of data is readily presented in graphs and tables. Other studies produce **qualitative data,** for example data from case studies or opinion surveys. It may not be helpful or even possible to present these data numerically in graphs or tables. In that case you need to describe the results in words rather than use descriptive statistics.

How much can descriptive statistics show?

Almost any study that you undertake will involve finding out about:

- **correlation** – the relationship between two sets of data; or
- the **difference** between two sets of data.

In the first case, you may be investigating the relationship between, say, GCSE examination performance and intelligence quotient (IQ) levels in a small sample of people. You are seeking to 'co-relate' the two sets of data. You probably expect the data to show that GCSE scores are better in people with a higher IQ score. You could show the relationship in a graph like this (invented) example:

Correlation of IQ with GCSE scores

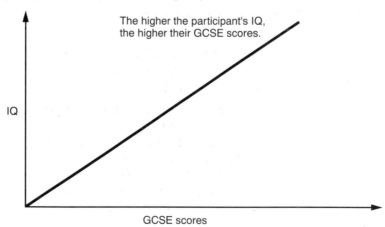

The higher the participant's IQ, the higher their GCSE scores.

IQ

GCSE scores

You have **hypothesised** (suggested the existence of) a certain relationship. Your descriptive statistics may show this relationship in your sample, but that is all. What you now need to know is whether, from your data, you can 'infer' the same result onto a wider population from just your **sample.** So, you need to apply an appropriate **inferential statistic** to your data. (See the next section for an explanation of inferential statistics.)

In the second case, you could be undertaking a study that is looking for a difference between two sets of data, say, for example, the effect that age difference has on Triplett's co-action effect (people working together will work faster than people working apart). Here you may hypothesise that a certain difference between the two conditions – working together or working alone – will be greater for either the younger or the older participants, so you set up an experiment to find out. Having conducted the experiment, you can present the data descriptively but, as with the previous study, you still need to know if you can infer from your results the same result onto a wider population than your sample. Again, the use of an inferential statistic allows you to do this.

Probability – how reliable are my results?

Before we discuss the choice and use of an inferential statistic, there is one more important decision that you will have to make and state in your research. You need to say – in statistical terms – how confident you are that your results are correct. You may be thinking that the whole point of using an inferential statistic is precisely to get the correct answer, and up to a point that is true. However, no researcher can ever be absolutely and totally confident that there is no error in a study. In the case of a study looking for a difference, your result may show that a difference exists, but to what extent can you be sure that the difference is a reliable conclusion from your calculations? How do you know that it hasn't occurred by chance? This is the study of **probability**. We must ask the question: what is the probability that the result happened by chance? For most psychological studies, we accept a 20 per cent (i.e. 0.05) risk that our result occurred by chance. We use a small p as an abbreviation and, by convention, the normal form for writing this is simply:

$$p = 0.05$$

Which inferential statistic should I use?

As you would expect, there are a number of different statistical tests to choose from. You decide between them by asking and answering the following four questions.

1. Am I testing for **difference** or **correlation**? (See above.)
2. What is the **level** of my data?
   There are three possible levels of data:

   - **interval data** are measured in recognised units, such as seconds, centimetres and so on;
   - **ordinal data** occur when your results are in a given order: first, second, third and so on;
   - **nominal data** are what is left – that is, just counting categories, for example 23 right-hand participants, three left-hand participants; ten males, six females and so on.

3. Does my data meet **parametric test assumptions**?
   Your data must meet three criteria to say 'yes' to this question:

   - The data must be interval (that is, measured in recognised units – see above).
   - The data must come from a normally distributed population (i.e. a representative cross-section).
   - The data must have homogeneity of variance.

The first two are straightforward. The third simply means that the variance – or variation – in the scores from the two groups are essentially the same. (This will almost certainly be true in the case of related samples, less so in unrelated samples – see below.)

4. Is my design **related** or **unrelated**?

This question is concerned with the design of your study. Are the two groups related in some way – for example, have you matched pairs of participants or have you a **repeated-measures design** (a situation where the same participants are tested under the two conditions)? Or, is your design unrelated (sometimes called an **independent-measures design**), in which case there is no connection between the two sets of participants?

Depending on the answers to these questions, you would use one of the tests indicated at the end of the two flow charts on page 15. The first chart is for a correlation study; the second chart is for a test of difference.

Having reached a decision as to which inferential statistic to use, you will need to refer to a book on statistics to find out how each of these tests works and for help with the calculation. (The selected reading list at the end of this unit recommends a useful statistics text.) The answer to the calculation is called the **observed value**, which you then use with reference to appropriate statistical tables to find the **critical value**. This tells you if your result is **significant** at the appropriate level (usually 0.05). Depending on the result, you are then able to make a statement either that you can accept the hypothesis (if the data is significant) or that you reject the hypothesis (if the data is not significant).

Planning and writing coursework

Choosing a topic

If you have been given a free hand in the choice of topic for your coursework, you may have to make a decision on what you will research. You may have a burning desire to investigate some particular aspect and cannot wait to get started. On the other hand, it is quite possible that you have no idea at all about what to do. There are several ways to solve this dilemma.

One is to look for ideas from your reading. Suppose that you are studying memory. As you read and study you will almost certainly come across classic studies which may generate ideas for your own work – the key is to prepare your mind to look for ideas. You can also find lots of ideas from the press, television and often from your non-psychological reading.

Bear in mind always that the work must be your own but that it is quite legitimate to base it on or model it on the work of others. This is the normal way in which much research moves forward.

Deciding on the research method(s)

How will you collect your data? There are four main methods:

- survey;
- questionnaire;
- experiment;
- observation.

The best method – or combination of methods – for your study will depend on the kind of information you are trying to gather. Refer to the section on research methods in Unit 2 (pages 41–6) to see which method(s) would suit your study best.

Statistical tests for
correlation

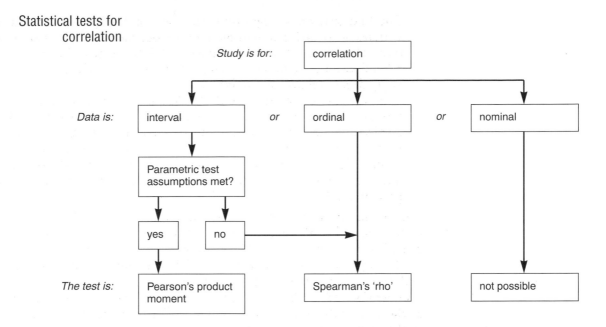

Statistical tests for
difference

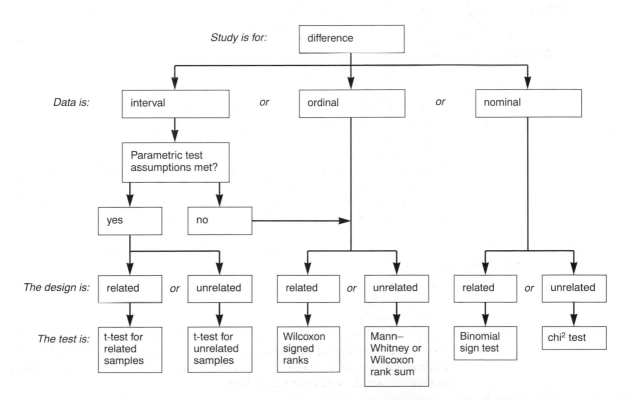

Action plan Suppose you have chosen to base your study on Triplett's work on audience effect but to investigate variations of the effect with change in age of participant. What do you do next?

1. **Design the research from start to finish** *before* **you start collecting data.** What this means is that you, the investigator, make the decisions about how to do the study. You have to answer the same four questions discussed on pages 13–14:

   - Am I testing for difference or correlation?
   - What is the level of my data?
   - Does my data meet parametric test assumptions?
   - Is my design related or unrelated?

   When you have worked through these questions, your answers will tell you the appropriate statistical test to use (see page 15).

   The easiest way to set out the design of your study is to use a form like the one shown below. This is filled in with typical answers and explanatory notes.

Form for coursework design (Triplett study)

Title	*A Study of Age Difference on the Audience Effect*	Obvious
Hypothesis H_A or (H_E)	*The audience effect will change significantly with age of participant*	H_E = Experimental hypothesis
Hypothesis H_0	*Age of participant has no effect on audience effect*	H_0 = Null hypothesis
1- or 2-tailed	*2-tailed*	2-tailed as H_E does not predict direction
Participants	*2 groups of 20 (10m, 10f)*	Spell out
	One group 8–10 yr. olds,	
	One group 14–16 yr. olds	
Design	*Independent Groups*	State type
Level of data: interval	✔ *(units = seconds)*	State. Include units when possible
nominal		
ordinal		
Test of: difference	✔	Obvious
correlation		
Parametric test assumptions met?	*yes* ✔ *no*	If 'yes' check all three conditions
Level of significance	*0.1* (*0.05*) *0.01*	Obvious
Statistical test	*t-Test for unrelated samples*	Check with flow charts on page 15 to establish
Ethical issues	*yes* ✔ *no* *maybe*	Play 'safe'
	will need to get teacher/parent permission	
Notes		

Something to do

• Redraw the coursework design form as a blank form ready for your own use.

---

2. **Use a checklist.**
   The following is a list of the major subsections of a research project:

   • Front cover/title page;
   • Abstract;
   • Contents;
   • Introduction/survey of the literature;
   • Aim;
   • Hypothesis;
   • Design;
   • Method;
   • Results;
   • Discussion/analysis;
   • Conclusion;
   • Bibliography/references;
   • Appendices.

   There are, of course, variations to this list, but the above is suitable for most research projects.

A good way to tackle your project is to start a loose-leaf file with 13 sections, each headed by one item from the above checklist. The advantage of this is that you can add work on the sections in any order, and so the whole project can move forward.

Staying with the Triplett study as the example, the above checklist can be clarified as follows:

• **Front cover/title page:** Include the obvious information – name, date, etc., but also give the title in an accurate and precise form.
• **Abstract:** This has to describe the whole project in one short paragraph. Include aim, method, results and conclusions. You normally write this last.
• **Contents:** Obvious, but remember to include page numbers.
• **Introduction/survey of the literature:** Think of this as a funnel. Start in broad general terms but rapidly focus on the precise topic area. It should lead naturally to your aim. The studies/research that you refer to should be selected to support the aim of your study.
• **Aim:** State the aim of your study in general terms.
• **Hypothesis:** (See also Unit 2, page 43.) There are three types of hypothesis; you need to state one of these:
  – **experimental hypothesis (H_E)** for an experimental design; or
  – **alternate hypothesis (H_A)** for all other designs – correlation, case study, observation, etc.
  You also need to state:
  – **null hypothesis (H_0)** in which you restate the H_A or H_E in null – or neutral – terms.
  You need to state whether your H_A or H_E is one- or two-tailed. (One-tail predicts a direction: 'Younger children will work significantly

faster than adults'; two-tail predicts only a difference: 'There will be a significant *difference* in the work speed of adults and children'.)

You also need to state the **independent variable (IV)** and the **dependent variable (DV)**. You set up the IV and then measure the DV; so, in the Triplett study, you set up the different age groups (the IV) and measure the time taken by participants in each age group (the DV).

- **Design:** State the type of design you have used and why you have chosen it. For example, 'This study uses a repeated-measures design. This replicates the method used in the original study.'
- **Method:** In this section you need to say exactly what you did. This includes details of participants, apparatus, etc. and the where, how, what and why of all you did. Your method needs to be so accurate and comprehensive that someone else could replicate your study with nothing more than your method to go on.
- **Results:** Here you present your results. You may choose to use summary tables of raw data, descriptive statistics or verbal descriptions. Note any strange results (for example, 'Participant 6 has an unusually high score as he dropped the apparatus halfway through the test'). Make sure you have accurately labelled all graphs and charts and given them a title and a figure number. You need to use the appropriate inferential statistic and also give the reasons for its use. Report the observed value (the 'answer' to the statistics calculation) and the critical value (obtained from statistical tables using the observed value). Finally, you need to make a concluding statement with respect to the significance of your results, and whether the results support (or reject) the hypothesis.
- **Discussion/analysis:** This is where you discuss the results that you have obtained with respect to the studies quoted in the introduction. You also need to discuss any limitations of the study, and the way that these may have influenced the result(s). This usually leads into a discussion on ways in which the study could be improved. You also need to comment on any implications that can be drawn from the result(s).

Using computer programs for analysis

There are now a number of computer software packages that will do all the statistics that you need for your coursework. Nice as that is, at the time of writing most examination boards expect you to show that you understand what you are doing. So by all means use a computer program, but in addition include in your report enough evidence – perhaps one worked example – to demonstrate your understanding.

- **Conclusion:** A conclusion is not always necessary if you have written a comprehensive discussion, but it is sometimes useful to state briefly the aim and general findings.
- **Bibliography/references:** References for *all* quoted sources must be given in conventional form.
- **Appendices:** Anything else that is relevant and not mentioned elsewhere goes in the appendix (for example: raw data, a word list, the questionnaire you used, and so on). Give each an appendix number and refer to it in the text.

Checklist: AS and A-level practicals

This checklist is designed to help you maximise your marks for practical work based on experimentation or correlational analysis. With a little ingenuity you can also adapt it for observational studies. Copy it and use one for each of your practicals, but remember that every question will not apply to every study.

Name _____

Title of practical work _____

_____

Abstract (summary)
Have you stated
- the topic area studied? ☐
- the aim/hypothesis? ☐
- brief details of the method used? ☐
- the principal findings? ☐
- the main implications of your findings? ☐

Introduction
Have you
- stated the general area of your study? ☐
- referred to relevant and carefully selected background studies? ☐
- reported your reasons for studying this topic? ☐
- precisely stated (i) the alternative hypothesis/es (ii) the null hypothesis/es? ☐
- stated whether the alternative hypothesis/es are 1-tailed or 2-tailed? ☐
- reported how you arrived at these aims/hypotheses? ☐
- justified the direction of your hypothesis/es? ☐
- organised your introduction in a logical way? ☐

Method
Have you divided this section into suitable subsections? ☐
Have you stated
- the design used? ☐
- why this design was chosen? ☐
- the nature of any experimental groups/conditions? ☐
- the nature of any control groups/conditions? ☐
- the IV and DV or the variables correlated? ☐
- the variables that you controlled and how you controlled them? ☐
- the minimum level of statistical significance that you will accept? ☐
- your number of participants? ☐
- the population from which participants were drawn? ☐
- how participants were selected/sampled? ☐
- how participants were allocated to experimental groups/conditions? ☐
- relevant characteristics of participants such as their age range and sex? ☐
- details of all apparatus and materials used? ☐
- any standardised instructions given to participants? ☐
- the procedure followed in such a way that someone else could replicate it precisely using your description? ☐
- any ethical issues which you took into account when designing and conducting your investigation? ☐

Checklist continues

Results

Have you
- provided a summary table of results?
- provided titles for all graphs, charts and data tables?
- labelled appropriately all axes and columns of your graphs, charts and data tables?
- used appropriate descriptive/inferential statistical techniques?
- stated full reasons why a particular statistical test was selected to analyse your data?
- reported appropriately your observed and critical values?
- reported your level of significance?
- reported the outcome of your study in terms of the hypothesis/es tested?

Discussion

Have you discussed
- your findings with reference to the studies quoted in your introduction?
- what your results mean in terms of your aim(s)/hypothesis(es)?
- the limitations of your study?
- how improvements could be made to the study if it was to be undertaken again?
- suggestions for follow-up studies?
- any wider implications of your findings?

Conclusion

Have you stated the main finding(s) from your study?

References

Have you
- provided full references for all sources used and all quoted by name in your report?
- written references in a conventional style?

Appendices

Have you
- provided copies of such things as stimulus materials and experimental layouts which are referred to in the text but not included elsewhere?
- provided a table of raw data?
- included specimen statistical calculations?
- provided appropriate titles and labelling for all appendices?

Presentation

Have you
- written your report in a concise scientific style?
- structured your report logically into sections?
- avoided unnecessary repetition or irrelevancy?
- provided a contents page and numbered your pages?
- presented your report in such a way that someone else could precisely replicate the study from your description?
- linked all graphs, charts and data tables into your text?

Source: Graham Davies, Association for the Teaching of Psychology, 1994

Ethics

An important area that you need to consider when planning and conducting your research is that of **ethics**. Ethical issues have become much more prominent in recent years, and need to be studied both for the written examination and for your coursework. There are now formal guidelines that everyone conducting psychological research with human beings or animals must follow (see Unit 2, pages 46–50). The British Psychological Society (BPS) has produced a booklet outlining all important ethical issues, as has the Association for the Teaching of Psychology (ATP). The essential issue is one of professional integrity, which comes down to not risking harm or discomfort to the participant in any way. In practice you must:

- request permission as appropriate;
- brief the participants;
- ensure no harm of any kind;
- allow participants the right to review their results, and withdraw if they wish;
- fully debrief participants.

If you have any doubt about any ethical issue, refer to the booklets mentioned above or seek further advice from your teacher or supervisor.

Presentation

In terms of the presentation of your report, most examination boards have their own requirements – so study these carefully. In general, always type or wordprocess if at all possible, double-space the lines and allow generous margins. Check your work carefully for technical mistakes.

Checking your work

A valuable tactic to ensure that you have completed all aspects of the coursework to the examination board's requirements is to mark your own work. To be able to do this you need to check your syllabus for the examination board's coursework mark scheme.

Writing essays

Essays are an important element of most courses and with most syllabi they are worth a high proportion of the final grade.

Basic tips for essay writing

- There is no formal rule that says a good essay has so many words; however, it is difficult to write a good comprehensive essay in less than three sides of A4 paper with normal line spacing and average handwriting.
- There are several standard instructions that examiners commonly use and you should make sure that you understand and take notice of these (see pages 25–6). For example, if required to 'discuss two or more theories', you may discuss either two in great detail or more than two in less detail.
- The standard of your grammar, punctuation and spelling can affect your marks, so check carefully – and have your practice essays checked.
- Essay questions are invariably a phrase from the syllabus presented as a question. Do this yourself to get used to the style and content of typical essay questions.
- Do not expect your essay-writing skills to reach grade 'A' standard the first time. It takes both time and practice to write a good essay.
- Write a practice essay each time you complete a block of work. This helps fix the information in your mind and develops essay-writing skills.
- File your completed and marked essays with the relevant notes.

Step-by-step guide to a successful essay

Let us suppose you have been given the following essay to write:

(a) Describe psychological explanations of forgetting. (8 marks)

(b) Discuss **two** practical applications which have developed from such explanations. (16 marks)

It is homework, not in an exam, so you have time to prepare carefully. There are four steps that you need to work through: preparation, planning, structuring and writing. Each of these steps is set out in detail below.

<u>Preparation</u>
- Do you know what 'describe', 'discuss' and 'applications' mean? Check to make sure.
- 'Explanations' and 'applications' are both plural. This means you need to cover either two in considerable depth or four or five in less depth. It is for you to decide.

Let's say that you have decided to discuss most explanations of forgetting and two applications, so:

- Study the relevant section(s) of this book (pages 180–3) and look back at any notes you have made on this topic.
- Go to the library and take out a couple of other general psychology texts. Make a list, with notes, of 'explanations of forgetting'. Use the different texts to help deepen your understanding.

  Now note the basics of each explanation and record the book titles and page numbers where you found the information. Note cards or file index cards are good for this (see page 6). On one side note the explanation, on the other the book title and the page numbers of each source. (The specific question will dictate how much detail you need.)

  One card, describing one explanation of forgetting (trace decay), might look like this:

Front

> FORGETTING: Trace decay
>
> A memory trace is a physical change – or path or series of connections – in neural tissue as a result of stimulation, in this case an attempt to learn something.
>
> The memory trace is assumed to be held or located in a sensory store or register.
>
> Involves both STM and LTM.
>
> Consider accessibility.
>
> Traces decay with time due to lack of use.

Back

> Twining, K., *Success in Psychology* (1998), pp. 180–3
>
> Cardwell, M., Clark, L., and Meldrum, C., *Psychology for A Level* (1996), pp. 324, 339
>
> Gross, R. D., *Psychology – The Science of Mind and Behaviour* (3rd edn 1996), p. 306
>
> Eysenck, M. W., and Keane, M. J., *Cognitive Psychology* (1990), p. 136

- You now have the raw information that you need to plan the essay.
- You have two main parts, (a) and (b) – so write two distinct answers, each complete in itself. Remember that part (a) carries 8 marks, part (b) 16 marks, so plan to write more for part (b).

<u>Planning</u>   This is a very important stage, but remember that in the exam you will only have about six or seven minutes to do it.

There are two basic ways of planning your essay:

- using a spider diagram or 'spidergram'; or
- using a list.

The spidergram is the more flexible of the two methods as it lends itself easily to expansion: you just add more 'legs' as you think of more points. We shall use a spidergram in this exercise.

For this essay you have to consider 'forgetting', 'explanations' and 'applications'. Your plan, or spidergram, should start something like this:

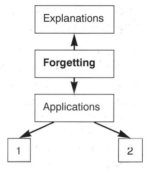

From your note cards you will have established that there are at least eight reasons or explanations for forgetting. Add these to your spidergram as you remember them – the order or position is not critical. The top of your plan now looks something like this:

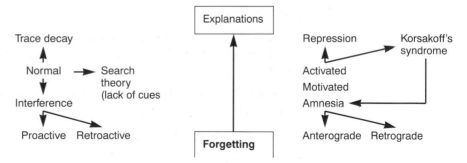

The bottom of your plan should look like this:

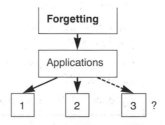

The bottom of your plan reminds you that part (b) asks for *two* applications. However, at this stage it is a good idea to include a third. You can then decide which two of these three you will write about when you have researed each of them.

<u>**Structuring your essay**</u>   Assuming a normal pattern of introduction, body and conclusion, each of the two parts of this essay will probably need to be structured as follows:

- part (a): an introductory paragraph, one paragraph for each explanation and a concluding paragraph;
- part (b): an introduction, a paragraph for each application and then a concluding paragraph.

Quickly add circled numbers on the relevant bits of your spidergram to indicate which bit is to go where in the essay. Doing this forces you to think about the order in which you will present the material before you write it.

<u>**Writing**</u>   Essay writing is more a case of hard, technical work than of 'inspiration'. Good essays require hard work and practice at all stages. Following the above step-by-step guide will help you to become a better writer.

Just before you start to write your essay, review the whole plan, get it into your mind and re-read the question. Now put the following tips into practice:

- Always write on alternate lines to allow for corrections later.
- As you write, imagine that you are talking to the reader.
- Try to write the whole essay in one go – or, in the case of split questions, write each part in one go.
- If fresh ideas come to mind as you write, add them on to your plan at the appropriate place straightaway – don't leave it until later.
- Stick to your plan. Making changes (as opposed to additions – see above) as you write creates complications.
- Draw a line through each part of your plan when you have written about it.
- Write convincingly – make points, clarify arguments, make comparisons, draw conclusions.
- Use all the supporting material that you have gathered.
- Put direct quotations from other writers in inverted commas and remember to include the reference (name and date in the text, full reference at the end).
- Remember to use transition phrases and sentences to join main ideas together in a coherent manner. Examples include: 'it can be seen that', 'on the other hand', 'Freud argues that', 'an alternative view is . . . '.
- Start each paragraph with a short, precise sentence.

When you have finished the essay, re-read it – critically:

- Does it answer the question?
- Does it flow?
- Is paragraph division correct?
- Do your arguments make sense?
- Are your comments/arguments supported by the appropriate evidence (theories, people, research)?
- Is the grammar correct?

Make any necessary corrections or small additions to complete the essay.

Examination techniques

The final section of this unit starts with an explanation of the terms used in examination questions. This is followed by some suggested revision tactics that you need to consider several months before the examination. The section concludes with a list of specific Do's and Don'ts about sitting the exam itself.

Terms used in exam questions

Make sure you are familiar with the terminology you will come across in exam questions: your syllabus will give you guidance on this. The following list from the 1998 syllabus explains the terms used in AEB papers, but check your current syllabus too.

Skill A terms

- **Consider:** requires the candidate to demonstrate knowledge and understanding of the stipulated topic area.
- **Define:** requires the candidate to explain what is meant by a particular term such as one used to identify a particular concept.
- **Describe:** requires the candidate to present evidence of his/her knowledge of the stipulated topic area.
- **Examine:** requires the candidate to present a detailed, descriptive consideration of the stipulated topic area.
- **Explain:** requires the candidate to convey his/her understanding of the stipulated topic areas and to make such an explanation coherent and intelligible.
- **Outline/state:** requires the candidate to offer a summary description of the stipulated topic area in brief form.

Skill B terms

- **Analyse/critically analyse:** requires the candidate to demonstrate understanding through consideration of the components or elements of the stipulated topic area.
- **Assess/critically assess:** requires the candidate to make an informed judgement about how good or effective something is, based on an awareness of the strengths and limitations of the information and argument presented. The candidate is required to present a considered appraisal of the stipulated topic area.
- **Criticise:** requires the candidate to critically appraise/evaluate the strengths/weaknesses of the stipulated topic areas.
- **Evaluate/critically evaluate:** requires the candidate to make an informed judgement regarding the value of the stipulated topic area, based on systematic analysis and examination.
- **Justify:** requires the candidate to consider the grounds for a decision, for example, by offering a supportive consideration of the logic behind a particular interpretation.

Skill A and B terms

- **Compare/contrast:** requires the candidate to consider similarities and/or differences between the stipulated topic areas (e.g. psychological theories or concepts). This may involve critical consideration of points of similarity and differentiation.
- **Critically consider:** as 'consider' (see Skill A terms), but in addition the candidate is also required to show an awareness of the strengths and limitations of the material presented.

- **Distinguish between:** requires the candidate to demonstrate his/her understanding of the differences between two stipulated topic areas (e.g. theories). Such a differentiation may be achieved at the levels of both descriptive and critical contrasting.
- **Discuss:** requires the candidate both to describe and to evaluate by reference to different if not contrasting points of view. This may be done sequentially or concurrently. Questions may instruct the candidate to discuss with reference to particular criteria, for example, by the use of the phrase '. . . in terms of . . .'.

Other terms
- **Applications:** actual or possible ways of using psychological knowledge in an applied/practical setting.
- **Concepts:** an idea or group of ideas. These are often the basic units of a model or theory.
- **Evidence:** material (empirical or theoretical) which may be used in support or contradiction of an argument or theory.
- **Findings:** the outcome or product of research.
- **Insights:** perceptions which facilitate an understanding or conceptual reappraisal.
- **Methods:** different ways in which empirical research is and may be carried out.
- **Model:** often used synonymously with 'theory' (see below) but, strictly, less complex/elaborate and often comprising a single idea or image meant as a metaphor. Explanation is often by analogy.
- **Research:** the process of gaining knowledge and understanding via either the examination of theory construction or the collection of empirical data.
- **Studies:** empirical investigations providing evidence which, through reference to the investigator's name and/or details of the investigation/outcome, should be recognisable to the examiner.
- **Theory:** a (usually) complex set of interrelated ideas/assumptions/principles intended to explain or account for certain observed phenomena.

Suggested revision tactics

At least three months before the exam

At least three months before the exam, and preferably earlier, you need to decide on which parts of the syllabus you will concentrate your revision. Whichever syllabus you are following, you will always be given a choice of question. You need to use this to your advantage. Study the syllabus carefully to find out on which areas you are guaranteed a question, and what choices you will have between questions on different sections. You then need to make up your own mind about which sections to make the focus of your revision. In doing this:

- concentrate on your strong areas; but also
- cover enough to be able to tackle the right number of questions.

Remember: You may be taking A level, AS level, modular assessment or terminal assessment – make sure you refer to the right part of the syllabus.

As the date for the exam approaches
It is worth doing at least one timed practice on the main written paper(s). Choose the same topic areas in each practice paper as you have already identified for the real exam. The same principle holds true for modular exams. You also need to increase the frequency of tackling essay questions. If you do not actually write the essay, at least develop an essay plan. You can't do too much of this practice.

Something to do

- Review the whole of this unit and put into practice the study skills and techniques that you think will help you.

Advice for sitting the exam

This short but vital section starts the day before the examination and assumes that your revision is complete.

The day before the exam

Do
- Eat well.
- Get a little exercise.
- Do some light revision.
- Get pens, pencils, exam number etc. ready.
- Get to bed at a reasonable time.

Don't
- Revise hard all day.
- Stay up late for that last bit of revision.
- Party.

The day of the exam

Do
- Have a good breakfast.
- Get to the exam room in good time.

Don't
- Get up early for some last minute revision.
- Arrive at the exam late.

In the exam

Do
- Ensure you are in the right exam with the right paper!
- Read – and note – *all* the instructions on the paper.

Vital
- Read *all* the questions.
- Assuming a three-hour, four-essay paper, decide which *four* questions you intend to answer.
- Start essay plans for *all four* questions.
- Re-read the questions several times – make absolutely sure that you understand what is wanted.
- Having started four plans, now concentrate on the first.
- On your plan, identify introduction, main body and concluding paragraphs.

- Ensure that you have identified and responded to Skill A, B requirements.
- Take about a minute to go over the essay in your mind – 'get it together'.
- Write rapidly, with frequent reference to the plan.
- As you write, it is almost certain that ideas, people, theories, etc. will come to mind concerning the other three essays. As they do, jot them on the plan immediately.
- Limit your time, as far as possible, to 40 minutes' writing per essay.
- Re-read your essay to check for silly mistakes and 'quality of language'.

Don't
- Panic! If you do, stop, close your eyes and breathe slowly and deeply for a full minute.
- Rush your choice of question.
- Skip the essay plans. If time is running out, it is even more important to plan – a complete plan will tell the examiner more about your knowledge than a half-written, badly structured essay!

Selected reading list

Coolican, H., *Research Methods and Statistics in Psychology* (Hodder and Stoughton, 2nd edn 1994)
Northedge, A., *The Good Study Guide* (The Open University, Milton Keynes, 1994)

2 An introduction to psychological perspectives and research methods

This unit has two main objectives. The first is to introduce and discuss **psychological perspectives** or schools of thought about psychology. The second is to give a brief explanation of different **psychological methods**. Both of these are fundamental to a good understanding of psychology. When you are referring to the work of a psychologist in your studies, essays or coursework, you need to understand:

- how the psychologist's work fits into the context of psychology – what was their **perspective** or **approach**? You may be asked, for example, to identify a behaviourist's likely approach to a particular set of observations or data;
- what **methods** the psychologist used to carry out his or her study. You may be asked to consider why they chose a particular method, and whether another method might have been more, or less, effective.

Perspectives

Knowing something about where psychology comes from helps in understanding where psychology is now. This unit therefore includes a brief outline of the background and development of psychology. You will soon discover that people have different views or **perspectives** on the subject – for example, they have disagreed over certain aspects of the developing theories. Some of these 'debates' – many of which have not yet been (and probably never will be) resolved – are outlined on pages 38–41.

Methods

Because psychology is all about people – how they 'work' and how they interact – psychologists need systematic **methods** to study them. Traditionally, thinkers, philosophers, theologians and others simply expressed their own thoughts, ideas or personal views. With the emergence of the scientific age, however, this was not thought to be good enough. Another debate emerged: is psychology a science and, if so, can it be studied scientifically? Most, but not all, argue that it is a science and so can be studied using the well-proven methods of science. As a consequence, there are a number of ways of studying, investigating and researching psychology. These are discussed on pages 41–6. The ethical issues that inevitably arise from many of these methods are discussed in the final section of the unit.

Something to do

- Ask a cross-section of people what they think psychology is. Compare their answers to the contents of this or any other psychology textbook. What conclusions can you draw?

You will probably find that most people have quite a limited view of what psychology is and what it does.

The development of psychology

Before we get into a detailed discussion of the specific approaches, we need to consider the origins of psychology. How and why did it develop? What were the forces behind it? What sort of time-scale is involved?

By trying to establish some of the roots, we can gain a better understanding of psychology, both in terms of its history and development and in terms of where it is at the moment. This, in turn, provides us with a solid basis as 'psychology' moves – at an ever-increasing rate – into the 21st century.

Early beginnings   Think classical Greek culture: the fourth and third centuries BC; people such as Plato and Aristotle and Socrates. These were the people who started asking the difficult questions. How does the mind work? Why do I think as I do? Why do I (and others) behave as I (we) do? How is the mind connected to the body? It was these same philosophers who started giving the answers.

Plato   Plato's Academy flourished in Athens from 380 BC to about AD 530. There was no syllabus as such; those who attended were the sort of people who enjoyed academic discussion and argument. The style was very much **dialectical**, following the practice of Socrates, who led his students forwards by asking *them* the difficult, challenging questions. Their knowledge grew as they struggled with the answers – only to be challenged by a subsequent and even more difficult question. In this approach, learning comes from reasoning, not from experience.

Think about it

• Compare a dialectical approach to learning with the other approaches discussed on pages 311–18.

The Church   In AD 530, the Emperor Justinian – who was a Christian – closed Plato's Academy. So now we see the early philosophies being challenged by the Church. As Roman Catholic **theology** spread throughout Europe, the early thinking that there are natural laws in the world that govern and operate at a physical level, was taken over by a theology that said that the mind, really the soul, is from God and cannot therefore be dependent on natural laws. The earliest of scientific approaches was pushed into the background.

The advancement of science

With only the occasional exception, the scientific approach did not emerge again until the 17th century at the time of the Renaissance. This was a time of general advancement in the natural and physical sciences, despite severe opposition from the Church.

The first significant influence in this period was from René Descartes (1596–1650). He was one of a number of **rationalists,** who believe (like the early Greek philosophers) that 'truth' can be established through a process of reasoning or rational thought. It is interesting that this was a Continental approach – Descartes was French. In Britain at this time **empiricism** was the main scientific strand, with people such as Hobbes (1588–1678) and others arguing that it is data that is important.

The emergence of psychology

Psychology was starting to emerge from philosophy. Back in France, Anton Mesmer (1734–1815) experimented with magnetism, while Jean Charcot developed and practised hypnotism. Franz Gall (1758–1828), a German physician with an interest in anatomy, was the first to show that the greater the area of cortex in the brain, the greater the intelligence of the human animal. This led him to believe that the shape of the skull was a suitable measure of intelligence and personality – the practice of **phrenology.** These strands and many others were moving psychology slowly and erratically from its philosophical beginnings into a scientific framework.

The birth of psychology as a science

Wilhelm Wundt

It is generally agreed that psychology was born in 1879 at the University of Leipzig. The professor was Wilhelm Wundt (1832–1920) and with him were two students, one of whom was G. Stanley Hall, an American, later to become a famous psychologist. The significance is that Wilhelm Wundt had set up the first formal psychology laboratory (Hunt, 1993). Wundt conducted experiments of a formal nature into almost anything and everything, which is one of the criticisms levelled at him. However, he was enormously influential and most psychologists of the early decades of the 20th century were influenced by him or by his writings.

Hermann Ebbinghaus

One such was a German, Hermann Ebbinghaus (1850–1909), who worked in Berlin and was influenced by Wundt's experimental methodology. Ebbinghaus worked in the field of memory and, in particular, in research using nonsense syllables or trigrams – vowel, consonant, vowel – for example *bix, cof, rab.* He conducted a huge number of experiments on himself using this method, and developed two important laws. The first of these showed that the more time spent *learning* material, the greater will be the success when recalling the material. The second showed that material, once learnt, is *forgotten* quickly at first and then more slowly. These laws (which we look at in more detail in Unit 4) are illustrated graphically over the page:

Ebbinghaus's laws of learning and forgetting

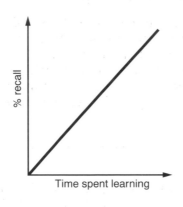

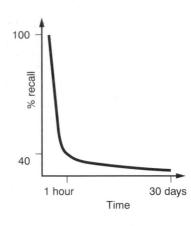

William James   Another very important psychologist of this time was William James (1842–1910), considered by most to have introduced experimental psychology to America. He worked at Harvard University and produced the first major psychology textbook, *Principles of Psychology*, in 1890. Possibly the major influence of James was in promoting **functionalism**, the idea that psychology should investigate the function or purpose of the mind and of behaviour in terms of their content. This was in contrast to **structuralism**, which had been the main approach of Wundt, and in which it is the structure of the mind, etc., that is the focus of the study. James had been influenced by Darwin, in particular by the theory of natural selection (see Unit 6), and argued that in order to apply this to humans we need to study the function of consciousness rather than its structure. In this respect, James coined the term 'stream of consciousness' to describe the non-stop flow of thoughts that we have.

Something to do

• Try to stop thinking! Is it possible?

In this broad division, structuralists (for example Wundt and Ebbinghaus) will naturally gravitate towards laboratory work, while functionalists (such as James) will want to know how people adapt their behaviour in the real world – outside the laboratory. As a consequence, new topics were introduced into psychology, such as intelligence, child development, sex differences and educational issues. The structuralists continued to work in the laboratory on topics such as sensation and perception, while the functionalists moved out into the 'real' world.

Psychological perspectives

In this section, we consider some of the main **psychological perspectives** or **approaches to psychology,** in particular some of the assumptions, and also the contributions, that they make.

There are a number of ways in which to consider the approaches or perspectives. Here, we stay within a traditional framework and consider what are usually thought of as the main five approaches in a roughly chronological order.

Something to do

• Prepare a chart on a large piece of paper (at least A4), which you can complete as you work through the unit. Use the headings shown below, and allow plenty of space for each category.

Approach	Assumptions	Contributions
Behaviourism		
Psychoanalytic		
Cognitive		
Humanistic		
Neurobiological		

The five major approaches have all been formulated in the 20th century. We deal with them chronologically, but what is more important than the order is to get an overall picture of the flow of these evolving and changing approaches. Behaviourism, which we shall look at first, and the psychoanalytic, cognitive and neurobiological approaches are foundational; while the humanistic approach, though very important, is not foundational to the same degree.

Other approaches are that of **feminism,** and also the relevance of **cross-cultural studies** (both of which are beyond the scope of this book). An **evolutionary approach,** with the emphasis on adaptiveness, is also considered by some as being relevant. Finally, **social constructionism,** which we discuss in a different context in Unit 3, is an approach that is currently gaining influence.

Behaviourism As the debate between structuralism and functionalism was raging, another school of thought emerged: **behaviourism.** John Watson (1878–1958) founded this school in the early 1900s based on the fundamental idea of the reflex, following the pioneering work of Pavlov in this area. We can say that behaviourism considers that the study of observable, measurable behaviour is the only scientific approach to psychology. Thoughts, feelings and emotions, while real, are not capable of being measured and therefore should not be considered as valid subject matter for a scientific psychology. According to Watson, psychology should become the scientific study of behaviour. The passion for behaviour raised the question of the cause of the behaviour; and so the concept of a **stimulus**, a cause in the environment, was linked to its resultant behaviour – leading to the concept of **stimulus–response**.

Inevitably this led to the argument that animals would make appropriate subjects to study. A key reason for this is that the experiment can be controlled much more effectively with animals than with humans.

Apart from the challenge of the functionalists, two other approaches were arriving on the scene at about this time. In Germany, **Gestalt psychology** was taking hold; while in Austria, Dr Sigmund Freud's analytical psychology, focusing on the unconscious, was beginning to make an impact (see page 35).

Behaviourism

Assumptions and basic principles	Contributions
• Behaviourism is scientific because it is 'done' in a laboratory under strict control. • Watson is considered a radical behaviourist. • Pavlov and Skinner are rather less dogmatic behaviourists (as are Hull and Tolman). • Behaviourism is more American than European. • What is important is not what people think, but how they behave. • The key notion is the **stimulus–response** (S–R) link. • Complex responses are merely a combination of smaller S–R links. • Responses to stimuli can be reflexive (as in a knee jerk) or learned. • Learning occurs through a process of conditioning, which is the mechanism by which behaviour is changed or shaped. • Watson and Pavlov use **classical conditioning** (that is, reflexive). • Skinner argued that the consequence of the behaviour is important. This is **operant conditioning**. • In operant conditioning, reinforcement plays an important part. • **Reinforcement** is the way in which a learned response is strengthened so that it will happen again. It can be positive – as when a child is given a reward for good behaviour – or negative – when bad behaviour is ignored (not punished). • Punishment can be seen as a positive reinforcer, as it pays attention to bad behaviour and therefore (may) reinforce it. • The basic principles of behaviourism hold for all species, therefore studying one species has relevance to other species.	• Behaviourism, in its various forms, has been a major influence in many areas; **motivation** and **therapy** are just two. • **Classical conditioning** approaches are used in therapy (see Unit 8). • **Systematic desensitisation**, where the person is slowly introduced to the thing that they fear in order to overcome it, is a classic form of classical conditioning. • **Flooding** and **implosion**, two techniques that are used in therapy, are applications of classical principles. They both 'flood' the person with the behaviour – particularly the phobia – which the client wishes to overcome. • **Operant conditioning** is used to shape desired behaviours, or to cause undesired behaviours to become extinct. • **Behaviour modification** (or behaviour therapy) uses operant principles. It is the process by which the person's behaviour is changed. • **Aversion therapy** is a form of behaviour modification. It uses unpleasant or painful stimuli to change the person's behaviour. • **'Token economy'** is an example of behaviour modification that can be used in education or therapy. It works by rewarding appropriate behaviour with a token – often a plastic counter – which can then be exchanged for the real reward. • **Programmed learning** relies on operant principles. In this method of learning, a predetermined number of steps require correct answers at each step before progressing. More able students can skip certain steps, allowing faster learning.

The psychoanalytic approach

While Watson and his colleagues in America and Pavlov in Russia were developing behaviourism, Freud (1856–1939) was practising as a medical doctor in Vienna and becoming interested in the unconscious. His image of the mind is as an iceberg, most of which is below the surface. Freud believed that a great deal of what goes on in the mind, or psyche, occurs in the unconscious. It operates below the surface and is a powerful influence on behaviour. Freud concluded that problems or difficulties are caused by conflict existing in the unconscious. His **psychoanalytic theory** is an attempt to explain these problems or disorders by analysing the forces at work in the unconscious, which drive our behaviour.

Initially at least, this was not a popular theory, because at the time the emphasis in psychology was turning towards the scientific exploration of behaviour. Interest in consciousness was decreasing and it was thought by many that an interest in the *un*conscious was just a passing fad. In fact, Freudian thinking became a major influence in the 1920s and 1930s and is still influential today. Much has changed in its theory and practice, but the fundamental issue of unconscious conflicts and drives remains central.

It is important to note at this point that **psychoanalytic** describes the theory, while **psychoanalysis** describes the practice of the theory. The term **psychodynamic** is sometimes used as a synonym for psychoanalytic, but more accurately describes theories that deal with that which is

The psychoanalytic approach

Assumptions and basic principles	Contributions
• The mind, or psyche, operates on two levels, the conscious and the unconscious. • The unconscious is much larger than the conscious. • The personality has three parts: the **id**, the **ego** and the **superego**. Each of these three is 'pulling' the personality in its own direction, thus creating a dynamic tension (hence 'psychodynamic'). • The two main drives or instincts are life (**Eros**) and death (**Thanatos**). • The drive for sexual gratification is also a vital instinct. • The personality develops through a series of psychosexual stages. • A person can remain fixated or 'stuck' in a psychosexual stage if that stage is not fully achieved such that the person can move into the next stage. • Fixation may produce neurotic symptoms. • These symptoms can only be dealt with by taking the person back to that stage of childhood where the fixation occurred, in order to gain 'insight' into the problem.	• The concept of the unconscious mind. • While some still hold strictly to Freudian views, many others have adapted or developed the approach (neo-Freudian). • Probably the main contribution is in the area of the 'helping' professions – counselling, social work, etc. • The value of the 'talk cure'. • The place of dream analysis. (Freud termed dreams 'the royal road to the unconscious'.)

dynamic. Hence it is perfectly correct to use the term psychodynamic when talking of Freud's personality theory, where the id, ego and super-ego are in dynamic tension (see Unit 7, pages 328–9 and 353 and Unit 8 pages 407 and 422).

The cognitive approach

In one sense, this approach developed as a result of advances in technology and in the understanding of brain function that started as a consequence of the rapid expansion of knowledge triggered by the Second World War. New ways of handling vast amounts of information were needed, thus boosting the development of information processing; while the training of pilots, for example, led to advances in perception. In quite another sense, the cognitive approach developed as a direct challenge to behaviourism.

In this perspective, people's behaviour *follows* their thinking, while thinking is a natural aspect of the brain.

No one person spearheaded the cognitive approach; rather a group of people, such as Piaget and Vygotsky, Chomsky and Simon and Newell, each contributed to one or more aspects of cognition.

The 'cognitive revolution' – as it is sometimes called – gathered speed after the Second World War and came of age in the 1960s. It brought together a number of fields, all of which were producing more and more information on how mental processes work: fields such as neuroscience, psycholinguistics, anthropology and, of course, computer science.

If cognition is all about the mental processing involved in acquiring knowledge, and if we think before we behave, then behaviourism, which involves studying just behaviour, must be incomplete.

The cognitive approach

Assumptions and basic principles	Contributions
• The cognitive approach is based on information-processing theory (the 'computer analogy'). • The cognitive approach studies the process of storing and retrieving information. • The cognitive approach relies heavily on the scientific method. • The cognitive approach argues that behaviour cannot be understood without referring to cognitive processes. • People are basically information processors. • Key areas are memory, perception and language. • Cognitive processes are needed to make sense of the world and to control behaviour. • Cognitive ability develops as the child gets older (see, for example, Piaget's stages of cognitive development – Unit 7).	• Cognitive psychology has made significant contributions to a wide area of psychology, for example child development, memory, language development. (This is also a problem, as there is, as yet, no integrated cognitive science.) • Creative thinking is the result of higher-order cognitive processes. ('Cognitive' comes from the Latin root *cogitare*, to think.) • Human beings, operating at a cognitive level, test experience (hypothesise) and draw conclusions – often with respect to survival. • The cognitive approach has made a significant contribution to modern therapeutic approaches. • Cognitive psychology is the dominant orientation at the end of the 20th century. • New trends may take more notice of meaning.

The humanistic approach

The humanistic approach, rather like cognition but for different reasons, emerged in the 1950s as a reaction to earlier approaches, particularly the psychodynamic and behavioural approaches.

Abraham Maslow (1908–70) is usually thought to have initiated this approach with his emphasis on the higher human motives. He reacted against the rather negative pathological focus of psychoanalysis, and the mechanical view of the human being in behaviourism. The emphasis in the humanistic approach concerns the person's ability to strive for and reach his or her full potential. The emphasis is essentially subjective – how you feel, rather than what you are thinking (cognitive) or what you have done (behavioural).

Carl Rogers (1902–87) has also been influential, particularly in terms of personal growth. It was Rogers who was the prime mover in the growth of client-centred therapy – usually practised in groups.

The humanistic approach	
Assumptions and basic principles	**Contributions**
• People have within themselves the capacity (sometimes with help) for **'self actualisation'** and for personal growth.	• The humanistic approach stresses the importance of subjective experience.
• The humanistic approach takes a holistic view of the person.	• It has added a new dimension to therapy.
• Each individual is quite unique.	• It provides an optimistic view of people.
• Human behaviour is influenced by the person's need to fulfil his or her potential.	• It has spawned many new therapies.

The neurobiological approach

This approach is also called the **biological approach**, and sometimes the **biogenic approach**. The reason we favour the term **neurobiological** is because of the emphasis it places on neuroscience, particularly the emphasis on understanding the functioning of the brain. Whichever term is used, this approach argues that it is our human biology that causes or influences our behaviour. By biology, we mean the action of genetics, the brain and the nervous system. It is interesting to note that this – the most recent of the approaches to develop – takes psychology back to its beginnings with the emphasis on physiology.

One of the most recent of emphases in this approach is that of **connectionism** or **parallel processing**. This argues that the brain is not like a computer (or at least the present generation of computers) that processes information in a linear or serial fashion, but rather that the brain can deal with many different inputs and processes at the same time and can therefore process data in parallel.

The neurobiological approach	
Assumptions and basic principles	**Contributions**
• Psychological and social phenomena can be understood in terms of biochemical processes. • Complex behaviours can be understood by analysing them into smaller, more specific, units. • All behaviour is determined by physical structures and largely hereditary processes. • Experience can modify behaviour by altering these underlying biological structures and processes (Zimbardo and Weber, 1994).	• The neurobiological approach is still in the early stages of development, but is likely to hold the most potential of all approaches. • It offers an understanding of the link between behaviour and brain activity. • It has identified brain areas associated with specific behaviour. • It has led to greater understanding of the relationship between hormone production and behaviour. • It is developing knowledge of the place of genetics in human traits and behaviours.

Something to do

• Review Unit 5 on bio-psychology. Can you add any more 'assumptions' and 'contributions' to the list given for the neurobiological approach?

Debates in psychology – the nature of the person

The previous section was concerned with the different ways in which we can 'approach' psychology. In this section, we deal with some of the issues or debates that surround the nature of the person, concentrating specifically on two major debates:

• Do you have **free will**? Or are you **determined** by some force or another?
• Can we operate on a **reductionist** principle such that all complex phenomena are capable of being 'reduced' to smaller units?

There are a number of other traditional debates that we do not discuss in detail here, but which appear in one form or another at other places in this book.

• One of the most important is the **Nature–Nurture debate**. Are we influenced more by **Nature** – genetics, or by **Nurture** – experience?
• Another is concerned with **idiographic** and **nomothetic** approaches, particularly with respect to personality theory. Do we consider people idiographically – as unique, or nomothetically – as a group?
• Yet another is the question of **consciousness**. What is it? And how does it function?

You might like to research these debates further for yourself.

Personality theory

'Personality' is one of those things that we all know what we are talking about until we try to define the term. Allport (1937) identified over fifty major different definitions. Definitions still vary today, depending on who you are reading: philosopher, theologian, psychologist, etc.

Having said that a generally acceptable definition is difficult to find, Child (1968) *has* produced a definition that many would agree with. Hampson (1988), quoting Child, says that personality refers to:

"... *more or less stable internal factors that make one person's behaviour consistent from one time to another, and different from the behaviour other people would manifest in comparable situations.*"

The key words in this definition are: stable, internal, consistent, different.

While this is a generally accepted definition, traditionally the subject is dealt with in terms of the personality theory under discussion. So, the definition will vary between say a behaviourist view and a Freudian view.

It is, however, possible to generalise some of these differences. We can consider the individual-ness of the person – the idiographic view; or the similarities between people – the nomothetic view. We can also consider a **trait approach** which is concerned with the person's traits or characteristic ways of behaving, thinking, etc.; or the person's **type** where a 'type' is a mutually exclusive group. A person can have traits in varying degrees, but can only be one type of person or another.

Free will and determinism

It is difficult to talk about **free will** on its own. If you argue that you do not have free will, then what replaces it? Something must direct your behaviour if you are not choosing to do so, and so we have the classic debate: free will versus determinism. The issue is important because it is not a stand-alone matter. What you believe about free will and determinism will affect what you think about other critical areas of psychology and vice versa.

Free will

The key idea in free will is that the individual has some degree of control over his or her behaviour. The individual is involved in decision making and action, and is not passive or simply responsive. In humanistic psychology, the central idea is that you can self actualise. This obviously supports the concept of free will. Those who oppose the concept of free will argue that the supporters – which includes those with humanistic views – only moderately support the scientific nature of psychology.

Supporters of free will have a number of quite legitimate problems to overcome. The first of these asks the question: just what is free will? Could you design an experiment to test it? Is it the opposite of determinism? If we say 'yes', then we are suggesting that behaviour has no cause, it is 'un-determined' – not a very tenable argument. A compromise has therefore to be found. The solution was first suggested by William James, who coined the term **'soft determinism'**. This means simply that behaviour is determined but only to a certain degree. It is a compromise position, and sits somewhat uneasily in psychological thought.

Something to do

• Draw up a chart that shows connections between the main psychological approaches and free will and/or determinism.

The second problem is that science is based on deterministic principles, so holding to a non-deterministic view is, by definition, not scientific. Most supporters of free will would have difficulty in accepting this view.

Another issue is the ethical or moral dimension. If we do not have free will, then something else is determining our behaviour. The logical extension of this is that 'I' am not responsible for my actions.

Determinism

If the concept of free will is difficult to support – which, in a literal or pure sense, it is – and we have moved towards a 'soft determinism', then it follows that what we are calling 'determinism' must be 'hard' or pure determinism. We started this discussion by talking about free will versus determinism, almost as if it were a bipolar continuum with free will at one extreme and determinism at the other. We have now positioned soft determinism on the continuum. Here, the behaviour of the person appears to be of their choosing but in fact is partly determined.

If we argue that behaviour has some degree of determinism, we can ask: where does it come from? There are two answers to this question.

- The first argues that it is the environment; thus we get **environmental determinism**.
- The second argues that it is from within the person, which is **biological determinism**. Internal, or biological, determinism can be caused either by genetic influences or by the unconscious. It has to be one or the other of these, or a combination of both.

We now begin to see the interplay between this debate and the various approaches: environmental determinism, for example, links with a behaviourist approach, while biological determinism links with both the neurobiological approach (biology is the cause) and the psychodynamic approach (the unconscious is the cause). In the case of free will, then clearly it is the humanistic approach that supports this view.

Something to do

- Draw a spider diagram showing hard and soft determinism, free will *and* the five approaches discussed above.

Reductionism

Reductionism is not as straightforward as at first it might appear. In this debate, the basic premise is that **reductionism** breaks down or reduces a complex whole into its component parts, with the purpose (usually) of aiding understanding. That is the basic theory. In practice, however, is it helpful knowing that, at the most 'reduced' level, turning over the next page is a matter of biochemistry? Does it add insight into the behaviour? Similarly, is 'reducing' a certain mental illness to a problem with a specific neurotransmitter in the brain (a case which can be made) helpful? It reduces mental illness to biochemistry, but ignores social factors and genetics.

Another problem is the question of cause and effect. Are we sure that behaviour is a result of chemistry and not the cause of it?

The early structuralists reduced perception to individual sensations; Gestalt theorists, on the other hand, argued an opposite view – the picture is more than the sum of its parts.

Perhaps the real issue in this debate is not about whether it is possible to take a phenomenon to bits by reductionism (which most would agree can be done) but rather about the extent to which this process adds to our understanding of the phenomenon. You know that your driving skill can be reduced to molecular activity of brain and muscle tissue. Does that help you to pass your driving test?

In a formal sense, there are a number of ways of applying reductionism to different areas within psychology.

- **Physiological reductionism** argues that because we are made up from physiological 'components' – neurons, chemicals, etc. – *all* behaviour, including perception, memory, etc., can be reduced to a neural level.
- **Biological reductionism** argues that we can follow a reductionary route from the human animal, the most complex, to much less complex animals, as a way to understand behaviour. This is based on Darwinian theory and assumes (a huge assumption) that there is a biological continuity from a simple animal, say a snail, to you and me.
- The **behaviourist** approach to reductionism attempts to break down behaviour into smaller and smaller stimulus–response links.
- A **computer-simulation** approach to reductionism argues that, as the computer can be considered similar to the brain (another huge assumption), then behaviour can be computer modelled and, as a consequence, analysed. This approach not only assumes that the brain is similar to a computer, it also ignores the fact that the brain is not an isolated item but a part of a bigger whole – you! When did your computer last feel that it needed a coffee break?

Something to investigate

- Reductionism relates to a number of different areas within psychology. Draw a spider diagram to show this. (Gross, 3rd edn 1996, has a good example of this.)

Methods in psychology

In this section, we discuss methods used to investigate psychological issues. With each method we give a typical application.

The debate about whether or not psychology (or any other subject matter) is 'scientific' rests not so much on the subject matter itself, but on the way the subject is studied or investigated. A very important assumption that we need to make is that the **scientific method** is used in all of the methods which follow.

The scientific method is fundamentally very basic. Issues relating to its philosophy and methodology, on the other hand, are extremely complex and beyond the scope of this section. At the most fundamental or basic level, the scientific method has a number of steps. These are:

- **observation**, which leads to the formation of a theory;
- **hypothesis**, which is an expression of what the theory could imply;
- **test**, which is steps taken to find out whether the hypothesis is correct;
- **conclusion**, which may involve revising the theory in the light of the result of the test.

As an example, consider the story (probably not true) that Newton discovered gravity when an apple fell on his head. Imagine Newton sitting in an orchard minding his own business when suddenly an apple falls on his head. He *observes* that the apple fell down and *theorises* that things released in space will fall *down*. He *hypothesises* that all objects released in space will fall to the ground. Therefore there must be a force that causes this, otherwise they might fly sideways or even upwards. He then *tests* the hypothesis by dropping various objects, perhaps from a tree or a ladder. He *concludes* that the hypothesis is true: objects released in space do fall down.

This, however, is not the end of the matter, as during these trials Newton made a fresh observation: that not all objects fall at the same speed. So a new hypothesis is formed, new tests are made and new conclusions are drawn; leading to yet another observation, and so on. And so science proceeds one step at a time, each step is rigorously tested and often – but not always – leads on to a new observation, hypothesis, test and conclusion. In other words, it is a cyclical process that continually moves forwards.

The important point to remember is that all science follows these key steps. Psychological investigations, including any work of this nature that you may have to do, does so also.

There are many ways in which science follows the scientific method, and psychology is no exception:

- You can **observe** the behaviour of football crowds.
- You can do a **case study** on the development of language in a baby.
- You can conduct an **experiment** to see if children sitting exams do better in the room in which they studied the subject or in the examination hall.
- You can investigate **cross-cultural issues**.
- You can **correlate** intelligence with, say, self esteem.
- You can **survey** attitudes towards smoking in children.
- You can do **qualitative research**, something that is becoming increasingly more common. (See page 46 for an example of the use of qualitative analysis.)

These examples are just some of the many possible variations of methods of investigating psychology. As we look at each of these in a little more detail, it is important to recognise that they fall into two groups:

- the **experimental** method; and
- **non-experimental** methods, with qualitative methods as a separate form of non-experimental methods.

They all follow the scientific method, but there is a critical difference between these two groups. This is described in the next section.

The experimental method

In this method (there is only one experimental method), the key factor is that *one* variable is deliberately manipulated while all other factors are held constant or **controlled**. As a consequence, with this method you can link cause and effect. You can say with a degree of certainty that because you changed one variable while holding others constant, any change in the outcome must be due to the change that you deliberately made. With no other method can you show a relationship between cause and effect.

Research methods

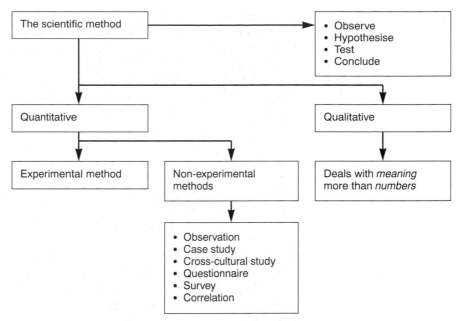

As an example, we work through the experiment mentioned on page 42. Let us assume we have **observed** that children, when taking a test, do better when they take the test in the room in which they studied the material rather than in the examination hall. How do we test this observation? We now formulate the **hypothesis** that we wish to test. It might read:

- 'Children examined in the room in which they studied the subject will achieve higher scores than children tested in a different room.'

Notice that a direction of result is predicted: 'higher scores'. This makes the hypothesis one-tailed (see Unit 1).

This then is the research question formulated as an hypothesis, in this case an **experimental hypothesis** (H_E). By convention, we now turn it into a **null hypothesis** (H_0), which means restating it in the null form:

- 'There will be no difference in test results between children tested in the room where they studied and those tested in a different room.'

We now test the null hypothesis to show that it is false. If it is, then, by implication, the experimental hypothesis must be true.

In this study, we manipulate the room where the test takes place: this is our **independent variable**; and we measure test scores: this is our **dependent variable**. All that remains is to **control** any other possible variables, sometimes referred to as **confounding variables**.

Still with the same study, let us suppose that we wish to conduct this experiment with 12-year-old children. These are our **participants**. In the school, there are 40 participants. We now need to divide the participants – the **sample** – into two groups: the control group who will be tested in the same classroom and the experimental group who will be tested in a different classroom. The key issue here is to have both groups as matched as possible. You could divide the sample into two by **random means,** or by matching, for example by age, sex or intelligence, or any other factors that are significant to the particular study.

We may now go ahead: the children are all taught at the same time (controlling another variable), and then tested at the same time with the same test, the same mark scheme and the same marker (more controls). If there *is* a difference in the results in the direction that we expect, we can reject the null hypothesis and accept the experimental hypothesis.

Something to investigate

• Refer to a statistics/methodology textbook, such as Coolican (1994), to find out more about the experimental method. Suggest ways to expand the above experiment.

Non-experimental methods

Observation

'Observation' is almost always a **naturalistic observation**, which simply means watching something, usually people or animals, in their natural setting. This may be, for example, children in a playground or adults carrying books from a library, or the way a family of elephants behave in the wild. You simply observe and describe the behaviour; you will not be able to explain the behaviour.

Case study

The case study is a classic form of investigation. It is used as a method of research to investigate one or more individuals over a period of time. You might, for example, want to study the development of language, or some other cognitive attribute, in very young children. In this case, you will arrange to see a child say once a week for a year, or you may get the parent to report each week for the year.

Freud based his theory of psychoanalysis on the results of case studies. Piaget also used the case study to develop his views of cognitive development in children.

Cross-cultural study

This is simply another way to investigate, or rather describe, differences between cultures. For example, one of my students is investigating the way English and Finnish students estimate intelligence. Initial findings suggest that English students estimate higher IQs for their parents than Finnish students do, and also that the English students estimate higher IQs for their father than for their mother – a form of stereotyping which the Finnish students do not show. In cross-cultural studies such as this, you are left with interesting data from which you can certainly draw conclusions.

Questionnaire and survey

These two terms tend to be used synonymously. The point in both cases is that public opinion is sought, usually by asking questions. These can be 'closed' with, typically, Yes/No/Don't know answers; or 'open', such as 'What do you think of . . . ?', where the answer has to be assessed or scored. The questionnaire, more technically the **instrument**, is designed with the objective of gathering a large amount of information. The wording of the questions is very significant, particularly when emotive issues are involved.

Correlation Correlational studies are interesting in that they show a relationship between two variables. Note, however, that they show only the relationship – a correlation does not show cause. For example, a current issue in education is what is called **value added**: how does each stage in a student's education add value to the student's examination success? It is possible to correlate a given student's GCSE scores with their A-level scores. A student with a certain GCSE score can be expected, on average, to achieve a certain A-level score. In this case, a correlation not only shows the relationship between two variables, it can also predict data.

As the diagram below shows, the correlation between two sets of data can be positive or negative. In the case of a positive correlation, as one variable increases, so does the other. In the case of a negative correlation, as one variable increases, the other decreases. An example of a negative correlation occurs when we consider self esteem and depression. People with low self esteem tend to show high depression.

Positive correlation

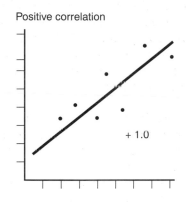

Negative correlation

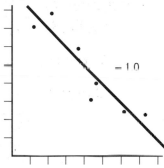

No correlation exists (but there may be a relationship)

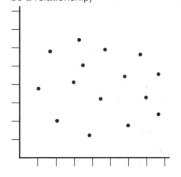

Correlation of zero

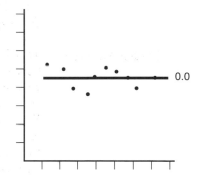

Correlation graphs

Qualitative analysis Qualitative analysis has been done for a long time. It lapsed in favour when behaviourism, with its emphasis on measuring, became the dominant methodology, but is currently becoming more common as researchers realise that not everything can be measured. Just because something cannot be measured does not mean that it cannot be studied scientifically. As the diagram on page 43 indicates, qualitative methods tend to focus on meaning rather than on the measurement of a given phenomenon.

An interesting example of qualitative analysis is a study of wall murals in Northern Ireland by Gerry P.J. Finn. This research is concerned with 'ideological dimensions of the conflict in Northern Ireland', and involves analysing the wall murals in a qualitative manner. The published study (Hayes, 1997) concludes with a helpful section on conducting qualitative analysis. Another useful text is Dey (1993), which discusses computer handling of qualitative data.

Something to do

- Draw up a table which lists (a) the advantages and (b) the disadvantages of each of the seven research methods (including the experimental) outlined above.
- Investigate what problems might arise in using a self-assessment method, for example keeping a diary (see also pages 158 and 174).

Ethical issues in psychology

As a general term used in philosophy, **ethics** can be defined as the moral values of human behaviour and the rules by which people govern that behaviour. In psychology, 'ethics' are the rules, or code of conduct, considered by the profession as the way in which the profession will conduct itself. We normally think of ethical issues as they relate to the conduct of research; in fact, the guidelines apply to all aspects of behaviour, and so relate also to other areas such as therapy. In this section, we consider ethical issues in two main areas: ethical issues relating to **human participants** and those relating to **non-human participants**. We conclude the section with a discussion of more general ethical matters.

Ethical issues with human participants

Ethical issues have become an increasingly significant aspect of the whole psychological scene. It takes only a brief review of some of the studies conducted in the past to see how unethical they were, at least by today's standards. It is impossible to be precise about why and when this change in ethical standards occurred. Probably the move towards a more ethical approach started in the 1960s when researchers began to discover that their 'subjects' (as they were called then) were not simply passive recipients but beings who interacted and reacted when a part of the experiment. Another possible factor with respect to the timing may be due to the decline in behaviourism and the rise in emphasis on cognition which was occurring at about the same time. It is not coincidental that, not long after this, the revival in interest in qualitative research began to have an impact.

Whatever the reasons, ethical issues are now considered to be of crucial importance. As a consequence, both the American Psychological Association and the British Psychological Society have produced detailed guidelines (the APA in 1992; the BPS in 1990 and 1993). Both codes outline essentially the same guidelines and constraints. These are summarised below:

Ethical guidelines for the involvement of humans in research

- **General**
  The value of the potential results from the experiment are to be considered with respect to ethical issues and possible harm to the participants.

- **Consent**
  Participants should be informed of the objectives of the research and give their formal consent.

- **Deception**
  Withholding information or misleading participants is to be avoided whenever possible.

- **Debriefing**
  Whenever possible, the participants should be fully debriefed.

- **Participant withdrawal**
  The option for the participant to withdraw from the research at any time should be made clear from the outset. Also, the participant has the right to withdraw their data or any consent previously given.

- **Confidentiality**
  Participant information is to remain confidential at all times unless specifically agreed in advance, and unless it contravenes any legal circumstances.

- **Protection of participants**
  The major responsibility of the investigator is to protect the participant from any kind of harm, physical or mental. If there is any kind of risk, it is to be no more than would normally be expected in everyday life. If research requires personal data, then the participant is to be assured that they have the right to refuse to answer. This guideline is particularly relevant to research with children, and investigators must be particularly careful when discussing results with parents, teachers or other responsible adults.

- **Observational research**
  Observational research is only acceptable when the participant is in a public place where they could be expected to be observed by strangers. In any other circumstances, the participant must give specific permission before the observation can take place.

- **Giving advice**
  If in the course of the investigation the investigator becomes aware that the participant has a problem, psychological or otherwise, then the investigator must inform the participant if by not doing so the participant might subsequently come to some harm. The investigator must refer the issue if it is beyond their own expertise.

- **Colleagues**
  Investigators have a shared responsibility with others to ensure that all investigations are conducted in accordance with the guidelines. They should encourage others to reconsider research that may infringe the guidelines.

Resolution of ethical issues

The essential element in the guidelines is the protection of the participants. This is paramount at all times. Having said that, there always have been and always will be times when, for the greater good, there needs to be a degree of relaxation of the guidelines to allow, for example, a mild form of deception to enable the investigation to proceed in such a way that it will work. This is only a last resort and all possible other means of remaining within the guidelines should be explored first. At all levels of investigation, from GCSE and A levels up to postgraduate and professional, there is always a higher authority to whom questions regarding ethical procedures can be referred. In the UK, the ultimate authority is the BPS Ethics Committee.

Ethical issues with non-human participants

The use of non-human animals in psychological investigations tends to raise even more complex arguments and ethical issues than does research with humans. For example, it is doubtful if there is much support for research into the possible harmful effects of make-up, tested by placing the substance in the eyes of rabbits. On the other hand, was Pasteur 'ethically correct', while experimenting with a cure for rabies, to inject the disease into dogs, thereby causing them pain? The outcome was a vaccine which has prevented thousands upon thousands of humans and animals from dying a horrible and agonising death, but does this justify the means? There are countless other examples of the use of animals in research, the outcome of which has benefited mankind in numerous ways. The often passionate arguments for and against the use of animals in this way have raged for a long time. The main issues that have emerged, when all the emotion is gone, are, first, the question of whether it is right to place the well-being of humans above the well-being of animals and, second, what are the ways in which we should protect animals.

Just as there are formal guidelines provided by professional bodies for research with human participants, so too there are guidelines provided for research with animals. The British Psychological Society (1985) has provided one such guide. Some of its main points are as follows:

Ethical guidelines for the use of animals in research

• **Ethical issues**
Does the potential outcome of the study justify the use of animals? Are there any procedures that would achieve the same results without using animals?

• **Species**
The researcher should choose the species least likely to suffer, consistent with the planned outcome. Endangered species are to be avoided unless the intended outcome concerns conservation of that species.

• **Conditions**
Animals should be kept in socially acceptable conditions with respect to the species. Animals should be obtained only from reputable suppliers.

• **Fieldwork**
In the case of field studies, the animal and its environment should be disturbed as little as possible.

• **Deprivation**
When animals are placed on deprivation schedules, these should cause as little distress as possible.

• **Stressful procedures**
Procedures that will or may cause pain or stress to the animals may be undertaken only if the establishment/researcher holds the necessary Home Office licences.

• **Surgical procedures**
These may take place only in appropriately licensed establishments and all possible post-operative care must be given.

• **Further advice**
If any question arises as to ethical issues or procedures, the appropriate authority must be contacted.

Constraints on using non-human animals

The ethical guidelines given above provide most of the constraints that researchers must consider as they design their experiment. The UK has what is considered as the most stringent legislation when it comes to animal research. The Animals (Scientific Procedures) Act of 1986 lays down very strict limits on what can and cannot be done in animal research. For example, the Act requires that all animal research is conducted under licence at recognised research centres and is carried out by researchers who hold an appropriate licence. A licence is only given if the research can only be conducted with animals, and if the potential benefits outweigh any costs to the animals. Other requirements that must be met include the conditions in which the animals are kept, research designed so as to use the minimum possible number of animals, and other similar criteria.

Arguments for and against the use of animals in research

The question over the use of animals in research tends to centre on whether or not the animal can experience pain and, if it can, to what degree. This is obviously a very difficult question since the animal cannot communicate how it feels. However, the behaviour of the animal is often sufficient to indicate to the observer quite clearly whether or not it is experiencing any discomfort or pain.

Bateson (1986) has proposed a model by which to judge animal research based on three key criteria:

- the quality of the research;
- the degree to which the animal will suffer;
- the value or certainty of the benefit of the research.

This model can be presented as a three-dimensional matrix, with each of the three criteria being rated from 'low' to 'high':

Model to judge animal research

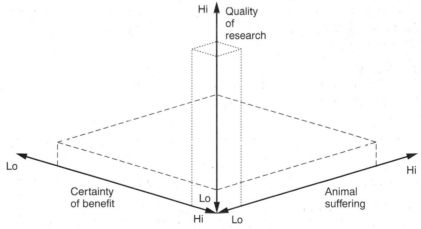

Source: Adapted from Bateson (1986)

For example:

	High quality research
plus	high certainty of benefit
plus	low animal suffering
equals	the best possible justification to proceed with the research.

Another relevant dimension in this debate, while not a question of principle, concerns the kinds or species of animals used in research and the frequency of the research. As the debate over the use of animals has moved from the laboratory and the university committee into the popular press, and with the rise of the animal rights campaign, there has been a dramatic drop in both the quantity of research studies undertaken and in the variety of species used in such research. In round numbers, from the mid-1970s to 1990, the total number of studies dropped from nearly 45,000 to just over 13,000, with 35,000 and 10,000 respectively using rats. In the 1970s, about 15 species were used; by 1990, this had halved.

Arguments *for* the use of animals are as follows:

- It is safer for humans to test new drugs on animals first, as there is a risk that new drugs may harm humans if tested on them.
- If we argue that there is a direct evolutionary link between animals and humans, then results of tests on animals can be extrapolated to humans.
- Animals, at least the kind used in laboratories, breed faster than humans. Animal testing is therefore quicker and more cost-effective.
- For the same reason, subsequent generations can be studied more quickly to test for long-term effects.
- As technology has advanced, it is now possible to conduct experiments on lower forms of life, for example flies.
- The question of causing pain and distress is central. The assumption is that lower forms of life do not experience pain.
- Knowing more about animals contributes to the well-being of animals on farms, in food production, in zoos and in wildlife conservation.
- The 'no-pain' argument is based on whether the animal has a sensory system that can respond to noxious substances, and a brain structure which has similarities to the human brain (Bateson, 1992). This is not a well-defined border, however.
- Sometimes there is an ethical dilemma which is in effect a moral choice, where the choice is between human suffering or animal suffering. In this case, Gray (1991) argues that it is right to allow animal suffering in order to avoid the suffering of humans – your own species.
- Studies undertaken on animals in their natural habitat do not harm the animals and can provide accurate and valid data on animal behaviour. Examples of such studies include those of Sir David Attenborough and Dian Fossey's studies of gorillas, as portrayed in the film *Gorillas in the Mist*.

Arguments *against* the use of animals are as follows:

- There is an intrinsic difference between animals and humans that makes valid extrapolation of data, from animals to humans, doubtful.
- Animals suffer pain and distress.
- Animals cannot be asked if they are willing to take part.

Social responsibility

A final dimension to the debate about ethics is the question of **social responsibility**. You could interpret all that has been said so far as being entirely within the psychological community; no field of science works that way, however. Psychology is not a discrete entity that has no contact with the real world. It touches it at many points and is influenced by the world 'out there'. In other words, all science works in a community that has its own value system; science needs to recognise this and be responsible for all the implications – particularly social, but other forms as well – that impinge on the world at large. In practice, this means that 'psychology' needs to look at itself and how it operates in the world and ensure that it operates ethically by recognising the value systems of society. It has to move away from the traditional values of white middle-class culture, and to recognise the much broader socio-cultural spread of humanity. We attempt to do just a little of this in the next section.

Something to do

• Before reading the next section, re-read the above section on social responsibility.

Wider ethical issues

So far the discussion on ethics has been concerned with what may be called the 'traditional' or 'normal' use of the term as it applies to the vast majority of investigations concerning humans and animals. As society has changed, however, particularly since the 1950s, what was once considered as 'normal' no longer seems quite so normal. Changes in patterns of behaviour have led to a reappraisal of what was considered as 'normal', and this in turn has led to a rethink of the relevant ethical issues.

Society has become more complex, its laws have had to follow suit and the moral and ethical codes, which have always existed in one form or another, have in their turn had to follow on. In the past, 'normality' was a fairly clear-cut issue, and the moral/ethical code was consequently also fairly clear-cut. With the changes in society, and a much wider understanding of what 'normal' might cover, the ethical issues have struggled to keep up. An interesting comparison is in the medical field, where medical technology has advanced rapidly but where ethical issues – really the controls – have lagged seriously behind.

Something to do

• Read the section on defining normality and abnormality in Unit 8 (page 387) and evaluate the term 'normal' with respect to the ethical guidelines given above.

Some of the issues discussed below do not have nice, tidy, clear-cut guidelines, but are complex issues posing questions that are very difficult to resolve. You need to bear in mind that in the following sections we are concerned with the ethical matters rather than a general discussion of any wider issues.

Socially sensitive research

It was noted above that society is changing rapidly and that this has major implications for wider and related issues such as ethics. It was also noted that our understanding of the way in which ethics 'work' in a given society is lagging behind the changes that are taking place. For a more detailed discussion of these changes, Toffler's book *Future Shock* (1970) is a helpful source. Toffler's thesis is that 'future shock' is an illness caused by an inability to cope with the accelerating rate of change of society.

Below we look at just a few of the issues facing society today which have social and ethical – and hence psychological – consequences.

Issues of social control

Social control is exactly what it says it is. It is controlling the social activity of people by the use – really abuse – of psychological, medical and other such practices. Over the years, there have been many examples of the exercise of social control. A classic example is the way in which some societies have sought to exercise control by using intelligence levels of the members of the society. The intelligence quotient (IQ) was developed in the early decades of the 20th century by a Frenchman, Binet, to help allocate children to the school most suited to them (see Unit 7, pages 337–8). This practice is still common in the UK today. It was soon believed that the IQ measure was both an accurate and a powerful 'tool'. Several American states passed laws in the 1910s and 1920s to limit people of low intelligence from having children. Other states introduced compulsory sterilisation for people with low intelligence; Terman, a prominent psychologist, strongly supported this view (Eysenck, 1994).

Other more recent examples of social control include similar practices in Europe and the imposition in China of a law limiting families to one child only.

Think about it

• Try to imagine the long-term consequences in China of the one-child policy.

Skinner was a strong advocate of social control. Since our actions are all a consequence of rewards and reinforcement, he argued, why not deliberately 'shape' society, using these operant conditioning principles, to produce Utopia? His book *Walden Two* (1948) describes an ideal society produced as a result of using these principles. The use of behaviour modification to change behaviour, often used in therapy, is discussed elsewhere in this text.

Think about it

• Read the section on behaviour modification in Unit 8 (pages 424–7). What are the *ethical* issues with respect to a token economy in a school setting? List the arguments for and against.

'Alternative' sexuality **Sexuality** is another area in which research needs to be conducted with extreme care, and where the ethical issues are complex. When we start talking about 'alternative sexuality', this is even more important.

'Sexuality' is the term used to describe a person's make-up and behaviour with respect to their biological sex. **Alternative sexuality** is more difficult to define because it deals more with attitudes and preferences. You can alter your sexual preferences – that is, the preferred sex of your sexual partner. It is also now possible to undergo a sex-change operation if the person is quite convinced that 'they' are a female but their body is male or, of course, the other way round. The procedure typically involves surgery and major hormone treatment, so in this sense you can change – some would argue only alter – your biological make-up.

Another aspect of the sexuality debate – if we may call it that – is the complex issue of **homosexuality**. If we use the term 'homosexual', then the general definition is simple: it describes a person whose sexual preference is for a person of the same sex. 'Homosexuality' has a rather broader use; while referring to sexual contact between two people of the same sex, it can mean anything from the most short-term, non-orgasmic contact to a long-term, permanent and dominant preference. Data suggest that while some 40 per cent of the population have had at least one homosexual experience, only 1 per cent are exclusively homosexual (Reber, 1995). In current popular usage, the term 'gay' is usually, but not always, reserved for a male homosexual, while 'lesbian' is the term used for a female homosexual.

In historical terms, homosexuality has been considered strongly anti-social; it has been referred to as a mental illness, and, more recently, as the result of a 'gay gene'.

There has, over the years, been considerable prejudice and discrimination against homosexuals, usually on the basis that homosexuals are not 'natural'. Current views are much more open and, for the most part, homosexuality is accepted simply as a preference, with no other connotation of 'illness'. This view changed somewhat, however, with the advent of HIV (human immunodeficiency virus) which, in the USA and the UK, is most commonly transmitted through homosexual practice (in 63 per cent of cases in the USA in 1988; Herek and Glunt, 1988).

Gender We can define **gender** as the term to describe male and female differences and their roles in society. It has become a preferred term because of the wide use and understanding of the term 'sex'. We can say that 'sex' refers to biology, while 'gender' refers to social and cultural differences between being feminine and being masculine.

Issues of gender are as complex as those of race and sexuality, and usually start with the assumption that maleness is the norm by which gender is measured. This, of course, is another form of prejudice, and in some ways can be considered to be, at least in part, responsible for the maintenance of sex-role stereotypes, as it is the gender of the person that is most frequently used to describe the role. Women are still frequently thought of in terms of the more domestic and service-orientated careers, with men expected to follow the more 'professional' careers. Lloyd and

Duveen (1992) suggest that it is school that both makes gender explicit and legitimises it: for example, children are often divided on the register by sex, with boys usually first, and play areas in the room are frequently associated with sex-typical activities for either boys or girls.

Something to investigate

• The October 1997 (No. 5) edition of *Psychology Teaching*, the journal of the Association for the Teaching of Psychology, is devoted to issues of the psychology of sexism and gender. Try to get hold of a copy and take notes for your file.

Race-related research

Another sensitive area, also often involving prejudicial views, is that of race-related research. Over the years, this has covered a wide range of topics, frequently dealt with in a less than sensitive manner and reflecting the middle-class white Western bias that has existed in psychology for a long time. 'Research' was often 'used' to show the superiority or inferiority of different races; we do not have to go back very far in history to find examples of such malpractice. Happily, this is now changing. There is now recognition that the white, middle-class, Western bias is false, and genuine efforts are being made to reflect the views and work of a much wider range of members of society.

The responsibility of the researcher to respect social and cultural diversity

In the preceding sections dealing with ethical issues, we have considered the theory and practice of research with human and non-human participants. We have also touched on some of the wider issues of what we have called socially sensitive research. The emphasis in this section is on the responsibility of the researcher.

Research of any kind with people or animals carries with it a significant responsibility. This holds true from the most basic research of a student working for a GCSE examination, through to the most sophisticated postgraduate work.

To avoid some of the horrendous research studies conducted in the past, professional bodies such as the British Psychological Society and the American Psychological Association have drawn up guidelines. In all cases of research, reference must be made to the guidelines *and* approval given by the researcher's immediate supervisor. Any question of doubt or uncertainty must be referred to a higher authority. In addition to the above formal rules, areas of research involving socially sensitive issues must receive particularly careful scrutiny before proceeding; for the lower academic levels such research should not be considered.

Psychological research is critically important in seeking to increase understanding of human behaviour and of the dignity and welfare of mankind, but the research must be so conducted as to respect and protect the dignity of the individual. It is a difficult task to balance these two guidelines, but it must always be remembered that it is the individual's integrity that counts above all else.

Examination questions

In this section we reproduce some typical examination questions on the topics dealt with in this unit: psychological perspectives and research methods. For some questions we have given sample answers with comments on the left-hand side. You might like to think about – or write – your own answer *before* reading the one given. Other questions we have 'unpacked'. This is intended to give you guidance and advice on how best to answer the question, and also to help you to analyse questions in terms of what they are requiring you to do.

The research-methods question is usually constructed with a number of short-answer questions based on one or more studies or topics. The approach you need to take is tactically different from that needed for the normal essay question. You do not need to spend as much time in planning your answer as you would in an essay question, so you can usually 'win' a little time which can be spent on other questions on the paper. You now need to make a decision as to whether to answer the question *first* so that you know how much extra time you have, or *last* in case you are running out of time. The best solution is to answer it first, for the reason just given, and also because most candidates do quite well on the question so you get a confidence boost right at the start of the exam. In tackling these short-answer questions, don't repeat the question in your answer, go straight into the answer, and use the number of marks as a rough guide as to how much you should write.

Research methods

Question 1

(a) Explain what is meant by the term *case study*.　　*(2 marks)*

(b) Briefly describe **two** research techniques that can be used to obtain information for a case study.　　*(4 marks)*

(c) Explain **two** advantages of the case study as it is used within pyschology.　　*(4 marks)*

(d) One limitation of the case study is its potential for research bias. Identify **one** possible source of researcher bias in a case study.　　*(1 mark)*

(AEB, Module Paper 7, January 1997)

Question 1: Sample answer

Comments
Good answer

(a) A *case study* is an investigation that studies in great detail either one individual or sometimes a small group. It is frequently used in psychotherapy to establish as much information as possible about the client, e.g. personal background and history, test results, results from interviews.

(2 marks)

Accurate but a bit too brief

A third possibility you may wish to use is an autobiographical account given by the person, usually with the assistance of one or more researchers.

(3 marks)

(b) (i) *Personal interview* with the person (the 'case') in question. This may involve note-taking during the interview, audio/video tape recording and questionnaire and testing.
(ii) *Observation.* Data may be collected by observing the person. This is often the case with small children or others who may not be able to communicate information.

Good answer

(c) (i) The case study can investigate individuals who are for some reason or reasons unique, e.g. the case recorded by Luria (1969) of the newspaper reporter with the exceptional memory.
(ii) A case study may contradict established theory. For example, the Czech twins (Koluchova, 1972) developed language and normal social skills despite severe deprivation in childhood, so disputing a 'critical period' theory.

Rather an obscure advantage but still accurate (see page 347 in this text)

(3 marks)

Good answer
Under this heading you could have discussed the selection of content for the report. There is likely to be too much material. Researcher bias may influence the choice of what is included and what is excluded.

(1 mark)

(d) The subject–researcher relationship is prone to researcher bias. By its very nature a case study requires a close relationship between the researcher and the person. As a consequence, unless the researcher is experienced and remains totally objective, researcher bias is almost inevitable.

Question 2

A group of researchers, interested in the feeding behaviour of birds, wished to establish whether members of a particular species would eat more when feeding in groups than when feeding alone. The research programme included approaches based on both laboratory experimentation and naturalistic observation.

(a) Explain **two** different ethical issues which the researchers would have needed to consider when planning such research, **one** which would apply to the laboratory experimental approach, and **one** which would apply to naturalistic observation.

(4 marks)

(b) Describe **one** disadvantage (excluding ethical issues) of adopting **each** of these research approaches to investigate feeding behaviour in birds. *(4 marks)*

(AEB, Module Paper 7, January 1998)

Question 3 Two researchers carried out a content analysis of television advertisements in order to establish whether women and men are portrayed differently.

The researchers made video recordings of all advertisements broadcast by one television company between 7pm and 9pm on weekday evenings for a three day period. A total of 220 advertisements was recorded. Ninety of these were found to be repeats of advertisements which had already been recorded, and these were discarded from the investigation, as were ten advertisements which did not contain any human characters. 5

Each researcher coded the following aspects of the advertisements:

(i) The gender of the central figure (operationalised as the gender of the per- 10 son who featured most prominently, either visually or vocally, in the advertisement).

(ii) Each of these central figures was classified as either 'product user' or, if primarily a source of information about the product, a 'product authority'.

Having checked for reliability of their coding, the researchers analysed their data using the chi-square test. They found that both their null hypotheses could be rejected. More men were identified both as central figures ($\chi^2 = 13.33$, $df = 1$, $p < 0.001$) and as product authorities ($\chi^2 = 8.53$, $df = 1$, $p < 0.01$). 15

(a) Explain what is meant by *content analysis* (line 1). *(2 marks)*

(b) In the context of the study outlined above, explain what is meant by the term *reliability* (line 15). *(2 marks)*

(c) Describe **one** way in which the researchers could have checked whether their coding of the advertisements was reliable. *(2 marks)*

(d) Suggest an appropriate wording for **one** of the null hypotheses referred to in line 16. *(2 marks)*

(e) Explain **one** limitation of restricting the sample of advertisements to those used in this investigation. *(2 marks)*

(f) Suggest **three** reasons why the chi-square test was used for analysis in this investigation. *(3 marks)*

(g) In the context of this investigation distinguish between the terms '$p < 0.001$' (line 18) and '$p < 0.01$' (line 19).

(AEB, Module Paper 7, January 1998)

Question 4 A researcher wishes to assess the perceived effectiveness of a course of psychotherapy. The course is for people suffering from depression or anxiety. The researcher wishes to examine both the clients' own perceptions about changes in their mood and the therapists' perception of changes of mood in the clients.

Ten people suffering from depression and ten people suffering from anxiety were allocated to different therapists and given a therapy programme lasting fifty sessions over a period of one year. At regular intervals throughout the treatment programme both the clients and their therapists were asked to estimate improvement in their condition by making a rating on a scale from 0–100.

The average ratings found at each interval by clients and their therapists are given in Figures 1 and 2 below.

Figure 1. Depressed clients' ratings and therapists' ratings of improvements in the condition

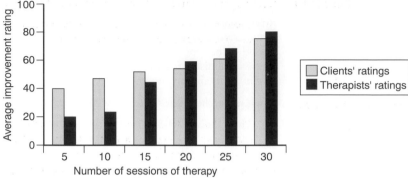

Figure 2. Anxious clients' ratings and therapists' ratings of improvements in the condition

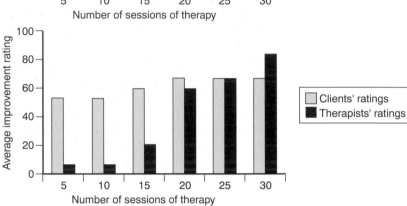

The researcher used Figures 1 and 2 when giving a talk about the findings of the study.

(a) Give **two** reasons why the researcher might have wanted to use bar charts to display the data. *(2)*

(b) (i) Name a different type of display that the researcher might have used. *(1)*
    (ii) Clearly present the data in Figure 1 in the way you have named in (b)(i) above. *(5)*

(c) (i) Interpret the summary data displayed in Figure 1. *(2)*
    (ii) Interpret the summary data displayed in Figure 2. *(2)*
    (iii) Outline differences between the patterns shown in Figure 1 and Figure 2. *(2)*

(d) (i) What statistical test might the researcher have used to investigate a difference in ratings between the clients and therapists after 20 sessions? Justify your answer. *(3)*
    (ii) What level of significance might the researcher use when testing for a difference using the test you have identified in (d)(i)? Justify your answer. *(2)*
    (iii) What is a Type I error and what is the probability of the researcher making a Type I error? *(3)*
    (iv) What is meant by a Type II error? *(2)*

(e) The researcher decided to interview a sample of the clients after the programme of therapy had been completed.

Discuss **one** strength and **one** weakness of **EITHER** a structured **OR** unstructured approach to interviewing. *(6)*

(30)

(NEAB, PSO2, February 1996)

Perspectives

Question 1   (a) Examine the use of the experimental method in psychology.   *(15 marks)*

(b) Assess the view that the experimental method may not be the most appropriate way of investigating human behaviour.   *(10 marks)*

(AEB, Paper 1, Summer 1997)

Question 1: Unpacked   Part (a)

- 'Examine' requires a 'detailed description', i.e. Skill A.
- You are required to examine the *use* of the experimental method – so don't spend too long on the 'how'.
- The experimental method is based on the scientific method – that is, observation, hypothesis, test, conclusion.
- The experimental method has been *used* from the time that psychology was recognised as a science in the mid-1800s (Wundt, Ebbinghaus) and still is the primary research paradigm.
- The principle value is that the experimental method can be *used* to show cause and effect relationship.
- Psychology *uses* the experimental method in situations ranging from the laboratory, where every effort is made to control every variable, to field and natural experiments where there is much less control over variables.

Part (b)

- 'Assess' is Skill B, requiring 'informed judgement ... strengths ... limitations ... appraisal.'
- This part now focuses on the use of the experimental method to investigate *human behaviour*, specifically the view that this method '*may not* be ... *appropriate*'. This should be your starting point.
- Weigh up the problems with using this method, then the advantages.

Question 2   (a) Discuss some assumptions of **one** psychodynamic orientation in psychology.
(12 marks)

(b) Critically consider the contribution of this orientation to **two** different areas of psychology.   *(12 marks)*

(AEB, Module Paper 7, January 1998)

The following student essay was written under simulated exam conditions in 45 minutes.

'Discuss' requires your answer to **describe** and **evaluate**. 'Critically consider' is also a standard examination term: you must give your opinion on the merits of the work in question, not just describe it.

Comments
Good introduction

Essay
(a) The psychodynamic approach is one of the major orientations with which to view psychology and like some of the other orientations, behaviourism or cognitive for example, is based on a number of major assumptions. The term 'psychodynamic' has a broad meaning

that refers to those approaches or orientations that have dynamic elements at their centre, for example internal-dynamic-drives or instincts. The term is sometimes used interchangeably with Freud's psychoanalytic view. The reason here is that in Freud's view the psyche has three components, the id, ego and superego that are considered to be in psychodynamic tension.

First assumption to be discussed

This needs further explanation

Second assumption

Assumptions made by Freudian psychodynamic theory are many. Perhaps the most significant is the assumption – and key to the whole structure of psychoanalytic theory – that the psyche can be considered as an iceberg, with ⅛th above the surface, representing the conscious self, and ⅞ths below the surface and representing the unconscious. The assumption is that we do not know how or when the unconscious forces act upon us, which means that we are helpless to direct our own affairs. A further major assumption in the pyschoanalytic approach is that our personality, and hence in many aspects our behaviour, is shaped by what Freud described as 'psychosexual' stages. These are stages that every child passes through in the early years of life and are how – according to Freud – the child gains sexual gratification. The assumption is that if the child passes through these stages successfully – although there is no scientific definition of what that means – then their psyche will be 'normal' and the adult will be a happy well-balanced individual.

Third assumption

For part (a) description is reasonable; evaluation is weak

A third assumption is that if the adult is not a happy and well-balanced individual and needs therapy to help, then psychoanalysis is required to take the person 'back' to their childhood so that they can 'work through' their problem and resolve the unresolved childhood conflict.

Good start; sets the direction

(b) Freud's psychodynamic, psychoanalytic theory has contributed to a number of areas of psychology. Probably the two most significant are child development and psychotherapy.

In terms of child development, Freud saw this as critical to the whole process of development. What happens in childhood, or does not happen, influences the remainder of the person's life. Freud divides the period of birth to puberty into five stages: Oral, Anal, Phallic, Latency and Genital. In this scheme – supported by Freudians and neo-Freudians but strongly opposed by other views, particularly the behaviourists – the child gets sexual gratification from each location and in the order given. If the child does not achieve a balance of sexual gratification then the child becomes fixated in that stage for life. This in turn will mean that the adult will show neurotic symptoms in adulthood related to the specific fixation from childhood. This view of the child has undoubtedly made a major contribution to the field of child developmental psychology and has been a major influence on many other theorists (e.g. Anna Freud, Erikson, Bowlby) who have developed dynamic theories frequently based on Freud's original work.

'balance' needs explaining further

Accurate

In terms of psychotherapy, Freud has again made a very significant contribution. Freud coined the term psychoanalysis for the therapeutic procedure which seeks to analyse the problem in terms of childhood development. The analyst seeks to gain insight into the

Good quote

Evaluation

problem by taking the analysand (the client) back into their childhood. The analyst uses techniques to 'get into' the patient's unconscious, for example dream analysis (Freud considered dreams 'the royal road to the unconscious'), free association and word association – techniques still used today.

Psychoanalysis has come in for serious criticism for a number of reasons. The whole system is based on very flimsy evidence from a very small, narrow sample of Freud's own patients. The terms used often have no general meanings and the process of analysis is lengthy and expensive. It has to be said, however, that it has made a major contribution to the 'helping' professions and still exerts considerable influence to this day.

General comments

The writer chose to discuss three 'assumptions': a good compromise between the minimum of two and a larger number.

Marks: part (a) 8
part (b) 8 = $\frac{16}{24}$

Question 3   (a) Outline ethical issues involved in psychological investigations using human participants. *(12 marks)*

(b) Critically assess attempts made by psychologists to overcome the problems raised by these. *(12 marks)*
(AEB, January 1997)

Question 4   Consider the following two examples of human behaviour.
(i) A car driver on approaching traffic lights brakes as the lights change to red.
(ii) A pair of identical twins obtain the same examination scores in school tests.

(a) Outline an explanation for each behaviour from a biological perspective. *(8)*
(b) Discuss the limitations of a biological perspective as the only explanation for the two behaviours. *(12)*
(20)
(NEAB, PS01, February 1997)

Selected reading list

Coolican, H., *Research Methods and Statistics in Society* (Hodder and Stoughton, 2nd edn 1994)
Dey, I., *Qualitative Data Analysis. A User-friendly Guide for Social Scientists* (Routledge, 1993)
Hayes, N., *Doing Qualitative Analysis in Psychology* (Psychology Press, 1997)
Hunt, M., *The Story of Psychology* (Doubleday, New York, 1997)
Psychology Teaching, 5 (Association for the Teaching of Psychology, October 1997)
Toffler, A., *Future Shock* (Bantam Books, New York, 1970)

3 Social psychology: how do we relate to others?

This unit covers the first of six major topic areas in psychology, which are dealt with in Units 3–8 of this textbook. We deal with the topic **social psychology** first for a number of reasons. The first and main reason is that, of the six, it is likely to be the area that you will already be most familiar with: you are already a social being; you have social relationships, you will have experienced social influence; and you may have come across pro- and antisocial behaviour. So you already know something about social psychology. What you now have to do is build on what you already know and give it an academic framework.

There are four main topic areas within social psychology:

- The first is **social cognition**. We can define this as the study of how we perceive, think about and interpret the actions of both ourselves and others. It is the mixing of cognitive aspects – thinking, perceiving, etc. – with the social activities of two or more of the same species.
- The second main topic area is **social relationships**. This is the study of the way we form, maintain and break up interpersonal relationships.
- The third topic is **social influence**. We discuss issues such as conformity and obedience, social power, leadership and aspects of group activity.
- Finally, in the fourth part of the unit, we look at **pro- and antisocial behaviour**. Why do people help each other? Why are some aggressive? What influences this and how do individuals differ in terms of pro- and antisocial behaviour?

We conclude the unit with a brief look at the relatively new area of **social constructionism**.

Something to do

- At the start of this unit (and all subsequent units), practise your study skills by doing the following three tasks:
    1. Make a contents list for your notes. If you are working towards an examination, use syllabus headings in your contents. Remember to add book page numbers as well.
    2. Start a 'word list'. Do this by writing down all terms that are new to you. Add a definition of the terms either as you write the word or later.
    3. Start a 'people list'. Do this by listing significant people/theorists/researchers, and adding a brief note about them.

- Review your word lists and your people lists frequently.

Social cognition

Here we are concerned with how cognition relates to social cognition. **Social cognition** deals with two main areas:

- the influence of social factors on perception; and
- attribution theory.

We also look at stereotypes, prejudice and discrimination; and include a brief discussion of personality.

Historical perspective

Before we get into the detail of the above areas, we take a brief look at the history of social psychology and see how it has evolved.

Early theories in social psychology were based mainly on the dominant paradigm of **behaviourism** (see Unit 2, pages 33–4). This was in the 1920s and 1930s when behaviourism was at its most influential, with the work of Pavlov, Skinner, Thorndike and others providing the theoretical base. The underlying theory was that of **reinforcement**: if you do something and it is 'rewarded' you will do it again. Later behaviourists, such as Bandura, modified the original and somewhat simplistic view by suggesting that, in addition to rewards, a person's beliefs and values, even feelings, needed to be taken into account to explain behaviour. One view is concerned with **interpersonal attraction** – we like those who 'reward' us; while in **social exchange theory** we weigh up the rewards and costs of a situation. Influence from **learning theory** has also modified behaviourism to suggest that an element of social modelling takes place – where we imitate the behaviour of others whom we like.

From this background of behaviourism emerged a change of emphasis. People began to be seen not just as a system responding to a stimulus or to a reward, but as having an involvement at an intellectual, or cognitive, level. As a result, in both psychology in the widest sense and in social psychology in a particular sense, **cognitive theories** began to modify and indeed replace behavioural theories. This shift in emphasis started in the 1930s with the rise of **Gestalt psychology** and the work of Kurt Koffka and Wolfgang Kohler. Koffka and Kohler were both assistants to Max Wertheimer, whose original work was to open the door to a fresh understanding of perception and the way that illusion occurs in the mind. Wertheimer used the German word 'Gestalt' (meaning 'shape' or 'form') to describe this form of perception (we see more of this in Unit 4).

Building on this early work, Kurt Lewin in the early 1950s developed **field theory**, which deals with cognitive representations of social situations. From this came **cognitive consistency theories**, meaning that people seek to resolve cognitive conflict within themselves – Aronson (1984), for example, uses this to explain how people can change their attitude in a given situation. This in turn led to the development of **attribution theory**, which is how we explain the causes of our own and others' behaviour. (We look at attribution theory in more detail later in the unit.)

Think about it

- Think back to a time when you found yourself in a new social situation. It may be the first meeting of your psychology class, your first time in the students' common-room, or some such similar situation.
- What impressions did you form of the people you were with? How did your teacher appear to you, and what about the other students? As you entered the common-room for the first time, how did you feel? What impressions did you make of the student body? What do you think they made of you?

The influence of social factors on perception

In all of these personal experiences you will have made or formed an impression of others, and others will have formed an impression of you. The process that you went through is one of **interpersonal perception**. Most research shows that first impressions do make a difference. Not surprisingly, the factors that seem to make the most difference are attractiveness, in both men and women and, in men, height. In general terms, people who are attractive are often assumed to have other positive characteristics such as being kind and likeable and more intelligent. Greater height in men is usually associated with authority and leadership; one study found a positive correlation between height and salary of male graduates – the taller you were the more you got paid. On the negative side, it has been found that in the case of women physical attractiveness can be a disadvantage, as some attribute the success of attractive women to their attractiveness – in other words, implying that their success is more to do with sexual issues than with intelligence or hard work.

Something to do

- The next few times that you meet someone new, carefully analyse your response in terms of the above discussion.

There is at this point a general principle in operation – the **primacy–recency effect**. This is a phenomenon that occurs in a number of areas of psychology; for example, in recalling a list of previously presented items or words, the first few and the last few will be remembered better than those in the middle (see Unit 4, pages 165–6 for a detailed explanation). In social psychology, information about a person that is perceived first will have a greater impact than information perceived later – lending weight to the well-known adage 'first impressions count'. This demonstrates the **primacy effect**.

A classic case of the primacy–recency effect

A study by Luchins (1957) involved the participants reading two versions of the same description of a fictitious person 'Jim'. In one version the personal attributes of 'Jim' were listed so that the 'friendly' ones came first, the 'unfriendly' ones later. In the other version, the personal attributes were the other way round. The **primacy effect** was evident in about 75 per cent of responses.

In a second part to the same study, Luchins found that by allowing time to elapse between presenting the paragraphs and asking the participants to assess 'Jim', the later information was more likely to be taken into account. This provided evidence for the **recency effect**.

Cultural differences in perception

As we talk about impression formation, one very important aspect is the influence that a person's **culture** can exert. We are often unaware of our own culture until we experience another culture at first hand. A British person on their first visit to the USA, for example, will see people driving on the 'wrong' side of the road or doing 'strange things' with their knives and forks when eating; or when visiting Japan for the first time, will find it 'very strange' being asked to take their shoes off when entering the house. What we are talking about are the normal rules that have evolved in a given society, but which are not common across all societies. It is interesting to note that these are learned rules and have no connection with genetic transmission.

Cultural norms are the accepted rules or standards of any one society that enable its members to go about their everyday business with the minimum confusion or misunderstanding. Problems start to occur only when people move between cultures without being properly prepared. Do you shake your Russian visitor's hand or kiss her on the cheek? And who makes the first move? Do I take my Japanese hosts a present? If I do, what should it be – or not be? How do I respond when the American visitor comments that our six-month-old son is a 'cute little bugger'? Clashes can occur in language, expressiveness, lifestyle, the speed with which we live our lives and even personal space. Genuine misunderstandings are all too easily taken as a personal affront. One of the goals of social psychology is to provide a greater understanding of the issues surrounding society and cultural differences.

Think about it

- Until relatively recently, social psychology has been almost entirely European or American. What does this mean in terms of cultural issues?

Self perception

What we are talking about when we consider **self perception** is the theoretical point of view that a person's attitudes and beliefs are determined by the person observing their own behaviour. In other words, attitudes follow behaviour. This, of course, implies that if we can change our behaviour then, as a consequence, our attitudes will also change.

Another way to assess your 'self' is to consider how others see you. This concept was formulated by Cooley in the early 1900s and is called the **looking-glass self**. In other words, you form a self image as a result of observing the attitudes which others have towards you. Cooley's input was significant in the sense that it came at a time when social psychology – at least in modern terms – was in its infancy. While an interesting concept, it suffered from a lack of empirical support.

A related issue to self perception is **self esteem**. However you establish a perception of your 'self' – whether by evaluating your own behaviour or by observing the attitudes of others towards you – you will then make a value judgement, which is the degree to which you value your 'self'. You can value yourself highly – high self esteem; or you can have a low opinion or value of yourself and consequently suffer from low self esteem. The level of a person's self esteem is not an abstract measure that has little relevance; in fact it has a significant bearing on a number of social psychological issues.

Carl Rogers argued that we all develop a need for positive self esteem. Our own self esteem first comes from the esteem in which others hold us, initially of course our parents. Parents do this by showing the child what Rogers termed **unconditional positive regard**, accepting the child as having worth irrespective of the child's behaviour. This is not a unique view: Festinger (1954), working in the area of social identity, concluded that people compare themselves with others (**social comparison theory**) in order to obtain a positive evaluation of themselves. This view goes some way to explaining juvenile delinquency. If we need positive self regard, and we don't get this from family, school or other significant structures, then the young person will look to their peer group for approval. Delinquency is usually a group activity, happening in public, which can provide the young person with a considerable degree of approval (Emler et al., 1987).

A classic case of self esteem

In a significant study conducted in America, Coopersmith (1968) studied the self esteem of 10–12-year-old boys. The boys were all considered to be normal, healthy individuals from middle-class families. Coopersmith grouped the boys into one of three groups: low, medium or high self esteem. He did this using self-report data, evaluations from the boys' teachers and data from personality tests. There were two main groups of findings:

- First, Coopersmith found that levels of self esteem correlated with other aspects, thus high self esteem correlated positively with successful, active, confident boys; and low self esteem correlated with poor levels of success, a degree of insecurity and, interestingly, poor physical fitness.
- The second main finding was that there was a positive correlation between the boys' self esteem and their parents' attitudes and behaviour. Boys who had high self esteem had parents who were strict, interested and had high expectations; whereas boys with low self esteem had parents with minimal expectations and who were less involved with their children.

The Coopersmith inventory is given opposite.

The Coopersmith self-esteem inventory

N.B. The key on the left and crosses in answers should be excluded when the inventory is presented to subjects; they are used for scoring.

If a statement describes how you usually feel, put a cross (✗) in the column 'like me'. If the statement does not describe how you usually feel, put a cross (✗) in the column 'unlike me'. There are no right or wrong answers. Mark every statement.

			like me	unlike me
GS	1.	I spend a lot of time day dreaming		✗
GS	2.	I'm pretty sure of myself	✗	
GS	3.	I often wish I were someone else		✗
SSP	4.	I'm easy to like	✗	
HP	5.	My parents and I have a lot of fun together	✗	
L	6.	I never worry about anything		
SA	7.	I find it hard to talk in front of the class		✗
GS	8.	I wish I were younger		✗
GS	9.	There are lots of things I would change about myself if I could		✗
GS	10.	I can make up my mind without too much trouble	✗	
SSP	11.	I'm a lot of fun to be with	✗	
HP	12.	I get easily upset at home		✗
L	13.	I always do the right thing		
SA	14.	I'm proud of my school work	✗	
GS	15.	Someone always has to tell me what to do		✗
GS	16.	It takes me a long time to get used to anything new		✗
GS	17.	I'm often sorry for the things that I do		✗
SSP	18.	I'm popular with kids of my own age	✗	
HP	19.	My parents usually consider my feelings	✗	
L	20.	I'm never unhappy		
SA	21.	I'm doing the best work I can	✗	
GS	22.	I give in very easily		✗
GS	23.	I can usually take care of myself	✗	
GS	24.	I'm pretty happy	✗	
SSP	25.	I would rather play with children younger than me		✗
HP	26.	My parents expect too much of me		✗
L	27.	I like everyone I know		
SA	28.	I like to be called on in class	✗	
GS	29.	I understand myself	✗	
GS	30.	It's pretty tough to be me		✗
GS	31.	Things are all mixed up in my life		✗
SSP	32.	Kids usually follow my ideas	✗	
HP	33.	No one pays much attention to me at home		✗
L	34.	I never get scolded		✗
SA	35.	I'm not doing as well at school as I'd like to		✗
GS	36.	I can make up my mind and stick to it	✗	
GS	37.	I really don't like being a boy/girl		✗
GS	38.	I have a low opinion of myself		✗
SSP	39.	I don't like to be with other people		✗
HP	40.	There are many times when I'd like to leave home		✗
L	41.	I'm never shy		
SA	42.	I often feel upset at school		✗
GS	43.	I often feel ashamed of myself		✗
GS	44.	I'm not as nice-looking as most people		✗
GS	45.	If I have something to say I usually say it	✗	
SSP	46.	Kids pick on me often		✗
HP	47.	My parents understand me	✗	
L	48.	I always tell the truth		
SA	49.	My teacher makes me feel I'm not good enough		✗
SA	50.	I don't care what happens to me		✗
GS	51.	I'm a failure		✗
GS	52.	I get easily upset when I'm scolded		✗
SSP	53.	Most people are better liked than I am		✗
HP	54.	I usually feel as if my parents are pushing me		✗
L	55.	I always know what to say to people		
SA	56.	I often get discouraged at school		✗
GS	57.	Things don't usually bother me	✗	
GS	58.	I can't be depended on		✗

Scoring an '✗' to match the crosses here indicates a score of 2 points. This adds up to 100 points as items on the lie scale are excluded.

Scores:
over 75: high
25–75: medium
under 25: low self esteem

Items measure general self (GS), social self/peers (SSP), home/parents (HP), school/academic (SA) and lie scale.

Source: Coopersmith, S. *The Antecedent of Self-Esteem* (W. H. Freeman and Company, USA, 1967)

The general conclusions that we can draw concerning self esteem are that high-level or positive self esteem is important to good physical and psychological health and that the process of developing good self esteem starts early in childhood.

Cultural identity What we are concerned with here is the relationship between culture and identity and how different cultures see the 'self'. The discussion centres on the degree to which a given culture practises an **individualistic** or a **collectivistic** view of itself (see the table below). Polarising this dichotomy, modern America is at the individualistic end, while rural Asia is at the collectivistic end. While this is true nationally, and we can describe whole nations as being at one extreme or the other, obviously individuals vary and it is quite possible for an American to be a collectivist and for an Asian to be an individualist.

The main differences between individualism and collectivism are summarised below.

A comparison between individualism and collectivism		
	Individualism	**Collectivism**
View of 'self'	Independent	Interdependent
Morality	Defined by the individual – based on self	Defined by social network – based on duty
Relationships	Many, often short-term	Few, usually close and long-lasting
	Disagreement acceptable	Harmony preferred
Behaviour	Reflects the individual's beliefs and attitudes	Reflects the society's roles
What is important	'I am.'	'We are.'
	Personal achievement	Social/group/family relationships
	My rights	

Source: Triandis (1994)

Think about it

- How do you see yourself? Are you an individual in the sense that you don't need all the social structures – family, work, etc. – to help you to maintain your identity; or would you find your existence very difficult if you were on your own and did not have family, work and all the other social structures, which form part of your lifestyle, close at hand?

The difference between the two systems does not imply a value judgement. We cannot say that one is better than the other, because in both cases individuals have grown up within that system and have not chosen which to be.

There almost certainly will have been a form of natural selection taking place, particularly in the case of America, a country populated by individuals who were excited about the possibilities of the 'New World'. (The family, friends and social structure in which the early settlers grew up would have been much more collectivist than the world to which they were going.)

Think about it

- Is the society of which you are a part changing in the terms discussed above?
- Interview older people and young people and compare their answers.

Social identity theory

Here we are concerned with social identity as opposed to cultural identity. Think for a moment of the friends that you have. What are they like? Why are these particular people your friends while others are not? How do you feel when you are in their company? It is questions like these that **social identity theory** seeks to explain.

Social identity theory is a relatively simple concept that says that you will seek out others – as friends, partners or just to be with – that are like you. The reason that you do this is because being with someone with similar tastes and interests makes you feel good; it enhances your self esteem.

If you think of your friends, you will probably find that they fall naturally into groups: sports teams, people you study or work with, and so on. All of these group relationships influence part of your self concept or social identity. Another part of self concept comes from personal identity, which has to do with your own personality traits and personal – rather than group – relationships. It is important to note that the value you place on a given social group or identity can change. For example, the group with which you play sport may change as the team improves (or gets worse) and you may move your 'membership'. Similarly, you may change your job and lose one group but gain – at least the potential for – another group.

Social identity theory overlaps the study of group behaviour, which we discuss in a later section (see page 104).

Social representation

This topic is related to the above discussion in that **social representation** is concerned with the way in which society has certain beliefs and views that are common to the majority of that society or major groupings within it. A key theorist in this field is Moscovici who, with others, has written extensively (see Moscovici, 1984, in the bibliography).

Taking it as given that you are an ordinary member of your society, where have you got your understanding of your society's values, norms, customs and behaviours from? Social representation theory would answer this question by saying from consensual understanding acquired by informal everyday experiences. It is the social interaction that is occurring most of the time as we go about our daily routines – working, playing, reading the papers, watching television, 'socialising' – that forms our ideas, opinions and understanding. We may have our own opinions and understanding of specific issues, but we have also formed certain reactions that are common to the society of which we are a part.

For example, in the UK, people greet each other with the phrase, 'Good morning, how are you?' and respond, 'Fine, thank you' when in fact they may feel terrible.

This is an example of the split or difference between European and American social psychology. The idea of the influence of society on the shaping of the individual comes initially from the French sociologist Emile Durkheim. The American emphasis is on the derivation of principles from the study of the individual. This is partly historical and stems from the great variety of people and races who came to America seeking their fortune; and is also partly due to a lack of social class structures and, perhaps as a consequence, the American idea of the worth of the individual.

Attribution theory

Attribution theory, still within the area of social cognition or perception, is specifically concerned with the way a person attributes certain traits or characteristics to him- or herself or to another. We all do this all the time in an effort to 'make sense' of what is happening around us, and humans have undoubtedly done so since time began.

Modern understanding of this aspect of social psychology can be seen in the Gestalt idea that we use past experience to deal with and understand new experiences. More modern theory has developed from the work of Fritz Heider in the 1920s and his understanding of **attribution of causality**. Heider, a European social psychologist working in America, first proposed the concept of 'attribution' in 1927. He pushed Gestalt views into the area of social psychology. For example, in **balance theory**, Heider (1958) says that we are motivated to maintain a balance, or state of harmony, between our beliefs and our perceptions of others. If these 'balance', then all is well; but if they do not, then a state of imbalance exists and the relationship becomes difficult. This is particularly so if the imbalance concerns a major issue between friends.

Before we look at the various theories that seek to explain the attribution process, there are two other concepts that we need to consider, both coming from the work of Heider. Heider argued that we analyse our own and other people's behaviour all the time, and try to determine the cause of a given behaviour. If we can understand the cause of a certain behaviour, then we are (up to a point) in the position of being able to predict the possibility of an event occurring and also of being able (again, up to a point) to control the event. For example, if a teacher sets a particularly difficult piece of homework (the cause), the teacher can predict that at least some of the class will be unable to complete the work. To control the situation, the teacher could set work at different standards for different members of the group.

Heider further argued that there are two questions that people ask when they are attempting to make attributions:

- Is the cause of the behaviour found within the person exhibiting the behaviour? (**internal causality**) or
- Is the cause found in the social context? (**external causality**)

The first question is sometimes referred to as **dispositional attribution**, while the second is sometimes referred to as **situational attribution**. Both are concerned with the **locus of cause**, or where we locate the cause of the behaviours. Let us suppose, for example, that you see across the busy students' common-room a student give another student a violent push in the back. Are they having an argument? That is the interpretation, or the attribution, that you are making. What you didn't see was that one student had stumbled over a bag that was on the floor and was simply trying to stop himself falling. Another, more serious, example is something that we all too frequently read about in the newspapers. A husband drinks too much and beats his wife. She fears for her life and kills him. In court, the defence argues that she acted in self defence, the prosecution that it is premeditated murder. The problem the jury then faces is a question of attribution.

Attribution theories There are a number of theories that seek to explain the attribution process. We deal with them in chronological order.

Something to do

• Redraw the summary chart on page 73 and add a short evaluation of each of the theories as you read about them.

The naive psychologist (Heider, 1958) Another aspect of Heider's work concerns the importance of what he called commonsense psychological theories. Heider argued that people have their own theories to explain behaviour, which in turn influence behaviour – they are in fact **naive scientists**. While they follow a simple scientific process, they are for the most part acting intuitively.

One of the main reasons for the development of Heider's naive psychology theory of attribution was the observation that we believe our own behaviour is motivated and so we attribute causes to the behaviour of others.

A classic case of attribution

Heider and Simmel (1944) showed that people will attribute human behaviour and causes to moving geometric shapes. In their study, participants saw circles and triangles moving around on a screen and almost always gave causal reasons to the movements: 'The large triangle is chasing the circle', 'The two triangles are competing for the circle' and other such causalities. This showed that we infer personal characteristics to situations that clearly do not have them.

Correspondent inference theory (Jones and Davis, 1965) In this theory, people infer that the observed behaviour corresponds to the person's general character. We infer that someone who is friendly to us when we first meet at a party has a friendly character – that is, is going to be friendly most of the time. We like it when this happens because that person's behaviour is predictable.

Covariation theory (Kelley, 1967 and 1973) There are some similarities between Kelley and Heider, in that Kelley also believes that people act like scientists when trying to make attributions. Kelley argues that people will analyse the behaviour and try to link – or 'co-vary' – other factors with it. This means that the two variables, behaviour and its cause, are linked in such a way that they vary (or change) in step with each other. So, for example, a certain behaviour may be linked to, and therefore vary with, a certain aspect of personality.

Kelley argues that we make this link by assessing the behaviour and its cause, and that we group the causal behaviour into three general classes:

- **Consistency:** Has the person always behaved in this way (high consistency) or only sometimes?
- **Distinctiveness:** Does the person behave this way in response to just one specific cause (high distinctiveness) or to all other similar kinds of cause?
- **Consensus:** Does everyone react to the cause in the same way (high consensus) or only that person?

Depending on the degree of the perceived existence of any or all of the above three classes, we will attribute cause to internal or external causality (see page 70). This is presented in schematic form as follows:

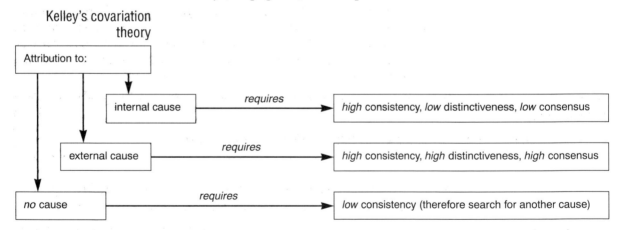

Kelley's covariation theory

Attribution to:

internal cause —*requires*→ *high* consistency, *low* distinctiveness, *low* consensus

external cause —*requires*→ *high* consistency, *high* distinctiveness, *high* consensus

no cause —*requires*→ *low* consistency (therefore search for another cause)

There have been a number of criticisms of this theory, all to the effect that to attribute behaviour in this way requires complex, even multiple, observations to ascertain the degree to which the three classes – consistency, distinctiveness and consensus – are present.

To overcome this, Kelley (1973) introduced the idea of **causal schema**. This means that you develop, over time and with experience, a schema of how a certain cause creates a certain behaviour. For example, a student might, over time, develop different causal schemas for different teachers. Teacher A will respond to late work with an extension of time, while Teacher B will always give a detention.

The stable/unstable dimension (Weiner et al., 1974 and 1986) Weiner et al. concluded that as well as making attributions about internal or external causes, people's attribution is also influenced by the stability of the cause. As a result, Weiner et al. suggested, there is an element of stability/unstability as well as internal or external causation. These four elements allow us to construct a two-by-two matrix, giving four types of attribution, as follows:

Weiner et al.'s theory of attribution

		Stable cause	Unstable cause
Internal cause		Ability Intelligence	Effort Mood Fatigue
External cause		Task difficulty	Luck Chance Opportunity

Source: Weiten (1972)

In this theory, Weiner et al. argue that people explain success or failure in terms of both stable or unstable elements, and internal or external causes. This is illustrated in the following example of selection for, say, a cricket team:

- You were picked for the team because you are a good player (internal–stable) or because you put in lots of extra training (internal–unstable). Or you were not picked for the team because there were too many other good players (external–stable) or because you had a row with the captain (external–unstable).

Think about it
- Think of another example of the use of Weiner et al.'s two-by-two matrix.

A little later Weiner added the further dimension of **controllability** to his model, thus doubling the number of possible attributional causes.

Summary of attribution theories		
Theorist	**Date**	**Known as/description**
1. Heider	1958	The naive psychologist
2. Jones and Davis	1965	Correspondent inference theory
3. Kelley	1967, 1973	Covariation theory
4. Weiner et al.	1974, 1986	Stable/unstable dimension

Attribution errors   In this and the following section we deal with errors and biases in the attribution process. It is not always easy to separate an error from a bias; but we can say that attribution errors are to do with the ways in which behaviour can be misinterpreted, while attribution biases are to do with who or what gets the blame. The **fundamental attribution error** (Ross, 1977) says that we are more likely to attribute someone else's behaviour to internal factors – for example, choice – than to external factors. It seems that we tend to overfocus on a person's behaviour and pay too little attention to the social context in which the behaviour occurs.

If we turn this around and consider how we attribute the cause of our own behaviour, the evidence suggests that we are more likely than an observer to attribute the cause to an external factor.

Attribution biases   One of the classic attribution biases is the **self-serving bias**. This occurs when we start to attribute our own success or failure in a given situation, tending to attribute our success to internal factors and our failure to external (or situation) factors.

Another bias is concerned with attribution in situations of misfortune. In these conditions the observer is even more likely to make internal attributions, tending to blame the victim for their own misfortune. This tendency is called the **defensive attribution**. Without it, we are faced with the possibility that the misfortune may happen to us.

Stereotypes, prejudice and discrimination

We often find it difficult to understand the precise differences between stereotyping, prejudice and discrimination. We need to consider their definitions and to look at the way in which they relate to each other.

Stereotyping   In simple terms, **stereotypes** are overgeneralisations about the members of a group of people held by members of another group. We usually think of stereotypes in negative terms, but it is possible also to stereotype in neutral or positive terms. There is a huge and continuing literature on stereotyping, the earliest contributor being Lippman (1922).

Key points concerning stereotyping include the following:

- There is a willingness to label groups of people with a few common attributes.
- These labels or generalisations remain for long periods of time.
- They change slowly, much as areas such as economics and politics change over long periods.
- They become more pronounced when groups become hostile.
- Children learn the labels and use them before they understand them.
- The labels or generalisations are difficult to modify.

Stereotyping inevitably follows the very human activity of putting people into categories, which we do in an attempt to simplify our world. The problem comes when we add to the categorisation value judgements about the person or group of people – in other words, when we make prejudiced stereotypes – as this leads quickly into discrimination. The psychological difference between the simple categorisation and the prejudiced stereotype is an increased emphasis on the differences between the stereotyped person or group and other groups. This distinction happens first because the issue has emotional relevance to the person concerned; and secondly because of the relative permanence, or resistance to change, of these differences.

<u>Prejudice</u>   The word 'prejudice' comes from the idea that we 'prejudge' someone or something and as a result end up with the wrong attitude about that person or thing. While the term is almost always used in a negative sense, technically it is possible to have a positive prejudice. In the sense that we are using the term here, we can define **prejudice** as a negative attitude that people in one group hold towards people in another group. As an attitude, it has cognitive, affective and behavioural components. For example, in the case of ageism, a young manager may not hire an older person because she thinks (cognitive) that he is too old for the job. She doesn't like (affective) old people and so refuses to interview (behavioural) the older applicant.

Prejudice can take many different forms. Racial prejudice is probably the most evident, but other forms are also common. Women, older people, homosexuals, people with mental or physical disabilities and other minority groups may all be victims of prejudice.

It is one thing to hold a certain – prejudicial – attitude towards another. If this attitude leads to behaving differently towards others, however, then we are talking about discrimination.

<u>Discrimination</u>   In a technical sense, **discrimination** means the ability to see the differences between various inputs or stimuli. In social psychology – in the context in which we are using the term – it refers to the unequal treatment of individuals or groups, usually but not always with a negative connotation. The relationship between prejudice and discrimination is shown diagrammatically below.

The relationship between prejudice and discrimination

		Prejudice	
		Absent	**Present**
Discrimination	**Absent**	No relevant behaviour	A restaurant owner who is bigoted against gays, treats them fairly because he or she needs their business.
	Present	A manager with neutral attitudes towards race doesn't hire black or Asian people because he or she would get into trouble with his or her boss.	A male teacher who is hostile towards women marks his female students unfairly.

Source: Weiten (1994)

In the two shaded cells, attitude and behaviour coincide; in the other two cells, there is a disparity between attitude and behaviour.

Explanations of prejudice

There are a number of theories, or explanations, for the existence and maintenance of prejudice. They can be divided into two main groups: those that are based on issues of **personality** and those that can be considered as **social psychological theories**.

<u>Innate component</u>   One of the earliest explanations, popular at the end of the 19th century and in the early decades of the 20th century, considered prejudice to be an innate or instinctive characteristic of human beings. Animals behave in this way and so, it was argued, do higher forms of animals – that is, humans. While this view has little empirical support, there is evidence that a small part of prejudice may be innate, although the fact that prejudice can increase or decrease as we develop seems to link it more to environmental than to genetic factors. For example, Zajonc (1968) found that the attitudes that people have towards each other improve with exposure to each other.

<u>Learned prejudice</u>   A second theory was proposed by Tajfel (1919–82). He argued that prejudice is learned at an early age, usually before the child understands anything about the society and culture of which it is a part. The learning occurs as the child observes its parents and their attitudes and behaviour and models itself accordingly. In some cases the child may even be actively encouraged to behave in a prejudicial way.

<u>Frustration–aggression</u>   A third form of prejudice was proposed by Dollard (1939). He studied the anti-Semitic behaviour in Germany prior to the Second World War, and as a result developed the **frustration–aggression hypothesis**. Strongly psychodynamic in nature, it argues that if your personal goals are frustrated you will become aggressive. If you are unable to express your frustration and the resulting aggression because, for example, the object of your frustration is too powerful, then you will seek a less powerful target against which to relieve the frustration. You have in effect displaced your frustration onto a scapegoat. Later research has suggested that the process is more complex than the simple frustration–aggression prejudice model.

<u>Authoritarian personality</u>   This major theory, proposed by Adorno (1950), is dependent on the person's personality. In this theory it is argued that some people are of such a personality that they are prejudiced against all minority groups – it is their personality not the group that is at the root of the prejudice. Like Dollard, Adorno also studied aspects of the Second World War. He concluded that much of the Nazi behaviour that led to the Holocaust could only be explained by an extreme type of authoritarian personality. Characteristics of this type of person include respect for authority, intolerance of those who are weak, extreme views of rank and power, and other related issues all usually taken to an extreme.

<u>Closed-mind theory</u>   This is another personality-based theory, and can be considered as similar to – perhaps even an extension of – the authoritarian view discussed above. Rokeach (1960) argued that, while the authoritarian personality certainly exists, there also exists a broader type of authoritarianism. This is described as the **closed mind**, and involves wider aspects of prejudice. The 'closed-mind' personality tends to stick with old-fashioned ideas, vigorously resists change despite the evidence,

and also is strongly authoritarian. As a theory, the closed-mind view places too much emphasis on the individual's personality and too little on the influence of social and cultural aspects of prejudice.

Theories of prejudice	
Theory/Theorist	**Description**
1. Innate component/Zajonc	Reduces over time with exposure.
2. Learned/Tajfel	Usually learned at an early age.
3. Frustration–aggression/Dollard	When our goals are frustrated we become aggressive.
4. Authoritarian personality/Adorno	Some people have an authoritarian personality and are prejudiced against all minority groups.
5. Closed-mind/Rokeach	A general intolerance of others.

The following two major studies demonstrate the way that prejudice can quickly form, take hold, become violent and abate, depending on influences and circumstances.

A classic case of prejudice

The brown eyes / blue eyes study (Elliott, 1977)

In this now classic study, Jane Elliott – who taught ten-year-old children in America – wanted the children to try to understand how it felt to be the victim of prejudice and discrimination. Her school was in a rural situation; the children were all white.

On the first day of her study, Elliott designated all the brown-eyed children as 'superior' and all the blue-eyed children as 'inferior', the two categories being arbitrary and having no basis in truth. The 'superior' children were given special privileges, while the 'inferior' children had to obey new rules that emphasised their inferiority. Within one school day, the blue-eyed children's school performance had deteriorated, the children became withdrawn and angry; while within the same time the brown-eyed children had begun to treat them as inferior, they looked down on the blue-eyed children and stopped playing with them. The next day Elliott told the children that she had made a mistake, and that it was in fact the blue-eyed children who were superior and the brown-eyed children who were inferior. Behaviour immediately reversed as the children changed their superior/inferior roles.

The study shows that all that is needed for prejudice and the resulting discrimination is the division of people into categories of in-groups and out-groups.

Another classic case of prejudice

The Robber's Cave study (Sherif, 1966)
In this famous study conducted by Sherif at the Robber's Cave State Park in Oklahoma, 22 white middle-class boys attended a two-week summer camp. The boys were randomly divided into two groups and called themselves the 'Eagles' and the 'Rattlers'. Competitions were organised between the two groups, with valuable prizes for the winning group.

As the first week progressed, competition turned into prejudice, with strong in-group and out-group tension, often resulting in fights and the destruction of the other group's property.

Having established a significant degree of prejudice and hostility between groups within the first week, the second part of the study concentrated on the reduction of prejudice. This was achieved by setting up a situation where the bus on which both groups were travelling for a much anticipated day out was arranged to 'break down'. The only solution to the problem was for all the boys from both groups to work together to push the bus. The experiment required both groups to work together, otherwise neither group would experience success (which they eventually did).

Think about it

• How would you categorise the approach of the above two studies in terms of social psychology theory?

The reduction of prejudice and discrimination

We have argued that there are two main approaches to explaining the cause of prejudice: one focusing on personality, the other on social psychological issues. It follows that in order to reduce prejudice and discrimination and the risk of conflict, any solution must first recognise the cause. In other words, knowing why something is wrong helps to put it right.

In the case of prejudice caused by a certain personality type, the solution – or means of reducing the prejudice – traditionally lies in education. The assumption is made (itself a pretty large assumption) that the cause of the personality problem is based, at least in part, on ignorance. If we can educate children, particularly young children, about prejudice, how it 'works' and how it feels, then there is less chance that those children will grow up with distorted and bigoted views of other groups. This, of course, is what Jane Elliott was attempting to do with her 'brown eyes / blue eyes' experiment. It is important to note that we are talking here about formal education – the kind that takes place in the classroom at school. While this has been shown to have made a difference, it ignores the influence of the informal education that goes on in the home, for example from bigoted parents or being the victim of prejudice.

Something to do

• Construct a chart with theories of prejudice on the left, and then fill in the right as we discuss possible ways to reduce prejudice. Use an adaptation of the chart on page 77 as a base.

Another experiment, also conducted in America, was known as the **jigsaw classroom**. The jigsaw classroom was set up in Texas following the desegregation of schools, in an attempt to reduce the prejudice between whites and blacks. Rather than showing children what prejudice was all about, as in the Elliott study, this study attempted to reduce existing prejudice. It aimed to do this not by education (even though the work was conducted in an educational context) but by co-operation through the setting of superordinate goals. This is sometimes called the **superordinate method** as it relies on both the in-group and the out-group co-operating to achieve a (superordinate) goal that neither group could achieve without the assistance of the other. (Sherif, in his Robber's Cave study, also set superordinate goals: working together when the bus 'broke down' was one; in another, it was 'arranged' for the camp water supply to dry up – only by both groups working together could the water be restored.)

In the jigsaw classroom, the 'jigsaw' came from the way in which co-operation in learning was required to achieve the goal. The children were divided into small groups, each group a mixture of blacks and whites; and each individual learned a part of a topic and then had to share this learning with the other members of the group. Marks were awarded on the basis of how much the individual knew about the whole topic, which obviously depended on how well the group worked together.

In general, this approach does succeed in reducing prejudice, but the results from these and other studies are somewhat variable, particularly if the common goal is not fully achieved.

Another method to reduce prejudice is for the groups concerned to get together and try to find ways forward simply by talking, perhaps using arbitration or negotiation. This social contact was first discovered by Allport (1954), who called it the **contact hypothesis**. It holds that the more contact there is between individuals and groups, the less prejudice there will be. An extension of this approach is **decategorisation**. This is a deliberate attempt to reduce the distinctiveness of the groups, whereby people in the groups start to consider other people first as individuals rather than as members of a specific group.

No one of the approaches discussed above is the answer to reducing prejudice. In general, methods which bring people into contact with each other, which provide a common goal and which allow people to interact as individuals show the most promise of effectively reducing prejudice.

Social relationships

As you work through the material in this section, you will see that just about everything you do involves some sort of **social relationship**.

Think about it

- Can you think of things that you do that do not involve a social 'relationship'? Make a list.

If relationships of one sort or another are a major part of our existence, the fairly obvious question to ask is: why do we make the relationships that we do? Think back to a time when you 'made friends' with someone. How did the relationship start? Why were you attracted to this person? Why did you sit where you did, or talk to who you talked to in a new class or in some other social setting?

Most theorists suggest that the answer to this sort of question hinges on the effect that the other person has on us. Their presence, or influence, causes a reaction within us and we respond to it. We are interested, perhaps intrigued, and so we respond and make a move towards them. We offer to show them where the cafeteria is or something similar. A relationship has begun to form. You have probably had hundreds of such relationships – you probably didn't even consider them as relationships, you were just being kind or helpful – but only a small number of these have developed into more lasting relationships. The relationship so far is in fact little more than a stimulus–response reaction. If, however, you enjoy the company of the new person in the class, you may arrange to meet in the cafeteria for lunch every day; or perhaps you find you have a common interest in sport and arrange to play, say, squash once or twice a week. Now the relationship is changing and is becoming much more *personal* than the initial purely *social* relationship. An important point to consider with respect to this developing relationship is the question of the sex of the two parties. What we have described so far can happen perfectly normally between two males, between two females or between a male and a female. All that has happened so far is the beginning of an interpersonal relationship.

Social psychology has long been interested in the way that humans (and animals – see Unit 6 on comparative psychology) relate to each other. The human animal has always wanted to be with others, whether this social grouping is a family, extended family, tribe or larger social community. Within these groups, individuals can **affiliate** with each other, be **attracted** to each other or **love** each other. There are times when people want to be on their own, but these occasions are likely to be rather few. (The study of those experiencing long-term isolation, forced or otherwise, is an interesting topic. Sole survivors of a catastrophe, for example, report experiencing severe stress, with some presenting symptoms of mental illness.) The much more likely situation is that people enjoy the company of others. We simply want to be with others, to affiliate with others.

There have been a number of attempts to explain *why* we need to affiliate. William McDougall (1871–1938), a famous psychologist who worked in the early decades of the 20th century, suggested that it was simply instinct. The behaviourists, emerging at about the same time, disagreed but were unable to come up with a satisfactory answer; while others looked (some are still looking) for a biological explanation.

How the human animal develops relationships is rather better understood.

Attraction

There are a number of reasons why people are attracted towards each other, and thence begin to develop a relationship:

- Probably the most obvious reason is **physical attractiveness**. Almost certainly the first thing you notice when a newcomer joins your class or when you meet someone for the first time is what they look like – their attractiveness to you. While individuals view attractiveness differently, attractiveness is seen by many to be important – that is, it does more for you than simply attract others. Studies by Dipboye et al. (1977) found that more attractive people were more likely to be offered a job following an interview. In an interesting study of couples dating and in long-term relationships, Walster et al. (1966) found that the attractiveness of each partner was similar. This gave rise to what is called the **matching hypothesis**, which holds that there is a significant positive correlation between the attractiveness of the male and the female in an established relationship. In a follow-up study, Murstein (1971) found similar data for married couples.
- A second reason why people become attracted to each other is **proximity**. Quite simply, you are more likely to become attracted to someone who lives nearby, who works in the same office or who plays tennis at the same club, than you are to someone whom you see less frequently. Proximity is part of a cluster which includes **familiarity** and **availability**.
- **Similarity of attitudes and values** is another reason for attraction. Byrne (1971) established a law of attraction which states that a linear relationship exists between attraction and commonality of attitudes.
- Another reason for attraction is **complimentarity**. We are attracted to, or seek out, those who can satisfy our needs. A typical example is the dominant person who is attracted to a submissive person.
- A final reason for attraction is **reciprocity**. We simply like people who like us!

Think about it

- Analyse your friendships in terms of the above reasons for attraction. Is there a common theme?

Theories of attraction

There are several theoretical views of attraction. The behaviourist theories and the cognitive theories are the two main groups; there is also a sociobiological view. Each of the theories is considered below.

Behaviourist theories

At a basic level, we like people who are present with us when we receive a reward. It is a case of classic reinforcement. The reverse is also true. We are likely to dislike people who are present when we are punished.

Social exchange theory   This behaviourist theory argues that we relate to others in terms of 'profit' or 'loss'. Profit represents reward or reinforcement and loss represents punishment or costs. The relationship proceeds if rewards outweigh punishments. It is a somewhat mechanical approach, but it does take into account the fact that both parties influence any outcome. Thibaut and Kelley (1959) suggested that there are four stages in the social exchange theory of a developing relationship:

- **Sampling:**   We 'check out' potential rewards and costs and compare them to other relationships.
- **Bargaining:**   As the relationship starts to develop, we try out giving and receiving rewards to see if the relationship is worth developing.
- **Commitment:**   The first two stages reduce as each party gets to know the other, and attention turns to the relationship itself. The costs decrease as familiarity with the other person increases and the costs involved become more familiar. Understanding increases.
- **Institutionalisation:**   The relationship settles down, the pattern of costs and rewards is known and is predictable.

While this pattern does explain or fit in with many relationships, there are many others where it does not fit and yet the relationship continues. This, of course, is the problem with any theory, particularly when dealing with people – there are always exceptions.

Think about it

- Using relationships that you know (yourself, friends, famous people), jot down the way some of these 'fit' the four stages outlined above and the way some do not.

Equity theory   Another behaviourist theory, **equity theory** in some ways evolved from social exchange theory. It argues that there is more to a relationship than a balance sheet of costs and rewards: the outcome of the balance sheet, or exchange, needs to be fair or just.

Equity theory was proposed by Adams in the 1960s and has been summarised by Walster et al. (1978) as follows:

- Partners will attempt to maximise rewards and minimise punishments.
- Rewards can be different for each partner. Rewards can be adjusted according to a given situation, and compensation agreed.
- A relationship that is not equitable or fair will produce distress in one or both partners.
- When a relationship develops a degree of unfairness, the loser will try to restore the balance. This assumes the loser wishes to restore the balance and is motivated to do so.

Cognitive theory   As you would expect, a cognitive theory of attraction focuses more on the mental aspects of the relationship than the objective or behavioural elements. Fritz Heider (who first proposed the concept of attribution – see page 70) was first to propose a general **balance theory**.

<u>Balance theory</u>   In balance theory it is argued that we like people similar to ourselves because it is easier to agree with such people, and agreeing has positive connotations – good feelings, affirmation and so on. However, when two such people disagree, negative elements occur in the relationship, resulting in a state of imbalance. The restoration of a good – balanced – relationship requires the operation of cognitive processes by either or both parties.

Balance theory also holds that it is unlikely that people with different views or attitudes will form a relationship. The difference will be recognised, at a cognitive level, from the start and so a relationship is unlikely even to begin.

Byrne (1971) argues that we can expect to have some cognitive dissimilarities. This is acceptable in general balance theory, providing that they are a significant minority.

Sociobiological theory   This theory follows the classic sociobiological view that the individual will do its utmost to see that its genes are passed on in the largest numbers to the next generation. As a consequence, a relationship will form in which both the male and the female seek to serve their own biogenetic ends.

Summary of three perspectives on attraction	
Theory	**Evaluation**
Behaviourist Social exchange theory	Definition of costs and rewards is difficult.
Equity theory	Assumes that people make choices based on personal satisfaction.
	Some criticism of methodology, definition of terms, etc.
	Considered by some to apply more in North America than in other societies.
Cognitive Balance theory	Theory only holds for some interactions. Difficulty is knowing which.
	Sometimes being deliberately different is rewarding.
Sociobiological	
	Based on views of animal behaviour.
	Possibly too deterministic.
	Assumes that heterosexuality is the norm.

Something to investigate
• Further develop the evaluation chart above, using other resource material (see guidelines in Unit 1).

Relationships – formation, maintenance and dissolution

Much of the above discussion has been concerned with the early stages of interpersonal relationships, in particular theories of attraction. We now turn our attention to the relationship itself, particularly the long-term relationship, looking at its formation, maintenance and dissolution. This is followed by a discussion of a variety of components that can exist within a relationship.

The formation of relationships

Individual interpersonal behaviour has a large element of reciprocity. We expect something from the other person, who in turn expects something of us, and so on. Most of our actions are in fact reactions. This holds true from birth, when we make our first relationship and first experience the expectation–expectation pattern (Schaffer, 1978). The classic example is the mother feeding her newborn baby. As the child grows and develops, the range of relationships will increase – parents, family, friends, more friends, same sex, opposite sex, and so on. All the time this is happening, the person is relating interpersonally. Long-term relationships, whether marriage or otherwise, usually start to form when the person reaches their early twenties. A long-term relationship may be one that has grown over time between two 'good friends' or it may be marriage (unique in that it involves both the making and giving of vows often in a religious setting, and a legal element) or any relationship that we may consider as an alternative to marriage, involving financial arrangements, parenting, and so on.

<u>Love</u>   Now may be the appropriate time to introduce the topic of **love**, for love obviously has an important bearing on all relationships. It is technically difficult to define: we can go back into classical Greek to find words such as *eros* for erotic love, *philia* for familial love or *agape*, which means a 'selfless giving love'; or we can use the Hatfield and Walster (1981) three-factor model, which suggests that romantic love requires:

- a cultural element: for example, in Western culture, 'falling in love';
- someone to love: in Western society usually an attractive person of the opposite sex;
- emotional arousal: experienced when with – or thinking about – the loved person.

If all these three are present, then the result is romantic love.

In another attempt to explain love, Sternberg (1988) produced a triangular model:

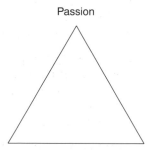

Passion

Commitment   Intimacy

For 'true love', in the traditional and common use of the term, all three need to be present. Other forms of love can exist with only one or two of the three elements – infatuation would have passion but not commitment or intimacy, while romantic love would have passion and intimacy, but no commitment.

There is thought to be another form of love, which long-established relationships and marriages often move into. This is **companionate love** or love that is based more on things such as security, friendship and trust, than on romance or passion.

The maintenance of relationships

Once a relationship – of whatever kind – is established, what forces act to maintain that relationship? Levinger (1980) suggested a model of a relationship that moved through five stages:

1. Acquaintance, which is the initial attraction.
2. Building up the initial relationship by trying out experiences.
3. Consolidation, where the relationship 'settles down' and usually involves commitment.
4. Deterioration, when things start to go wrong.
5. Ending.

In Levinger's stage model, there are no set periods of time for each stage or for between each stage. The model is helpful in that it suggests the order in which the various stages are passed through. Many long-term permanent relationships stop at stage 3 and remain that way until the death of a partner. Stages 4 and 5 are the alternative ending and occur when the relationship is breaking down.

Think about it

- In terms of the maintenance of a relationship, what do you think might be the differences in the maintenance effort needed to sustain a married relationship and that needed to sustain a non-married relationship?
- Make a list of the differences.

The dissolution of relationships

There are two main theories which seek to account for the stages that a long-term relationship will go through as it is breaking up. In this context we are considering a 'normal' breakdown of a relationship, usually over a period of time, and not one where, for example, one party faces a terminal illness, thus bringing the relationship to a forced ending.

Levinger (1980) has suggested that there are likely to be four main factors which indicate that the relationship is in trouble:

- A new lifestyle appears to be the only solution.
- There are other alternative partners available.
- There is a general understanding or expectation that the relationship is failing.
- There is no real commitment to making the relationship work.

An alternative model was proposed by Duck (1988 and 1992). This model is called the **relationship dissolution model** and also has four stages that a failing relationship will pass through. Duck's theory argues that there is a threshold level for each of the stages; when this threshold is reached a series of subsequent behaviours will occur. The process is outlined below.

Duck's relationship dissolution model		
Phase	**Threshold**	**Resulting behaviour**
1. **The intra-psychic phase** Little obvious evidence. Hoping things will get better. Possible involvement of third party.	'I can't take any more.'	Thinking about breaking up. Focus on partner's performance. Weighs up costs of breakdown.
2. **The dyadic phase** 'Something must be done but I'm not leaving yet.' Arguments emerge. Attribution of responsibility.	Justifies withdrawing.	Confrontation or avoidance dilemma. Discussion of problems. Attempts to put things right.
3. **The social phase** Involvement of others for support and assurance. Friends take sides. Allocation of blame.	'This time I mean it.'	Partners discuss *post*-breakdown conditions. Openly involve others. Create face-saving stories.
4. **The grave-dressing phase** Partners know the relationship is over. Financial/childcare arrangements discussed. Partners build own self image with view to future.	Breakdown inevitable.	Starts 'getting over it' activity. Post-relationship attribution. Partners make public their own 'acceptable' version of the break-up.

Valuable though these stage models are, it is important to appreciate that they are very Western in orientation, being particularly appropriate to North American society. Reading them in London or Los Angeles, the various stages, comments and behaviours seem, if not personally familiar, then certainly the sort of things that could well happen. However, to someone from a non-Western culture, the models would have very little in common with their own experience or understanding. Similarly, the models would have had little relevance in Western societies earlier this century.

Think about it

• What other life experience is similar to the breakdown of a long-term relationship?

One answer to the above question is the death of a partner or friend. This is covered in Unit 7 in the section on bereavement (pages 362–4).

Something to do

• Read pages 362–4 on bereavement. Draw up a cross-curricular connection chart listing the similarities and differences between the stages in bereavement and in the breakdown of a long-term relationship.

Components of relationships

The word 'component' has a nuts-and-bolts ring to it, as if we are taking something to bits and ending up with a heap of components. In this section we discuss some of the bits or components that make up a relationship, bearing in mind that each component can have a different impact in different relationships. There is no clearly observable pattern.

Think about it

• Make a list of 'components' in a relationship.

The components discussed below are: goals, rules, roles, power and conflict. Did you have these in your list?

In general terms, social psychology believes that the main determinant of the way an individual behaves is the situation that the individual is in. This can overrule experience, training and even personality. So, as we consider the five components listed above, we need to remember that a given situation can influence the behaviour of an individual more than we think.

Goals   'Goals', as we are using the term here, means that there is an intended aim, or future direction or result, usually agreed by those involved. Reber (1995) points out that it is important not to confuse 'goal' with 'purpose' – goal being the end and external element, while purpose is the internal.

Of the five components, goals probably come first in terms of what happens in a relationship. Two people might plan (set a goal) to get married, to change job, to move house. All of these behaviours have a goal, whether implicit or explicit. The goal sets the direction either for the short term or for the long term: the other components then follow. It may be that both partners agree a goal, set rules, agree who does what in terms of power and what role each has, and there is no conflict. On the other hand, it could be that conflict arises from the first, roles are not clarified, people break the rules and try to exert power over the other.

In a relationship, because it is dynamic and never static, goals are being set all the time. The crucial aspect of this process is the degree of honesty of each partner in their agreement of the goal. If the goal is agreed, then both parties can work together towards achieving it. If, on the other hand, the goal is not agreed or there is a degree of uncertainty – or worse, resentment – then the relationship is heading for trouble. Equally, if the relationship has no goals of any kind, then it will not know where it is going and both parties will introduce their own agendas, which also leads to difficulties.

Rules   Rules can be defined as a set of guidelines, or a code, that tells us how to behave in a given situation. Think of the rules that exist in an institution or workplace that you are a part of. You will almost certainly have rules that are defined for you, perhaps contractually, and unwritten rules that are just as well known and obeyed.

The same applies in a relationship. There are contractual rules as in the case of a marriage; there are formally agreed rules, but perhaps not written; and there are unwritten and unspoken rules that have never been explicitly agreed, but both parties in the relationship are fully aware of them and practise them.

Roles   Roles are all to do with what is expected of someone. There is evidence to suggest that a child's social experience will help it to develop its own social understanding of who does what – for example, pre-school children can understand authority relations within a familiar setting (Laupa and Turiel, 1993).

A role is a socially defined way of behaving. As with rules, certain roles are well understood. For example, a headteacher will behave in a certain way when taking a school assembly, but may behave differently when helping with the lower school camping trip, and differently again when playing golf at the local country club. The role the person plays will depend in part on the person, but in greater part upon the social setting. The general idea is that a person can be expected to behave in a certain way.

Again, the same holds true in a relationship. As the relationship develops over time, each party 'takes on' certain roles. These are sometimes discussed at length, or perhaps argued about, or just evolve naturally. There is no one 'right' way for roles to be developed, each relationship will evolve its own way of relating and of playing these roles. As time goes by or as circumstances change, so an individual role may change, again by agreement with the other party or just by evolution.

Roles will most certainly have to change because a relationship is never static – at the very least it grows older, but it may also have to cope with the birth of children, children growing up and leaving home, and all the other developmental changes that occur in life. If the members in a relationship can cope with these changes and adjust to them, either by arrangement or by implicit means, then the relationship will – or is more likely to – remain stable. If, however, one member or perhaps both are unwilling or unable to change, then the relationship itself becomes threatened.

Power   There are a number of definitions of power, depending on the context, but in social psychology power is usually defined as the control that one person has over one or more others.

In a relationship, power can be expressed in a number of different ways. The most basic is simple physical power. In a heterosexual relationship the man is usually the more powerful and can exert this power in a physically threatening sense if he chooses to do so. The less powerful person in the relationship is powerless to do anything about it. The use of power implies control, and certainly the physically stronger can control the physically weaker.

Physical power is by no means the only power at work in a relationship. A threat of some kind to affect the behaviour of another so that they act out of fear and contrary to what they would normally do is a form of power or control. If, however, in this situation the weaker party seeks to distance themselves *emotionally* from the one attempting to exercise control, there is not a lot the one attempting to control the relationship can do. It is rather like the smaller boy walking away from the playground bully. It can be very effective. This kind of emotional distancing is often at play in a relationship, particularly when the relationship is starting to break down.

A classic case of power in relationships

An old but classic study by French and Raven (1959) suggests that it is possible to distinguish six different types of power:

Power type	Action	Relationship
1. Reward power	Power to reward	Parent/child
2. Coercive power	Power to punish	Father/child
3. Referent power	Influences	Style/dress of pop star, for example, is copied
4. Expert power	Greater knowledge	Teacher/pupil
5. Legitimate power	Accepts norms	Civic/legal authority
6. Informational power	Independent of social setting	Influenced by unknown source

The consensus of this work, supported by later studies, suggests that power in relationships rarely operates on one level or in one form; much more common is a mix of tactics and responses.

We pick up the topic of 'power' again on page 102, where we consider power in a wider setting than interpersonal relationships.

Something to do

- Skim-read the section on power in a wider context (pages 102–4) and identify key differences between that and power in interpersonal relationships.

Conflict   Perhaps the best phrase to define conflict within a relationship is 'mutual antagonism'. When we consider a relationship in conflict, we usually imply that each party is antagonistic towards the other.

There *are* states of conflict that an individual can experience on their own but these are not usually considered in the context of relationships. Briefly, these are:

- 'approach–approach', which means conflict between two equally pleasant goals;
- 'avoidance–avoidance', which is conflict between two equally unpleasant goals;
- 'approach–avoidance', where the conflict is between a pleasant goal with unpleasant consequences, for example an increase in pay which brings a huge increase in workload.

In a relationship where 'mutual antagonism' exists, the conflict can be over a number of causes – behaviour, attitudes or goals, for example. Conflicts of this type can arise when one or usually both parties follow what to them is a perfectly reasonable course of action, but which because of its self interest ends up in conflict with the other. What is sad in the context of relationships is that invariably the person initiating the action is not looking for conflict – usually that is the last thing on their mind. It tends to occur because of a lack of trust between the two parties, and as a consequence they can end up in a **social trap** (see over).

The figure below demonstrates a game for two players in which both players can win or lose. The purpose of the game is to show that by being selfish you may in fact 'lose', but by thinking of the other person as well as yourself you may both 'win'. Each player will receive the amount shown after you have each chosen 'A' or 'B'. You choose knowing what the possible outcomes are but *not* knowing what choice your partner is making. The outcome is one of the four boxes – the first person getting the amount above the diagonal, the second person the amount below it. The only sensible outcome is for each player to think of the other player and choose 'A'. You then each make £5. If you choose 'B' thinking that you will make £10, the other player will choose 'B' so that they don't lose. As a consequence you don't lose but neither of you gain. If, on the other hand, you act less selfishly and think of the other player, you choose 'A' and make £5 (top left box), and the other player does the same. You both make £5 and neither of you lose. If you are both selfish, you end up with nothing; if you both think of the other, you end up with £5 each.

Social trap matrix

The top left box is the optimum outcome, but the bottom right box is the most probable outcome.

Source: Myers (1996)

Think about it

• Think of an example of the social trap on a national or global scale. (One example on a global scale is the way that some fish stock has been over-fished. With no fish left in the ocean, nobody 'wins'.)

In personal relationships, a false or distorted perception of the other person can, and usually does, lead to conflict. If John believes that Jane is cross with him about something (whether it is true or not), then he may retaliate by 'forgetting' to do the washing up. This causes Jane to act in such a way that the action justifies the original misconception.

Individual, social and cultural variations in relationships

The place to start here is very basic – we are all different. However much we think that we are like someone else, we are not. We may have certain similarities in intellectual, physical or personal aspects, but that is all. You are your own person, you have your own fingerprints, voice print and DNA pattern. Even if you are a monozygotic twin, you share only certain things with your twin – you are still different in many ways. Such differences exist between people who live close together in a given region, where they may have a similar accent or similar social norms;

even in a relatively close society, there are still huge individual differences. If we take these individual differences and consider them in different social and cultural settings, then the number and type of variations between people expand enormously.

Think about it

• Make lists to compare the similarities and differences between you and your friends, and a similar group of, say, Inuit (Eskimos).

In this section, we limit the discussion to the differences that exist between individuals, societies and cultures only as they apply to individual relationships. In all of these cases it needs to be said that these differences are changing rapidly with time. Within a given society, standards and customs once understood and acceptable now no longer exist. For example, in Western societies, the traditional daily family meal is becoming a rarity, with parents and children frequently eating at different times or in different places. In more rural societies, where traditionally the eldest son would automatically follow in his father's footsteps, this too is becoming less common. Major changes have occurred in many Western societies, and with the availability of worldwide communications the impact and influence of these changes are felt elsewhere.

Individual variations You need to be aware that 'individual differences' forms a major subdivision in psychology. A quick look at the contents of a general psychology text will show that this topic normally covers areas such as intelligence and personality, and often abnormality and therapy. In social psychology, and particularly in the context of this text, the topic is much more focused, more concerned with outcome, and only deals with the way individual *relationships* differ. As stated above, people are different, but so too are relationships (see also Units 7 and 8).

Social variations There is a wide variety of elements of social interaction in any relationship. Many of these will vary between cultures as well as within a culture. For example, there are often differences in the way that relationships start and begin to become established. These differences can be noted both within the British Isles – northerners are supposed to be more friendly, southerners more aloof – and between the British Isles and, say, America – the British (or, at least, the English) being more formal, distant, and with more social conventions, while the Americans are more open and quick to start a relationship.

Another social difference is that British people will rarely speak highly of themselves, preferring almost to play down or denigrate their own performance; Americans are less likely to do this; while in some Middle Eastern countries, speaking highly of oneself is considered quite normal.

Another significant social variation is the place of women in a society, and therefore in relationships. Women in most Western societies are, for the most part, relatively 'liberated', while in many other countries women are clearly second-class citizens, and in extreme cases still legally a chattel owned by the husband.

Cultural variations

Relationships do not take place in a vacuum, they take place in a setting and in a **culture** (see page 65). Any given culture is likely to have a number of subcultures. A subculture is an identifiable group, within the main culture, which has its own additional rules and ways of behaving and interacting with others and the environment. Some sociologists define a subculture only when it is easily identifiable, such as a major religious or ethnic group; while others are happy to accept a subculture of much smaller size, for example a 'punk' subculture.

When we consider just what it is that varies culturally, we need to consider the individual elements that make up a given culture. Argyle (1983) suggests the following:

• Language is a very important element in a culture. Think for a moment of the differences in language between cultures in the British Isles. As you do, you will appreciate the wide differences that exist in accent, vocabulary, syntax, colloquialisms and so on. There are also cultural differences in meaning, for example British understatement and American openness.
• Non-verbal communication also varies between cultures. Gestures have the widest variation of use, and things such as touch can be particularly sensitive. The distance that we stand from each other, and the way that we look at each other, also vary between cultures.

If we accept that cultural variations exist between individuals, and that relationships are usually formed between people of the same culture, then it follows that there will be differences between relationships across cultures. Some of these will be due to the nature and culture of the individuals, others will be due to the way that the specific cultural issue is handled in the relationship. So, for example – and generalising broadly – an upper-class British couple would be likely to be given to understatement, while an American couple would be much more likely to speak to each other frankly and literally and make less use of innuendo and suggestion.

Note: In the above sections on individual, social and cultural variations, we have made some rather extreme stereotypical statements about different people! While there is truth in the statements, we have exaggerated them to make a point.

The effects of interpersonal relationships

This topic overlaps a number of others. For example, the section on happiness has obvious links with the section on stress and the way we cope with stressors (Unit 5). Likewise, the section on relationships and mental health has some overlap with abnormal psychology (Unit 8); while health psychology (Unit 9) also touches on happiness and mental health issues.

Something to do

- As you read this section, make a note of other related areas, so that you can study them later. *Or*;
- Make a spider diagram of all the related topics, showing the connections.

The question that we need to ask here is: how does a relationship affect the individual(s) in that relationship? (This question implies another question: why do people make a relationship in the first place? This, however, is too big a question for the present discussion.) Assuming that the individuals in a relationship entered the relationship voluntarily and because they chose to do so – which isn't always the case – what are the effects that the relationship can or will have on the individual(s)?

Happiness

Probably the most important effect that an individual hopes to gain from a relationship is happiness. They hope that they will be more happy in the relationship than not in the relationship. Most people would accept that if you are happy, at a fundamental level, then you are much more able to deal with the normal pressures of life.

So, you have decided to enter a relationship. It is significant, it is important, and you and your partner in the relationship are happy. What happens next? Obviously your personal happiness is directly related to the health of the relationship. Taking out any other factors that may have a significant effect on your happiness but which are not a consequence of the relationship (such as the death of a parent), the health of the relationship is most likely to be the most significant indicator of your own personal health. The two are inextricably linked. The 'happy relationship – happy person' link holds for most long-term relationships.

There are two general psychological principles concerning happiness that can be related to this discussion:

- The **adaption-level principle** suggests that happiness is relative to our previous experience. We judge things against previous similar experiences. For example, if you start getting Bs instead of Cs for your work you are initially very pleased, but you will rapidly adapt to this new norm and then start looking for As to give you another boost in happiness.
- The **relative-deprivation principle** says that happiness is relative to others. We are always comparing ourselves to others, so despite personally getting good grades (or a better job or a pay rise), we can always find someone doing better than us, and as a consequence we feel 'deprived' and therefore less happy. We 'forget' that we are doing much better now than we were two years ago.

Recent studies in this area are scarce, but available data suggest that when unhappiness occurs, then the relationship is in trouble. The problem is determining which came first. Did the person become unhappy and then the relationship suffered? Or did the relationship start to go wrong and as a consequence the person became unhappy? As is often the case, it is usually 'both/and' rather than 'either/or'.

A summary of happiness	
Happy people tend to:	**Happiness is NOT generally correlated to:**
• have high self esteem; • be optimistic and outgoing; • have close friends; • have a satisfying marriage; • have work that recognises their skills; • have leisure activities; • have meaningful religious faith.	• age; • race; • gender; • educational achievement; • parenthood.

Source: Myers (1996)

Mental health If the happiness of an individual is linked to the health of their relationship, can the same be said of the mental health of a person? Is mental health also linked in some way to the relationship? And does happiness feature in this? These questions indicate the complexity and interrelatedness of the issues involved.

Accepting, then, that this is a complex issue, we need to focus our attention on the question of the influence or effects of the relationship on the mental health of the person in the relationship. What is it, in the relationship, that can cause one of the partners to experience mental illness?

The approach that we take is to review briefly the recognised criteria for defining 'mental illness' or 'abnormality', and then to consider if or how a relationship may be a causal factor in the development of a mental illness or disorder.

Something to investigate

• For more detailed discussions of the criteria for defining abnormality, refer to Unit 8, pages 387–8.

The criteria used to define mental illness or abnormality are as follows:

- **Deviance:** This is differing from an accepted standard or norm. The person is not behaving as they should, or as they ought.
- **Dysfunction:** Put very simply, this is to do with whether the person is functioning normally in their society.
- **Distress:** Is the person experiencing a more than normal level of personal distress or anguish?
- **Danger:** Is the person developing a personal lifestyle that is dangerous to themselves or to others?

It is important to recognise that the four criteria above need to be understood from the viewpoint of a given culture. Note also that there is no rank order of seriousness. The four terms starting with D have been chosen deliberately as an *aide-mémoire*.

In the case of **deviance**, there may be what some would call a deviant relationship, but it is unlikely that the relationship is the cause of the deviance. It is more likely that two people with similar 'deviance' form a relationship.

With **dysfunction** we immediately get into problems with value judgements (what is 'normal'?). If we ask what normal functioning is, then most of us could be considered at some point to be abnormal. One definition of normal is the ability to love and be loved. Often in a relationship this is absent or at least not operating normally (another value judgement), but it is difficult to say that it is the relationship that has caused the problem.

In the case of **distress**, we can perhaps say that the relationship is to blame. If the relationship is not working – in that the parties are not communicating properly, are finding fault with each other, practical aspects are not going well, there is not enough money, physical relations are not as they were, the children are not doing as they should, etc. – then it is a relatively short step for an individual to 'not feel well', to feel things are 'getting them down', followed by a gentle slide into a state of personal distress. To say that the relationship has caused the distress is too simple, but it has to be considered as a factor.

The final criterion is **danger**. Has the person become dangerous to themselves or to others? This has long-term and short-term implications. Probably most people at some time have been tempted to hit out, to be physically violent. Newspapers often report incidents of parents finally 'breaking' and harming their baby. Such instances may have causes that are from outside the relationship, but many are relationship-related – in other words, they would not or could not happen if there were no relationship. The issue of danger can also build up over the long term. It may take decades for a person to become 'dangerous'. Their public behaviour may be perfectly normal; or they may be exhibiting bizarre incidents or behaviours. The same may be true in the relationship, both parties slowly adjusting to new ways of relating, however unsatisfactory. Then something becomes just too much, giving rise to small incidents of dangerous behaviour, self-inflicted or on others; or there may be a major and very severe event. As before, it is difficult to be categorical about the cause. However, the mere fact that the person was in a relationship implies that the relationship may, at the very least, have contributed to the cause.

So far, in considering the effects of a relationship on a person's mental health, the implication has been that it may contribute to *ill* health. There is of course the other side of the coin: being in a relationship may contribute to the long-term positive mental health of an individual. When an individual may otherwise start becoming mentally ill, being in a close, supportive, positive relationship may be sufficient to prevent the development of illness. In other words, the relationship, far from causing mental illness, has the opposite effect and causes a healthy state to exist. A good example of this is the way that family support can reduce the effect of stress.

Something to do

• Read the section on stress in Unit 5.

Social influence

Having considered social cognition and social relationships, we now turn our attention to **social influence**. We can define social influence as the area in psychology concerned with the way that people influence the thoughts, feelings and behaviour of other people. We shall look at **conformity, obedience** and **independent behaviour.**

Conformity

We probably all like to see ourselves as free, independent spirits, who think and behave as we choose to. The truth is that while we may like to think that, in fact almost all of us conform to the social norms of our culture and society. We conform when we yield to social pressure, either real or imagined.

Something to do

- Make a list of all the ways that you conform. Consider both attitudes and behaviour.
- Read or re-read the section on free will and determinism in Unit 2 (pages 39–40)

Three classic cases of social influence and conformity

The literature dealing with conformity is extensive. Here we consider three classic studies:

- the Bennington study of the 1930s, because it produces evidence for the long-term effect of conformity;
- the Sherif study (1935), because it illustrates the development of group norms; and
- the Asch study of the 1950s, because of its emphasis on compliance.

The Bennington study
This is interesting because it illustrates the slow and subtle influence of group norms, an influence that in this case lasted for decades. Newcomb started the study in the 1930s at Bennington College in America, a small women's college in New England. Newcomb observed the changes in the political and social attitudes of the students, who were mostly from wealthy, conservative families. In contrast to the students' home backgrounds, the staff at the college fostered an atmosphere of political and cultural liberalism. Newcomb observed that over the four years at the college the political views of most of the students changed from traditional right-wing views to more democratic and socialist views. Newcomb concluded that it was the existence of group norms within the college that influenced the change. The significance of the study is that students who changed their views to the widely accepted 'college' group norms were more likely to be accepted and given approval. The pervasiveness of the influence is shown by the fact that twice as many Bennington students as a comparable group continued to support democratic views 20 years later (Newcomb et al., 1967).

The Sherif study (1935)
While still concerned with social influence, the Sherif study focused on the way that a group norm is established, particularly with people who are uncertain; and how, once established, the people involved will stay with the norm.

In this study, the **autokinetic effect** was used. This is where participants are asked to estimate the movement of a spot of light, which in fact does not move, while seated in a totally darkened room. When a person is on their own, they will make an estimate of the movement, remaining reasonably consistent over several trials, even though different individuals' responses vary widely. However, in the Sherif study, when the participants were grouped to view the spot and then asked to report aloud their estimate of the movement, the amount of movement reported by any one participant became very similar to that of others in the group. Individuals reporting extremes rapidly reduced their estimates to the average of the group. As evidenced in the Bennington study, group norms, once established, are frequently long-lasting and may even be passed on from one generation to the next. Insko et al. (1980) found that norms could still influence the individual long after the group had ceased to exist.

There are a number of areas in psychological research that have validity in the laboratory but which later researchers argue have no **ecological validity** – that is, they have no relevance to the real (ecological) world. The Sherif autokinetic study is a good example. How often do you sit in a dark room and watch a spot of light? Asch (see below) argued that what was needed was a study that investigated conformity under real-life conditions, or at least as near to real life as possible.

The Asch study (1951)
In this classic study, participants, who were male undergraduates, were recruited for studies in visual perception. Seven participants were seated round a table and were shown a large card with a vertical line on it (see the figure on the left, below). They were then shown a second card with three vertical lines on it (see the figure on the right, below) and were asked to say which of the three lines 1, 2 or 3 was nearest in length to the first, single line. The lines were drawn such that there could only be one answer.

Stimulus figures in the Asch conformity trials

The point of the study was that six of the seven participants were accomplices of the experimenter, and only one was a naive or 'real' participant. He was seated in position 6. For the first two trials, all seven gave the correct answer; for the third trial onwards, the first five 'participants' – in fact accomplices – all gave the wrong answer. The point of the study centres on how the 'real' participant will respond. If he is honest, he will disagree with the first five answers; but if he agrees with a clearly wrong answer, then he is conforming. In the original study of 50 real participants, Asch found that they conformed in 37 per cent of the trials. Subsequent trials revealed that conformity peaked when there were seven accomplices; also that if just one accomplice hesitated or gave the correct answer, the participant's conformity dropped significantly.

This type of conformity is usually known as **compliance**, as it occurs when the person conforms but does not believe in what they are doing.

Three key terms are important to an understanding of conformity:

- **Norms**, sometimes **social norms**, are those behaviours or rules that a given society accepts as normal.
- **Normative social influence**, sometimes **normative processes**, describes the need to belong or be approved of or liked. It is to do with belonging.
- **Informational social influence**, sometimes **informational processes**, occurs when the person is anxious to do the right thing in a given social setting, to accept the opinions of others about what is real. It is to do with knowing.

There have been a number of interesting studies of follow-up work on conformity. Crutchfield (1954) argued that the presence of the other people in Asch's trials influenced the participant. He arranged his study so that participants answered questions with very obvious correct answers in private but with a panel of lights to show how the others in the study answered the questions. Crutchfield found a similar rate of conformity to Asch's. A criticism of this study is that Crutchfield used military personnel as his participants, and it can be argued that the military can be expected to conform and be obedient.

Two other later but related studies were carried out by Perrin and Spencer (1980) and Dom and Avermaet (1981). Perrin and Spencer did Asch-type tests and found a lower rate of conformity. They argued that the difference was to do with the culture and attitudes of the 1980s as compared with the 1950s. Dom and Avermaet did much the same but found similar conformity rates to the original Asch studies. The Perrin and Spencer study used maths and engineering students as participants, hoping to avoid anyone who may have heard about 'conformity'. Dom and Avermaet made no such selection and used a wide cross-section of participants.

Think about it

- Perrin and Spencer argued that the low rates of conformity achieved in their study were to do with different cultural attitudes. Can you think of another reason for the low rates of conformity in their study? (For Dom and Avermaet's answer to this question, see the end of the unit.)

Obedience   Another element of social influence is **obedience** – acting to obey orders. There is a great deal of similarity between obedience and compliance (discussed above) which carries with it the idea of not believing in what you are doing. The most famous study into obedience was carried out by Milgram (1965 and 1974) (see page 100) and concerns the degree to which people will follow orders even if the orders are contrary to what the person believes is 'right'. There have been some horrific examples of this in recent history: Hitler and the Holocaust; Bosnia and prison camps of the worst kind; and in 1993 in Waco, Texas the death of almost 100 members of the Branch Davidian Sect, as the members appeared to commit group suicide. The outcome of Milgram's work shows that such behaviour is more the result of **situational factors** than of **dispositional characteristics**. In other words, it was not a particular kind of personality of the German people that allowed the Holocaust to happen, rather it was situational forces that were responsible. The implication is that anyone, given certain situations, will 'obey'.

A classic case of obedience

Milgram's research into obedience is highly significant in that it demonstrates the degree to which a person will obey. The study is also highly controversial in terms of its ethical issues.

The experiment

The work was carried out at Yale University, ostensibly to research the effect of punishment on learning. Participants were paid $4.50. They were allocated either a 'teacher' role or a 'learner' role – except that this was rigged such that the 'learner' was always an accomplice and the 'teacher' always a participant.

The learner is seated in a 'electric' chair and wired in; the participant (teacher) is seated next door in front of a machine with a row of switches, each labelled with a voltage level (he does not know the 'machine' is only a row of switches and is not connected to anything). The task is to teach the learner word pairs and then test his recall. Wrong answers receive an 'electric shock'. (Before beginning the task, the teacher is given a real shock of 75 volts – so he knows that this produces a noticeable pain.) After each successive error, the teacher moves to the next highest voltage – 15 volts higher each time – and flips the switch. The switches are labelled in groups, from 'mild shock' to 'danger – severe shock' at 450 volts.

As the experiment proceeds, the teacher is instructed by the university experimenter – the authority figure – to increase the level of shock at each mistake. As the learner makes mistakes, the level of the electric shock given to the learner increases. At around 100 volts, the teacher can hear the learner reacting with considerable discomfort. At 150 volts, he cries out and demands to be released. The teacher naturally becomes confused and is unwilling to continue, except that the researcher – the authority figure – insists that he carry on. At higher voltages the cries of the learner become more distressing, and he insists he be released. At 300 volts, the learner becomes hysterical, cries out and insists he can take no more, the experimenter must stop. By now the teacher is really confused and most unwilling to continue and is himself clearly in a state of some distress and ambivalence, but is urged on by the researcher to increase the voltage. Silence from the learner is treated as a wrong answer and shocked. The teacher is told the experiment requires him to continue, it is 'absolutely essential' to go on to the 450-volt level.

In 20 such experiments, involving almost 1000 participants, all of whom were men aged between 20 and 50, 63 per cent complied fully, up to the final 450 volts.

Conclusions

A number of conclusions can be drawn from the experiment. Perhaps the most fundamental is that ordinary people will be obedient to a very high degree under certain conditions, namely:

- when the authority figure has high status or respectability (these studies were conducted at Yale University);
- when the authority figure giving the orders is close;
- when the victim is not in view;
- when there is no objection from a third party;
- when the 'punishment' starts very small and builds in small increments (the 'foot-in-the-door' phenomenon);
- when the teacher is one stage removed from administering the punishment (by telling someone else to flip the switches, obedience went up to 93 per cent!);
- when other teachers (really accomplices) are present and refuse to continue giving shocks, only 10 per cent of teachers (participants) can be persuaded by the researcher to obey to the 450-volt level.

The ethical issues

If you have not met Milgram's study before, you are quite likely horrified by the ethical issues. Most of today's ethical guidelines would have been broken or at least violated to some degree. In defence of Milgram's study, guidelines in the 1960s were not as clearly defined as they are now. To counter what criticism there was, a psychiatrist, a year after the experiment, interviewed a sample of participants and found no permanent harm had been done.

Something to do

• With respect to today's ethical guidelines, list problems with the Milgram study.

In another study on obedience, Hofling et al. (1966) set up a study in a hospital. The participants were the nurses, but they did not know this until being debriefed after the trial. A nurse on a busy ward received a telephone call from a hospital doctor whom he or she did not know. He instructed the nurse over the telephone to administer to a hospital patient 20 milligrams of a drug – he would sign the authorisation when he arrived. The label on the bottle containing the drug stated that the normal dose was 5 milligrams, with 10 milligrams an absolute maximum.

The purpose of the study was to investigate obedience: whether the nurse would obey and in so doing break a number of fundamental and serious hospital rules, namely:

• taking a clinical order over the telephone;
• acting on the orders of someone he or she did not know;
• administering an 'overdose' without checking.

In the study, 21 out of 22 nurses started to prepare to administer the drug before being stopped. In an interesting preliminary to the real trial, nurses were asked what they would do if put into the trial situation. They responded such that ten out of 12 said they would disobey.

In studies such as these, there are always a few, usually a very few, who do not conform or who do not obey. So the next topic to consider is why it is that some do not conform or obey. We call this **independent behaviour**.

Independent behaviour

One way to tackle this topic is to look at the reasons why people obey and then to identify strategies that resist or counter these pressures:

Reasons why people do and do not conform or obey	
Reasons why people conform/obey	**Strategies to resist the pressure to conform/obey**
• The authority figure is close at hand.	• Be aware that situational forces can and do affect everyone.
• The person giving the orders is assumed to have authority/status.	• Be prepared to analyse the situation critically.
• The setting lends weight (e.g. a prestigious university).	• Take time to think before obeying.
• The victims are far away, or at least out of sight.	• Take advantage of any 'cooling off' period (a legal requirement in most sales contracts).
• No one objects. There are no role models to defy orders.	• If you do start to succumb, conform or obey, be willing to recognise it and back out.
• We have all been trained from childhood to obey authority.	• Finding one other person willing to *not* obey strengthens defiance significantly.
• The orders can be passed on to another person.	• If you value being right more than being liked, you are more likely to defy orders.
• The authority uses 'foot-in-the-door' techniques.	• Clarify procedures necessary to disobey.

As you study the above lists, you will see that the points are not nice and tidy opposites: 'This is why, therefore this is why not'. Rather they are reasons culled from the classic studies discussed above; and the ways to resist inappropriate demands to conform or obey are for the most part implicit responses to the 'why' list. Sitting reading them when not under any pressure, they seem quite obvious and just the sort of thing that we would all do – wouldn't we? *All* the evidence, however, is to the contrary. Our personality has very little to do with independent behaviour, the situation has almost everything to do with it. You have been warned!

Something to do

- Extend the chart on page 101 by adding elements from the major studies to illustrate the reasons and strategies. For example:

Reasons	Strategies
• In the Milgram study, there was no procedure to allow the teacher to stop giving the shocks.	• Clarify procedures necessary to disobey.

Social power

The way that power is used in interpersonal relationships was discussed in the previous section. Here power is looked at in a wider social context.

Something to do

- Re-read the section on power in relationships (pages 88–9) and reduce to a few key notes. Identify issues which refer to one-to-one relationships and those which are more general.

One kind of social power, usually called **coercive compliance**, is manifested in the rather extreme examples of conformity and obedience (see above). Another kind of social power is what is sometimes called **persuasive influence**. Turner (1991) refers to this as a **dual process dependency model**. The model distinguishes between the two main types of social influence. People are influenced by others because of **dependency** or because they need **social approval**. Another, relatively common, form of social power is a direct pressure to **comply** with a request – for example when someone asks a friend for a lift or when a salesperson is trying to get someone to buy something. Strategies used in such instances are:

- **ingratiation:** the more they like you the more they will comply;
- **reciprocity:** if you do them a favour, they are likely to comply with a request from you;
- **multiple requests:** you start with an easy request, and build up to what you really want. This takes three forms:
  - The foot-in-the-door: compliance with a low-level, easy request first; subsequent requests get more demanding.
  - The door-in-the-face: the first request is outrageous with certain refusal. You follow up with easier requests.
  - The low-ball tactic: the request is accompanied with inducements. Compliance will remain even when the inducements cease.

Source: Hogg and Vaughan (1995)

Think about it

- Think of everyday examples of when you have been faced with attempts to get you to comply. Make a list.
- Can you identify the three strategies given on page 102?

Leaders and followers   The use of social power is perhaps best illustrated in the context of leaders and followers. For the purposes of this discussion, the term 'leader' refers to the person who holds authority in a group, while 'leadership' refers to the exercising of that authority.

Popular opinion holds that certain people are 'born leaders'. This is called the **great person theory**. It holds that great leaders are born not made. There have been sustained efforts to identify a personality type that correlates with great leaders – but without success. Neither is there an accepted list of skills that 'makes' leadership. Leadership, like many of the issues discussed above, depends on situational factors (Reber, 1995).

Most research in this field has come to believe that the situation in which the leader exists and leads is more important than his or her personality and that a good leader in one situation may not be a good leader in a different situation. A classic example of this is Winston Churchill. His personality characteristics were recognised as well suited to leadership needs in wartime, but not in peacetime. We can conclude that effective leadership is more a matter of task and situation than personality or leadership style.

Something to investigate

'Good leadership is *not* dependent on the leader's personality; it depends more on the situation.'
- Research the above statement in the light of leaders that you know something about. Think of those you know personally and those in the media spotlight. For example, pick a current political situation, then compare your findings with theoretical models of leadership.

Contingency theory   One of the classic studies in the field of leadership was conducted by Fiedler (1967 and 1971). His **contingency model** is concerned with leadership effectiveness and the way that the leadership style fits the situation. He argued that the effectiveness of a leader is contingent upon the fit between the leader's style and the quality of the leader–follower relationship, the task structure or complexity of the task, and the position-power of the leader (for example the rewards and punishments available to him or her). In other words, the effectiveness of a leader is contingent upon situational factors.

As a consequence of this work and that of others, two main types of leader have been identified:

- **Task-oriented leaders:**   those who set goals and can keep the group working towards the goal. The style is typically directive.
- **Social leaders** (sometimes referred to as **relationship-oriented leaders**):   these leaders tend to mediate conflict and seek to build team morale. Their style is usually democratic, with a lot of delegation.

<u>Leadership style</u>   In an early but influential study, Lippitt and White (1943) trained co-workers in three distinct leadership styles. The co-workers were then placed as leaders of after-school boys' clubs, where they operated as a leader in the style to which they had been trained:

- **Autocratic leaders:** organisers, gave orders, aloof, task-oriented.
- **Democratic leaders:** welcomed suggestions, got involved, discussed issues.
- **Laissez-faire leaders:** minimal intervention, let it all happen, casual, non-directive.

To rule out the possibility that the personality of the leader may have been influential, each group had three leaders, all trained in the same leadership style.

Conclusions from the study were as follows:

- Autocratic leaders were liked less; the group atmosphere tended to be aggressive; and group efficiency was high with the leader present, but low when absent.
- Democratic leaders were liked more; the group was friendly and task-oriented; and efficiency was relatively high and unaffected by leadership absence.
- Laissez-faire leaders were liked rather less; the group was friendly and group-centred; efficiency was low but increased with leader absence.

Collective behaviour

Having started with the individual, then moved on to the individual in a group setting, we now move further to **collective behaviour**, or the behaviour of a very large group, a crowd or a mob.

There is no formal numerical definition of when a group becomes a crowd or mob. We can think of a **crowd** as a temporary coming together of a large number of people, usually with some kind of purpose – for example to watch a football match, to attend a religious gathering or to make a peaceful protest. The key terms are 'large' and 'temporary'. In other words, a crowd is a large number of people gathering for a specific one-off planned occasion such as a football match, or a large number of people gathering spontaneously at, say, the scene of an accident.

A **mob** is also a large group of people, a crowd, but the distinction is that, for whatever reason, the emotional level of individuals in the mob has become so high that the almost inevitable outcome is violence against other persons and the destruction of property. Again, the mob may gather for a specific purpose or it may be a spontaneous gathering that 'turns nasty', resulting in mob behaviour. A mob may also be formed when a peaceful group or crowd is deliberately taken over by those intent on causing mob-like behaviour. Their intent is deliberately to manipulate the crowd into acts of violence.

All aspects of collective behaviour are of interest to the social psychologist, including the study of bizarre and extreme examples of hysterical behaviour such as the religious fervour expressed through dancing in the Middle Ages. Here we consider only the more usual forms of crowd behaviour.

Theories of collective behaviour

What does the hit show *Les Misérables* have to do with crowd theory? The answer to this question is that Hugo wrote *Les Misérables* (1862) at least in part as a social comment on crowd behaviour in Paris at the time of the French revolution and after. Probably the earliest theory of crowd behaviour was formulated by the Frenchman LeBon in 1908, having both read accounts of crowd behaviour and experienced it at first hand. From his experiences and observations, LeBon suggested that there are three main reasons why a crowd may come together almost with one mind and act in a base, primitive manner:

- In a crowd, individuals are in effect anonymous and as such lose a sense of personal responsibility.
- The crowd allows ideas and suggested actions to spread rapidly.
- Unconscious antisocial motives and forces are released.

Hogg and Vaughan (1995) make the point that LeBon's view, that crowd behaviour is pathological, was a major influence on subsequent theorists such as McDougall and Zimbardo. These early theorists placed considerable emphasis on basic instinctual drives that are released when the person is in an anonymous state in a crowd. It can be said that the person loses his or her individuality such that the crowd (or group) is seen to 'take over' the responsibility for antisocial actions. Festinger et al. (1952) coined the term **deindividuation** to describe this process.

The 'prisoners and guards' study by Zimbardo et al. (1973), conducted at Stanford University, found that the 'guards' when dressed as guards – that is, deindividuated – behaved in an excessively brutal manner. A number of other studies support these general findings – that anonymity allows an increase in aggressive antisocial behaviour.

There are two related issues to consider. The first is the **emergent norm theory** (Turner, 1974), which holds that initially there is no norm within the crowd. Because of this lack of a norm, the crowd does not know how to behave – until a norm emerges. A problem with this theory is that more often than not people come together for a specific purpose which implies the existence of a norm. It is quite 'normal', for example, if you join a crowd waiting to see the Queen, to wave a flag and cheer. In the second, Reicher and Potter (1985) suggest an **intergroup action**. Other 'norms' would apply when one group (crowd) of football fans meets another group (crowd) of rival fans, or when the protesters at a nuclear weapons base confront security forces. This view suggests that the group or crowd has a very definite group identity, which in turn sets limits on the way the group can be expected to behave.

Pro- and antisocial behaviour

This final section within social psychology starts on a positive note, with a discussion on altruism, very much a pro-social behaviour. We then move on to antisocial behaviour and aggression, before considering issues that surround the influence of the media on behaviour. Finally, we look at individual, social and cultural diversity in pro- and antisocial behaviour.

In terms of the development of pro-social behaviour, most of the evidence suggests that childhood is the key stage. Critical areas are the actual experiences that the child undergoes, and the way in which the child comprehends the experience. During later developmental stages, individual differences and a wider range of social circumstances come into play, making pro-social development very much an individual issue.

Altruism and bystander behaviour

It is important to distinguish **altruism** from other forms of pro-social behaviour. Altruism can be defined as putting the interests of another person before your own, with no expectation of reward – in other words, behaving selflessly. **Helping behaviour** is more common than altruism; it is behaviour that is likely to cost little and may be rewarded. **Co-operation** is doing something with another for mutual benefit.

Something to do

- Altruism is discussed in Unit 6, page 289 and pages 300–1, in the context of comparative psychology. Skim-read these sections and note any differences from what you read here.

Theoretical approaches

Any consideration of pro-social behaviour has to involve motive. Do we or do we not get involved? What is it that makes us help or just walk away? There are a number of theoretical approaches to consider as we try to answer these two questions. The four main approaches are:

- **decision-making theory**, a process approach;
- **social learning theory (SLT)**, a learning approach;
- **sociobiological theory**, a genetic approach;
- **social norms**, a rules approach.

<u>Decision-making theory</u>   In the decision-making theory – also known as the **cognitive model** – the classic work was done by Darley and Latané (1968). The essence of the model is a series of steps in the process of deciding to help, each step requiring a 'yes' or 'no' answer. The process is illustrated diagrammatically on page 107.

In the model at each stage the potential helper has to make a decision. The option exists to withdraw at any stage with a degree of justification or to carry on to the next stage and become more fully involved. This model is generally considered to be the most realistic in explaining pro-social behaviour on the basis that responding to a need requires a considerable amount of cognitive processing in a relatively short time span.

The decision-making process

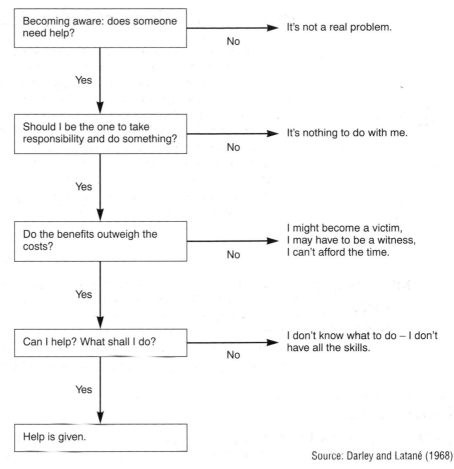

Source: Darley and Latané (1968)

Social learning theory In this approach, classic learning theory is given as the reason for helping. As children grow up they are usually taught to share and to help, both in the home and at school. They receive rewards – perhaps verbal praise, perhaps extra sweets or pocket money. They also see adults role-modelling pro-social behaviour. In a study in which six-year-old children watched selected episodes of the television programme *Lassie* (Sprafkin et al., 1975), those who had seen helping behaviour responded significantly more quickly to a staged need for help immediately following the viewing than those who had not. This and other studies show that reinforcement and modelling are powerful ways to shape pro-social behaviour. An advantage of this theory is that it can account for individual differences.

Sociobiological theory Sociobiology is discussed in Unit 6 on comparative psychology in the context of the helping or altruistic behaviour of animals. The theory holds that a parent will sacrifice itself in the interest of the survival of its young because in doing so more of its genes will be passed on than if the offspring died and the parent lived. (See also page 112).

Something to do
- Read the sections on sociobiology and altruism in Unit 6, pages 287 and 300–1.

The key question to ask here is: does this form of helping behaviour occur in the human animal? A dramatic example by Harcourt (1991) reports that in traditional Inuit (Eskimo) families, when food is in seriously short supply, elderly grandparents will 'stay behind' in the almost certainty of death to enable the other, younger family members to survive. While this example supports traditional sociobiological theory, there are countless other examples of helping, altruistic behaviour where life is lost or at risk yet there is no family connection and hence no genetic argument. These are examples of **reciprocal altruism** (see also page 293). The argument goes that if I help another member of my species, then perhaps another time I will receive help when I need it.

This theory is useful, but it does not explain why some people are altruistic and others are not, or why in a given person their altruistic, pro-social behaviour can change with time.

<u>Social norms</u> This fourth approach is in some respects the result of the work of critics of sociobiology, who argue that genetic evolution may well operate at a basic social level, for example within the family, but that it does not explain helping behaviour directed at complete strangers.

Campbell (1975) suggests that it is social evolution that is at work. He suggests that social evolution describes the way that human societies slowly evolve behaviours that are for the benefit of the whole group. Pro-social rules thus become the norms of a given society. Examples of such norms are as follows:

- social responsibility, whereby certain people – parents, teachers, doctors, religious leaders and so on – are expected to help others;
- reciprocity: it is well established that when someone has been helped, they are more likely to help others;
- justice or equity: we are uncomfortable if we get paid more than someone else for the same job and will frequently try to put the inequity right. Societies tend to have rules about fairness.

All of these provide a cultural 'push' towards pro-social behaviour.

Examples of pro-social behaviour There are a number of oft-quoted reports that provide examples of pro-social behaviours, and also others that introduce the concept of **bystander behaviour**. Among them are the following:

- An extreme example of pro-social behaviour occurred when a passenger aircraft crashed into the partly frozen river Potomac in Washington DC in 1982. An anonymous observer jumped in and rescued several drowning passengers.
- In another incident, Lisa Potts, a nursery nurse in Wolverhampton, in 1996 put herself between a man with a machete and the children in her charge, taking the blows from the weapon herself in the process.

- Possibly the most famous report of bystander behaviour is the case of Kitty Genovese. It occurred in the late evening in New York in 1964. For about 30 minutes, 38 respectable citizens observed Kitty Genovese being repeatedly attacked and stabbed and as she called for help. Twice bystanders' voices and lights going on frightened the attacker so that he stopped – only to start again when nothing happened. Not one of the 38 observers called the police during the attacks. The police were eventually called, but only after Kitty Genovese was dead.

The murder of Kitty Genovese gave rise to a great deal of research into **bystander behaviour**. Why were people so indifferent to what was going on? Why do people ignore a violent attack when all that is needed is a telephone call to the police? Or, on the other hand, what is it that causes people to intervene at considerable risk to themselves? Darley and Latané (1968), working in this area, were interested in the effects that the number of observers to an incident had on the behaviour of the observers. They argued that the presence of others influences how we behave. The more bystanders there are, the longer it will be before any one of them helps. This is known as the **bystander effect**. They were able to show that when there was only the one bystander, attempts to help were made in 85 per cent of incidents; this figure dropped to 30 per cent with four others present. As a result of their work in this area, Darley and Latané formulated a decision-making process for bystander intervention:

The decision-making process for bystander intervention

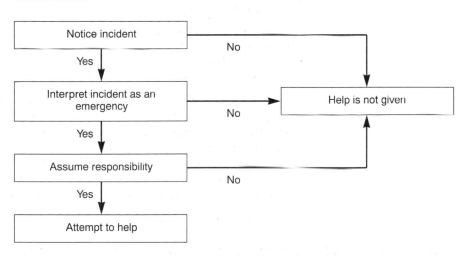

Myers (1996), summarising helping and altruistic behaviour, suggests that the odds of our helping someone are best when:

- we have observed someone else being helped;
- we are not in a hurry;
- the victim is perceived as deserving help;
- the victim is similar to us;
- we are in a small town or rural area;
- we are feeling guilty;
- we are focused on others and not preoccupied with something else;
- we are in a good mood.

Social-psychological theories of aggression

Aggression is at the root of much antisocial behaviour. Defining it is not as straightforward as it would appear.

Think about it

- How would you define 'aggression'? Write down your definition.

You probably used words such as 'violence' or 'hurting others' in your definition. This is perfectly correct except that it ignores the *intent* of the aggressive behaviour. The issue of intent in aggressive behaviour is a classic problem in the literature, which is why there is no real agreement on a definition. It is further complicated because the theoretical orientation of the person making the definition will influence the definition. For example, an ethologist is likely to define aggression as an evolutionary determined instinct, while a social learning view would say that aggression is a learned response as a result of observation and reinforcement.

Something to investigate

- Using all the resources that you have available, list all the definitions of aggression that you can find.
- Now combine them into one.

You may have found the second part of the above task quite difficult. The generally accepted simple definition of aggression within psychology is: 'the intent to harm'. Check this against your list of definitions and keep it in mind as we discuss various theories that seek to explain aggression. See if you can make this definition 'fit' each of the theories.

Theories of aggression can be divided into two broad groups, with a degree of overlap. One group are basically of a social nature, the other of a basically biological nature – another example of the Nature–Nurture debate. The theories can be outlined as follows:

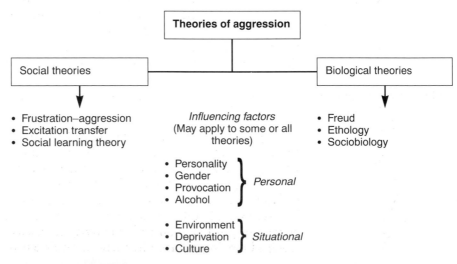

Social theories
Most social theories hold that some kind of arousal has to come before the aggression. The fundamental cause is considered to have a significant learning element, with some social theorists accepting that there may be an instinctual component as well.

The frustration–aggression hypothesis   In this theory (see also page 76), it is argued that whenever frustration occurs then aggression is likely to follow. The initial work was conducted at Yale University in the 1930s. Dollard, an anthropologist, worked with psychologist colleagues to arrive at the hypothesis (Dollard et al., 1939). The theory was popular for a time, but was subsequently considered too simplistic, particularly in the lack of definition of 'frustration'. Critics also pointed out that frustration can frequently lead to depression and other conditions, including illness; and that aggression can be caused by a wide variety of causes, of which frustration is only one.

The excitation-transfer theory   In this model, Zillman (1979) suggests that there are three prerequisites for aggression to occur:

- learned aggressive behaviour;
- an arousal event;
- an interpretation of the arousal event resulting in aggression.

The basic idea is that there is a transfer of an aroused state onto a situation that results in aggression. Aggression would not normally be the outcome of the situation if the prior arousal was not 'available' to be transferred. For example: you are late for work because someone delayed you (initial arousal); driving to work, another driver cuts in front of you (the situation); you (over)react in an aggressive manner. You have transferred the initial excitation onto a later situation.

Social learning theory   The basic notion in this theory is that aggression can be learned. The most famous example is Bandura's experiment with the bobo doll (Bandura, 1963 and 1973) – see also Unit 8, page 392. In this experiment, groups of children between three and six years old watched different examples of an adult behaving aggressively to a large rubber 'bobo doll'. Following this, the children were allowed to play with a variety of toys, including a bobo doll. Hidden observers watched and noted aggressive behaviour in the different groups of children. Results from the study show that children readily learn to model their behaviour on the behaviour of role models. This is true, whether the modelling occurs live, on television or in cartoon form.

Biological explanations of aggression
In these theories, the basic assumption is that aggression is a genetically controlled instinct.

Freudian theory   This is the oldest of the theories discussed here. Freud proposed that we all have two basic instincts that are in opposition: Eros is the instinct towards life, Thanatos is the instinct towards death. Freud proposed that the death instinct is initially directed at the self, but is later redirected against others in the form of aggression. Modern Freudians still hold to the instinct concept, but suggest that people engage in positive, controlled activity to release this built-up aggression (such as playing squash after school on Fridays).

Something to do

• Read the sections on Freud in Units 2 (pages 35–6), 7 (pages 328–9) and 8 (pages 407 and 422) and integrate this view into Freud's main ideas.

The ethological view   The ethological view of aggression is also instinctual, but with the key difference that while the aggressive instinct is innate – there, waiting to emerge – it needs the appropriate signal or releaser stimulus before it happens. Lorenz (1966) suggested that this is an evolutionary aspect linked to the survival of the species. In terms of the human animal, Lorenz suggested that we too have an innate fighting instinct that can emerge as aggression.

Something to do

• Read the section on ethology in Unit 6, page 286, and integrate the above view into that account.

The sociobiological view   This is the most recent of the theories and follows generally accepted sociobiological thinking. The essence of the argument, which is classic Darwin, is that a behaviour has evolved because it allows the survival of the animal's genes such that they can be passed on to successive generations. Aggression is helpful to the individual and to the species, particularly when resources are limited, when social systems are in disarray, and when in the presence of strangers (Barash, 1982). The view suggests that human beings can be expected to be aggressive because of the way that these circumstances threaten the person's survival.

Influencing factors on aggression   There are a number of other factors which can be considered to influence aggression. These may be divided into two broad groups: personal and situational (Hogg and Vaughan, 1995). The various influencing factors are listed in the chart on page 110. It is important to appreciate, however, that it is virtually impossible to separate personal factors from situational factors – in any instance of aggression both will inevitably be involved, the only question is that of degree.

A long-term study of aggression

In a long-term study, Eron et al. in 1960 studied nine-year-olds in terms of aggression. In a follow-up study reported in 1987 with the sample now 27 years old, an association was found between high aggressiveness and low IQ for both sexes. In the case of the males only, it was found that those with high aggressiveness and low IQ were more often in trouble with the police when adults. The clear implication is that aggression in childhood can have consequences that reach into adulthood. This is particularly significant in the context of media influence (see pages 113–15).

The reduction and control of aggressive behaviour

At a theoretical level, the approach that you take towards the reduction of aggression must depend on your view as to the cause of aggression. Social explanations of aggression require social solutions to reduce aggression, and biological explanations require biological solutions.

In terms of the biological theories, if the drive is there, then it must go somewhere. If it is not to be released as aggression, then it must be released elsewhere. Freud's term for this was **catharsis**. We might say that we 'let off steam' to 'get it out of our system'; we might engage in strenuous aggressive action (such as playing squash). Most evidence suggests that this approach is not very successful in reducing aggression; it can in fact increase aggression due to the heightened state of arousal of the person.

In terms of the social theories, if aggression is learned, then it can be unlearned; many programmes have been developed to teach behaviours that are appropriate responses. Some of these involve attempts to alter social norms by changing perceptions of what is acceptable, and by actively encouraging pro-social behaviour.

Punishing aggression is rarely successful, as the punishment is seen as a form of legitimised aggression. However, Baron (1977) found that punishment can be effective if it is strong, consistent and directly related to the inappropriate behaviour.

Media influence on pro- and antisocial behaviour

Probably no one would argue with the proposition that television affects people. The issues centre more on how and how much. Most studies have focused on the influence of television on children and young people, and the following text looks at this area.

In a study conducted by Williams (1986), the residents of a rural area of Canada were studied immediately before the community was able to receive television broadcasts and again two years after the arrival of television. There were some interesting conclusions. Children of school age showed a decline in both reading ability and creativity, and an increase in stereotyped beliefs. This age group also showed an increase in both verbal and physical aggression during play. The teenage group also showed negative changes, with a significant drop in community participation. While this is a particularly interesting study, there are thousands of other studies, just about all of which show that television has a major impact on society. This is of course a reflection of the programme content, coupled with viewing habits, particularly of parents with children.

In terms of the amount of television that is watched, a very general conclusion is that most children spend more time watching television than they spend in school, and certainly more time than they spend in family activities. These figures are of greater significance with children from more deprived homes, living in overcrowded housing and from lower-income families.

As far as the effects of television on children are concerned, general conclusions are that for the pre-school and young school-age child, information is piecemeal, with little comprehension of reality and no ability to exercise any critical evaluative skills. This is thought to increase the likelihood of imitation of television characters, and to cause the children to believe what they see (Berk, 1997).

Something to investigate

Media violence is a hotly debated topic. One of the most recent studies has been conducted on the island of St Helena in the South Atlantic (Charlton, 1998). The islanders have only recently been able to receive TV broadcasts. A naturalistic pre-TV/post-TV study was conducted (and is still on-going) on the effect of TV on the island's children.
• Read up about this study and compare your findings with other recent studies into the effects of watching media violence.

In another dimension, there is evidence to suggest that television presents a stereotyped view of society. While this may not lead to aggression or violence, it can certainly lead to the reinforcement of prejudicial stereotypes. Archer et al. (1983) coined the term **face-ism**. This describes the difference in the way that males and females are portrayed in the media. They observed that in almost all the examples where males were portrayed the head was prominent, while in the case of females the body was prominent. In another study, Manstead and McCulloch (1981) analysed the sex-role stereotyping in British television commercials and found considerable evidence of blatant stereotyping. Males were shown as having expertise and authority, women were more often shown as consumers.

Television, violence and aggression

In terms of aggression, research suggests that television provides children with specific lessons in how to initiate aggression (Comstock and Paik, 1994). Donnerstein et al. (1994) report that findings such as these are consistent across many different studies which take into account a wide range of variables, such as IQ, socioeconomic group, school achievement and so on. This is a finding of some significance as it suggests that reduction of aggression by means of catharsis (see page 113) and the view that aggression is an internal drive are *not* supported by these findings.

With the mass of available evidence, it is relatively easy to conclude not only that television does have an effect of major significance but that for the most part it is negative. We need to ask: why? Why does television violence cause violence in viewers? Some of the reasons given are as follows:

• **Modelling**   Children will simply copy what they see. Adults as well as children will often imitate a particularly bizarre or extreme behaviour modelled on a television character.
• **Arousal** can be such that the viewer becomes aggressive.
• **Desensitisation** is where viewers repeatedly exposed to violence simply get used to it. It no longer has an impact, and so the suffering caused by the aggression is not seen as serious.
• **Distortion**, whereby – particularly in conflict resolution – it is seen as easier to hit than to talk.

On a positive note, with respect to aggression as a consequence of watching television, Huesmann et al. (1983) have demonstrated that there are ways to minimise the harm that can be done. The study found that young people who regularly watch television programmes portraying violence are rated by their peers as being less violent in their own behaviour when they have been taught the following:

- that the violence in the television programme is not typical of most people;
- that the violence they see is not real, it is a result of special effects;
- that most people resolve problems in a non-violent manner.

The discussion so far has concerned main-channel television in the UK, which for the most part is monitored for violence and other extreme 'adult' behaviours; the more responsible broadcasters observe the 9.00pm watershed – programmes suitable for children are shown before 9.00pm, after which time the guidelines are relaxed. In terms of violence, aggression and explicit, often sadistic, sexual activity, programmes on cable television and satellite stations are significantly less restricted. For the most part these are not regulated, programmers making the not unreasonable assumption that it is the parents' responsibility, not theirs, to monitor what children watch. In ethical and moral terms, this is a weak argument; they know full well that parents rarely exercise complete control over what is watched, particularly when many children have a television set in their own bedroom. The situation gets worse still when we consider the type of film available from video-hire shops. The murder of the toddler James Bulger by two ten-year-old boys in 1994 provided a horrific example, with the trial judge commenting that the boys' habit of watching 'video-nasties' possibly influenced their behaviour.

There are a number of points that need to be made concerning the methodology of studies concerning the media and aggression:

- Due to the nature of these investigations, most are correlational, which means that cause and effect are not shown.
- With respect to experimental studies, there is a problem in deciding how to define and measure aggression – notoriously difficult.
- There is also the problem of ethics. You cannot deliberately show children violence and then let them be violent.
- Even if the above problems can be overcome, the sample will be small and it will only be possible to conduct the experiment over a short period of time – both serious design problems.

Something to do

- Draw up a chart showing some possible research ideas and the problems each may have. An example is given below:

Possible research	Related problems
• Measure violence watched on TV by different age groups	• Defining 'violence'
	• Gathering data

We finish this section with some figures:

- In the UK in 1987, four- to seven-year-olds watched an average of 2.8 hours of television every day; eight- to 11-year-olds watched an average of 3.3 hours per day.
- Children's television averages 25 incidents of aggression every hour.
- By age 16, the average child will have watched 13,000 television murders.
- There are now more than a billion television sets around the world.
- The film *Die Hard* (a popular video rental) has 264 deaths.
- In American 'cop' films the 'cops' fire their guns frequently – in Chicago the average police officer fires a gun once in 27 years.

The media and pro-social behaviour

We have seen that watching television influences behaviour. We have also noted the high incidence of aggressive and violent behaviour portrayed on television, which engenders aggression and violence in the viewers. The reasons why television presents so much aggression and violence is an altogether different issue. The fundamental question concerns whether television reflects what is happening in society or whether television leads what happens in society who watched them.

There have been far fewer studies exploring the positive effects of watching television. In a study by Gunter and McAleer (1990), they reported that programmes showing kindness, generosity and general helping behaviour had positive short-term and long-term effects by producing the same behaviours in the children who watched them.

Pressure from concerned parents and others is having a positive effect in reducing – albeit by only a small amount – the degree and frequency of violence in children's television programmes. There is also the political issue of censorship. If a definite link between televised aggression and aggression in children is proved (which thus far is not the case), should strict censorship of programmes be applied? That is a hugely complicated question to resolve, something that social psychologists will perhaps have to grapple with in the future.

Individual, social and cultural diversity in pro- and antisocial behaviour

We have discussed pro- and antisocial behaviour in terms of altruism and helping behaviour (pro) and aggression (anti). We then considered the effects of the media on these behaviours, and recognised that there can be influences for both pro- and antisocial behaviour. We now turn our attention to the diversity of individuals in terms of their pro- and antisocial behaviour, and how society and culture affect their pro- and antisocial behaviour.

It takes only a cursory glance at the influences shown in the following chart to see just how many and diverse these are. It is important to realise that the various factors can influence behaviour in both pro- and antisocial ways. For example, your mood can be happy and positive with the potential for pro-social behaviour, or it can be angry with the potential for antisocial behaviour. There is also, of course, considerable overlap between individual, social and cultural aspects of a given situation. The environment, for example, can influence the individual, social and cultural aspects for both pro- and antisocial behaviour.

Factors influencing diversity in pro- and antisocial behaviour		
Individual	**Social**	**Cultural**
• Mood	• Situation	• Tradition
• Personality	• Environment	• Expectation
• Competence	• Learned response(s)	• Subcultures
• Environment	• Social norms	
• Heredity	• Social learning theory	
• Biological (Darwin, Freud, the ethologists)		
• Personal distress		
• Empathy		

Note: Most of these factors can influence behaviour in a pro- *or* antisocial way.

In the case of social diversity there is an obvious relationship between antisocial behaviour and aggression – the issues just discussed. We have seen (pages 110–11) that there are three main theories for the social cause of aggression:

- the frustration–aggression hypothesis;
- the excitation-transfer theory; and
- social learning theory.

Social diversity can be considered as the range – or diversity – of social experience, whose outcome can lead to aggression, when, for example, rates of frustration reach breaking point. On the other hand, in a situation where someone has retired early, has a good pension, and gives up several mornings a week for volunteer work at their local hospital, we see typical pro-social behaviour. The danger is that at this point we drift into a stereo-typical view that antisocial behaviour occurs only in those from lower social classes, living in poor housing, etc., with the inference that pro-social behaviour occurs only in 'better' situations; both situations are clearly not true.

When it comes to cultural diversity, there are many examples from around the world. For example, a culture or people that have had to defend themselves against aggressors, perhaps over centuries, will need to be aggressive to survive. On the other hand, a people or tribe in a remote valley are less likely to have developed aggressive behaviour. A recent example of how circumstances can effect change is seen in the Jewish people. Having practised a peaceful non-aggressive lifestyle since Old Testament times, the Israeli nation is now aggressive and in one sense actually fighting for survival. The culture of the people has changed radically, with the Holocaust perhaps being the turning point.

Something to do

- Review this unit and see if you can add any other individual, social or cultural influences to the chart above.

Social constructionism

The purpose of this section is to explain briefly what **social construc-tionism** is, and to consider its relevance to psychology and its usefulness. We start by saying that the focus is not on 'social' but on 'construction-ism'. The essence of the subject is more philosophical than practical; it argues that what we know comes from the mental constructions of the people in a given social system. The idea is essentially the same as Gre-gory's view of perception – we 'construct' our view of the world from what we see and from what we know (see Unit 4, page 131).

Burr (1995) suggests that while there is no one generally agreed defini-tion of social constructionism, there are a number of basic notions which are fundamental to a belief in social constructionism. She lists these as:

- a critical stance towards taken-for-granted knowledge;
- historical and cultural specificity;
- knowledge sustained by social processes;
- knowledge and social action together.

The field of social constructionism has grown out of an attempt to explain the way that social psychology works, or rather does *not* – at least in a scientific manner – work. Social psychology has been criticised for being too **positivistic** – that is, accepting uncritically that science is the only way to establish fact. The problem comes because the social psychologist inevitably involves himself in whatever is being studied and therefore the study is not, and almost by definition cannot be, objective and hence scientific. Other criticisms of social psychology, which have helped to create the climate in which newer ideas such as social con-structionism can flourish, are that social psychology cannot make cause-and-effect connections, despite the fact that it tries to (think of attribution theory, for example), and that by trying to stay within the limits of traditional research methodology, many of the unique elements of the human participant are lost.

The emergence of social constructionism has not been sudden; it has evolved over the last 30 or so years, with Gergen (1973) contributing an early paper of some significance. The approach does not dispense with the scientific method, but rather tries to be as objective as possible, while recognising that people, however carefully they try to be objective about their behaviour, are still individuals. As such they bring with them to the laboratory their own ideas, feelings and so on, all of which are, at least in part, a result of social forces, culture and other historical antecedents.

Something to investigate

- Investigate social constructionism further by reading Burr, *An Introduction to Social Constructionism*.
- Consider how a social constructionist would view 'personality'.
- What part does 'language' play on social constructionist thinking?
- What does social constructionism have to say about psychological research?

Revision and practice

• •

Coursework opportunities

1. Replicate the study by Luchins (1957) into the primacy–recency effect (see page 64). Present participants with a description of a fictitious person by listing a series of personal attributes. Half the participants have the list ordered so that the good, positive attributes come first, the less good later; the other half have the list in the reverse order. Test participants on how they assess the fictitious person.
2. Using the Coopersmith self-esteem inventory (see pages 66–7), correlate the data with, for example, behaviour, school success, etc. Take particular care with ethical issues.
3. Investigate attribution by observing participants playing video games. Do they attribute human characteristics to the 'characters' in the games?
4. Many sixth forms and colleges recruit students from different schools, resulting in a number of different groups of students who know each other but do not know members of groups from other schools. Usually, over time, any intergroup prejudice disappears. Design a study to measure changes in attitudes towards other groups of students that occur over time. Be particularly careful with related ethical issues.
5. Investigate the effects of long-term isolation or the effects on sole survivors of catastrophes (see page 80). See if you can identify or isolate any personality characteristics of those who survive. This might lend itself to qualitative analysis (see page 45).
6. Use face-ism (Archer et al., 1983) to analyse televised interviews (see page 114). As an alternative source of data use, for example, Sunday newspaper magazines.
7. Replicate the Manstead and McCulloch study (1981) into sex-role stereotyping in British television commercials (see page 114).
8. If you argue that television influences behaviour, then children who watch violent behaviour may display violent behaviour. Investigate this idea by correlating children's playground behaviour with the TV programmes they watch. Take particular care with the ethics of this investigation.

• •

Examination questions

Question 1   Discuss psychological insights into the behaviour of crowds.   *(24 marks)*

(AEB, Module Paper 4, January 1997)

Question 1: Unpacked   This essay requires you to 'discuss', i.e. a Skill A and B term meaning 'describe and evaluate by reference to different if not contrasting points of view'. In this case, there is only one main subject: the behaviour of crowds.

- The introduction should refer to 'collective behaviour' and include a definition of 'crowd', and the distinction between a *crowd* and a *mob*.
- You now have the familiar problem of whether to discuss each 'insight' in turn and then do an evaluation of them all, or to discuss one 'insight' then evaluate it, a second 'insight', evaluate it, and so on. It is really a question of your preference. Whatever you decide, however, work it out on your plan, and then stick with it. Probably it is better to make *one* general evaluation following the presentation of various 'insights', as in this way you can more easily relate, or argue, one view versus another.

- 'Insights' that you could discuss are:
  - Lebon (1908) gave three reasons for why a crowd forms.
  - Hogg and Vaughan (1995) argue that Lebon was influential.
  - Festinger (1952) – deindividuation.
  - Turner (1974) – emergent norm theory.
  - Reider and Potter (1985) – *inter*group action.
- Now evaluate the 'insights'. As always, provide as much evidence as possible from other studies, theories, etc.

Question 2   Describe and evaluate research studies of conformity.   *(25 marks)*

(AEB, Paper 1, Summer 1997)

Question 2: Sample answer   The essay that follows was written by a student in 45 minutes in a practice exam situation. It has been typed verbatim including any mistakes.

Comments

Essay

Good introduction. Relevant, accurate and good use of supporting evidence.

Defined by Taguin as 'yielding to group pressure', conformity occurs for many reasons. Insko ('60s) said that conformity is the result of 2 types of influences: normative social influence – the desire to be liked, and informational social influence – where we look to others for ways in which to behave. Numerous studies have been carried out. The main ones were by Sherif, Asch, Crutchfield and Zimbardo. Each revealed explanations for conformity.

Needs a little more explanation.

Sherif ('35) used the autokinetic effect to look at the emergence of group norms. It was found that when people make their own estimates on how far a stationary spot of light appears to move, the estimates differ considerably whereas when people worked in groups and gave their answers aloud, estimates became closer together and gradually produced a group norm. The emergence of group norms is faster when people work in groups in the first place because people's actions and opinions are affected by others. This study was criticised by Asch in '46 who said that the task was ambiguous, therefore there was no right or wrong answer and that conformity was not being tested, just group norm formation.

Accurate comment/evaluation

Date wrong ('52)

In '46, Asch carried out his line study – the Asch paradigm. Having 3 lines of obviously different lengths on one card and a line the same length as one of the lines on a different card, Asch was sure to be measuring conformity because the answer was unambiguous and clearly if anyone did conform to the confederates, they were ignoring their own eyes. Asch found that there was 32% conformity – quite surprising considering the answer was obvious. In producing the results, Asch put forward 3 psychological explanation to explain findings. These were (1) distortion of perception – people believed they perceived the lines wrong and so conformed, (2) distortion of judgement – people were not aware they were being influenced by the group, and (3) distortion of action – these people couldn't stand being in a minority and being ridiculed. 13 out of the 50 participants in this study never conformed – Asch therefore found evidence for independent behaviour. By interviewing the participants after the study, Asch found that people behaved independently for 2 reasons. (1) independence based on confidence – these people saw

Explanation of the study is not very clear

Accurate

the confederates as wrong and were unaffected by the 'group' opinions, (2) independence based on withdrawal – people avoided eye-contact with the group as a result of not conforming, and the third reason being that people felt obligated to say what they saw even if this meant they were stressed, nervous and rejected by the group – independence based on tension.

Good description. Some evaluation evident

Asch varied his technique and found that different variants can affect conformity. In a 1 participant : 1 confederate situation, there is a 'my word against yours' scenario and there was little or no conformity. By having a confederate who acted as a dissenter, conformity levels dropped dramatically – the participant didn't feel so pressured because there was someone else who wasn't conforming. Asch found that the mode of response affects conformity – if asked to write down their answer rather than say it aloud, conformity levels dropped. This illustrates the difference between public compliance – seen as agreeing with others – and private acceptance – not internalising the group's view.

Good description. Some evaluation evident

Zimbardo's controversial prison simulation study showed how people can conform to social roles. Ordinary people, assigned the role of prisoners or guards were transformed in the study. Guards were very authoritative and aggressive towards the prisoners who, it is argued by Savin ('73), were treated inhumanely and did not give full consent for the study (although did volunteer for it when advertised from Stanford University).

Description rather too short

Evaluation

Explanations for this quite shocking conformity to behaviour of typical roles could be that the guards were acting in a way that they thought typical of prison guards – stereotyped ideas, or were just trying to please the experimenters.

Evaluation

Ran out of time   Talk about ethics in study
Other criticisms by Savin
Conclusion

General comments
A good essay with accurate, relevant comments. Some areas needed more explanation/clarification. Evaluation was a bit patchy and rather weak.

Marks: Skill A 9

Skill B 7 $= \dfrac{16}{25}$

Question 3   Discuss some of the effects that interpersonal relationships have been shown to have on a person's psychological well-being (e.g. happiness and health).   *(24 marks)*

(AEB, Module Paper 4, Summer 1997)

Question 4   Describe and evaluate **two** theories of interpersonal relationships.   *(24 marks)*

(AEB, Module Paper 4, January 1997)

Question 5   Discuss psychological explanations of the breakdown of relationships.   *(25 marks)*

(AEB, Paper 1, Summer 1996)

Question 6   (a) Distinguish between any **two** named components of an attitude.   *(3 marks)*
(b) Outline **one** method of measuring attitudes used by psychologists.   *(3 marks)*
(c) Describe how an individual might show compliance in a social situation.
(2 marks)
(d) What is meant by the term *group polarization*?   *(2 marks)*
(e) How might a *democratic* leader differ from a *laissez-faire* leader in their behaviour towards a group?   *(3 marks)*
(f) Outline **one** criticism of experimental studies of the primacy effect in impression formation.   *(2 marks)*
(g) What do psychologists mean by the term *self-esteem*?   *(2 marks)*
(h) Outline **one** way in which inter-group conflict can sometimes be reduced.
(3 marks)
(Total: 20 marks)

(NEAB, PSO5, February 1996)

Selected reading list

Duck, S., *Human Relationships* (Sage, 2nd edn 1992)
Durkin, K., *Developmental Social Psychology: From Infancy to Old Age* (Blackwell, 1995)
Hogg, M.A. and Vaughan, G.M., *Social Psychology: An Introduction* (Prentice Hall, 1995)

Answer to question on page 98
Dom and Avermaet suggested that maths and engineering students should be expected to place greater emphasis on accuracy and less on social conformity.

4 Cognitive psychology: how do we think?

A simple definition of **cognitive psychology** is that it studies what goes on in our minds – in other words it studies thought processes or cognitive functions. As such it is central to psychological study.

Think about it

• What do you think your own thought processes or cognitive functions are? Make a list.

You probably came up with most of the following: thinking, problem solving, learning, speaking, perception, remembering (and forgetting), forming concepts (ideas) and information processing. These are the areas that form the body of cognitive psychology. We look at them in this unit as follows:

• We begin with a discussion on **information processing**, with a brief look at problem solving and artificial intelligence (which we return to in more detail at the end of the unit).
• We then consider **perception**, which holds a key place in psychology.
• Following perception, we consider **attention**, both divided attention and focused or selective attention.
• We then look at **memory** and the processes involved in remembering and forgetting.
• The next topic is **language** and, closely linked to it, the development of **thought**.
• Finally, we discuss **problem solving** and **artificial intelligence** as a model for our own thinking processes.

The mind–body debate

Before we consider the above in detail, there is a classic debate that you need to be aware of. It is called the **mind–body problem**. It has been debated by philosophers since the time of Plato, who first raised the question of dualism, and it still generates interest and fresh debate. In essence, the problem concerns the relationship between the *body*, that which is physical, and the *mind*, that which is mental. Solutions to the problem of the relationship fall into three main groups: a **dualism** view, a **monism** view and, thirdly, a compromise of dualism *and* monism. This is an important issue, and we have to ask the question: what does it have to do with psychology? The answer is a great deal, because we have defined psychology as 'the scientific study of mind and behaviour', which implies a relationship between mind and behaviour. At the very least then, the debate will have a bearing on behaviourism, which in terms of mind–body is a **materialistic** or, more specifically, a **peripheralist** view; that is, the idea that having a mind means little more than engaging in some kind of special, sophisticated **behaviour**. This is more a matter of philosophy than of psychology, but it is still relevant to psychology.

A more recent view of the mind–body debate as it relates to psychology is the materialistic, centralistic view that argues that the 'mind' is in fact a physical process occurring in the central nervous system. This view, called **central-state materialism** or the **identity view**, allows the existence of internal mental processes which can interact with, and therefore influence, the body, something which the behaviourist view does not allow (Gregory, 1987).

Something to investigate

- Research the mind–body debate as it applies to psychology, and summarise different views in a simple flow chart. Include the terms used above and add: interactionism, psychophysicalism, parallelism, subjective idealism, phenomenalism, double aspectism, epiphenomenalism.

Information processing

Almost all of what you do cognitively – that is, your thought processes – requires or uses some form of information processing, in other words:

> "... *organising, interpreting and responding to incoming stimulation.*"
> A.S. Reber, *Dictionary of Psychology* (Penguin, 2nd edn 1995)

Cognitive and perceptual processes take place in stages and can be shown as follows:

These processes are in action in a range of activities as diverse as translating a foreign language and riding a bicycle.

Much of the early work in this area was done by cognitive researchers such as Broadbent and Neisser in the period after the Second World War when there was a great surge of research and development in communications science and in the technology that made it possible. Their work led to the concept of the brain as an information-processing system and to the idea that the basic model of input/processing/output could be used to explain mental, or cognitive, processes.

A more recent theoretical approach, particularly as information processing is applied to problem solving, is the **production systems approach**. This is a theoretical model that provides a set (or sets) of rules on how to deal with a given situation (the 'production'); it deals with the rules and their application.

Connectionist theory also has a part to play, particularly as information processing is applied to systems. This moves us beyond a linear approach to the processing of information: it deals with the information to be processed as a network, where different stages (or parts) of the process can be dealt with at the same time. (We look at examples of 'linear' and 'networking' models in the context of memory in the section beginning on page 159.)

Models of information processing

There are three main ways of looking at information processing:
- the lens model;
- the cognitive approach;
- the process-tracing approach.

The lens model

The way this model works is to consider both the task and its environment. It looks at how the situation or environment provides information about the cognitive task or problem that has to be attended to and recognises that this influences the processing that occurs. Since the information gained from the environment is not always very good or accurate, the individual has to develop a range of strategies to cope with it. The lens model is particularly relevant to how people make decisions and solve problems.

The cognitive approach

The emphasis of this model lies with the individual person. The theory holds that it is possible to classify the individual according to the way that that person uses information, in particular in decision making. The classic work by Hudson (1966) in dividing schoolboys into **convergent thinkers** and **divergent thinkers** (see page 198) is a good example of this model.

The process-tracing approach

In broad terms, both the lens model and the cognitive approach concentrate, in different ways, on the input and output stages of information processing. The process-tracing approach (as the words suggest) looks in detail at the way the information is processed. It looks, microscopically, at how processing occurs.

With the lens and cognitive models, it is possible to infer or deduce the processes by considering the relationship between the input and the output. With process tracing, the interest lies in the detail that goes on between the input and the output. Typically, you would be asked to describe, in detail, the thought processes that you went through to solve a particular problem.

A classic case of information processing

An information-processing approach that concentrates on the way children process information was proposed by Pascal-Leone and Case in the 1970s. It focused on children's memory, particularly memory capacity, and the children's cognitive functioning. The theory suggests that the frequent failure of children to carry out certain tasks (failure which, according to Piaget (see Unit 7), is caused by or is a reflection of the child's development of *thought*) may in fact be due to the lack of development of the child's *memory*, particularly the short-term memory. A typical problem or task given to the child would require a number of steps which would relate to the number of 'chunks' or bits of information that the child would have to hold in short-term memory while it is working on the next part of the problem. The average adult can hold seven, plus or minus two, chunks. An average three-year-old can hold one chunk; a five- or six-year-old two; and this improves to seven, plus or minus two, by about 15 years of age.

Information-processing models

Lens	Cognitive	Process tracing
Considers the environment of the problem.	Considers the cognitive style of the problem solver.	Considers details of the problem-solving approach.
key word: **problem**	*key word:* **person**	*key word:* **process**

Important links from information processing to problem solving and artificial intelligence are discussed in more detail at the end of this unit. As we turn now to a study of **perception**, keep in mind the main ideas discussed in information processing and look for cross-curricular connections.

Something to do

- Look up 'bottom-up' and 'top-down' in the glossary.
- Write a short paragraph on their relevance to information processing.
  (Also see pages 128–31 for a more detailed description of how the terms apply to perception.)

Perception

As stated at the beginning of this unit, **perception** has a key place in the study of psychology. A broad definition of perception is that it refers to the processes that enable us to make sense of the world around us. This in turn means that we 'perceive' the following:

- the **physical** – the room you are in;
- the **sensory** – are you feeling rather warm?
- the **cognitive** – are you making sense of what you are reading?
- the **affective** – the mood you are in at the moment.

Think about it

- What sensory inputs are you experiencing now? Make a list.

The key word is, of course, 'sensory', so your list should have five items at least – one for each sense.

In the context of psychology, you are required to study **visual perception**. Two things need to be said. The first is that you do not need to have a detailed biological understanding of the human visual system. And secondly, you may, if you wish – in the context of examination question answers – refer to other human sensory systems. As far as this text is concerned, we limit our discussion to the human visual system of perception.

Visual perception – the human visual system

To understand visual perception you need a basic grasp of how the human visual system works. A simple representation is shown on page 127. (Further information is given in Unit 5 in the context of neurophysiological explanations of visual perception – see pages 247–50.)

The human visual system

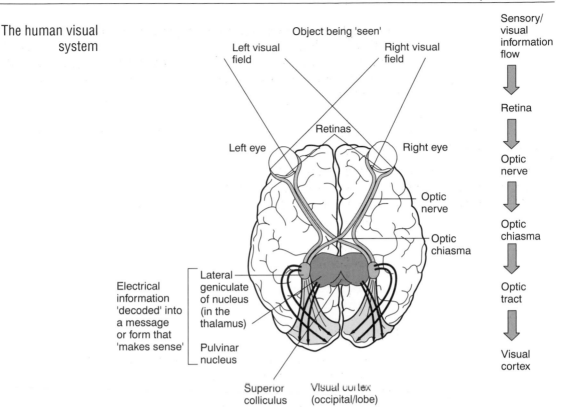

Basically, what happens is that information from each eye travels via the optic nerves to both sides, or hemispheres, of the brain. The crossover point – the optic chiasma – allows information from both 'ends' of the object being seen to be transmitted to and to register in both hemispheres of the brain. The result of this crossover means that you have, to put it crudely, the maximum possible options for partial eye and partial brain damage to occur before becoming completely blind. Partial eye damage or partial brain damage need not mean more than partial blindness.

The human visual system is a good example of information processing. Because of the type of processing that occurs in the lateral geniculate nucleus, where information is received from the retinas *and* from higher visual centres in the brain (in the visual cortex – see Unit 5, pages 227 and 249–50), which is *based on previous information*, we have a system of information processing which can be considered as both 'top-down' (the brain's previous knowledge) and 'bottom-up' (retinal information). This in turn blurs the distinction between **sensation** (a purely physical process) and **perception** (the psychological 'making sense' of perceived perceptions) (Coren, Ward and Enns, 1994). The concept of 'top-down' and 'bottom-up' is important and occurs in a number of contexts. See the section beginning on page 128 for a more detailed explanation.

Something to try

• Look at something straight ahead. (It makes no difference where you are.) Now rotate your head rapidly – with your eyes still open – about 90 degrees left or right. How do you know that it was your head that moved and not the object you were looking at?

Perceptual processes – theories of perception

The task of perception is to make sense of the world around us, all the time.

In terms of the above experiment (page 127), all your retina 'saw' was a rapidly changing picture. Something else was necessary for you to make sense of the experience (in this case, information from your neck muscles and information from the balance system of your ears). Perceptual processes, or theories of perception, attempt to provide answers to how you make sense of, or understand, the information that your senses are receiving.

Making sense of experiences is more than simply processing information. It must involve interpreting, combining, synthesising, making judgements about size, shape, distance, colour and intensity; sorting out things you know from things you do not know; remembering past experience and so on. What has to happen, then, is a complex set of problem-solving computations, the result of which are **percepts**. These can be considered as the result or outcome of the perceptual processes – in other words the psychological sense or end product of the experience, which you (really your brain) can comprehend; because you *know*, don't you, that you were moving your head and that it was not the room revolving around you.

There are occasions when you cannot make sense of the world you are in – this is **spatial disorientation**. It occurs when you do not have sufficient information or input to be able to make sense of the world around you. It sometimes happens to pilots flying small aircraft in thick cloud and turbulent conditions. In these conditions *and* with a loss of instruments, a pilot can become spatially disorientated and quite literally not know which way up he or she is.

Bottom-up, top-down theories

What are the clues, or cues, that give us the information that enables us – our brain – to make sense of a given situation? Or, to rephrase: how do I get from **sensation**, which is a purely physical process, to **perception**, which is the psychological 'making sense' of received perceptions? These are key questions and have given rise to two main theories:

- **Theory 1:** Our understanding of the world is based purely on sensory information.
- **Theory 2:** Our understanding of the world is the end product which starts with sensory information but also draws on higher mental processes such as inference, memory, experience and so on.

Both theories must start with you as a person interacting with the world around you at any given moment in time, and must end with the interpretation of that scene or experience. They start and end at the same place, but they get there a different way.

We can represent the two theories diagrammatically as follows:

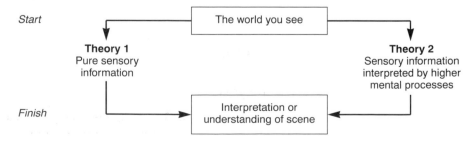

Something to do

- Redraw the diagram of the two theories (remember this is a valuable study skill you will need to practise).
- Now consider the relevance of the Nature–Nurture debate (see page 38) as it applies to perception and add the labels 'Nature' and 'Nurture' to your diagram – one to each theory.

You should have added 'Nature' to Theory 1 and 'Nurture' to Theory 2, so the two theories can now be represented briefly like this:

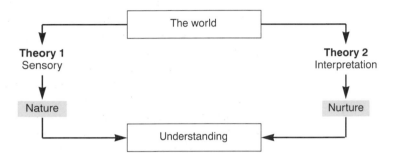

We can go on developing our understanding of these two main theories in this way. Remember that Nature theories, sometimes called **nativism**, concentrate on our innate abilities; while Nurture theories, **empiricism**, concentrate on empirical processes – those based on learning and experience. One of these two sets of theories is called 'bottom-up', the other 'top-down'. Can you work out which is which?

Something to do

- Redraw the diagram of the two main theories, this time adding 'Nativism' and 'Empiricism' *and* 'Bottom-up' and 'Top-down'.

You should now have arrived at the following:

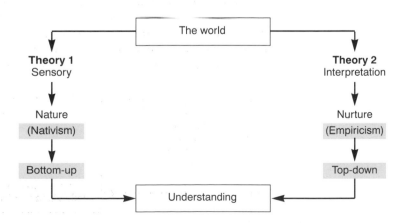

Next we need to add to the diagram the names of key psychological theorists and a few important variations on the Nature and Nurture approaches:

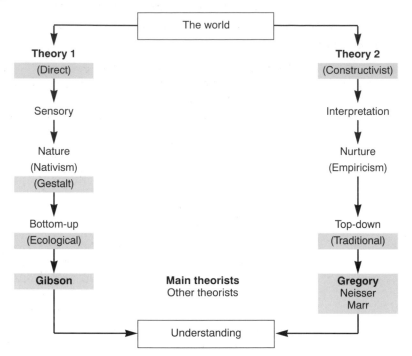

You also need to be aware of the following:

- The Gestalt theorists (see below) are nativist.
- Theory 1 (Gibson) is also sometimes known as 'ecological'.
- Although Gibson is nativist/ecological in his thinking on cognitive processes, he takes an empiricist approach in his thinking on some other aspects of psychology.
- Top-down is also sometimes referred to as the 'traditional' approach to cognitive psychology.
- 'Direct' = Gibson (see below).
- 'Constructivist' = Gregory (see below).

Summary of the two main theories of perception

- **Theory 1** starts with direct sensory information, is called 'bottom-up' and is linked with Gibson.
- **Theory 2** starts with prior knowledge and experience, is 'top-down' and is linked with Gregory.

We now need to discuss the two main theories in more detail. We look at each of them in turn below.

Direct perception ('bottom-up'): Gibson (1966 and 1979)   The essential idea in this theory is that the sensory information arriving at the retina, the **optic array**, contains sufficient information to enable us to make complete sense of what we perceive and that our brain and nervous system do not need any other information. The optic array contains all the information we require in the form of:

- **optic flow patterns**, which have to do with the way we move relative to what we see; and
- **texture gradients**, which are the distance clues that we get from changes in the texture of what we see.

Something to try

- It is easy to demonstrate texture gradient. Stand on the edge of a lawn or a playing field and notice that you can identify individual blades of grass close to your feet, but only a mass of green further away – the texture changes with distance.

In evaluating Gibson we need to remember that his theory is fairly old and that it has flaws. He is not explicit in all the concepts he uses, and while he explains 'optic array' and other theoretical concepts, it is likely that in reality the process of perception is rather more complex. The theory does not adequately explain, for instance, why we are fooled by illusions (see pages 140–3).

Constructivist ('top-down'): Gregory (1972 and 1980)   The essential idea in this theory is that our perception is constructed; it is built up, starting with the sensory information and adding to this our knowledge and experience and sometimes hypotheses about the sensory input. While you obviously have to start with the sensory, that is only the beginning; it is the higher-order functions of the brain (the 'top') that are used to make sense of what we see. Gregory argues that sensory information alone is insufficient for making sense of perceptions.

When we evaluate this theory a key problem is that we are nearly always correct in our perceptions. A notable exception is the Müller-Lyer illusion (see page 140) when we are almost always wrong. If, as Gregory's theory suggests, we are always inferring and hypothesising about what we see, it would be reasonable to expect more errors more often. In general, we tend to be accurate about real-life perception and when we have time to consider what we see, but less so when tested in the laboratory or when our perception is, for whatever reason, sensorarily incomplete or very brief.

A general conclusion on the bottom-up/top-down debate is that the process of perception is not fully explained by either one or the other, but by both. The diagram on page 135 shows how the theories overlap.

Other theories of perception   We now need to discuss other related theories, in particular the **Gestalt** view, Marr's **computational theory** and Neisser's **'analysis by synthesis'** model.

The Gestalt view   'Gestalt' is a German word with no direct English translation, the nearest being 'form', 'whole' or 'shape'. You will find that most references are to the German 'Gestalt' rather than any English equivalent. Perhaps a better way to consider the term is to say that *the whole is more than the sum of its parts*, a principle at the heart of the Gestalt view of psychology. Under 'Gestalt', we consider those things that go towards making up the whole: figure/ground; similarity and proximity; the way things are grouped.

> *"If the key process in Gregory's theory is inference and in Gibson's direct perception of invariants, then the key concept in the Gestalt approach is that of organisation."*
> R.D. Gross, *Psychology. The Science of Mind and Behaviour*
> (1996)

Max Wertheimer (1923) is generally considered to be the 'father' of Gestalt psychology. He presented his subjects with groups of shapes or figures, and then moved or altered one of them in order to see how the change affected the way that the subjects perceived the whole. From this he developed a number of laws:

- The **law of proximity** says that we see objects that are closer as being grouped together.

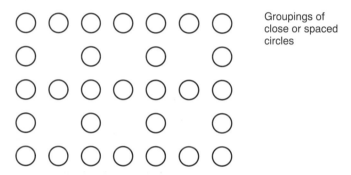

Groupings of close or spaced circles

- The **law of similarity** says that similar shapes will be seen as groups.

The circles are all the same; we 'see' horizontal lines because of the similarity of open and filled-in circles.

- The **phi phenomenon**, first described by Wertheimer in 1912, is familiar to all of us. It is the illusion of movement which is created by the rapid presentation of stimuli – for example, fairground lights that switch on and off rapidly create the impression of movement. If you watch a film, you are seeing slightly different pictures presented – in the case of home movies – at 24 frames per second. Television works the same way: you 'see' smooth movements, but you are in fact being presented with rapidly moving individual pictures.
- **Figure/ground** concerns which part of an image is background and which is the figure. In the famous example illustrated on page 133, do you 'see' two faces (in silhouette) or one vase?

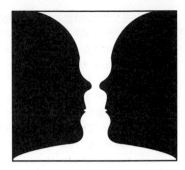

- The **principle of closure**: what do you see in the illustration below?

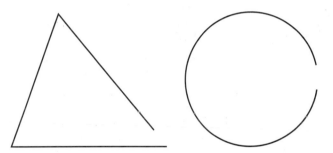

You will almost certainly say a triangle and a circle. In fact what you see is two lines, one with two bends, the other a curve. You 'closed' the figures, making them *whole*.

- **Continuity**: if you are presented with a series of dots in a pattern, what you see is the most obvious continuous arrangement of dots:

In this case you 'see' the 'line' shown to the right of the dots.

Gestalt psychologists believe that all these 'laws' are examples of a general principle: the **law of Prägnanz**, which translates as 'meaningfulness' or 'good form'. This means that the simplest organisation, requiring the least cognitive processing, will always represent the end product.

Thus far we have discussed the three Gs of perception: Gibson, Gregory, Gestalt. Now we turn to computational theory.

Marr's computational theory (1982) In some ways this is not a separate theory, as Marr is concerned with a problem that occurs in Gregory's theory – that of defining precisely just what the mechanism is for dealing with the sometimes ambiguous or incomplete information hitting the retina. (Gibson believes that all the information needed is present in the optical array, so he does not have this problem.) Marr's theory is an attempt to solve the problem of precisely how we extract useful information from the retinal image of the scene. In other words, he looked at the question: how do we extract the information that is useful in helping us understand, from a hugely complicated image often involving other senses?

As a mathematician, Marr took a computational approach to solve this problem. He attempted to develop a computer programme or model that would simulate the perceptual process – a form of **artificial intelligence**. He argues that the main purpose of perception is to make sense of a 3-dimensional (3D) world; he sees this occurring in stages, as almost a linear process, with the 'picture' being built up by successive stages. It is a classic form of information processing, with the output of each stage becoming the input of the next.

Marr's starting point is shape and how our visual system derives information from the shape impinging on the retina.

- The first stage is the most basic, and is concerned with taking retinal information and converting it into, in Marr's words, a **primal sketch**. This sorts out light and shade, edges or boundaries and generally organises the image – rather akin to the Gestalt laws of organisation.
- The second stage takes this 'primal sketch' and converts it into a **$2\frac{1}{2}$D sketch** – between 2D which is 'flat' and 3D which is fully pictorial or contoured and with depth. So in this mode, $2\frac{1}{2}$D is additional processing to the first stage (the primal sketch), adding the beginnings of 3D such as surface form and contour, variation of texture and of relevant movement information. If you think of this in a wider context, this is about as far as 'bottom-up' processing can go; it is also where memory will hold the $2\frac{1}{2}$D sketch in store while additional processing takes place.
- The third and final stage is full **3D representation** and is the completion of the processing from $2\frac{1}{2}$D to 3D. This is done by using 'top-down' information. The second ($2\frac{1}{2}$D) stage requires more information to make detail precise or explicit so that the object is fully recognisable. If you were looking at a dog, for example, the first stage would be rather like seeing a child's crude model in plasticine – little more than cylinders stuck together. For the second stage you would start to see more detail such as size, proportions and colour; while for the third stage – drawing on past experience – you would see a St Bernard, say, and not a dachshund!

You will notice, however, that this still has not fully explained the way in which these processes act or occur – particularly the way in which 'top-down' mixes with, or influences, 'bottom-up' processing.

Analysis by synthesis: Neisser (1976)   This is rather like Marr, in that it starts from existing theory. While Marr picks up from a detail of Gregory's work, Neisser is unhappy with both Gregory and Gibson *alone*, and so develops a view that seeks to show the interaction *between* bottom-up (Gibson) and top-down (Gregory) processing. He starts with a bottom-up analysis and then brings to bear a top-down approach that looks for, or analyses, expected features that could be expanded or clarified to make 'better sense' or synthesise the input. If this does not happen, fresh analysis takes place, leading to fresh synthesis.

Integration of top-down and bottom-up

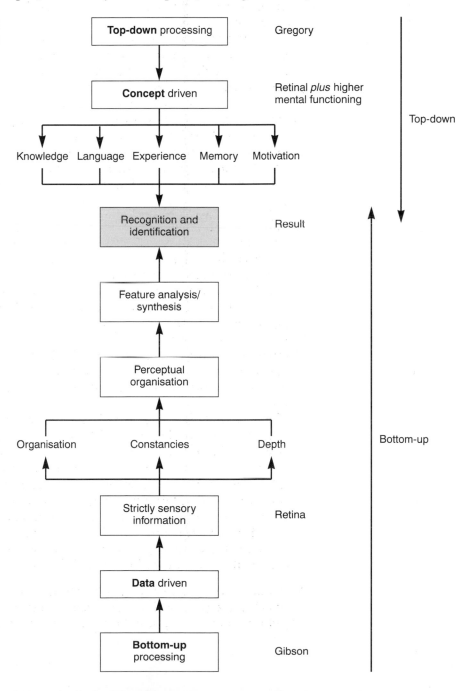

How do we recognise things?

The way we perceive things visually varies according to a wide range of factors – how far away something is and the angle from which we see it are two obvious examples.

Perceptual constancy

Our ability to recognise things is due to what psychologists call **perceptual constancy**. Constancy, in all its various forms, has to do with perceived objects remaining constant, or providing the same perceptual experience, despite the fact that the input can vary widely. If we did not have perceptual constancy, it would be extremely difficult to make sense of our world – doorways would change size as we approached them (size constancy); your car would change colour in twilight conditions (colour constancy); your coffee mug would look flat if viewed straight on (shape constancy). These examples are just some of the constancies that we experience continually.

- **Size constancy** is the tendency to see the same object as always being the same size, however far away it is. For example, the size of the retinal image of, say, a football player viewed from the top of a stand is much smaller than the football player you are about to tackle, but you 'know' they are the same. Putting this into real numbers, the retinal image of your pet cat at 5 metres is the same size as a 10 pence coin in your hand.

A classic case of perceptual constancy

One of the classic studies in this area is the work done by Turnbull (1961). He studied the perception of an African tribe who lived in dense forest, and who therefore had no experience of open spaces. Turnbull took one of the Africans to the edge of the forest and showed him buffalo grazing far away on the plains. The African was convinced that the animals were ants because they 'looked' so 'small'.

- **Colour constancy** is the ability to 'see' an object as the same colour, in varying lighting conditions.

Something to try

- Collect several sheets of coloured paper. Use a room where the lighting level can be changed from bright to almost dark. Ask a helper to identify the colour of the paper sheets as you vary the lighting level.

You will find from the above experiment that white paper is always called 'white' even when, as in poor lighting conditions, it looks grey.

- **Brightness constancy** works in a similar way. Again, it is relatively easy to conduct a simple experiment. Look at the following two squares:

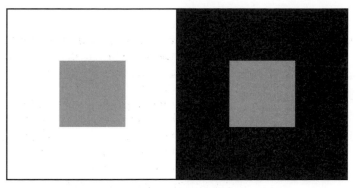

and say which of the two inner grey squares is the darker. You will find that your perception of the strength or darkness of the grey area depends on its surroundings.

- **Shape constancy** is fairly easy to demonstrate. Look for a moment at the door of the room you are in. What shape is it? You will probably say rectangular, but unless your eyes are at a position exactly in front of the centre of the door, the door will not be rectangular *on your retina*, it will almost certainly be trapezoidal. The following diagram shows a door in three positions. The shapes shown here are what the retina sees, but if you were asked the shape you would say rectangular, whatever position the door was in.

Similarly, you could look at your coffee mug. What shape is the top? It is a circle, of course; but unless you are looking straight down into the mug, what your retina sees is in fact an ellipse.

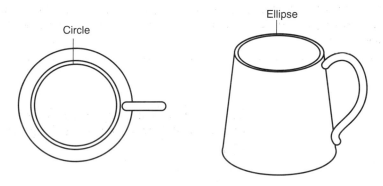

Circle

Ellipse

Depth perception   This concept is related to perceptual constancy. Because what we look at is usually a picture made up of a combination of objects, some nearer than others, there are a number of clues – or cues – that provide information for our **depth perception** of the view to be accurate. If you did not have this ability, you would not know whether to run towards the pitch or the boundary to catch a high cricket ball, or when in traffic you might stop too soon or run into the vehicle in front.

Something to try

- Close one eye. Put your hands in front of you at arms' length with forefingers extended and pointed towards each other. Bring them together until they touch. You will find that it is not easy – they sometimes 'miss'. Try this again with the person you are sitting next to, each of you with one finger – you will probably be even more inaccurate.

<u>Monocular and binocular cues</u>   There are two main **cues** that provide us with the necessary information:

- **monocular cues**, which can be interpreted with only one eye; and
- **binocular cues**, which require the use of both eyes.

If you did the above experiment with both eyes open, you would be accurate every time. Why? The answer is that you need two eyes for accurate depth perception, particularly close up (within about 3 metres). In general we use binocular cues for distances less than 3 metres and monocular cues to interpret data further away.

Binocular cues include convergence and retinal disparity:

- **Convergence:**   when you move the focus of your eyes from something in the distance to something say 2 metres in front of you, the eyes converge. The **ciliary muscles** cause the lens to change shape or **accommodate,** and your brain uses this information to assist in the distance judgement.

 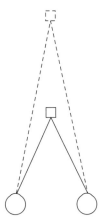

- **Retinal disparity** is somewhat similar. Look back at the diagram on page 127 and you will appreciate that each eye 'sees' the object from a slightly different position (because the eyes are about 6cm apart). The brain uses the difference in views – the disparity – to help judge the distance of the object.

Monocular cues are as follows:

- **Clearness** is our experience telling us that the clearer or more detailed the view the closer it is.
- **Interposition** has to do with the relative position of objects. An object that partially covers up or overlaps another is obviously in front of it. If you draw two circles the same size so that one overlaps the other, one will be seen as in front of the other:

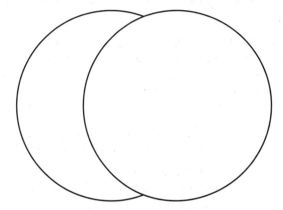

Colouring or shading the circles makes no difference:

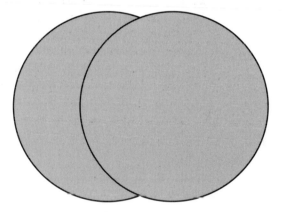

Size also makes no difference to this monocular cue:

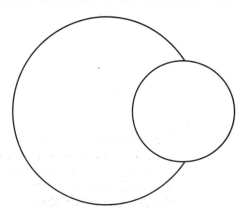

- **Perspective:** this is when two parallel lines appear to converge as they get further away – for example railway lines. They do not of course actually get closer together, they just appear to do so.
- **Shadow:** this monocular cue is more than just shadow, it is also linked with the way that light can produce a 3D effect. Look at the three stages in the following diagram, where the circles are all the same size:

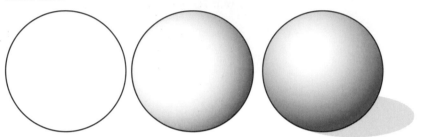

- **Texture**, usually called **texture gradient**, is similar (see also page 131). The coarser or rougher the texture, the closer the object is. If you were standing on a pebble beach and looked along it, the effect far away would not be a texture made up of a 'rough' surface – it would have merged into a general impression of distance.

This discussion on depth might suggest that the binocular and monocular cues occur one at a time. This is not the case. The visual information that you are taking in, that is arriving and making an impression on your retinal surfaces, amounts to a mass of information that your perception makes sense of. At any one point in time you can be using any one or any number or perhaps even all of the binocular and monocular cues described above, simultaneously or in rapid succession.

Think about it

- Go outside and just look. Try to 'freeze' an image of what you see. Now analyse that scene for binocular and monocular cues.

Illusions

Visual illusions are another interesting aspect of our perception. What is it that fools us into 'seeing' what is not there, into misjudging angles and lengths of lines and sizes of similar circles?

An **optical illusion** is a conflict between what is 'seen' and its reality. The Müller-Lyer is a classic optical illusion. Look at the diagram below. Which of the two vertical lines is longer?

The Müller-Lyer illusion

Both verticals are the same, but they *look* different. Why? The traditional answer is that of Gregory, who argues that one drawing looks like the outside corner of a building, while the other looks like the inside corner of a room:

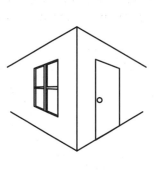 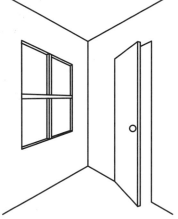

The logic of this argument is that we see buildings as farther away than a room, so the room appears larger. If this is the case, how is it that even once we know this we are still fooled by the illusion?

Something to do

- Construct the Müller-Lyer illusion from stiff card such that it looks like this:

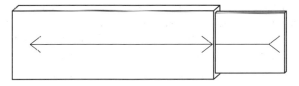

The right-hand piece slides into the left-hand slot.

The left-hand part is a flattened cylinder.

The centre line must appear continuous, and the 'fins' should be drawn as shown.
On the reverse side, draw another centre line indicating degree of error, plus and minus, from the position where the two centre lines are *in fact* equal.
- To demonstrate the illusion, ask a friend to slide the inner piece in or out of the outer until the two lines (the distances between the arrow heads) are equal.

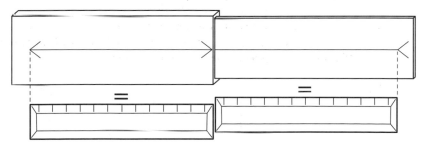

Now, without moving the slider, turn over and read off the error. Can you find anyone who is not fooled by the illusion?
Note: 'Pym' software allows you to test the Müller-Lyer illusion on screen.

What about the Nature–Nurture debate? Is the illusory perception due to our innate perceptual processes, or is it affected by 'Nurture' – external influences?

A classic case of perceptual illusions

Segall et al. (1963) were intrigued by this question. They tested the illusion on the Zulu people of Africa, who live in an environment of mostly curves with no square buildings or square corners to rooms, or even perspective (sometimes called a **carpentered environment** and typical of a Western environment). Consequently the Zulu people were *not* fooled by the illusion.

Some more perceptual illusions

The Ponzo illusion

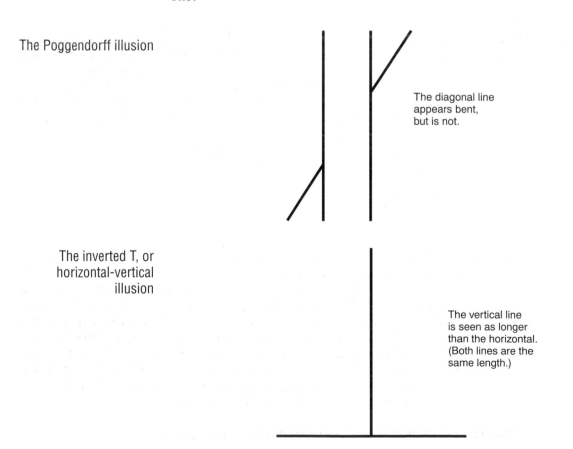

The top horizontal line is seen as longer than the bottom one, but they are both the same length.

Which of the horizontal lines is the longer, the top one or the bottom one?

The Poggendorff illusion

The diagonal line appears bent, but is not.

The inverted T, or horizontal-vertical illusion

The vertical line is seen as longer than the horizontal. (Both lines are the same length.)

The Zöllner illusion

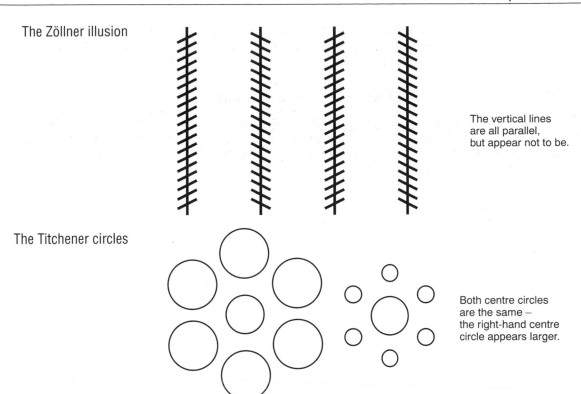

The vertical lines
are all parallel,
but appear not to be.

The Titchener circles

Both centre circles
are the same –
the right-hand centre
circle appears larger.

Influences on perception

We have looked at what we can crudely call the 'mechanics' of perception – that is, aspects of the optical and biological systems. We now turn to factors external to the optics and biology of perception that can influence perception. The work done in this field shows that we have a **perceptual set**, which is a state in which we are influenced by these other factors. They 'set us up' to be influenced by the 'set' or setting, or mental state, that we are in.

These factors, or influences on perception, are:

- motive;
- emotion;
- expectation;
- culture.

Motive

Motive, or **motivation**, can be regarded as a process or internal state of arousal that drives an organism into action (see Unit 5, pages 261–4). How does this relate to perception, and how do you test this? Many of the studies that have been conducted in this area concern the use of food. For example, Sandford (1936) presented his subjects with pictures that could be interpreted in a variety of ways. He found that subjects who were hungry were more likely than subjects who were not hungry to interpret, or perceive, the pictures as representing food. Other similar studies have come to the same conclusion: if we want or need something, our perception is influenced by that need.

Emotion

Emotion is difficult to separate from motivation.

A classic case of emotion as an influence on perception

A study conducted by Solley and Haigh (1958) has become something of a classic. They were interested in the way that a major emotional event affected perception. Their subjects were children who were asked to draw pictures of Father Christmas arriving with presents. The children were asked to draw the pictures several times in the weeks leading up to Christmas and after Christmas. Analysis of the pictures showed that Father Christmas got bigger and the presents more numerous as Christmas approached; and reduced in size in the weeks after Christmas.

Expectation   Our perception can also be affected by what we *expect* to see. The work of Bruner and Minturn (1955) demonstrates this. They showed their subjects a series of numbers, then an ambiguous figure, then a series of letters followed by an ambiguous figure. In both cases the ambiguous figure was reported as being a number or a letter depending on the series being shown: a number when numbers were shown, and a letter when letters were shown. This is easy to demonstrate:

Something to try

• Copy the following numbers/letters onto a piece of paper:

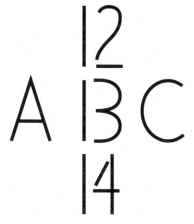

Now cover up the '12' and '14' and ask someone to read horizontally. Do the same with A and C covered up and ask the person to read vertically.

Culture The work of Segall et al. (1963), testing Zulus with illusions (see page 142), is an example of the influence of culture on perception.

A classic case of culture as an influence on perception

Brislin (1974 and 1993) studied the effect of culture when he investigated the response to the Ponzo illusion of participants in Guam (in the Pacific) and Pennsylvania (in the USA). He argued that the residents of a Pacific island would not have experienced the effect of perspective, since the island has no long straight roads or buildings, while the residents of a major, modern society would have grown up with perspective all around them. The findings confirmed this for the adult population, but the children in the study showed a similar, but less marked, effect, suggesting that *experience* of perception has an effect also.

"Walk into the painting did we..?
...yes, first did down on the left."

Perceptual development

It is inevitable that we shall need to consider Nature–Nurture issues as we study perceptual development. As we do so, it is important to remember that Nature–Nurture is not an either/or situation, rather two extremes of one continuum.

One of the earliest studies to investigate perceptual development was carried out by Stratton in the 1890s. He wore an inverting lens over one eye so that everything appeared to be upside-down and an eye patch over the other. After about a week he found that he was able to make sense of the world which was now, for the most part, 'appearing' normal. When he removed the lens, the world appeared upside-down again; but then slowly returned to normal. (The Wellcome Trust provides a series of experiments to investigate perceptual development.)

Think about it

- Does the work of Stratton support the Nature or the Nurture view?

Something to investigate

- Research and take notes on one of the Wellcome Trust's experiments.

Two classic cases of perception and the Nature–Nurture debate

A famous study investigating perception and Nature–Nurture by Blakemore and Cooper (1970) involved the use of kittens. The kittens were reared in the dark except for a period each day when they were placed in an apparatus with only vertical lines. It was found that the kittens had adapted very well to a vertical environment, but when they were confronted with a horizontal object (a rope or pole positioned horizontally), it appeared that they did not 'see' the object.

Another study, by Held and Hein (1963), also using kittens, stressed the importance of action in developing perception. They designed an apparatus which allowed one kitten to walk in circles, while another was positioned so that it was static yet receiving the same visual input. The active kitten was judged to have a much better developed perception.

Think about it

- The above study by Held and Hein was conducted in 1963. Read the section on ethical issues with non-human participants (pages 48–9). Would this study meet today's guidelines?

Turnbull's study with pygmies in Africa investigating size constancy (look back at page 136) and the work of Segall et al. with the Müller-Lyer illusion (see page 142) also have significance for perceptual development with respect to the Nature–Nurture debate. Other areas that are often studied when investigating perceptual development include:

- studies of people who are congenitally blind (that is, born blind);
- studies of those whose sight has been lost and then restored; and
- studies of very young children (neonates).

Results from the first set of studies frequently show (Von Senden, 1932) that some aspects of visual perception may be innate (Nature). Precise conclusions are difficult, however, because of the learning that may have taken place in other perceptual modes which may have influenced the person's perception.

A classic case of depth perception

As far as neonatal studies are concerned, probably the best known is Gibson and Walk's study (1960) using the visual cliff apparatus. This requires the baby to crawl over a 'visual' cliff, a 'cliff' simulated by a glass-topped table. If the baby hesitates or refuses, despite encouragement by its mother, it can be concluded that an awareness of depth perception is present. We cannot conclude positively that this is an innate (Nature) feature, however, because of other perceptual learning that has taken place since birth.

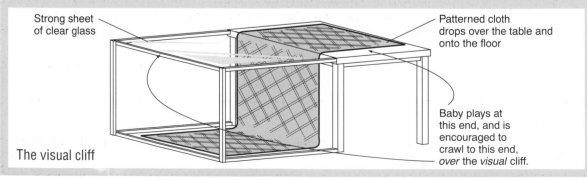

Strong sheet of clear glass

Patterned cloth drops over the table and onto the floor

Baby plays at this end, and is encouraged to crawl to this end, *over* the *visual* cliff.

The visual cliff

The development of perception, as we implied at the start of this section, is almost certainly a mix of Nature and Nurture, with some perceptual abilities being innate and others developed with experience.

Perceptual organisation

In the Gestalt approach or theory of perception (see pages 131–3), the emphasis is on the interpretation of the whole. You will remember that the Gestalt theorists developed the law of Prägnanz. Look at the diagram:

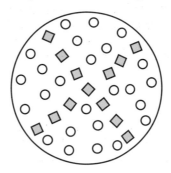

Your eye and brain will immediately try to make sense of what it sees: just some squares and circles? A pattern in a large circle? A diagonal cross of squares? A pizza? All of these? None of these? Some of these?

Perceptual organisation is more to do with how we organise what we see than with how we interpret what we see. It is perceptual organisation that 'puts together' the purely sensory information arriving at our retinas so that it makes sense.

Something to try

- With a television (or computer monitor) switched on, look at the screen *very* closely – perhaps even using a magnifying lens. Do this only for a short period, preferably when the screen is not moving. What do you see?

Close up to the television screen you will see hundreds of small dots or pieces of information (called 'pixels'). This is crudely similar to your retina, which has something in excess of a million **retinal receptors**, each one of which carries information to the brain which then organises this flood of information.

The primary, or initial, sorting out of this information occurs in the way you see colour and texture. If there is any change in either – or both – of these, your brain recognises the change and searches for other (top-down) information to make sense of what it is 'seeing'; the changes are represented as divisions or boundaries.

Look again at the diagram. Do you see how you use 'boundaries' to help sort out the picture?

Something to do

- You have just completed the section on perception. Draw up a list of headings or a spider diagram to show key ideas, theories, etc.

Attention

Something to do

• Wherever you are, sit still for about a minute. Then make a list of what sensory input you experienced.

Theoretically your list should have included something from each of your senses: what you saw, heard, tasted, felt and smelt. The question that this section deals with is which of all this sensory input you attend to and why. Did you attend to one sense more than any other?

If you now methodically attend to each of your senses in turn:

• you can see the book;
• you can hear the radio or perhaps the traffic noise;
• you can taste the wine-gum you are eating;
• you can feel the chair you are sitting on;
• you can smell the flowers, furniture polish, etc.

But what happened to the other sensory inputs when you attended to just one?

Attention was first studied seriously by the nineteenth-century **introspectionists** such as William James in America and Wilhelm Wundt in Germany. Their work was overtaken and even neglected by the **behaviourists** – Pavlov, Watson and others – who argued that psychology should only concern itself with objective, measurable data. This all changed with the renewed emphasis on cognitive psychology that came with the explosion in technology created by the Second World War.

Something to investigate

• One of the study skills suggested in Unit 1 was that you make your own biography of important people in psychology. Use your list of key people to make a 'family tree' of the way psychology has developed. If you start it on a large piece of paper you can add to it as you read and learn more. It might begin something like this:

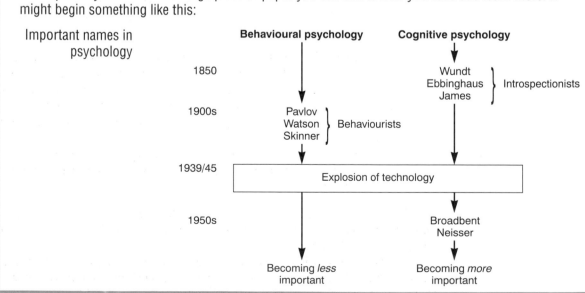

Models of attention

Before we get into detailed models of attention, it is worth spending a moment reconsidering information processing. In the section beginning on page 124, we inferred a parallel between the brain and a computer, arguing that both process information – which of course implies that this analogy is true of all aspects of cognitive psychology. The relevance of the information-processing approach to attention will become obvious as we consider different theories. Think back also to the discussion on perception, where we observed that it is not possible to make sense of all that we perceive: in some manner much is not 'seen' or, in the context of this section, not 'attended to'.

There are two types, or ways of considering, attention:

- **selective attention**, sometimes called **focused attention**, where some information is registered and some not; and
- **divided attention**, which is the capacity or limit of what can be meaningfully attended to.

We can go back to William James's work in his book *Principles of Psychology*, written in 1890 (rewritten in 1892 as *Psychology – The Briefer Course*. Students of that day referred to the books respectively as 'James' and 'Jimmy'). James is well worth reading; he is a giant of his age. His understanding and insight:

> " . . . have the steadiness of a polar star . . . The present day student is a wiser scientist and practitioner if he is acquainted with this beacon."
> Allport (writing in the introduction to a new edition of James (1892), *Psychology – The Briefer Course*)

Definitions of attention – from James onwards – have all made the distinction between selective or focused attention and divided attention. We shall look at each separately, but before we get to the inevitable theories we need to ask the question: *how* do we study attention?

The classic answer was formulated by Eysenck in 1984. He identified two experimental approaches:

- In the case of selective attention, participants are asked to '**shadow**' one of two messages they are receiving. Experimentally, this is usually achieved by a modified pair of headphones feeding separate messages to each ear. The participant is instructed to indicate some response to one of the messages, for example tapping when a key word is heard.
- For divided attention, the **dual-task** or **split-span technique** is used, where participants are told to respond to both messages or, in some cases, more than two inputs.

The logic here is that shadowing forces the attention on to a specific message, while the dual-task method deliberately divides the attention being given to the task.

The usual modalities in which attention is studied are auditory and visual. The following discussion centres on auditory attention; visual attention is considered in the section beginning on page 156.

Selective attention The key questions in understanding selective or focused attention are the 'what' and the 'how'. What is it that is attended to, and therefore what is not; and precisely how does this happen?

Something to try

- For this to work you need to be in a situation where groups of you are standing around chatting. Position yourself so that you are with a small group, and someone you know is in another small group within conversational hearing range. In the course of your group's conversation, mention something moderately personal – like a name – about a person in the nearby group.
What should happen is that the person referred to in the other group will stop dead in their conversation to attend to what you are saying about them, despite being in conversation in their own group.

This is called the **cocktail party effect** and was devised by Cherry in 1953. The question it raises is what is the mechanism by which a person who is listening to one conversation can suddenly, with no cue or instruction, switch attention to another? The other conversation, as with all the others in the room, was present all the time, but when something personal was mentioned attention switched. This has to imply that you were hearing the other conversation(s) but your attention was focused on 'your' conversation, which means that the other conversations were stopped from reaching your consciousness until something very meaningful to you occurred and 'broke through'. This brings us to the earliest of the models prepared to answer the question as to the mechanism involved.

Broadbent's filter model (1958) Based in part on the work of Cherry, who investigated the cocktail party effect by using **dichotic listening tasks** such as shadowing and split-span, Broadbent developed a model that appeared to explain this phenomenon. It works by filtering out unwanted information.

Broadbent's single-channel filter model of attention

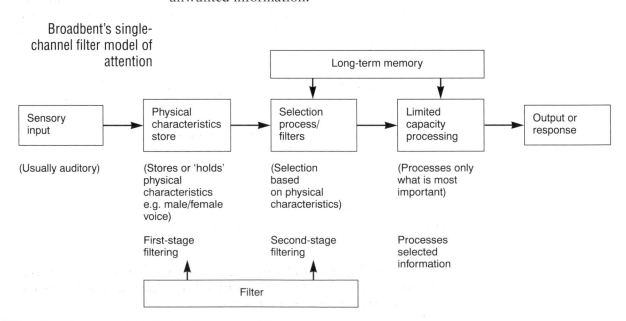

If we argue that there is a mass of input – true even if limited to an auditory mode – then somewhere in the process there has to be a filter that blocks unwanted input and allows the wanted input to proceed. In Broadbent's filter model, the filter (sometimes called a bottleneck) occurs early in the processing. It is in two stages and works primarily on physical characteristics of the message, such as pitch, volume or brightness. It is unable to identify content, the language of the message and other non-physical properties.

We need to bear in mind that Broadbent provided this model in 1958, around the birth of cognitive psychology. Its genius lay not so much in the detail but rather in the fact that it was the first model of attention and, as is the way of science, spawned a number of other models. Most of these follow Broadbent's single-channel filter model, but position the filter in a different place or change the way it works.

Some of the impetus for new models came from criticism of Broadbent's filter model by, for example, Gray and Wedderburn (1960) – see below.

There is evidence both for and against Broadbent's model. Evidence in support of it includes the following:

- Remembering that this is a single-channel theory, the model supports Cherry's (1953) finding that subjects were able to process effectively *one* channel.
- Broadbent's own evidence also suggests that the filter mechanism selects only one input at any one time.

Several strands of thought provide evidence that the model is too simplistic, however:

- When Gray and Wedderburn (1960) tested participants using Broadbent's split-span method they found that the subjects responded to a message that was meaningful, even if presented alternately to each ear with the subjects instructed to attend to only one ear (as illustrated in the diagram below). They found that when using a split-span method which switched between numbers and a message with meaning (Broadbent used only numbers), the brain ignored the numbers and mixed the bits of message from both channels – the ears – to make a coherent whole.

Broadbent

Input	Left ear:	1 2 3	Result:	Ear by ear	Pair by pair
	Right ear:	4 5 6		'123, 456'	'14, 25, 36'

Gray and Wedderburn

Input	Left ear:	OB 2 TIVE	Result:	'OBJECTIVE'
	Right ear:	6 JEC 9		

or

Input	Left ear:	1 THE 3	Result:	'PASS THE TEA'
	Right ear:	PASS 2 TEA		

Gray and Wedderburn's findings effectively refute the model, which argued that it is the physical nature of the signal and not meaning which determines what is attended to.

- Allport et al. (1972) studied the effect of several different modal inputs, for example visual *and* auditory. They found that, contrary to the theory, both sensory inputs were processed at the same time.

The above and other related studies (Eysenck and Keane, 1990) suggest that the filter is not limited to physical characteristics; also that there is not a clear division between the attended and non-attended messages.

Summarising the debate, there was general agreement that some sort of filter or bottleneck existed; the focus of further research was on just where in the process this occurred.

Attenuation: Treisman (1964)   The next major model to be proposed was by Ann Treisman in 1964.

Treisman's attenuation model of selective attention

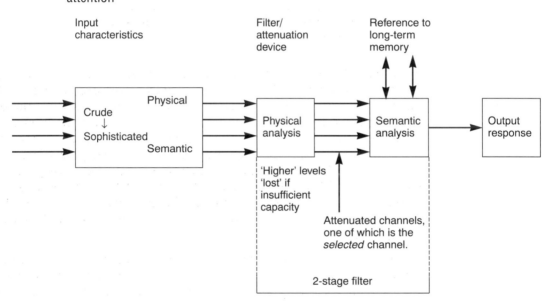

Rather than a filter, Treisman suggested that the unattended message was **attenuated**, or 'turned down', much as you turn down the volume on your radio or television. This is a significant departure from Broadbent, as it suggests some sort of progression from attenuation of physical perception to the attenuation of meaning, in effect from crude to sophisticated filtering. Whatever message survives this first-stage filter – where capacity limit forces the weaker signal(s) to be lost – is then processed **semantically** (in terms of its meaning) with reference to the long-term memory data.

This model, therefore, is capable of explaining the cocktail party effect whereby the non-attended input is processed by being 'switched on' *if* the message has meaning. The problems not fully explained by the model are concerned with the 'how' of attenuation – how precisely does it work and how precisely does semantic analysis work? Is it possible that some subjects do not 'parallel process' (that is, process more than one sequence of information at the same time), but switch between channels?

The pertinence model: Deutsch and Deutsch (1963) Deutsch and Deutsch provided a similar single-channel model.

Deutsch and Deutsch pertinence model of selective attention

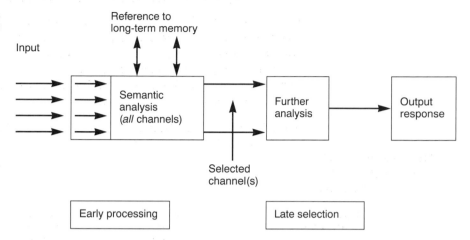

They placed the filter arrangement later in the processing, so in this model all incoming information is initially processed, selection then takes place semantically by reference to long-term memory, but only information which has relevance – or is pertinent at that point in time – is selected for further, final analysis. If circumstances change, then other initially processed data will be 'switched' into the later processing.

This model by Deutsch and Deutsch, the pertinence model, was subsequently modified by Norman (1969 and 1976). It recognises all incoming information unconsciously, initially parallel processes on both the physical and semantic characteristics and then filters on the basis of pertinence.

You should note at this stage that the three main models – Broadbent's, Treisman's and that of Deutsch and Deutsch – are similar in that they all have a form of filtering, but differ in where they place the filtering in the process.

In terms of evaluation, work by McKay (1973) using ambiguous words to each ear supports this pertinence model; but work by Treisman and Riley (1969) using a shadowing task does not. A reasonable conclusion is that Broadbent and Treisman's work can account for most of the research into selective attention (Eysenck and Keane, 1990).

Divided attention Divided attention is nothing more or less than doing two things at once. We do it all the time: reading and drinking coffee, driving and talking, and so on. The question we are concerned with here is *how* we attend to two things at once.

It is important to recognise that there is no sharp distinction between focused attention (one task) and divided attention (two tasks), and also that we switch quite naturally between the two conditions. A driver will stop talking, mid-flow, when some kind of traffic situation requires more attention, for example. Once past this immediate short-term problem, he or she switches back to the conversation as if it had never stopped.

The single-channel models of selective attention discussed above require a single process. Work on divided attention, however, suggests that there is a need for either several parallel processes, or one central processor that has sufficient capacity to allocate capacity as the need arises to several 'channels' at the same time. Allport et al. (1972) had skilled musicians shadow a story at the same time as playing. Shaffer (1975) conducted a similar study with skilled typists, typing a foreign language while shadowing a story. Both suggest that we can divide our (total) attention between quite different tasks.

Think about it

• Think of a few examples of divided attention in your own experience. Remember that both 'tasks' need to demand more than just awareness. One example might be carrying out a conversation while continuing with a piece of typing or drawing.

Kahneman (1973) devised a model which allocates attentional resources depending upon demand.

Kahneman's model of divided attention

Notes

Model assumes a finite limit in capacity.

Affected by arousal.

Monitors demand. How well you handle things depends on demand(s) and how interested you are in the task.

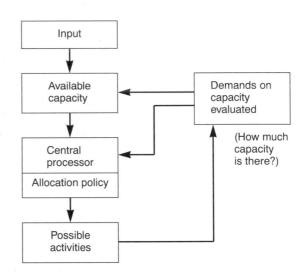

Automatic processing   How much of what you do, do you do without either awareness or intention? This moves the discussion into **automaticity** or **automatic processing**. Are you, for example, like the musicians or typists mentioned above, who were *very* skilled at one of the two inputs?

There seems to be fairly general agreement as to the meaning of automatic processing (Eysenck and Keane, 1990):

• Automatic processes are fast.
• Automatic processes do not reduce the capacity for performing other tasks.
• Automatic processes are unavailable to the consciousness.
• Automatic processes are unavoidable (that is, they will always happen if stimulated).

The Stroop effect (Stroop, 1935)

The Stroop effect is a classic example of automatic processing. The participant is required to read the colour of the ink the word is printed in from a list of words of colours. For example:

- RED (printed in, say, green);
- BLUE (printed in, say, yellow);
- GREEN (printed in, say, red);
  and so on.

The control is a list of words of colours printed in the same colour:

- RED (printed in red);
- BLUE (printed in blue);
  and so on.

What happens is that the participant automatically processes the *word*, realises they should have processed the colour, and consequently takes longer to read the first (disparate) list.

The main problems in discussing automatic processing are:

- defining precisely what automatic processing is;
- spelling out exactly how it works;
- explaining how and why practice produces automaticity.

There have been a number of theoretical approaches which attempt to clarify these issues:

- Shiffrin and Schneider (1977) proposed a model that distinguished between controlled and automatic processing. In their model, controlled processes are of limited capacity and require attention, whereas automatic processes have no capacity limits, do not require attention and are difficult to change once learned. Evaluation of this model shows no real answer to the question of how practice produces automaticity, only that practice leads to a situation requiring progressively less processing.

- Norman and Shallice (1980) provided a similar but significantly different model by suggesting that there are two separate control processes, one for fully automatic and the other for partially automatic processing.
- Finally, Logan (1988) attempts to answer the problem of precisely how and why practice produces automaticity. His theory centres on the idea that performance of a task requires knowledge *and* attentional resources and that it is the knowledge of the task that improves with practice. This requires only the retrieval of relevant information concerning past experiences from long-term memory.

Focused visual attention

All of the above discussion on attention has been concerned with auditory attention. We now turn to **visual attention**.

Think about it

- Think of the differences and similarities between the human auditory system and the human visual system. In what ways are they different? In what ways are they similar? Make lists.

Your list of differences probably includes the fact that ears can provide two input channels, which you can choose between, while eyes visually combine to form only one input. Another difference that you may have noted is that you can move the focus of attention visually by moving your eyes, your head or both; but you cannot do this to any significant extent with your ears, however much you move your head.

You will also have noted that you have the capacity visually to focus deliberately on a relatively small area, almost a pinpoint, with detail of the input rapidly decreasing with distance from the focal point. Look, for example, at the pattern on the wallpaper across the room. You will find that the area 'in focus' is very small, but your **peripheral vision** is huge, virtually a hemisphere.

Something to try

- You can easily test your peripheral vision. Focus on a point directly to the front across the room. Stretch out both arms in front of you, with your thumbs sticking up. Now watch the point but slowly move your arms outwards from the shoulders. You should be able to see, peripherally, your two thumbs until they move out of your vision when your arms are about 180° apart. You will note that the amount of detail you can see rapidly decreases: you soon start to see only major shape features.

The illustration most often used to demonstrate the focus is a torch or a spotlight. Point a torch with a narrow (focused!) beam and you will see whatever is in the spot and not much outside the spot. If your torch has the ability to widen the area the light beam falls upon, this too is like visual attention. LaBerge (1983) investigated this and concluded that visual attention is indeed like such a torch beam.

Trying to measure the size of spot is rather more difficult. Humphreys (1981) concluded that the beam varies from less than half a degree to a little over one degree, the smaller area occurring when the focused object is in the centre of the **fovea** (the part of the eye's retina that focuses images).

Something to try

• When you hold your arm out straight in front of you, the distance between your knuckle joints is approximately one degree. Using this very rough guide, see if you agree with the above.

1 degree between knuckles

Continuing with the comparison between auditory and visual attention, in the auditory mode it is reasonable to think in terms of multi-channel input; but this is not possible when considering the visual mode. This implies that visual capacity is limited by the number of 'bits' of input (letters, numbers, shapes, etc.) that can be processed at any one time.

Working in this area of visual attention, Neisser (1964) developed the visual search task. This comprised visually searching for a target letter or shape located in a pattern of many other similar or dissimilar letters or shapes. A classic example is looking for a letter V set in a matrix of other angular letters such as W, X or Y; then setting a V in a matrix of curved letters such as C, B or S. As a result of these and other related studies (Neisser, 1967; Gibson, 1969; Johnston and Dark, 1986), the concept of **feature detection** (or feature recognition) was accepted. The implication of this in visual processing is that some form of crude visual recognition is the first stage in visual processing.

There are several lines of argument, however, that provide evidence that feature detection is too simple an explanation. Try, for example, this experiment:

Something to try

• Read the following once through, counting the number of Fs:

The following sentence is made up of frequently used letters which are the product of famous filmstars' first names.

You will almost certainly have counted one, possibly two, Fs too few. If your counting depended simply on feature detection, why did you get it wrong?

One possibility is that we automatically process familiar words as whole units; another is that as we read the words we in effect say them silently and so the likelihood in this task is that you said 'ov' not 'of', and missed counting the Fs in the two OFs.

What is most likely is that visual processing involves expectation and memory in addition to feature detection.

Flaws in attention   The final topic in the section on attention is concerned with when attention goes wrong. It is interesting to consider how much we can learn when things do not work as they are supposed to. For example, Piaget was very interested in why children gave the wrong answers to questions. Similarly, a lot has been learnt about cognitive functions such as memory, by studying subjects who have had accidents or illness resulting in brain damage.

Here we consider what can be learnt about attention by investigating the common errors that we all make when we don't 'pay attention'. These errors are variously known as absentmindedness, attentional slips, attentional errors and – a more general catch-all – **performance deficits**.

Something to do

- Think carefully backwards in time from 'now' over the last few days and list those things that you had intended to do but – for whatever reason – forgot to do. For example, did you forget to make a phone call? Did you mis-dial a phone number? Did you leave your notes somewhere?
- Gather similar data by starting a diary now of things that you forget to do. When you have a reasonably long list, see if you can devise a system of categories or types of slip.

This diary technique – despite the accuracy problems that come with self assessment – is the method most often used to collect data. Reason (1979), in a major study, had participants complete a diary over a two-week period. This gathered over 400 slips from 35 participants (or approximately one slip per day per participant). In his analysis of his findings he suggested that attention operates at three levels:

- superficial, mostly automatic/routine;
- deeper than superficial and requiring more attention – implying awareness of error/correction;
- deepest – requiring full attention/knowledge.

A more general finding is that lapses of all kinds increase both with tiredness and in situations of high stress.

If you did the above task you will probably have noticed that most, if not all, of the slips you made were when you were doing very routine tasks. Reason (1979) suggests two ways in which information processing 'controls' our behaviour such that we either make a slip or not:

- **Closed-loop feedback**, where feedback from visual and/or other modes feeds back via your information processing to monitor and control your behaviour. An example might be the control you exert when riding your bicycle.
- **Open-loop feedback**, which is experienced in very well-practised behaviour, rather like engaging a personal 'auto-pilot'. This frees up space in the information processing that allows other non-related tasks to operate. For example, when pouring a cup of tea you might momentarily turn to talk to someone and stay 'open loop', resulting in your filling up the saucer as well. In closed loop you would have watched the tea rising in the cup and, with visual feedback, stopped pouring when the cup was nearly full.

Application of 'action slips theory' is often applied to the analysis of accidents and disasters that have a significant human element in them. By recognising that these slips occur, engineers and designers can 'design in' features which help to reduce the likelihood of a slip. This is particularly true in work situations in which serious consequences might result from a slip – for example, in the cockpit of an aircraft.

Memory

Memory is perhaps one of the most important of our cognitive functions. We use it when we answer examination questions, telephone our friends, read, play sports, or engage in any one of hundreds of other everyday activities.

Think about it

- Think for a moment of any situation where you do not involve the use of your memory. What would your life be like if you had absolutely no memory? What could you do and what could you not do? If you think about that, you will probably find that virtually everything you do requires the involvement of your memory.

This section begins with a brief look at the history of the study of memory and introduces two important early theorists. It then covers the kinds, processes and stages of memory, before examining the various models of memory. This is followed by a discussion on how information is organised in the memory. We then look at forgetting; and conclude with a consideration of the practical applications of memory theory.

The study of memory

Before we go on to consider some of the models of memory used by psychologists to help explain the way the memory works, it is useful to consider the historical context.

The Ancient Greeks

We can trace the history of the study of memory right back to the classical Greek period – around 400 BC when the Ancient Greeks investigated memory. Having discovered that boring a hole in the skull and looking for something that might resemble memory – whatever that is – did not really help, the Greeks came up with what they called the **spatial metaphor**. (A metaphor is a figure of speech in which one idea is represented by another.) The metaphor in this case is a birdcage, with many birds flying around inside the cage. The cage represents the memory store, the birds the memories, and reaching in to capture a bird (a memory) is the retrieval of the memory. In many respects this is a remarkably accurate picture. The Ancient Greeks seemed to like it, as there were no further advances during the extent of their culture; in fact virtually nothing changed in the study of memory until the mid-19th century – when science had finally emerged from philosophy as a distinct discipline, and psychology was establishing itself as a scientific discipline in its own right.

Hermann Ebbinghaus

Hermann Ebbinghaus is generally considered to be the first psychologist to use a scientific approach to the study of memory. His main work was published in 1885 in Berlin where he worked as a lecturer. His theories and methods are still current. He was concerned that previous learning would affect the way that he tested memory and so in order to avoid this he made up nonsense words to use in his memory tests, usually **trigrams** – consonant, vowel, consonant – for example, *cex*, *sar*, etc. He was very meticulous and precise in all his work, and frequently used himself as a prime subject in his experiments.

- One of his earliest and most important findings was that there is a direct relationship between the time spent learning the material and the amount that can be recalled. (That is worth remembering when it comes to examination revision!)
- He also suggested that there are different ways in which we forget. (We consider forgetting in more detail later in this unit.)

If you try to remember what you saw on television on Wednesday evening last week, or what you had for dinner yesterday, how are you retrieving that information? The chances are that you are using all sorts of other details – memories – related to those events: who you were watching television with, the time, where you were. Can you still recall the smell of yesterday's dinner? Did that prompt your recall or follow the recall?

Frederick Bartlett These are the sort of questions that challenged another early theorist – Frederick Bartlett. He did much of his work in the 1930s, nearly 50 years after Ebbinghaus, while professor of psychology at Cambridge University in England. His book *Remembering* was published in 1932.

Bartlett believed that the memory is constructed of structures or **schemas** on which, or into which, individual memories dealing with 'real life' can be fitted or accommodated.

A classic case of the use of schemas in memory: 'The War of the Ghosts'

Bartlett investigated this model of memory by devising a story and reading it to his subjects and then testing their ability to recall details of the story. He called the story – which has became quite famous – 'The War of the Ghosts'. Briefly, it is about a battle between two Indian tribes, one of which is made up of ghosts. The whole story relies heavily on Indian culture, with the description of the battle being quite vague and with much of the story being very symbolic – all of which was deliberate on Bartlett's part. When his subjects were asked to recall details, Bartlett found that they had great difficulty remembering the story, particularly the more strange parts. He argued the reason for this was because they had no schema into which, or by which, the story could be understood and made to fit or make sense. He further found that his subjects did recall some of the detail, but also that they were equally likely to 'make up' answers or details of the story, or get the order of events muddled. Bartlett concluded that his subjects were trying to make sense or create meaning from what they had memorised of the story, even if they were in error. He called this process **effort after meaning**, something he believed that we do all the time.

The 1960s onwards Later still, in the early 1960s, evidence was growing to support the view that the memory could be considered more as a system, with distinct subsystems or stages. Although much of the work of the early theorists has been superseded, they nevertheless have had a profound effect on the general development of psychology, particularly cognitive psychology and its recognition as a science.

An outline for the study of memory

Note that most of the main sub-topics – kinds, processes, stages, forgetting – are divided into three. It is worth learning this list as it is the key to your study of memory.

Three kinds of memory
1. Episodic
2. Semantic
3. Procedural

Three processes of memory
1. Encode
2. Store
3. Recall

Three stages of memory
1. Sensory
2. Short-term
3. Long-term

Models of memory
1. The two-stage or modal model
2. The levels of processing model
3. The parallel distributed processing model
4. The working memory model
5. The ecological approach

Everyday memory

Organisation of information in memory

Three ways of forgetting
1. Normal
2. Amnesia
3. Activated

The physiological and biochemical bases of memory

Practical applications of memory theory

Something to investigate

- Go to your library and make a chart of all the subsections under 'memory' from the index of as many books as possible.
- This is useful in two ways:
  1. You will become more familiar with the subsections of memory.
  2. You will see that different authors add, omit or link topics in different ways. This in turn will help your general understanding of the subject.

Three kinds of memory

The mind is able to store several different sorts of information. Psychologists generally group these into three kinds of memory, based on the way the memory deals with the information.

Episodic memory

Episodic memory deals with episodes or events that happen in your life or take place in your presence. For example, can you remember a particularly happy birthday and the presents you received? Or can you remember the emotions you felt when you moved house? These memories are stored as episodic memory.

Semantic memory

Semantic memory deals with more generalised knowledge or memory. Semantics has to do with the meanings of words or things. You know that the height of Mount Everest is 8854 metres, even though it is doubtful that you have been there. The fact that 8854 metres is nearly 9 kilometres also means something. You can remember how to spell 'psychology', and you know something of what the word means.

Procedural memory

The third kind of memory is **procedural memory**, sometimes known as **skill memory**. This involves knowledge of how you do something. You have both learnt and remembered these skills in lots of ways. These memories tend to last a long time. Your tennis may get quite rusty if you have not played for some years, but the minute you pick up a racquet again you will remember how to hit the ball. Riding your bicycle is another example of procedural memory.

Think about it

- Identify two examples of each of these kinds of memory from your own experience.

Three processes of memory

Before we turn to the processes that occur in our memory we need first to consider just what a process is or, more accurately, what **information processing** is.

Encoding

Think again about riding your bicycle. If you have to make a sudden stop, or change of direction, the first stage in the processing of the information to enable you to do this is to **encode** the information reaching you through your senses (in the case of avoiding a bus, through your eyes). Your eyes and brain do this by converting visual sensory information into a psychological form that can be mentally represented. You have in effect already begun to process this information.

Encoding can be considered to have its own three parts or stages. Memorise this group of letters: TNL WHN URH T PK.

- You would almost certainly start to encode by using a *visual code*, by looking at the set and attempting to acquire a mental image of the letters. This is the first stage.
- To help your memory retain this set you will then almost certainly find yourself reading the set, or at least trying to read the set, either aloud or silently to yourself. This is an attempt to encode the information *acoustically*, and is the second stage.

- The third stage of encoding is to try and make meaning from the letters by saying them as a word, even if it is a nonsense word or set of nonsense syllables as in our example. Try saying them to yourself, or even aloud. What you are doing is trying to encode the material *semantically* by giving the words some sort of meaning. Try 'Turn Left When You Reach The Park'.

Storing Once the information to be remembered is suitably encoded, the second process is to **store** the encoded information, so that it will be available over a period of time – perhaps a very long period of time. One way of storing the set of letters is by **rehearsal**, sometimes called maintenance rehearsal, by mentally repeating the list or saying it over and over again to yourself. You have undoubtedly used this technique many times, and you are now becoming more aware of how – and why – this works. Your awareness of how your memory works is referred to by psychologists as **metamemory**. This becomes more 'clever' or sophisticated as we develop, and certainly as we learn to improve our memory.

Recalling The third of the three memory processes is **recall**, sometimes referred to as **retrieval**. However much or however perfectly you have encoded and stored information, unless you can get back to it, it is only so much electrical activity in your brain. If someone asks you to tell them your name and address, recall is virtually effortless, but when you are asked to recall large and perhaps complex data for an examination then it is not so easy.

When you need to retrieve a file from your computer or a book from the library, you need to know the name or code of the file on your computer or the author's name or the title of the book. The file code, or the author's name, are **cues** to assist recall or retrieval. Similarly, to retrieve data from your memory you need to use the proper cue. To give you an example, see if you can recall from your memory the meaning of the following well-known sequence of letters: R O Y G B I V. It is of course the initial letters of the colours of the rainbow. You may have 'remembered' the cue phrase 'Richard Of York Gave Battle In Vain' and linked or associated this to the real meaning: Red Orange Yellow Green Blue Indigo Violet.

Think about it

- The three processes of memory are: encode, store, recall. Think of something you have done recently that required these three processes.

Three stages of memory

The three stages of memory are:

- sensory memory;
- short-term memory; and
- long-term memory.

Models of memory

Psychologists have come up with various models of memory which help to make clear the meaning of these three stages. A model, as used here, is simply a way of representing reality. The Ancient Greeks' spatial metaphor mentioned on page 159 was just such a model.

The two-stage or modal model

Atkinson and Shiffrin, in 1968, proposed a system that is sometimes called the two-stage theory but is also known as the **modal model**. The **sensory input**, according to Atkinson and Shiffrin, first enters the sensory memory (or sensory registers). The sensory memory converts sensory information into perceptions that make psychological sense. If the information is attended to, it continues on into the **short-term memory** (usually abbreviated to STM), which is the first stage. STM has a capacity for about seven bits of information but it can only hold, or remember, these seven bits for about 20 seconds.

The Atkinson and Shiffrin two-stage model of memory

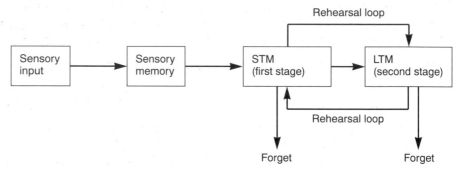

Something to try

• An easy way to demonstrate the capacity of STM is to do a simple experiment. Read the following sequence of numbers to a friend and ask them to write them down in the correct order immediately you have finished reading out each set. When they finish writing, read the next set, and so on. You will see that the series starts with three digits and increases by one digit each time. Here is the series:

$$
\begin{array}{l}
8\ 2\ 7 \\
6\ 4\ 1\ 9 \\
2\ 8\ 3\ 6\ 4 \\
7\ 0\ 2\ 8\ 6\ 3 \\
5\ 9\ 1\ 5\ 0\ 9\ 4 \\
2\ 7\ 3\ 1\ 8\ 5\ 0\ 6 \\
1\ 8\ 0\ 9\ 2\ 4\ 7\ 3\ 2 \\
3\ 2\ 6\ 8\ 5\ 1\ 9\ 2\ 6\ 4
\end{array}
$$

You will probably find that your friend will remember up to the seven- (plus or minus two) digit span.

The above is a good illustration of how short-term memory works. Your STM ran out of storage space at about seven bits because you did not have time to *rehearse* the memory input, or digit span, to enable it to pass on through your memory and on into the second stage, the **long-term memory** (LTM) store. This is also very easy to demonstrate:

Something to try

• Ask your friend – without looking at the numbers they have just written down – to recall the six-digit span, which was the fourth set of numbers. Even if you give a prompt by saying it starts with a '7', it is doubtful that your friend will be able to recall the six digits. This is because there was no rehearsal and therefore the six digits were not passed on into LTM.

The key to the way the two-stage model works, or at least how it gets information into the long-term memory – or second stage – is **rehearsal**. In other words, if I give you a ten-digit span and also give you time to repeat or rehearse the numbers over and over again, which of course you do in your short-term memory, you are much more likely to remember the ten digits, as the rehearsal aids transfer into long-term memory.

Something to try

Another simple experiment – this time recalling words – can provide evidence of the distinction between STM and LTM. First do the experiment, then we shall discuss the results. Again, you need a friend to help you with this experiment. It is very easy and (almost) always works.

- Read the following list of 20 words to your friend, allowing a two-second pause between each word.

coin   hat   tree   button   pencil   sky   paper   shoe   book   cake   boat
knife   desk   leaf   mug   key   torch   ball   flower   string

- When you come to the end of the list, ask your friend to write down as many words as s/he can remember – the order s/he writes them in is unimportant.
- Repeat this procedure with at least ten different friends. (If you were to do this experiment in a more formal way, you would read the list to all ten participants at the same time.)
- To put the data into the correct form, construct a table as follows:

Word (in order presented)	Number of times recalled
1 COIN	
2 HAT	
3 TREE	
4 BUTTON	
5 PENCIL	
6 SKY	
7 PAPER	
8 SHOE	
9 BOOK	
10 CAKE	
11 BOAT	
12 KNIFE	
13 DESK	
14 LEAF	
15 MUG	
16 KEY	
17 TORCH	
18 BALL	
19 FLOWER	
20 STRING	

- Using the answer sheets from your friends, tally the number of times each word is recalled.
- To make the results clearer, plot the data as a graph. You should end up with a roughly U-shaped graph. It may not be a very even curve; and you will find that the more people who take part in the experiment the smoother the graph is likely to become.

This experiment is a good way to show the **primary–recency effect** and the distinction between the STM and LTM (see page 166).

In the above experiment, assuming that you get the typical U-shaped curve, you can see that the first words you read out were remembered by most participants, as were the last words. This shows us that information presented first (in a list) is remembered – the **primacy effect**; and that information presented last (in a list) is also remembered – the **recency effect**. The participants in your experiment will almost certainly have rehearsed the early words in the list, the primacy, (despite not being told to) and this data will have transferred through STM and into LTM. The last words in the list, the recency, will still be in STM and available for recall. The badly remembered words in the middle were not adequately rehearsed to enter LTM, but were too many and taking too long (before recall) to remain in STM; they were therefore forgotten.

We can now label the graph as follows:

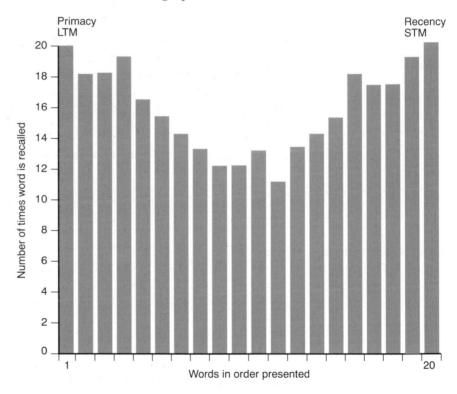

This is called the **primacy–recency effect** and is useful evidence to support the STM/LTM model.

Before we discuss a method whereby it is possible to remember more than the seven (plus or minus two) bits in STM, try to remember the following series of letters:

C I A P O I B M F A G M T P C

The method by which it is possible to increase the amount of data that the STM can store is usually called **chunking**. If we accept that there are seven 'slots' in the STM, then if we can chunk or group the to-be-remembered data into seven sets of data, we can place each set into one of our seven slots. Using the same series of letters, an example of chunking would be to look at the letters in six groups:

C I A   P O   I B M   F A   G M T   P C

Another example of the use of chunking, that you have probably been using since you first learnt to spell, is the way you divide up a word to help your spelling. If I ask you to spell what some schoolchildren think is the longest word in the English dictionary – antidisestablishmentarianism – it is highly unlikely that you will remember a sequence of 28 letters that start with 'a' and end with 'm'. It is much more likely that you chunked the word, for example: anti–dis–establish–ment–arian–ism.

The Atkinson and Shiffrin two-stage model of memory, like all models, is only one way to represent reality, but it does seem to be the most widely accepted model of the 'stage' variety.

Criticisms of the 'stages' model   There are a number of criticisms of the stages or modal model:

- Studies by Shallice and Warrington (1970) provide neuropsychological evidence of problems with the model, mostly to do with patients with limited short-term capacity which – if the stages model theory holds – should indicate subsequent problems with long-term memory. LTM problems did not, however, exist with their patients.
- Another problem area is the assumption that material processed in the STM will – almost by definition – be passed on into the LTM. An example of this not happening is given by Baddeley, who observed that the campaign by the BBC in 1980 to prepare listeners for the introduction of major new radio wavelengths, despite providing about 1000 occasions to hear the new details, had virtually no effect in registering these details in listeners' LTM.
- A final problem area is the oversimplification that STM uses acoustic coding, while LTM uses semantic coding.

The levels of processing (LOP) model

Fergus Craik and Robert Lockhart (1972) put forward an alternative view or model of the working of the human memory. They suggested that rather than stages, our ability to remember depends upon the degree to which we process the to-be-remembered information. Hence their model is called the **levels of processing model** of memory. If we think of the two-stage model as a horizontal flow, then we can think of the levels of processing model as a vertical structure: the key idea with this model is that the more ways and the more varied the ways in which we process the data-to-be-remembered, the more will be the effectiveness of that memory.

Craik and Lockhart's levels of processing model of memory

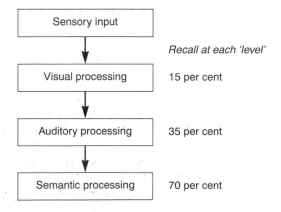

The levels of processing or LOP model does not ignore or reject the idea of stages and rehearsal; rather it sees them as a whole, or entity, whose effectiveness varies depending on its depth of processing.

A classic case of levels of processing

Craik and Lockhart's classic study of 1972 explored this concept of depth by asking three groups of participants to study – remember – word lists. As they did so, they were prompted by being asked questions about the word list.

- One group was asked about the way the words looked visually – size of print, style of lettering and so on – in other words **visual processing**.
- The second group were asked about the way the words might sound, whether they might rhyme with each other or with other similar words – this is **auditory processing**.
- The third group were asked to think about the meaning of the words on the list and how the words could be used. This is **semantic processing**.

Later, when the subjects were tested for recall, Craik and Lockhart found a significant difference between the recall scores of the three groups. Group 1 recalled 15 per cent, Group 2 recalled 35 per cent and Group 3 recalled 70 per cent. They explained these results as being directly due to the level of coding, or the amount of processing, that had occurred.

An important point is that each level implies that processing has already occurred at previous levels. Group 1 had simply looked at the words; Group 2 had looked at the words and then processed them by sound; Group 3 had looked and said the words and then thought about their meaning (hence the vertical representation of the LOP model).

Criticism of the LOP model Craik and Lockhart's work on levels of processing provided two important generalisations. The first is that deeper semantic processing leads (usually) to better learning; and secondly that rehearsal, as well as maintaining data over a short time, will incorporate new information into old. However, a criticism of the model is that it does not offer a very detailed explanation of the way it functions, and this has given rise to a degree of controversy, despite its very obvious advantages.

Something to do

Before we discuss significant further developments in our understanding of the way memory works, try this activity:

• Consider the following question and as you do so think of the process that your mind goes through as you answer it:

What is the name of the British Prime Minister who was male, smoked cigars, enjoyed painting and led the country during the Second World War?

• Now, before you have forgotten how you did that, write down an analysis of how you came up with the correct name (Winston Churchill). In other words, how did you use the clues? Keep your analysis handy, and see if it fits what follows.

The parallel distributed processing (PDP) model

The **parallel distributed processing** model, or **PDP model**, was proposed by McClelland in 1981. The idea here is not a stages or levels-type model; the key to understanding PDP is the notion of **parallel learning**. 'Parallel' learning is more than one process occurring at one time, and 'distributed' is the processing occurring in a number of different locations at the same time. As you would expect, there are several variations of this model, but there are assumptions which are common to most of them.

The PDP model is quite different from the models already discussed. These, in general, involve the memory having a vast number of **memory traces** and the recall of a memory means accessing the relevant memory traces. (For more on memory traces, see page 181.) The memory trace is assumed to be in the nervous system (in one unified place or store) and is the result of some stimulus. Most theorists argue that the memory traces are held in a sensory store long enough to allow them to be processed or passed on into memory proper (or long-term memory). In contrast, with parallel distributed processing (PDP) it is assumed that information is stored in several, perhaps many, different but interconnected units or places, and learning occurs when the strength of the connections between these various units is increased. The PDP model would explain your answer to the question about Churchill by suggesting that each of the clues – Prime Minister, male, smoked cigars, painted, British, Second World War – would activate its own unit which in turn would activate other units associated with it; as a result 'Winston Churchill' is activated more than say 'Harold Wilson' or 'Margaret Thatcher'. If you consider this task using a serial or stages model, retrieval of the correct answer can only occur by following one clue at a time, however rapidly (such as 'male', then 'smoked cigars', and so on); if any of the clues were wrong, interpreted ambiguously or even partially incorrect, then you could come to a dead end or a wrong conclusion. The PDP model overcomes this.

Another advantage of the PDP approach is something that McClelland calls **spontaneous generalisations**. This involves, at its most basic, 'remembering' something that you have not specifically learned. A good example of this is given by Eysenck and Keane (1990). Suppose you were asked whether right-wing people tend to be older or younger than left-wing people. PDP theorists would argue that you might be able to come up with the correct answer simply on the basis of answers about specific individuals. The cue 'right-wing' activates information about all the right-wing people you know, including information about their ages; and the same happens for the cue 'left-wing'. In other words, novel or spontaneous generalisations can be produced readily even though the specific sought-for information is not actually stored in your memory.

McClelland in 1986 developed the idea of what he called **default assignment**. This is similar to spontaneous generalisation and is where the PDP model allows missing information to be filled in on the basis of knowledge of related circumstances or objects. Suppose, for example, you forgot someone's age. Default assignment in the PDP model will take or activate units of information that you know about similar people, for example job, ages of children and so on, and the information that you require will be 'filled in' on the basis of this knowledge. It is quite possible that you are not aware that this is happening. For example: tell me the age of your best friend's father. You probably don't know his age but, if the PDP theorists are correct, particularly with respect to default assignment, your thinking would go along the following lines: I am 18, so is my best friend. My father is 42. My friend's father is a bank manager, that means a lot of training, so he is probably a bit older than my father – that will make him about 46.

There is experimental evidence to support default assignment. Bower, Black and Turner in 1979 presented stories about everyday events. On subsequent memory tests participants gave information which would naturally form part of such events – but which had not been explicitly given – in their responses. The reason for this, PDP theorists argue, is that participants 'fill in' the extra and missing information by means of default assignment.

Something to do

- Think of the word 'dog'.
- Now write down your response – in as much detail as you want – to this word.

You have probably written down information about specific dogs that you know and more general information about the concept of 'dog-ness'. What has happened, according to PDP theorists, is that presentation of the word 'dog' has led to the activation, in parallel, of many memory units relating to specific dogs that you know, which in turn leads to an averaging process of a group of attributes about a typical dog – the number of legs, colour, size and so on.

More evidence for the value of the PDP approach to memory concerns work carried out by McClelland and Rumelhart in 1986 and its relevance to the question of **amnesia**. We deal with amnesia in more detail later; for the moment we need to consider amnesia simply as total or partial loss of memory. Memory problems of amnesiac patients can be both varied and complex; it tends to be the case, however, that amnesiacs are better able to learn the common features of a number of situations rather than individual or specific features found in only one situation. For example, an amnesiac would be better working at a repetitive task, say opening and distributing the office mail, than at the more complex task of taking visitors round and dealing with questions. If we argue that learning causes a strengthening of connection paths between many and various units, the evidence has shown that this process of strengthening connections happens more slowly for amnesiacs than for other people but that it does nevertheless happen; as the PDP model would suggest. This means that amnesiacs learn more slowly and therefore show poor memory for non-repeated features of situations precisely because connection strengths remain low or weak in these areas.

Evaluating the PDP model   Evaluation of the PDP model – sometimes called a **connectionist model** – is difficult, not least because the model is relatively new. It appears to have value because of the powerful conceptual framework which it provides. Put crudely (and because the brain is so complex, this is a gross simplification), a theory which suggests that lots of activity can happen in parallel – at the same time – seems to offer more than a theory in which processing occurs in a linear fashion, one event happening after another.

The working memory model   Yet another model of how the memory works, proposed by Baddeley and Hitch in 1974, is called the **working memory model**. Baddeley and Hitch tackled the problem of how memory works by starting with the question: what is the memory for? And so we can consider this model as a functional approach.

Think about it

- Jot down your answer to the question that troubled Baddeley and Hitch: 'What is the memory for?'
- Hold your answer in mind as we discuss this model.

The original working memory model (1974) has been modified a number of times; in its current form it consists of four major elements, as shown below.

The working memory model

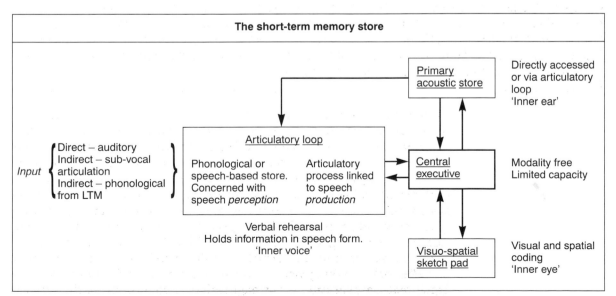

Source: Adapted from Baddeley and Hitch (1974), Baddeley (1986)

- In terms of the way the model works, the key is the **central executive** which controls and directs the other three components. It is the most important component because it is used when handling any cognitive issue. It is also very flexible in that it can process information in any modality and in a variety of ways.
- The **articulatory loop** is used when we try to remember things in the short term, for example a new telephone number: you repeat it to yourself as you dial it. It is also used to hold the words which we are getting ready to speak – our 'inner voice'.
- The **visuo-spatial scratch pad** (or sketch pad) deals with visual input. It can rehearse the visual pictures and relate them to space. For example, if someone asks you to describe the way from your school to the centre of town, you will picture the different roads, turns and traffic lights in your mind's eye, using a visual spatial code.
- The **primary acoustic store** is the fourth element of the model. In this part of the working memory model, the input is in an acoustic or auditory form, entering either directly or after being converted via the articulatory loop from a visual to an auditory form. This acoustic or **phonemic code** is in the form of pitch and loudness and is in our 'inner ear', just as the visuo-spatial sketch pad is represented by the 'mind's eye'. If you choose to, you could 'remember' a tune in your mind without hearing it, or singing or whistling it aloud.

As Alan Baddeley, the proposer of the working memory model, says:

> *"We have a long way to go before we can be sure of the details of the model."*

However, perhaps the best way to consider the model is as a central executive with a number of subsidiary systems working with it.

Criticisms of the working memory model
- Eysenck and Keane (1990) suggest that there is general agreement that the component about which least is known is the central executive – the most important component of the model – and that this may be the model's greatest limitation.
- It is also thought that the central executive is capable of carrying out a large number of processing activities under a variety of conditions, which makes it very difficult to describe its precise function.
- Eysenck and Keane further suggest that it is possible that there is more than one central executive.
- Baddeley suggests that while the functions of the other elements are fairly clear, it might be that the central executive handles the rest of the processing, which the other elements, due to their specific function, cannot.
- Not so much a criticism as an evaluation, is the notion that any one component of the system is likely to be involved in a wide variety of tasks and not just a main function.
- Further uncertainty is concerned with the central executive. Baddeley and Hitch claim that one of the major characteristics of the central executive is its limited capacity. Thus far all attempts to measure the capacity have failed.
- One final criticism is that this model has little to say about changes that take place as a result of time or practice.

The ecological approach

Our final theory about memory is significantly different from the others, and is based on recent work in the cognitive field. It is very important to realise that this whole area is advancing at a rapid rate; if you wish to find out more about these advances then you will need to turn to the academic journals for your information, as much of this work has not yet been written into book form.

The start of this change in emphasis or approach can be traced to the late 1970s. It was argued (particularly by Neisser) that cognitive psychology had become far too laboratory-based and was ignoring, implicitly if not deliberately, the fact that human cognition takes place not in the laboratory but in everyday situations, encounters and conversations. The arguments raged on between the pure, scientific laboratory-based work on the one side; and, on the other side, the out-of-the-laboratory work which came to be known in general terms as the **ecological approach**. This approach deals with most areas of cognitive psychology, and is ecological because, according to Neisser, it is based on real situations and real environments and as a consequence any results or findings have 'real' significance or value. Within this context we find the concept of the **everyday memory** (see below).

Everyday memory

Work on everyday memory has grown dramatically over recent years, even if these advances have been greeted rather less than rapturously by the laboratory-based researchers. Laboratory work on memory will always have an important part to play in research; it is the mechanisms of memory that can be studied in the laboratory, while the contents of memory are best studied out of the laboratory. This raises the question of how then do you study memory in everyday terms? The answer is by asking people to describe the way they see or understand their memory to work, and by designing experiments which try to simulate real-life situations.

Discourse analysis

Some of the early work in this area is called **discourse analysis** or **DA**. Supporters of DA argue that naturally occurring discourse or conversation is the obvious object of study. The central idea of DA is how people use knowledge of past events to generate new meanings and to use these to communicate with each other. In other words, DA is concerned more with how people use knowledge of the past (our memories) in the present (as we discourse or discuss), rather than how such knowledge was acquired, stored and recalled. This is the essence of the difference between previous models and discourse analysis.

Metamemory

We have already mentioned **metamemory,** or knowing what you know; it also means having the ability to assess your own memory and this is one way to study everyday memory outside the laboratory. It is done simply by asking people how well they remember or forget things – by means of self-assessment questionnaires. An example of such a questionnaire is given on page 174. You might want to expand this to include more items and then use it on yourself and others – but don't forget: this measures not memory ability but what you *believe* about your memory ability!

A self-assessment
questionnaire

	Very often	Quite often	Sometimes	Rarely	Never
How often do you forget a telephone number?	4	3	2	1	0
How often do you forget an appointment?	4	3	2	1	0
How often do you forget the way to a particular place?	4	3	2	1	0
How often do you forget an assignment?	4	3	2	1	0
How often do you forget a friend's birthday?	4	3	2	1	0
How often do you forget to get something when you go shopping?	4	3	2	1	0
How often do you forget someone's name?	4	3	2	1	0
How often do you forget to take correct books/kit/ papers to class or to work?	4	3	2	1	0
How often do you forget the score when playing games?	4	3	2	1	0
How often do you forget the author of a book?	4	3	2	1	0

You can, of course, add more questions of your own making.

Your score reflects what you *believe* your memory to be like; not the effectiveness (or otherwise) of your memory.

You might like to have someone who knows you well complete the questionnaire *for you* and then compare scores; what might be the significance of any difference?

Self-assessment tests of this kind have been shown to have high reliability and validity, and they can be used to study differences between groups – age groups, for example – as well as on an individual basis.

Schemas, scripts and frames

Another question studied by those interested in everyday memory is: why do we remember certain things and forget others? This is usually studied in the context of **schema theory**, which emphasises the fact that it is what we know already that influences what we remember. We discussed schemas in the context of Bartlett's work in the 1930s (see page 160). Current thinking has more closely defined or subdivided a schema (the whole) into:

- **scripts,** which are general knowledge about particular kinds of events; and
- **frames,** which are made up from general knowledge of specific objects and places.

In other words a schema is broken down into a hierarchical form of parts in order to assimilate knowledge or memories more effectively. By breaking down the schema in this way, it is possible to study more precisely just what is assimilated into the schema and is therefore remembered, and what is not assimilated and is therefore forgotten.

A related issue is the question of default assignment or default values – the idea that certain 'bits' of information will trigger the recall of much larger memories (see page 170).

Everyday memory has sparked a considerable amount of work outside the laboratory, in contrast to the models discussed earlier which were formulated and tested under laboratory conditions. By its very nature, everyday memory has to be studied where and when it is happening – and that is in real situations.

It is obviously very difficult to measure and control all the variables or even make reasonably accurate observations. However, it is quite possible that in the not too distant future these things will be capable of being measured much more precisely, and that theoretical models to account for everyday memory will be formulated.

Classic cases of everyday memory

The classic studies in this area were conducted in the 1970s by Elizabeth Loftus, based on work by Bartlett from the 1930s. Bartlett had been working on reconstruction in memory and concluded that interpretation plays a large part in remembering past events. We reconstruct the event by making it – or trying to make it – fit an existing schema, searching for 'effort after meaning'. To do this, our memory – rather than our conscious self – reconstructs the events to make the whole thing more 'tidy', with no loose ends and more coherent. Because of this process of 'tidying up' the event, or in the words of Bartlett because of 'imaginative reconstruction', our memory of an event is, or can be, highly suspect.

Elizabeth Loftus took this work of Bartlett and applied it to **eye-witness testimony**. Her argument was that when questioned about past events the *way the question is presented* – worded, if you like – has a significant effect on what is remembered. In a court of law, for example, a lawyer may ask leading questions which deliberately suggest the answer the lawyer wants the witness to the event, now maybe a year or more ago, to provide and which the witness believes to be accurate but which may not be.

In another classic study, conducted in 1975 by Loftus and Zanni, participants saw a film of a car accident and were then asked questions about the accident. Some were asked, 'Did you see a broken headlight?' Others were asked, 'Did you see the broken headlight?' The 'the' group said 'yes' twice as frequently as the 'a' group. In fact there was no broken headlight or even broken glass in the film.

This, with other subsequent related studies, shows that our memory reconstructs events from the past, and does not just forget detail. However, later research conducted on witnesses to real events suggests that leading questions are not as likely to influence our memory as Loftus and Zanni found in their study.

Face recognition

Another important aspect of the way we use memory is **face recognition**. This is something that we do many times each day. It is a part of the more general object- or pattern-recognition aspect of cognitive psychology, which we discussed in the context of David Marr's computational approach (see page 134). Perhaps the most comprehensive and well-developed model of face recognition is that of Bruce and Young (1986). They developed an eight-point model and, in addition, have distinguished between the recognition of familiar and unfamiliar faces. The eight components of this model are:

- structural encoding (similar to Marr's, 1982, 3D model);
- expression analysis;
- facial speech analysis;
- directed visual processing;
- face recognition units;
- person identity nodes;
- name generation;
- cognitive system.

In terms of evaluation, most current theory supports this model in terms of its general approach, with certain limitations – noticeably the lack of preciseness of the final stage which, as Bruce and Young agree, is something of a catch-all, and also the lack of detail of the processing of *un*familiar faces compared to familiar faces.

Spoonerisms

Everyday memory looks at a great variety of aspects of our memory, including absentmindedness, slips of action and spoonerisms. Perhaps the best-known spoonerism is the phrase supposedly said by an Oxford academic, Reverend Spooner, to a lazy student:

"You have hissed my mystery lectures and tasted the whole worm."

Hence the term 'spoonerism' refers to the accidental transposition of the initial letters of two or more words.

Autobiographical memory

The last aspect we shall consider is **autobiographical memory**. These memories are essentially 'episodic', referring to events or experiences usually relating to specific times or places. Episodic memory is of course closely linked to semantic memory, as Tulving first described in 1972 (he argued that episodic and semantic were two separate systems), but while episodic refers to specific events, semantic refers to the meaning behind or implied in the event, and this can be, and usually is, of a more general nature. To illustrate the difference: I *know* that Snowdon is the highest mountain in Wales and has a cog railway to the top and I understand what this means; but last weekend I walked with a group of students to the top of Snowdon. It was blowing, raining, and there was still a lot of snow about. The feelings (wet, windy, etc.) are still with me as a powerful 'episode' in my memory. This autobiographical memory is very distinct, mainly because I have not been to the top of Snowdon for some years. If, however, I repeat that experience several times in the reasonably immediate future, the individual episodes will tend to lose their individuality and will merge into a series of common features (a schema) within my semantic memory. As a part of this whole process, it is important to note that trivial events – what I had in my sandwiches – tend to be forgotten, while emotionally significant events are remembered in vivid detail – these are sometimes called **flashbulb memories**.

Everyday memory, at least for the moment, appears to be the way to move the study of memory forward. In this context it seems probable that a schema-based approach can provide the best theory or concept. However, there is a downside to the schema approach: distortions, or even mistakes, can be made as the schema is evolving. Schema theory, then, good as it is, does not as yet fully explain everyday memory.

Organisation of information in memory

So far in our study of memory we have discussed kinds, processes, stages, and models of memory, all of which imply, directly or indirectly, that the memory, really the long-term memory, handles large amounts of information: everything from mathematical formulae to German verbs. The question that we now need to discuss is: just how does the long-term memory *organise* this huge range of information?

A convenient parallel is to consider the organisation of a large library. If you were looking for information on, say, public education in Great Britain in the 19th century, you could track down the information by using the index and following a number of 'leads': Education, Great Britain, Nineteenth Century, and so on. The index would tell you precisely where to look to access the information.

Most of the research in this area suggests that our memory *does* organise information, but that it is not as efficient as a library system. Some of the methods that we use are discussed below, but remember that these will overlap and that none of them is totally precise or accurate. The methods of organising information are:

- hierarchies;
- schemas;
- semantic networks;
- clustering.

Hierarchies

A hierarchy is simply a structure that starts with a topic at the top and then breaks it down into more and more detail at each new level below. For example, a hierarchy of plants would look like this:

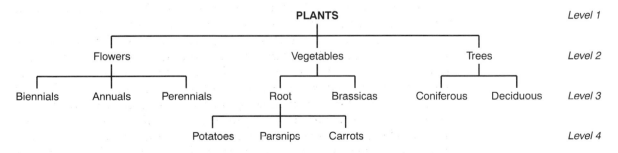

The point with a hierarchy is that it organises information into classes or groups which have a common element. Each item has a 'home' or location determined by logic. As a consequence, individual items can be retrieved by following the logic inherent in the hierarchy. It also means that, following the same logical system, new items have a home to go to. For example, you may have learned the 'plants' hierarchy in biology; you have recently learned that coniferous trees are softwoods, while deciduous trees are hardwoods; a little later, as your interest has grown, you have learned that not all trees fit neatly into these categories – there is a degree of overlap. You also need to learn the Latin family names of some of the trees, and so on. So the hierarchy in your memory, or at least one part of it, now looks like this:

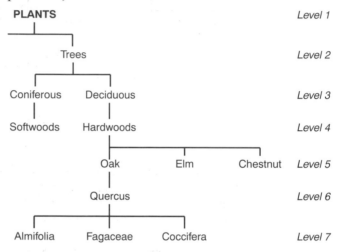

Precisely because you have organised the new information into an existing hierarchy, retrieval is (relatively) easy: you mentally follow the hierarchy, up or down, to locate the required detail. You do not have to rely on **rote memory** from a long-gone biology lesson, an episodic memory; rather you are using the much more reliable semantic memory. You will appreciate that accurate recall only holds true if there has been accurate learning. If you have learned – stored – the information incorrectly, you will either recall it incorrectly or not be able to recall it at all.

Schemas   A **schema** is knowledge that is organised around, or associated with, a place or event. It is often based on what you *expect* to find in a given context. For example, if I invited you into my office and then later asked you to make a list of what you saw there, you would list the desk, paper, pens, books, etc. You would probably forget to list the umbrella, the ice-axe, the pile of photographs. The reason for what you recall and what you forget is based on your schema – or mental representation – of 'office'. You *expect* to see a desk, paper, pens, etc.; you do not expect to see an ice-axe or an umbrella, so you would 'forget' these. This can, of course, lead to other errors where you 'remember' things that were *not* in the office you visited – for example, a hole-punch or stapler – things that would fit a general schema of 'office', but which were not in the office that you visited.

Something to do

• Take a photograph of an office that includes one or two items that you would not expect to see in an office. Show the picture to your friends, and later test their recall. Do the results support schema theory? (You could extend this into a piece of coursework.)

Semantic networks

A **semantic network** is an association of concepts or ideas which are independent but related. A semantic network involves a central node to which are joined associated concepts (Collins and Loftus, 1975) – for example, the semantic network for *bus* would look something like:

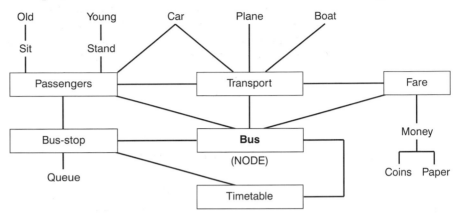

'Bus' is the main concept or node. Transport, fare, timetable, bus-stop and passengers are related concepts, and each one of these has its own related *but meaningful* concepts. The network can also show associations between these sub-concepts.

Collins and Loftus suggest a process of **spreading activation**, by which a given concept can cause a spreading out of related concepts, gradually becoming weaker as it moves further from the original concept. For example, if you were asked to write down the ideas or concepts that come into your mind when you hear the word 'sandwich', you might come up with words (related concepts) such as: bread, butter, tomato, cheese, mayonnaise, lunch, midday, canteen, friend, hungry, me, others, and so on.

Clustering

Something to do

• Read the following once, and then from memory recall as many of the words as you can.

Cat   River   Daffodil   Fox   Rose   Hill   Peony   Contour   Primrose   Estuary   Rabbit

Sparrow   Mountain   Eagle   Pansy   Saddle   Lupin   Cow   Scree   Cliff   Lion   Orchid

Donkey   Coast   Dog   Crocus   Valley   Horse   Sheep   Dalsy   Lake   Badger   Stream

Tulip   Mouse   Lily   Iris   Rat   Bluebell   Gerbil   Daisy   River   Begonia   Hare   Poppy

As you tried to recall the list of words in the above activity, it is almost certain that you 'clustered' the words; that is, you remembered them in **clusters** or groups – in this case, groups of animals, flowers and land features. What happens is that your memory 'likes' to organise data and so it will tend to organise the material that has to be remembered into clusters with a common theme. Because organisation is so important to memory, even if a long list of words has no obvious clusters, your memory will still try to impose some form of cluster or grouping.

Forgetting

A vitally important part of understanding how our memory works is the matter of **forgetting,** which we can also study in the form of a threesome:

- normal forgetting;
- amnesia; and
- activated forgetting.

Normal forgetting

'Normal' forgetting is concerned with **trace decay** and **interference.** The first suggests that the memory simply fades away with time. The second suggests that new material to be remembered interferes with, or gets in the way of, old material, perhaps confusing and obscuring it.

A classic case of forgetting – Ebbinghaus's curve of forgetting

The classic work on forgetting was conducted by Hermann Ebbinghaus, the German psychologist, in the late 19th century. In his study – which he carried out on himself – he learnt lists of nonsense syllables until he could recite them twice without error. Then over intervals of time ranging from minutes to 31 days, he re-tested himself. The result was his now famous **curve of forgetting**, which is shown below.

Ebbinghaus's curve of forgetting

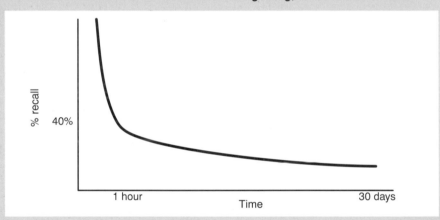

Note that the rate of forgetting is non-linear, almost logarithmic in shape, with forgetting occurring rapidly over the first hour, down to about 40 per cent recall, after which the rate of forgetting slows down.

Subsequent studies have shown that the Ebbinghaus curve will vary depending on the material memorised; it can vary from the classic curve when using nonsense syllables to almost perfect recall over many years with other material such as how to ride a bicycle or play tennis.

Trace decay We suggested earlier that trace decay is a fading away of memory as a function of time. William James, the American psychologist, suggested this in 1890 and there are modern supporters of this view. To accept that our memory 'fades' must imply that learning new material – material to be remembered – causes some sort of physical change within the brain; this change is called a **memory trace** and the theory suggests that it is subject to decay with time. Time, of course, can also implicate disuse – the passage of time, coupled with lack of practice of knowledge or a skill that you have learnt, will cause the memory traces to fade and the memory of that knowledge or skill will be impaired or lost.

There are obvious limits to this theory. For example, I can think back to my childhood and, without a lot of effort, remember things that I have not – consciously at least – rehearsed. If you start, deliberately, in your mind to go back to your childhood you will almost certainly be able to recall events and people that you have not thought about for a very long time. Perhaps this is more a case of accessing weak memory traces? On the other hand, there is a huge amount that we do forget about events of long ago – and so there is evidence both for and against the theory of trace decay.

The concept of a 'trace', whatever the actual form that it takes, is nevertheless generally accepted as part of the theory of memory, especially short-term memory.

Interference Even if we do not lose memory through trace decay, we can lose it through the interference of other information or memories. For example, think of the party game of going round the group remembering, say, items to take on holiday, each person reciting the list and then adding a new item. The key idea is that interference results not just from simple overcrowding of the memory, but also from a lack of suitable retrieval cues to distinguish one memory from another.

There are two main types of interference:

- **retroactive interference** (sometimes called retroactive inhibition) when new learning interferes with the recall of old learning; and
- **proactive interference** (sometimes called proactive inhibition) when the older learning interferes with the ability to retrieve the more recently learned information.

Both are forms of forgetting, and both indicate that our learning or our experiences are rarely isolated. The more similar they are the more likely they will interfere or inhibit each other. Often (indeed normally) this can be helpful, since new learning can build on the old, but problems occur when you need to separate out different memories – for example when asked to respond to a questionnaire or to provide eye-witness testimony. It is then that you are likely to experience forgetting in the form of retroactive or proactive interference.

Search theory Another theory of forgetting, similar to interference, is the **search theory**. This suggests that the recall of a memory involves a problem-solving approach. Russell, in *The Brain Book* (1979), gives a good example of how this works. This is demonstrated in the following activity.

Something to do

- Write down your thoughts or the stages that your thinking goes through as you attempt to answer the question: *What were you doing on Monday afternoon in the second week of September two years ago?*
- If we now apply the search theory to this question and to your answer, your first thought was probably, 'I haven't got a clue', meaning you have forgotten. But if you persisted your next thought may have been, 'OK, two years ago in September I had just moved here with my family. Oh yes! I started at my new school in the second week. On the Monday I remember we had an induction day, and in the afternoon we played silly games', and so on. As you search for more clues, more and more clues come together, and it becomes easier to find the answer to what initially was an impossible recall task.

The key to understanding interference and search theories of forgetting is that as more and more memories accumulate without sufficient cues to differentiate between them, it becomes harder to recall an individual memory, so we say we have forgotten it.

Amnesia

Like interference theory, this has two aspects: **anterograde amnesia** and **retrograde amnesia**.

- In **anterograde amnesia**, there is memory failure for a period of time following a traumatic event such as being knocked over and sustaining a head injury. The degree of forgetting can vary from very temporary and very mild to a more serious state when all the memory functions are impaired: attention, encoding, rehearsal and recall. There are, of course, degrees of memory failure anywhere between these two extremes.
- In **retrograde amnesia**, on the other hand, the trauma prevents the individual from remembering events that took place before the accident.

Activated forgetting

The third form of forgetting is **activated forgetting**. Here we shall look at two types: **repression** and **Korsakoff's syndrome**.

<u>Repression</u>   This hypothesis was put forward by Sigmund Freud and is one of the earliest of the forgetting theories. Freud contributed a great deal to our understanding of the unconscious. He suggested that our mind is like an iceberg with one-eighth conscious and the other seven-eighths unconscious but still working. His repression hypothesis is as follows: If you go through an incident or a period of time in your life that you find very stressful, then your unconscious mind will repress or not allow these memories back into your consciousness for fear of causing you more distress or anxiety – you have 'forgotten' them. Freudians believe that repression is the main cause of a disorder called **psychogenic amnesia**. We know that amnesia is damage to the brain, psychogenic amnesia is when there is no known accidental damage or blow to the head; the 'forgetting' is caused by a mental state, rather like a psychosomatic illness. Its onset is sudden and usually involves loss of memory of personal details.

Korsakoff's syndrome This is caused by severe alcoholism – sufficiently severe to cause brain damage. People with this problem – Korsakoff amnesiacs – usually experience both anterograde and retrograde amnesia. They suffer loss of memory because of impaired semantic encoding of new information and a failure or difficulty with retrieval.

Summary of forgetting

Ways of forgetting can be grouped under three main headings:

- **normal forgetting**, which involves trace decay and interference;
- **amnesia**, which is forgetting due to some kind of injury to the brain, whether permanent or temporary; and
- **activated forgetting**, of which the two main types are repression (a Freudian concept) and Korsakoff's syndrome (which is alcohol related).

Think about it

- Think of at least one example of forgetting, that you have experienced or witnessed, for each of the above categories.

The physiological and biochemical bases of memory

This aspect of memory study is in its infancy, in that we know very little of the biology of memory. It is also one of the fastest growing areas of research, and holds the most potential for a full understanding of how our memory functions.

A starting point might be the assumption, made by many psychologists, that mental processes – the encoding, storage and retrieval of information (involved in, for example, memorising a new telephone number) – are accompanied by changes in the brain.

This notion of some sort of change taking place in the brain has been in place for many years. In the early part of the 20th century, psychologists hypothesised that tiny electrical currents or circuits were formed in the brain which corresponded to memory traces – a neurological process that occurred whenever memory processes were taking place. These tiny electrical circuits were called **engrams**. Karl Lashley, in the 1950s, spent much time searching in various parts of the brain – unsuccessfully – for these engrams.

A little later James McConnell thought that he had located the engram in **RNA (ribonucleic acid)**. While **DNA (deoxyribonucleic acid)** carries the genetic code from one generation to the next, it was thought that RNA changed with experience so that a person's experiences – which included learning and hence memory – were stored and could be recalled from RNA. McConnnell's experiments included teaching worms to respond to or learn a stimulus, and then feeding a new batch of worms on chopped up pieces of the first batch to pass on the RNA. (Needless to say, students at the time proposed chopping up and eating their professors as a short cut to learning!)

However, this research was inconclusive and – as is the way of science – the focus of further research turned in other directions. One of these new directions focused on the activity of neurons, neurotransmitters and hormones. The first section of Unit 5 deals with the technicalities of the human neurological system, but a very detailed discussion on this in the context of memory and learning is beyond the scope of this book. You may want to find out more from your own reading (see below).

Something to investigate

- Read up about the following areas of recent and continuing research:
  (a) The structures and re-structuring of the brain following learning – for example, research with rats has shown that a high level of visual stimulation is associated with more dendrites and synapses in the brain than are found in rats who do not experience as high a level of stimulation.
  (b) Research using sea snails, who have about 20,000 neurons (you have billions!), has shown that changes take place at existing synapses when learning takes place, the transmission of neurotransmitters becoming more efficient with more learning.
  (c) The effect on memory of hormones.

Practical applications of memory theory

We started this section with a discussion on the place of memory in our everyday lives and how virtually everything we do depends in some way on our memory. We now look at some practical applications of memory theory, which could help you to make better use of your memory.

Mnemonics

The general term for memory aids is **mnemonics**. Almost every technique you use is a mnemonic and has as its basis some kind of association or connection. A mnemonic that I often use, for example, is to tie a knot in the end of my tie if I want to remember something when I get home – perhaps a book I promised to loan someone. When I do get home and take my tie off, I find the knot and that prompts me to remember – or associate the knot-tying with – the book that I said I would loan.

The von Restorff effect

We can use this phenomenon – also sometimes called the **isolation effect** – to improve our memory (see also Unit 1). You are probably already doing so. Do you use a highlighter pen? Do you underline in your textbook? Both of these are examples of the von Restorff effect. If used selectively – and that is a key point – they will help you to retain material. The idea is that any way in which you can exaggerate or isolate things to make them stand out will help you to remember them. The more extreme or fantastic you make the imagery, the better, as it then stands out more from the material, or word list, of which it is a part.

Photographic or eidetic memory

A specific form of imagery in memory is popularly called a **photographic memory**. The correct term for this is **eidetic memory**. The word comes from the Greek word *eidos*, which means 'that which is seen'. People who have this ability are able to recall whole pages of information after only a few seconds: they seem to be able to make a photographic image of the material in their mind and then recall it at their leisure. A lot of work was done in this field from the 1880s to the 1930s, but since then very little formal research has been conducted. One conclusion is that eidetic memory is much more common in children than in adults; this might suggest that we unintentionally educate children out of this attribute by placing a strong emphasis on formal learning. A second conclusion is that this attribute or skill can be reinforced or strengthened by practice.

Something to try

Here is an experiment to demonstrate the role of **imagery** in memory. To be theoretically correct you should have two groups of participants, one for each 'condition'. Below is a list of pairs of words – for example, PENCIL / CUP – which you need to read, with five seconds between each pair, to each group of participants.

train / grass	washer / coal
monkey / sun	desk / racquet
table / alligator	shirt / piano
shoe / boat	hammer / case
ink / book	bag / snake
ball / nail	pencil / cup
key / button	angel / tie
pen / rain	cloud / sweet

- **Group 1**
  The task of the first group of participants is to remember the pairs of words purely by rehearsing them by saying the pairs silently to themselves. Immediately at the end of the list, ask them to recall the pairs of words, in order. Prompt them by giving one word of each pair, either the first or the second.
- **Group 2**
  You now need to repeat the procedure with the second group of participants. Their task, or condition, is to remember the word pairs using imagery, not rehearsal.

To score your answers, count only strictly correct word pairs. Simply add up the totals of correct pairs for the two conditions. If the difference is not very great, it is probably because in the first condition members of the group used mental imagery even though told not to. However, you should find that the 'imagery' group (Group 2) scored higher than the 'rehearsal' group (Group 1).

The conclusion that we can draw is that imagery – and the more dramatic or extreme the better – provides stronger connections than pure rehearsal.

Acronyms Another mnemonic is the use of **acronyms**. The classic example of this is the phrase 'Richard Of York Gave Battle In Vain'; R O Y G B I V being the first letters of the colours of the spectrum or rainbow. The key to this method, again connectionist, is to link the to-be-remembered material to a phrase that you can recall with 100 per cent reliability.

Method of loci Closely related to acronyms is the **method of loci**. This method requires a personalised series of actions that you take perhaps every day and can recall with 100 per cent accuracy. For example, suppose that you were learning names of psychologists, and suppose also that you decided to use your getting-up-in-the-morning routine as the loci (locations). The result would look something like this:

Loci (morning routine)	Words to be remembered (link) (names of psychologists)
Alarm sounds	Pavlov (bells)
Slippers on feet	Sigmund Freud (SF same initials)
Shave	Skinner (skin)
Wash	Westheimer (same initial)
Breakfast	Broadbent

The point with this method is that the loci have to be your own and ones which you know extremely well. You then make associations – the more extreme the better – between your list of loci and the to-be-remembered list. You can, of course, use your loci list with various sets of to-be-remembered information.

Peg-words The final mnemonic that we look at are the **peg-word systems**. These work rather like the method of loci but with the locations replaced by a set of objects, each of which is connected to a specific number. The objects are then linked by imagery to the information that needs to be remembered.

- The number–rhyme system might look like this:

  1 Gun —   2 Shoe —   3 Me —

  The way it works is to link simple words that rhyme with a number in a sequence – say 1 to 10. You then need to link the words (Gun, Shoe, etc.), using imagery, with the to-be-remembered material. Again, as with the method of loci, you need to make your own personal list.

- A variation on this is the number–shape system, where the number looks like the shape. For example:

  1 Pole —   2 Swan —   3 Breasts —

  As before, you then link the word, using imagery, to the to-be-remembered list.

Both of these systems can be considerably expanded, but the third peg-word variation is capable of almost unlimited extension:

- In this variation, each number, from 1 onwards, is associated either with an individual consonant or with a group of similar sounding consonants. The fairly standard connections for the first few numbers (with the reason in brackets) are as follows:

1	=	t, d, th	(all have *one* downstroke)
2	=	n	(has *two* downstrokes)
3	=	m	(has *three* downstrokes)
4	=	r	(last letter of 'four')
5	=	l	(Roman for 50)
6	=	j, sh	(j is mirror image of 6; sh is six when drunk!)
7	=	k	(two 7s joined)
8	=	f	(8 looks like f in script f)
9	=	p, b	(p and b look like 9 rotated)
0	=	z, s	(zero – sounds the same)

  You now need to come up with your own key words – images that you link with the number/consonant list. For example:

1	(t)	tie
2	(n)	notebook
3	(m)	mattress
4	(r)	rope
82	(f, n)	fun (by adding a vowel)
994	(ppr)	paper (by adding two vowels)

And so on. Make up your own 50 or so peg-words, on to which you can add your to-be-remembered words – using dramatic imagery.

Language and thought

In this section we consider what language is, how we acquire language, and how we produce and comprehend language. We also look at definitions of thinking, different ways of thinking and models of thought. Finally, we consider the relationship between language and thought, including social and cultural variations.

Defining language

A useful starting point for this section is to ask ourselves just what it is that sets us apart as human beings from all other animal life-forms. When philosophers, and later psychologists, discussed this question, the almost universal answer was that it is the ability of the human animal to use language that sets him apart from all other animals. But what exactly *is* language?

Think about it

- You may have been *using* language all your life. Now try to define accurately what it is that you have been using.

You will probably discover that while you know what you mean by language, you find it difficult to define. For example, the term 'body language' is much used today but is it really a language? What about 'sign language' for people who are deaf? Is this a language? And how about 'computer language'? What about animal communication? Is this language also?

During the 19th century three main theories were proposed for the origin of language. There was no real scientific base for any of them, and they all dealt only with single words.

- The first started with natural sounds, animal and otherwise, and was known as **onomatopoeic**.
- The starting point for the second was the natural exclamation, for example the sound you make when you hit your thumb with a hammer – 'Ow' (actual words such as 'Blast!' do not come into this category). This was known as **interjectional**.
- The third, known as the **natural response** theory, held that there was an automatic vocal reaction to environmental stimuli.

None of these theories was ever taken very seriously due to the lack of scientific evidence. Their critics knew them respectively as the 'bow-bow', the 'poohpooh' and the 'ding-dong' (Reber, 1995).

Trying to define language in animals can be more difficult than defining language in humans. It can be argued that all social behaviour – whether in goldfish or gorillas – requires and is organised by a form of communication, but is this language? How do we describe behaviours – social, aggressive or sexual – that affect or alter the behaviour of another animal? And what about the notion of intention? Is it possible to identify intention in animals, and if it were, could we call it language?

Think about it

- Think of typical animal 'communications' and make a list.
- Try to classify these into groupings, for example: warnings, social, etc.

If you look at your list you will probably see that the communications are species specific and all are innate. They may be learned behaviour, but this is not language.

Brown, a leading **psycholinguist,** suggested (1973) that there are three key properties which separate language from other communication systems:

- **semanticity,** which is the way that words can be symbols for all sorts of things from simple objects to complicated philosophies;
- **productivity,** which is the way that the human animal can combine words in original ways;
- **displacement,** which is what you are using when you tell someone today what you did yesterday, or when you discuss what you are planning to do next week. Displacement is the ability to use language across time and space.

Now go back to your list of animal communications and see if any fit the above three elements.

Brown (1970) also suggests that the essence of language is the ability to know much more about things than is possible by individual experience. You know about other periods in history or places in the world which you wouldn't unless you – and others – had language.

Language and the uniqueness of the human animal

Is there something unique or special about the human animal that enables him to acquire language? Simply in terms of brain power or brain capacity, a human brain is certainly the most advanced of any animal and would have the potential to cope with language. But this does not answer the long-debated question as to whether there is a uniqueness about the human animal that exists nowhere else. The philosophical and sometimes theological issues that are raised in the course of this debate are interesting, but beyond the scope of this book. Where we can go is into the Nature–Nurture issue. It is generally agreed that children are born with innate language abilities – a readiness to acquire language – but that social circumstances play an important role in the actual acquisition of language.

Language acquisition theories

If we take as our starting point the fact that we *acquire* language (see above), then we need to ask: how does this happen? Here we discuss the major theories of language acquisition:

Language acquisition theories		
Nurture	Learning theory	Skinner (1957)
Nature	Nativist theory	Chomsky (1959)
Cognitive	Interactionist	Piaget (1974)
Social	Social theory	Bruner (1983)

Nurture – or the learning theory

In his book *Verbal Behaviour* (1957), Skinner describes how **operant conditioning** (see Unit 6, pages 315–16) explains language acquisition. The emphasis is on behaviour, and Skinner treats language as any other behaviour. He argues that the child acquires verbal behaviour by **selective reinforcement**. The theory holds that pre-linguistic vocalisations are innate, but that the parent reinforces appropriate vocalisations, such as when the child says 'dada' or 'mama' or something that to the parent *sounds* like 'dada' or 'mama'. There is evidence that the resulting attention that the child receives encourages further vocalisation, and by the same token sounds that the young child is babbling, but which do not 'sound' like English (to English parents, or Russian to Russian parents), drop away due to lack of reinforcement. The arrival of early vocabulary is thus explained by the behaviourist as a matter of **shaping**. The same holds true of phrases and sentences. 'Correct' combinations of words are rewarded; while incorrect combinations are first corrected, then imitated and then rewarded.

As language development becomes more complex as the child develops, the learning theory approach tends to develop some cracks. For example, Brown (1973) suggests that parents reinforce the 'truth' of a child's statement rather than the correct grammar or syntax. Thus 'I drinked my drink' is likely to be enthusiastically rewarded (reinforced) despite its grammatical inaccuracy. Nelson (1973) demonstrated that children whose parents strictly correct their poor pronunciation develop vocabulary more slowly than children whose parents are more tolerant. Other criticisms of the learning theory approach are that it is unable to explain the fact that children's language develops in much the same way across languages, cultures and societies; and also that there is no satisfactory behavioural explanation for the irregular rate at which children acquire language. It also cannot explain how children – or adults – can recognise the difference between a complex sentence when it is correct and when it is incorrect *and* know which is correct.

On the other hand, there is evidence that children who grow up in an environment where they are talked to a lot, have large vocabularies – and this theory does explain the acquisition of the meaning of words.

Nature – or the nativist view

The essence of this view is that while learning may have a part to play in language acquisition and development, the innate, inborn factor 'allows' this to happen. In other words, children are neurologically and biologically prepared to acquire language. There are three main proponents of this view: Noam Chomsky and D. McNeill who hold a **psycholinguistic theory**, and E. Lenneberg who believes in a **sensitive period**.

<u>**Chomsky and McNeill**</u>   Chomsky, a linguist not a psychologist, argued in the 1950s and 1960s that the behaviourists' nurture theory was inadequate to explain the acquisition of language. This was a major turning point away from what was then current thinking. Chomsky's view was that while nurture certainly exerts an influence on language acquisition, this alone does not account for the almost universal way that language is acquired and develops. If it doesn't, Chomsky argued, then what does? He came up with the only other option: that the ability to acquire language must be innate. In 1970, McNeill referred to this innate capability as the **language acquisition device (LAD)**.

At a superficial level, different languages are highly dissimilar, but Chomsky argued for a 'universal grammar' – a general set of rules for creating structure and sentences from the raw material of ideas. It is this universal grammar that makes up the LAD. If we draw a parallel with the computer, the universal grammar (the essential part of the LAD) is the operating system of the computer that 'allows' the programme to work, while the computer software corresponds to the language the child acquires and develops.

<u>Lenneberg</u> Lenneberg also proposed a nativist view, but one significantly different from the LAD. He suggested that the child enters a **sensitive period**, during which neural maturation occurs such that language acquisition and development is possible. This sensitive period, he suggests, lasts from about 20 months until puberty. (See also the discussion on sensitive periods – sometimes called critical periods – in Unit 6.)

Evidence to support Lenneberg comes from studies with brain-injured pre-pubertal children, who were able to regain substantial speaking ability. Brain-injured older people were less able to regain speaking ability. This reinforces the generally (but not universally) held view that the brain can 'adjust' to damage up until about puberty; after this time the brain is less flexible in its ability to cope with damage.

The cognitive or interactionist view

This theory is not so much a different theory, as an extension or variation of the nativist view. The main difference is that cognitive psychologists, particularly Piaget, stress the importance of the maturation of the child in the acquisition and development of language. 'Maturation' in this context includes both cognitive readiness and the development of thought processes (more on this later) and the ways these interact.

There are a number of different notions within this theory. These include the natural development of analytical abilities, and the recognition that children are active in the language learning process. In other words, language doesn't just 'happen'; children are motivated to express more, as they grow more.

Social theory

Social (learning) theory is also an interactionist view, but one which stresses the importance of the child's early social development in its acquisition of language. The theory argues that simple exposure to language is not sufficient. Active motivation through social interaction – play and early games, for example – is required for effective acquisition and development of language.

Bruner (1983) suggested a **language acquisition support system (LASS)**, which allows the child to make sense of its social interactions.

Most researchers would argue that none of these theories is 'right', but that normal and successful acquisition of language requires elements of all of them.

Something to do

- Develop the outline of language acquisition theories (given on page 188) to include key ideas, people and evaluations.

Production and comprehension of language

Thus far we have considered theories of the acquisition of language. We now turn to the questions of how we produce language and how we comprehend language.

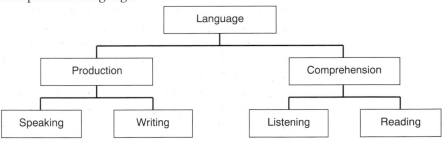

Think about it

It is equally possible to have a discussion on language the other way round – starting with the questions of production and comprehension and then moving into language acquisition.

- Where would *you* start a chapter on language and why?

Speech production

This section starts with a brief look at the building blocks of language and the way that they can be fitted together in an infinite number of ways.

The building blocks of language

Phoneme
Phonemes are the smallest of our building blocks and represent the sounds in a specific language. In English there are 26 letters, but a much greater number of sounds. In the words 'tone', 'to' and 'gone', for example, the letter 'o' has three different sounds.

↓

Morpheme
A morpheme is the smallest unit of meaning (not necessarily a word) and is made up of a number of phonemes. There are two main kinds of morpheme:
- **free morphemes**, which can stand alone, for example 'book';
- **bound morphemes**, which can only be used in conjunction with another morpheme, for example 'ed' or 'ly'.

↓

Word
This is the smallest unit that can stand alone and have meaning both in written and spoken form.

↓

Syntax
Syntax is to do with the rules of language concerning the way words are arranged into phrases and sentences.

↓

Semantics
This is the relationship between language (phonemes, morphemes, words, syntax and sentences) and what the language represents – in other words, the study of meaning. Chomsky has suggested two 'levels' of meaning:
- **surface structure** can allow for ambiguous statements, for example: 'Please make me a jam sandwich', implying that you can be turned into a jam sandwich;
- **deep structure** refers to the 'real' meaning which is, I would like a jam sandwich made from bread and jam.

Think about it

- Hold a brief conversation with a friend.
- Working together, think about why and when you said what you said. Try to analyse your conversation.

In the above, you will probably come to the conclusions that (1) you were trying to communicate and (2) you were following some unspoken rules – rules that involved aspects of language (you were both speaking good English) and co-operation (you took turns to speak).

Grice (1967) summed up and formulated what is essentially obvious: that for successful communication, both parties to the communication – the speaker and the listener – must co-operate. He called this the **co-operation principle**.

Typical language development in a child – the major milestones

There is an almost universally common progression across all languages. The major stages are as follows:

- **Birth:** crying.
- **3+ months:** 'cooing'-type sounds.
- **6 months:** 'babbling' possibly one-syllable sounds: 'ma', 'da'.
- **12 months:** repetitive-type words: 'dada', 'mama'. Signs of understanding words.
- **18 months:** vocabulary now between 10 and 50 words, but no real communication.
- **24 months:** 50 or more words, two-word phrases, communication emerging.
- **36 months:** vocabulary now about 1000 words, with most utterances intelligible.

The two main, current theories of speech production are those of Garrett (1984) and Dell (1986). The following table shows that there are considerable similarities between the two theories or models.

Models of speech production

Garrett	Dell
1. **Message level** Meaning is worked out.	1. **Semantic level** Meaning of what is to be sent – as a whole – is worked out.
2. **Functional level** Ideas, but not actual words, are worked out and decided.	2. **Syntactic level** Grammatical structure is planned.
3. **Positional level** Root morphemes are worked out in sequence.	3. **Morphological level** The basic meaning in terms of sounds (morphemes) is planned.
4. **Articulatory level** The final stage where the message is prepared for speech.	4. **Phonological level** The basic sound units are planned.

Issues such as feedback, where the speaker modifies a sentence mid-flow because it is not 'coming out right', are not adequately dealt with in either theory.

Dell adds the idea of **categorical rules** at each level, which limit what is being represented at that level. He also suggests that a form of networking occurs at each level, the processing of which is concurrent at all four levels. The network has key points, or nodes, which, when activated, activate nodes in related networks. When a node – say a verb – is selected, it shuts down, which avoids repetition.

Arguably the key difference between these two theories is that Dell provides more detail on the precise nature of the mechanisms, or workings, at any given point, particularly with respect to speech errors, which, as noted below, can provide clues as to the way that we produce speech.

Speech errors We now need to consider what exactly is involved in speech production. When considering any complex system, whether in psychology or another field, one way to understand the system is to investigate mistakes or errors that commonly occur. For example, Piaget – the cognitive psychologist – was interested in why children made mistakes in the tasks he set them.

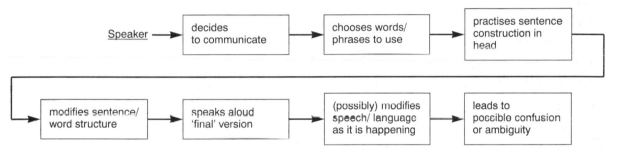

Errors can occur at any or several of the (rather arbitrary) stages of speech production shown above. An analysis of these errors is the usual method used by linguists to help understand the processes of production of language.

- We mentioned **spoonerisms**, and the famous Oxford academic who gave his name to this particular speech error, in the context of everyday memory (see page 176). According to Garrett, a spoonerism will occur at the stage when the root morphemes are being worked out (positional level), and the switching of these in a clause stresses the importance of the clause in grammatical construction. Dell finds that spoonerisms occur at the phonological level, where the phonological representation is created.
- Another speech error that we are all familiar with is the **tip-of-the-tongue** phenomenon (sometimes abbreviated to **TOT**). The phenomenon occurs when there is a discrepancy between the concept or idea to be expressed and the specific word needed to express it. In Garrett's theory this happens at the final, articulatory level.

Think about it

- Both spoonerisms and TOT have a direct connection with memory theory. Can you work out what it is?

- A third form of speech error is the **exchange error**. 'Exchange' can occur at both morpheme and word levels. In word exchange, the exchange is normally between the same parts of speech – for example two nouns are switched – within the same clause: 'The *mat* sat on the *cat*.' In morpheme exchange, the roots or suffixes of the two words are exchanged, while the rest of the two words remains the same: 'The children came runn*ed* in and were seat*ing*' (suffixes exchanged).

Think about it

- Can you identify where, in both Garrett's and Dell's theories, these two exchange errors occur?

A related and interesting aspect of speech production errors is that of errors made by brain-damaged patients. This, however, is beyond the scope of this book.

Writing production

How do you go about writing? Not whether you are right- or left-handed, or whether your writing slopes backwards or forwards, but how do you go about planning what you write?

Writing is in effect another form of language production. For a theoretical framework, we turn to Hayes and Flower and the work they did in the 1980s. Their model (1986) proposes three main processes:

- planning – ideas organised to meet the goal or task;
- sentence construction – the production of sentences to meet the goal;
- revision – at both the word and structural levels.

Much of the work done by Hayes and Flower uses **protocol analysis** (thinking out loud). While this provides considerable data, it can only provide data about what the writer is doing consciously and not about what happens unconsciously or automatically.

An interesting distinction can be made between 'expert' and 'non-expert' writers:

- At the planning stages, an expert will use key knowledge in constructing the plan, sometimes called **strategic knowledge**. Kellogg (1988 and 1990) found that an outline plan improved quality and reduced the time spent moving between the three stages.
- In terms of sentence construction, the expert is more likely to use longer sentences (Kaufer et al., 1986), which implies that the expert can think using larger units to achieve the goal.
- At the revision stage, the expert will not only spend more time than the non-expert, but the extra time will focus on sense and structure rather than on phrases and words.

Think about it

- Compare your own writing method and style with the 'expert' approach outlined above.
- Is there scope to improve?

Comprehension: listening and reading

We now turn our attention to **comprehension**, which we break down into listening and reading. In some ways this is a false dichotomy – they are both forms of comprehension, it is just that they use different sensory input modes.

<u>Listening</u> Views of how we listen, how we perceive speech, are broadly divided into either serial or parallel processing.

- The **serial view** (Forster, 1979) suggests that to comprehend speech, analysis of the message occurs at several consecutive stages.
- The **parallel view**, more accurately described as **interactionist** (Marslen-Wilson and Tyler et al., 1980), means that various knowledge sources, such as words, syntax and semantics, are interrogated and interact with each other to analyse and therefore understand the spoken message. The model therefore uses bottom-up processing (direct word recognition) and top-down processing (the listener's input or understanding, based on the topic or context of the message).

An interesting element of this discussion is the part that lip-reading plays in speech comprehension. The general view is that lip-reading is used by people with normal hearing more than is sometimes thought.

Studies of brain-damaged patients suggest that, in the case of listening, a number of different routes or pathways exist within the brain between hearing a word and repeating it aloud (Ellis and Young, 1988).

<u>Reading</u> This is another term that is easy to define superficially, but difficult to define precisely and is not by any means fully understood.

The first stage in the reading process is to understand the **orthography** – that is, the written format. Are you reading a word in English, or an ideogram in Chinese, or a technical drawing in engineering, or a score in music? In each case, the marks on the page require different cognitive and perceptual processes. Secondly, the system of syntax and semantics employed by the writer needs to be understood.

In practical terms, studying the eye movements of readers provides data on the process of reading. It is now known that under normal circumstances a reader's eyes fixate, then jump to the next fixation point. Each fixation lasts for about a quarter of a second, while the 'jumping' movement is known as **saccadic movement**. A related element is the **perceptual span**, or field of view. For normal left-to-right reading, the span is three or four letters to the left and 15 letters to the right of the fixation point. The fixation time is influenced by the complexity and similarity of the words and their context.

In a similar vein to their work in listening, Ellis and Young have proposed three routes between a written word and a spoken word; much of their work here was with patients with **acquired dyslexia**. We can consider it as the cognitive neuropsychology of the processing of words.

Eysenck and Keane (1990) point out that in the Ellis and Young (1988) model (see above), there are in fact three different ways or routes between hearing a word (or words) and repeating the same word (or words) aloud:

1. The normal manner of speech production by those with no brain damage: the input is analysed in auditory terms, the auditory lexicon recognises the word, the semantic system identifies meaning, and speech output goes via the output store of spoken words.

2. Those with 'word-meaning deafness' take a route that excludes or by-passes the semantic system. As a consequence, patients with this deficit can usually understand written sentences but not spoken sentences.

3. This is the most serious condition, and most rare. In this route, both the auditory input lexicon and the semantic system are bypassed, meaning that only auditory analysis and the production of speech sounds remain in the processing. Virtually no higher-order processing is involved. In this condition, a person could hear a word, but comprehend very little.

Word recognition at sight appears to depend on letter recognition, but evidence (McClelland and Rumelhart, 1981) suggests that the word can influence letter recognition. Work by Reicher (1969) resulted in the **word superiority effect**, which says that a word is more readily recognised than a series of letters which do not form a word.

Evidence to suggest that reading is a multi-skill activity comes from many different remedial reading programmes, each of which deals with a specific reading problem and has proved successful in its own right.

Something to do

- Draw a spidergram showing the connections between:
  – word recognition;
  – reading;
  – writing production;
  – speech errors.

Thinking

"Thinking, broadly defined, is nearly all of psychology; narrowly defined, it seems to be none of it."
Reber, quoting G.C. Oden, *The Penguin Dictionary of Psychology* (1995)

You may not find the above quotation very helpful, but Reber goes on to define thinking as:

"a term used so that it encompasses all of the mental activities associated with concept-formation, problem-solving, intellectual functioning, creativity, complex learning, memory, symbolic processing, imagery, etc."
Reber (1995)

Something to do

- Make a cross-topic chart with 'Thinking' at the centre (see Unit 1, page 9). Add page numbers to your chart so that it looks something like this:

Add more boxes as you go along.

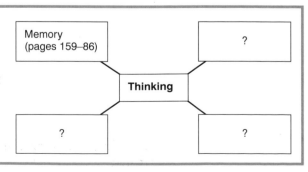

Ways of thinking   There are various ways in which people think. We look at two cognitive processes involved in thinking – **reasoning** and **decision making**; and then at some specific styles of thinking – **insight thinking, convergent thinking, divergent thinking** and **lateral thinking**.

Reasoning   This is a process that we all follow many times each day. In a very real sense, it is the application of thinking skills in a logical and purposeful way, usually aimed at solving some kind of problem. The emphasis is on the cognitive processes that are going on, rather than the logic behind them.

Decision making   Also a cognitive process, this is similar to reasoning. It is generally divided into two types, particularly when applied to organisations: **programmed decision making** and **non-programmed decision making**. 'Programmed' tends to refer to repetitive issues with well-defined options; 'non-programmed' refers to non-routine, unique or unstructured situations.

We turn now to the specific ways of thinking that theorists have identified. As we do so, bear in mind that we are talking of symbolic processes, dealing with ideas and concepts, and often focused on solving some sort of problem, practical or otherwise.

Insight thinking   Calling this 'thinking' is not strictly correct, for insight is more a process of apprehending something – perhaps a solution to a problem – intuitively.

A classic case of insight thinking

Köhler (1925) studied problems set to chimpanzees, which involved obtaining fruit beyond their normal reach. The chimpanzees would jump to reach the fruit, but soon stop when unable to reach it. At this point the chimpanzees would appear to have given up. However, Köhler had positioned boxes and sticks inside the chimpanzees' cage which could be pulled into position and used to climb on to reach the fruit. Köhler described the chimpanzees' behaviour first as 'dispirited', then 'sudden action' as the chimpanzees pulled the boxes into position to enable them to reach the fruit. He described this action as **insight**. It is an experience with which we too are familiar – for example when working on a problem which we cannot solve and then *suddenly* the solution is obvious – 'A-ha, I've got it!' Psychologists refer to this as the A-ha moment, for obvious reasons.

We could call this form of thinking insight, problem solving or even just learning.

<u>Convergent thinking</u>   In this form of thinking, the activity is focused on a solution and involves the bringing together of all relevant data to solve the problem – which usually has only one correct answer.

<u>Divergent thinking</u>   This can be seen as the opposite of convergent thinking. Rather than focusing on a 'target', which is the problem, divergent thinking seeks to draw in all possible relevant – and some not so relevant – ideas that *may* have a bearing on a particular problem. It is quite possible that novel or unique solutions may occur as a result of divergent thinking.

A classic case of divergent and convergent thinking

A classic study in thinking was conducted by Hudson (1966). He asked schoolboys to list as many uses for a housebrick as they could. He established that divergent thinkers had more possible uses and were more likely to be arts students; while convergent thinkers had fewer uses and tended to be science students.

<u>Lateral thinking</u>   This term was coined by De Bono (1977) and in some ways is an extension of divergent thinking. De Bono was interested in novel or creative approaches that would still give the 'right' answer. As an example, imagine the problem that you are faced with when you go to undo your bicycle lock and find the key does not work the lock:

- convergent thinkers might concentrate on making the key work;
- divergent thinkers might try to break the lock;
- lateral thinkers might get the bus home.

Concept formation

This is another aspect of thinking that we need to consider. We can define **concept** very loosely as a grouping of things that share some of the same attributes, that results in a mental representation. The relevance to thinking concerns the way that we form and use concepts. As an example, your concept of psychology has probably changed since you started reading this book. It has changed because you already had a concept of 'psychology'. What has happened is that you have added new words, terms, ideas, etc., to the basic concept of psychology which has now grown to include these new ideas.

There are generally considered to be two main types of concept:

- **classical concepts**, where all aspects of the concept are shared by all its members; and
- **probabilistic concepts**, where not all aspects are shared by its members.

'Chair' would be a classical concept, while 'government' would be probabilistic. Note, however, that the two types of concept are more the extreme ends of a continuum than opposites.

Think about it

- Decide if 'spoon' is a classical or probabilistic concept.
- Make a list of examples of both types of concept.

Models of thought In discussing 'thinking', we continually refer to problem-solving activity and learning. It is doubtful that you can think without doing so in the context of problem solving, which in turn implies that learning has occurred.

The first formal ideas on thinking were developed in the 17th century. John Locke (1632–1704), the philosopher, suggested a linear model of thinking, in which one idea led on to the next that was associated with it and so on. So the first model of thought is one of **association**.

A different view was proposed by Tolman. He was working in the 1930s, some 20 years before the birth of cognitive psychology and at the height of behaviourism. If you have linked Locke with associationism, you need to link Tolman with **cognitive maps**. Tolman's view is that we form a 'map' within our mind of any given activity, and we can then 'apply' this map as and when the need arises. Tolman worked mostly with rats running mazes, but argued that this form of **latent learning** applied to any animal, including humans. Tolman's approach is already far more complex than Locke's simple association.

Other attempts to 'explain' thinking were proposed by Freud, who suggested that thinking is the result of attempting to satisfy our biological drives; and Piaget, the Swiss psychologist, who argued that thinking occurs when we have to adapt to new demands made on us by the situation or environment that we are in. In Piaget's terms:

- Knowledge results from **adaptation**, which is an active process.
- **Assimilation** is the process by which the child adapts to the new situation in the light of interpreting new experiences.
- **Accommodation** is the modifying of an internal and familiar schema to enable it to fit new experience and fully adapt.
- **Equilibrium** is the balance of organised structures. When in balance, they aid ways of interacting with the environment.
- **Disequilibrium** occurs when a change in the organism or the environment requires a revision of the basic structures.
- To attain equilibrium, the child develops new **schemas**.

Another view is held by John Dewey, who argued that thinking occurs when we are faced with any kind of discrepancy or mismatch in what we expect. You expect, for example, water to come out of a tap when you turn it on: if it does not, then there is a mismatch or discrepancy and so thinking occurs. Dewey's view is also known as the **trouble theory** of thinking.

The relationship between language and thought

The essential question that this section seeks to answer is: which comes first – language or thought? There are three main views:

- Language comes first.
- Thought comes first.
- Language and thought develop together.

We can expand this outline a little further by adding more detail and including theorists who have worked in this area:

Language and thought		
Theory	**Main theorists**	**Other theorists/theories**
Language comes first	Wittgenstein Whorf	Whorf and Sapir (the linguistic relativity hypothesis – strong and weak forms) Watson (peripheralism) Bernstein (restricted and elaborated codes) Labov (black English)
Thought comes first	Piaget	The cognitive view or the developmental view
Language and thought develop together	Vygotsky	Initially separate (until about age two), then together. Importance of social context.

Something to do

- Copy out the above outline on a large (A3) piece of paper, and add additional notes or connections as you read about them (here and in parallel sources).

Language comes before thought

This view was proposed by Whorf and Sapir (1956). It is generally called the **linguistic relativity hypothesis**, and comes in three 'strengths':

- the strong hypothesis, which says that language determines thought;
- the weak hypothesis, which argues that language affects only perception;
- the weakest hypothesis, which argues that language affects only memory.

In terms of the strong version, Whorf and Sapir argue that if you do not have the vocabulary, then you have no 'tools' to comprehend new concepts. Evidence against this version comes from a wide range of studies. For example, Heider (1972) studied a primitive tribe of people from Indonesia who had only two main words for colours. He tested them for memory of many colours, and found not that they remembered them all equally, which would be the case if language came before perception, but that they remembered some more than others. Most of the evidence suggests that it is thought that affects language. This evidence against the strong position provides support for the weak position, the consensus being that language may influence thought. The weakest position (language affects memory) seems to be the best-supported linguistic relativity hypothesis.

A classic case of linguistic relativity

Perhaps the best-known evidence for this comes from Carmichael et al. (1932). They divided their subjects into two groups and gave each group the same series of pictures or stimulus figures. However, the stimulus figures were labelled differently for each group. For example, the figure '0–0' was labelled 'eye-glasses' for one group, but 'dumb-bells' for the second group. Participants were tested later by being prompted with a word ('eye-glasses' or 'dumb-bells') and asked to draw the figure they had been shown. Each group drew a figure which closely resembled the prompt word, rather than the simple figure as it had been given to them. Carmichael et al. argued that this showed that language does affect memory. Other studies support this view.

Thought comes first This is the developmental view supported by Piaget, since thinking begins at an earlier developmental stage than language (Piaget, 1967). The very fact that Inuit have many words for snow, Arabs many words for camel, and Philippinos many words for rice, while other cultures do not, must suggest that it is thinking that precedes language: their words depend on their experience.

Language and thought develop together Also a developmental view, the argument here is that language and thought develop in the child separately until about two years of age, when they 'merge'. Before two years, thought is pre-verbal. It is experienced more in action (Piaget's sensorimotor stage – see Unit 7, pages 330–1), and the child's utterances are more automatic reflexes – crying when uncomfortable – than thought-based. At about two years, the child is able to express thought verbally, and speech reflects rationality. While this view is essentially that of Vygotsky (1962), it overlaps Piaget's view.

Social and cultural variations in language in relation to thought

Bernstein

Under the heading of social and cultural variations, we need to consider the work done by Bernstein on restricted and elaborated codes, and Labov on black English.

Bernstein was more sociologist than psychologist and so was interested in the social rather than individual aspects of language. During the 1960s, he studied the relationship between social class and the use of language in children and concluded that there were significant differences in the way that children from different social classes used language. Children from lower social classes used a **restricted code**, while children from upper classes used an **elaborated code**.

- The restricted code, as the name implies, is limited in its use of vocabulary, is less technically correct, uses more slang and rarely expresses abstract thought.
- Elaborated language is essentially the opposite: varied, with correct use of grammar, vocabulary, and so on.

There are a number of quite serious implications that can be drawn from this work, particularly with respect to education. If we argue – as we have been doing, although not explicitly – that language is crucial to normal development, then in its extreme form a child with restricted language will face a serious problem in terms of its education and is unlikely to reach its full potential, intellectually or otherwise. On the other hand, a child with an elaborated code of language is much more likely to reach its full potential.

Something to do

- Write a short paragraph in two ways, (a) using an extremely (to make the point more clearly) restricted code and (b) using an extremely elaborated code.

It does not take much thought to realise just how serious a handicap a restricted code is.

Criticisms of Bernstein's work are that reducing language use into only two categories is much too simplistic, and that within the theory there is an inherent value judgement – that elaborated is better.

Labov

Rather later than Bernstein, Labov (1970) studied cultural and ethnic variations in language. He found that in black cultures the language spoken was significantly different from standard English, yet, in its social context, the communication was clearly understood. Labov showed that there is a danger in suggesting that black English is 'wrong' or 'incorrect', and that it should be seen as a dialect of English rather than as a poor version of standard English. The view that black English is wrong has implications for education, in particular intelligence testing. An implication of Bernstein's view, repudiated by Labov, is that children speaking in a **restricted code** are less able to develop and communicate in abstract terms. Labov's conclusion is that these children are able to communicate effectively with each other, possibly because of basic assumptions rather than explicit use of vocabulary and grammar.

Problem solving

Problem solving is one of the themes or concepts that keeps re-occurring in cognitive psychology. One extreme view (Boden, 1987), for example, is that all thinking involves problem solving. We therefore bring into the discussion of problem solving some topics previously discussed and some yet to be discussed.

Approaches to problem solving

There are a number of ways of approaching problem solving. One of the earliest theories is the **Gestalt approach**, while the latest is the use of **artificial intelligence**. In between come a variety of methods or sets of rules, all of which have been delineated by theorists to provide a handle on just how the human animal goes about solving its problems.

The Gestalt approach

One of the main notions of the Gestalt school is that human beings do things in certain ways according to a set, or sets, of principles that are innate and rigid. The word for this is *Einstellung*. In terms of problem solving, this implies that human beings will look at a problem in only a certain number of ways. You will remember that we discussed the Gestalt principle of closure in the context of perception (see page 133). This says that we see things as wholes, or complete figures, with clearly defined boundaries even if the boundary does not exist. Boundaries are the clue to 'puzzles' such as the **nine-dot problem**:

The nine-dot problem

The task is to join all the dots with four straight lines without going over the same dot twice or lifting your pen from the paper.

The only way in which this problem can be solved is by going outside the imaginary boundary set by the square of dots – the principle of closure suggests that you will not look for the solution outside the square.

A similar problem is the equally well-known **match problem**:

The match problem

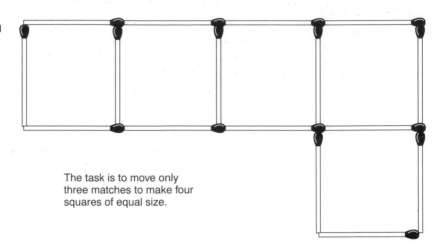

The task is to move only three matches to make four squares of equal size.

(The solutions are given at the end of the unit, on pages 211–12.)

Functional fixatedness A similar limiting factor when it comes to problem solving is the way in which we get stuck by restricting our approach to considering only the usual function of an element (or elements) in the problem. The work of Hudson (1966) with his housebrick experiment is a good example of this (see page 198). If you were asked to list as many uses for a housebrick that you could think of and you limited your thinking to the normal uses of housebricks – mainly building – then you would have exhibited **functional fixatedness**: you thought only of the brick's *function*. If, on the other hand, you could think of the brick as a heavy object, as rectangular, as absorbent, and so on, you would be more likely to think of a greater number of uses.

Brainstorming This technique for problem solving is carried out by a group. The rules are simple. Once the problem is defined, members of the group call out any possible idea – however silly it may appear – that may have a bearing on the problem. A scribe very briefly writes down the ideas. No discussion of the ideas is allowed until later. **Brainstorming** is a form of divergent thinking as a group, with one idea prompting the next.

The risky-shift effect An interesting aspect of group decision making applied to problem solving is the way a group will tend to make a different decision from an individual. This is known as the **risky-shift effect**: a group will often be willing to solve a problem or make a decision that involves more risk than any individual in the group might be prepared to shoulder on their own.

Think about it

• Can you link the *reasons* for the risky-shift effect to your understanding of *social* psychology?

Adversary and non-adversary problems

If we attempt to categorise problems, we find that they fall into two main groups: **adversary** and **non-adversary** (Garnham, 1988):

- Adversary problems are those in which you are competing against one or more opponents, for example in games like chess.
- Non-adversary problems are those you solve on your own, for example the nine-dot problem.

Something to try

The munchies and crunchers problem
Crunchers eat munchies. On one side of the river there are three munchies and three crunchers. All six have to cross the river. There is only one boat and it has room for two only. At no time must two crunchers be left with one munchie or the munchie gets eaten.

- How do all six cross the river?

Heuristics and algorithms

Two other important concepts that we need to consider in this discussion on problem solving are **heuristics** and **algorithms**.

Consider the problem of the munchies and crunchers. How did you tackle it? You probably thought of a number of options, guessed a bit, tried a few options, maybe something intuitive seemed worth a try, and so on. Any and all of these are **heuristics** – ways of reducing the possible number of solutions. They are directed thinking, but – and this is a key point – they do not guarantee a solution.

An **algorithm**, on the other hand, is a method that is guaranteed to solve a problem. It does this by setting up a procedure that will investigate or try every possible solution in a logical manner. For example, when doing long-division sums, you know a set of rules that will always lead to the correct answer. If you used an algorithm to solve a chess problem, it would go through every possible move you and your opponent could make. This is a good example of where an algorithm will work, but where it is hugely inefficient.

In summary, heuristics are a 'rule-of-thumb' technique, while algorithms methodically try every possibility.

Means–ends analysis

Because of the essential nature of the two techniques, it is generally heuristics that are of more interest to psychologists. For example, an important heuristic developed by Newell and Simon (1972) is **means–ends analysis**. This is a problem-solving technique that breaks down the problem into a number of steps and solves these smaller steps one at a time.

Problem–space theory

Another technique proposed by Newell and Simon (1972) is their **problem–space theory**. This views the problem as having a number of alternative states within the 'space' between the problem and the solution. The problem is solved by exploring each of these alternative states – usually using heuristic devices – within their own space, and moving from one state to the next until the final goal or state is reached.

Computer technology

Not surprisingly, psychologists became interested in the use of computer technology to solve problems. As we have already noted, the 'birth' of cognitive psychology in the 1950s coincided with an increase in the availability of computer technology.

The development of psychology and computer technology	
1940s and 1950s	During and following the Second World War, technology made great strides; the electronic computer was developed.
Pre-1950	Behaviourism was the main approach or **paradigm** used in psychology.
1950s	Cognitive psychology took over as the main psychological paradigm.
Mid-1950s	Psychologists started to rethink cognitive psychology in information-processing terms. This led naturally to attempting to develop a **computer-analogy**: **artificial intelligence** was born.

The general problem solver

The **general problem solver** was a computer program written to simulate the way that humans solve problems (Newell and Simon, 1972). The information for the program was obtained by asking people to describe the mental processes that they were going through as they tackled a problem. This method is called **protocol analysis**. There are difficulties with protocol analysis, however (Garnham, 1988):

- It is impossible to know just how accurate the commentary is in terms of what is really happening in the brain.
- A similar difficulty is the fact that in some instances unconscious operations take place that simply are not available to our conscious state, and we are not consciously aware of it.

It was also found that the general problem solver was not very effective when it came to solving problems that were not very well defined.

As a result of these difficulties, what was once thought to be an approach with almost unlimited possibilities quickly lost favour.

Artificial intelligence (AI)

Some aspects of **artificial intelligence** were discussed indirectly in the context of **computer simulations** or the use of the computer to solve problems. It is important to be clear that the two concepts are related but different:

- Computer simulation is about using computers to test theories, the intelligence is in the programmer.
- In AI, the goal is to develop an artificial system (usually using computer science) that has, in some form or other, the ability to think or have intelligence much like a human.

An early attempt to use AI focused on **interactive programs**. This is where you sit at a keyboard and have a 'conversation' with the computer (you interact with it). An early version of this was ELIZA: a therapeutic program where you discussed your problem with the computer, the computer being programmed to respond to key words.

Expert systems

Here we are concerned with the difference that knowledge can make in problem solving. In human terms, an average chess player may know the rules as well as a grand master, but the grand master has the intelligence – perhaps better described as awareness – of the overall situation and the experience to win the game.

Put simply, the 'expert' program has a huge database from which the human expert can draw to enable him or her to make a better decision.

The problems with expert systems are typical of the differences between artificial (machine) and real (human) intelligence: the human expert can draw on higher-order functions – the ability to synthesise material and use intuition or 'guestimates' to shorten processing – which the 'system' cannot.

Strong and weak AI

This discussion centres on the argument: do computers think for themselves, can they behave intelligently, and therefore can they be considered to be like their human counterparts? Or, on the other hand, are they simply simulating or copying human thinking and do not have any of those attributes which can be considered as intelligence? The issue hinges on whether the computer is a tool.

- **Weak AI** supporters argue that however powerful the computer and its programs, it is still only a tool. It may be able to be used in many different ways, for example to test certain hypotheses in a very precise and accurate manner; and is certainly better than human participants in particular circumstances. However clever, though, it does not have its own intelligence.
- **Strong AI** supporters argue that the computer is more than a tool; a computer, suitably programmed, does have its own 'mind' which can 'understand' in certain, if limited, cognitive states. Supporters of strong AI argue that if the computer and its program can do things that an intelligent human being can, it therefore must have intelligence.

The argument between weak AI and strong AI could be seen to be centred on the issue of whether or not the human mind is merely an information or symbol processor (granted, of huge complexity); if it is, then a suitably complex computer with a suitably complex program, which can also manipulate the same information or symbols, could therefore be said to have its own mind.

The whole question of AI is currently very much in the forefront of research. Areas that are likely to be considered fruitful, and indeed are already being investigated, are parallel distributed processing and other connectionist theories. Perhaps the fundamental problem is that we still don't know exactly how the brain works, so successful attempts to model it with a computer – however powerful – remain in the future.

Revision and practice

• •

Coursework opportunities

1. Investigate the Müller-Lyer illusion. Use either a model (as described on page 141) or use a computer software package. Try varying the angle of the fins, replace the fins with circles, squares, etc.
2. Replicate, or design a variation of, the Solley and Haigh (1958) study to investigate the effect of emotion on perception (see page 144).
3. Investigate split-span attention (Gray and Wedderburn, 1960; see page 151) by making your own audio-cassette tape and playing the two messages, one to each ear. (The Wellcome Trust provide just such a tape.)
4. Investigate the Stroop effect (1935) (see page 155). Design your own variations using colour patches and/or other changes.
5. Investigate the place of lip-reading in speech comprehension. If possible, video-film a speaker full-face and have participants tested or self-report on comprehension (a) viewing the whole screen and (b) viewing with the speaker's mouth concealed.
6. Replicate the Hudson study (1966) on convergent/divergent thinking.
7. Investigate the risky-shift effect as follows.
   Devise a series of problems, the solution to which involves a degree of risk. For example, you have received a small inheritance: do you invest it safely or do you gamble on horses or possible high-gain stocks and shares? Ask your participants individually to rate the degree of risk in each decision on a scale of, say, 1 to 10. Then ask a group of participants to solve the same problems, on the same scale, giving a group decision.

• •

Examination questions

Question 1   (a) What is meant by bottom-up perceptual processing?   *(5 marks)*

(b) Describe and critically assess **one** theory that explains perceptual processing in this way.   *(20 marks)*

(AEB, Paper 1, Summer 1996)

Question 1: Unpacked   Part (a) is a straightforward Skill A question, requiring a description of bottom-up perceptual processing. As a rule of thumb, 5 marks = 20% = about two-thirds of a page with average writing.
      You will need to cover:

- sensory input as 'raw' data;
- definitions;
- (some) supporting evidence;
- two main theories, Gibson and Gestalt.

Part (b) requires Skill A and Skill B in your answer. A logical approach would be to describe your chosen theory and then 'critically assess' it, i.e. 'make an informed judgement of strengths and limitations' and 'present a considered appraisal'. To do this you will need to:

- focus on your chosen theory, say Gibson, and refer to Gestalt;
- describe it in some detail;
- spell out its strengths and weaknesses, using supporting evidence for both.

Question 2   (a) What is meant by the information processing approach to the explanation of cognitive processes?   *(5 marks)*

(b) Outline information processing explanations of any **two** cognitive processes.
(10 marks)

(c) Critically assess these explanations.   *(10 marks)*

(AEB, Paper 1, Summer 1997)

The following essay was written by a student under simulated exam conditions.

Comments	Essay
	(a) The information processing approach is used by psychologists to explain the mental and active processes of the brain.
Rather weak and lacking in definition	It has often been compared to the workings of a computer system. The information is taken in, sorted and later retrieved. This shows that the processes can be broken down into a series of stages.
	(b) Information processing can explain many different cognitive processes and the two outlined here are focused auditory attention and focused visual attention.
Defines *two* relevant areas	
Weak and unclear	By focused auditory attention we mean that we pay attention to one piece of information and pick it out from a whole lot of other information that we hear.
Date? Essential detail missing	This was suggested by Cherry who asked participants who were played the message once, to repeat one message and ignore the other one. He found that there were some points that people remembered from the ignored message, like whether the speaker was a man or a woman, but not much else. This is sometimes called the cocktail party effect, because at parties we can be listening to one conversation but we can switch our attention to another conversation if we like the person speaking or if our name is mentioned.
Generally accurate	
	Broadbent put forward the theory of a filter model of selective attention.
	He used a method called a split-span procedure, where participants were told a set of 6 numbers, 3 numbers to one ear and 3 to the other. Then some people were asked to recall the numbers in pairs[1] and others were asked to recall ear-by-ear[2], e.g. 258176 [1]21 57 86 [2]258 176.
Very unclear	
	The second group found it easier to remember.
	Broadbent's theory followed an information processing system, e.g. input (senses) into sensory store, filter selects some information and rejects other, this is processed in a limited capacity store and passed on to the response process.
Getting better!	
	This model was known as a single channel model. Other models suggested more than one channel is used in the process.
Correct	In focused visual attention the information comes in through the eyes, information is processed and some is rejected.

Date?

Neisser carried out a visual search task in which people had to pick out a straight letter from a background of curved letters (1) or against a background of straight letters (2). Group 1 found the task easier as the features of the letter were different from the background letters and stood out.

Again, generally correct but badly presented

The other group (2) had to process all the letters. This shows we can either shift our attention and focus on an item that is different or we can process each item in turn so that the right item is matched.

Date?
How does this fit?

La Berge suggested that visual attention was like a spotlight where the items in the beam were in focus but items could still be glimpsed outside the beam.

(c) Broadbent's model had problems which happened when too much information clogged up the filter store and caused a bottleneck – Treisman came up with a solution and suggested that the information passes through several filters getting weaker slowly, unless it triggers off a match in the person's memory and then becomes important. This made the model more flexible.

Some evaluation evident

Needs further explanation

Another criticism of Broadbent's model was that it didn't account for 'meaning'.

Date?

Gray and Wedderburn found that by using words instead of numbers for the dual listening task they could remember by meaning instead of ear by ear.

Some evaluation

Cherry's experiment showed we do listen to some physical parts of the message we don't attend to. Also we listen more if it has some meaning.

Which 'experiment'?

In visual attention Neisser's experiment suggests that in order to recognise an item or letter we look for the features of it. Sometimes we have to search through the information; at other times we 'spot' it right away. Sometimes the sound of the letter can add to the confusion, for instance F and V sound similar.

Relevance not explained

Also, if words that had meaning were presented, participants were more likely to identify the letters than in words that had no meaning, e.g. NEAT and ATNE.

General comments
In part (a) the material is essentially accurate, but badly presented; in places very muddled/unclear. In part (b) same muddled presentation, but evaluation is evident. The essay suffers from poor quality of language.

Marks: Part (a) $\frac{3}{5}$ (poss 2)   Part (b) $\frac{6}{10}$ Part (c) $\frac{5}{10}$

$$= \frac{14}{25}$$

Question 3   Describe and critically assess psychological explanations of why we forget.

(25 marks)
(AEB, Paper 1, Summer 1997)

Question 4   (a) Explain what is meant by the term *performance deficit* in relation to attention.

(4 marks)

(b) Outline the findings of **two** experimental investigations of this phenomenon.

(8 marks)

(c) Evaluate the contribution of such studies to our understanding of attentional processes.

(12 marks)

(AEB, Module Paper 6, January 1998)

Question 5   (a) Outline Whorf's theory about the relationship between language and thought.

(3 marks)

(b) Describe **one** study which appears to support Whorf's theory.

(5 marks)

(c) Evaluate Whorf's theory. Refer to alternative theories and evidence in your answer.

(12 marks)

(Total: 20 marks)

(NEAB, PS07, February 1997)

Selected reading list

de Bono, E., *The Use of Lateral Thinking* (Penguin, 1967)

Eysenck, M.W. and Keane, M.J., *Cognitive Psychology* (Lawrence Erlbaum Associates, 1990)

Gross, R.D., *Psychology. The Science of Mind and Behaviour* (Hodder and Stoughton, 2nd edn 1992, 3rd edn 1996)

Solutions to problems

Solution to the nine-dot problem

Solution to the match problem

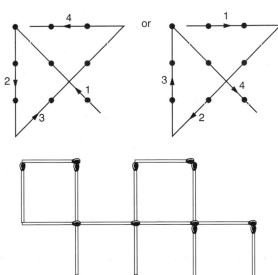

Solution to the munchies and crunchers problem

Left bank	River	Right bank
m m m c c c	(boat, empty)	
m m m c	c c (boat) →	
m m m c		c c
m m m c	← c (boat)	c
m m m c c		c
m m m	c c (boat) →	c
m m m		c c c
m m m	← c (boat)	c c
m m m c		c c
m c	m m (boat) →	c c
m c		m m c c
m c	← m c (boat)	m c
m m c c		m c
c c	m m (boat) →	m c
c c		m m m c
c c	← c (boat)	m m m
c c c		m m m
c	c c (boat) →	m m m
c		m m m c c
c	← c (boat)	m m m c
c c		m m m c
	c c (boat) →	m m m c
		m m m c c c

5 Bio-psychology and the psychology of health: how do our systems function?

Bio-psychology is to do with the way the body 'works', particularly the relationship between behaviour, mental processes and physiology. In this unit we look at the following topics:

- the human body's nervous systems;
- hormonal processes;
- the effect of drugs on human behaviour;
- the way the brain works;
- the way the human body has certain rhythms;
- motivation, emotion and stress.

All of these are topics within the field of bio-psychology, and can be grouped under three main headings: **biological processes, mental processes** and **behaviours**.

We can start thinking about what this means by asking the basic question: just who are you? The answer can be expressed in biological terms; you are a result of the coming together of two biological or physiological components – a living (which is what *bio* means) **biological** or **physiological organism**. You also have the capacity to think, and you are an individual with ideas, feelings, creativity – **mental processes**; and you have certain characteristics (some inherited), actions and reactions – **behaviours**.

Bio-psychology is the study of how these factors combine and influence each other; it studies the relationship between the way the brain and nervous systems work, and the resulting behaviours.

The unit is divided into five main sections:

- The first section looks at the **nervous systems**, the way neurons and hormones work, and the influence they have on behaviour. These are, in a sense, the 'building blocks' of the body.
- This is followed by a discussion on **psychopharmacology**, or the effect that certain drugs have on behaviour.
- The third section looks at the **brain**, its different parts and functions, and includes a neurophysiological explanation of visual perception.
- The next section concentrates on some specific **bodily states** or **awarenesses**: biorhythms, sleep, dreams and hypnosis.
- The final section looks at the relationship between the brain and certain other aspects of the way we work and behave – **motivation, emotion, stress** and **illness**.

Something to do

- Start a new word list and a new people list for this unit.

Organisation of the human nervous systems

Bio-psychology is a complex subject. We approach it by applying the principle used in SQR4 (see Unit 1, page 4): starting with an overview of the whole of the body's nervous systems, and then filling in the details.

Suppose that you are sitting at your desk, getting ready to read this new material. You have just made a mug of coffee, and you have a packet of your favourite biscuits at hand:

- You take a mouthful of coffee – but burn your tongue as it is too hot.
- Your chair is too far from the desk – so you pull it in a little more.
- The telephone on your desk rings – it makes you jump, but you reach out and pick up the receiver.
- You start reading the material – as you do, you think about the meaning of the words.
- Unconsciously, you reach out for another biscuit – and without thinking start to nibble it.

If we analyse the different **behaviours** in these everyday events, we will see that they depend on sensory systems and information processing, followed – usually, but not always – by a reaction. The instant the too-hot coffee touches your tongue, you rapidly withdraw the mug. The first ring of the telephone makes you jump, and you react automatically:

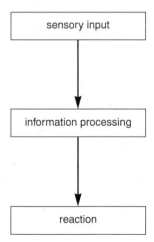

These examples of behaviour are both:

- **involuntary** (reacting to hot coffee); and
- **voluntary** (making yourself more comfortable, deciding to answer the telephone).

In each example, the *process* of sensing–reaction–behaviour is almost instantaneous. In each case, and indeed in just about every other behaviour all day and every day, it is your body's **nervous systems** that are doing the information processing.

This section of the unit looks at the way the human nervous systems work and how they interact with each other. Look at the diagram:

The human nervous systems

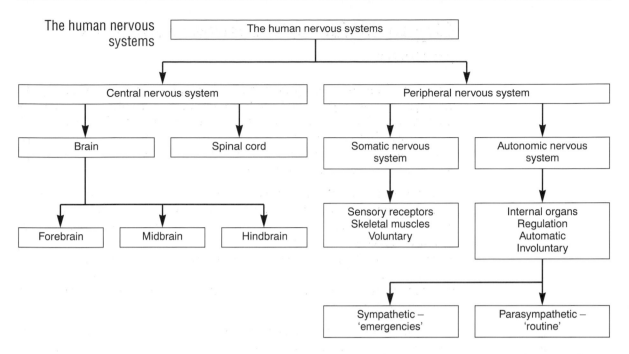

You will see that there are two main nervous systems: the **central nervous system** or CNS, and the **peripheral nervous system** or PNS.

- 'Central', obviously meaning in the centre, refers to the spinal cord and the brain.
- 'Peripheral', meaning on the edge, refers to most of the rest of our nerve activity.

Note that the brain has a number of sub-systems, while the spinal cord is a system in itself.

There are two main peripheral systems:

- the **somatic nervous system**, which deals with voluntary activity, for example when you move your chair to get more comfortable or reach out and pick up the telephone; and
- the **autonomic nervous system**, which generally (but not strictly) operates automatically. This includes sending messages to keep your heart pumping, your lungs working and your digestive system dealing with the biscuits and everything else that you have eaten.

You will also see from the diagram that the autonomic system is in fact two systems:

- the **parasympathetic**, which in general terms deals with the routine as described above; and
- the **sympathetic**, which deals with the 'emergencies', telling your body to prepare for 'fight or flight'.

You need to hold this diagram in mind, as it is the framework within which most of bio-psychology fits. The human nervous system is an incredibly complex series of systems, all interconnected and all operating at high speed. What follows is a description, in fairly basic terms, of how this 'works'.

The neuron

If we take a **reductionist** approach to the body, we can say that the nervous system is made up of its own structure, sub-systems and parts. Following the reductionist approach, the smallest component or building block within the nervous system is the **neuron**.

Neurons themselves are complex structures. Look at the diagram showing the various parts of an individual neuron:

The neuron

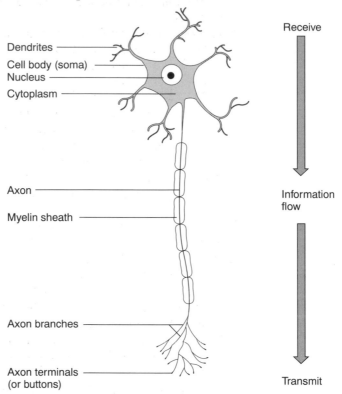

Dendrites

Cell body (soma)
Nucleus
Cytoplasm

Axon

Myelin sheath

Axon branches

Axon terminals
(or buttons)

Receive

Information
flow

Transmit

You have in your body billions of neurons, and they were all present when you were born. Most of these neurons are in your brain. An interesting fact is that the neurons you are born with are all you ever get – the neuron is the only cell in your body that does not reproduce itself. It does, however, grow in size and complexity. With billions of neurons, losing a few here or there may not seem to be very important, but there are many ways in which you lose neurons. These include blows to the head and drinking alcohol. You also lose neurons at a rate of approximately 10,000 every day of your life as a result of natural causes.

The purpose of neurons

Before we get into a detailed discussion on how neurons work, let us focus on two broad questions:

- What is the purpose of the existence of neurons?
- What exactly do they do?

The answer to these questions is that the brain and the nervous systems, which are composed of all these neurons, provide the body with its **communication system**. Neurons function to transmit information within the body's nervous systems.

Sizes and types of neuron

If you refer to the diagram of the neuron, you may get the impression that neurons are all alike. This is not the case, as neurons come in a variety of shapes and sizes; however, just about all neurons have essentially the same construction and the same key parts.

- In terms of size, neurons located in the spinal cord can be up to a metre long, while neurons located in the brain are rarely more than a millimetre long.
- In terms of neuron function, there are three main types:
  - **Sensory neurons** are those that transmit signals *from* sensory receptor cells, for example the eye, *to* the brain. These are also called **afferent neurons**.
  - **Motor neurons** or **efferent neurons** are those that carry messages *from* the brain *to* muscles and glands.
  - **Interneurons**, sometimes called **connectors**, most of which make up the billions of nerve cells in your brain, are the means by which the other two types of neuron 'talk' to each other.

  If you need help to remember which of the first two is which, remember that they are nearly the SAME: Sensory Afferent Motor Efferent!

Glial cells

With a head full of brain cells and the rest of the body busily sending signals to and fro, you might well ask: what is it that stops the 'wires getting crossed'? The answer to that problem comes in the form of the other major cell that makes up the nervous system – the **glial cell**. There are about ten times as many glial cells as there are neurons. They hold together neurons that need to be held together, and serve as an insulator between other neurons that need to be kept apart.

In the case of the latter, glial cells form an insulating cover along the neuron's axon, called the **myelin sheath**. These neurons are **myelinated neurons**. As well as insulating the axon, the glial cells which form the myelin sheath also speed up the transmission of information (or electrical signals) along the axon. This is done by means of small gaps, or nodes, in the sheath called **nodes of Ranvier**. The 'action potential' (or signal – see page 221) can jump from node to node and thus travel faster. This is called **saltatory conduction**.

(As an interesting aside, **glia** comes from the Greek word for glue. That bit of information may give new meaning to the slang term of someone 'coming unstuck'!)

Neurotransmission and synaptic activity

This section considers the way in which the electrical signal is passed from one neuron to the next. The section could equally correctly be called the **'neural impulse'** or **'synaptic transmission'**. We look at what is in fact a highly complex electro-chemical process in a fairly simple manner. Any good biology textbook will provide more detail.

The reason we need to understand something about the way in which neurons pass on electrical signals (which, remember, are not just electrical signals, but signals which represent facets of the outside world) is that the point at which the signal moves from one neuron to the next critically affects the *content* of the message. The transmission of the signal between neurons is essentially chemical, and is arguably the most critical point in the whole chain of information processing. If this process is not working properly or is affected by drugs, then the messages that involve and often control emotion, thought and behaviour – the very keystones of psychology – are going to be affected. As a result, the person's 'psychology' – whether their normal or abnormal behaviour – can be altered. This can be both for ill, as in the case of illicit drug taking; and for good, as in the case of properly prescribed drug therapy. (See pages 231–7 for more on the psychological effects of drugs.)

Synaptic activity, then, plays a crucial role in the transmission of signals from one neuron to another. The question we need to consider now is: just how does the message move from one neuron to the next?

Synaptic transmission

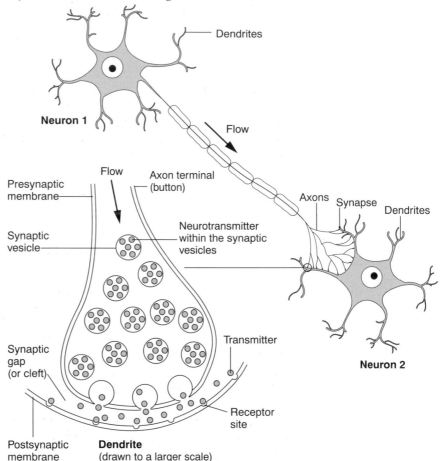

Look at the diagram 'synaptic transmission'. The **synapse** or **synaptic gap** is the point at which two neurons 'meet'. The neurons do not exactly touch; rather they transmit signals across a very small space between them – about 25 nanometres wide (25 billionths of a metre). This is the synaptic gap. (The word 'synapse' comes from the Greek and means junction or contact.) The reason for this gap is that it allows the nervous system to be *selectively* active, depending on what messages need to be transmitted. If there were no gap between the neurons, the whole of the body's nervous systems would be permanently connected. This in turn would mean that a given signal, whether to or from the brain, would (or at least could) flow down every neuron and so the whole of the nervous system would be 'active' at all times.

What happens in synaptic activity, in simple terms, is that incoming information is received at the dendrites of a neuron, passed on through the cell body or **soma**, along the axon to the axon terminals or **buttons**, and then via the synaptic gap (sometimes also called the **synaptic cleft**) to the dendrites of the next neuron.

The basic principle of neurotransmission can be represented as follows:

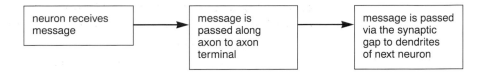

It is of course rather more complicated. As noted above, not all neurons are the same in their physical make-up, and the same applies to the way they transmit to other neurons. For example, some neurons have a great number of axons, all passing on messages. Remember also that any one neuron will be connecting with many other neurons – so the process forms a network rather than a chain.

Something to do

• Remember to enter new terms into your own vocabulary list.

So, let us assume that the signal that is to be transmitted has arrived at the 'end' of a neuron. In front of it is a very small fluid-filled gap. On the other side of the gap is the next neuron in the chain. In other words, the message needs to move across the synaptic gap from the axon terminal on the transmitting neuron to the dendrite on the receiving neuron (see the diagram on page 218).

The **neural impulse** is electrical, but it does not jump across the gap as does the spark in, say, a car's spark plug. Rather it triggers the release of a series of chemicals called **neurotransmitters** – biochemical material – which have the job of stimulating other neurons. It does this as follows: When the signal arrives at the end of the axon of the transmitting neuron, it causes small round sacs called **synaptic vesicles** to move down to the membrane of the axon terminal or button, where they fix themselves. Inside these vesicles are the neurotransmitters. The vesicles now rupture and the neurotransmitters move into the synaptic gap: they have left the **presynaptic membrane** and are moving across to the **postsynaptic membrane**.

The neurotransmitters now attach themselves to receptor sites on the postsynaptic membrane. There are two key conditions for this to happen:

• There should be no other chemical of any kind on the receptor site.
• The neurotransmitter must fit exactly the shape of the receptor site – rather as you might position a piece in a jigsaw puzzle or fit a key into a lock.

If both of these conditions are met, then the neurotransmitter locks into the receptor site and is able to stimulate the postsynaptic membrane. It then initiates an **action potential** (see page 221), and the message is moved down the axon of this neuron and on to the next in either a positive or a negative direction. Once the neurotransmitter has 'locked in' and the message has been relayed, it has done its job. It then 'unlocks' itself from its receptor site and either returns to the presynaptic membrane for reuse, or remains in the synaptic gap and slowly decomposes.

A historical note

In historical terms, the first neurotransmitter to be identified was acetylcholine in the late 1920s. By the mid-1950s, three other compounds had been identified. As research continued, other types were isolated. Today we know of six types or groups, with a total of some 50 different neurotransmitters.

Described above is the action across one synapse. In reality, any one neuron may be dealing with perhaps 10,000 connections or synapses from many thousands of other neurons and passing messages on to many thousands of other neurons.

Something to do

• Reduce the above section to a few key statements on how neurotransmission and synaptic activity work.

A classic case of neurotransmission

Probably the earliest work done in this field was that carried out by the Italian physiologist Galvani in 1791. He connected the spinal cord of a frog to a Leyden jar (an early device for producing electricity). At the point of electrical discharge, the frog's legs violently 'kicked'. Galvani called this 'animal electricity' and argued that it flows from the brain and spinal cord to cause muscle movement. Initially it was thought that nerve impulses were purely electrical, but by 1870 Helmholtz and Du Bois-Reymond had shown that they were electro-chemical in nature.

We now know that messages move at varying speeds along chains of neurons, the difference in speed being mainly due to whether or not the neuron is myelinated (look back at page 217). If it is, then the speed is about 200 miles an hour; if not, it can be as slow as 2 miles an hour. This means that a message takes about one-fiftieth of a second to get from finger tip to brain.

The electro-chemical process

It is the chemical change at the *receptor* of a neuron that generates the electrical charge that is transmitted along the neuron. To describe the process of neurotransmission in electro-chemical terms, we start with a neuron in a quiescent (at rest) state. The neuron has an overall internal negative charge with respect to the outside. This gives the neuron a negative **resting potential** of around minus 70 millivolts.

Now imagine many other neurons transmitting signals to our 'at rest' neuron. As they stimulate the 'at rest' neuron, the signal, or change in potential, might be large enough on its own to fire the neuron, or several small **graded potentials** may summate to reach the response threshold. As these other neurons stimulate the 'at rest' neuron, the cell membrane of the 'at rest' neuron changes its permeability to allow positively charged ions (of sodium and calcium) to enter. The inside of our neuron now has a positive potential, called an **action potential**, of plus 110 millivolts. The membrane now 'closes', allowing no more positive ions through. The result of the −70mv at rest and the +110mv action potential is a positive charge of +40mv.

This charge now affects the next section of the cell in the same way and as a result the difference, still +40mv, is 'passed along' the neuron, with the charge remaining at +40mv.

This describes the process for a non-myelinated axon. It is slightly different for a myelinated neuron, in that the charge 'jumps' from node to node, which, as stated above, allows the charge to travel faster.

The diagram below shows the state of charge and the development of the action potential.

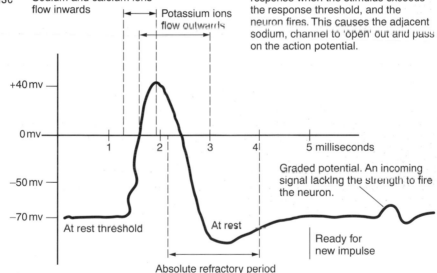

The neural impulse

Sodium and calcium ions flow inwards

Potassium ions flow outwards

Action potential is the electrical response when the stimulus exceeds the response threshold, and the neuron fires. This causes the adjacent sodium, channel to 'open' out and pass on the action potential.

+40mv

0mv

1   2   3   4   5 milliseconds

Graded potential. An incoming signal lacking the strength to fire the neuron.

−50mv

−70mv

At rest threshold

At rest

Ready for new impulse

Absolute refractory period

- −50mv is the response threshold, below which the neuron will not fire.

- The neuron will not fire again during the absolute refractory period.

Once the action potential has been reached, then its size will not change *and* it will move at a uniform speed along the axon. Note also that once the action potential has completed its journey to the synapse (or synaptic gap), the neuron will then return to its 'at rest' potential and will be totally unresponsive for a period of time – up to 2 milliseconds. This period is called the **absolute refractory period**; even if a new stimulus arrives, the neuron will remain unresponsive until this period of time has passed. The process is sometimes referred to as the **'all-or-none' principle** as the neuron will either fire or not fire, there is no in-between state. When the action potential reaches the synaptic terminals, it triggers the release of the chemical transmitter across the synapse. This excites the receptor of the next neuron and the whole process repeats itself.

Types of message

There is one other important point to make in this discussion on synaptic transmission. It concerns the message that is transmitted. There are two types of message:

- **excitatory messages**; and
- **inhibitory messages**.

Both are essential to the normal functioning of the nervous system. For effective control within the nervous system, there clearly has to be a system whereby messages get relayed and then excite or activate a muscle or some other gland or function; but without inhibitory messages the excitatory message would go out of control – you would have a 'run-away' situation where the body would lose control of some organ or muscle group, possibly with catastrophic results. For example, the poison strychnine works by disabling inhibitory messages, often resulting in fatal convulsions.

We described above the way the neurotransmitter, when locked in to a receptor site, creates a potential – sometimes called a postsynaptic potential – which can move in either a positive or a negative direction. If the voltage moves in a positive direction, then the neuron is prepared to fire; it does so when the voltage reaches the necessary threshold. On the other hand, if the voltage moves in a negative direction, then the neuron will not reach the threshold, will not fire, and the message is inhibited.

The central nervous system

If you refer back to the diagram on page 215, you will recall that the human nervous system consists of two main sub-systems, the central nervous system and the peripheral nervous system, each of which breaks down into further sub-systems. We look first at the central nervous system, and then at the peripheral nervous system.

The central nervous system has two major sub-systems: the **spinal cord** and the **brain**. Both are critical to normal functioning of the body.

The spinal cord

The spinal cord consists of a column of nerves about 2 centimetres in diameter, which runs the length of the backbone and merges into the brain stem. It exists to transmit messages, using the peripheral nervous system, both *from* the brain to muscles and glands, and *to* the brain from receptors. The column of nerves consists of longer myelinated neurons which make up the **white matter**, together with non-myelinated neurons which make up the **grey matter**. The spinal cord is housed in a hollow part of the backbone called the **spinal column**. The spinal column is made up of 33 vertebrae.

Messages enter and leave the spinal cord via 31 pairs of **spinal nerves**, each pair of which connect with a specific part of the body.

In the event of an accident where the spinal cord is severed, paralysis of the trunk or legs usually follows. The degree of paralysis depends on the precise point at which the spinal cord is severed. The higher up the spinal cord the fracture is, the greater the part of the body that is likely to be paralysed.

The spinal cord is also capable of **spinal reflexes**. These are reflex actions in response to external stimuli. They are unlearned reactions. Examples include the 'knee-jerk' reflex when tapped just below the knee, swallowing, the desire to urinate and defecate, and male and female sexual response. Spinal reflexes do not involve the brain and are, for the most part, aimed at maintaining basic body functioning.

The brain   We have taken the traditional model of the nervous system and shown the brain as a sub-system of the central nervous system. In reality the brain is the key element in any animal and particularly so in the case of the human animal. It is the size of a human brain in proportion to the body, and its complexity, that sets us apart from the rest of the animal world.

There are a number of different approaches to studying the brain. We could start either by discussing modern methods of analysing brain function, or by identifying the major parts of the brain, or by looking at the historical development of our understanding of the brain. Here we look first at the three main parts of the brain as it develops during the foetal stage, and then go on to use this three-way division as the basis for discussion of other parts of the brain.

Something to investigate

- Choose a selection of general psychology textbooks from your library. Outline the different ways the authors deal with the brain.

The diagram on page 215 shows the brain as having three major sub-systems:

- the **forebrain**;
- the **midbrain**; and
- the **hindbrain**.

We can expand these three parts of the brain as follows:

Sub-systems of the brain

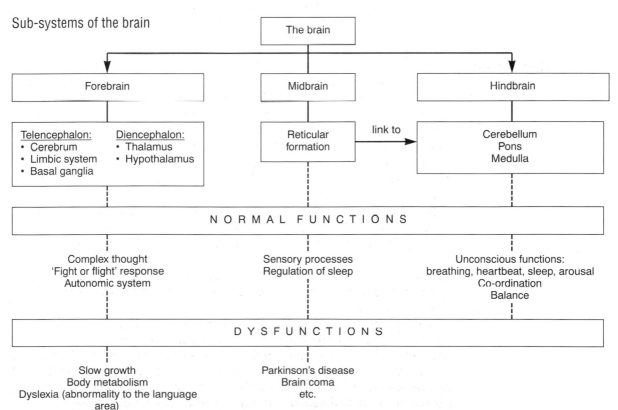

In terms of the development of the three main parts of the brain, as early as four weeks the spinal cord has developed and the top has grown and thickened such that the three parts can be identified. The top of the spinal cord turns into the hindbrain, above this comes the midbrain, and above that the forebrain. As the foetus develops, the forebrain grows the most rapidly and 'covers' or absorbs the midbrain and the hindbrain. At birth, the brain is about 65 per cent of its final weight; it continues to grow until about the age of 20.

The diagrams below show a developed human brain. They show the respective position of the spinal cord, the brain stem and the mid-, hind- and forebrain; and identify the major parts of the brain.

Areas in the human brain

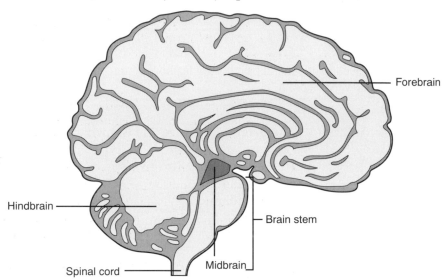

Cross-section of the human brain: key structures and functions

Cerebrum
Responsible for sensing, thinking, learning, emotion, consciousness and voluntary movement

Corpus callosum
Bridge of fibres passing information between the two cerebral hemispheres

Thalamus
Relay centre for cortex; handles incoming and outgoing signals

Amygdala
Part of **limbic system** involved in emotion and aggression

Hypothalamus
Responsible for regulating basic biological needs: hunger, thirst, temperature control

Cerebellum
Structure that co-ordinates fine muscle movement, balance

Pituitary gland
'Master' gland that regulates other endocrine glands

Brain stem

Hippocampus
Part of **limbic system** involved in learning and memory

Spinal cord
Responsible for transmitting information between brain and rest of body; handles simple reflexes

Reticular formation
Group of fibres that carry stimulation related to sleep and arousal through brainstem

Medulla
Responsible for regulating largely unconscious functions such as breathing and circulation

Pons
Involved in sleep and arousal

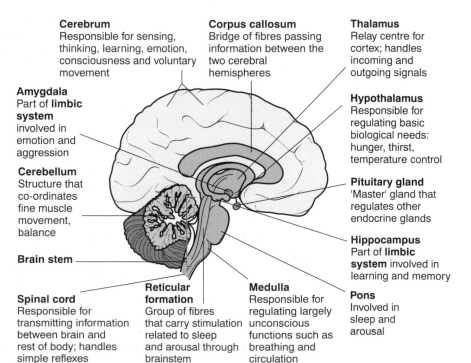

The hindbrain   In evolutionary terms, this is the oldest part of the brain and includes the **cerebellum** and, lower down on the brain stem, the **medulla** and the **pons**.

- The cerebellum, which means 'little brain', is involved in the co-ordination of movement and of balance. Specific instructions to move muscle groups come from higher brain centres, but the cerebellum assists – indeed is vital to – the actual operation of these commands.

Something to do

- Next time you play table-tennis or squash, analyse your return of serve. You will find that your reaction occurs faster than you can think about it. It is your cerebellum that controls this reaction.

- The medulla, more accurately known as the **medulla oblongata**, is attached to the spinal cord and is responsible for mostly unconscious bodily functions such as breathing, circulation and blood pressure. It is also involved with sleep, and when you sneeze.
- The pons, or **pons varolii**, is positioned on the brain stem and connects with the cerebellum and the medulla, and with higher parts of the brain. (The word *pons* means bridge, and is often used to describe matter that joins two or more parts together.) In terms of its function, the pons is involved with aspects of sleep and arousal.

The midbrain   The **midbrain** is positioned between the hindbrain and the forebrain.

- The **reticular formation** is a group of fibres in the centre of the brain stem that run between the midbrain and the hindbrain. The reticular formation is active in the regulation of sleep, and in maintaining alertness in the brain. Damage in this formation can cause brain coma.

The midbrain itself is concerned with sensory processes, particularly vision and hearing.

The forebrain   The forebrain is larger and more complicated than either the hindbrain or the midbrain. It subdivides into the **telencephalon** and the **diencephalon**, which in turn divide into – in the former case – the **cerebrum** (of which the key part is the **cerebral cortex**), the **limbic system** and the **basal ganglia**; and in the latter into the **thalamus** and the **hypothalamus** (refer back to the diagram on page 223).

In terms of position, the thalamus, the hypothalamus and the limbic system form the centre of the forebrain at the top of the brain stem, while the cerebrum is above these three (see the diagram on page 224).

Because of the complexity of the forebrain, we look at its structure and functions in more detail in a separate section (see below).

Structure and functions of the forebrain

The thalamus   The thalamus is rather like a relay station where messages are received, processed and then passed on. The messages that the thalamus processes are from all the senses except the olfactory, the sense of smell, which has its own relay station in the **limbic system** (see below). The processing that takes place involves integrating messages before they are passed on to the **cerebral cortex** (see below). In physical terms, the thalamus is a two-lobed shape with each lobe attached to either side of the top of the brain stem.

The hypothalamus   The hypothalamus is below (*hypo* means below or under) and a little forward of the thalamus, and serves the function of controlling the body's basic biological needs. It is about the size of a peanut. The hypothalamus plays a key role in controlling the autonomic nervous system, and also regulates many of our basic bodily drives, such as the 'fight or flight' mechanism, and eating and sex drives. For example, it is the hypothalamus that reminds us that we are hungry when the body's energy levels start to get low. It also regulates the **endocrine system** and works to maintain the body's balance or equilibrium. If, for example, the heating goes off and you start to get cold, then body sensors will signal this and, via the hypothalamus, will initiate corrective action – you will shiver (which is the body's way of warning you that you are getting cold). In the opposite case, when you get too hot, you will perspire. In other words, the regulatory systems of the body (such as controlling temperature or energy) are controlled by the hypothalamus. The process by which regulation occurs is called **homeostasis** (meaning 'in the same state').

Much of this control is exercised as a result of the influence of the **pituitary gland**, which is situated just below the hypothalamus and connected to it by the **infundibulum stalk**. It is the pituitary gland that controls the rest of the body's endocrine glands. (See pages 229–30 for more on the endocrine system.)

We have described the thalamus and the hypothalamus, which form the **diencephalon**; we now turn to the other major part of the forebrain, the **telencephalon**, which includes the cerebrum, the limbic system and the basal ganglia.

The cerebrum   The cerebrum is the largest part of the brain and consists of two hemispheres separated by a longitudinal fissure, but joined below the fissure by the **corpus callosum.**

The **cerebral cortex** (*cortex* means bark) is a thin covering over the cerebrum, about 3 or 4 millimetres thick. This is the key part of the cerebrum, and is where the brain deals with complicated mental processes such as thinking, learning, memorising and language – in other words, what are sometimes called the higher mental processes. The cerebral cortex is the most recent part of the brain in terms of evolution. As it develops from birth, it tends to fold back and forth upon itself, so forming convulsions and giving the brain its distinctive folded, almost crumpled, appearance. The cortex consists primarily of cell bodies – about 15 billion – and appears greyish in colour; hence the term 'grey matter', often used when speaking of the brain.

Each hemisphere of the cerebrum is divided into four areas called **lobes:**

The four lobes of the cerebrum

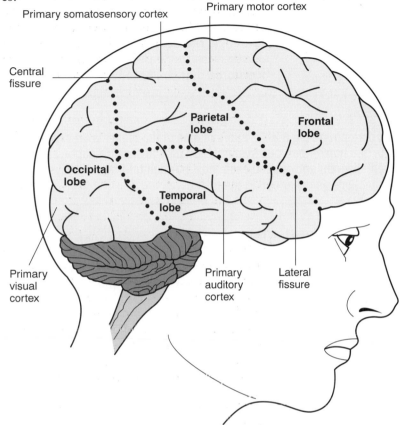

- The **frontal lobe** is the largest of the four lobes. It is also called the **primary motor cortex**, as it deals with the control of muscles. More of this lobe deals with small muscles which require precise control, and less with the control of large muscles.
- The **temporal lobe** – so called because it is near to the temples – is lower down and further back. This lobe is concerned with auditory processing. Damage to the left temporal lobe causes problems with speech and language.
- The **parietal lobe** is situated above the temporal lobe and to the rear of the frontal lobe. It is involved in visual input and spatial awareness, and also deals with the sense of touch.
- The **occipital lobe** is found at the rear of the brain, and deals with most visual processing.

<u>The limbic system</u>   The limbic system ('limbic' meaning 'on the edge') is, in evolutionary terms, an older part of the brain, and is situated in the forebrain below the corpus callosum (see the diagram on page 224). The structures that form a part of this system include the hypothalamus, the anterior thalamus, the **amygdala** and the **septum**. This system is not well defined, however, and sometimes other structures are included within it.

In general terms, the limbic system is involved with motivation and emotion, with the amygdala and septum both dealing with aggression.

The basal ganglia   The basal ganglia are three large nuclei, situated below the cortex and in front of the thalamus. The primary function of this structure is the control and co-ordination of arms and legs. Another key function of the basal ganglia is the production of most of the brain's output of the neurotransmitter dopamine. It is the degeneration of the neurons in the basal ganglia and the consequent lower output of dopamine that has been linked to Parkinson's disease.

Something to do

• The diagram on page 223, 'sub-systems of the brain', is an expansion of part of the diagram on page 215, 'the human nervous systems'. On a large sheet of paper, sketch out the 'sub-systems of the brain' diagram and expand each 'box' by adding further sub-systems. Make the appropriate connections as described in the text.

The peripheral nervous system

The diagram on page 215 may give the impression that the **peripheral nervous system** is larger and more complicated than the central nervous system. In fact, this is not the case. The peripheral nervous system serves the function of transmitting messages to and from the central nervous system. It is what 'connects' the outside world to the brain. As the diagram shows, there are two major sub-systems: the **somatic nervous system** and the **autonomic nervous system**.

The somatic nervous system

The somatic nervous system is made up of sensory (afferent) and motor (efferent) neurons; it works voluntarily – that is, it is under the direct command of the brain. For example, when you finish reading this page, your eyes tell your brain and your brain sends the message to your fingers to turn the page.

The autonomic nervous system

The autonomic nervous system connects the central nervous system – and hence the brain – to internal organs such as glands and certain muscles over which we have virtually no direct control. The primary function of the autonomic system is to maintain and regulate internal bodily functions; it deals only with motor control.

The autonomic nervous system is subdivided into two sub-systems: the **sympathetic** and the **parasympathetic**. These two systems work together, usually on the same organs of the body, but in opposition. This can be exemplified as follows:

• The parasympathetic system controls 'normal' or everyday activities such as keeping your heartbeat at normal levels as you read this section.
• If, however, it is late at night and you hear a strange noise and convince yourself that a burglar has broken in and that any minute you may be attacked, then the sympathetic system starts to work. It does so by speeding up your heartbeat, dilating the bronchial tubes to allow more air to your lungs, secreting adrenaline and generally preparing the body for 'fight or flight'.

The following diagram shows a simplified version of the classic diagrammatic layout of the autonomic nervous system.

The autonomic nervous system

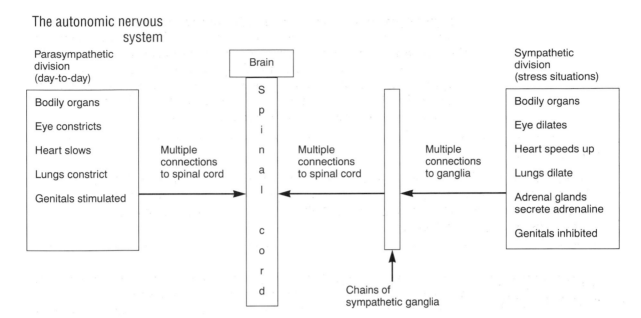

Parasympathetic division (day-to-day)

Bodily organs

Eye constricts

Heart slows

Lungs constrict

Genitals stimulated

Multiple connections to spinal cord

Brain

Spinal cord

Multiple connections to spinal cord

Multiple connections to ganglia

Chains of sympathetic ganglia

Sympathetic division (stress situations)

Bodily organs

Eye dilates

Heart speeds up

Lungs dilate

Adrenal glands secrete adrenaline

Genitals inhibited

The endocrine system: glands and hormones

One way to consider the nervous system is as a hugely complex communication system, using neurotransmitters to carry the messages. In addition to this system, the body has a second communication system – the **endocrine system**, which uses **hormones** to carry the messages.

The endocrine system consists of a series of glands in different parts of the body, each with a specific task. Males and females have some glands in common and some specific to their sex.

Endocrine glands are ductless and secrete the gland's 'output' directly into the body. The output of endocrine glands consists of different types of **hormone** (the word means 'urge' or 'excite'). To complicate things a little further, some hormones, produced by some glands, also function as neurotransmitters. Examples are norepinephrine and endorphin.

As you would expect, it is the brain that controls the endocrine system. The centre of this control is the hypothalamus, which, you will remember, is situated at the base of the brain and is involved in the control of the autonomic nervous system, other parts of the brain and the endocrine system. When called upon to do so, special cells in the hypothalamus direct the release of a number of different hormones to the pituitary gland, which then either stimulates or inhibits the release of other hormones. So, in simplistic terms, the brain (hypothalamus) controls the pituitary gland which in turn controls the endocrine system of glands.

The exocrine system

Not all glands belong to the endocrine system, some belong to the **exocrine system**. Glands in the exocrine system also have a specific purpose, but the secretion from these glands does not pass into the body's circulatory system (as is the case in the endocrine system). In the exocrine system, the gland's secretion performs the specific purpose of the gland. Exocrine glands have **ducts**, and it is these ducts that are used to deliver the secretion to its destination. Examples of this type of gland are tear ducts and sweat glands.

The table below lists some of the glands and hormones in the endocrine system, together with their function. Even a superficial glance at this list will indicate the vast range of bodily functions influenced and controlled by the endocrine system. Just as the other systems discussed above seek to keep the body functioning normally and responding to demands made upon it, so too does the endocrine system. In fact all the body's systems are working with each other to maintain control and to respond when the body calls for specific action – be it in normal activities like getting hot when riding your bicycle, responding to sexual desire and activity, or simply ensuring that the body is growing normally and that the hamburger and chips you had earlier are thoroughly digested.

The endocrine system: its glands and hormones		
Gland	**Hormone**	**Purpose or function**
[Hypothalamus	Several hormones that cause the anterior pituitary gland to secrete other hormones]	

Pituitary
  Anterior
  Posterior
	Growth hormone
	Oxytocin
		Stimulates growth in all parts of the body.
		Causes uterine contractions during labour.

Thyroid	Thyroxin	Body metabolism – growth development
Parathyroid	Calcitonin	Controls calcium levels.
Adrenal	Adrenaline Noradrenaline	Controls 'fight or flight'. Body metabolism – sexual desire in females
Ovaries	Oestrogen Progesterone	Development of female sexual characteristics
Testes	Testosterone	Development of male sexual characteristics Sperm production – sexual desire in males
Pancreas	Insulin Glucagon	Increases glucose uptake.

The immune system

The primary function of the **immune system** is to protect the body from infection. The agent that fights the intruding infection is the white blood cell (lymphocytes) which is manufactured in bone marrow. The **thymus gland** is located above the heart and secretes the hormone thymosin.

The immune system		
Gland	**Hormone**	**Purpose or function**
Thymus	Thymosin	Acts in support of the immune system.

The immune system works in co-operation with the brain and the endocrine system. The total system works in two ways:

- The brain tells the immune system directly.
- The immune system is triggered by the endocrine system on receiving messages from the brain.

The disease Acquired Immunodeficiency Syndrome (AIDS) is caused by a number of related viruses that severely affect the efficiency of the body's immune system to combat infection. As a result, AIDS is invariably fatal. While AIDS is a specific disease linked with the immune system, many studies, both with animals and with humans, have pointed to stress as a cause for lowered effectiveness of the immune system. (We look at stress in more detail in the final section of this unit.)

Something to do

• Draw flow charts to show how each of the above systems work.

Psychopharmacology: the effect of drugs on perception and behaviour

In this section we are concerned primarily with the *psychological* effect of drugs, hence the term **psychopharmacology**.

Think about it

• From what you have learnt so far in this unit, on which part of the body/brain/nervous system do you think a drug 'works'?
  – the limbic system?
  – neurotransmitters?
  – the spinal cord?
  – hormones?

Your answer to the above question should be neurotransmitters. In the simplest of terms, most drugs work by affecting the transmission of information across the synaptic gap. They do this by altering the ways in which the natural production and operation of neurotransmitters function.

Drugs have been used for thousands of years both for medical use and for the psychological effect that certain substances produce. The earliest drugs were produced from a variety of plants – for example mescaline is derived from a cactus called peyote; opium, morphine and heroin were (and still are) produced from a poppy.

We discuss the use of drugs for medical purposes in Unit 8 when we look at chemotherapy (see pages 420–1). Here we focus on non-medical drug use, which has variously been called 'drug abuse', 'substance abuse' and even 'recreational drug use'.

Psychoactive drugs

The following table shows that psychoactive drugs fall into four main groups – depressants, stimulants, opiates and hallucinogenics – according to the action or effect that the drug has. Almost all of these drugs have a legitimate use when prescribed by a doctor (and, of course, they work in exactly the same way), but the thrust of this section is the illegitimate or illegal use of these drugs.

	Psychoactive drugs				
	Name of drug	**Medical use**	**Length of effect* (hours)**	**Dependency**	
				Psychological	**Physiological**
Depressants	Barbiturates	Anaesthetic, sleeping pills	1–15	Moderate/High	Moderate/High
	Benzodiazepines	Antianxiety, sleeping pills	4–10	Low/Moderate	Low/Moderate
	Alcohol	Antiseptic	1–15	Moderate	Moderate
Stimulants	Amphetamines	Sleep disorders	2–6	High	High
	Caffeine	Stimulant, weight disorders	4–6	Low	Low
	Cocaine	Anaesthetic	1–2	High	High
	Nicotine	None	1–2	High	High
Opiates	Morphine	Painkiller	2–6	High	High
	Heroin	None	3–6	High	High
	Codeine	Painkiller	2–6	Moderate	Moderate
Hallucinogenics	LSD	None	8–12	Moderate	None
	Cannabis (marijuana)	Some	2–4	Moderate	Low
	Mescaline	None	4–6	None	Low
	Psilocybin	None	4–6	None	Low

* The 'effect' depends in part on the dosage.

A note on terms used

Before we get into further detail, there are a number of terms that you need to become familiar with:

- **Psychoactive drugs:** This is the basic term for the drugs discussed in this section. It refers to any drug or substance that has an effect on the perception or behaviour of a person by changing their conscious awareness of the world around them.
- **Narcotic:** Used correctly, this term refers to any drug that has both sedative and analgesic or pain-relieving properties, a definition which limits the term to opiate drugs. In other words, if used in a technically correct sense, 'narcotic' applies only to opiates.
- **Drug tolerance:** When someone takes the same drug over a period of time, their body can become accustomed to the drug such that the drug has progressively less effect. This is 'drug tolerance'.
- **Drug addiction:** Frequent use of a drug can lead to 'drug addiction' – an internal drive or craving for the drug that can be extremely strong.
- **Drug dependency:** This describes the condition, developed after a long period of drug use, in which a person literally becomes dependent on the drug to be able to function from day to day. Dependency can take two forms: psychological dependency and physiological dependency.
- **Withdrawal symptoms:** When a person stops taking a drug after a period of use or even dependency, they can experience 'withdrawal symptoms' as the body adjusts to the absence of the drug.

Any or all of the last four conditions may exist in a person who is taking drugs on a regular basis – do you ever feel that you just *have* to have a cup of coffee?

Depressants   This group of drugs tends to depress or slow down both the mental and the physical aspects of the body. They work by decreasing the rate of nerve impulses in the central nervous system.

- **Barbiturates** (usually called tranquillisers) are used to sedate. Their effect is similar to alcohol (see below), as they depress sympathetic nervous activity. Barbiturates are often used as sleeping pills; when these are taken following the consumption of alcohol, then the severe depression of the nervous system and hence bodily functions can quite literally be fatal.
- **Benzodiazepines**, for example Valium, are used as tranquillisers.
- **Alcohol** is by far the most common drug in this group. When taken in small amounts, it relaxes the sympathetic nervous system and as a consequence the person relaxes also. With larger amounts (about 0.1 per cent alcohol in the blood), speech becomes slurred, reactions slow and any action requiring skill or co-ordination deteriorates rapidly. Alcohol-related research has identified an interesting and significant principle. The *effect* of a psychoactive drug is influenced by the *expectation* of the user, which explains why drug experience can vary with culture (Ward, 1994).

Stimulants   Drugs in this group are the amphetamines (for example, Benzedrine and Dexedrine), cocaine, nicotine and caffeine. These drugs work by speeding up body functions by stimulating the heart and breathing rates. Stimulants also increase self confidence and can give the user greater energy and a heightened degree of alertness; they can also produce moods of great euphoria. On the down side, stimulants can rapidly become addictive and frequent and heavy use can induce classic symptoms of **paranoid delusions**. When the effect of the drug wears off and the body slows down, the user may experience extreme tiredness and frequently depression.

- The slang name for **amphetamines** is 'speed'. They are also called 'uppers' or 'bennies' (for Benzedrine). The main legitimate use for these drugs is to help people stay awake, improve physical performance and sometimes to lose weight. Amphetamines work by causing an increase in the release of the neurotransmitter norepinephrine (see nicotine, below).
- **Caffeine** is found in tea, coffee and chocolate. A large mug of tea or coffee has enough caffeine to provide a significant effect in about 15 minutes. The drug – because that is what caffeine is – works as a general stimulant by allowing an increase in synaptic activity, particularly dopamine. It is thought to prevent the reabsorption of neurotransmitters.
- **Cocaine** is extracted from the coca leaf. It can be taken by eating, injection or smoking. It works by blocking the re-uptake of dopamine, which in effect leaves lots of neurotransmitters in the synaptic gap, thus intensifying the experience or 'trip'. When the supply of cocaine to the synapse drops, it is the *absence* of these neurotransmitters that causes the 'crash' or depression at the end of the 'trip'. Addiction to cocaine can develop rapidly. In the 1980s a particularly nasty drug arrived on the drug scene – 'crack'. Crack is a highly

purified form of cocaine. Its effect is extreme – a fast and high 'high', quickly wearing off with a resultingly more severe 'crash'.

- **Nicotine** is a stimulant present in tobacco, and in terms of addiction can be as difficult to give up as any drug. Nicotine causes the release of the neurotransmitters epinephrine and norepinephrine, which removes hunger and increases mental alertness. It also releases neurotransmitters that create a calm, anxiety-free mental state.

> *"Given current smoking habits, half a billion people alive today will be killed by tobacco."*
>
> World Health Organization Report, 1994

Opiates This group of psychoactive drugs acts to depress neural functioning. Opiates are those drugs which derive from the opium poppy: morphine and its derivatives heroin and codeine.

- When taken intravenously, **heroin** produces feelings of euphoria, the pupils constrict and breathing and other bodily functions slow down. Addiction follows rapidly. Under repeated doses, the brain stops producing **endorphins** – opiate-like peptides produced naturally by the brain (the pituitary) – which is its own way of controlling pain, anxiety or fear. As a result, when the person starts to withdraw from heroin, the brain lacks the natural opiates – hence the withdrawal process is extremely painful.
- Opiates are often prescribed as painkillers, and the derivative **codeine** is used as a cough medicine.

Hallucinogenics The final group of psychoactive drugs that we need to consider are the hallucinogenics. These drugs produce hallucinations, which are extreme sensations and perceptions that have no physical cause – the effect is caused by the drug. Other effects produced by these drugs can range from extreme euphoria to absolute panic. Users of hallucinogenics may become psychologically dependant on them, but physiological dependence is unlikely. These drugs are also called **psychedelic** (from *psyche*, meaning mind and *delos* meaning visible), as one of the primary effects of a psychedelic drug is to produce vivid images in the mind.

Natural substances that are hallucinogenic are marijuana, mescaline and psilocybin (which comes from 'magic mushrooms'); while the synthetic drugs that have a hallucinogenic effect are LSD (lysergic acid diethylamide), otherwise known as 'acid', and PCP (phencyclidine thiophene), known as 'angel dust'.

- **LSD** was first synthesised in 1943. It is chemically similar to the neurotransmitter serotonin and blocks the action of naturally produced serotonin (Jacobs, 1987).

The hallucination typically starts with geometric shapes and patterns and develops into 3D images. It progresses into unreal scenes where the user often feels detached from his or her body. There is an interesting parallel between this experience and that described by people who have had 'near death' experiences (that is, having 'died' and then been resuscitated on the operating table). Moody (1976), a medical doctor, collected written accounts from many patients who went through near death experiences. They almost all describe the same kind of sequence of events, including apparent detachment from the body, watching themselves being frantically resuscitated, experiences of hovering, and looking and moving along tunnel-like structures – all of which are reported by LSD users.

- The drug **marijuana** comes from the hemp plant *Cannabis sativa*, which for at least 5000 years has been cultivated for its fibre, which is used to make rope. The drug is found in most of the plant, but is concentrated in the resin of the female plant. It is from this resin that hashish or hash is derived.

Smoking gets the drug into the brain in seconds, while eating it takes much longer. Once taken, the drug can stay in the body for several weeks, making it possible for subsequent doses to achieve the same effect with smaller amounts. Marijuana has effects similar to alcohol in that judgement and reaction times suffer, but in addition it can also affect memory recall. Marijuana does have medical uses, including the reduction of symptoms associated with Parkinson's disease and glaucoma and the reduction of nausea associated with chemotherapy treatment of cancer.

The who and why of substance abuse

The American system of classification of mental disorders, the DSM (version IVR), defines **substance abuse** as the use of a substance for at least one month to a degree such that its use affects or causes problems in the user's lifestyle. The key to this definition is not so much the amount of the drug, but its effects.

The who of substance abuse

No one person, sex or socioeconomic group is immune to substance abuse. Tobacco and alcohol are used by a very wide spectrum of the population; addiction often starts in childhood, particularly in the case of tobacco. Alcohol abuse also often starts with the younger person; alcohol has become the single most abused substance of the older teenage population. It is used by 80 per cent of older secondary school students. It is estimated that one in ten social drinkers becomes an alcoholic.

Cannabis, the plant from which marijuana (also known as hash, hashish and a number of other slang terms) is derived, is the most widely used of the illegal drugs. It is also the drug used by the widest range of the population.

In terms of hard drugs, most users start when in their teens. No one group is particularly vulnerable, but evidence does suggest that there is a progression from legal to soft to hard drugs. (Soft drugs are drugs such as cannabis, while hard drugs include cocaine and heroin.)

The why of substance abuse

The following data were presented in a newspaper article on the behaviour of 11–13 year olds.

It is certainly the case that younger people, who come under peer pressure at school, form one category of substance user – initially the drugs are tobacco and alcohol, but increasingly harder drugs are used at earlier ages. But why, apart from peer pressure, do people abuse drugs?

As you would expect there are different views, depending on the psychological approach that you take.

Drug use by 11–13 year olds				
	11–12s		12–13s	
	Yes %	No %	Yes %	No %
Have you ever smoked a cigarette?	13	87	24	76
Do you like the taste of wine?	39	61	38	62
Have any of your friends smoked marijuana?	3	97	11	89
Have you ever been offered any drugs?	3	97	23	77

(The sample was 204 children from five state schools.

Source: *Telegraph Magazine*, 6 September 1997

Think about it

• Before you read on, refer back to Unit 2 on psychological perspectives.
• What reasons do you think the psychodynamic, the cognitive and the neurobiological approaches might give for substance abuse? Make a list.

• In the **psychodynamic approach**, the basic theory is that we have unconscious needs that either have to be kept under tight control or have to be expressed. In this context, drugs – and their effects – may reduce the effort required to control emotional conflict or to deal with what are in effect unconscious urges.
• In the **cognitive approach**, the 'why' of substance abuse centres on the expectation of the drug. As noted earlier, the expectation of an effect has a powerful influence on the effect itself. Most people drink alcohol because of what they expect to happen; the principle is the same with other drugs. Stimulants enhance performance and so they are taken for this reason – 'reason', of course, being a cognitive function.
• **Biological** reasons for substance abuse tend to focus on addiction. As the body becomes used to the drug, it needs more of it to give the same effect, so the user takes more. This downward cycle leads to dependency and addiction.

Generally, the reasons for drug abuse are extremely complex. Parents, with the best intention, may start the process of dependency by allowing alcohol use as a part of growing up. Most studies indicate that both parents and peer groups influence drug use. Personality differences also affect drug use. Finally, teenagers experiencing difficulties in areas such as personality identification, gender role, sexual problems, academic differences, etc. are all, at some point, likely to experiment with drug taking. For the adolescent, drug abuse is the major delinquent behaviour.

Treatment and prevention of drug abuse

Since we are talking about illegal use of drugs, then treatment implies the total withdrawal of the use of the drug. In extreme cases this can mean hospitalisation, often followed by treatment which may include the use of drug-like substitutes. For example, methadone is sometimes used with heroin addicts, but can itself lead to addiction. Other treatments include counselling, either on a one-to-one basis or in a support group.

In terms of prevention, the task is difficult – not least because the reasons for taking the drugs are hugely complex (see above). However, most if not all of the abuse suggests that the best prevention is early recognition of a *potential* difficulty or problem, coupled with sensitive handling at an early stage. 'Prevention is better than cure' is a particularly appropriate adage at this point.

Note that in the context of this text, only superficial treatment can be given to this vital topic. There are many excellent resources devoted to the treatment and prevention of drug abuse, which you can consult for more detailed information.

Cortical functions

The first section of this unit looked in some depth at the way the body works, particularly in terms of the body's nervous system and the way that different parts of the body communicate with each other. We saw that the brain has a key role in all of this. We now concentrate our attention in more detail on the brain, more specifically the **cerebral cortex**, which contains about 90 per cent of the brain's cells – some 15 billion – and which is where most of the higher-order processing takes place.

We start this section with a discussion on how we study the brain: what techniques or equipment are involved? Do we literally have to 'dig in' to the brain; or can we measure brain activity from outside the skull? Next, we look at which brain functions occur in what part of the brain, and consider the significance of the two hemispheres. Finally, we discuss brain activity with respect to visual perception.

Investigating cortical activity

Observations over thousands of years have led us to the conclusion that the head of an animal, human or otherwise, has a key function in the behaviour of the animal. Lose an arm in battle, and the soldier – whether a Stone Age fighter with a club, a Roman legionary in a chariot or a twentieth-century army recruit in a tank – will, probably, be able to carry on. But lose your head, and it is all over. The Greeks of classical times, 2500 years ago, realised the importance of what went on inside the head; they used **trephining**, which is little more than drilling a hole, to investigate the innards of the human skull. What has also been observed over the centuries is that damage to certain areas of the head results in certain types of behaviour. You have perhaps seen this yourself, or even experienced it, when playing football or some other sport and someone has been knocked unconscious. A hard knock on the head produces a state of unconsciousness or mild confusion, while a hard knock on the shin may produce little more than a swear word or two.

Whilst this type of observation is one way of investigating brain activity, it lacks an essential element of science – control. A more scientific method is surgery. This has advanced significantly since the time of the Ancient Greeks; modern surgical techniques allow very sophisticated procedures to be conducted on both animals and humans. With advances in technology, mostly since the Second World War, new and very sophisticated techniques have been developed for investigating brain activity from outside the skull.

Major methods of investigating cortical activity

1. Observation of the effects of accidental damage.
2. Surgery or invasive techniques.
3. Non-invasive techniques.

Observation of accidental damage to the brain

In terms of understanding the brain, the first observations were made possibly as long as 5000 years ago. The Greeks certainly made observations about 2500 years ago, and also attempted basic surgery. It all went rather quiet after the classical Greek period until the beginning of the 1800s, when the medical profession started to bring together and formalise observations. It was noticed that damage to one side of the head resulted in impairment to the opposite side of the body. Damage to the back of the head was likely to cause problems with vision, and that damage to the front left side produced problems with speech. As these observations were slowly built up, so the medical profession started to understand more about the brain and the localisation of functions. While the method provided useful data, the process was rather haphazard as the medical profession had to wait until some poor unfortunate had an accident to the head! From a scientific point of view, the process lacked control, which made the data of only moderate value.

During the late 19th century, much of the emphasis was on analysing the brain tissue from dead people who had previously been diagnosed with a specific illness. Freud fell foul of this process when working in Paris with the neuropathologist Theodore Meynert. The medical profession at that time was interested only in formalising the symptoms of mental illness and classifying specific brain pathology. Freud upset the establishment by asking the question: 'How then do we help these patients?'

Surgery or invasive techniques

Also during the 19th century, others were working with animals using invasive techniques – cutting into the brain surgically. While this did not give specific answers that could be applied to the human brain, the knowledge of brain functioning that it gave rise to, together with the practical skills of operating on a brain, pushed medical knowledge forward.

Invasive surgery on the human brain has been conducted for perhaps as many as 150 years. Initially the surgery was crude, with large portions of the brain being cut away or connecting tissue between parts of the brain being severed. With time, however, and as knowledge of brain localisation and function grew, procedures improved and became much more precise. In terms of today's knowledge and techniques, brain operations of only 30 or 40 years ago read like horror stories.

> *Something to do*
> • Read the section on psychosurgery in Unit 8 (page 420).

The earliest technique involved in invasive surgery is **ablation**, which is the surgical cutting of brain tissue. **Lesions**, in practice small areas of removed tissue, are made either by a knife cut or, more commonly, by applying an electrode to the area and then passing current through the electrode such that the tissue is burned away.

A more recent technique involves introducing **neurotoxins** by injection into a localised part of the brain. The word 'neurotoxin' means nerve poison, which is an exact description – the neurotoxin poisons or kills the neurons producing the neurotransmitter that is causing the problem.

Non-invasive techniques

The third method for investigating cortical activity is non-invasive – everything is done from *outside* the head. There are a number of non-invasive techniques, all of which require extremely high-tech equipment.

- The earliest of these is the **electroencephalogram** (EEG). Since brain activity is essentially electrical, if we can measure this then we can begin to understand what is happening in the brain. The EEG works by placing electrodes at a number of key positions on the head and then recording the electrical activity or brainwaves at each of these electrodes when the patient is asked to respond in certain ways, for example by speaking, blinking their eyelids, and so on. The graph below is an EEG recording of an eight-year-old boy thought to have a mild form of autism. Modern EEG equipment is so precise it can detect an individual neuron when it fires.

An EEG recording of brain activity during speech

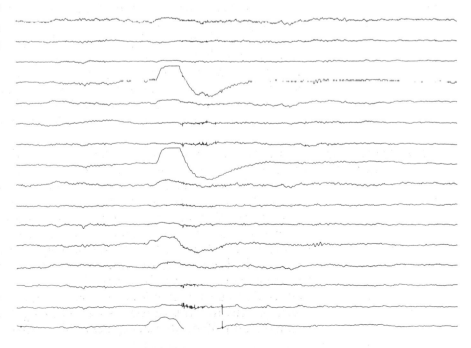

- A second technique makes use of X-ray technology. The **computerised axial tomograph** (or **CAT scan** or sometimes **CT scan**) takes a series of X-ray pictures with a very narrow beam; a computer is then used to 'mix' the pictures and so provide a 3-dimensional image of the brain.
- Another technique is **positron emission tomography**, also known as the **PET scan**. In this procedure, the patient is injected with a very mild radioactive dose of glucose. Glucose is the fuel that energises the brain's chemistry, so what the PET scan does is to record which parts of the brain are burning most glucose and hence are most active. As the glucose is burned, and since the glucose is radioactive, the radioactivity will be given off and can be measured. The resulting data are plotted by a computer and provide a picture of the brain which shows where most activity is taking place. As with other techniques, the patient can be asked to do sums, read aloud, or do other tasks, which can then be related to the picture or scan taken at the same time.
- Yet another non-invasive technique is **magnetic resonance imaging** or **MRI**. In this procedure, which is rather more sophisticated than PET, the patient's head is put into a machine – which looks rather like an enormous ring doughnut – and a powerful magnetic field is generated which causes the nuclei of some molecules to spin. While this is happening, radio-waves are generated which act on the nuclei; these in turn emit energy that can be picked up by the machine's sensors and is then processed by computer to produce a picture of the 'slice' of tissue which is being investigated. The MRI can produce pictures at the rate of several a second, almost giving a moving picture of brain activity. As with the other procedures, the patient is given various tasks while scans are being taken. Significant advantages of the MRI technique are that the resultant picture is more detailed and the patient does not have potentially damaging X-rays transmitted through the brain. The MRI machine is also capable of taking pictures in a variety of planes.

These techniques are very complex and are contributing significantly to the advancement of our knowledge of the brain.

Localisation of brain functions

With the ever-increasing sophistication of procedures for investigating brain activity, and the rapid acceleration of technology, our knowledge of what goes on where in the brain is becoming well established. This section discusses localisation of brain functions: it maps out which part of the brain controls which part of the body or mind.

First, though, for a broader perspective and an understanding of the advances in our knowledge of the brain, we need to go back a little in time and look at the work of Broca and Wernicke (see page 241).

Phrenology

While the work of Broca and Wernicke laid the foundations for the study of the localisation of function, another related theory was already up and running. This approach, called **phrenology**, holds that the shape of the skull, and hence the brain inside it, influences our personality and behaviour. This work originated with Franz Joseph Gall (1758–1828), a German anatomist.

Two classic cases of language and the brain

Two early studies of the localisation of brain functions, and perhaps the best known, are those of Paul Broca, published in France in 1861, and Carl Wernicke, published in Germany in 1874. Both are concerned with language.

Paul Broca

Broca observed that patients with severe speech production problems (not speech understanding problems) had damage to the lower part of the left frontal lobe. He therefore concluded that this part of the brain is critical to successful speech production. Patients with this problem – understanding but no speech – have **motor aphasia**, sometimes known as **Broca's aphasia**. 'Aphasia' is a general term meaning any partial or complete loss of language ability. The area on the frontal lobe first identified by Broca is known as **Broca's area**. While Broca's area is involved in speech production, it is now known that this is not the only area involved with speech. Also, while this area on the left frontal lobe affects most people with this problem, some left-handed people are affected by the equivalent area on the right hemisphere.

Carl Wernicke

Around the same time, Carl Wernicke was working in Germany as a neurologist and psychiatrist. He trained under the neuropathologist Theodore Meynert (as did Sigmund Freud). In 1874 (when he was only 26), he published details of his work on aphasia. The condition described by Wernicke was similar to that described by Broca. Whereas Broca was working with **motor aphasia**, the inability to speak even though the patient had understanding, Wernicke was working with **sensory aphasia**, which is a severe defect in the understanding of speech.

Wernicke went on to identify an area in the left temporal lobe responsible for sensory aphasia, which has been named after him.

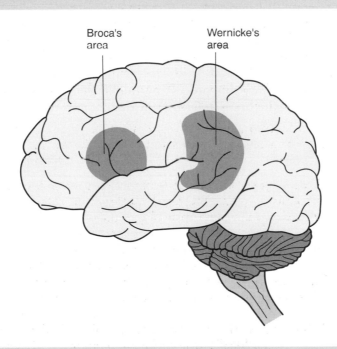

Broca's area   Wernicke's area

Quite apart from identifying a specific area of the brain and linking it to a specific behaviour, Broca and Wernicke opened the door to the concept of different functions or behaviours in different hemispheres of the brain.

Phrenology is based on three principles:

• There is a specific relationship between brain area and mental function.
• The more developed the function, the larger the associated brain area.
• The skull shape reflects the brain size.

The theory was very popular until the mid-19th century. Gall's classification of the head identified some 35 specific areas, many of which had two parts, left and right. Despite the fact that phrenology has no real scientific basis, Gall's concept of brain area being related to function is true. It is also worth noting that it was Gall who first distinguished between grey matter and white matter.

An interesting modern development suggests that the brain is organised into 'modules' which carry out complex mental functions (Foder, 1983). The old term was 'mental faculty' – for example the faculty of will or the faculty of memory. The new term is **modularity theory**, which assumes the mind has a number of relatively independent 'modules', each dealing with a specific cognitive function. This is more of a philosophical approach, however, with little supporting empirical evidence.

We have established that specific areas of the brain are linked to different functions – behaviour, thought, emotion, etc., and that this is the theory of **brain localisation**. We now need to identify more precisely just what and where these areas are.

Something to do

• Review the names and relative positions of the four lobes found in each hemisphere of the brain (see page 227).

We can start this process by thinking in very general terms and representing the brain in terms of its functions thus:

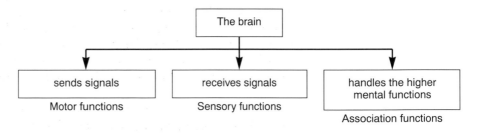

There are three main areas of the cortex that deal with these functions as follows:

• Motor functions are carried out in the motor cortex.
• Sensory functions are carried out in the sensory cortex.
• Association functions are carried out in the association area of the cortex.

In terms of size, the motor and sensory parts of the cortex take up about 15 per cent each, and the association area about 70 per cent.

Motor functions The **motor cortex**, where motor functions are carried out, is an arch-shaped area of cortex situated at the back of the frontal lobe (as illustrated below).

In general terms the motor cortex runs from ear to ear across each hemisphere. The left hemisphere controls the right side of the body, and the right hemisphere controls the left side of the body. Immediately behind the motor cortex is the **central fissure**, which is a fold in the cortex and which forms a natural division between the frontal lobe and the parietal lobe (see the diagram on page 227).

The cerebral cortex

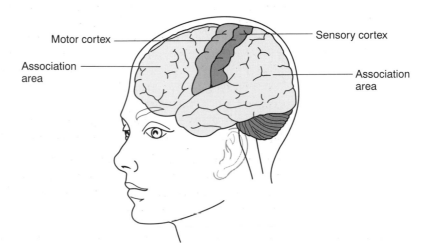

Motor cortex — Sensory cortex

Association area — Association area

Sensory functions The **sensory cortex** lies on the other side of the central fissure at the front of the parietal lobe and forms an arch from ear to ear parallel to the motor cortex and immediately behind it.

The following diagram of the left hemisphere of the brain (page 244) shows the specific areas involved with a specific function. Functions of the body that require very precise control and are very sensitive take up a proportionally larger area of cortex than functions that are less complex or sensitive. Your fingers, for example, require a lot of motor cortex area to enable them to operate very precisely when you are writing or painting a very delicate picture, for instance. Taking a step or kicking a football are less delicate functions and therefore use less cortical area. Similarly, the sensory cortex has relatively more space devoted to the more sensitive areas of body functions, such as the lips.

Association functions As stated earlier, the sensory and motor areas of the cortex take up about 15 per cent of the cortex each; the remaining 70 per cent of the cortex is called the **association area**. It is in this area that all the wider aspects of mental functioning take place, for example learning, thought, memory and language. It is in the association area that the brain integrates data or information from other parts of the brain, bringing all the parts together to 'make sense' of things. Some areas of the association cortex have a specific function, for example areas on the frontal lobe are involved in making judgements, while an area on the right temporal lobe is involved in recognition. Aspects of cognition such as memory, however, do not have a clearly defined area, they occur over a wide range of the cortex.

Left hemisphere,
showing areas of the
motor cortex and the
sensory cortex devoted
to specific body parts

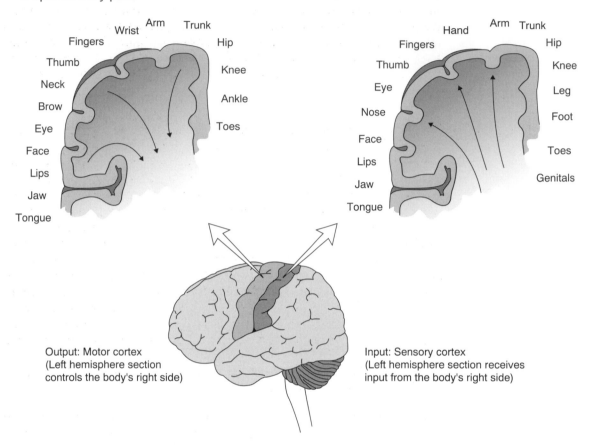

Output: Motor cortex
(Left hemisphere section
controls the body's right side)

Input: Sensory cortex
(Left hemisphere section receives
input from the body's right side)

Hemisphere asymmetry

As knowledge of the brain has filtered into the popular literature, so the idea that there are differences between the left and the right hemispheres that can significantly affect our personalities and behaviour has gained appeal. As is often the case, there is some truth in this proposition. Here we discuss these differences and their effects, and then consider the effect of split-brain operations – where the hemispheres are surgically separated.

Evidence to date suggests that it is the left hemisphere that is usually, but not always, dominant; and that it is the dominant hemisphere that is more involved in functions such as logic, problem solving, speech and mathematical calculation. The non-dominant hemisphere has more to do with visual, aesthetic and emotional aspects and with creativity (Levy, 1985). For 'dominant', read 'mildly dominant', since in a healthy, normally functioning brain, both hemispheres are working all the time, with the functions of both frequently overlapping. It is important to realise that there are areas of specialisation *and* functions that require integration.

Most bodily tissue, if damaged or destroyed, will regenerate to heal the wound. However, it is usually thought that brain cells, once destroyed, are not replaced. Essentially this is true, as brain *cells* do not reproduce. What can happen – and whether it does or does not depends on a number of different factors – is that if an area of the brain is damaged, nearby neurons may start to 'take over' the damaged area by making new connections (not new cells). This is termed **brain plasticity**, and work in this area is opening up possibilities of brain tissue transplants. Transplants on patients with diseases such as Parkinson's or Alzheimer's have already shown significant progress in terms of their success (Myers, 1996).

The split brain
The two hemispheres of the brain are joined by the **corpus callosum** (the tissue made up of several hundred million nerve fibres). If the tissue of the corpus callosum is severed, then the result is a **split brain**. Operations of this kind – called commisurotomy – have been conducted on human patients since the 1960s; on animals for much longer. Commisurotomies are usually performed, for perfectly proper medical and ethical reasons, on patients who are suffering from extreme and intractable epilepsy. A patient who has undergone such an operation becomes a very interesting and very unusual individual, and one who, if willing, can provide invaluable information on aspects of left–right brain functioning. It is patients such as these that Roger Sperry and others investigated. Sperry, one of the earliest researchers in this field at the California Institute of Technology, worked on how brain circuits or pathways are formed and what happens when they are severed.

The following is a brief outline of the stages involved in the research that led to split-brain surgery.

• Our starting point is patients suffering from severe epilepsy. The researchers are Sperry, Vogel and Bogen, who are all American. Sperry, working with Myers and Gazzaniga, also conducted research in this area on animals.
• Epilepsy occurs because of abnormal electrical discharges generated by groups of brain cells. There is a wide range of epileptic disorders. In serious cases the patient suffers a seizure, can lose consciousness, has fits, and can lose control of autonomic functions. (Drug therapy today is quite effective, but was not available in the 1960s when Sperry and others were researching the disease.)
• The spurious electrical discharges were shown to move between hemispheres in the brain, possibly even gaining power in the process.
• If the electrical discharges are responsible for the disease, and they move between hemispheres, then why not – the argument went – separate the hemispheres by severing the corpus callosum?

A commisurotomy is clearly a drastic remedy. It was first tested on animals and then on human patients. The results were encouraging in that, in most cases, the severity of the epileptic fit reduced and there appeared to be very little other malfunctioning of the brain in spite of the radical surgery. Why was this so?

To answer this question, Sperry and Gazzaniga devised an ingenious test. Before we consider this test, however, we need to review the signal pathways within the brain.

Think about it

• A split-brain patient has a coffee mug placed in their left hand, without being able to see the mug. Why would the patient deny the mug was there?

The answer to the above is that information from the left hand goes to the right hemisphere, which normally sends the information to the left hemisphere which (as we have learned) usually controls speech. With the connections between the hemispheres cut, the information could not be passed to the left hemisphere speech area.

The following diagram shows the pathways for *visual* information between the eye and the brain.

Pathways for visual information between the eye and the brain

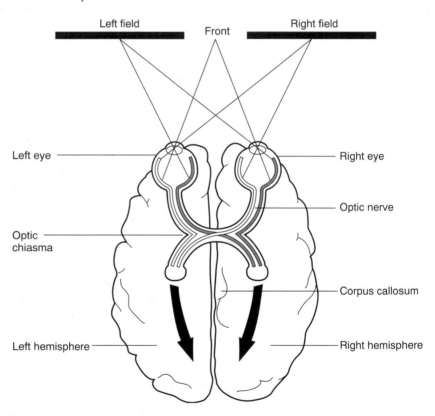

You will see that visual information from left of centre goes via both eyes to the right hemisphere; while visual information from right of centre goes via both eyes to the left hemisphere. You make sense of the information because it is transmitted both ways via the corpus callosum. However, when this is severed to give a split brain the information is not passed between hemispheres. As a result, only the part of the picture that one eye has seen is recognised. To test this phenomenon, Gazzaniga (1983) devised a simple but very telling practical demonstration.

A classic case of split-brain perception

A patient with a split brain is seated in front of a screen with a dot in the centre, and told to focus on the dot. The word HEART is then projected onto the screen for a split second such that it straddles the dot: H E · A R T. The patient is asked to say what they see. The patient reports seeing only ART, which is the part of the word transmitted to the left hemisphere.

The patient is then shown a card with the words HE and ART on it, and is asked to point with their left hand to what they see. The patient points to HE, which is of course the part of the word HEART seen by the left eye and transmitted to the right hemisphere. Each hemisphere is reacting only to what it has seen.

A non-experimental example of this is reported by Oliver Sachs in his book *The Man Who Mistook His Wife for a Hat* (1985). He reports the case of a lady in her sixties who had suffered a massive stroke which had severely affected her right hemisphere (not her right eye). She would often complain to the nurse that there was no coffee on her meal tray. When her head was turned so that the coffee came into view of the working right half of her visual field, she would comment, 'Oh, there it is. It wasn't there before.' The lady had lost her concept of 'left'.

Neurophysiological explanations of visual perception

We looked at visual perception in Unit 4. Here we discuss neurophysiological explanations of visual perception. We start with the structure of the visual system – that is, the component parts that give you the ability to see and perceive visually, and then go on to consider the processes by which this happens.

Structure of the visual system

As we think of the structure of the visual system we need first to consider what it is that the structure has to deal with – which, of course, is light. Light arrives at the eye as **electromagnetic energy** in the form of light waves, with the wavelength (or frequency) determining the colour and the wave amplitude (or size) determining brightness. The wavelength of red, for example, is longer than that of violet and your eye is so constructed to be able to tell the difference.

Look at the diagram of the human eye (page 248). Light enters the eye through the **pupil**, the size of which is adjusted by the **iris**. The light then passes through the **lens**, which focuses the light onto the **retina**, but with the image – whatever you are looking at – upside down.

A cross-section of the human eye

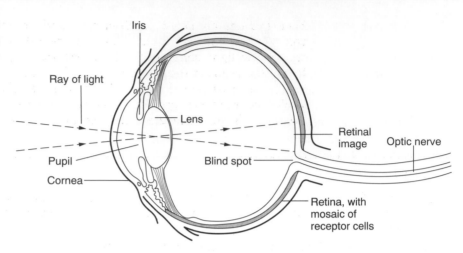

The **optic nerve** assembles the information from the retina and takes it to the brain in millions of 'bits' of information. The brain then reassembles the bits back into the image, but the right way up. The **blind spot** is the small area on the retina where the optic nerve leaves the eye. It is 'blind' because it has no receptors.

Something to try

- Try this to 'test' your blind spot. Close your left eye and stare at the black dot (below) with your right eye. Start with the page, and hence the dot, close to your eye. Slowly move the page away from your eye. The boat will disappear at about 30cm and reappear shortly after.

The change from visual to electrical information takes place at the retina, the surface area at the back of the eye onto which the image is presented. The retina is extremely complicated, with as many as ten layers of nerve cells. For practical purposes, we can divide these into three main layers, starting from the front:

- first, the layer of ganglion cells;
- then a layer of bipolar cells which join the ganglion cells to the receptors;
- then the photoreceptor layer, which is made up of rods and cones.

Each eye has about 120 million rods and about 5 million cones. The cones enable the eye to see colour and fine detail, the rods help you to see in low light conditions. The cones are very densely packed in the **fovea** (the point at the centre of the retina and what you are looking at, and most sharply in focus) and less dense further out from the fovea; while the rods are present in large numbers just outside the fovea. Because it is the rods we use more at night, we see less in colour.

Something to try

- Go outside when it is dark or when the illumination is very low. Focus on an object a little distance away and try to identify detail. Rest your eyes for a moment, now look just to the left or right of the object and try again to identify detail.
- You should be able to 'see' more detail when looking with the periphery of the eye because the rods are packed more tightly outside the area of the fovea. Did you see any colour in what you were looking at?

Nocturnal animals often have a retina made up mostly of rods, with only a few cones, so while they see very well at night, they see colour less well.

When light energy enters the eye, it passes through the first two layers of the retina and hits the rods and cones. Chemical changes then occur in the rods and cones which generate signals that go via the bipolar cells to activate the ganglion cells. The message, which is now in electrical form, moves along the axons of the ganglion cells; these join together to form the optic nerve, which takes the message to the brain.

Cross-section of the retina

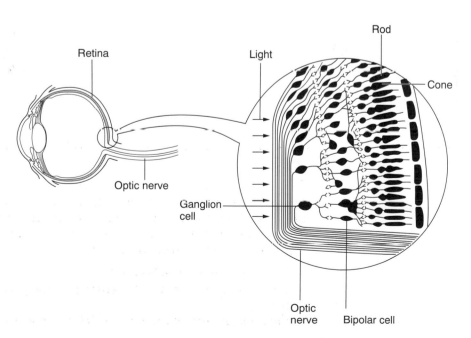

Processes of visual perception

As we have seen, the image enters the eye, is processed by the retina and is sent via the optic nerve to the brain. The question we now need to consider is: what is the visual information processing that occurs in the brain?

Each eye has something like 125 million receptors – 120 million rods and 5 million cones – which initially analyse and encode the incoming signal. The coded electrical message then gets passed on to the roughly 1 million ganglion cells which come together to form the optic nerve. The optic nerve from each eye goes via the **optic chiasma** and then the **optic tract** to the visual cortex at the rear of each hemisphere. This is where most of the processing takes place.

In a classic piece of work conducted in 1979, David Hubel and Torsten Wiesel demonstrated that when cortical neurons receive information from the optic nerve – a 'bit' of the picture – they respond to certain very limited aspects of the picture. For example, a specific neuron might respond to lines at a certain angle, or the edge of an object, or some detailed feature. Consequently these neurons are called **feature detectors**. The brain then assembles, or rather reassembles, all the features of the seen image by taking information from each feature detector and adding it to information from other neurons that only operate at a higher level. This process of building the picture continues until the picture is complete and the brain 'sees' what the eye has seen.

One very significant aspect of the process is that the brain operates as a parallel processor. This means that when you look at, say, a moving car, your brain works in parallel or simultaneously on perceiving the movement, the colour, the shape (as an outline) and the 'three dimensionality' of the car.

The final stage of this process is when you *recognise* the image. The now assembled picture of the car is recognised because your brain has compared the incoming, assembled image with similar images in its memory store.

The visual information process from image to recognition

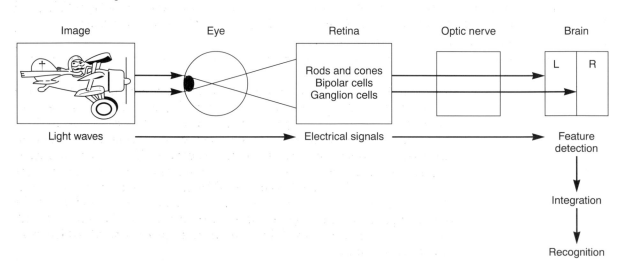

Image	Eye	Retina	Optic nerve	Brain

Rods and cones
Bipolar cells
Ganglion cells

L   R

Light waves ⟶ Electrical signals ⟶ Feature detection

↓

Integration

↓

Recognition

Human states of awareness

What time of day is it? You are obviously working on your study of psychology or you would not be reading this. Have you developed a habit of working late at night, or is it early in the morning? What sort of state are you in? Hopefully you are naturally alert, perhaps helped with a mild intake of the drug caffeine. Or is your **awareness** affected by the drug alcohol or even by a hard drug? On the other hand, you could – even now – have drifted into a state of day-dreaming, yet another state of awareness or **consciousness** (the two terms are virtually synonymous).

Think about it

- What do you understand by 'consciousness'?
- Write out a definition in your own words.

This section of the unit focuses on human states of awareness: we discuss body rhythms and consider the different states of being asleep and of dreaming; then look at the nature and function of sleep; and finally discuss a variety of aspects concerning hypnosis.

Consciousness: a historical perspective

Before we get into the details of awareness, consciousness and other related topics, we take a brief look at the subject in its historical context. Much of the psychology that was studied in the 19th century involved states of consciousness; at that time consciousness was one of the key topic areas. William James (1842–1910), writing in 1892 (*Psychology – The Briefer Course*), devoted a key and substantial chapter to 'The Stream of Consciousness'.

Something to investigate

- Read James. He is probably one of the most important American psychologists of all time. He studied and then taught at Harvard University. His main work was *Principles of Psychology* (1890), which he shortened to *Psychology – The Briefer Course* (1892). (As noted in Unit 4, students referred to these books as 'James' and 'Jimmy'.)

As psychology became more scientific, difficulties emerged with defining 'consciousness'. At the turn of the century, Sigmund Freud and **psychoanalysis** became centre stage; this in turn was overtaken – particularly in America – by **behaviourism**. Psychology was moving away from an emphasis on consciousness, or mental aspects of life, towards a greater emphasis on the scientific study of behaviour. Then, with the technological push provided by the Second World War, the new emphasis on information processing and the rapid increase in our understanding of the brain, **cognitive psychology** came to prominence. While not quite full circle, the emphasis turned back to mental processes, of which consciousness is a part.

Defining consciousness

While it is very difficult to define consciousness formally, a satisfactory definition is: 'our own awareness of ourselves and our environment'. This can, of course, include aspects such as attention and introspection. Alternatively, you could ask what it is you have lost when you are unconscious.

If we argue that consciousness has a variety of states, we need to consider the range that these states cover. At one extreme, you are dead and consciousness has ceased to exist. At the opposite extreme, you are in a state of heightened consciousness when, say, you have just had a severe fright and are running away from danger. On a bipolar continuum, consciousness would look like this:

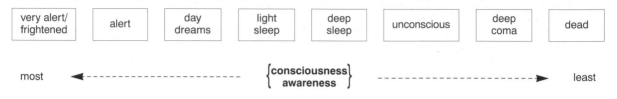

Think about it

- Where and why on the above scale would you position (a) someone in a hypnotic state; and (b) someone hallucinating due to a psychoactive drug?

As you consider the continuum, you will see that we quite normally move between different states of consciousness. The 'normal' range is between deep sleep and alertness. You can also say, quite accurately, that we move *rhythmically* between states of consciousness: we move daily between deep sleep and alertness; other rhythms occur as we sleep; and yet other rhythms have much longer cycles.

Body rhythms

We now turn our attention to the concept of **body rhythms** or, to use the more general term, **biorhythms**, or, the up and coming term, **chronobiology**.

- The most basic body rhythm is the **circadian rhythm** (from the Latin *circa*, meaning about and *dies*, meaning day), a rhythm which occurs daily, every 24 hours.
- Rhythms that have a frequency of less than 24 hours are called **ultradian**; examples of this are the rhythms that occur when we are asleep.
- Rhythms that have a frequency of more than 24 hours are called **infradian**; an example of this is the menstrual cycle.

Most of the human body's functions operate on a circadian or 24-hour cycle. Physiological activities such as heart rate, body temperature, metabolism and hormonal activity all operate on an approximate 24-hour cycle. Most of us, in terms of performance, tend to peak around midday or early afternoon. Some people prefer the morning and function better by getting up early, while others seem to peak later in the day. While much of this follows natural timings, workers on permanent shifts can adjust to other patterns, given time. Workers on rotating shifts, however, never really adjust and consequently suffer disturbed sleep patterns, loss of concentration and other knock-on effects.

An interesting question arises if we ask why humans operate on a 24-hour cycle. Has it evolved simply as a response to the earth's 24-hour day and night and so we respond to light and dark? In other words, is it externally driven? Or do we operate **endogenously** – that is, driven from some internal biological clock?

A classic case of circadian rhythms

In a now classic study conducted in 1972, a researcher spent six months underground, totally separated from the world outside and with no means of telling the time, apart from what he felt like. He was allowed to eat and sleep whenever he wanted to, and put lights on and off when he wanted to. All of his activities were monitored remotely from the surface.

In terms of sleep habits, after initial quite wild fluctuations he settled down into a routine of sleeping and waking of a little over 25 hours.

Other research along the same lines also suggests that a 'natural' cycle is about 25 hours.

<u>Jet lag</u>   While less extreme than the above experiment, jet lag is a fairly common experience, disrupting our natural cycle. Flying from north to south or from south to north has minimal effect because you remain in the same time zone, but fly east or west and it is a different matter. For example, flying west from London to New York crosses five time zones. If you leave London at 10.00 in the morning, you will arrive in New York seven hours later – your body thinks that it is 5.00 in the afternoon, time for tea. However, subtracting the five time zones means that you arrive local time at 12.00 midday – time for lunch! Not too bad, just a long day. Coming back is rather worse, however. If you leave New York at, say, 5.00 in the evening, add the seven hours' flying time and you arrive in London at what your body thinks is midnight – time to go to bed. In fact, taking account of the five time zones, it is 5.00 in the morning, time to get up – except you haven't been to bed! In both cases, your body time is five hours different from local time. Flying west is not so bad, it just seems a long day; but flying east, when the day is shortened, is more difficult to adjust to.

Seasonal mood disorder   Another form of time change that can affect the human animal is **seasonal mood disorder**. This is a general term for any mood disorder caused by the changing seasons. Seasonal affective disorder (SAD) is the most common form and is caused by lack of sunlight in the winter months. Sufferers typically display depression, lethargy and sleep disorders. There is a simple therapy – exposure to bright light.

Rjukan, in southern Norway, lies at the bottom of a valley with very steep sides, rising about 3000 feet almost vertically. From mid-October to mid-March, the sun never reaches the town at the bottom of the valley. The town has high alcoholic and suicide rates.

Rjukan, southern
Norway

Sleep and dreaming

Sleep

Sleep is in fact more than just a stage on the continuum of consciousness. We now know that there are a number of **sleep stages**, each of which has its own physiological characteristics. Bodily systems such as heart rate, muscle tone and metabolism all vary depending on the stage of sleep, as do our eye movements and genital arousal.

The key research tool in understanding sleep is the electroencephalograph (EEG), which measures brainwaves, or brain activity, via sensors stuck to the head in key positions – depending on what is to be measured. Other sensing devices are attached to other parts of the body to measure activity such as heartbeat, respiration or other physiological functions. Suitably wired up, you go to bed!

In a typical night's sleep, most people follow a regular cyclical pattern which moves in and out of four stages of sleep. This is shown below.

Activity in a typical night's sleep

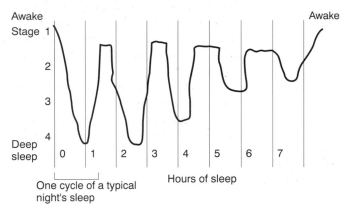

One cycle of a typical night's sleep

The activity during one cycle of a typical night's sleep is shown here:

Activity during one cycle of a typical night's sleep

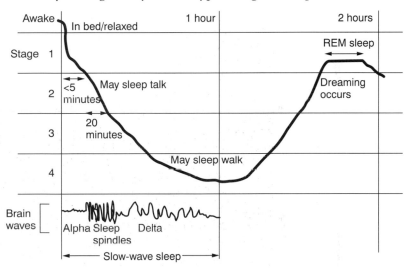

Under normal circumstances, you will move through the cycle about every one-and-a-half hours. At various times in your sleep the brain produces electrical waves – alpha waves and delta waves.

Refer now to the diagram as we discuss in detail one cycle of a typical night's sleep:

- Imagine that you are in bed and in a relaxed, sleepy state. At this point most bodily functions start to slow down. Your brain produces **alpha waves**. You are in Stage 1 sleep, which only lasts a few minutes. It is at this stage that you sometimes 'jump' or wake up with a start.
- You sink deeper into sleep and spend about 20 minutes in Stage 2. In this stage, the EEG may record a short burst of brain activity called **sleep spindles**. If you talk in your sleep, you are most likely to do it in Stage 2.
- As you move into Stage 3, your brainwaves slowly change to **delta waves,** which have larger amplitude and slower frequency.
- Delta waves continue as you sink into deeper sleep in Stage 4. If you are a sleep walker, you will usually do so in Stage 4, when you are most deeply asleep.

- During these four stages the brain shows slow-wave patterns.
- Whatever stage of sleep you are in, routine noises such as the central heating switching off or traffic noise are ignored, but critical sounds like the baby crying or a door opening will cause you to wake up.
- So far you have been asleep for about an hour and you are in Stage 4. You now proceed back up the stages and into a new condition where you will remain for about 15 minutes. During this period, a situation develops where you experience **rapid eye movement** or **REM**. Your brainwaves become more rapid and sharper in profile. During REM sleep not only do your eyes move, your heart rate and breathing rate increase, and both sexes experience genital arousal – males an erection, females increased vaginal lubrication. During this REM stage, your muscles are relaxed and you are most difficult to wake.
- It is also during REM sleep that you dream.
- While in REM sleep, the brain stem blocks messages trying to reach the motor cortex, which is why the muscles of your body relax. This is called **paradoxical sleep**. The paradox is that the body is aroused internally, but if viewed externally you appear very peaceful and calm.
- Note that for each succeeding cycle the REM period gets longer and depth of sleep gets less.

In terms of the length of sleep, in the animal world predators generally sleep longer than their prey – they have less to worry about! In humans, there are wide differences in the amount of sleep that individuals need. Generally, evidence suggests that those who regularly sleep for a long time have faster reaction times and slightly higher daytime body temperatures.

All of the above raises the question: what is the purpose of sleep? The short answer is that there is no clearly defined purpose. Old-fashioned ideas, since discarded, included the idea that the brain needed to rest and sort itself out from the day's activities. One physiological aspect that occurs rather better during sleep than when awake is the synthesis of protein. In humans, growth hormones are released at a higher rate during sleep – particularly during **slow-wave sleep** – than during awake periods. Tissue restoration also occurs rather better during sleep than when awake. We can sum up by saying that, in general terms, sleep provides time for the body to restore itself, although at present there is no formal proof of this, at least not in terms of specific chemical processes.

Dreams and dreaming

As we have seen, dreams occur during REM sleep. This is not to say that they occur only during REM sleep, but that the two coincide most of the time. REM dreams tend to be vivid, coherent and clear in terms of detail; while dreams in non-REM sleep are much more likely to be vague and indistinct. Dreaming usually occurs in real time; that is, a five-minute event in a dream will take five real minutes to dream.

Most research on dreams suggests that the dream is an extension of the person's real-life experiences. So if you are concerned about health, family or some other life event, particularly if stressful, then your dreams are most likely to be based on these issues.

It is also possible that while you sleep your brain continues to work on problems encountered during the day. Whether or not this has anything to do with your dreams is still unclear. It is, however, possible to use this phenomenon to your advantage. You may, for example, have been working on a piece of creative writing and, as the evening wears on, you get stuck. The tactic is to review the problem immediately before you go to sleep. In a sense you have primed your brain to worry about the problem. On waking, you may find that a number of possible alternatives will now occur to you. This is not a 'magic' solution, it is simply a matter of using what we know about brain activity during sleep.

Theories of dreaming

- In 1978, Hobson and McCarley proposed the **activation–synthesis model** to explain dreams and dreaming. In this model, dreams reflect biological activity. The 'activation' is of the **reticular activating system** (**RAS**), which is a part of the brain stem involved in arousal. During REM sleep, motor activity is inhibited so we don't move, but we do dream movement. The RAS also connects to the cerebral cortex, which 'synthesises' various inputs to provide information for the dream. This model is supported by the fact that most dreams reflect daytime events, which can be assumed to be the latest information that the cortex has been dealing with.

- Another theory of dreaming is provided by Crick and Mitchison (1983). This model suggests that during REM sleep and dreaming, the brain sorts out information that it is holding in memory and discards surplus material. This in turn provides capacity for the coming day's events. There is little experimental evidence to support this view, however.

- On a rather different tack, Sigmund Freud believed that dreams – in his words – were 'the royal road to the unconscious'. He was concerned not so much with the mechanism of dreaming as with the interpretation of dreams. Freud himself believed that his book *The Interpretation of Dreams*, published in November 1900, was his most significant work (Jones, 1953). Freud's theory was that dreams reflected the unconscious desires of the person. These were too damaging or embarrassing to be expressed practically, and so were repressed into the unconscious, emerging as dreams. Dreams have a **manifest content,** which is on the surface and therefore known to the dreamer; and a **latent content,** which is the deep or hidden meaning of the dream. Psychoanalysis involves the interpretation of dreams, particularly the symbolism.

Sleep deprivation Another aspect of sleep and dreaming is sleep deprivation. This can be defined as any change in sleep patterns such that the time asleep is significantly reduced. The current world record for the longest period of wakefulness – according to *The Guinness Book of Records* – is held by Randy Gardner, who in 1964 stayed awake continually for 11 days. He suffered only short-term problems of a relatively minor nature, quickly recovering his normal sleep pattern. This raises an interesting question concerning the purpose of sleep. If serious sleep deprivation causes minimal problems to the body or brain, as appears to be the case with Randy Gardner, what then *is* the purpose of sleep? These data suggest that the purpose of sleep is *not* to restore the body.

A further dimension to this debate concerns the effects of deprivation of REM sleep. This can be tested in a relatively straightforward manner. The person is monitored by an EEG and, the instant REM sleep starts, they are woken up. After a short time awake, they are allowed to go to sleep again – until they move into REM sleep, when they are again woken up. When then allowed to sleep normally, but still being monitored by the EEG, the person will sleep for extra-long periods of REM sleep. The body, then, is naturally making up whatever is lost. This is called **REM rebound**. The generally accepted view is that during normal REM sleep the body is producing more neurotransmitters to make up for those lost over the course of the day. Evidence for this comes from the fact that when patients are given antidepressants (one of the purposes of which is to increase neurotransmitter activity), they show shorter periods of REM sleep because the medication is providing the shortfall.

Sleep learning or hypnopaedia

One aspect of sleep of obvious interest to students is the question of whether it is possible to learn while asleep. The method usually followed is to tape-record notes and then play them back while asleep. You do not of course actually learn while you sleep: to learn you have to give attention to the specific task or the content of the material to be learned, and when asleep it is impossible to pay attention to anything. The only way that you *may* learn in this fashion is by playing the material immediately before you go to sleep. (For more efficient methods to learn material, see Unit 1.)

Insomnia

Insomnia can be defined as a serious inability to sleep normally. Most research suggests that insomnia is usually caused by a number of factors rather than by any one, and that anxiety and depression are two key causes. Physical pain can also give rise to problems with sleep.

The usual 'cure' is to take a sleeping pill, most of which work by reducing levels of arousal. Problems with this can include dependency and tolerance to the drug, which then requires a higher dosage to get the desired effect. Used with alcohol, the result can be lethal. Other successful, and perhaps more positive, strategies include relaxation exercises, use of **biofeedback** (see page 278), and deliberately allowing fantasies to occur and develop as you start to fall asleep. Trying to make yourself sleep almost never works.

Hypnosis

Although we did not include it on the bipolar continuum of states of consciousness (see page 252), **hypnosis** is one of a number of states of awareness. The word itself comes from Hypnos, the Greek god of sleep.

Historical perspective

The earliest roots of hypnosis in Western civilisation can be traced to the Viennese physician Anton Mesmer (1734–1815), from whose name we get the English words 'mesmerism' and 'mesmerised'. Mesmer did not actually use hypnotism; he practised what he called 'animal magnetism', which he describes as a form of energy to which the human nervous system can respond. The term 'hypnotism' was invented by James Braid (1795–1860), who practised as a doctor and surgeon in Manchester. Having been introduced to mesmerism, Braid believed that the trance which the patient exhibited was caused by the patient fixating on a bright coloured object used by the 'mesmeriser'. Braid used the term 'nervous sleep' for this trance-like state. He found that functional nervous disorders could be treated when patients were in this state. He called this **neurhypnology**; while the practice of getting the patient into the trance-like state he called **neurhypnotism**, rapidly shortened to 'hypnotism'. Braid himself used hypnotism in his own medical practice, and even performed major surgery on patients under hypnosis (Gregory, 1987).

There is no doubt whatsoever that a person can be hypnotised. The evidence is irrefutable. The question that we need to answer is: just what does this mean in psychological terms?

Probably the earliest formal scientific work investigating hypnotism was carried out by C.H. Hull at Yale University in the early 1930s. In general terms, he was able to confirm the efficacy of many hypnotic practices, such as anaesthesia and pain relief; he was also able to refute claims that people when hypnotised were able to carry out extraordinary feats, for example of strength and memory.

Since the 1930s, research into hypnosis has expanded considerably. One outcome of this was the development of a standardised scale for hypnotic susceptibility: Weitzenhaffer and Hilgard's **The Stanford Hypnotic Susceptibility Scale** (1961) (Hilgard, 1965).

The Stanford Hypnotic
Susceptibility Scale

---

(1) **Arm lowering:** It is suggested to the participant that an outstretched arm is getting heavier and heavier. The arm should be gradually lowered.

(2) **Moving hands apart:** The participant sits with arms outstretched in front. The suggestion is made that the hands are repelled from each other as if by magnets. This should lead to them moving apart.

(3) **Mosquito hallucination:** The suggestion is made to the participant that an annoying mosquito is buzzing around. This should lead to the participant trying to 'shoo' it away.

(4) **Taste hallucination:** The participant should respond to the suggestion that a sweet substance and then a sour one is being tasted.

(5) **Arm rigidity:** Following the suggestion that an arm held out straight is getting stiffer and stiffer, the participant should be unable to bend it.

(6) **Dream:** The participant is told to have a dream about hypnosis while remaining hypnotised. The contents of the dream should be released by the participant.

(7) **Age regression:** The participant is told to imagine being at different school ages. For each of the ages selected, realistic handwriting specimens should be provided.

(8) **Arm immobilisation:** Following the suggestion made by the hypnotist, the participant should be unable to lift an arm involuntarily.

(9) **Anosmia (loss of smell) to ammonia:** Following suggestions made by the hypnotist, the participant should report being unable to smell household ammonia.

(10) **Hallucinated voice:** The participant should answer questions raised by a hallucinated voice.

(11) **Negative visual hallucination:** Following suggestions made by the hypnotist, the participant should report the inability to see one of three small coloured boxes.

(12) **Post-hypnotic amnesia:** The participant should be unable to recall particular information after hypnosis until given a prearranged signal.

Hypnotically susceptible people are those who become very involved in imaginary activities; they will become totally involved with the character of a novel or film, for example.

Theories of hypnosis   We saw earlier (page 254) how useful the electroencephalogram (EEG) is in understanding sleep. Using the EEG on a hypnotised person has shown that the pattern of brainwaves is not at all like that of someone asleep, but much more like that of someone in a normal state of wakefulness. In other words, in terms of brain activity, the person in the hypnotic trance is awake.

Several times in the discussion of hypnosis we have used the word 'state'. It is the idea of being in a state, or not being in a state, that provides the basis for the main theories that seek to explain hypnosis – so we have **state theory** and **non-state theory**.

<u>State theory</u>   State theory holds that hypnosis is a special state of dissociated consciousness. Evidence for this is provided by subjects who will carry out commands when hypnotised even when they are on their own and believe no one else is present. The Hilgard view is that hypnotic dissociation is little more than a more extreme form of the kind of thing that we all do when we do two things at once: drive and talk, take notes in a lecture while planning an evening date, and so on. An important element in Hilgard's theory is what he calls the 'hidden observer'. This is a part of the mind which remains aware of what is going on, and is not in a hypnotic state. State theory, or divided (or dissociated) consciousness, does have a degree of empirical support, but there are still gaps in our understanding of it.

<u>Non-state theory</u>   The other main theory proposed to explain hypnosis is non-state theory. In this theory, it is suggested that the hypnotised person is simply acting out the role that has been suggested. It is for this reason that non-state theory is sometimes called the **social influence theory**. This of course implies that the hypnotised person is functioning in a normal state of consciousness and not in some altered state or hypnotic trance. Parallels can be drawn with certain similar kinds of behaviour, as for example when a person has extreme religious experiences. Evidence in this area suggests that similar behaviours can be produced both in subjects who are in a hypnotic state and in those who are not in a hypnotic state (Spanos and Coe, 1992). Spanos argues that the 'hidden observer' of the state theory – one of the main supporting pieces of evidence for state theory – is merely carrying out the hypnotist's instructions. The person is acting out two *roles*, not demonstrating two different *states*.

Evidence for a conclusive theory of hypnosis does not at present exist. It may be that it is a both/and solution; although current research seems to be moving more to the support of non-state theory (Alden, 1995).

Think about it

- What is the evidence for and against each of the two main theories of hypnosis? Draw up a chart to show this.
- What ethical considerations do you think should be taken into account with respect to hypnosis? Write a brief paragraph.

Motivation, emotion and stress

This is the final main section under the heading of bio-psychology. What follows is a discussion of three major, linked aspects in psychology:

- **Motivation** asks the *why* question.
- **Emotion** has more to do with how we *feel* about things.
- **Stress** has to do with the *response* we make to stimuli that upset our equilibrium and coping mechanisms.

We deal with the three terms in the order given, noting that motivation and emotion go together (they even have the same root meaning in Latin, *movere*, which means to move); it is almost impossible to deal with one without the other.

Motivation

Motivation is a hypothetical construct: we cannot see motivation itself, only its resulting behaviour. We can think of motivation as the drive or the need that energises behaviour to reach a goal. You spend time studying because you are motivated to achieve the goal of exam success. That is an example of motivation to *achieve*. We are also motivated by hunger, sex, the need to belong, and perhaps a number of other things.

There are generally thought to be three basic ways to classify motivation:

- **physiological**, which is concerned with neurological and biological aspects, and which operates at the level of primary drives such as hunger and sex;
- **behavioural**, which complements the physiological drives, and is concerned with less basic behaviour, for example learning to drive a car;
- **psychosocial**, which is to do with the explanation of more complex learned behaviours.

When it comes to studying motivation, one of the earliest researchers was Tolman (1932). He described motivation as a process that bridges, or comes between, a stimulus and a response. An example might be the motivation of hunger, which comes between possible psychological or physiological conditions and which may lead to a response or output such as searching for food or eating – an output activity that can be observed or measured.

Theories of motivation

Instinct theory

Motivational theory takes a number of different forms.

The earliest of these is instinct theory, based on Darwin and evolution. It soon collapsed as a theory, mainly because all it did was to label motivation and behaviour as instinctual; it did not explain motivation.

Something to do

- As a cross-curricular connection exercise, compare instinct theory of motivation with the discussion on instinct, fixed action pattern and imprinting in Unit 6, comparative psychology (pages 288–9, 290 and 303–5).

Drive-reduction theory

With the effective demise of instinct theory, the next approach was the **drive-reduction theory**. The basic idea here is that whenever there is physiological need, it creates a psychological state that then drives the organism to reduce the need by satisfying it. This theory incorporates the concept of **homeostasis**, the body's way of maintaining stability. If you become too hot (physiological), you feel (psychological) uncomfortable and seek to return to normal. When you become hungry, you seek food to reduce this motivation or drive.

Arousal theory

The **arousal theory** of motivation holds that people are motivated to do things that may be considered dangerous – for example mountain climbing, watching a horror film or feeding sharks – in order to increase arousal. We have a basic drive to experience stimulation. George Mallory, for example, when asked why he wanted to climb Mount Everest, answered: 'Because it's there'.

This climber is undoubtedly experiencing a state of high arousal

Other people are similarly motivated to solve crossword puzzles or complex mathematical problems. Arousal can take another form when, for example, we are motivated for action in the case of fear or anger.

There is an interesting relationship between arousal and performance, represented graphically in the shape of an inverted U (see below).

The Yerkes–Dodson law

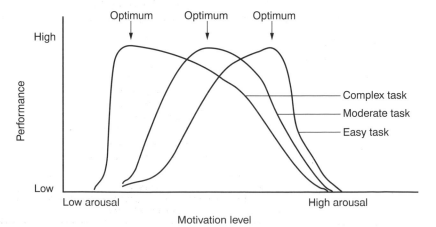

These data imply that there is an **optimal arousal level** depending on the degree of task difficulty. This is known as the **Yerkes–Dodson Law**, which says that on difficult tasks low arousal improves performance, while on easy tasks high arousal improves performance. In other words, if you are solving a very difficult mathematical problem, low arousal is better than being in a state of high arousal. If, on the other hand, you have a (relatively) easy task, for example making a tackle in rugby, you need a high degree of arousal to do the job properly.

Think about it

- What causes you to be in a high or low state of arousal? Compare your answers with friends. How do you account for the differences?

Social motivation

Social motives are different from physiological motives in that they are acquired through learning. They arouse us, and lead to behaviour that is directed towards achieving a social goal, such as a better job, more money, power seeking and, frequently, aggression.

An early researcher in this field was Murray (1938). He defined social motives in psychological terms, expressed as needs – for example the need for autonomy, the need for acceptance or the need for power.

In Murray's day, it was thought that social motives were secondary to physiological motives, because a social motive is rarely essential to maintain life. In practical terms, the distinction is difficult to maintain as in many cases – for example sexual drive – it is difficult to separate the physiological from the social.

In terms of social performance, one of the most powerful of motives is the need for achievement, sometimes abbreviated to **n Ach**. People who are always striving for the better job, for more power, to achieve difficult tasks (such as climbing Mount Everest), to achieve higher grades in exams, and generally pushing themselves to achieve more than the next person – are people with a high n Ach.

Maslow's hierarchy of needs

Another psychosocial theory of motivation, also discussed in Unit 2 and Unit 6, is that of Abraham Maslow and his hierarchy of needs (1954). The principle behind this is that human motivation can be organised as a hierarchy, with basic needs forming the base of a pyramid, psychological needs next, and self-fulfilment needs at the top.

Maslow's hierarchy of needs

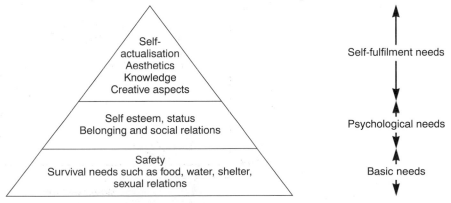

Something to investigate

• Search your library for different variations of Maslow's hierarchy and draw up a composite version.

The basic motivations of biological or physiological needs, while not ignored by Maslow, are seen as lower-level motivations. Maslow believed that as humans we also have higher-order motivations – we are driven towards a psychological state of well-being. Once this is achieved, we are driven towards the even higher level of **self actualisation.**

Maslow's hierarchy of needs has received only moderate empirical support. While in principle a hierarchical structure to motivation seems to make sense, often people will go for the higher levels and ignore the lower – Mother Theresa, for example.

Sigmund Freud In some ways Freud's theory of motivation bridges the psychosocial and instinct theories. Freud argued that as humans we have two main drives or instincts: towards life and towards death (see also Unit 3, page 111). If these motivations are not satisfied, then tension builds up until they are satisfied. This approach is similar to drive-reduction theory. However, Freudian theory has its critics; a key problem is its lack of scientific rigour.

Think about it

• What is the relevance of Nature–Nurture issues to the question of motivation?
• Look at the summary chart below of the primary motive of hunger in terms of its physiology and psychology, showing the division between Nature and Nurture.
  (a) Think about how you could expand both sides of this table.
  (b) Draw up a similar table for, for example, thirst or sex.

Hunger – its physiology and psychology	
Physiology (Nature?)	**Psychology (Nurture?)**
• Causes of feelings of hunger. • Empty stomach pangs. • Body chemistry – in normal circumstances regulation is automatic. • Stress-related cravings. • Low blood-glucose causes hunger. Signals to the brain from stomach, intestines and liver tell the brain to tell the body to eat. • Hunger control is within two areas of the hypothalamus. Works by influencing how much glucose is converted to fat, and how much is used to reduce hunger. Acts like a control to keep body weight at its set point. Weight control is exercised by food intake and energy output.	• Culture significantly affects tastes. • Some tastes are conditioned both by liking and by aversion. • Repeated exposure to different perceived unpleasant foods can result in acceptance (an involuntary response). • 'External' information, e.g. visual or smell information, can influence people more than 'internal' hunger signals.

Emotion

What did you feel as you came to this new heading 'emotion'? Were you reminded of a new relationship, or perhaps a relationship coming to an end? Maybe the word triggered the feelings of fear that you felt when walking home alone late at night, with your heart pounding as the footsteps behind you grew closer; or maybe you remembered an argument you had yesterday and the way your friend looked at you and then slammed the door.

The term **emotion** has traditionally been difficult to define, particularly in a scientific manner. What is generally accepted, however, is that emotion has three components:

- physiological arousal – for example your heart pounding;
- behaviour or situation – for example your physical expression;
- cognitive awareness – for example hearing and interpreting the footsteps (and feeling afraid).

The question is: how do these three components fit together and which comes first (the pounding heart and then feelings of fear, or feelings of fear followed by a pounding heart)? We discuss the three components, and then consider theoretical attempts to explain emotion in terms of which component comes first.

Something to do

- At this point you may want to re-read the earlier section in this unit on the sympathetic and parasympathetic systems of the autonomic nervous system (pages 228–9), as these play an important part in understanding how emotion 'works'.

We shall take the emotion fear as an example. As perhaps you have experienced, fear causes a fairly uniform set of responses: heartbeat increases, respiration rate increases, muscles become tense and you start to perspire. All this is as a result of the arousal of the sympathetic system. Physiologically, your body is preparing itself to meet the cause of the fear. Your liver provides extra sugar to the blood; faster breathing provides more oxygen to 'burn' the sugar to provide extra energy; perspiration cools you down; digestion slows to allow more blood to the muscle tissue; and blood clotting will occur faster than normal if it is required to. Most of this action is triggered by the adrenal glands which produce and release the stress hormones adrenaline and noradrenaline. You are now ready for 'fight or flight'.

In behavioural terms, emotion is expressed in **non-verbal communication**, for example facial expressions of fear or sadness, or perhaps clenched fists. Facial expressions are thought to 'be innate, as people who have been blind from birth smile and show fear just as sighted people do. There is evidence to show that feedback from facial muscles to the brain exerts some degree of influence over the way that we experience emotion (Adelmann and Zajonc, 1989).

The cognitive component is essentially evaluative, as people describe how they interpret and then how they feel about an emotional experience.

We all experience the same situations that can cause emotion, for example a wedding or a funeral, but we do not all experience or express the felt emotion in the same way. The exception to this is the way that we respond physiologically. We all tend to respond in a similar manner because the response is controlled by the autonomic system. This is the basis for the lie detector test.

Components of emotion			
Emotion	Component		
	Physiological	Behavioural or situational	Cognitive
Fear	Sympathetic arousal	Threat	Awareness of danger
Anger	Sympathetic and parasympathetic arousal	Frustration	Confusion Retaliation

Think about it

• Look at the table, 'components of emotion'. How would you break down into their three components a number of other emotions? Add to the table.

Theories of emotion

There are a number of theories that seek to explain emotion. As we discuss these, you will come to realise that there is no consensus of opinion as to which theory is 'best' or most accurate. The problem of deciding which is the most accurate is unlikely to be solved easily, since this is a sensitive area in terms of ethics. While it is entirely ethical to ask someone to tell you about their emotions, it is not ethical to set up a situation in which emotions are caused or manipulated – thus making it impossible to test theories of emotion empirically.

Charles Darwin

The first modern work of significance was by Charles Darwin, in his book *The Expressions of the Emotions in Man and Animals*, published in 1872. While not a theory as such, Darwin wrote that certain emotions are expressed in the overt behaviour of humans and animals. For example, the 'commonsense' view is that when we are sad we cry; when angry we hit out; when afraid we shake.

The James–Lange theory

This theory was first proposed at the end of the 19th century by William James, who thought the exact reverse of the above commonsense view (James, 1890). James's argument is that our emotions follow our behavioural response to an event. Lange (1834–1900), a Danish physiologist who lived at about the same time, came independently to the same conclusion as James. The **James–Lange theory** argues that some external event or stimulus triggers instinctively arousal and response. We then become angry *because* we have acted in an aggressive manner, or we become afraid *because* we have run away from something. In this theory, physiological and behavioural components come first and are followed by the cognitive:

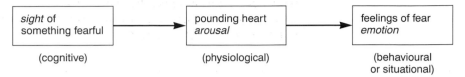

sight of something fearful		pounding heart *arousal*		feelings of fear *emotion*
(cognitive)		(physiological)		(behavioural or situational)

The Cannon–Bard theory This theory was proposed in America by another physiologist, Walter Cannon (1871–1945). He too had a colleague who agreed with him – another physiologist, Philip Bard. (As an interesting aside, it was Cannon who first developed the concept of the body's regulatory system of homeostasis, discussed above. This early work also led to the development of **cybernetics**.) Cannon, working in the 1920s, was critical of the James–Lange theory and, with Bard, published an alternative version – in effect a critique – of the James–Lange theory.

The thrust of the Cannon–Bard theory is that physiological arousal and emotional experience occur at the same time:

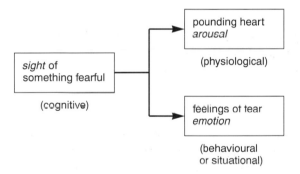

Several factors led Cannon and, later, Bard to this view. Cannon believed that the body was not capable of behaving in different ways for different emotions. For example, your heart will pound when you are aroused due to the emotions of both fear and sexual attraction. Cannon and Bard also believed that some bodily behaviours, for example increasing heart rate and perspiration, occur too slowly to set off emotions. As a consequence, Cannon and Bard proposed their model in which emotion and arousal occur at the same time. The model relies on our cognitive interpretation of an event as well as the physiological changes to our body.

The major criticism of the Cannon–Bard theory relates to its assumption that our bodily response of arousal and our emotions occur simultaneously. An example of when they do not might be a 'near-miss' in a road accident. You step off the pavement and a 10-tonne truck screeches to a halt only a metre or two away. Some time later – maybe minutes, maybe hours – you go into shock, start trembling, experience rapid shallow breathing and a pounding heart. It is this sort of evidence, where emotion and arousal do not occur simultaneously, that casts doubt on the Cannon–Bard theory.

The Schachter–Singer or two-factor theory

The clue to understanding this theory, by Schachter and Singer, rests on the two factors of bodily arousal and the situation. The theory is also known as the **cognitive theory** or the Schachter–Singer theory. Schachter argued that when you experience arousal at a **visceral level**, you search for an explanation. For example, as you prepare to sit an exam you will most likely label your arousal as 'nerves' or anxiety; on the other hand, arousal caused by a traffic jam is likely to be labelled as anger. In this theory, then, emotion follows arousal, as in the James–Lange view, but the theory also reflects the Cannon–Bard view that different emotions give rise to similar patterns of arousal.

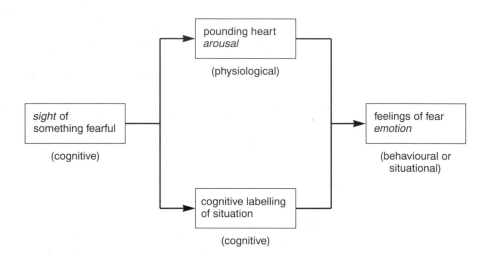

Evidence from studies investigating this theory provide conflicting answers. A study by Dutton and Aron (1974), for example, supports the theory. In this study it was 'arranged' that the researcher, a young woman, would ask individual young men to answer a questionnaire. There were two different conditions. In both cases the interview took place on a footbridge, but in the first it was a rather precarious, narrow, high bridge over a deep ravine; in the other it was a very solid concrete bridge only a few feet from the ground. In both cases the woman researcher gave the men her telephone number with the pretext to phone her if they wanted to know the outcome of the research. If the two-factor theory was true, then more men interviewed on the high bridge would phone than would those interviewed on the low bridge – the logic being that the high, slightly dangerous bridge would have created a heightened autonomic arousal, which the low, safe bridge would not. In fact this is what the study found. It was concluded that the heightened emotional arousal was attributed by the men to the woman and not to the fear created by the height. This supports the two-factor theory by demonstrating that people experiencing emotion from physiological causes will explain it in cognitive terms. Generally it has been found that evidence in support of this theory occurs only in novel situations – like a high bridge!

Contradicting the theory is the view that often, when aroused, the person will look beyond the immediate situation to similar experiences stored in memory.

While the above theories outline the major options, there are a number of other researchers who add to our understanding of emotion. Zajonc (1984) believes that in certain circumstances our emotional reactions are quicker than our interpretation of a situation – in other words we do not need to identify and label the arousal before experiencing emotion. We feel before we think! Neurological evidence lends support to this view. For example, one neural pathway goes from the eye to the thalamus, and then to the amygdala. This pathway does not involve the cortex, so the process of thinking – the cognitive component – is not possible. As a result, a rapid emotional response is possible, which may be modified later after you have thought about it (Ledoux, 1994).

One other view that needs to be considered is that of Lazarus (1990), who argues that no matter how fast the emotion is generated there is always an element of cognition required. We may not be conscious of it, but it is there.

Summing up the discussion on emotion, it is impossible to say precisely how emotion 'works'. Perhaps the best approach is to remember that there are three components to emotion and no one of them is necessarily more – or less – important than the other two. There is also the fact that people are all different and bring to a given situation widely differing experience.

Stress

There are obvious links between the above topics – motivation and emotion – and stress. Stress and the results of stress often follow strong feelings or emotions, and there is now much evidence linking our health to our state of mind. These links can be minor and short-term, like needing to use the toilet several times just before making a presentation or not sleeping very well following a row with someone; or they can be major, as for example when the stress is not dealt with and as a result may give rise to anything from skin problems and stomach ulcers to heart problems and cancer.

Think about it

• What links can you make between stress and health, illness, therapy, etc.?

Defining stress

As we attempt to define stress, we need to distinguish between cause and effect. In the widest sense, stress can be considered as a force applied to a system or structure which causes change. Aircraft designers need to consider the stress imposed on an aircraft in the form of changing air pressure and other forces. The wing tips of one large aircraft (the B52), for example, move up and down by about 5 metres between being stationary on the ground and the point of take-off – next time you fly, watch the wing tip of the aircraft as you take off. Chairs in the students' common-room frequently suffer broken or bent legs due to being over-stressed. Notice that in these examples we consider stress to be the cause, while the effect is damage or distortion. In psychological terms, it is different. In this case, stress is the effect that occurs as the result or cause of some kind of force or pressure, usually called the **stressor**.

Stress

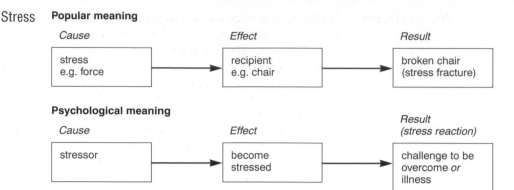

When you first came to this section, you probably thought of stress in psychological terms. You may have thought of someone you know, or even yourself, as 'stressed out', by which you mean under a lot of pressure and not coping very well. This raises an important concept concerning stress in terms of how we see, or perceive, the stressor and how we then deal with it. We said above that the stressor is some kind of force or pressure that leads to the resulting stress. But what happens when we see the stressor not as inevitably leading to a pathological condition called 'stress', implying illness or failing to cope, but rather as a challenge to be met and dealt with? In this case, the arousal that comes from the stressor now becomes a force for good, a challenge to rise above the circumstance. In the aircraft example, the flexibility of the aircraft wing allows it to move up and down, thus accommodating the external pressures. If the aircraft did not have this capability, it would not do its job (or it would have to be made so heavy and so strong that it would never get off the ground!).

In summary, then, stress involves external forces that cause, or are likely to cause, change. A general definition of stress might be: any situation or circumstance that threatens or that we believe will threaten our normal functioning and our ability to cope.

Think about it

• Using any resources available in your library, think about how you would define 'stress' in your own words.

The effects of stress on the body

In this section, we are concerned with the kind of stress that affects the health of people – the negative side of things – but not forgetting that stress can also have a positive side that provides the motivation to achieve great things in both the physical and the mental realms. It is important to bear in mind that stress can affect people differently. Some people will see a stressor as nothing more than a temporary irritation, while for others the same stressor becomes a major and perhaps long-term, serious problem.

Inevitably, issues concerning stress overlap into what is generally called **health psychology** – how psychosocial factors influence our well-being (see Unit 9, pages 444–5).

Stress and illness   If you analyse frequency and type of common diseases in Western society during the 20th century, you will see that there has been a major shift. The following diagram shows, very crudely, what has happened in terms of the frequency of different types of illness and deaths caused by them. Death rates from serious contagious illness have steadily decreased, while death rates from stress-related disease have steadily increased. This coincided with a major shift in the way in which disease and illness is viewed.

During the 20th century, there has been a move away from the view that physical illness is a physical problem and purely a question of biology, to an awareness that illness is caused not just by biological factors but by a combination of biological, psychological and social factors – and so we have the **bio-psychosocial model of illness.**

Death rates and frequency of illness, by type of illness (Western societies)

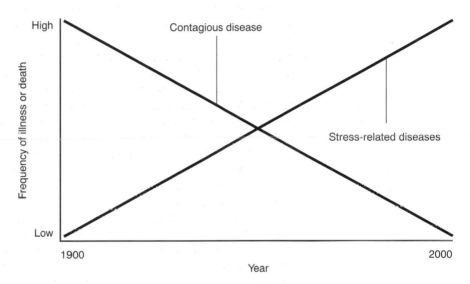

At this point we need to be careful in drawing conclusions, for, despite the above general trends, the biological element in illness is still present; so stress-*related* illness is a better term than stress-*caused* illness.

It was the American physiologist Walter Cannon (who proposed the Cannon–Bard theory discussed above) who first concluded that stress reaction involves both body and mind. His books *Bodily Changes in Pain, Hunger, Fear and Rage* (1919 and 1929) and *The Wisdom of the Body* (1932) were very influential. In his work, Cannon observed that the sympathetic nervous system responds to stressors by releasing into the blood stream from the adrenal glands the hormones epinephrine (adrenaline) and norepinephrine (noradrenaline). When this happens, the body is prepared for 'fight or flight' (the term was originally coined by Cannon). Whether intended or not, the term 'fight or flight' suggests the two responses to stress – on the one hand, a challenge to be fought and overcome or, on the other hand, the beginnings of 'flight', which may lead into illness.

Somewhat later, in 1976, the Canadian researcher Hans Selye (who first used the term 'stress') built on the work of Cannon and showed that the body responds to stressors in a very general way, no matter what form the stressor takes. The stressors used by Cannon and Selye were both physical and psychological, for example heat and cold, electrical shock, physical restraint, lack of oxygen and emotion-arousing situations. Selye observed that the reaction to this variety of stressor was the same. Not surprisingly, he called this the **general adaption syndrome**, or **GAS** for short.

The general adaption syndrome (GAS)

The general adaption syndrome has three stages or phases:

- When experiencing a stressor, the first thing to happen (Phase 1) is that your body activates the sympathetic nervous system, which you experience as 'alarm'. You are now ready for fight or flight.
- Phase 2 is 'resistance'. Your body remains at a high level of arousal – although not as high as the initial reaction – as you start to cope with the stressor.
- If the stressor remains present, you move into Phase 3, 'exhaustion', which occurs when the body runs out of its ability to cope with the stressor. Taken to its extreme, the body will run out of coping resources, collapse and may ultimately die. As the ability to cope decreases, vulnerability to illness in general increases – possibly leading to collapse or death.

Modern research is now able to distinguish differences in response to stressors, so the 'general' in Selye's GAS is not quite so general as Selye thought. However, the principle of stress causing illness remains.

Stress appraisal

We have said that stress comes from circumstances that threaten our coping behaviour, which some see as a challenge, others as a threat; and we have said that there is a general adaption syndrome in that, in general terms, we all react physiologically in essentially the same manner. We have also said that stress can seriously damage your health. We now need to consider ways in which we appraise stressors. Just how do we evaluate or interpret events?

Most theorists agree that there are three major groupings of stressors. In order of highest to lowest degree of stress, they are:

- major catastrophes;
- significant life changes; and
- daily hassles.

Flying can be very relaxing when everything is working as it should be. Stress levels increase dramatically when problems arise, when the weather is bad, when you are flying into a busy airport, and so on

<u>Catastrophes</u> Catastrophes are for the most part unpredictable, major events, perceived by all involved as threatening, perhaps even life-threatening, and of such major force that reaction or 'fighting back' is just not possible. Major aircraft crashes, earthquakes, tidal waves, war and other such disasters – some of which may require moving home and separation from family – all qualify as catastrophes. The effects of such catastrophes include a significant increase in stress-related illnesses, such as heart disease, depression and anxiety. In some cases, stress symptoms emerge immediately following the event; in other cases, prolonged separation or living in temporary housing causes a slow onset of stress reaction. Paton (1992) investigated the effects of the Lockerbie jumbo jet disaster on the emergency services and reported a 38 per cent increase in short-term illness. Other studies indicate that figures of 20 per cent are quite normal for increased stress-related illness rates.

Significant life changes Another major form of stressor is any change to existing daily life patterns. Changes to the way we live, particularly if sudden, can cause considerable stress. It is also interesting to note that events that are positive, such as getting married, the birth of a baby, promotion at work, can all create stress.

In an attempt to be more objective in defining and measuring stress, Holmes and Rahe (1967) developed a Social Readjustment Rating Scale (SRRS) (see page 274). The scale gives a numerical value (a 'life-change unit' or LCU) to a large number of life events, the value for each event having been determined by the analysis of medical records of patients with a diagnosed stress-related illness. Normal practice with the scale is to add the LCUs experienced by a person over a period of a year. A figure in excess of 300 usually shows a small but significant correlation with the onset of mental and physical ill health.

The Social Readjustment Rating Scale (1967)

Life event	Life-change units
Death of spouse	100
Divorce	73
Marital separation	65
Jail term	63
Death of close family member	63
Personal injury or illness	53
Marriage	50
Fired at work	47
Marital reconciliation	45
Retirement	45
Change in health of family member	44
Pregnancy	40
Sex difficulties	39
Gain of new family member	39
Business readjustment	39
Change in financial status	38
Death of close friend	37
Change to different line of work	36
Change in number of arguments with spouse	35
Mortgage for major purchase (e.g. a house)	31
Foreclosure of mortgage or loan	30
Change in responsibilities at work	29
Son or daughter leaving home	29
Trouble with in-laws	29
Outstanding personal achievement	28
Wife begins or stops work	26
Begin or end school	26
Change in living conditions	25
Revision of personal habits	24
Trouble with boss	23
Change in work hours or conditions	20
Change in residence	20
Change in schools	20
Change in recreation	19
Change in church activities	19
Change in social activities	18
Mortgage or loan for minor purchase	17
Change in sleeping habits	16
Change in number of family get-togethers	15
Change in eating habits	15
Vacation	13
Christmas	12
Minor violation of the law	11

The Social
Readjustment Rating
Scale (student's
version)

Life event	Life-change units
Death of close family member	100
Death of close friend	73
Divorce between parents	65
Jail term	63
Major personal illness or injury	63
Marriage	58
Being fired from job	50
Failing an important course	47
Change in health of family member	45
Pregnancy	45
Sex problems	44
Serious argument with close friend	40
Change in financial status	39
Change of major academic subject	39
Trouble with parents	39
New girl- or boyfriend	38
Increased workload at school	37
Outstanding personal achievement	36
First quarter/semester in college	35
Change in living conditions	31
Serious argument with instructor	30
Lower grades than expected	29
Change in sleeping habits	29
Change in social activities	29
Change in eating habits	28
Chronic car trouble	26
Change in number of family get-togethers	26
Too many missed classes	25
Change of college	24
Dropping of more than one class	23
Minor traffic violation	20

In a modification of the SRRS, a new scale was produced for use with college students (see above). On this scale, an LCU score for a year in excess of 300 is likely to indicate serious health problems. Below 150 LCUs, you have a 1-in-3 chance of illness.

On a slightly lighter note, most students at some point complain of being 'stressed out', some more frequently than others. This raises the possibility of self-induced stress. The point here is that if the student is faced with several demanding pieces of work, perhaps with deadlines within a few days of each other, and keeps putting off getting down to work, then the student will inevitably become 'stressed'. Whether this should be called 'stress', with the negative connotation; 'good stress', implying a pressure to achieve something positive; or simply 'guilt' – is a moot point.

Daily hassles The third and least serious group of stressors was described as 'daily hassles'. These are the ordinary everyday types of minor problem or irritant – getting stuck in rush-hour traffic, not getting the letter or telephone call you were expecting, a minor row with someone at home or work, losing a book, knowing that you have not had time for . . . , etc.

Different people respond in different ways to these daily stressors. For some it is all too much and daily events build up into major problems; while others seem to be able, if not to ignore the problem, at least to shrug it off or cope with it in some other way.

Most of the work done on the effects of stress in both animal studies and with humans shows that the effect of the stressor is more serious if the recipient perceives the problem both as having a negative effect and as being uncontrollable. In other words, simply having to take whatever is thrown at you, with no hope of being able to take any kind of avoiding action, is likely to lead to serious, negative effects. People caught in a poverty trap, the long-term unemployed, those living in overcrowded situations, people having to cope with long-term ill health in themselves or a family member, those coping with long-term family problems – are all likely to experience stress-related illness. On the other hand, people with some control over their own circumstances fare better.

- Circumstances where there is loss of control, coupled with a pessimistic outlook, can lead to health problems.
- An optimistic outlook, coupled with some degree of control, tends not to lead to health problems.

The physiology of this is now well documented from both animal and human studies. In a situation where the animal or human loses control of their personal situation, then the body starts to produce high levels of stress hormones (see page 265).

Stress reaction We stated above that people react to stressors in different ways and that those who have a more positive outlook and a more relaxed manner tend to suffer less stress-related illness. So what are the mechanisms or reasons for this?

A classic case of stress reaction

In what has now become a classic study investigating reaction to stress, Friedman and Rosenman (1974) investigated more than 3000 male participants over a nine-year period. Following initial interviews, the participants were classified as Type A or Type B personalities.

- **Type A** characteristics included: competitiveness, forcefulness, time-consciousness, impatience, high motivation, verbal aggressiveness and argumentativeness.
- **Type B** characteristics were essentially the opposite of Type A, and included a tendency to be easygoing, relaxed, and so on.

At the end of the nine years, 257 men had suffered a heart attack, 69 per cent of whom were Type A men. This meant that Type A men were more than twice as likely as Type B men to suffer a heart attack. The other key finding to emerge from the study was that not one of the men at the extreme end of Type B suffered a heart attack.

The following chart gives a brief summary of the major studies investigating stress.

Research into stress		
1956	Friedman and Rosenman	Discovered that women consumed similar amounts of cholesterol and fats as their husbands but suffered half the number of heart problems as their husbands.
1962	Friedman and Rosenman	Measured cholesterol levels and blood clotting speed of 40 accountants. Noted dangerous levels in both measures at peak work loads, which returned to normal after work peaks. Concluded that stress caused the problems.
1974	Friedman and Rosenman	Nine-year study of 3000 men (described on page 276).
1991	Kamarck and Jennings	Type A men tend to be in a heightened state of arousal for most of the time – as if expecting to do battle. This leads to higher levels of cholesterol and more fatty deposits around the heart, in effect weakening it. When the next stressor arrives, the weakened heart cannot cope and a heart attack follows.
1988	Matthews	Type A problems centre on negative emotions rather than just a busy lifestyle. Anger is the key negative emotion.
1993	Williams	

Stress and the immune system

Another dimension to the link between stress and illness is the part played by the body's immune system. As noted on page 230, the immune system works in co-operation with the brain and the endocrine system. Its fundamental job is to defend the body by identifying and destroying harmful viruses, bacteria, etc.

There have been many studies which show that in animals there are direct links between high levels of stress and reduced levels of immune efficiency; other studies have shown the same positive correlation with humans. One such study showed reduced levels of immune efficiency during the final examination period of a group of medical students, normal levels having been recorded before and after the examination period.

Stress reduction   Accepting that stressors exist and affect us all, what can be done to reduce the effects of stress? There are a number of factors that have been shown to reduce the effect of stress on humans.

- **Social support** is seen to be crucial. Having a group of family members or close friends in regular contact has a positive effect; while the 'loner' is much more likely to suffer from ill health – both physically and mentally.
- **Physical exercise:**   Research shows that individuals who engage in aerobic exercise on a regular basis are less likely to suffer illness than those who do not. Precise reasons why this is so are still unclear. What is known is that exercise strengthens the heart and lowers stress-caused blood pressure.
- **Biofeedback:**   This is the ability to control 'bio' aspects of the body – heart rate, respiration, etc. – by the deliberate use of 'feedback'. This can be done either by using sensing equipment in which the person tries to reduce a signal of some kind, or simply by willing the desired change.
- **Relaxation**, either coupled with bio-feedback or on its own, is another established technique.
- **Personality:**   This aspect of the way people cope with stress, deliberately or otherwise, has been researched by Suzanne Kobasa (1979). The starting place for this work is that personality affects response to stressors, therefore those who cope must be hardier than those who do not. According to Kobasa, hardiness involves three 'C's:
  – seeing the issue as a **challenge**;
  – having a sense of **commitment** towards an active solution; and
  – believing that you have **control** over your own actions.
- **Anxiolytic drugs:**   A more traditional way of dealing with stress is to use drugs, specifically anxiolytic drugs whose purpose is to reduce levels of anxiety. Most of the symptoms of stress can be controlled, at least to some degree, by drug treatment.

Something to do

- Make a list of the symptoms of stress, then link to each symptom an appropriate drug. The first is done for you:

Stress symptom	Drug treatment
Anxiety	Valium

- **Humour** is also thought to have a positive effect on recovery from illness, implying that a good dose of humour, taken regularly, will keep you from becoming unhealthy. This is not a frivolous matter – there is now research that indicates that humour can decrease tissue inflammation, increase circulation and reduce the release of stress hormones (Fry, 1986).

All of this gets us into the rather new field of **psychoneuroimmunology**, which is the study of the way that the brain, emotion, the body and the immune system work together for the good of the whole.

To conclude this section on stress we can now develop a schematic diagram as follows:

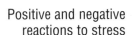

Positive and negative reactions to stress

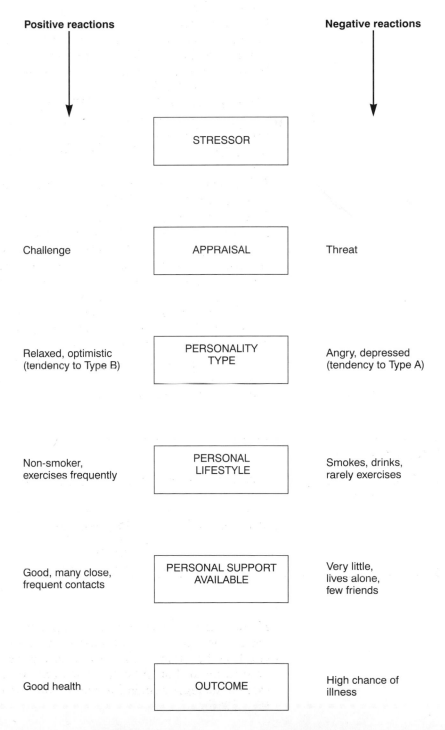

Positive reactions		Negative reactions
	STRESSOR	
Challenge	**APPRAISAL**	Threat
Relaxed, optimistic (tendency to Type B)	**PERSONALITY TYPE**	Angry, depressed (tendency to Type A)
Non-smoker, exercises frequently	**PERSONAL LIFESTYLE**	Smokes, drinks, rarely exercises
Good, many close, frequent contacts	**PERSONAL SUPPORT AVAILABLE**	Very little, lives alone, few friends
Good health	**OUTCOME**	High chance of illness

Revision and practice

● ●

Coursework opportunities

1. If you have access to a mirror box, it is possible to conduct a number of experiments testing various aspects of cerebral dominance. For example, you can study 'handedness' by comparing left-hand and right-hand dominant people. To do this, create a shape such as the star shown below. The task is to draw a line that stays within the parallel lines of the shape. By using the mirror box, you are providing a situation that is new to each hand–eye combination. Most left-hand dominant people are better with their right hand at new tasks than right-hand dominant people are with their left hand. Test this hypothesis by counting the time taken and number of mistakes for each hand.

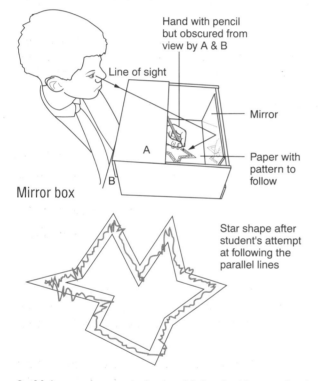

Hand with pencil but obscured from view by A & B

Line of sight

Mirror

A

B

Paper with pattern to follow

Mirror box

Star shape after student's attempt at following the parallel lines

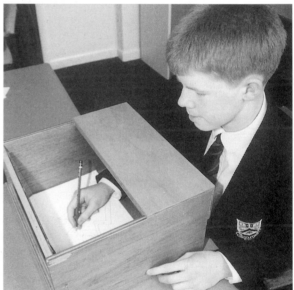

So designed that you can only see your hand and pencil *via* the mirror

2. Males are known to have a higher incidence of colour blindness than females. There is also a view that males and females 'see' colours differently. Explore and test these ideas.
3. Investigate evidence that length of sleep can have an effect on reaction times and daytime body temperatures.
4. *Either:* Investigate dreaming by correlating dreams of participants with their daily activities. *Or:* Investigate problem solving while asleep.
5. Assess and measure levels of arousal on different tasks. Try to demonstrate the Yerkes–Dodson law (see page 262).
6. 'Arousal affects our emotion.' Gather evidence to support this. Using naturally aroused participants – say players at the end of a football match – and a totally unaroused control group – say students at the start of a normal day (with no tests!), ask both groups to rate their feelings of elation on receiving some imaginary good news. You might need to run a pilot study to establish ratings that distinguish between conditions. Remember to consider carefully the ethical issues.
7. Investigate the concept of 'good stress' – that is, when stress acts as a pressure to achieve something positive.

● ●

Examination questions

Question 1   Describe and analyse research into some of the major sources of stress.

(25 marks)

(AEB, Paper 2, Summer 1997)

Question 1: Unpacked   This is a straightforward essay incorporating Skill A 'describe' and Skill B 'analyse'. Your main decision hinges on the word 'some'. You need to decide whether to deal with two or three sources in considerable depth, or rather more sources at a less significant depth. Your answer will depend on how much research evidence you can marshal to support your comments.

- Some of the major groups of sources of stress are: major catastrophes, significant life changes and daily hassles. (Don't get side-tracked into issues concerning stress reaction or stress reduction. Stay focused on sources of stress.)
- You must focus on research in your chosen areas.

Question 2   (a) Describe the organisation of the autonomic nervous system.   *(12 marks)*

(b) Assess the influence of the autonomic nervous system on any **one** behavioural function.   *(12 marks)*

(AEB, Module Paper 5, Summer 1997)

The following student essay was completed in 45 minutes under simulated exam conditions.

Comments

Good start in general terms

Useful background to the question

Good accurate description and good use of correct terminology

Essay

(a) The nervous system is the body's primary form of communication, it consists of billions of specialised cells called neurons. The function of a neuron is to transfer information throughout the body via electrical impulses.

The nervous system is divided into two component parts, the central nervous system and the peripheral nervous system, where nerves lead from the brain and spinal cord to all parts of the body. The peripheral nervous system also subdivides into two components, the somatic system and the autonomic system, which usually operates without conscious control. However, we are able to learn to control some autonomic functions, for example, urination. The nervous system is highly organised, with no one subsection working independently, in fact the autonomic nervous system is neither structurally nor functionally independent of the central nervous system. It is regulated by centres in the brain, in particular by the cerebral cortex, hypothalamus and medulla. The autonomic nervous system is entirely motor, which means the electrical impulses are transmitted from the central nervous system to internal (visceral) organs, such as blood vessels and the digestive system. There are two divisions within the autonomic nervous system, the sympathetic and the parasympathetic nervous systems. Most of the internal organs that

Terms need basic definition

are stimulated by the autonomic system receive an input from both these divisions. The sympathetic and the parasympathetic branches are structurally different and operate in different ways, they are known as an antagonistic system. Together they are able to maintain homeostasis within the body. The sympathetic system prepares the body to use energy, it increases the body's internal activity, for example, it releases sugar stored in the liver into the blood to increase energy levels. It also increases blood flow to muscles so that they can be used for physical action.

The parasympathetic system works in the opposite way, therefore it aims to conserve energy and is known as a rest-response system.

'interact' needs explanation

Relevant example

How?

(b) The autonomic nervous system concentrates on our internal environment, and as previously mentioned is an automatic process. In order to evoke a behaviour, the ANS will interact with the central nervous system and another system, known as the endocrine system. Should we find ourselves in fearful situation, e.g. being chased by a angry dog, we experience both an initial emotional and physical reaction – fear and avoidance. The hypothalamus will activate the ANS to respond appropriately. The action of the sympathetic system will increase energy levels, known as the 'fight or flight response', Walter Cannon (1927). Blood flow to the muscles will be increased to enable the body to run to safety. The released sugar from the liver will provide the necessary energy needed to implement an avoidance behaviour. You are not immediately aware of your behaviour until after you have reacted, when you will feel your heart beating faster, you may be breathless and feel anxious.

Once you are safe, the parasympathetic system will return the body functions to normal. The autonomic nervous system enables us to react to a changing environment, the sympathetic system acting as an accelerator, whilst the parasympathetic acts as the decelerator.

General comments

Part (a) is well written and accurate. Some areas are a little limited, and would benefit from further explanation. Part (b) has good description but if one is to 'assess' in terms of 'strengths and limitations', is a bit weak.

Marks: part (a) 8

part (b) $7 = \dfrac{15}{24}$

Question 3 Discuss the influence of the nervous system **and** the endocrine system upon homeostasis. *(25 marks)*

(AEB, Paper 2, Summer 1996)

Question 4 (a) Describe the *biomedical model* in health psychology. *(6 marks)*

(b) Discuss how the *bio-psychosocial* perspective offers an alternative to the biomedical model. Refer to appropriate research to support your answer. *(14 marks)*

(Total: 20 marks)

(NEAB, PSO8, February 1997)

Selected reading list

Bloom, F.E. and Lazerson, A., *Brain, Mind and Behavior* (W.H. Freeman & Co., New York, 2nd edn 1988)

Gregory, R.L. (ed.), *The Oxford Companion to the Mind* (Oxford University Press, 1987)

Gross, R. and McIlveen, R., *Biopsychology* (Hodder and Stoughton, 1996)

6 Comparative psychology: what makes our behaviour human?

Comparative psychology is concerned with the similarities and differences between **species**, particularly as these differences relate to behaviour. 'Species', as used here, includes both human and non-human. In this unit, we look at:

- **evolution** and the way that it determines behaviour;
- **reproduction strategies**;
- **kinship** and **social behaviour**; and
- **behavioural analysis**.

Something to investigate

- Skim the contents pages of a selection of psychology textbooks in your library. You will find that some have a separate section devoted to comparative psychology (as in this book), while others do not. In the latter case, most or all of the topics discussed in this unit will almost certainly be included elsewhere in the text.
- As you do this, you may notice that most British and European textbooks have sections dealing with comparative psychology or ethology; while most American textbooks do not. Why do you think this is?

Evolution: an introduction

Fundamental to an understanding of comparative psychology (and indeed most other areas of psychology) is the need to understand **evolution**. Evolution is a fact. Things do evolve. The evolution debate centres on explanations as to how and why things evolve. The popular and rather loose definition of evolution has to do with the processes by which plant and animal life develop and change from earlier forms.

Charles Darwin   Charles Darwin (1809–82) is the key figure in evolution theory. His book *On the Origin of Species* (1859) created a huge impact. It was the result of his extensive and detailed observations while on a five-year voyage (1831–36) on the ship HMS *Beagle*, and his own research into selective breeding.

    Darwin argued that if breeding could be controlled to develop or strengthen positive traits and to weaken negative traits – which was precisely what he was doing with domestic animals – then why couldn't nature do the same? In this case, it becomes the traits necessary for survival that will be strengthened or developed, and traits that contribute little to the survival of a particular species that will weaken and disappear. As a result, species with the positive traits will produce more offspring and those with less positive traits fewer offspring. This is what Darwin called **natural selection** – the ability of organisms to adapt to their environment.

Despite the enormous significance of Darwin's theories, it was not until much later, and until much more was known about **genetic transmission** (see page 294), that some of the questions that Darwin was unable to answer became more fully understood.

Something to investigate

• Read up on 'Darwin's finches'. It is a classic example of how natural selection occurs. (Ridley, 1995, is a good source.)

Terms and ideas relating to evolution

There are a number of ideas relating to evolution that we need to consider briefly.

• **Phylogeny** is the term used to describe the origin and evolution of a species.
• **Ontogeny** refers to the origin and evolution not of a species but of an individual organism.
• **Phenotype** refers to the features and behaviour by which an organism can be identified.
• **Genotype** refers to the genetic construction of an organism, which of course means its heredity.

The usage of these terms will become more obvious as the unit proceeds.

Something to do

• Start your word list and people list for the topics in comparative psychology.

Evolutionary determinants of behaviour

Theories and approaches

While evolution has been a major force in the development of psychology, behaviour has an equally important place. At its simplest level, behaviour can mean any kind of action that can be measured. As we saw in Unit 2, the behavioural approach is one of several theoretical approaches or schools of thought in psychology (others being psychoanalytic, cognitive, humanistic and neurobiological; see pages 33–8). Current debate concerns whether or not some of the newer branches of psychology, such as neurological processes, can be considered in behavioural terms. It seems that as areas such as this get increasingly complicated, 'behaviour' becomes a less appropriate term to use. Perhaps the real issue has more to do with the question of psychology as an objective science, in which things and behaviour can be measured; or whether psychology can legitimately move into areas such as neurophysiology on the basis that these areas cause organisms to behave in certain ways.

Nature or Nurture? Before we start thinking about non-human animals, think for a moment about yourself and some of your behaviours. A good example would be to consider your musical abilities. It may be that the nearest you get to playing is to 'play' your tape or CD player. On the other hand, you may be extremely competent and have achieved success in the high grades in your chosen instrument. Perhaps you have a gift for musicianship. Now bring the classic Nature–Nurture issue to bear on you as a musician. Is your musical ability all Nature, all Nurture, or a mix of both? How do you know? How do you decide? Answers to these questions will depend in part on such things as how musical your parents are; if they are musical, is there a possibility that you have received a genetic predisposition to good musicianship? Or, on the other hand, do you simply like music and have spent a lot of time learning and practising how to make music?

In terms of comparative psychology, the above example can be linked to the Nature–Nurture issue as follows:

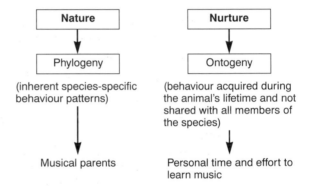

If we expand the above to include important theorists, we get:

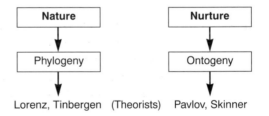

We discuss the work of Pavlov and Skinner on pages 312–16 in the context of learning theories. Lorenz and Tinbergen are discussed below.

Ethology Lorenz (1903–89) and Tinbergen (1907–88) worked in the field of **ethology**, which is essentially the study of behaviour using naturalistic techniques. The main reason for this shift towards naturalistic methods was the belief that psychology had moved too much into the laboratory and needed to be balanced by more observation of behaviour in its natural setting – where it evolves naturally. Ethology is a part of comparative psychology, which – as noted above – tends to concentrate on observing comparisons between species and uses non-experimental techniques.

Lorenz and Tinbergen are usually considered to have been responsible for the emergence of ethology as a distinct discipline. The field has since moved from this classical position to a more social-biological approach.

Sociobiology

Sociobiology is the study of genetic and evolutionary behaviour as the basis for explaining social behaviour. This definition applies to all organisms including humans, and is an attempt to explain the behaviour of the organism in terms of its social behaviour.

The field of sociobiology came alive in 1975 with the publication of *Socio-Biology: A New Synthesis* by Edward Wilson. The essential argument in sociobiology is that natural selection favours the kind of social behaviour that leads to maximal reproductive success and the resultant passing on of the organism's genes. The contentious part of the theory concerns the argument that evolution influences – if not directs – motivation, including in the human animal. As a result, the approach is by no means universally accepted.

Game theory

Much of our understanding of animal behaviour comes from the traditional approach of direct observation in a natural setting. In 1972, Maynard-Smith used a mathematical technique called **game theory** to attempt to model animal behaviour mathematically. Game theory tries to analyse the decision-making process, which itself takes account of the actions of the other 'player' in the 'game'. The purpose of this work is to attempt to show how a species population may behave in such a way so as to maximise its chances of survival – that is, to determine the best evolutionary option or, in the jargon, the **evolutionary stable strategy**.

Criticisms of this approach come from theorists who argue that it is simply impossible to categorise animal behaviour in such a way as to reliably model it mathematically. A second criticism is that it is trying to analyse an individual behaviour when in fact behaviour is the result of a whole host of factors. However, it is possible that with time and ever more 'clever' models this approach may at least help in our understanding of animal behaviour.

Motivation

As we saw in Unit 5, the term 'motivation' is difficult to define in a technical sense: what happens, in psychological terms? In the general sense of the word, motivation means an internal drive or force that impels the organism into action. For example, the desire or need to pass a psychology exam motivates you – or drives you – to spend hours studying the subject.

In human terms, probably the most well-known theory of motivation is the **hierarchy of needs** first proposed by Abraham Maslow in 1954 (see also Unit 5, page 263). Maslow was a humanist. He believed that behaviour is motivated by a desire for personal growth and that people will put up with discomfort and even pain in order to achieve their personal goals. His pyramid of needs is hierarchical in that a person moves up the various stages in order and only when the lower stage has been achieved.

It is interesting to note that you can move in and out of self actualisation. It is quite possible that at 20 years old you may have achieved or fulfilled your potential for that stage in your life; in other words, you have achieved all you want for a 20-year-old. At say 21, however, you may realise that there is a lot more 'out there' that you are capable of achieving, and so you move down the hierarchy and start climbing up again.

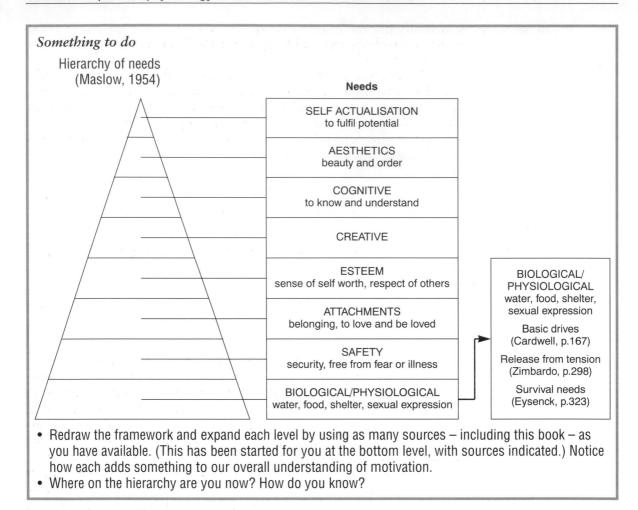

Something to do

Hierarchy of needs
(Maslow, 1954)

Needs

- SELF ACTUALISATION
  to fulfil potential
- AESTHETICS
  beauty and order
- COGNITIVE
  to know and understand
- CREATIVE
- ESTEEM
  sense of self worth, respect of others
- ATTACHMENTS
  belonging, to love and be loved
- SAFETY
  security, free from fear or illness
- BIOLOGICAL/PHYSIOLOGICAL
  water, food, shelter, sexual expression

BIOLOGICAL/
PHYSIOLOGICAL
water, food, shelter,
sexual expression

Basic drives
(Cardwell, p.167)

Release from tension
(Zimbardo, p.298)

Survival needs
(Eysenck, p.323)

- Redraw the framework and expand each level by using as many sources – including this book – as you have available. (This has been started for you at the bottom level, with sources indicated.) Notice how each adds something to our overall understanding of motivation.
- Where on the hierarchy are you now? How do you know?

Instinct

If Maslow's humanistic theory of motivation is concerned primarily with the human animal, then **instinct theory** is concerned primarily with animals. Lorenz has defined instinct as

> *"behaviour which is to a large extent determined by the nervous mechanisms evolved in the phylogeny of the species."*
>
> Lorenz, cited in Reber (1995)

What this means is that a given species will act instinctually when a given stimulus – the **innate releasing mechanism** – occurs. An innate releasing mechanism is the suggested means by which instinctive behaviour is triggered. Tinbergen, in the 1950s, suggested that each inherited behaviour has its own innate releasing mechanism, which is activated by an external stimulus which he called a **sign stimulus**. An animal will have a number of latent sign stimuli, which, if triggered by an innate releasing mechanism, result in a **fixed action pattern**.

The original definition for the term 'fixed action pattern' suggests a behaviour that occurs in a fixed, almost stereotyped way. It occurs, or is 'released', when the appropriate **species-specific stimulation** is present. Since the term was originally coined, however, the elicited behaviour has been found to be less typical than was first thought. The concept has now been replaced by **species-specific** or **species-typical behaviour** (Reber, 1995).

In the context of reproduction strategies, the fixed action (really re-action) pattern of sexual response is released by **pheromones**, which are chemical secretions used by the species to indicate sexual readiness. (Pheromones are also used to mark territory – see page 290.) Fixed action patterns are much more common than just in sexual responses, however.

Something to do

- 'Instinct' is used as a term in a number of other areas in psychology. Make a list of different uses for the term.
- Find out more about fixed action patterns (see also page 290).

Altruism

We can define **altruism** simply as putting someone else first. It can be extended to the point where an organism puts the survival of another before considering its own welfare. The theory holds that by acting in this manner other members of the organism's family will benefit, and as a result the organism's genes will be passed on. This is called **kin selection** and is one of the evolutionary methods that provide support for sociobiological theory. (We look at this in more detail later in the unit.) The term was coined by Maynard Smith (1964) to describe the way in which certain of an organism's characteristics are favoured because of the positive effects that they have on the survival of close relatives, even if the organism itself fails to survive. For example, Sherman (1981) established that unrelated ground squirrels (a species found in the western states of the USA) kill each others' offspring, while relatives do not. (For further discussion on altruism, see also page 300.)

Looking at the approaches described above, we can say with some confidence that some behaviour is genetically determined, some behaviour is solely a result of learning, and some involves both. As we turn to look at specific behaviours of non-human animals, we see the same pattern: some are primarily genetic, others primarily learned, others a combination of both.

Evolutionary explanations in non-humans

Genetic influence

An obvious example of genetically controlled behaviour is the way in which animals behave as they mature. If it can be shown that a given behaviour occurs at a certain stage in the animal's maturation – without any possibility that it learned it or observed it from another member of its species – then that behaviour can only have come from the animal's genetic make-up. A considerable number of studies have confirmed the genetic influence on maturational behaviour.

Something to investigate

- For the purpose of this unit, we consider only a small selection of animal behaviours. Use your library resources to research and classify a wider range of behaviours.

A classic case of genetic influence

An example of genetic influence was documented by Lorenz in the 1950s: the **fixed action pattern** (see page 288). In this behaviour, the animal goes through a fixed series of actions when appropriately triggered. The classic example is the behaviour of ducks engaging in courtship display. The duck will always go through a fixed action pattern that involves neck stretching and bobbing and diving in the course of the display. The interesting question then becomes: just what is the triggering mechanism that can cause an animal to go through a fixed action pattern?

"As soon as he sees you Maggy, he just goes crazy"

Competition for resources

Under this heading we can consider a number of different but related areas. **Territoriality** is a fundamental concept, and is often linked to **resources**. This in turn can imply **competition**, which in its turn may involve **aggression**.

<u>Territoriality</u>   In a formal sense, this simply means defending one's own space. Ethologists would agree with this, but take the meaning rather further. They would distinguish between **territory** and the **home range**.

- **Territory** is the general area that an individual or animal or a group of animals or a family or an extended family will defend against others.
- The **home range** is the area that the animal or family have or use or frequent – the area in which they live and hunt.

Territory and home range are not the same – the home range of one animal, for example, may well overlap the home range of several other animals of the same species.

With many species, territoriality changes with the seasons. This factor is further influenced by the breeding needs of the species. For animals to breed successfully, their territory needs to be able to support the mating pairs in terms of food supply and to be appropriate for rearing the young. Even before courting and mating, the animal needs to be strong enough to defend its territory; if the territory has all the required needs for a given species, there will always be a demand and the 'resident' must be ready to see off intruders.

A classic case of territoriality

Krebs (1976) studied territorial behaviour in great tits. He found that if a resident was removed, another great tit would take over the territory within only a few hours. He concluded that the species was constantly looking for better territory and observed that the great tit used its song as a means to identify and defend its territory. If the bird is able to defend the territory successfully, it invariably means that it is stronger than the intruder. This fact makes it a good mating prospect – and so we have **reproductive fitness**, which is the link between an animal's territory and sexual selection.

Resources   Territory can and often does include resources, such as food and appropriate conditions for the rearing of young. What if these resources are in short supply? The answer is that competition becomes more serious, and ritualistic behaviours turn into acts of real **aggression**, with – as you would expect – evolution playing its part.

Aggression   Aggression, in psychological terms, has an extremely wide usage. In ethological terms, the definition is (usually) limited to evolutionary instinctual reactions involving territory, survival and care of young.

Something to investigate

- 'Aggression' is a term used in a number of different areas of psychology. Research and list definitions for 'aggression' taken from these different areas.

Ritualistic aggression tends to occur within certain species, often involving lengthy procedures that exhibit dominant/submissive roles – the outcome of which is that one party 'wins' and the other 'loses' or submits, but no real damage or harm has occurred to either. The fight – the aggressive act – has been mostly ritualistic play acting.

Should, however, the aggression occur between different species, the outcome is usually more serious – particularly if the species are in a predator–prey relationship (see below).

In certain circumstances, aggression takes on an even more serious role. Calhoun (1962) allowed rats to breed freely but with limited food and limited space. As the population grew, and with food and space remaining static, aggression increased – ultimately resulting in **infanticide** and then **cannibalism**.

Predator–prey and interdependent relationships

Here we consider two types of relationship and the resulting evolution of behaviour:

- the relationship between a **predator** and its **prey** and the effect that that relationship has on the evolution of the behaviour of the two;
- the evolution of behaviour in **symbiotic relationships** – that is, those relationships between members of different species who live together because each needs the other.

<u>Predator–prey relationships</u> Most species in the animal world exist in a predator–prey relationship. Obvious examples, frequently seen in filmed nature programmes, include lions preying on antelope or owls catching mice; another example is your domestic cat catching birds in the back garden.

Think about it

- Draw a flow chart showing a series of predator–prey relationships. Is there a related order – i.e. A eats B, B eats C, and so on?

What is interesting in evolutionary terms is that the behaviour of both the predator and its prey develop simultaneously. As the prey develops stronger musculature to speed flight, so the predator does also. As the prey evolves new escape strategies, so the predator develops successful means to overcome them, and so on. The whole process, however, is rather more complicated than this suggests. Endler (1991) suggests a series of different stages with any and all of these stages responding to evolutionary change so as to avoid the final stage, being eaten!

An example of this is the octopus who, when about to be consumed, emits a cloud of 'ink'. Alternatively, the prey can adapt in such a way as to deter the predator – for example the syrphid fly, which is harmless but has adapted by mimicking the wasp and evolving black and yellow stripes on its body.

This gives rise to the complex evolutionary questions of why it is that predators do not become so efficient that they drive their prey into extinction, or – the opposite of this – why prey do not become so efficient at not being eaten that it is the predator that becomes extinct. Krebs and Davies (1993) suggest that it is the prey that is always one step ahead. This view is based on the 'life/dinner principle', which says that rabbits run faster than foxes because for the rabbit its life is at stake but for the fox it is only its dinner. Because the rabbit cannot reproduce its genes after it has been eaten, but the fox can reproduce its genes even when hungry, the selection process has favoured the rabbit.

<u>Symbiotic relationships</u> In one sense symbiosis is the opposite of a predator–prey relationship, for in a symbiotic relationship the health and security of each partner depends upon the other. Another term used

for this relationship is **reciprocal altruism**. There are two main ways in which symbiosis is expressed:

- between members of the same species; and
- between members of different species.

In the former case, the relationship is basically selfish, as both animals are 'using' the relationship in a selfish manner and to their own advantage. For example, Packer (1977) has observed this in baboons. Often two males will co-operate to fight off a third male intent on mating with the partner of one of the baboons. Clearly this is to the advantage of the female's partner and not the other male. Later, when the other male needs the same kind of help to fight off another single male, he will call on the male that he helped earlier.

In the latter case, there is still a fundamentally selfish motive but the relationship has evolved to the point where each animal needs the other for its own survival. A good example of this is the pairing of the cleaner fish with a much larger fish – say the shark. The cleaner fish has so evolved that it gets its food by 'cleaning' its host – taking scraps from its teeth and sometimes parasites from its skin. The larger fish is therefore healthier and accepts – perhaps welcomes even – the attention of the cleaner fish. As well as gaining its food from its host, the smaller cleaner also gains protection – who else is going to swim into the mouth of a shark? Certain types of cleaner have further evolved so that they have the facility to attach themselves to their host, thus getting free transport as well as food.

Caribbean Reef Shark with cleaner fish hitching a lift: a good example of symbiosis

Symbiotic relationships can also occur between animal and plant species. For example, the fig tree needs the fig wasp to pollinate it, while the fig wasp needs the fig tree for its food.

Think about it

- Watch critically the next few nature programmes on television.
- Which of the behaviours discussed above can you identify?

Reproduction strategies

To understand the motivational drive associated with reproduction and reproduction strategies, you need a basic understanding of **genetic transmission**. This is a complicated subject and what follows is a brief review of the general principles necessary to make sense of what comes later in this unit.

What is a gene? A gene is a specific region of a chromosome which is capable of determining the development of a specific trait or characteristic of an organism.

Genetic transmission The key issue is that sexual reproduction is the joining together or fusing of two **haploid cells**, one coming from each parent and each having half the number of **chromosomes** present in the parent. This means that the offspring has half the genetic structure of the mother and half the genetic structure of the father. The **inherited** characteristics of the individual are carried by **deoxyribonucleic acid** (**DNA**) in the cell. This 'genetic blueprint' is what makes you you.

Each individual has a different arrangement of genes and is therefore genetically unique. It is this uniqueness that has led to **genetic fingerprinting**, which is the ability to identify an individual from a piece of tissue – blood, skin, hair, etc. – however small the sample, since each of our cells contains our unique genetic 'code'.

Knowledge of genetics also allows **genetic engineering**, which is the process by which the genetic structure of an animal is altered by the addition or removal of certain genes. In the future – and probably not very far away – it is likely that it will be possible to engineer out of a person the specific gene or genes responsible for a specific illness and so correct, or at least alleviate, the illness. For example, people with Down's syndrome have an extra chromosome in the twenty-first pair of genes. Just as it is now possible to detect the syndrome while the child is still in the womb, it is entirely possible that 'corrective genetic intervention' may one day be available to correct the problem.

Think about it

• What are the pros and cons of genetic engineering? Concentrate on ethical issues. Write two lists.

Sexual selection in evolution Krebs and Davies (1993) defined sexual selection as selection for traits which are solely concerned with increasing mating success. Sexual selection can act in two main ways, often at the same time:

• by favouring the ability to compete, for example by fighting better. This is usually male (intra-sexual selection); or
• by favouring traits which will better attract the other sex (inter-sexual selection).

The question that we attempt to answer in this section is: how do animals select a sexual mate? What is it that causes one animal to choose another? How has the mechanism evolved? Are there any 'ground rules' that apply, irrespective of species?

The issues surrounding sexual selection are of major importance because of the influence that the production of offspring has on the future evolution of the species. The instincts of the animal to mate are directed not just to reproduce, but to reproduce in such a way that the offspring survive, and survive in as large numbers as possible so that they in turn may reproduce. There is also the desire – also instinctually driven – to widen the range of genetic material from which offspring are derived, because this is the best strategy to meet the goal of maximum surviving healthy offspring. If a parent is carrying an 'unhealthy' gene, then by mating with a large number of sexual partners the chances of that unhealthy gene meeting with an unhealthy gene from a sexual partner (and thus producing offspring which will develop the unhealthy attribute) are reduced. Some unhealthy offspring are still likely, but with a wide range of partners there will be a higher proportion of more healthy offspring. This is because when an aberrant gene joins with a healthy gene, the healthy gene 'wins'; the unhealthy or aberrant gene does not then reproduce and the potential for unhealthy young is reduced.

We see the opposite of this in the breeding of pedigree animals. Here, particular genetic traits are deliberately strengthened and traits not normally considered a feature – or at least a desirable feature – are deliberately bred out of the species. As a result you see bulldogs, for example, with even flatter faces – this is considered a desirable bulldog trait, but can lead to breathing problems precisely because of the flatness of the face. It would be reasonable to assume that if the bulldog species was allowed to reproduce naturally in the wild, with the bulldog choosing its own mate, then because difficulty with breathing is not a healthy or indeed helpful trait, with time the very flat face would disappear.

The assumption in the bulldog example suggests that the species knows what is best for itself, and that this is instinctual and evolutionarily driven. In some species, for example the elephant seal, choice of mate rarely exists: it is more a question of simple availability, followed by brute force of the male – in this species the male weighs twice as much as the female. This pattern of mating is fairly unusual, however. Much more normal is the pattern in which the female makes the choice of whom to mate with.

In general terms, the female will wait to mate until she is sure that the male is suitable. Suitability means, first, that the male must be of the right species. This is usually shown by the male going through the appropriate courtship displays and rituals. Secondly, in the case of there being more than one male who displays correctly, suitability will be determined by which male takes the display rituals to the extreme – showing the most vivid colour, extreme plumage or other innate releasing mechanism. This is the male with whom the female will mate.

This process explains the evolution of the peacock, for example, with its manner of displaying its enormous and colourful tail to any peahen that should pass by.

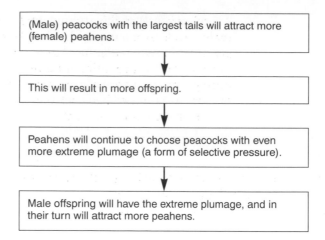

An interesting question raised by this discussion is why it is the *female* that makes, in most cases, the choice of a mate. The reason for this is fairly straightforward if we consider the investment made by each sex in the production of young.

Parental investment in rearing their young

Having reached the point of mate selection, we now take the discussion on reproduction strategies further – that is, into parental investment in terms of what is usually called **reproductive effort** and then in the actual rearing of the young.

Reproductive effort

The main point here concerns the differential effort invested in reproduction by the male and female parents.

Think about it

- How would you describe parental investment in reproduction in human terms?
- List the aspects of male and female 'investment'.

In terms of the human animal, there are a number of places where we could begin to consider this issue. We could start with the coital act, for example, or with the birth of the baby. Probably better, however, is to start earlier with the beginnings of courtship, since the first 'effort' is to find a partner. The natural progression towards reproduction is then:

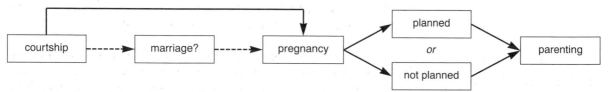

The issue of a planned or non-planned pregnancy is a particularly human one, and may have an influence on 'parental investment' – the male may run away or the female, with or without the male, may choose to abort. These issues, however, are more relevant to social psychology than to comparative psychology.

Following courtship, then, to take one extreme, the male can quite literally walk away while the female has a lengthy pregnancy and then gives birth. On the other hand, the male and female may have spent much effort on providing a home, and the male may support the female during the pregnancy and assist at the birth. Either of these two extremes, or somewhere between, may occur because of the freedom of choice of the human animal.

Think about it

• How has the pattern of human reproductive effort changed (evolved?) over the last 50 years? In evolutionary terms, this is a very short period.

Rearing of human young

The same extremes in terms of differential effort may occur in issues surrounding the rearing of the human young. The female may be left to do it all on her own, the male may make very significant contributions, or a situation somewhere between these two extremes may occur. These wide extremes of human behaviours occur mainly because of the social and cultural development of modern society.

Parental investment in non-human animals

In the animal world, species have evolved to act instinctively, and so behaviours are more set – within a given species – and reasons for the behaviours more readily available.

In many animal species, male investment in reproduction is much higher than a few moments of mating. The male may first have to find a suitable territory, he may have to defend his chosen territory by fighting off other males, and he may have to drive off an existing male. This is a considerable investment in terms of time, energy and risk. The male may be harmed or even killed in the process and thus not be able to pass on his genes which, as we have seen, is a major driving force.

Following mating, the male role decreases; the female takes on the principal investment. She now has to carry the young, give birth and then expend time and energy in bringing the young to maturity.

This pattern is quite common in mammals. In general terms, the male puts most effort into mating, while the female puts most effort into having and then nurturing the young. Measured crudely, the female expends more effort than the male. The generally accepted reason for this is that, since the female invests more in the production of offspring, she has more to lose if the young die and she has to go through the whole process again. It is a circular pattern which forces the female into the role of care giver, protector and nurturer of the young.

Mating patterns and parental care

The fundamental differences between males and females have implications for the different behaviour of the sexes in terms of social organisation and parental care. For example, basic biology predisposes females – in most species – to perform fundamental parental care; while males tend to be predisposed to show parental care by defending the territory and, in some species, sharing some of the parental care with the female. These differences are frequently linked with the mating pattern of a particular species.

Mating patterns Mating follows one of several distinct patterns:

- **monogamy**;
- **polygamy**; and
- **promiscuity**.

<u>Monogamy</u> This has two forms:

- In **pair-bond** or **annual monogamy**, the relationship between one male and one female lasts for only one season. In succeeding years, different pair-bonding takes place.
- The other form is permanent or **perennial monogamy**, where the pair-bond is a permanent relationship which lasts for the lifetime of the partners. In this case, if one partner dies before the other, the surviving animal will refuse new sexual partners.

Traditional human 'mating' tends to follow the perennial monogamy pattern, but with **serial monogamy** becoming more common.

<u>Polygamy</u> This is where one member of one sex mates with more than one member of the other sex. This also has two forms:

- **polygyny**, where one male mates with several females but each female mates with only one male; and
- **polyandry**, the opposite of polygyny, where one female mates with more than one male, either at once or in succession. Polyandry may be characterised either by male–female role reversal or by male–female co-operation. Male–female role reversal occurs when, in the case of the jacana bird, the female (who is bigger than the male) lays a clutch of eggs for each of 'her' males and it is then the role of the male to incubate the eggs and care for the young. She also forcibly stops other females mating with 'her' males. In co-operative polyandry, the care of the young is usually shared by both male and female.

<u>Promiscuity</u> In this case, there is no bonding between male and female: the two come together, mate and then separate. Frequently, an individual animal – male or female – will mate several times.

Mating patterns, and examples of species that follow them

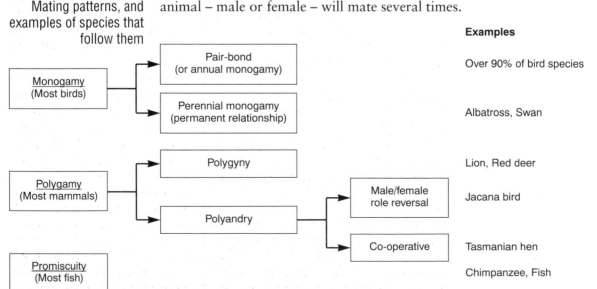

Something to do
• Redraw the diagram of mating patterns and add other examples of species.

Parental care

While the mating system of a species does not necessarily imply a specific form of parental care, the two are, as stated above, frequently linked. There are no hard and fast rules, but in many cases mating and parental care do follow a set pattern. For example, species that practise biparental care tend to be monogamous, while species where only the females care for the young tend to be polygamous. Where only the male takes care of the young, the mating pattern tends to be polyandrous.

Notwithstanding these links, there are many exceptions and variations. A related factor which has significance is the form in which fertilisation takes place. Parents that care for their young tend to practise internal fertilisation, while parents that practise external fertilisation are less likely to care for their young.

Evolutionary explanations of parent/offspring conflict

The general assumption is that parents look after their young. We do see on television, all too often, examples of parents leaving their children to fend for themselves as 'street children' in South American cities or, as documented in a Channel 4 programme *Innocents Lost* (9 December, 1997), as 'sewer children' in Romania. However, these examples, awful as they are, are usually caused by poverty and other social pressures. They are not normally caused by **parent/offspring conflict.**

As we have seen, in the animal world there is a wide range of parenting strategies, involving lengthy parent care at one extreme to parents who leave their young to fend for themselves immediately after birth at the other. The amount of care that is provided usually depends on the number of young – more young generally means less care.

One area of parent/offspring conflict occurs where the normal birth pattern is the production of just one offspring. In this case, conflict centres on when the young should 'leave home' and fend for itself. From the parents' point of view, the sooner the young has gone (assuming that the young can survive by itself) the sooner they can have more young. Also, the sooner the young is independent and able to support itself, the sooner it can mate and produce its own offspring.

A different parent/offspring conflict occurs when the parent(s) is feeding newly born young. In this case, each individual will attempt to get more than its share of the available food and so ensure its own survival. It is thought that the exaggerated feeding behaviour patterns displayed by the young have evolved so that the young will get its food at the expense of its siblings, particularly when there is not enough food and the parent has to decide *which* of the young gets the food – hence the parent/offspring conflict (Trivers, 1974). As a consequence of this type of conflict, patterns have evolved where some of the young are not weaned. This allows greater shares for the 'chosen' young and reduces the likelihood of them dying before maturity. In such cases, the weakest is allowed to die and often becomes food for the survivors. This issue becomes one of costs and benefits (see Unit 3, page 82, social exchange theory), usually with respect to the parents but sometimes to the offspring as well.

Kinship and social behaviour

Much of the discussion so far has been concerned with the individual animal and its evolutionary behaviour and reproduction. In this section, we consider the animal in a social context. While much (but not all) of what we have talked about has no direct equivalence to the human animal, the minute we start discussing social behaviour, the parallels are everywhere.

Think about it

- Consider your own existence in social terms. What social contacts have you made over the last 24-hour period?
- List parallel animal behaviours as you work through this section of the unit.

Apparent altruism

We defined altruism on page 289: at its most basic level, it is putting the other person – or animal – first. **Apparent altruism** is rather different. In this case, it appears as if the animal is putting the welfare of another animal before its own; while this may appear to be the case, however, the fact of the matter is that the one appearing altruistic is in fact selfish. It has in effect weighed up all the options and decided that the altruistic act provides the best possible option for its own genes to be passed on. A classic example of this is the wild rabbit, who, if threatened by a predator, drums its feet on the ground to warn others of the approaching danger. Many other species behave in a similar manner: one individual sounds the warning which, as well as warning others, inevitably draws attention to itself, thus making it more vulnerable to the danger. The question is whether this behaviour is altruistic or selfish.

To work out the answer, we need to go back to Darwin's principle of natural selection, which says that an individual will act in such a way as to *enhance* its own survival – in other words, just the opposite of altruism. Far from solving the problem, this makes it seem even more complicated. The only possible solution is that while the behaviour appears altruistic, it is in fact selfish on behalf of its species, and will in fact meet the Darwinian principle of natural selection. To make sense of this, we need to think in sociobiological terms (see page 287) and concentrate on genetic issues. Consider the altruistic rabbit, not as a furry, friendly little animal, but rather as a collection of genes. If we argue that the main goal of the animal – the rabbit – is to propagate its own genes in as many ways as possible, then – if we assume the altruistic rabbit is a parent (which is most likely) – by sacrificing itself it allows its own offspring to escape. Since every one of the offspring has half the parent's genes, if four offspring escape and the parent does not, then the 'account' stands at a profit: one whole set of genes lost, four half sets of genes saved. This is what sociobiologists call **kin selection** (see also page 289). It takes Darwin's theory of natural selection and, rather than looking at the survival of the individual, looks at the survival of the genes which are repeated in its kin. The animal acts in order to ensure that the maximum possible number of its genes survive. This is the concept of **inclusive fitness** for survival, and differs from individual fitness for survival. Other forms of altruism exist where, for example, one animal will do something for another fully expecting the behaviour to be reciprocated at some later date. Finally, there is reciprocal behaviour, as for example in the symbiotic relationship between the cleaner fish and the shark. While this is not altruistic behaviour in the strict sense, it does imply a form of working together.

Social co-operation in non-human animals

We now move one stage further from altruism, but still recognising that animals can work together for a common goal. We consider **social co-operation**, also sometimes called **mutualism**, in three specific contexts:

- co-operation in defence;
- co-operation in attack; and
- co-operation in what we can call general helping behaviour.

The 'bottom line' for all animals is to stay alive as long as possible and to produce as many offspring as possible. In contrast to the predator–prey relationships discussed above, we now consider the ways in which animals co-operate in a social manner to assist each other in terms of defence from predators. There are two forms of co-operation: the first within a species, the second between species. The principle at work in both cases is that co-operation provides a higher chance of survival than remaining alone.

<u>Co-operation in defence</u>   This is a common tactic which many species practise. The principle is simply that large numbers provide protection, can confuse or daunt a predator, and an individual within the group will always 'think' it won't be the one that gets eaten.

<u>Co-operation in attack</u>   The classic example in this situation is the co-operation between female members of a pride of lions when tracking and making a kill. An extension of this principle is the case of a pack of hyenas co-operating to drive the lionesses away from the kill so that they may feed.

<u>General helping behaviour</u>   This can take a variety of forms. Some species will co-operate in feeding – an individual honey-bee, for example, will return to the hive to give direction and distance information to a good food source. Other species – deer, for example – will wander and forage in groups. In this case, the weaker animals are likely to be led to food that they might otherwise not find. There is also the question of vigilance – with many pairs of eyes and ears, a group feeding or just travelling is more likely to become aware of danger than is a sole individual.

Think about it

- Observe a flock of starlings descend on crumbs you have thrown out in the winter. Is this a case of group vigilance?

Another example of helping behaviour occurs in certain species, such as the dwarf mongoose, where some individuals act as 'helpers' to others, usually with respect to the care of the young. In most cases, the helper is a close relative and will breed in later seasons.

Attachment
In the context of this unit, **attachment** has to do with the relationship between a newborn and its parent. It (almost) always involves a relationship that has within it elements of emotion and dependency. The key words in discussing these early relationships are: **precocial**, **altricial**, **imprinting** and **bonding**.

Precocial and altricial species

- **Precocial** species are those whose young are born in a stage of development such that they can survive with no or very little support from the parents. Examples are many species of birds, primates, horses, chickens and ducks.
- **Altricial** species are those whose young at birth are totally dependent on the parents for survival. Examples include rabbits, rats and the domestic cat.

Think about it

- If you have not met these two terms before, devise a memory aid to ensure you remember which is which.

There are a number of other significant differences between precocial and altricial species which are generally true (but there are exceptions):

- Precocial species usually have long gestation periods, a long life span and a large brain. As you would expect, this leads to a more complex set of social behaviours. Typical examples are the primates – monkeys, chimpanzees, apes.
- Altricial species, on the other hand, tend to be the opposite. They have a short gestation period, large numbers of young who are very dependant immediately post-birth and for some time after birth, a short life span and a small brain – all of which lead to less complex social behaviour. Examples are the domestic cat, rabbits and rats.

Think about it

- What about the human animal? Are we precocial or altricial?
- List the features of precocial and altricial mammals, then circle those features which apply to the human newborn.

If you now refer to the chart on page 303 you will see that, with one or two exceptions, the human infant fits the precocial criteria.

The exceptional feature is that the human newborn requires attention for a considerable period of time following birth. Children remain totally dependent for several years.

Think about it

- Think of young children you know. At what age would you say they could survive without their parents or some other adult?
- Why is it that the human child needs so much attention?

Features of precocial and altricial species		
Feature	**Precocial**	**Altricial**
Gestation period	Long*	Short
Brain size	Large*	Small
Life span	Long*	Short
Social behaviour	Complex*	Simple
Number of young	Few*	Many
Dependency post-birth	No	Yes*
Able to move independently at birth	Yes	No*
Senses	Developed	Poorly developed
Examples	Primates, horses, chickens, ducks	Cats, rabbits
Attachment process (see pages 302–5)	Mostly imprinting	Bonding*

*Features of the human infant

Gould (1978) suggests that the reason the human child needs so much attention is due to the size of the human brain. Because the brain is large, the head is also large, but other parts of the body are not as well developed. If the child were to be born more fully developed, then the brain and the head would be proportionally larger – which would make birth virtually impossible. As a result, the child is born with a well-developed brain, but is underdeveloped in other areas.

Imprinting and bonding

To recap, **precocial** species bear young that are virtually independent at birth, while **altricial** species bear young that are virtually dependent at birth. **Imprinting** is usually associated with precocial, while **bonding** is usually associated with altricial species.

<u>Imprinting</u>   In ethological terms, imprinting is the development of the relationship of the newborn to its (usually, but not always – see below) mother. It is a pattern of learning that occurs quite rapidly during the **critical period** and which is exceedingly hard to break. The critical period – the time span when imprinting can take place – is usually only a few hours long; it starts either at birth or shortly after birth. If the animal is isolated for this period of time, it is possible for it to imprint later. If isolated for a longer time, imprinting is highly unlikely and it is possible that the animal's subsequent behaviour will not develop normally.

The term 'critical' suggests a strictly limited time span, and that imprinting can only occur in this period. For this reason, the term **sensitive period** is sometimes used, but this term is less accurate and has a number of other applications. It does, however, allow for a more flexible period in which imprinting may occur.

A classic case of imprinting

The classic study (though not the first) was conducted by Lorenz, an Austrian ethologist, in the 1930s. He set up an experiment where he took a clutch of goose eggs and allowed half of them to incubate and hatch with the mother goose; the other half he allowed to incubate and then hatch in his presence, so the first thing the goslings saw was Lorenz himself. The 'normally' hatched goslings followed the mother goose, on whom they had imprinted; while the other half followed Lorenz, on whom they had imprinted, wherever he went. In the case of goslings, the critical period starts when they are able to move and ends when they develop a fear of strangers. These limits hold true for most species.

Bonding   This is similar to imprinting in that it concerns the relationship between a parent and its young. The main difference is that bonding, which is more often used in the case of primates, takes a longer time to form – often several years. Bonding serves the same purpose as imprinting, in that it is an attachment mechanism of the newborn to its parent. The mechanism has evolved to provide protection for the newborn to enable it to survive.

A classic case of bonding

Classic studies in attachment and bonding include work by Harlow (1959) with rhesus monkeys. He set up a number of conditions where the newborn monkeys were reared with and without parents, and with 'parents' made either of plain steel mesh with a feeding bottle or of the same mesh but covered with soft fabric and no feeding bottle. The thrust of this work was to see if the bonding depended on feeding – that is, does the newborn attach to the animal feeding it? Harlow concluded that attachment had more to do with the comfort that the newborn gained rather than the feeding. This was based on his observation that the newborn monkeys went more readily to the 'soft' parent.

We have seen that there is a certain overlap between the four terms precocial, altricial, imprinting and bonding, and the division between them is not sharp. In the context of attachment, there is one other dimension to consider. What is the connection between the stage of the animal's development at birth and bonding mechanisms? The answer is fairly straightforward:

- The offspring that are mobile immediately following birth – precocial species – are very vulnerable to predation and other forms of harm. Imprinting therefore evolved as the mechanism by which these young identified and stayed close to their parent, who could then look after them.
- Species which are altricial (that is, the offspring are born at an earlier developmental stage, are not mobile, often cannot see and have only limited development of their senses) need much more parental attention and nurture, often for an extended period. In the case of these species, attachment takes the form of bonding.

To sum up, attachment is an evolutionary relationship between parent and newborn. This involves the development of a bond between the parent and the newborn and may take up to several years to develop fully. A specialised form of bonding is imprinting, which occurs in only some species. Imprinting takes place during a sensitive period, usually a matter of hours or days immediately following birth. Imprinting normally occurs in precocial species, bonding in altricial species. This is shown schematically as follows:

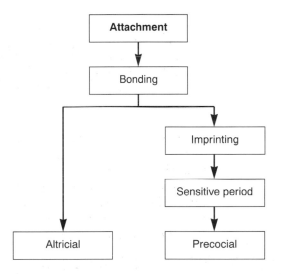

Signalling systems in non-human animals

This section is about communication in animals. At the most basic level, communication is sending something from one location to another.

In more formal terms, **communication theory** holds that there is a sender, a message to be sent which is then encoded, a medium over which the message is transmitted, and a receiver who can decode the message. As an example: I am the sender, the message is about comparative psychology, the medium is the printed word, you are the receiver. The code we are using is the English language, which is understood by both parties. That has described the mechanics of communication. It says nothing, however, about why I am sending the message in this way and what you are going to do about it.

There are many other communications which also send messages which, by definition, must also follow the same stages, but which also can be automatic and ritualised. The rabbit's thumping the ground with a foot, for example, is a clear means of communication. Another example is the bird's call when its territory is being invaded. A different form of animal communication is that of the whale: whales have the capability to communicate up to three miles underwater; they also use sonar to identify underwater objects and to detect prey.

A relatively sophisticated system of warning sounds has evolved in vervet monkeys (Byrne, 1991). They have different warning calls for different predators: a bark for a leopard, a cough for an eagle and a chutter for a snake. Whenever they hear the warning, they act in an appropriate way to escape the danger:

Communication system of the vervet monkey		
Predator	**Warning sound**	**Means of escape**
Leopard	Bark	Climb tree
Eagle	Cough	Hide in bushes
Snake	Chutter	Stand up to look, then run away

This is clearly a very effective means of species-specific communication.

An important point in the evolution of communication systems in animals is **coevolution behaviour**: the way that the evolution of, say, courtship behaviour and hence communication by the male coevolved with the responding female behaviour. They both evolved together, with one influencing the other (as in the predator–prey relationship – see page 292).

The question that we attempt to answer in the following pages is: are these examples of effective species-specific communication examples of *language*?

Natural animal language

Picking up on Unit 4 and the discussion on communication in this unit, we now discuss what we can call 'natural' animal language.

Something to do

• Review the section on language in Unit 4. Pay particular attention to the discussion on defining language (see pages 187–8).

It is reasonable to argue that if we look at our nearest relatives in the animal kingdom in terms of the way that they communicate, and see how – or indeed if – they use language, then we are most likely to establish whether or not any animal possesses language naturally. Genetically speaking, the chimpanzee is the closest to the human animal. For this reason, it is the chimpanzee that is most usually chosen for animal 'language' investigations.

The problem in trying to establish whether or not the communication system of chimpanzees – and, for that matter, other species – can be considered as 'language' is that it is us, the human animal, that is trying to define animal language in terms of human language, which is of course a hugely complicated system. So maybe we are asking the wrong questions when *we* study animal language? The whole point of animal communication is that it has evolved, more precisely coevolved, to enable the organisation of the communication to influence the behaviour of the receiver of the communication. It can be argued that evolutionary forces have positively influenced the effectiveness of the communication.

Another danger when discussing animal communication is to assume we are only talking about auditory vocalisation (which is perhaps an example of the problem of trying to place animal language into the same framework as human language). The animal world is able to communicate using a much larger range of 'channels' than the human animal. Depending on the species, animals are able to communicate using auditory, chemical and visual means, and sometimes also touch. In each of these cases, there is a trade-off between the effectiveness and the cost, usually in terms of energy used. The general rule in all forms of communication is that while the communication has, in most cases, a specific purpose, perhaps to attract a mate or threaten a rival, the very process of making the communication advertises the presence of the initiator of the communication, and this can pose a serious threat.

If we try to sum up the various elements of natural animal communication, we would find that for most (if not all) species the communication system would involve:

- vocalisation that was meaningful, which involved various sounds, but was not linguistic (that is, it did not have a system of grammar or syntax); and
- a range of non-verbal communication, including facial expressions, bodily movements, chemical 'marking' and touch, that were intentional but were learned behaviour and for the most part fixed in terms of their use and interpretation.

Think about it

- The animal world uses a variety of 'channels' (auditory, chemical, visual, touch) to communicate. How many 'channels' does the human animal use? Make a list.

Attempts to teach animals language

We have accepted that animals communicate, and can do so in quite sophisticated ways. What we have not yet shown is whether animals can learn language in the sense of what we as humans mean by language.

The debate over this matter has been long, and at times furious. Some psychologists argue that studies with animals clearly show 'language'; while others reject that and say that yes, animals do communicate, but it is not language – a view which may imply more about the human–animal distinction than about language itself. Is the human animal unique or not? This is another aspect of the great debate, with the answer usually 'yes' *because* we are able to use a very complex language to communicate with each other. If we were to move the debate into philosophical and theological areas – as some do – then it becomes even more complicated (see Lea, 1984, for a brief but wide-ranging discussion on this topic).

In the context of this debate, we shall concern ourselves with the attempts to teach animals language. 'Language' here means spoken English, American sign language (ASL or Ameslan) or symbols. The table below lists some of the major studies that have been conducted in this area.

Animal language studies				
Date	**Animal's name**	**Species**	**Researchers**	**'Language'**
1933	Gua	Chimp	Kellogg and Kellogg	English
1950	Vicki	Chimp	Hayes	English
1969	Washoe	Chimp	Gardner and Gardner	ASL
1972	Sarah	Chimp	Premack and Premack	Symbols
1977	Lana	Chimp	Rumbaugh	Keyboard
1978	Koko	Gorilla	Patterson	ASL
1978	Austin & Sherman	Chimps	Rumbaugh et al.	Keyboard
1979	Michael	Chimp	Patterson	ASL
1979	Nim	Chimp	Terrace et al.	ASL
1980	Cody	Orang-utan	Laidler	English
1983	Alex	Grey parrot	Pepperberg	English
1984	Akeakamai	Dolphin	Herman et al.	Symbols
1988	Kanzi	Chimp	Savage-Rumbaugh et al.	Symbols/ keyboard

However, before we discuss these studies we need first to return to the question of a definition of 'language'. See page 309 for an outline of what defining language involves. Without some form of definition we cannot determine whether or not the animal is using language.

Think about it

- Refer to Hockett's list of the design features of language (page 309). Which of these apply to animal 'language'? Make a list.

Having discussed definitions of language, we now return to the research studies conducted in the field of teaching language to animals. In the interests of clarity, we consider just a few of the studies listed above.

Defining language

The definition usually centres on **intentionality** – the intention deliberately to communicate a message (for example: 'Please pass the jam', 'What do you make of the present government?' or 'Discuss the view that animals possess language') – and **displacement** – the ability to communicate about things displaced in time or space (for example, last year's holiday, the Christmas story or pre-historic development of tools).

In Unit 4, we considered the three key properties that language has, but a communication system does not (Brown, 1973):

- **semanticity:** the language can express complex meaning;
- **productivity:** the language is capable of infinite expression;
- **displacement:** the language can communicate information displaced in time and space.

Considerably earlier than Brown, Hockett (1959) devised what he called the design features of language. He proposed 16 features which are required to define language and which are found in human language.

The design features of language		
1.	Vocal/auditory	Sounds are transmitted.
2.	Broadcast/direction	Listeners can tell direction.
3.	Rapid fading	Sound fades quickly.
4.	Total feedback	Sender can hear what they are saying.
5.	Interchangeability	Sender and receiver can both send and receive.
6.	Specialisation	The language can stand alone.
7.	Semanticity	The language has meaning.
8.	Arbitrariness	The language units (words) do not resemble their meaning.
9.	Traditional transmission	The language is capable of being passed to later generations.
10.	Learnability	Variations of the language can be learnt.
11.	Discreteness	Meaning is communicated by rules, e.g. words, grammar.
12.	Duality	Sentences are made up from words; words are made up from morphemes.
13.	Displacement	Things displaced in time and space can be understood.
14.	Productivity	The language is capable of infinite novel expression.
15.	Prevarication	The language can be used to tell lies.
16.	Reflexiveness	The user can use a language to talk about themselves.

The fact that Hockett's work pre-dates most of the studies into animal language makes it free from the criticism that it was designed to show that animals are not capable of language. That may seem a strange comment, but the study of animal language has come in for fierce criticism both from within the field and from outside.

- **Washoe** (Gardner and Gardner, 1969) In this study, the Gardners trained Washoe to use American sign language (ASL) by using a number of different techniques, for example modelling the sign and reinforcement; they also placed Washoe's hands into the appropriate positions. Washoe learned over 100 signs and could use them to construct two- and three-word sentences.
- **Sarah** (Premack and Premack, 1972) Sarah was taught to use a different 'language': plastic symbols that stuck magnetically to a board. Again, reinforcement was used, sometimes in the form of a symbol (a banana), sometimes verbal encouragement. Sarah was able to use some complex forms of speech – 'if', 'then', 'same' – but never initiated a 'conversation'.
- **Nim** (Terrace et al., 1979) Nim's full name was Nim Chimpsky – a play on words. Terrace spent five years working with Nim and concluded that while chimps may be capable of learning a large vocabulary, they are not able to produce original sentences. Terrace further argued that in studies where an animal did produce apparent sentences it was more a case that the animal had been operationally conditioned, than that it was able to create language.
- **Kanzi** (Savage-Rumbaugh et al., 1988) In this study, Savage-Rumbaugh and her colleagues tried to eliminate criticisms of previous studies. Kanzi, a pygmy chimpanzee, was taught to use an electronic keyboard with symbols which, when touched, produce the relevant word. The trainer used spoken English to talk to Kanzi, who responded using the keyboard.

As noted earlier, the arguments for and against animal language have been heated. Many have centred on methodological issues within a study. Terrace (1979), for example, based on his work with Nim, was critical of earlier studies. He argued that the animal trainers were giving the animal clues and that the animal was simply imitating – this despite double-blind conditions. (Double-blind is a research procedure where the participant and the researcher are both in the dark concerning the real purpose of the experiment.)

Perhaps a general conclusion (after Terrace) is that animals are capable of achieving a certain ability in terms of language, but that this rapidly plateaus and may be related to cognitive functioning as much as to the language itself.

Something to investigate

- Research other animal language studies (refer to the list on page 308).
- Write a paragraph on the ethical issues involved in training animals to use language.

Behavioural analysis

The final section of our study into comparative psychology concerns the analysis of behaviour. We look first at learning theory; then learning in the natural environment; and finally evolutionary explanations of human behaviour.

Think about it

- What is 'learning'? How would you define it?

Learning theories

In a technical sense, there are generally thought to be four elements present in the process of **learning**. These are:

- relative permanence – not just short-term changes;
- potential – the learning may not be immediately obvious;
- reinforcement – to learn, reinforcement is needed; and
- practice – the learning needs to be repeated.

As a result of these four elements, learning can be defined as: 'a relatively permanent change in behaviour due to experience'. There are other ways to define learning, such as: 'acquiring knowledge' or 'knowledge gained by study', but the above definition, or some variation on it, is the most frequently used technical definition.

Something to investigate

- The FIDO principle of learning is outlined below. Take each of the four elements and expand the explanation by cross-referring to other theories/principles. Use as many sources as you have access to.

The FIDO principle of learning

FIDO is an acronym. Words refer to the process of learning:

- **Frequency** The more frequently the material to be remembered is repeated, the better the learning.
- **Intensity** The more visual, intense, bright, personal, etc. the message, the better the learning.
- **Duration** Short, focused, relevant items are better attended to and therefore better learned.
- **Over again** Learning occurs with repetition – particularly in smaller, manageable bits.

The next question to consider is why it is that humans are so well equipped to learn.

Think about it

- Think of the reasons why *you* are so well equipped to learn. Draw up a list.

Your answer should have been based on the notion that the human animal has a huge capacity to adapt to different situations or environments. For example, one minute I can be sitting reading a book on the beach; minutes later I can be swimming 30 metres down in the ocean; while the next day, or perhaps when on my next holiday, I can be 5000 metres up in the mountains, speaking a different language and dealing with temperatures of minus 30° Celsius.

It is doubtful if any other organism can adapt to the enormous variety of conditions and environments that the human animal can.

There are a number of different theories that account for the way that we – humans and non-humans – learn. In this section we consider four:

- classical conditioning;
- operant conditioning;
- social learning theory; and
- cognitive behaviourism.

While it is important to recognise these as four separate theories, in practice there is considerable overlap. The order in which we discuss these theories is more or less chronological.

Something to do

- Prepare a summary chart into which you can insert the relevant data as we discuss the four learning theories. The chart should look something like this:

Summary of learning theories				
	Classical conditioning	**Operant conditioning**	**Social learning theory**	**Cognitive behaviourism**
Theorist/date				
Main points				

Classical conditioning The key to understanding classical conditioning is that once conditioned you cannot help it (unless, of course, you are reconditioned). It is an automatic or, more accurately, an **autonomic response**. The conditioning is also sometimes called **Pavlovian conditioning**.

A classic case of classical conditioning

Ivan Pavlov (1849–1936) worked in Russia as a physiologist. He was studying the digestive system of dogs (in 1901) when he made the observation that was to lead to what we now call Pavlovian conditioning or, more usually, classical conditioning. What Pavlov discovered (quite by accident, as is so often the case in science) is that a *response* can be controlled by changing the *stimulus* that causes the response.

In the course of his investigations into the digestive system of dogs, Pavlov was measuring the saliva that the dogs produced under a number of different conditions. What Pavlov observed was that the dogs salivated when they were fed – which is quite normal and to be expected. What he went on to observe, however, and what was not expected and which went on to provide the basic proposition of classical conditioning, was that the dogs in his laboratory started to salivate when they heard the clanking of the food pails, even when there was no food present and hence no cause for them to salivate. The dogs had *associated* clanking pails with food, and as a consequence had started to salivate.

Pavlov now turned his attention to this new phenomenon and started to investigate it more fully. In the now classic study, a dog was strapped into a harness in the laboratory and meat powder was placed on its tongue. This caused the dog to salivate. In the next stage, a bell was rung just as the meat powder was placed on the dog's tongue; and of course the dog salivated. This pairing of bell and food was repeated many times. For the third stage, the bell was rung, but no meat powder was placed on the dog's tongue – despite this, the dog salivated.

Pavlov's terms for these various conditions are as follows:

- the food – unconditioned stimulus (US);
- salivation – (before and during conditioning) unconditioned response (UR); (after conditioning) conditioned response (CR);
- the bell – (during conditioning) neutral stimulus (NS); (after conditioning) conditioned stimulus (CS).

Drawing this conditioning process schematically, we get:

The process of classical or Pavlovian conditioning

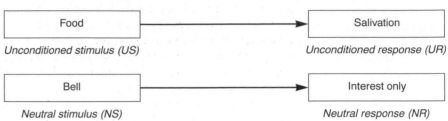

Before conditioning begins

| Food | → | Salivation |
Unconditioned stimulus (US) — Unconditioned response (UR)

| Bell | → | Interest only |
Neutral stimulus (NS) — Neutral response (NR)

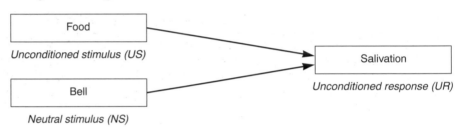

During conditioning

| Food |
Unconditioned stimulus (US)

Salivation
Unconditioned response (UR)

| Bell |
Neutral stimulus (NS)

After conditioning

| Bell | → | Salivation |
Conditioned stimulus (CS) — Conditioned response (CR)

The learning process that the dog underwent is explained in two different ways:

- Classical conditioning is explained by **behaviourists** as a simple form of learning in which a stimulus (bell) causes a response (salivation) usually brought on by another stimulus (food). This occurs as a result of the two stimuli being repeatedly paired.
- More recently, **cognitive psychologists** have come to view classical conditioning in a similar but significantly different way. Pavlov's bell and the resulting salivation occurred because of the way the bell *represented* the meat powder.

The behaviourist focuses on the mechanical aspects, the cognitive on the information being processed.

Something to do

- As a cross-curricular activity, read the section on therapies in Unit 8 (pages 419–30) and identify applications of classical conditioning.

Operant conditioning If the key to classical conditioning is association between a stimulus and a response, and a recognition that it functions via the animal's autonomic system; the key to understanding **operant conditioning** is 'trial and error'. In this system of learning, the emphasis is on the consequence of learning. Operant conditioning is sometimes also known as **instrumental conditioning**, although there are differences: the main one being that in instrumental conditioning the organism must respond in a very specific manner. This makes instrumental conditioning a special type of operant conditioning.

If we associate Pavlov with formulating classical conditioning, then we need to associate the American Edward L. Thorndike (1874–1949) with operant conditioning.

A classic case of operant conditioning

Thorndike conducted his early research in America in the 1890s by studying the way that domestic cats 'escaped' from a cage. He observed (note again that observation is always the first stage in the scientific process) that the cats made fewer and fewer random efforts to escape and that their behaviour became more and more deliberate and directed at 'operating' in such a way as to escape. Thorndike called this the **law of effect**

The essence of the law of effect is that in a given situation a behavioural response is strengthened by being rewarded. Another way of looking at it is to say that an organism's responses that are voluntary will be strengthened by **reinforcement**. A key difference between classical and operant conditioning is that the response in classical conditioning is involuntary, whereas in operant conditioning it is voluntary.

Another important researcher in this field is B.F. Skinner (1904–90). His emphasis was on precisely documented empirical data on the behaviour of animals. He conducted much of his work with pigeons. One of his better-known experiments involved teaching pigeons using operant techniques to play table tennis! Important contributions made by Skinner include:

- the **Skinner box**, in which he placed animals, that was so designed to enable him to study and record precisely their behaviour;
- the design of the first **programmed teaching machine**, a piece of equipment – still in use today – in which learning occurs in small, very precise steps which do not progress until the previous material has been fully learned and, in most cases, the learner has passed a test demonstrating their understanding of the material being studied.

Reinforcement A key concept in operant conditioning is **reinforcement**. This can be defined as any stimulus that increases the probability that the response will be repeated. There are two main groups of reinforcers: positive and negative.

- **Positive reinforcers** are such things as food or perhaps approval.
- **Negative reinforcers** work in that the rate of response increases when they are removed. Electric shock is often used as a negative reinforcer.

A **reward** is a term that is sometimes used synonymously with reinforcer. However, 'reward' suggests that the organism understands – cognitively – that it is being rewarded for some sort of action. Skinner did not approve of this concept and so preferred 'reinforcer'.

Punishment is not the same as a negative reinforcer in that it uses aversive behaviours to decrease the frequency of the undesirable behaviour.

Other aspects of operant conditioning are **schedules of reinforcement** and **shaping**.

Shaping This is the process of breaking down a complex behaviour into a number of component parts and then using reinforcement to learn each component before moving on to the next. A classic example of shaping is the way parents teach young children to use the toilet. The first (component of) behaviour to be reinforced might simply be to get the child to ask to use the toilet; a second might be to get the child to use and flush the toilet; and so on until the whole process is learned.

Schedules of reinforcement This has to do with the frequency that a desired behaviour is reinforced.

- **Continuous reinforcement** is when every time the behaviour occurs it is reinforced. This leads to rapid learning, but can also lead to the loss or extinction of the behaviour once the reinforcement is stopped.
- **Intermittent reinforcement** is when reinforcement occurs often, but not on every occasion. This usually leads to more long-term learning.

Something to do

- As you did with classical conditioning, read Unit 8, pages 419–30, and identify applications of operant conditioning.

Social learning theory

Social learning theory (SLT) is usually associated with the work of Albert Bandura and Robert Walters (1963), who stressed the place of observation and imitation of role models in the learning process. Also used in SLT, is direct instruction, which in turn relies on cognitive processes.

Social learning theory grew out of a behaviourist tradition, where learning is important in terms of human behaviour; but SLT theorists see a major role for cognitive processes. While the behaviourists focus on the environment and learning through repetition and reinforcement, SLT theorists believe that the individual is capable of changing their own behaviour and so emphasise intentional learning by direct observation. SLT theorists are also influenced by the humanist tradition in that they believe – as do humanists – that our values and expectations play a significant role in what we choose to do.

As the theory has developed, it has emerged that some role models are more influential than others. People will imitate those they like or respect, and those they consider attractive and powerful. Imitation is also powerful for same-sex models. Role models do not only influence social aspects of behaviour, they have also been shown to have a powerful influence on personality development, particularly the personality development of children.

A classic case of television watching and behaviour

In a now classic study, and incidentally one of the first to show a direct link between watching television and behaviour, Bandura et al. (1963) showed nursery-aged children a film of aggressive behaviour. The film had two endings: one where the aggressor was rewarded, the other where the aggressor was punished. Having seen the film, the children were allowed to play freely, but under observation. Children who saw the aggression rewarded acted significantly more aggressively with the toys than did the children who saw the aggression punished.

Cognitive behaviourism

In classical and operant theories of learning, the emphasis is on a mechanical relationship between the environment and a response. Social learning theory emphasises aspects of these theories, particularly the observation and imitation aspects and the place of the role model, and started to involve cognitive processes. **Cognitive behaviourism** continues this trend and places much more emphasis on the cognitive processes taking place when learning occurs.

Edward Tolman (1886–1959), an American, came from a behaviourist background. He is one of a number of theorists who based their work on the scientific nature of behaviourism but who believed that there was more to learning than the mechanistic views of behaviourism. Tolman was concerned with what happened in the process of learning a new behaviour – for example, the place of expectation and purpose, and also belief and value, but more particularly spatial representation in the form of **cognitive maps**.

Evidence for the existence of cognitive maps came from Tolman's work with rats running mazes. It was shown that if a learned pathway to a goal – the food at the end of the maze – was shut off, the rat would choose the shortest alternative route to the goal. In other words, the rats had a picture – a spatial representation – of the maze, rather as you do if your normal route to school or work is barred by roadworks.

Something to investigate

- Why do you think behaviourism was primarily an American movement? What was happening in Europe at about the same time (the first half of the 20th century)? Do some research and write notes.

We can sum up cognitive behaviourism by saying that it involves all the other forms of learning, but in addition it brings to bear on the process of learning the learner's own value system, expectations and motivation.

Learning in the natural environment

Foraging

The term **foraging** has to do with animal feeding behaviours in a natural setting. It includes the search for food and also aspects such as storing food and avoiding predators. The essential idea concerns the balance between costs and benefits (a principle that applies to many animal behaviours). The principle of natural selection operates to provide the maximum benefits.

A classic case of foraging

In a study by Lima et al. (1985) (cited in Krebs and Davies, 1993), the trade-off between feeding and danger was studied by feeding chocolate-chip cookies to squirrels in a park. In their study, Lima et al. observed the behaviour of squirrels being fed large pieces of cookie and small pieces of cookie. In the case of large pieces, the squirrel would take the piece up a tree and eat it, thus avoiding being vulnerable to predators while out in the open. With small pieces of cookie, the squirrel did the same – which is obviously not efficient in terms of energy intake (the cookie) balanced against energy loss (running down and back up the tree). The point is that if energy were the only concern, then the squirrel would eat the food where it was; but the squirrel also has to balance danger with food value – hence the constant to and fro from the food source, which equals energy but danger, to the tree, which equals security but hunger.

Homing and migration

Homing behaviour can be described simply as the ability to return to where you started from. **Migration**, on the other hand, tends to concern the movement of large groups of animals for reasons such as climate, breeding or food supply. The two are essentially the same, any difference being more to do with numbers than principle. Classic examples are the salmon and the homing pigeon. The question that we need to discuss concerns the mechanisms by which animals are able to 'home' or migrate.

In the case of the Atlantic salmon, it starts its life in small streams and rivers in Europe, travels downstream and then some 4000 miles to the Sargasso Sea in the Atlantic to feed, returning to the same stream where it was born. It then swims upstream to spawn; then, in a weakened state, it usually dies. Some fish make the journey once or twice, others three or even four times. This describes what the salmon does, but not how it finds the same small stream that it left a year before.

In the case of the homing pigeon, the bird can be taken hundreds of miles away and within a few hours it is back in its own loft in the back garden of its owner. Again, how does it manage this difficult navigational feat?

The short answer is that we still do not know with any degree of certainty exactly how the pigeon, and other homing animals, navigate with such precision. The longer answer has a number of different possibilities. Homing pigeons have been shown to have **magnetite** within their skull, which is a material sensitive to magnetic fields. It is rather like having a compass in your head. Also, the sun is a reliable device for navigation, providing you know the time of day. Since it has been shown that pigeons have an internal 'clock', this is not a problem.

In sum, the evidence that animals can 'home' over long distances is irrefutable. We still do not know exactly how they do this. It is most likely a combination of the sun, magnetic fields, terrain, smell and possibly extremely low-frequency sound. All or some of these are likely to contribute to the explanation.

Evolutionary explanations of human behaviour

Why are we the way we are, and does this influence our behaviour?

It is almost impossible to use the word 'evolution' without thinking 'Darwin'. We have discussed Darwinism in terms of animal behaviour; here we discuss the evolution of human behaviour. To do this we need to go back a very long time and in the process identify those aspects which set the human apart from the animal. This is a huge and complicated topic, but for our immediate purposes we shall note three basic aspects:

- First is the fact that when we move we are upright – we are **bipeds**.
- Second is the size of our brain – we really do have a huge brain.
- Third, as discussed above, we have language, an ability which is linked to **encephalisation** which, put simply, means that as the brain has evolved and grown it has taken over more and more of the control functions of the body, and due to its size and complexity has 'allowed' higher-order skills, such as language, to develop to their current state.

These changes were mostly to do with human biological development; but with the advent of language, cultural evolution took place. (An interesting question to consider is whether we should speak of cultural *evolution* or cultural *development*.) With the ability to communicate, societies grew culturally, and while biological evolution is measured in very long time-periods, cultural development is not. To make the point: the human brain has taken perhaps 2 million years to reach its present size; someone who is 50 years old will have seen major cultural changes in their lifetime; and someone born in the year 1900 will have experienced more cultural change in their lifetime than has occurred in all of history before 1900, the year they were born.

Toffler, in his book *Future Shock* (1970), which is concerned primarily with how people cope – or, more frequently, do not cope – with change, talks about what he calls 'the 800th lifetime'. He takes the last 50,000 years of man's existence, takes an average lifetime of 62½ years, divides one by the other and comes up with 800 lifetimes. Of these 800, he argues that as much has happened in the last one, as has happened in the first 799. His book is compelling reading and shows enormous insight into the culture and social and psychological implications of the changes (evolution?) that have occurred in the 20th century.

In evolutionary terms, man is at the apex of a huge variety of other species. The main reason for this is the size and complexity of the evolved human brain, which permits man to carry out ever more complex functions. Taking as an example the speed of a neural signal or message: in a worm, transmission moves at something like 100 centimetres per second; in man, it is something like 50,000 centimetres per second (and even this is slow compared to a computer). This gives man a huge evolutionary advantage in terms of his behaviour (Toffler, 1970).

Limitations of human behaviour

Notwithstanding the above, man is still limited when environmental input exceeds the rate at which all the data can be handled – which it frequently does (see the section on attention, Unit 4, pages 148–58). In this case, our image of reality – the world outside – becomes increasingly distorted and as a result reality and illusion are difficult to separate.

Think about it

• When you are next at a disco or rave, try to analyse all sensory input – noise, lights, visual, etc. – that is hitting you in a period of, say, 10 seconds. Can you sort out the real from the imaginary?

A second point concerning the limitation of behaviour as it has evolved is that while in the past evolution was slow and man adapted at the same rate, now evolution in cultural terms is much more rapid and man is not keeping up with it.

A suitable point to conclude this section is to return to the basic unit of evolution – the gene. Today, at the end of the 20th century, we are capable of engineering or manipulating that most basic unit. We have cloned a sheep, 'Dolly'. We have identified genes that cause illness and disease and are able to 'engineer' them in and out of the body to control the illness. We are living what only a few short years ago was called 'science fiction'. The 'bottom line' is that humankind, having been ruled by evolution for our total existence on this planet, now has the opportunity to control evolution, to shape our future.

Think about it

• If we are technologically capable of controlling genetics, do we have the moral ability to do so ethically? Have a discussion on the issues involved.

Revision and practice

● ●

Coursework opportunities

1. Carry out some naturalistic observation on territoriality in your back garden. Both blackbirds and robins are territorial. Observe their behaviour, particularly in winter when food is short and in spring when mating occurs. Write up your observations.

2. Investigate the effect of sound on chickens before hatching. Before you begin, you may like to read the original study: *Pre-Natal Imprinting* (Grier, J. B., Counter, S. A. and Shearer, W. M., 'Prenatal Auditory Imprinting in Chickens', *Science 155*, 1692–3, 1967). Think through the ethical implications very carefully before embarking on this project.

   Method: Obtain fertile chicken eggs and place in an incubator. About one week before hatching, expose the eggs to a regularly repeated auditory signal of some kind. The control group of eggs is handled in exactly the same way but do not 'hear' the signal. Upon hatching and when the chicks are mobile, expose *both* groups to the pre-natal signals and, from a second speaker, a different sound. Chicks in the experimental (exposed) group should move towards the familiar sound. The control chicks should show no preference for sound. Does this imply imprinting?

   (For more details of this practical, see Flanagan, C., *Psychology Practicals made Perfect*, Richard Ball Publishing, Birkenhead, 1993.)

3. Similar studies to the one described in 2 above have been conducted on human infants before birth, with the mother repeatedly reading aloud a set passage. Design your own study based on this idea.

4. Read Lima et al.'s study on foraging in the original source (see page 318). Then use their study as a model for an original piece of research on another aspect of 'learning in the natural environment'.

5. Construct a study to investigate lateral cradling of an infant. Does a/the mother/father cradle a baby in the left or right arm? Why? Write up the results of your investigation.

6. For additional coursework possibilities, refer to Krebs and Davies (1993). Suggestions are given at the end of each chapter.

● ●

Examination questions

Question 1 (a) Describe the nature of both predator–prey **and** symbiotic relationships in non-human animals. *(12 marks)*

(b) Assess the significance of these relationships to the animals concerned. *(12 marks)*

(AEB, Module Paper 4, Summer 1997)

Question 1: Unpacked Part (a) requires you to 'describe', i.e. 'to present evidence and knowledge of . . .' – clearly a Skill A question. Part (b) requires you to 'assess', i.e. 'an informed judgement based on strengths and limitations . . . a considered appraisal'. Clearly a Skill B question.

Keep your plan to one side of A4, make separate 'sub-plans' for parts (a) and (b), and show *how* you intend to use the plan.

Part (a) needs to cover both predator–prey and symbiotic relationships, so the introduction to part (a) could introduce both topics and briefly show how they relate:

- explain the evolution of the process;
- Endler's (1991) four stages;
- give examples;
- Krebs and Davies (1993) 'life–dinner principle';
- transition into symbiosis/reciprocal altruism;
- two topics, same species, different species;
- describe *how* the relationship works;
- describe evolutionary aspects.

Leave a couple of lines' space between the two parts in case you add something to the first part that you may have missed. (It is a good idea to do this between *paragraphs* too, for the same reason.)

Part (b) requires the assessment of *both* types of relationship.

In the predator–prey relationship:

- Coevolution is of key significance.
- This can involve the evolution of warning coloration, e.g. caterpillars with orange and black bands. This has advantages and disadvantages.
- Other adaptations and counter-adaptations occur, some of which have been tested, e.g. Sargent 81 on the wings of moths.

In symbiotic relationships:

- In a strictly symbiotic relationship, neither party could survive without the other.
- The relationship is open to exploitation by either party.
- The behaviour is not true altruism as each party gains without caring about the other.
- Weigh up the advantages and disadvantages to each party.

Question 1: Sample answer	This essay was written by a student under simulated exam conditions.
Comments	**Essay**
	(a) Both predator–prey and symbiotic relationships show interesting aspects of evolution and also the impact that evolution has on a
Good start	wide range of animal development.
	In the case of predator–prey relationships natural selection occurs as with all species, but the driving force for this is the relationship
Recognises key point	between the predator and its prey – the fact that they co-evolve. When the prey evolves stronger muscles and longer legs, it starts to out-run its predator. If this was to continue then the predator would catch less and less prey and as a consequence die off. However, natural selection operates by enabling the predator to evolve – really
Accurate description, but not very well expressed	co-evolve – so that natural selection in its case occurs to enable it to evolve in new ways so that it can catch the prey. This may occur in such a way to enable it to run faster so that it can keep up with the prey, or by developing new skills or strategies in other ways for example more cunning, better camouflage or working in packs. Sev-
Who/when?	eral writers have drawn parallels between this aspect of evolution and the 'arms-race' that occurred between east and west following the second world war.

Accurate

Accurate

In the case of symbiotic relationships the evolutionary aspects have less to do with predation and more to do with reciprocal altruism. Altruism in a literal sense means doing something for another without expecting anything in return. Reciprocal altruism is altruism but with the expectation that the other will 'return' your altruism.

Symbiosis exists within species, between different animal species, and between plant and animal species.

Generally a good description, but a little brief

One example of a symbiotic relationship is the shark or other large fish, and the cleaner fish. In this example the cleaner fish stays with the larger fish and 'cleans' scraps of food from its teeth and also small parasites that attach to the skin of the larger fish. In this case the cleaner has its meals provided and also gains from the protection of the larger fish. The larger fish 'recognises' this and does not eat the cleaner fish. There is one example of this that is more parasitical than symbiotic which is where another small fish *acts* like the cleaner fish but in fact takes a bite from the larger fish.

Opening sentence is a useful way to remind yourself of where you are going

Accurate, but needs to explain relevance to question

(b) The significance of these relationships to the animal concerned is very important. In the case of the predator–prey relationship the key factor is the co-evolution of the two species. If this did not happen then either the predator would go hungry and either evolve in a different direction or the prey would all be eaten and the species would die out, this in turn would have consequences for the predator as their food source would disappear. Endler (1991) has suggested that there are five stages in the process of predation: encounter, detection, identification, approach, and consumption. In all of these stages evolutionary processes have taken place between the two species to maintain the balance between the predator and its prey. When it comes to symbiosis the relationship between the two animals or species is equally significant. At the most basic level each animal gains from the relationship. The smaller fish gets food, protection, and often free transport, while the host or large fish gains by having its teeth cleaned and frequently harmful parasites removed from its skin. It is interesting that the 'cost' to each species in the relationship is nil and both gain from the attention of the other. This is a feature of the evolution of the process and is not recognised as such by the other animal.

Good general point

Rather untidy ending

General comments

Style/structure is good. Part (a) has good accurate description with some omissions; part (b) is fair with *some* strengths and limitations of the topic discussed.

Marks: part (a) $\dfrac{8}{12}$

part (b) $\dfrac{7}{12} = \dfrac{15}{24}$

Question 2 Critically consider the role of both genetic **and** environmental factors in adaptive behaviour of non-human animals.
(25 marks)

(AEB, Paper 1, Summer 1997)

Question 3   (a) Outline some of the main features of the ethological approach to animal behaviour. *(15 marks)*

                (b) Critically assess ethological explanations of animal behaviour. *(10 marks)*

                         (AEB, Paper 1, Summer 1997)

Question 4   Discuss the nature and consequences of sexual selection as it relates to mate choice **and** mate competition. *(24 marks)*

                         (AEB, Module Paper 4, January 1998)

Question 5   Describe and evaluate evolutionary explanations of **two** different aspects of **human** behaviour (e.g. altruism, mate choice and xenophobia). *(24 marks)*

                         (AEB, Module Paper 4, January 1998)

Question 6   (a) Describe different ways in which males and females invest in the rearing of their young. *(12 marks)*

                (b) Assess the implications of these sex-differences in parental investment. *(12 marks)*

                         (AEB, Module Paper 4, Summer 1997)

Question 7   (a) Consider the nature of parent–offspring conflict. *(12 marks)*

                (b) Assess the implications of this conflict. *(12 marks)*

                         (AEB, Module Paper 4, January 1997)

Selected reading list

Clamp, A. and Russell, J., *Comparative Psychology* (Hodder and Stoughton, 1998)

Krebs, J.R. and Davies, N.B., *An Introduction to Behavioural Ecology* (Blackwell Science Ltd, 3rd edn 1993)

Ridley, M., *Animal Behaviour* (Blackwell, 2nd edn 1995)

7 Developmental psychology: how do we become who we are?

This unit begins with a look at two basic issues in developmental psychology, followed by an explanation of the different approaches to, or perspectives on, developmental psychology. The Freudian view of psychosexual development is expanded in a separate section. The unit is then divided into three main sections, covering:

- **cognitive development** (make sure you are familiar with Unit 4, which will be referred to quite often in this section);
- **early socialisation** and **social development**: the psychology of how we learn to function as human beings;
- **adolescence**, **adulthood** and **old age**.

The main emphasis in developmental psychology is on childhood development; less emphasis is placed on what happens in developmental terms after childhood. The term 'developmental psychology', when G. Stanley Hall (1844–1924), a prominent American psychologist, first used it, meant development 'from womb to tomb'. Recently, however, developmental psychology has come to be almost synonymous with child (developmental) psychology, with terms such as 'adolescent psychology' and 'psychology of the aged' being used for other age groups. 'Life span' is still used by some in the original sense of developmental psychology.

Something to do

- Refer back to Unit 1, page 4, to remind yourself of the SQR4 study skill of getting to grips with a large section of new material. Put it into practice as you work through this unit.

Basic issues in developmental psychology

There are two main issues, sometimes called controversies, in developmental psychology that we need to consider:

- the Nature–Nurture debate; and
- the question of whether development occurs continuously or in stages.

The Nature–Nurture debate

In the context of developmental psychology, we can ask two questions:

- What aspects of our behaviour are genetically controlled and what happens as we grow? That is the **Nature** view.
- What aspects of our behaviour can we attribute to the way in which we are brought up – what are the environmental, social, perhaps human, influences on us? That is the **Nurture** view.

In the early 20th century, psychologists' opinions tended to polarise over this issue. People such as Watson, who was a founder of the behaviourist school, came down firmly on the Nurture side. Others, such as Piaget, favoured the Nature view. As we approach the end of the 20th century, there is just about universal agreement that both Nature and Nurture are involved in the child's development.

Development: continuous or in stages?

Rather like the Nature–Nurture issue, the debate over whether human development occurs in a steady, regular manner, or in an irregular, staged fashion, is less focused now than it once was.

- The behaviourists, for example Watson et al., believe that our development is a steady, continuous process based on the rate at which we learn new behaviours.
- Stage theorists such as Freud, Piaget, Erikson et al. (see below), all believe that development or maturation is an uneven process, with periods of little development followed by dramatic changes over a relatively short time. These theorists argue that however good or enriched the environment, however keen parents are that their child should speak, walk, or whatever – until the child is ready or has matured enough for the next stage, it will not happen. In other words, until the child has matured biologically, the next stage will not occur. Biological change precedes or prepares us for psychological change.

As with the Nature–Nurture issue, the behaviourists' view of steady continuous development came to be overtaken by stage theories.

To sum up, Nature theorists tend to be stage theorists, while Nurture theorists tend to hold to the continuous view.

Theoretical perspectives in developmental psychology

We now turn to a brief overview of four major theoretical perspectives that have shaped our understanding of human development. These are:

- the psychoanalytic approach (theorists: Freud, Erikson);
- the behaviourist approach (theorists: Watson, Bandura, Skinner);
- the cognitive approach (theorist: Piaget); and
- the ethological approach (theorist: Gesell).

A basic understanding of these theoretical approaches will enable a better understanding of many of the finer points discussed in the rest of the unit.

There are also a number of newer theories and approaches, which are only now emerging. These include **behavioural genetics**, which emphasises hereditary aspects; and an **information-processing approach**, which emphasises intellectual development. (For a more detailed discussion of these approaches, refer to Unit 2, Perspectives.)

The psychoanalytic approach

Sigmund Freud (1856–1939) originated psychoanalysis at the beginning of the 20th century. The emphasis, as far as development is concerned, is centred on the child's psychosexual development and the resolution of instinctual drives, all of which is conducted in the unconscious where the forces of the id, ego and superego are in dynamic conflict. (We look at Freud's stages of psychosexual development in more detail in the next section.) Early (childhood) experiences, particularly sexual, will have great influence on later behaviour (and personality).

The behaviourist approach

The behaviourist approach, sometimes called the learning approach, of theorists such as Watson followed the philosopher John Locke, who believed that children are born as a *tabula rasa*, literally a 'blank slate'. The child gradually develops over time and through learning and new experience. The child's environment will influence the direction, speed and kind of learning, and hence the child's development.

The cognitive approach

In this approach, cognitive development, with the child active in the process, is the key to the child's development. Piaget delineated four main, invariant, stages:

- sensorimotor;
- pre-operational;
- concrete operational; and
- formal operational.

As cognition develops, so the child is able to interpret the world around it and will learn and will develop its social behaviour and personality.

The ethological approach

The view in this approach is that development is mainly due to the way we mature biologically. Ethology, used in this context, is interdisciplinary and is concerned with the behaviour of animals in their natural setting. The theory is that children follow a timetable that is genetically controlled and development will occur when the genetic clock says so. Environment, learning and parental influence are of little consequence. As a theory, it has only minimal support today.

To conclude this section, it is worth noting that most developmental psychologists today are eclectic: they will not stick strictly with one approach, but will absorb into their theoretical stance elements of other approaches.

Freud's stages of psychosexual development

In this section we discuss the classic view of the psychosexual development of the child as proposed by Sigmund Freud.

We can define **psychosexual development** as that part of psychodynamic theory that deals with the developmental stages of childhood, each of which has a sexual focus, the satisfactory resolution of which is required for a normal and healthy **personality** in adulthood.

The following chart outlines the stages of psychosexual development.

Freud's stages of psychosexual development			
Stage	Age (approximate)	Sexual focus	Developmental task
Oral	Birth–1½ years	Mouth	Suck, bite, weaning
Anal	1½–3 years	Anus	Retention and elimination of faeces
Phallic	3–6 years	Genitals	Sexual gratification through self-stimulation
Latency	6–12 years	None	Sexual feelings are repressed
Genital	Puberty onwards	Genitals	Sexual feelings towards others

Freud came to the conclusion that childhood development was crucial to healthy adult functioning. To Freud it seemed that problems with an adult could frequently be traced back to the adult's early childhood experiences. From this he formulated the view that the child passes through a series of stages, each of which has a sexual focus and a corresponding task or action that requires a satisfactory resolution. In each of these stages the id, which is the pleasure-seeking part of the psyche, is focused on a pleasure-sensitive part of the body. The degree to which the child deals with these different tasks will determine the adult personality. The key factor in this process is **fixation**. In Freudian theory, fixation occurs when the child becomes 'stuck' in a given stage and fails to move onto the next stage. Fixation is caused by one of two extremes: either by excessive gratification, that is, put crudely, too much gratification; or by excessive frustration, which is the opposite, where the child lacks normal gratification. Fixation in any of the stages leads to related behaviour in the adult. Thus, Freud believed that, for example, fixation in the oral stage leads to overeating, dependency and other oral, or 'mouth', related conditions in adulthood.

The oral stage

This lasts from birth until the child is about 18 months old. The erotic gratification in this stage comes primarily from stimulation of the mouth. The child receives food through its mouth, but also contacts its environment by placing objects in its mouth. Freud considered that feeding the child is critical: the way the child is breast-fed, bottle-fed and later weaned, is of major importance.

The anal stage

At some time in their second year, the location for the child's erotic pleasure moves from the mouth to the anus – specifically bowel movements – and is achieved through either the retention or the expulsion of faeces. Just as feeding is crucial to the oral stage, toilet training is the key to the anal stage. The child quickly learns that it can exert some influence on its environment. It can become **anal-retentive** and delay expulsion of faeces, or the reverse and become **anal-expulsive**. Both of these extremes can – in Freudian theory – lead to related traits in adulthood. The anal-retentive personality may show excessive self control or extreme cleanliness. The anal-expulsive personality may imply a sloppy lifestyle, messy behaviour and possibly even **sadistic** traits.

The phallic stage

At about three years old, the child moves into the phallic stage in which the genital regions, the penis and the clitoris, become the focus for erotic stimulation and pleasure. At about the same time, the **Oedipus complex** emerges. In this the boy will develop an erotic preference for his mother and see his father as a threat. The girl will develop a special attachment to her father and see her mother as the threat – the **Electra complex**. This is complicated for the girl as she now realises that she has no penis and develops **penis envy**, blaming her mother for her lack of a penis. (Freud named these complexes after the Greek story of Oedipus who unknowingly kills his father and marries his mother.) For Freud, successful completion of this stage requires the child to resolve these conflicts and develop healthy relationships with both parents.

The latency stage

By about six years old, the child has started formal schooling and its sexuality becomes suppressed or **latent**, often because of an increasingly wide range of interests and friends, all of which are important to healthy development.

The genital stage

As puberty occurs, the child enters the **genital stage**, with a renewed interest in stimulation of the genital regions. The focus of the sexual energy is now outwards and onto the peer group of the opposite sex rather than inwards and onto the self as in the phallic stage. The genital stage comes to an end either during or at the end of adolescence.

For Freud, the psychosexual stages are absolutely critical to a proper understanding of the development of the psyche and equally crucial to an understanding of adult psychopathology. It is interesting to note that Freud would not tolerate opinions that contradicted his view of childhood development. As a consequence, he parted company with others of his period, such as Jung and Adler who both went on to develop their own psychodynamic theories: Jung's analytic psychology and Adler's individual psychology (see page 391).

Something to do

• Redraw the chart 'Freud's stages of psychosexual development'. Expand the 'developmental task' column and add a new column which lists adult pathology associated with each stage.

Cognitive development

In this section, we discuss theories of cognitive development; practical applications of these theories, including new research in the field; and finally intelligence and the development of ways of measuring it.

Theories of cognitive development

Jean Piaget

As we have seen, Piaget is the most prominent and perhaps the most influential of the cognitive developmental psychologists. Jean Piaget (1896–1980) was born and worked in Switzerland. He published his first paper – on the behaviour of an albino sparrow he observed in his garden – when he was only ten years old. He went on to study zoology and **epistemology**. He also studied in Paris under Alfred Binet, and worked with him on the first standardised intelligence tests. It was in this context that he became interested in why children gave the wrong answers to questions; he observed that children of the same age would frequently give the same wrong answer. Piaget used the clinical interview method to study children's development and came to the conclusion that younger children getting wrong answers were not necessarily less intelligent, but rather their thought processes were different or at a different stage of cognitive development.

Piaget's four stages of cognitive development relate to age as follows:

- Sensorimotor: birth to two years;
- Pre-operational: two to seven years;
- Concrete operational: seven to 11 years;
- Formal operational: 11 years onwards.

Something to do

- Make connections across topic areas such as cognition, intelligence, development and so on. On a large sheet of paper, draw a spider diagram and 'grow' it as you read about topics that fit into it. You could start it like this:

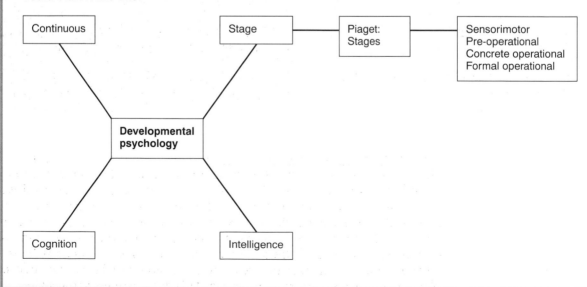

Piaget's four stages of cognitive development

There are two ways of approaching Piaget's four stages: the first is to outline the stage and then describe something of the way that Piaget arrived at it; the second is to discuss Piaget's approach, from which he developed the stages. We adopt the former of these two. (For a more exhaustive treatment of the subject, you will need to consult a specific developmental psychology textbook.)

<u>The sensorimotor stage (from birth to two years)</u> Piaget termed this first stage 'sensorimotor' because the child's development is concerned primarily with learning to co-ordinate itself with its environment. Essentially, the child at this stage is perceiving the world and responding to it in a motor or physical manner. What the child is doing during this stage – also often called 'infancy' – is developing its own behavioural schemas by acting on and getting to know something of its world. At the start of the period, at birth, the child is mainly reflective; while at the end, at two years old, the child is purposeful, a limited problem solver and has knowledge of itself, others and the environment.

Because of the huge cognitive gains the child makes during this stage, Piaget divided it into six sub-stages, outlined below:

Piaget's sub-stages of the sensorimotor stage

1. Reflex activity (birth to one month)	Little more than reflex actions.
2. Primary circular reactions (one to four months)	Child discovers it can repeat simple acts.
3. Secondary circular reaction (four to eight months)	Child discovers it can make things happen, e.g. shake a rattle.
4. Co-ordination of secondary schemas (eight to 12 months)	Child can co-ordinate two actions with intent, e.g. hold and squeeze. Represents earliest problem solving.
5. Tertiary circular reactions (12 to 18 months)	The child invents new ways of doing things. Uses trial and error. Emergence of curiosity.
6. Invention of new means to solve problems (18 to 24 months)	Problem solving becomes internalised. Emergence of insight. Able to form mental images.

<u>The pre-operational stage (two to seven years)</u> This stage is also subdivided. The first period, from two to four years, is called the preconceptual period; the second period, from four to seven years, is the intuitive period. It is at this stage that the child is able to form mental categories. During this stage, the child uses words and symbols in a representative way. The child is also very **egocentric**, and firmly believes that he or she is centre-stage and that all else revolves about him or her. The child will also attribute life to inanimate objects. The small stones or beads the child is playing with really are a row of insects. This demonstrates **animism**.

Something to try

• Ask a four-year-old child the following type of questions and note their answers. For example:

About egocentrism	*Type of answer*
Why is the sky blue?	Because Daddy painted it.
Why does it get dark?	So I can go to sleep.
About animism	*Type of answer*
What does the car do at night?	It goes to sleep.

This stage is *pre*-operational because Piaget believes that the child is not yet capable of logical thought.

Another classic test at this stage is to test for **conservation**. Conservation is the ability to conserve a knowledge of the shape, volume or other properties of something even if it appears to change. For example, Piaget would show the child a tall, thin beaker of water and, while the child watched, would carefully pour the water into a short, fat beaker. The child would be asked: 'Which beaker has the most water?' The pre-conservational child would say the tall, thin beaker. If the child has the ability to think simultaneously about two elements in a problem – that width can compensate for height in the beaker problem – then the child has the ability to conserve. This stage is marked by the emergence of the ability of the child to think symbolically.

A classic case of egocentricity

One of Piaget's classic tests at this stage was to show the child a table-top model of mountains, with a church and some houses. The child would be asked to view the scene from a position where the church and houses could be seen, and to report what he or she could see. The child was then asked to describe what someone else on the other side of the mountains would see. A young, egocentric child would say the same, as they could not take another person's view of things.

The concrete operational stage (from seven to 11 years)   In this stage, the term 'concrete' refers to the way that the child is more likely to deal in concrete than abstract issues; while 'operational' refers to the fact that the child is able to operate in adult logic using concrete terms. The child's ability to conserve now becomes more evident and the child becomes much less egocentric; it is able to understand and appreciate that others also have views. Also at this stage, the child is developing its own value system; its moral thinking is also beginning to develop independence.

The formal operational stage (11 years onwards)   Formal operation, in Piaget's child development theory, occurs when the child can deal mentally with ideas and concepts; and the child can talk in terms that include ideas that are not based on reality. The child can think and solve problems abstractly, in the process handling a number of different elements used in arriving at the solution. The child in this stage can also reason deductively.

Vygotsky – a challenge to Piaget

Another main theorist in this area is Lev Vygotsky (1896–1934), the Russian psychologist. (See also Unit 4, page 201, where he is referred to in the discussion on language and thought.) Vygotsky's research on childhood development, particularly in the 6–12-year age range (Piaget's concrete operational stage), came to some of the same conclusions as Piaget – for example the importance of children being actively involved in their learning. The main difference between Piaget and Vygotsky is that Vygotsky places much more importance on the part that social interaction with others – particularly older children or parents or other adults – plays in the cognitive development of the child.

Vygotsky uses the term 'zone of proximal development' to describe the area or context in which a child is working on a problem with the help of an older person. What happens is that the 'helper' provides support, encouragement and, if necessary, clues as to how to solve the problem. In this way, with this social help, the child develops. Recent research (Freund, 1990) strongly supports this social approach to development.

The information-processing approach to cognitive development

Piaget, and to a lesser extent Vygotsky, sees the child as a developing organism that can acquire information as it develops. The information-processing approach, on the other hand, seeks to draw parallels between the child and a computer. It is interested in how the growing child acquires, stores and retrieves information. It asks questions like:

- What are the 'programs' that the child uses to handle information? and
- How do these programs develop?

Crucial to the debate is the fact that while the child does develop the skill to 'process information' similar to the way a computer does, the child is clearly not a computer. One aspect of the debate is therefore to consider ways in which the child is different.

Piaget argued that the child develops the ability to think in increasingly complex ways as he or she grows older. The information-processing view, and researchers such as Pascal-Leone and Case, suggest that the increasingly complex thought processes are due more to the developing memory and the increasing capacity of the memory for storage and recall. Viewed from this perspective, some of the explanations given by Piaget are equally capable of explanation from an information-processing viewpoint.

Practical applications

The following chart summarises the key points of the three main theoretical approaches to developmental psychology, together with some practical applications in terms of educational principles.

Summary of cognitive development theories and their implications for education		
Piaget	**Vygotsky**	**Information processing**
Emphasis		
• Child at centre	• Interaction (of teacher/learner) at centre	• Rules at centre
Role of teacher		
• To create an environment for child to discover	• To prompt and guide	• To know what information the child needs
		• To analyse the child's mistakes for incorrect 'rule'
Learning		
• Child 'adapts' to the environment	• Interaction between children can be good for learning	• 'Active'
		• 'Uses' incorrect answers
Method		
• Small steps	• Children working together	• Child learning how own cognition develops
• Structured in simple processing stages	• Learning from older models	
• Learning by doing		

Something to do

• Expand the above summary chart onto a large piece of paper and add to it as you read this and other units. Include information from parallel reading sources.

Piaget and the implications for education

An important consideration when we attempt to evaluate Piaget's work and draw implications for education is the place of current evidence. Post-Piagetian work suggests that there are some fairly serious flaws in Piaget's original work; we must take this into account when evaluating and seeking implications for education. There is not space in this book to detail these differences, but the general thrust of recent work suggests that Piaget underestimated the ability of children, particularly pre-school children, mainly because his questions were too complicated. (Remember he used the case-study, clinical interview method.) In other words, the questions often did not allow the child to express the child's understanding. Piaget pushed the child to provide not just the answer, but the reasoning behind the answer.

Vygotsky had less to say about the pre-school child than Piaget had. The information-processing approach, however, which is also mainly post-Piagetian, suggests that the reason that younger children may have difficulty in answering questions and solving problems is not because the child is egocentric so much as because the child's other cognitive functions (attention, memory, problem solving, etc.) are not sufficiently advanced to cope with the necessary 'data-handling' that is required to answer the question. The child simply does not have the memory capacity and the ability to cope with several strands of thought in parallel.

The educational implications of Piaget's work, particularly for the younger child, are then as follows:

- Keep the content of any teaching/learning in simple steps.
- Keep questions in single stages, so that they do not require elaborate multi-processing.
- Stay within Piaget's framework but, with the above in mind, expect considerable variation.
- Children are naturally inquisitive, so provide a 'teaching' environment that allows slow and steady learning. Do not expect large jumps in understanding.
- 7–11-year-olds can think, but they do better with concrete objects.
- Children learn by doing (rather than by listening).
- The teacher's job is to provide an environment that creates curiosity and allows the child to discover.

Vygotsky and the implications for education

With Vygotsky, the implications for education are similar but there are some significant differences. The main difference is that Vygotsky, while also believing in 'discovery learning', further believes that the discovery is best done in a social rather than a solitary context. The educational implications of Vygotsky's work are as follows:

- Children learn best when working together on a problem. (Remember Vygotsky's phrase 'zone of proximal development'.)
- When a child is young, it is an adult or older child who can best provide the social input (guiding, prompting).
- As the child gets older, the age differences can reduce.
- The teacher then provides the prompts and encouragement, but steps out of the learning process as the child gets closer to the solution.

Piaget and Vygotsky   For both Piaget and Vygotsky, as the child reaches early teens, 'formal operation' becomes possible. At this stage, the implications for learning are as follows:

- The learning environment needs to provide opportunities for the systematic, logical development of learning.
- Much more emphasis can (should) be placed on abstract processes.
- Learning can follow the 'scientific method': observation–hypothesis–test–conclusion.
- In terms of language development, Piaget believed that language follows cognitive development; Vygotsky believed that children use language to help construct solutions to problems and that this process develops into verbal thought.

More recent research supports Vygotsky rather than Piaget. The implication is that language plays a very important role in learning.

Something to investigate

Piaget and Vygotsky are pivotal figures in psychology, and are still hugely influential. Both concluded that 'knowledge is constructed within a specific material and social context' (Tryphon and Vonèche, 1996). Bearing in mind their different backgrounds, research and write a paragraph:

- Bearing in mind their different backgrounds, research and write a paragraph:
  (a) explaining the above quotation; and
  (b) summarising the post-Piagetian/Vygotskian theory of early cognitive development.

  (Start with the above reference.)

Implications for education from the information-processing viewpoint   As we consider the educational implications of the information-processing approach, we need to keep in mind that no matter what approach, learning is an active, cognitive process. That does not change just because we consider 'learning' from an information-processing viewpoint.

Something to do

- Review the section on information processing at the start of Unit 4.

We have argued that the information-processing approach involves the cognitive skills of attention, memory and problem solving. So, with this in mind, the implications of this approach for learning are as follows:

- Active learning is important.
- Learning depends on cognitive development – particularly attention, memory and problem solving.
- With younger children, recognition memory is better than recall memory.

- Children need to be encouraged to rehearse facts to ensure accurate and complete transfer from short-term memory to long-term memory (rehearsal is done more efficiently as the child gets older). Play 'memory' games to facilitate this.
- Teaching/learning should reflect the increasing capacity of children to use cognitive information-processing skills as they grow older.
- Children will use different rules or strategies for problem solving at different ages.
- Analysis of a child's 'rule' enables more effective diagnosis of incorrect processing.
- Build new work on incorrect answers.
- Encourage children, particularly when older, to learn more about their own attention, memory and problem-solving strategies.

In view of recent research in this area, the future appears to be in **cognitive processing**, which is not any one of the above three theories but rather a combination of them all.

The development of measured intelligence

Intelligence is probably one of the most difficult concepts to define – despite the fact that intelligence tests have been used since 1905 when Alfred Binet, a French psychologist, started work on the first test to help identify children who have special educational needs.

Think about it

- What do you think 'intelligence' is? Try to write a precise definition.

There are various reasons for the general lack of agreement on a definition of **intelligence**. These include different views on matters such as the stability of a given attribute (does it change with age or with other factors?) and, more importantly, the fact that there is no agreement on just what attributes make up intelligence. In other words, there is no agreement on *what* to measure.

Most theorists would agree, however, that intelligence is all about problem solving, adapting to change and thinking in abstract terms.

Measuring intelligence

Despite difficulties of definition, and lack of agreement on what exactly to measure, there are several main views of intelligence and how it should be measured.

Binet and a colleague, Theodore Simon, produced the first intelligence test in 1905. It was intended to identify children in French schools who were below average in intelligence and who would need remedial help. The first Simon–Binet test was trialled on children of all abilities, and questions that failed to discriminate between able and less able children, according to their teachers, were dropped. Using this process, the resulting test achieved a reasonable degree of reliability. Subsequent developments included tests that were age-graded, and the term **mental age (MA)** came into being.

The next major development occurred in 1916, when Lewis Terman (1877–1956) of Stanford University in America translated the Simon–Binet test and published the **Stanford–Binet test**. It was Terman who introduced the term **intelligence quotient (IQ)**:

$$IQ = \frac{\text{mental age}}{\text{chronological age}} \times 100$$

This means that the IQ of a ten-year-old child with a mental age of ten (as established by the Binet tests) is as follows:

$$IQ = \frac{10}{10} \times 100 = 100 \text{ (which is the average IQ)}$$

The concept of IQ is still widely used, but it is being superseded by what is known as **deviation IQ**, where children of the same age are compared.

Another major development occurred when Wechsler, of New York University, developed what is now known as the WISC (the Wechsler Intelligence Scale for Children). The WISC-R and then the WISC-III were revised versions. The essential difference from the Stanford–Binet test is that the WISC and the WPPSI-R (a test for pre-school and primary children) rely much more on non-verbal test items and are not just verbal tests. Subsequent versions of the Stanford–Binet test now also use more non-verbal items.

New tests of intelligence are continually being developed, but further discussion is beyond the scope of this book. We now need to turn our attention to the factors that affect performance on intelligence tests. We consider intelligence in the context of the Nature–Nurture debate, particularly as it applies to heredity, environmental issues and sociocultural issues, particularly home and family.

Intelligence and the Nature–Nurture debate

The issue at the centre of this debate concerns variations in IQ scores. How much of the variation is due to genetic influences and how much to environmental factors? Since both of these elements exist and will inevitably influence intelligence, some argue that the debate is meaningless.

<u>Heredity</u>   Much of the work done on the influence of heredity on intelligence is done by studying children in families. This traditionally has involved studying identical and fraternal twins, and adopted children.

One argument in support of the view that intelligence is the result of genetic factors is that there is a high correlation of IQ between identical twins and that this correlation weakens with relationships that are, in genetic terms, further apart. So if in the same family and home situation you had identical twins, fraternal twins, and other brothers or sisters, the correlation is highest with identical twins and lowest between brothers or sisters.

In terms of adoption, it has been established that the IQs of adopted children are more highly correlated with the IQs of their biological parents than with their adoptive parents. This, therefore, is another strand in the argument that a child's genetic structure shapes its intelligence.

Environmental issues Turning now to environmental issues, we consider extremes of environmental factors on intellectual development.

Klineberg (1963) proposed the **cumulative-deficit hypothesis** to explain findings that show that children brought up in poverty-stricken surroundings score well below average on IQ tests. The essence of the hypothesis is that the longer the child spends in a deprived environment the lower will be his or her IQ – the effect of deprivation is cumulative.

In terms of environmental enrichment, there is evidence that a rich environment does make a positive difference to intellectual development. One of the often reported studies is of an isolated and very poor mountain community in eastern Tennessee (Wheeler, 1932 and 1942). Children tested in 1932 averaged an IQ of 82. Tested again in 1942 after major improvements in communications, schooling, availability of radio and other environmental, social and economic factors, the same children scored on average 11 points higher. The child's own home environment can also be said to influence intellectual development along similar lines. However, this also points to failings in what IQ tests measure; i.e. *acquired* knowledge (rather than environmental influence alone).

We can sum up by saying that both genetic and environmental factors affect IQ test performance. A general conclusion is that about half the variation between individual IQ scores can be attributed to hereditary factors.

Sociocultural issues In terms of sociocultural aspects of intelligence testing, political decisions taken at the beginning of the 20th century make very uncomfortable reading. For example, immigrants to the USA were given an intelligence test and those found 'mentally defective' were excluded. By the start of the First World War, Lewis Terman, the prominent American psychologist, claimed that lower IQ scores were the result of 'racial dullness'. At the same time, Goddard and others were associating low IQ with not only hereditary but also racial and ethnic causes.

More recently, Jensen (1969) caused an uproar when he claimed that cultural differences in IQ results are due mostly to heredity, his evidence suggesting that about 80 per cent of intelligence is inherited. Even if the figure is accepted, as many do accept it, it does not mean that the differences between groups are due to heredity. Most accept that differences are due to environmental issues and cultural disadvantages.

When we consider specific cultural effects on IQ scores, the evidence is fairly conclusive. The IQ scores from lower socioeconomic groups tend to be ten or more points lower than IQ scores from higher groups. Reasons for this include, for lower-group children, fewer books and other source materials, less privacy for study, role models that do not encourage learning and often need to earn to help the family. Since minority groups tend to be over-represented in the lower socioeconomic groups, some sources (for example Weiten, 1994) suggest that ethnic differences in intelligence are simply a reflection of 'social class' differences.

A final cultural issue that we need to consider is the question of cultural bias. Generally, IQ tests are written by white middle-class psychologists, who inevitably have only minimal knowledge of cultural and ethnic minority languages or concepts. As a consequence, those groups do less well than the equivalent white middle-class children. However, later evidence, perhaps linked with test construction, has shown that cultural bias exerts only a minimal influence (Kaplan, 1985).

Early socialisation

The emphasis in this section is twofold: first on the early socialisation of the child, and second on the place and effect of others on the child's early development.

Something to do

• Look at the nine topics dealt with in the main subsections of 'early socialisation' and draw a spider diagram showing the links between them. (There is no 'correct' order in which to deal with these topics.)

Early emotional and social development

Emotional development

The first question to consider is: when do babies begin to show **emotion**? There is evidence to suggest that mothers believe that their babies can express emotions when they are as young as one month. You may wish to question whether 'emotion' is the correct word, but the evidence suggests that a very young baby is capable of expressing, or communicating, a variety of experiences and emotions and feelings.

It is also interesting to note that there is a progression of expressed emotions that is common across cultures. According to Izard (1982), **primary emotions** emerge between three and six months; typical of these are distress, happiness and other extreme emotions. Izard believes that these emotions are more biologically than socially prompted. Secondary or **complex emotions** start to occur from about 12 months; these include embarrassment, pride and similar emotions. Lewis et al. (1989) believe that there is a connection between the appearance of these emotions and the child's cognitive development.

Another stage is reached when the child can recognise itself as an individual; this normally occurs at about 18 months and when the child can evaluate a situation where an emotion requires both an awareness of rules and a self awareness.

Coming up to 24 months, the child's emotional development is such that all the above are now commonplace and in many instances the child has learned to deliberately manipulate its own emotions to control others.

The Nature–Nurture debate is very much at the centre of emotional development. As we turn our attention to aspects of social development, we see that it plays an equally significant role.

Socialisation

Socialisation can be defined simply as the process by which we learn the things we need to know to enable us to fit into the society to which we belong. **Early socialisation** refers to those things which occur first in this process. The connection between the developing emotions and early socialisation is fairly obvious. As the baby expresses its emotions, it is clearly communicating with its parent or care giver: the socialisation process has begun.

It is at this point – when socialisation begins – that we need to consider the theoretical frameworks that have been suggested to account for the development of (early) socialisation.

Theories of early socialisation   We consider the following approaches:

- the psychoanalytic approach (Freud, Erikson, Bowlby);
- behaviourism or learning theory (Bandura);
- the cognitive view (Piaget);
- the cognitive view (Vygotsky);
- the ethological view (Lorenz); and
- the ecological or environmental view (Bronfenbrenner).

Something to do

- As you work through these six approaches, draw up a table or chart to show the key factors of each.

The psychoanalytic view   As we have seen (pages 328–9), Freud's theory has a great deal to say about a child's early development, in particular the way the child has innate drives that it will seek to satisfy. The place of the parent or care giver in a social sense is not seen to be as powerful an influence on the child as the child's own drives. An important exception is when the child suffers either from an older person's abuse, particularly sexual, or when the child's natural curiosity about its own body and bodily functions is stifled. Erikson, also from a psychoanalytic viewpoint, places more emphasis on psycho-social processes.

Bowlby, a very influential figure in the 1950s and 1960s, also came from a psychoanalytic background. Much of his work centred on **maternal deprivation** – the effect that the separation of the child from its mother will have on the child's development and socialisation.

Behaviourism or learning theory   Also known as social learning theory or **SLT**, learning theory follows classical behavioural theory in that the parent or care giver is the reinforcer (see also Unit 6, page 316). The baby, instinctually to begin with, deliberately later on, exhibits a behaviour – say hunger – which, if met, reinforces in the child a positive view of the provider. A variation, which is in effect a development of this, is the approach of Bandura (1963), known as **observational learning**. (See also Unit 3, page 111, and Unit 8, page 392.) The key elements in this view are that the child will observe and then copy or model this behaviour, but particularly so – and this is an important point – if the 'model' is someone important to the child. Bandura argues that observational learning is more efficient than learning by trial and error, or by reinforcement, and that some behaviours, language for example (see Unit 4), would never be learned solely by reinforcement.

The cognitive view (Piaget)   We discussed Piaget's views in some detail at the beginning of this unit. In the context of early socialisation, we simply need to remind ourselves that Piaget argued that the child's development will only occur at the rate of the child's cognitive development; this has to occur before any other function.

The cognitive view (Vygotsky)   We also discussed the work of Vygotsky, as a challenge to Piaget. Almost reversing Piaget's view, Vygotsky argued that a child's understanding must first occur in a social context before it can be assimilated at a cognitive level.

The ethological view   In psychology, ethology is the study of animals in their natural setting. Lorenz and Tinbergen (see Unit 6, page 286) stressed the innate behaviour of the newborn and developed the concepts of imprinting and the critical (or sensitive) period. The relevance for early socialisation is hard to assess, particularly as it is difficult to show if imprinting occurs in human infants. However, Bowlby concluded that early bonding between mother and child was important for successful early socialisation.

The ecological or environmental view   The starting point in this view is that the most realistic place to study child development is with the child in all of its natural settings or environments. Bronfenbrenner (1979 and 1989) further believes that there are a number of different environments all interacting with each other and with the child, who is at the centre of them. At the heart of this model is the triangle, child–mother–father. This triangle is located in the home. Influences on this inner dynamic are such things as school or peer group. Continuing to expand outwards, the next area of influence is the social setting of the family, the school and so on. The whole point of this ecological approach is that the only sensible place to study environmental influence is in the natural setting.

Development of self

- At what point does the developing child come to realise that it is a separate entity?
- How does it know?

In non-psychological language, these are the questions that concern us here. Let us skip a few years and ask *you*: 'Who are you?' You will probably answer by giving your age, gender, what you do, what you look like, and quite likely a series of personality traits – kind, honest and so on. It is equally likely that what you know about yourself comes from what others know about you and from the social interactions that you involve yourself in (your *self* and not *yourself*) – what is sometimes called the **looking-glass self**.

Classic theory at this point has held the view that the development of a child's **self concept** is closely allied to the child's social development. They go together. (This also suggests that the child's social development requires the development of a healthy self concept, but that is not the issue under discussion here.) If we argue that these two develop together, at what point in the developing child do they become separate?

If we argue that the self concept *starts* to develop when the child can separate itself from its surroundings, then logically we can say that the child is *beginning* to perceive as an individual.

Think about it

- Look back to Piaget's developmental stages (pages 330–2). When, do you think, does Piaget suggest the emergence of self?

The answer is not spelled out in Piaget's scheme, but if you consider the sub-stage of primary circular reactions – about one to four months – during this stage the child is repeating actions that provide pleasure. That may be instinct or coincidence, but it is more likely that there is at least a degree of intention present in the action. As the child goes through this stage, it can be observed acting deliberately on its immediate surroundings – shaking a rattle to obtain the effect – and moving into Piaget's sub-stage of secondary circular reactions at about four to eight months. By now the child has begun to realise that it can 'act on' and not just respond to its environment. We have the beginnings of self concept.

Next we need to find out at what age the child can recognise itself. Lewis and Brooks-Gunn (1979) developed a technique of placing the child in front of a mirror and observing the child's reactions. They concluded that self recognition started to occur at about 16 months; but they believed that it was not until 18–24 months that the child was fully able to recognise itself as an individual. These data were confirmed when photographs of the child were shown to the child. Note that this is the age in Piaget's scheme that the child is able to form mental images.

The next stage in the development of the self occurs when the child is able to put itself into different categories – the **categorical self** – for example the category of 'boy' or 'girl' or of 'age'. It is at this stage and thereafter that researchers are not in agreement. The debate centres on whether the four- to five-year-old has any psychological awareness. It is agreed that at this age the child has views that are basically physical, but does the child have the beginnings of a psychological self concept? The research is beginning to accept that maybe it does.

Something to do

• Draw up a chart to show the connections or 'parallelness' between Piaget's view of cognitive development and the development of self as discussed above.

Gender identity

The discussion in the previous section on the development of self lays the foundations for a discussion on gender identity. Immediately from birth, parents and others will treat the child based on its biological sex, and this social input begins the process of gender identity. The child at about 24 months is able to recognise categories such as different ages: 'me *big* boy now' and sex differences: 'me big *boy* now'.

The acquisition of sexual identity – the child knowing its own sex – starts at about this time. This learning continues over a period, with some muddled thinking by the child in the early stages; for example associating the sex of someone with their appearance. During this time, the child also learns that certain behaviours are associated with boys, other behaviours with girls; so as well as learning about its sex it learns a **gender role** as well.

Our sex is determined by the chromosomes that we inherit from our parents. There are two kinds of male spermatozoa, produced in equal numbers. One contains 22 matched chromosomes and one X chromosome; the other contains 22 matched chromosomes and one Y chromosome. The X and Y chromosomes are the sex chromosomes. The X chromosome is about three times as large as the Y chromosome. The mature ovum, on the other hand, always carries an X chromosome. When the ovum is fertilised by the spermatozoa, the result will be either two X, or one X and one Y chromosome. XX will result in a girl, XY in a boy.

The segregation of X and Y chromosomes: the determination of sex

parental phenotype:	female (♀)	male (♂)
parental genotype:	XX	XY
gametes:	Ⓧ Ⓧ	Ⓧ Ⓨ

	$\frac{1}{2}$X	$\frac{1}{2}$Y
$\frac{1}{2}$X	$\frac{1}{4}$XX	$\frac{1}{4}$XY
$\frac{1}{2}$X	$\frac{1}{4}$XX	$\frac{1}{4}$XY

| offspring genotypes: | XX | XY |
| offspring phenotypes: | ♀ | ♂ |

Theories of gender identity

While our sex is determined genetically, there are several theories of gender acquisition:

- biological and biosocial explanations;
- the psychoanalytic view (Freud);
- cognitive theories (Kohlberg);
- social learning theory (Bandura);
- gender schema theory.

<u>Biological and biosocial explanations</u> Traditionally this theory started life as a purely biological view. **Gender** (also **gender role, sex typing** or **sex role**) was everything, and the developing child's gender 'happened' as a result of their genetic structure – their sex. More recent understanding couples the social element now seen to be present in gender development with the genetic – so we now have a **biosocial theory** of gender development.

Money and Ehrhardt (1972) proposed a biosocial approach that started with the purely genetic (XX or XY chromosomes), as of course every theory must, and recognised that developing sexual characteristics continued to influence gender role, but then added to the purely sexual the importance of social input. This social input consisted of both the child's view of or reactions to its own developing sexual characteristics and the child's awareness of other people's awareness of its physical (sexual) characteristics. This dual process results in the development of gender identity and continues into adulthood. So this theory accepts that early biological development affects the way others treat the child and that this has an intrinsic effect on the child's behaviour and therefore sex-role development. It also stresses the way that the biological and social interact with each other.

The psychoanalytic view   The central idea in Freud's view of gender development, which is essentially social theory, is that it is initially determined during the phallic stage in a child's psychosexual development – between about three and six years old. During this stage, boys develop an **Oedipus complex**, which is sexual desire for their mother and jealousy of their father; while girls develop the **Electra complex**, which is love for their father and hatred of their mother. This theory is given very little credence now in terms of the two complexes, but what does remain significant is the importance of the father in the development of the child's gender, and this is true for both boys and girls.

Cognitive theory   As you would expect, this theory places the child's cognitive development at its centre. Kohlberg's (1966) theory has three stages, which are based on the view that gender development depends primarily on the child's cognitive development, and that children are actively involved in their own socialisation. The theory has it that the child establishes its own identity and then, and only then, looks for same-sex role models. The three stages of acquiring gender identity are as follows:

1. Basic **gender identity**, where the child has adequately identified itself as a boy or girl. This occurs by about three years of age.
2. **Gender stability**, where the child acquires the view that their gender is fixed over time. This occurs usually by about five or six years of age. For example, the child might say, 'I'm a boy now, but when I grow up I'll be a man.'
3. **Gender consistency**, where the child, now about seven years old, realises that its sex is fixed. For example, the child might say, 'I wear trousers and like to play with a hammer and nails, but I am still a girl.'

Other studies have shown that there is a correlation between the child's ability to conserve (see page 332) and their understanding of gender. Munroe et al. (1984) found that Kohlberg's stages are common across children in a number of different cultures.

One problem with this theory, however, is that sex-typing happens well before significant cognitive development – the cornerstone of the theory – so, despite supporting evidence, the theory may be too simplistic.

Social learning theory   This theory of gender identity was proposed by Bandura (1977) and Mischel (1970). You need to think of it from both a social and a learning theory approach.

Something to investigate

• Add the theorists Bandura and Mischel to your biography notes. In what other areas of psychology do they occur?

The essence of this theory is that the child acquires its gender and sex-typed behaviour in two main ways:

- direct teaching; and
- learning by observing others.

The first of these argues that the teaching comes directly from older siblings and friends, parents, teachers and others who have social contact with the developing child. The 'teaching' occurs when the older persons show, encourage and sometimes teach the child the required behaviour. In this context, the teaching is achieved by reinforcing the appropriate behaviour and punishing the inappropriate – in other words, classical learning theory. One interesting aspect of this is that it has now been established that **peer pressure** – even with children as young as 20 months – can be a significant influence.

The second method for acquiring the appropriate behaviour is by observation – observing the same social contacts as in direct teaching, but in this case same-sex models. One reason why the same-sex person is observed and copied is precisely because he or she is of the same sex as the child. However, most of the evidence suggests that this observational process only starts to happen when the developing child reaches the relatively late age – for gender development – of six or seven years.

Another dimension to this theory is the consideration of the family as a social unit. The argument goes along the lines that in a family the behaviour of any one member will affect all the others, no one member is immune to this, and the sex-role typing of a developing child will be influenced more by the dynamics that are occurring in the family as a group than by any one other member of the family.

<u>Gender schema theory</u>   This is the latest model to appear on the sex-typing scene. Martin and Halverson (1981 and 1987) have suggested a model which is cognitive based and draws on information-processing theory. The basic idea within the theory is that the child has an intrinsic drive to acquire values and behaviours, but that this aspect of the child's development only occurs when the child has reached a relevant stage of cognitive development of the self. This stage starts at about three years of age, when the child has begun to make sense of its own gender identity. What happens next is that the child, now with a basic understanding of its developing gender identity, is motivated to learn more about the sex roles of itself and others. This information is incorporated into **gender schemas**, which are organised mental structures about males and females, and which will in turn influence the child to process information that he or she attends to and therefore remembers.

The first schema that the child forms is an in-group/out-group schema. This allows the child to classify objects and behaviour as suitable to either males or females: dolls for girls, guns for boys; girls can cry, boys should not. A second early schema is an own-sex schema, which contains information about how the child should behave in sex-typed ways. As the child does so, he or she will continue to add to the schema(s) appropriate sex-type information, while for the most part ignoring sex-type information and behaviours appropriate to the opposite sex.

Deprivation effects

In terms of early socialisation – the broad topic under discussion – deprivation can occur in a number of ways. The question as to what is the worst form of deprivation a child can experience is difficult to define and depends on many factors. If we go back to the work of the psycho-analyst Bowlby (see page 341), he argued that maternal deprivation was a form of deprivation that caused psychological damage that the child never recovered from. We need to remember, however, that Bowlby was working in the 1940s. More recent research, particularly Rutter (1981), has shown that when deprivation occurs there are invariably other, additional factors present which at least in part contribute to the situation, which is therefore not as simplistic as Bowlby suggested. Another issue concerns the permanence of such deprivation. Whatever the cause of deprivation, is the child permanently harmed? Again, post-Bowlby research, particularly with severely deprived children, has shown that these children, given an improved, enriched and loving environment, are capable of almost complete recovery.

A classic case of deprivation effects

An extreme example of this is a study by Koluchova (1972), who reported the case of twin boys from Czechoslovakia. From about 18 months until they were seven years old, they suffered terrible deprivation and isolation. At seven, when they were found, they were severely physically and mentally retarded – so much so that they were incapable of even taking an IQ test; they had no language and had suffered almost continual beatings and lack of food. They were hospitalised until they were well enough to attend a special school and then, when they had developed basic social skills, they were placed in foster care where the foster mother created an environment of a happy, loving, caring home. There is a happy ending! By 11 years of age, their speech was normal and by 15 their IQ levels were also normal. Coupled with this, their general emotional health was also considered to be virtually normal.

Although this is a striking case, it is important to realise that it is scientifically inappropriate to draw general conclusions from just one or even a small number of cases.

What seems to happen (there are other recorded cases of severe deprivation) is that children brought up under extreme conditions *are* able to and do make successful recoveries – made possible because of a much wider range of coping skills and adaptability than the more traditional studies would suggest. The fact that these children, once found or identified, often have huge amounts of special attention and care shown to them, may also have a significant bearing on their recovery. In the case of the twins studied by Koluchova, there is also the possibility that – even though very young – they were able to support each other emotionally. They did not have to suffer terrible deprivation and ill-treatment on their own, as have children in many other recorded cases.

Something to investigate

• A number of examples of deprivation are cited above. Research other examples and then try to identify areas such as recovery rates, long-term outcome, and so on.

Enrichment effects

We have argued that depriving a growing child of normal opportunities for physical and emotional experiences can cause serious developmental problems. So we can also argue that providing an enriched physical and emotional environment does the opposite. At the very least, an enriched environment enables the child to mature in a normal way, while in some circumstances and with some children an enriched growing experience enables the child to accelerate through certain developmental stages.

It is interesting to note that while there is a mass of research on children in deprived circumstances, there is a lot less on children in enriched circumstances. Perhaps the reason for this is that the difference between normal and deprived is much greater and more dramatic than the difference between normal and enriched.

The Headstart programme

The Headstart programme in America is a deliberate attempt to enrich the lives of pre-school children. It does this by providing special pre-school educational facilities for underprivileged children, to encourage more normal learning and social development. Over the years, the programme has met with a mixed response: initial results indicated resounding success, later results suggested that this was overly optimistic. The latest long-term follow-up results show that while long-term IQ gains may be limited, other social and cultural advantages, such as improved positive attitudes, are gained.

Interactions between infant and care giver

Here we discuss the ways in which the infant reacts and interacts with its care giver, whether the mother or other care giver. What is perhaps the major interaction – **attachment** – is dealt with separately in the following section.

'Interaction' between infant and care giver here means the effect that the one has on the other. This implies that some form of communication is taking place. What form does this communication take and how early does it start?

Think about it

- Imagine for a moment that you are a very young baby, with no language or motor control. How would you express yourself?

Something to do

- With a partner, attempt to express yourself using only facial expressions. Show happiness, sadness, joy, anger, frustration, discomfort, etc. Swap roles and see if you can guess what feelings your partner is expressing.
- If you can, spend some time with a very young baby and try to identify the child's expressions. Ask the mother (or father or other care giver) what they think their child is expressing.

You will probably find it very difficult to express or identify a variety of emotions where only facial expressions are involved. Izard, working in the 1980s, used a videotape to record a baby reacting to a variety of events, such as having a toy taken away or seeing its mother return. An independent panel of viewers watched the videotape and were asked to identify the emotions expressed by the baby. There was general consensus between the viewers who, independently, identified the same emotions. As a result of this kind of research, it is possible to identify a number of commonly expressed emotions which occur universally at approximately the same time.

Attachment

We now turn to a specific interaction between infant and care giver that is highly significant and has created a lot of research – that of **attachment**. It is doubtful that you can remember any very early experiences in your own life that influenced *your* early attachments. It is useful, however, to think about how you view attachment now, so try the following exercise:

Think about it

- What 'others' do you feel an attachment to? Make a list.
- Put the list in order of strongest to weakest degree of attachment.

Ainsworth (1973) proposed a general definition of attachment. She suggested that attachment has elements of emotional ties and dependency. In terms of behaviour, for the younger child **separation anxiety** occurs when attachment breaks down. Both older children and adults seek to avoid separation anxiety by deliberately seeking to maintain contact with the person who is the object of the attachment. Bowlby did a lot of the early work on attachment. He suggested that the essential aspect of attachment behaviour is that the child will actively look for or move towards its primary care giver – it will want to be *with* the person. However, much of this work was done in the 1940s and 1950s when the prevailing general view was that the **maternal instinct** was a crucial factor in making attachments. Another element in Bowlby's theory is that infants have a biological need or instinct for close attachments and if these are not formed then the child will suffer with emotional problems later. (Remember that Bowlby came from a background of psychoanalytic work.)

Ainsworth has identified three stages that a child will progress through in the normal course of forming attachments:

1. **Initial pre-attachment** (birth to three months), where attachments are not focused on a specific person.
2. **Attachment-in-the-making** (three to four months) At this stage, the child shows a preference towards specific care givers.
3. **Clear-cut attachment** (six or seven months), depending on the primary care giver.

Theories of attachment   We consider three theories:

- the behaviourist view;
- the contact view; and
- the ethological view.

As is often the case when there are a variety of views on a specific topic, the views are rarely clear-cut. It is the same with attachment.

The behaviourist view   This is the earliest theory of attachment and simply says that attachment is learned through conditioning. The child gets food, comfort and other needs provided by the care giver and so associates with – becomes attached to – that care giver.

The contact view   This is sometimes also referred to as the 'comfort' view and is based on classic work by Harlow (1959) (see also Unit 6, page 304). Although he did the initial work on monkeys, usually baby monkeys, he argued that the results can be transposed to children.

A classic case of attachment

Harlow had observed that baby monkeys on their own would become attached to pieces of soft material placed in their cages. He then conducted the now classic study in which he constructed two 'adult monkeys', one from a steel wire framework but which had a baby-bottle of milk, and the other from soft materials with no baby-bottle. Baby monkeys would cling for hours to the soft 'mother' and only rarely go to the wire mother briefly to drink. From these and other similar studies, Harlow concluded that babies – monkeys and human – have an innate (unlearned) need for contact and comfort that is as basic as the innate survival need for food.

You will notice that the above two theories provide another example of the Nature–Nurture argument.

The ethological view   In this view, attachment is a **fixed action pattern** which is innate and will occur at or during the **critical period** for that species. In other words, the newborn baby will become attached (usually) to the object that it first sees after birth, that is close to it *and* that moves. This process of forming attachment is **imprinting** (see Unit 6, pages 303–4).

Social and cultural variations in child rearing   The first thing to note here is that the variation in social and cultural child-rearing practices is enormous. The second thing to note is that by the time the child has reached its late teens, the effects of these wide differences have reduced significantly.

In the context of social and cultural variations, it is difficult to separate the social from the cultural, mainly because any one culture will affect its social aspects and mores while social practices help shape the culture.

Social variations However, there are certain specifically social aspects. One of these has to do with the differences in child rearing across 'social class', also known as **socioeconomic status** (SES) or a person's position in society. For example, the UK has a class society based on a long history and tradition, India has a strong caste system where your position is determined by your birth, while the USA is a more open society with little tradition or caste but which tends to emphasise wealth as a determinant of position.

In a major study reviewing literature of child-rearing practices, Macoby (1980) identified differences between high- and low-SES families in a variety of societies and other groupings. Some of these differences are as follows:

Low-SES parents	High-SES parents
Emphasis on respect, neatness.	Emphasis on ambition, curiosity, independence.
Restrictive, arbitrary, power exerting.	Permissive, discuss problems.
Reason less.	Reason more.
Use simple language.	Use complex language.

It is easier to see why there are these differences if we look at the extreme cases. Living in poor housing, with little money and probably inadequate food and medical attention, will create problems that have a bearing on child rearing. Life for lower-SES families is much more insecure, perhaps even dangerous, with higher stress levels on a day-to-day basis and less time – and perhaps patience – to relate to children. This scenario is likely to be self perpetuating, with children from low-SES families marrying earlier and repeating their parents' patterns.

Life for high-SES families is usually less problematic in terms of life's basic needs, and the children of those families are – as we have seen – more likely than low-SES children to have a higher IQ. However, having more independence and freedom can bring its own problems. As with low-SES families, children of high-SES families also tend to repeat their parents' lifestyle.

Cultural influences We now turn our attention to cultural variations in child rearing. The term 'culture' refers to the systems of meanings and behaviours that are shared by a group of people and are transmitted from generation to generation (by teaching/learning, not genetically). It can be broken down into:

- **physical culture,** to do with technology and artefacts (significant objects); and
- **social culture,** to do with beliefs, values and customs.

If evolutionary theory places great emphasis on the **genotype** (see Unit 6, page 285), cultural theory places the emphasis on the environment, particularly its cultures, as the primary shaping influence of the child's development. **Cross-culture theory** attempts to analyse the behavioural patterns of groups rather than those of an individual in a group.

Think about it

- If you have only lived in one culture, list what you think makes that culture your culture. Think in terms of
  - family life;
  - religion and conventions of behaviour;
  - art forms.
- If you have lived in more than one culture, list what you think are the elements that make the two cultures different.

The value in taking a cross-cultural approach is that it increases awareness not only of other cultures but of our own as well. **Cultural determinism** argues that it is the culture that the child is in that determines the context and rate of development. Biological factors in this theory are seen as relatively insignificant. A major study in this field was carried out by Whiting and Edwards (1988). They observed 12 different cultures to assess the place of culture in determining childhood behaviour. Their conclusion was that the cultural environment did affect the development of the child.

The existence of **subcultures** within a given culture is widely recognised. Subcultures can be of various kinds: ethnic, religious and – perhaps less prominent – sexual or youth 'gang' cultures.

Depending on the culture in which the stages of human development occur, certain events may have a stressful, even painful effect, or may be passed with almost no awareness at all. For example, the onset of puberty in some cultures is accompanied by certain rites which may be celebratory or, at the other extreme, painful or kept secret. Different cultures have different expectations and different timings, as well as different values in such things as personal qualities. For example, Western cultures tend to expect adolescents to make choices concerning such things as work, marriage and religion. As these, in Western cultures, are often complex issues, the adolescent stage of development can take a long time. This is in contrast to other cultures where such choices are limited, frequently making the transition through adolescence short and (relatively) painless.

A final rather salutary thought is that if we are arguing that culture affects our understanding of development – which we are – then the scientific base on which we have made this judgement may be seriously flawed. This is simply because almost all studies so far have concentrated on Western civilisation, which is not only a small sample but an unrepresentative one. So any attempt to propose universal principles of development must be regarded as unsafe (Nsamenang, 1992).

Moral development

A very basic definition of **morality** would be 'that which is right or wrong behaviour'. The definition will often include, or at least imply, a **moral code**, which attempts to describe right or wrong behaviour as understood by those who support, or agree with, that particular code. This in turn implies that someone who behaves in a moral way has **internalised** these moral codes and will conform to them even when on their own or with no authority figure present.

Theories of moral development

We consider five theories of moral development: those of Freud, Piaget, Kohlberg, Gilligan and finally the social learning theory. This order corresponds roughly with their chronological order.

<u>Freud (psychoanalytic)</u>   While Freud was the first to suggest a theory of moral development, much of what he proposed is now considered inaccurate. He argued that the personality consists of three parts: the id, the ego and the superego (see also pages 328–9 and Unit 8, page 422).

- The **id** seeks to satisfy instinctual urges.
- The **ego** controls the id on the reality principle (that is, until a realistic solution to the id's urge can be created).
- The **superego** is concerned with moral issues or the ego-ideal, a kind of internal censoring system.

The Freudian view of the place of internalising moral codes is important, but the structure of this theory, particularly the place of the Oedipus complex, is now thought to have little value or relevance. Erikson, also a psychoanalyst, was among those who rejected the Oedipus complex, arguing instead that the child internalises the moral views of both parents.

<u>Piaget (cognitive)</u>

A classic case of moral development

Piaget published much of the work he did in his book *The Moral Judgement of a Child* (1932). One of the main methods that he adopted was to get children to teach him how to play their games, as opposed to games taught to children by adults. He reasoned that children who made up games would also make up the rules about how to play them. From this approach, he observed that there were differences in the rules and their application that changed with the age of the child, and he further observed that the child's use of rules develops in parallel with the child's intellectual development.

We can link Piaget's moral development to his developmental stages thus:

Age	Developmental stage	Moral development
Birth to two years	Sensorimotor	—
Two to seven years	Pre-operational	Child copies rules of older children (still ego-centric). Rules 'fixed'.
Seven to 11 years	Concrete operational	Child realises it can make its own rules. Intention becomes increasingly important.
11 years onwards	Formal operational	Child begins to think for itself – develops its own morality. Becomes autonomous.

It is important to realise that while Piaget and others define stages in terms of the child's age, all children develop at different rates. Some pass quickly through the early stages and then their development slows down, others start more slowly and then catch up.

Kohlberg (cognitive)   Kohlberg derived his theoretical structure using a different approach. Instead of trying to establish a progression of moral development from children's games and their rules, as did Piaget, Kohlberg presented his subjects – who ranged from young children to adults – with a series of stories which presented moral dilemmas; he then asked the subjects to solve these dilemmas. The thinking that the subjects went through to provide the answer enabled Kohlberg to classify the answers into the following levels and stages.

Kohlberg's theory of moral development

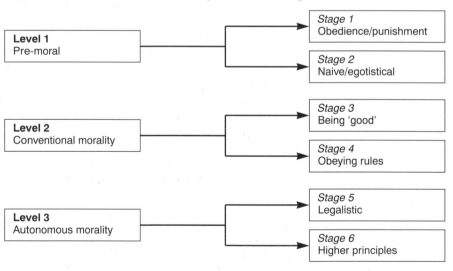

It is important to realise...

An interesting implication that can be drawn from Kohlberg's model is that as cognition develops so does the level of thinking, but also so does the behaviour of the person.

Kohlberg's theory is precise in the order and content of each level, but it should be noted that the stories which contained the moral dilemmas were fictitious and, however plausible, were still not 'real' moral dilemmas. Subsequent research has suggested that in the real world children's behaviours will be more varied. Also of interest is the fact that Kohlberg did most of his work on boys. While from a methodological point of view this is acceptable, it does leave open the question as to how girls deal with moral dilemmas.

Gilligan (social)   Carol Gilligan (1977) studied the moral development of both boys and girls, and developed a theory that recognises differences between the way that males and females develop morality. The key distinction between the morality of boys and girls, according to Gilligan, is that boys develop a morality of justice, a moral legalistic system; whereas girls develop a morality of care, a morality of concern for others.

Gilligan's theory, which she based in part on a study involving decisions about the moral issues in abortion, has females progressing through three stages:

- first, **self interest**, which is purely selfish;
- second, **self sacrifice**, putting others first; and
- third, **non-violence**, being fair to everyone.

Evidence for and against Gilligan is sparse, with most finding very little difference between male and female morality.

Social learning theory   The final theory we consider is SLT (Bandura, 1973). The essence of this theory is that children develop their morality in two ways: by observing others, and as a result of rewards and punishments. As the child observes others, it learns the effects or results of violating the moral codes of its society. The goal of rewards and punishments is to reward, or reinforce, appropriate behaviour and to punish inappropriate behaviour. Most of the evidence suggests that when 'punishment' is part of a reasoned cognitive approach, explaining to the child the implications of the wrong behaviour, such that the child internalises accepted moral codes and behaviours, then the method is effective.

Research evidence supports both of these methods for learning morality, but there is also general evidence that adults show some degree of consistency in moral behaviour over a variety of different situations, which a behavioural approach would find difficult to explain. The theory, as with much behavioural theory, does not explain precisely the mechanisms by which people develop their morality.

Theories of moral development				
Psychodynamic	**Cognitive**		**Social**	**SLT**
Freud	**Piaget**	**Kohlberg**	**Gilligan**	**Bandura**
Moral development occurs in the phallic stage (3–6 years) by internalising the moral views of the same-sex parent.	Heteronomous Discipline imposed by others Autonomous Child can think for itself	*Level 1: Pre-moral* Stage 1: Obedience/punishment Stage 2: Naive/egotistical *Level 2: Conventional morality* Stage 3: Being 'good' Stage 4: Obeying rules *Level 3: Autonomous morality* Stage 5: Legalistic Stage 6: Higher principles	Self interest Self sacrifice Non-violence (A particularly female view)	Observation Rewards and punishment

Adolescence, adulthood and old age

As stated at the start of this unit, the emphasis in developmental psychology is on childhood development. This has been the traditional approach, mainly because major theorists have stressed the importance of childhood to the rest of life. More recently, however, there has been a drift towards the view that 'development' continues through the whole of life. As a result, more emphasis has been placed on what is now often called **life-span development**.

Major issues in life-span development

There are three major questions on which life-span development research tends to be centred:

- **The Nature–Nurture issue:** Is your development the result of your genetic structure (Nature) or your experience (Nurture)?
- **The continuity or stage issue:** Is your development a gradual and continuous process or does it pass through stages which have to be negotiated one after the other?
- **The stability or change issue:** Is your personality stable over your life span or does it change as you develop?

Looking at the first of these, and whenever the Nature–Nurture argument comes up, we can always say that it is a mixture of both. But how much of each? And how does the 'mixture' come about? In things such as size or colour of hair, genetics play a major (total?) role, but what about behaviour? Or, more contentious, intelligence (see pages 337–9)? The study of twins and adopted children provides some of the answers, but asking how much of Nature or Nurture – or which is the most important – is asking the wrong question. Much more accurate is the suggestion that 'genetic structure shapes experience'. Our nurture is nature-driven.

With respect to continuity or stages of development, the issue is less clear. Major stage theorists, such as Piaget, Kohlberg, Erikson and others, have all received criticism; mainly to do with the timing of stages rather than their content, but in some cases relating to their methods. Despite problems with the stage approach, to say that life is one long, smooth progression is equally suspect. So again we have a mixture: development does occur throughout life, but often in stages and in an uneven fashion.

Finally, with respect to the question of personality: is it stable or does it change with development? The answer again is a bit of both. There is a lot of evidence supporting the view that children and young people often change as they mature, but also that some aspects of personality continue through life.

Stage and non-stage theories of development

As with many of the debates or issues within psychology, the issue of whether development is in stages or continuous is quite complex. You will find that here as with other issues many theorists, while predominantly on one side or the other, do accept certain aspects of the other view.

Think about it

- Think of all the major personal changes that you have passed through since you were about 15.
- Now think of all those that you think you will pass through during the rest of your life.
- Make a chronological list of all these major changes.

Stage theories of development suggest that we pass through a series of 'stages'. At each stage there are specific characteristics that explain certain behaviours *and* certain other characteristics that need to be achieved or mastered before we can pass on, successfully at least, to the next stage. Now look back at your list of major changes in your life and see if you can identify specific stages that have already occurred or that you are expecting to occur.

It is important to remember that we are talking about models – 'ways of representing reality' – and however good our model, it is still only a model or a way of helping us 'see' what is happening. In trying to make all of human development 'fit' a model, it is inevitable that there will be limits. However, despite these difficulties, developmental models are still very helpful.

One way of looking at the continuity or stage issue is to consider the **non-stage** or **continuous view**. In this view, development occurs in a smooth manner, and change can only be noticed over a period of time because of the 'smoothness' of the development. If there are steps, then they are very small. Whether smooth or with small steps, the process is seen as cumulative. On the other hand, stage theorists – sometimes known as discontinuity theorists – view development as occurring in abrupt changes that are quite major and usually quite obvious.

Related to this issue is the nature of the change, irrespective of the way that it occurred. Is the change **quantitative** or **qualitative**? Quantitative has to do with the amount of change – you might almost say you could measure it – for example height change or increase in knowledge. Qualitative has to do with the kind of change that is taking place – for example changes before and after language development, or before and after reaching sexual maturity.

The third aspect of this issue is whether change, however it takes place, is connected to other changes or whether it occurs in isolation with no connection with what has gone before or with what is yet to take place (in other words, one change does not prepare us for the next).

The following chart is an attempt to summarise the above issues. They are not isolated categories, however; they may merge or overlap.

Summary of issues in the stage or non-stage debate	
Stage	**Non-stage**
• Discontinuous development	• Continuous development
• Qualitative change	• Quantitative change
• Changes take place in isolation	• Changes are connected

A number of stage theorists have produced their own model of developmental stages. We consider these in general terms before going on to discuss some specific issues in developmental psychology.

Just as we considered the work of theorists such as Freud and Piaget, with models that apply mostly to children, so we now turn our attention to a number of specific life-span theories of development. We consider, briefly, the developmental tasks model of Havighurst, and then models by Erikson, Levinson and Marcia.

Something to do

- As we consider each of these theories, draw a chart of the major points. Use the same style for each theory so that you can make comparisons.

Havighurst's developmental tasks model

Havighurst, writing in America in the 1950s, developed what he called **developmental tasks**. He proposed a series of tasks that stretched from birth to death. He defined a developmental task as:

> *"a task which arises at or about a certain period in the life of the individual, successful achievement of which leads to his happiness and to success with later tasks, while failure leads to unhappiness and difficulty with later tasks."*
>
> Havighurst (1953), cited in Hurlock, *Developmental Psychology* (1959)

Developmental tasks – Havighurst (1953)

1. Developmental tasks of adolescence

- Accepting one's physique and accepting a masculine or feminine role
- New relations with age-mates of both sexes
- Emotional independence of parents and other adults
- Achieving assurance of economic independence
- Selecting and preparing for an occupation
- Developing intellectual skills and concepts necessary for civic competence
- Desiring and achieving socially responsible behaviour
- Preparing for marriage and family life
- Building conscious values in harmony with an adequate scientific world picture

2. Developmental tasks of early adulthood

- Selecting a mate
- Learning to live with a marriage partner
- Starting a family
- Rearing children
- Managing a home
- Getting started in an occupation
- Taking on civic responsibility
- Finding a congenial social group

3. Developmental tasks of middle age

- Achieving adult civic and social responsibility
- Establishing and maintaining an economic standard of living
- Assisting teenage children to become responsible and happy adults
- Developing adult leisure-time activities
- Relating oneself to one's spouse as a person
- Accepting and adjusting to the physiological changes of middle age
- Adjusting to ageing parents

4. Developmental tasks of later maturity

- Adjusting to decreasing physical strength and health
- Adjusting to retirement and reduced income
- Adjusting to death of spouse
- Establishing an explicit affiliation with age group
- Meeting social and civic obligations
- Establishing satisfactory physical living arrangements

Havighurst gave three main reasons for the arrival of a given task:

- physical maturation (for example learning to walk);
- cultural pressures of society (for example learning to read);
- personal values and aspirations of the individual (for example choosing a vocation).

Most developmental tasks arise as a result of these three forces working together.

While the model is comprehensive, we need to remember that it was structured in the 1950s primarily for an American population. However, despite these possible limitations, the concept of developmental tasks is an interesting one and still features in developmental schemes, particularly those with a psychosocial emphasis (see Newman and Newman, *Development Through Life. A Psychosocial Approach*, 6th edn 1995).

Erikson's 'eight stages of man' Erikson's concept differs from that of Havighurst in that he divides up the life span into eight stages and suggests that a **psychosocial crisis** has to be resolved at each stage for healthy development. Despite being a life-span approach, Erikson's theory places great importance on the early stages, distinguishing five distinct stages between birth and adolescence. Erikson comes from a psychoanalytic tradition, so the heavy emphasis on childhood can be expected.

Erikson's psychosocial development, 'the eight stages of man' (1959)			
Stage	Age	Psychosocial crisis	Favourable outcome
1	Birth to one year	Trust vs. mistrust	Hope, trust, optimism
2	Two to three years	Autonomy vs. doubt	Self control, adequacy
3	Four to six years	Initiative vs. guilt	Purpose, initiates own activities
4	Seven years to puberty	Industry vs. inferiority	Developing intellectual, social, physical skills
5	Adolescence	Identity vs. role confusion	Awareness of self as a unique individual
6	Early adulthood	Intimacy vs. isolation	Forming close relationships; making career commitments
7	Middle adulthood	Generativity vs. stagnation	Concern for family and society
8	Old-age to death	Integrity vs. despair	Satisfaction with life

Think about it

- What are the connections between Erikson's stages and Freud's psychosexual stages? Draw up a chart.

Levinson's 'stages of
male adulthood'

Moving on roughly chronologically, we come to Levinson's 'stages of male adulthood' – 'male' because he developed his scheme from an in-depth study of a male-only sample. You may also find this model described as 'seasons' of male adulthood. Levinson proposed a series of stages (seasons), each followed by a transition stage before the next stage or season. This structure is a key element in the model (see the chart below).

Levinson's stages of male adulthood (1978)

Age (years)	Stage	Activity
17–22	Early adult transition	Preliminary adult choices
22–28	Enters adult world	Lifestyle choices made
28–33	Age 30 transition	Crisis and change likely
33–40	Settling down	Making progress – career, family, etc.
40–45	Mid-life transition	Questions existing lifestyle
45–50	Entering middle-adulthood	New crises and choices, commitments
50–55	Age 50 transition	Modifications to lifestyle Possible time of crisis
55–60	Culmination of middle adulthood	Consolidation, fulfilment
60–65	Late adulthood transition	Fluctuations between pride and despair
65–80	Late adulthood	Acceptance
80 plus	Late late adulthood	Preparation for death

Marcia's model of
adolescence

Yet another model is proposed by James Marcia (1966 and 1980). This work is with adolescents and is based on the framework provided by Erikson for this stage.

If you refer back to Erikson's model, you will note that he sees the issue of identity versus role confusion as the psychosocial crisis for this age. Marcia takes this conflict and, using a structured interview technique, seeks to establish whether the adolescent has explored a number of alternatives, which result in either a commitment or a crisis. Marcia sees this process as giving rise to four different degrees of **identity status** (for a fuller discussion on this see page 369). It is interesting to note that Marcia's data show a resolution of the identity crisis rather later than Erikson proposed.

Identity status during adolescence (Marcia, 1966 and 1980)

Status		Commitment or crises
1.	Identity confusion	No evidence of future identity, no commitment
2.	Identity foreclosure	Commitment to new identity is made without a crisis
3.	Moratorium	In crisis, searching for a new identity but no commitment (Erikson – identity crisis)
4.	Identity achievement	Crisis is resolved Personal commitment to a new identity is made

Life events and their impact

We discuss below some of the major events that occur in adulthood and the impact that the event has on the individual. It is important to realise that positive or happy events can have just as much of an impact on the individual as negative or sad events. Marriage, for example, or the arrival of a new family member can create as much impact as losing your job or the death of a close friend.

A classic case of measuring the impact of life events

One of the classic studies is the development of the Social Readjustment Rating Scale (SRRS) by Holmes and Rahe in 1967 (see Unit 5, page 274). This was an attempt to quantify the impact of life events. The researchers derived the data from an analysis of the medical records of a large number of patients. The scale can be used to predict possible illness. Their data suggest that there is a correlation between the number of points a person accumulates in a given year and the possibility of illness.

The Social Readjustment Rating Scale (SRRS) – selected life events grouped as topics

Rank	Event	Points	Topic group
1	Death of spouse	100	Bereavement
5	Death of close family member	63	
17	Death of close friend	37	
2	Divorce	73	Divorce
3	Marital separation	65	
12	Pregnancy	40	Parenthood
14	Gain of new family member	39	
23	Son or daughter leaves home	29	
8	Lose job	47	Unemployment
26	Spouse begins or stops work	26	
30	Trouble with boss	23	

Source: Adapted from Holmes and Rahe (1967)

While the concept is useful, there are a number of problems with the SRRS. It was developed in 1967, and in the field of psychology the 1960s is a long time ago. It deals with life events – that is, isolated events – and while individual events can be accumulated, there is no provision for rating ongoing daily stressful situations. For example, it has been suggested that driving your car is one of the most frequent, constant causes of stress. Another problem is that there is no provision for positive, stress-reducing events.

Something to do

- Make your own personal life-events chart covering the last 12 months. Indicate what events occurred and when, and whether they were positive or negative. Include ongoing, daily stressors as well as one-off events. Give each event a rating.

We turn now to a consideration of the topics or groups of life events listed in the extract from the SRRS and discuss their impact on the individual. We consider each of these in turn in the order presented in the chart, which in general terms is in decreasing order of impact.

Bereavement The main life events that involve bereavement are the death of a spouse (100 points on the SRRS); the death of a close family member (63 points) and the death of a close friend (37 points). A son or a daughter leaving home is also a form of bereavement, as are any other kinds of permanent or long-term separation, for example divorce or marital separation. However, we deal with these separately under 'Divorce' and 'Parenting' below.

When bereavement takes its normal form of expression, it usually involves an emotional reaction that *needs* to be gone through in order for the grieving person to adjust to the experience and return to a degree of personal stability even if their situation has changed because of the death.

Another aspect of bereavement is the question of how expected or sudden was the death. If both partners in a marriage are elderly, then death can be expected. It may be that the person has been diagnosed as having a terminal illness, or it may be that the person dies suddenly as a result of short-term illness, accident or even violence. The degree of emotional reaction may depend on the circumstances of the death.

In all of these circumstances, however, someone dies leaving someone bereaved. What does this mean and what does the surviving person experience?

At the most basic level, it means that the survivor has to adjust to or cope with the loss of someone who was very close, part of their family, perhaps someone with whom they had shared their life for 50 or 60 years.

In terms of the survivor's experience, it has been shown that for almost all cases there is a series of stages of bereavement or grief that the survivor goes through, however the death of the other person happened.

Societies throughout history have practised certain rites for the dead. However, modern understanding of the process of dying, and hence bereavement, began only when Elizabeth Kübler-Ross published a book *On Death and Dying* in 1969. Her work is based on interviews with the terminally ill, with the emphasis on the stages that the dying person passes through. There are, however, clear implications for those who are bereaved. The stages identified by Kübler-Ross are as follows:

1. denial and isolation;
2. anger;
3. bargaining;
4. depression;
5. acceptance;
6. hope.

This series of stages needs to be considered in the same way as all stage theories – the stages are not clear cut and individually identifiable, they often merge and the rate at which an individual passes through them may vary considerably.

Something to do

- Go to your library and skim-read *On Death and Dying*.

A classic case of the psychology of bereavement

Just as Kübler-Ross is considered to be the first major theorist on stages of dying, so Lindemann (1944) is considered an early theorist on the stages a bereaved person goes through. He formulated his theory after working with the surviving relatives of those who died in the Coconut Grove fire in Boston, USA. (This was a major fire in a large apartment block; many residents died.) Lindemann observed that there were common stages that many of the bereaved went through. He defined these as:

1. release from ties to the deceased;
2. adjustment to the absence of the deceased;
3. the development of new relationships.

He concluded that if the bereaved person can work through these three stages, usually over a period of a year or more, then a healthy adjustment can be made. The 12-month period is significant because within that period all major events that have emotional ties to the deceased – birthdays, anniversaries, Christmas and so on – have to be negotiated.

In a more recent study, Parkes (1972) identified three stages of bereavement:

- First is **denial** – denial that the death has occurred.
- The second is a period of **longing**.
- The third is **depression**.

Each of these is 'normal', together they will take about a year to move through, and can be expected in a healthy grieving situation.

All the above refers to what we can call 'good' grief. There is of course the opposite – when the bereaved does not move through the grief process but, for whatever reason, becomes stuck at some stage. The problem causing the 'block' may resolve itself with more time, but often some kind of help is needed to enable the bereaved person to complete the grieving process. Newman and Newman (1995) suggest that the central process in adjusting to bereavement in late adulthood is introspection. To achieve integrity at this stage the individual needs to engage in deliberate self evaluation and reminiscence. Through this process the person is able to build a mental and emotional bridge between the past and the present (Merriam, 1989).

Divorce The life event second in significance on the Holmes and Rahe scale is divorce. Marital separation is third. This is perhaps not surprising as divorce and separation have obvious similarities to death and bereavement – you sometimes hear people say things like, 'Oh, that marriage died a long time ago.' Couples who divorce or separate can therefore be expected to go through a series of stages of emotional reaction and adjustment similar to the stages involved in bereavement. Length of marriage prior to divorce and separation may have an effect on the way the participants react to the divorce or separation – a longer marriage often indicating a more difficult adjustment post-divorce. Some couples will go into divorce or separation in what they themselves regard as a rational, intelligent manner, implying that everything is under control and that they are not going to fight over who has what. In fact divorce rarely happens like this and the process usually ends in acrimonious squabbles. Even if it does go smoothly, with no fights or serious argument, there is still almost certainly going to be a reaction akin to bereavement. The increasingly common practice of a couple living together without being married and then separating can also trigger a greater or lesser degree of emotional trauma at and following the separation.

In terms of statistics, over the 1980s and 1990s divorce rates have moved from one in three marriages to one in two marriages; while for the same period something like one in two children are likely to be involved in a broken marriage and to spend some time in a one-parent family.

As with other staged situations, the person experiencing divorce or separation is likely to have certain emotions or reactions occurring at certain times. An important difference in the case of divorce, however, is that there is a very significant cumulative or long-term effect. Divorce does not just happen and then it's all over. The marital discord may have started some time before the divorce, and all kinds of after-effects, many very stressful, will continue for years to come. These may include anger, loneliness, despair, reduced income, moving house, loss of old friends, making new friends, and so on. There are a number of stress-related illnesses that correlate with divorce. Examples include a general increase in health problems, an over-represented population of divorced people in psychiatric hospitals, and a higher than average suicide rate (Stack, 1990).

While a number of theorists have attempted to delineate stages for divorce, Hetherington (1981 and 1989) suggests a **crisis period** of a year or more, in which the lives of all of the family are seriously disrupted. The 'bottom' occurs about a year after the divorce. This is followed by a long period of reorganisation, the precise length of which may be only a few years but the nature of the reorganisation may affect negatively the remainder of the person's life.

The effect of divorce on children has also been studied (Hetherington et al., 1982; Fauber et al., 1990). The custodial parent – the mother in 90 per cent of cases – is likely to become more punitive, insensitive and impatient; while the non-custodial parent, usually the father, will become overindulgent and permissive while the children are with him. Divorce has been found to be harder on boys than on girls in both the short term and the long term. The most likely cause for this is that boys normally identify with their father, but then stay with their mother after the divorce, often with no father present. It is also possible that these findings are influenced by the way that boys and girls react to divorce: boys more overtly, girls more covertly. Children and adolescents of both sexes seem to suffer less when they live with their parent of the same sex (Zimiles and Lee, 1991).

The traditional view of parents staying together in an unhappy relationship 'for the sake of the children' is generally not the best solution (Hetherington, 1981). Recent evidence suggests that divorce, however painful and however long-lasting the effects, is on balance better than maintaining an unhappy relationship.

Parenting   If you refer back to the chart on page 361, you will see that the life events grouped under 'Parenthood' are the third most stressful of the four groups we have chosen to consider. This group contains pregnancy (40 points), gain of new family member (39 points) and a son or a daughter leaving home (29 points). From the parents' perspective, this period can last for up to 20 years or more.

In a broad sense, parenting in different cultures shows many similarities – for example, whether the parent and child are in Tokyo, Tonga or Twickenham, a caring, stimulating environment will produce a well-balanced child; whereas if the same parents are rejecting, cruel or punitive, then the child will grow up hostile and with a poor self image (Scott et al., 1991). During the 1970s, LeVine studied parenting and child-rearing practices from many different cultures. He concluded that despite the culture or society all parents have three basic goals for their children:

- **survival:**   to do what is necessary to ensure the survival of the child until it reaches maturity. (Is there a 'survival of my genes' argument here?);
- **economic:**   to teach the necessary skills and behaviours to enable the child to reach economic independence;
- **self actualisation:**   to encourage the development of cultural values leading to personal self actualisation.

Within a given society or culture, however, there are quite different approaches to parenting.

Something to do

• Go to a large supermarket and observe differences in parenting methods. (If you intend to do this in any way other than a casual walk round, ask the manager's permission first.) See if you can categorise parenting styles.

One of the best known research studies in the area of parenting styles is work done by Baumrind (1967 and 1971) with pre-school children. She concluded that there are three main approaches to parenting:

• **Authoritarian:** This is very rule based, requiring strict obedience.
• **Authoritative:** The child is expected to comply with the rules, but with moderate freedom. The parent is willing to discuss reasons for the rules.
• **Permissive:** Few demands are made on the child. The child is allowed to 'express' itself. Parental monitoring is minimal.

While much of the above concerns childhood, parenting – as already stated – can last for 20 years or so.

As adolescence approaches, the parent–child relationship changes significantly, mostly due to the developing maturity and search for autonomy of the adolescent. This can cause difficulties that require considerable skill and willingness to give and take by both parent and teenager, as a new and more mature relationship is forged. (Adolescence is discussed in the next section.)

The relationship changes again when the 'child', now 18 years old or more, leaves home, perhaps for college or – usually a little later – to marry.

Unemployment Referring back to the Holmes and Rahe scale, you will see that 'Unemployment' includes losing your job (47 points), a spouse beginning or stopping work (26 points) and trouble with the boss (23 points).

Something to do

• Ask a number of adults to tell you something about themselves. How many of them, very early in the conversation, tell you what they do?

The above task provides evidence – albeit somewhat unscientifically – that the average adult considers the job they have as fundamental to who they are. Most of the evidence suggests that while employment is important, it is satisfaction with what the employment is that is more important. In this context, unemployment can be catastrophic to the individual who loses his or her job. Fryer and Payne (1986) have identified three main areas where unemployed people are at greater risk than the population as a whole:

• Unemployed people show higher rates of depression.
• Suicide rates are higher for unemployed people. (Fryer and Payne add the caution that unemployment may not be the only cause.)
• Some unemployed people have difficulty with cognitive functioning, for example concentration span.

Our discussion of developmental psychology has made frequent reference to stage theory – the idea that change occurs in a series of discrete stages. Stage theory can also be applied to unemployment. Some theorists argue that the stages an unemployed person passes through are similar to those of a bereaved person.

The impact of unemployment can vary considerably – from being a minor inconvenience to being the cause of major distress and serious mental illness. For an individual with a job that is fairly common, and a general employment situation that requires that kind of work, the likelihood is for a short period of unemployment before a return to work. The impact or effect of this is little more than a minor disruption. On the other hand, for the older person in a higher-status position, with the likelihood of similar employment slim, the impact can be very serious. Argyle (1989), comparing unemployed people with people in employment, found that for the unemployed depression is common and gets worse with length of unemployment, alcoholism and suicide are more frequent, and general emotional and physical health suffer.

The impact of unemployment also inevitably affects the family of the unemployed person, increasing the pressure on what may be an already fragile situation. Even in the most secure and stable relationship, there can still be a severe impact. This may involve loss of earnings, which may necessitate a house move, change of school for the children, loss of friends and social acquaintances. All these pressures and changes can further deepen the depression, which in turn can lead to reduced possibilities of re-employment. In general, the longer the person is unemployed, the higher the likelihood of serious problems; and the more the person enjoyed or found satisfaction from work, the more will be the possibility of serious problems following the loss of their job.

A small number of people will accept unemployment as 'the best thing that ever happened' and go off and manage a pub or something similar, swearing never to work for anyone else ever again. This is a small minority, however, and they usually have a highly supportive family and reasonably secure financial stability.

Some theorists argue that retirement is a form of unemployment, and in one sense it is. The unemployment we have discussed here could be regarded as *forced* retirement. We look at retirement in the usual sense of the word in a later section in the context of adjusting to old age. Next, however, we turn to a consideration of development through adolescence and adulthood.

Personality change and social development: theories and research

Adolescence

In this section, we consider personality change and social development for the periods of **adolescence** and **adulthood**. We take a developmental view and consider personality and social issues as they occur during these periods.

G. Stanley Hall, the nineteenth-century American psychologist, described adolescence as a time of '*Sturm und Drang*', of storm and stress, which in his view was caused by biological change. Modern understanding rejects this view as the sole cause, and argues instead that the changes that occur in adolescence are due as much to cultural issues as to biology – another instance of both Nature and Nurture rather than one or the other (Ben-Amos, 1994).

The word 'adolescent' comes from the Latin *adolescere*, which means 'to grow up' or 'to develop to maturity'. This is quite close to modern usage, as today we think of adolescence as the period which starts when the young person reaches puberty (about 13 for girls and 14 for boys) and ends when the adolescent reaches 'maturity', which, in Western cultures, can mean 15 or 16 in sexual terms or 18 or 21 in legal terms. Maturity could also mean when the young person reaches 'emotional and psychological maturity' – the term is not clearly defined (Simmons et al., 1987). Some theorists see the period of adolescence as being divided into two distinct stages, early and late adolescence, with different developmental tasks and characteristics in each stage.

Think about it

- Consider Havighurst's developmental tasks of adolescence (see page 358). How would you divide them into early or late adolescence?

You will find that it is quite difficult to identify some tasks or stages in terms of their starting and stopping points, never mind the subtlety of a change-over from early to late adolescence. Havighurst's first developmental task, for example, is 'accepting one's physique and accepting a masculine or feminine role'. For some people this task is never resolved, however, and for others it may take until early adulthood.

For a different perspective, consider Erikson's psychosocial developmental stages (see page 359). You will see that 'adolescence' is the fifth of the 'eight stages of man'. Erikson defines adolescence as the resolution of the crisis 'identity versus role confusion', the ideal outcome of which is an 'awareness of self as a unique individual'. This awareness is arrived at by the person – consciously or unconsciously – trying out different roles and then integrating them into a single identity. If the person does not achieve this, then the result is that they become confused about their identity. The resolution of the crisis rarely occurs suddenly; it usually takes several years, sometimes many years.

Personality change in adolescence   The key question here is: 'Who am I?' At the start of adolescence, the young person is still a child; by the end, the child has become an adult. One thing is certain, and that is that under normal circumstances the child will grow – growing up simply cannot be put off. The child may want to cling on to the familiarity of childhood, but the growing and changing body pushes the child into new and unfamiliar territory with impending crises all around: 'Do I follow the gang and ignore my parents?' 'Me a prefect?' 'I hate school – or do I?' 'Of course I drink – see you in the pub tonight – do I look old enough to get in? What happens if I drink too much? How does it feel?'

All of these questions, dilemmas, pressures and new experiences occur over a very short time span, many of them causing conflict in the home as the adolescent seeks to achieve independence, in many ways wanting to grow up, in other ways fearful. It is through the impact of these social and cognitive processes that the adolescent comes to attribute stable psychological, social and personality characteristics to him- or herself (Damon, 1983).

One reason for the intensity of this conflict is the speed at which society and culture are changing. The world now is significantly different from the world in which those who are now parents were adolescents themselves. Their adolescent world was quite different from their child's, they have not experienced the same situations and pressures and are therefore flawed as role models. How often do you hear an older person saying, 'I just don't understand you young people today'?

So how does the young person learn to cope and how to behave? To resolve their identity crisis? To develop their new personality? The young person's own friends are in the same boat, they too are struggling to make sense of this period – so they may not be in a position to help but at least they talk the same language. Where young people often turn is to the media – television and magazines.

Something to do

• Analyse a selection of teenage magazines in terms of the way they may help to resolve an adolescent's identity crisis.

Social development in adolescence   Social development obviously occurs at the same time as the personality develops and in many ways the two cannot be separated. The fact that girls mature earlier than boys adds another dimension to the issue. In Erikson's model, the goal is 'identity'. Gilligan (1982), however, sees a different emphasis at this stage. She believes that while boys may be primarily interested in an identity which implies individuality, girls are more concerned with an identity which has a large relationship component. Many other theorists support this view and see this difference starting with the child and continuing through adolescence and into adulthood.

James Marcia (1980) developed a framework that started with Erikson's concept of the adolescent's search for identity, but he developed the concept further by suggesting that the adolescent's identity can be assessed (see page 360). The process he employed involves a personal interview using two criteria: crisis and commitment. These two terms indicate the state of the person's identity. Is it in crisis, in that the young person is still experimenting or trying new roles but with no conclusion or decision? Or is it in a state of commitment, with the young person having reached a decision? Marcia uses the term status to indicate the various possibilities of the adolescent's identity (see again page 360). While it is possible to consider Marcia's model as sequential, it is important to realise that a young person could move in and out of each status in a non-sequential manner.

- Initially there is **identity confusion**. This status may imply a degree of crisis, but equally it may not. It will display a lack of commitment, and the young person may give the impression of not caring and lacking interest.
- The second status, that of **identity foreclosure**, suggests a situation where there is a moderate degree of commitment – to an ideal, a vocation, or something similar; but very little or no crisis involved in reaching the commitment. It is likely that the identity taken on will be similar to a parent or other significant adult.
- The third status, **moratorium** (sometimes referred to as **psychosocial moratorium**), sees the adolescent in a state of ongoing crisis, which has not been resolved, and so there is no commitment.
- The final status is that of **identity achievement**. In this status, the person has dealt with any crisis, has made significant commitments, and as a result has achieved a new identity.

Adulthood   As with adolescent development, we consider adult development, primarily in terms of personality and social development, from the perspective of several developmental theorists:

- Havighurst's developmental tasks span the whole of life, so we consider the developmental tasks of adulthood (see page 358).
- Erikson also deals with the whole of life, so we consider his sixth and seventh stages – early adulthood and middle adulthood (see page 359). We consider his eighth stage – old age – in the final section of the unit.
- Finally we consider Levinson's stages of male adulthood.

Remember to keep in mind the differences between developmental *tasks* (Havighurst) and developmental *stages* (Erikson and Levinson).

Something to do

- On one sheet of paper, outline the three approaches mentioned above in as parallel a fashion as possible.

An obvious difference between adolescence and adulthood is the time span that each takes. Adolescence lasts about six or seven years, adulthood up to 60 years. Equally obvious is the fact that in adulthood developmental change takes place much more slowly. Perhaps as a result of this, different theorists have divided up the period into a number of substages, sometimes determined by major events or turning points such as Levinson's 'mid-life transition'.

Think about it

- How would you define adulthood? Does it start at the end of adolescence? Do you become an adult just by growing older, by maturing physically (as the literal meaning of the word implies) or is there some other criterion to identify an adult?

The answer to the question of how we define adulthood has a number of strands. Can the person cope with the world in which they exist? Are they moving reasonably smoothly through Havighurst's developmental tasks, or are they not? In terms of Erikson's stages, are they resolving the successive stages satisfactorily? Or, if we consider Levinson, are the transitions going smoothly? Most theorists would argue that if the person is coping with most of the demands placed upon them as they deal with life and living as an adult, they are indeed 'adult'. Cunningham and Antill (1984) argue that the fact that the adult lives in the real world of family, social and work environments, demands change and development, and that these will occur alongside changes and development in cognitive and intellectual development. All of the above implies, of course, the presence of maturity, responsibility and other like attributes.

- Referring to parts 2 and 3 of Havighurst's developmental tasks (see page 358), 'early adulthood' can be considered to extend approximately from 20 to 40 years of age and 'middle age' from 40 to 60 years of age.
- For approximately the same total period, Erikson (see page 359) also has two periods or stages: 'early adulthood' (stage 6) and 'middle adulthood' (stage 7).
- Levinson (see page 360) uses a different approach. At around 22 years of age, the adult enters adulthood and 'transitions' through various stages until age 60–65, when the adult moves into late adulthood.

If you completed the task on page 370 which asked you to outline these three theories in parallel, you should begin to see where the similarities and differences lie. Hold this in mind as we consider them.

Havighurst's model of adulthood   We can see that for early adulthood Havighurst's developmental tasks centre on adjusting to new situations, a new lifestyle and new social expectations. For middle age, the tasks centre on transition and readjustment. Middle age is the age about which least is known or understood, and about which there exist the most (usually unfavourable) stereotypes.

The most important developmental tasks of early adulthood are adjustment to marriage, parenthood and vocation. In each of these the focus is on sex-role adjustment. In marriage and parenthood the role that each partner plays must not only satisfy the individual, but their partner as well. Adjustment to an appropriate sex-role in the vocational choice of the individual is no less important. The woman may feel the need to cope with the demands and pressures of both family and work. This can induce guilt when, for example, work pressures mean that the family takes second place. For the man, too, vocational choice is critical. The increasingly common trend of the woman having the 'better' job, with the husband in a 'less good' job, also calls for considerable adjustment; this can be compounded if one partner needs to take care of the children while the other works, particularly if the traditional roles are reversed, such that the woman stays in work while the man stays at home. While these trends are becoming more common, Jackson (1987) has found that both males and females have their own constraints about what the partner is 'allowed' to do in the house.

In terms of middle age, personal and social adjustments are difficult, but vocational and family adjustments are even more difficult. For men the problems generally centre on work, while for women family relationships are the most difficult. Changes in family patterns at this age include children moving out of the home and increasing responsibility for ageing parents, possibly involving one or both parents moving into the home.

<u>**Erikson's model of adulthood**</u>   As we have seen, Erikson's view of development involves the successful resolution of a series of eight psychosocial crises over the whole life span. For adulthood the first of these is 'intimacy versus isolation', the second 'generativity versus stagnation'.

The individual must first resolve the intimacy versus isolation crisis by the development of close and meaningful relationships, often with just one other person but not necessarily so. Also, and as a part of this crisis, the individual needs to resolve career or vocational issues. This process will be severely hampered if the individual has not fully negotiated the adolescence crisis of achieving ego identity, for without a strong ego it is difficult to commit to another person in a meaningful way or to make a success of a career.

The second of Erikson's stages of adulthood is the crisis of generativity versus stagnation. This is resolved through the experience of care, caring for both family and society. Generativity implies doing things that we believe in. Stagnation on the other hand can be understood quite literally as standing still, of achieving little, and of focusing effort on oneself. Some theorists are of the view that many adults never fully resolve this crisis and remain in a state of stagnation. This of course implies difficulty with the next – and final – stage.

<u>**Levinson's model of adulthood**</u>   Levinson's approach is different from that of both Havighurst and Erikson. His is a 'male-only' model, in that he developed his theory from working extensively with a small group of mostly middle-class, professional men. The key idea is that at any point in the person's life, the person is involved in the world of which they are a part, particularly in the form of family and work situations. As the person gets older, their 'world' changes and a new set of structures comes into play, at least for a period of time, until a new transition stage is reached, which is negotiated, and the next structure emerges. Perhaps the most significant of these transitions is the mid-life transition, which occurs at 40–45 years. This is also sometimes referred to as the **mid-life crisis**, a term coined by Levinson in 1978. Levinson sees the crisis as pivotal. Up to the age of 40 we see our life in terms of the years that have passed, from 40 onwards we see our life in terms of the years remaining. Realisation finally comes that you will not be selected for the Olympic athletics team, nor will you ever make captain of industry or some other goal that only a few years ago seemed like a real possibility. Some theorists, however, believe that Levinson places too much emphasis on this particular transition.

Adjusting to old age

In this last section on developmental psychology, we consider issues surrounding the final stage in the life span – that of growing old and adjusting to old age. We look mainly at:

- the impact of retirement; and
- issues surrounding health, fitness and illness in elderly people.

We then take a brief look at some theories of ageing, before concluding with a few words on death itself and the related issues of spirituality and immortality.

Both Havighurst and Erikson provide a framework, in their different ways, of events and processes at the end of life. At this stage, perhaps more than any other, we should beware of stereotyping, for there is no one way that people react to or deal with the events of the final stage in life. For example, Hummert (1990) has found that there are multiple stereotypes ranging from the positively complimentary ('a perfect grandparent') to, at the negative end, 'vagrant'. People react very differently when they are actually 'in' this stage. However much the person has planned for the final years of their life, there are many things that can happen to upset the planning, any one of which can have a serious effect. Also, the impact of several things happening at any one time has a compounding effect, the result of which is much more serious at this stage than at any previous stage. Havighurst's developmental tasks of later maturity (see page 358) outline the tasks that have to be achieved. In general terms, the tasks of old age relate more to the individual's personal life than to the way the person interacts with others. In Erikson's psychosocial development stages (see page 359), old age is the eighth and final stage and requires the resolution of the crisis 'integrity versus despair'. The ideal outcome of this is 'satisfaction with life'. As with Havighurst, notice that in terms of the ideal outcome the emphasis is on the individual's adjustment.

Something to do

- Draw up a chart which shows the similarities and differences between Havighurst and Erikson in relation to old age. Expand your chart by including other theories.

The impact of retirement

There are obviously a large number of factors that affect the individual's adjustment to retirement. We discussed earlier the question of unemployment, which for the older person can run into retirement if the retirement age is reached before the person finds re-employment. Many people 'can't wait for retirement' and 'wonder how I ever found time to go to work'. For these people, retirement is thought about, planned for and in most cases comfortably adapted to. There will certainly be adjustments: a lower level of income, loss of working environment and routines, much more discretionary time, and possibly at some point death of spouse and, frequently, new living arrangements. For the person looking forward to retirement, the early retirement years can give a whole new lease on life, allowing the individual to move smoothly through Havighurst's developmental tasks *and* to resolve Erikson's eighth stage, demonstrating integrity not despair and achieving satisfaction with life.

In contrast, the person forced into retirement on reaching 'retirement age' may take this very personally and suffer a loss of self esteem. Extra free time will push couples together more, which can itself create more pressure and this, with reduced income, raises still further the pressures the couple feel and have to deal with. In this case, the individual may not negotiate successfully Havighurst's developmental tasks; and may, in Erikson's terms, not resolve the integrity versus despair crisis and as a result slowly become more and more despairing.

There is wide variation in the way that individuals react to retirement; most studies find that something like one-third of adults indicate some problems in adjusting to retirement (Fletcher and Hansson, 1991).

A key psychosocial element in making a satisfactory transition into retirement involves coping with the loss of a usually clearly defined role associated with employment. As noted earlier, the typical adult will frequently define who they are by reference to what they do. If the person has 'lived' this role for all their working life, loss of it is a major issue, the consequences of which are potentially serious to the functioning of the person in both cognitive and social areas.

The three major factors that are most influential in assisting in the adjustments to retirement are as follows:

- first, the person's acceptance of the fact that retirement is going to happen and that plans can be made for it;
- second, and also highly significant, the person's view or perception of retirement – is it perceived as something threatening or as a new opportunity that is about to open up?
- third, finance (on average, income reduces by 50 per cent). If this has been thought about and planned for, then the adjustment is likely to be at least reasonably smooth.

The key to all these aspects is whether the retiree is exercising some degree of control over what is in effect inevitable.

An important point in the context of retirement is that the retired person is likely to experience change as the retirement proceeds. In this respect, retirement is a process rather than an event, with the psychological and social state of the person fluctuating from an initial 'honeymoon' period, through some degree of upset or depression, and levelling off somewhere in between. This process may take up to about two years.

In summary, preparing for and moving into retirement can be a difficult time, with major personal adjustments needing to be made. Early preparation for retirement can do much to smooth the transition. This can be meaningful in two ways: retirement, looked forward to positively, can be planned for or at least thought about during earlier developmental stages; this, in turn, can bring greater meaning to these earlier stages as the person looks forward to retirement.

Pratt and Norris (1994) draw an interesting parallel between adolescence and those approaching retirement. People approaching old age and retirement are likely to be aware of both the positive and negative aspects and as a consequence enter a psychosocial moratorium as they seek to form a new identity. The retiree will search out new options, try a new activity of some kind and generally make adjustments; just as the adolescent does on moving into adulthood.

Health, fitness and illness in elderly people

Health and physical fitness in elderly people is generally considered to be dependent on four major factors:

- heredity;
- temperament;
- living style; and
- environment.

Of these, heredity is in most cases the most significant, but all four usually play a part. In addition, sex, race and education are also factors that influence health and longevity.

Heredity as the primary cause of health and longevity can be seen by the fact that different species have different life spans, and within a given species different families and individuals age at different times.

Secondary causes are much more variable and can significantly affect the onset of ageing and its length. Poor diet, frequent illness, excesses of almost any kind, high levels of stress and living in extremes of climate can all have a marked effect on a person's health and length of life. Problems with the endocrine system can complicate or speed up physical changes in old age, as can deficiency of the sex hormones. Hormone replacement therapy (HRT) can help to correct this situation.

Other physical changes include decreasing efficiency of all the sense organs, a process that starts earlier than old age but which becomes much more noticeable during old age. The visual and auditory sensory systems are those most affected by increasing age. Sexual changes also occur in old age, affecting both men and women. Sexual potency declines during the sixties, as does sexual desire – but not in all cases. While physical changes are influential, the effect of culture on attitudes to sexual change are at least of equal importance, particularly today as those who are elderly now grew up in a society that was much less liberated. The anxiety elderly people often feel about engaging in sexual activity may have a negative effect on their lifestyle in general, with some evidence indicating that those who are married live longer than those who are single or widowed. Possibly the key point is that to be happy and well adjusted in old age, a positive attitude about one's own gender and sexuality is required. Physical illness also becomes more critical in old age. Older people succumb more frequently and with more serious effects than younger people. Because the body takes longer to repair itself, the older person will suffer more seriously and for a longer time than a younger person. Problems such as physical disability, accidents and poor eating habits contribute significantly to illness among elderly people.

Elderly people also experience changes in mental abilities. These too start in middle age but become more pronounced with age. Again, as with physical aspects, there is a wide variation in mental decline in different individuals.

Theories of ageing

Over the last few decades there have been a number of attempts to provide some sort of theoretical model of what happens during retirement and ageing.

- A biological theory of ageing is the **cellular-ageing theory**. This suggests that the person's DNA breaks down to the point that the body becomes unable to repair itself.
- A more socially biased theory, popular in the 1960s and 1970s though less so now, is the **disengagement theory** (Cummings and Henry, 1961). This suggests that the older person gradually withdraws or 'disengages' from society. This theory may also have a biological basis which, in a clock-like fashion, allows the person to 'run down' biologically as age increases.
- Havighurst (1964) has proposed an **activity theory**. Somewhat the reverse of disengagement, in activity theory the older person is encouraged and supported – an important aspect – throughout their old age to stay involved as much as possible for as long as possible. This view has provided evidence that elderly people who are active have a healthier old age and are more satisfied with their lives.

Death, spirituality and immortality

As is often said, the only sure thing about life is death. As this 'final stage' draws nearer, the individual is likely to react in a number of different ways, depending for the most part on their attitudes and beliefs. For those with no particular belief, death means the end, nothingness, extinction; and this approach can colour the whole of the later stages of life. In Erikson's terms, the psychosocial crisis of integrity versus despair has not been resolved and the person remains in a state of despair. For the person who has accepted retirement and old age, however, and who has engaged in life to the fullest degree possible, the likelihood is that despite some ambivalence the person will be 'ready' for death. They will have talked to others about past times, good and bad, and about fears and perhaps certainties for the future. Kübler-Ross, from her work with the terminally ill, called this process **anticipatory grief**.

If the person has strong religious convictions, then the spiritual dimension becomes paramount and hope is kept alive in a very real way. Here Erikson's final crisis is successfully completed to the very end as the individual demonstrates ego-integrity.

It is, of course, entirely possible for the individual to demonstrate ego-integrity without religious belief. In this case, the person is likely to experience a psychological sense of immortality. They will 'live on' through their children or perhaps through the involvement they have had with others. This is perhaps the 'hope' that Kübler-Ross saw as vital.

> *"It is the feeling that all this must have some meaning, will pay off eventually if they can only endure it for a little while longer."*
>
> Elisabeth Kübler-Ross, *On Death and Dying* (1969)

Revision and practice

● ●

Coursework opportunities

1. Study the cognitive development of a young child. The opportunities here are almost endless, so plan carefully in advance what aspect(s) you intend to study. You could, for example, study language development over, say, a six-month period; or you could study motor development or intellectual development. You could test children (take care here with ethical issues) using some of Piaget's tests, for example of conservation.

2. *Either:* Observe small children from about three months to a year old. See if you can identify Piaget's stage of 'secondary circular reactions'. *Or:* Replicate the Lewis and Brooks-Gunn (1978) study. How do you identify 'self recognition'? Does it start at about 16 months?

3. Carry out a study along the lines of that done by Martin and Halverson in 1981 and 1987 (see page 346). Show five- and six-year-old children schema-consistent pictures (boys/guns, girls/dolls) and schema-inconsistent pictures (boys/cooking, girls/lorries). A week later, test the children's memory. Schema-inconsistent activities will most likely be found to be remembered – in error – as schema-consistent. The theory predicts that children use and will remember gender-consistent activities, and if the information is inconsistent, it will be distorted to 'fit' the correct schema. As always with a research task, take care with the ethics of this study.

4. Develop a series of questions along the lines suggested on page 332 and ask children aged between three and five years for their answers.
   - Can you identify egocentrism and animism?
   - Do these stages overlap?
   - Are there identifiable differences between boys and girls?

● ●

Examination questions

Question 1 Discuss psychological explanations of the development of the self concept in

(a) infancy and childhood *(15 marks)*
and
(b) adolescence. *(10 marks)*

(AEB, Paper 2, Summer 1996)

Question 1: Unpacked
- The injunction used at the start of the question: 'Discuss', requires *both* description and evaluation.
- There are two areas to be discussed.
- In 'parted' questions, it is generally better to plan and answer in parts.
- You now have two basic options to cover four areas in terms of the question:
  - (1) describe stage (a), then stage (b);
    evaluate stage (a), then stage (b).
  - OR (2) describe stage (a), then evaluate stage (a);
    describe stage (b), then evaluate stage (b).

There is no obvious best solution, this is more a question of personal choice. However, since there are fairly significant differences between the 'psychological explanations' of the two age groups, it is slightly more logical to go for option (2).

- As with most 'describe' questions, you will need to present the material first, then evaluate.
- Essay *content* should include, for both stages:
  - (i) a *brief* description of consciousness and self consciousness; the self concept: self image, self esteem, ideal self; theories of self; theories of mind.
  - (ii) Focus on the *development* of self concept: the 'I–me' debate   James (1980); the 'looking-glass' self   Cooley (1902); the eight stages of man (first four stages)   Erikson (1959); psychosexual development   Freud (1910).
- Evaluation in part (a) should focus on the difficulty of researching this topic in children and a lack of empirical data.

Question 2   Discuss psychological research into the effects of **two** life events in adulthood.

(24 marks)

(AEB, Module Paper 6, Summer 1997)

Question 2: Sample answer

Key points to watch for in this essay include a discussion (describe and evaluate) of relevant research, and the identification and effects of two life events in adulthood.

The following student essay was written under simulated exam conditions in 45 minutes. It is given below verbatim.

Comments

Essay

'Life events' is a relatively modern term and is generally seen as something that happens in the course of a person's life that has a major impact. It's usually thought of as having a negative impact, but some events are positive.

Relevant start

Accurate definitions and supporting evidence

Adulthood can be defined as the period in a person's life from 19 years (Erikson 1980), or in Levinson's (1978) terms transition into early adulthood takes place from 17–22 years. Adulthood itself is sub-divided – early, middle, later – and ends at death.

Needs expansion

While stage theories are helpful in understanding adult development, the life events or sometimes critical life events is another approach.

Good way to lead into the two chosen life events. Good evaluation

One of the earliest attempts to quantify life events is the Social Readjustment Rating Scale (SRRS) developed by Holmes and Rahe (1967). This approach has been criticised for several reasons. The fact that it's now 30 years old is a major criticism, while a second is that it does not take account of daily hassles which over time can have major impact on mental health.

Relevant to question as both are 'adult'. Accurate reference

The two life events that Holmes and Rahe consider most significant are death of a spouse and divorce.

Death of a Spouse
Elizabeth Kübler-Ross (1969) is considered by many to be the first psychologist to attempt to define the stages of grief that a person goes through. Her work was more concerned with the stages that a dying

Good distinction

Needs expanding/explaining

person faces than someone dealing with the death of their spouse. Murray-Parkes (1972) suggests four stages of grieving: Shock, Coping, Intermediate stage, Recovery. The whole process taking about two years, at which point the person may have come to accept the death.

Need to show relevance
Who/What?

While Erikson's 'Eight stages of man' is concerned with human life-span development, his final stage 'Integrity versus Despair' does suggest that to achieve or maintain 'integrity' it may be necessary to cope with the death of one's spouse. Other research suggests that the person will be able to cope with this event if there is a variety of significant support and help available, i.e. other family, friends, clubs, etc.

Another major life event is divorce. Rated second on the Holmes and Rahe scale.

Good start to this topic

Divorce can be defined as the ending of a marriage. It can also refer to the ending of a long-term relationship, although the term 'separation' is more usual here. In both cases the psychological impact can be similar, and there are also similarities between the psychological effects of death of a spouse and divorce.

Good point/evaluation

Accurate use of evidence

Duck (1988) suggests that there are four main reasons that can lead to divorce: marriage at a young age, marriage between people from lower socio-economic groups, often linked with lower education, marriage between people from different religions or races, and marriage between children of divorced parents. The fourth point is significant as it suggests that if your parents are divorced, you are likely to divorce, which means your children are likely to also – and so on.

Interesting point

Needs expanding

Duck (1988) has proposed four reasons that lead to the breakdown in relationships – including divorce. The intra-psychic phase, the dyadic phase, the social phase, the grave-dressing phase.

(Ran out of time: Was going to expand above para' and make point that recent research focuses more on changing dynamics than static state of relationships.)

General comments
A reasonably good essay with relevant/accurate supporting evidence, but a little short on evaluation. The final paragraph in brackets is worth adding if you are running out of time as it will indicate to the examiner your intention and *may* be worth a mark.

Marks: Skill A $\frac{9}{12}$ Skill B $\frac{7}{12}$ Total $= \frac{16}{24}$

Question 3 Describe and evaluate studies of the effects of enrichment **and/or** deprivation on the child.
(24 marks)

(AEB, Module Paper 6, January 1997)

Question 4 (a) Describe **one** theory of cognitive development.
(12 marks)

(b) Assess the extent to which this theory is supported by psychological studies.
(12 marks)

(AEB, Module Paper 6, January 1997)

Question 5 (a) Outline **both** the social learning theory **and** psychodynamic explanations of moral development. *(15 marks)*

(b) Evaluate **one** of these explanations of moral development. *(10 marks)*

(AEB, Paper 2, Summer 1997)

Question 6 (a) A psychologist is investigating how children think. She shows pictures of animals, people, toys, and machines to the children and says to them she was thinking of one of these pictures. The child has to work out which picture she is thinking of by asking questions that can only be answered by 'yes' or 'no'.

(i) Identify **two** ways in which 6-year-olds and 12-year-olds may differ in the reasoning they use to discover which picture the psychologist is thinking about. *(4 marks)*

(ii) According to Piaget, what other differences would the two age groups given in (i) above show in cognitive ability? *(6 marks)*

(b) With reference to more recent research, evaluate Piaget's view of the *pre-operational stage* in cognitive development. *(10 marks)*

(Total: 20 marks)

(NEAB, PSO6, February 1996)

Selected reading list

Bruner, J. S., *Child's Talk: Learning to Use Language* (Oxford University Press, 1983)

Durkin, K., *Developmental Social Psychology: From Infancy to Old Age* (Blackwell, 1995)

Newman, B.M. and Newman, P.R., *Development Through Life. A Psychosocial Approach* (Brooks/Cole, California, 6th edn 1995)

8 Atypical development and abnormal behaviour: what makes an individual different?

It is important to understand that **atypical development** and **abnormal behaviour** are significantly different.

- The term **atypical development** is applied mainly to children who have one or more learning difficulties. Learning difficulty in this context is taken to mean any difficulty or disability, either physical or mental, associated with problems in the development of the child. The term is also used of children who are atypical in a way that makes them outstanding – in other words, children who are exceptionally gifted.
- **Abnormal behaviour,** on the other hand, means behaviour that is considered abnormal – different from what is accepted by the majority. The terms **maladaptive, maladjusted, deviant** or **mentally ill** are also used. The word 'abnormal' is the traditional, historical word, but is going out of favour as it is difficult to define.

So 'atypical' concentrates on developmental issues, usually in children; while 'abnormal' concentrates on behaviour, which can apply to both children and adults.

Having made that important distinction, we can outline this unit as follows:

- The first part looks at atypical issues.
- The second part deals with abnormality, looking first at definitions and then at various models, including implications for treatment and ethical issues.
- The third section attempts to describe and explain specific abnormal conditions.
- The final section discusses treatments and therapeutic approaches.

Atypical development

Definitions and criteria

As a starting point for this section, and to get you thinking about some of the problem areas of what 'atypical' means, try the following:

Something to do

- Describe, say, a ten-year-old 'typical' child.
- What were some of the words or phrases that you used?
- Ask one or two others to do the same and then compare your answers – they are likely to be quite different.

If we accept the proposition that children who are atypical will require atypical help, education and training, we immediately come up against the problem of definition. Just what is atypical? What do we use as criteria – intelligence, behaviour, physical or mental disability or handicap, a combination of one, some or all of these? In the above task, you probably said that the typical ten-year-old has average intelligence, is inquisitive, sometimes misbehaves, prefers same-sex friends, and collects things. You may also have said or implied an absence of any kind of disability. You may have struggled at this point, as no one wants to 'label' children who have either mental or physical disabilities, but the fact remains that they are atypical.

Something to do

• Read the section on definitions of 'normal' and 'abnormal' (pages 387–8). Which of these criteria can be used to distinguish between 'typical' and 'atypical'?

If we argue that the atypical child needs to be identified so that it can be given all possible help – in the widest sense – then some sort of criteria must be used to identify such children. Although we tend to think of atypical as meaning some sort of condition which makes the child less able than the typical, we need to include in our discussion those children at the other end of the scale who are atypical because they are extremely gifted.

We suggested above that the atypical child may be atypical in physical or mental terms, which makes a broad distinction between mental and physical problems. It is important to note at this stage that atypical mental development is *not* mental illness; mental illness is discussed in the section on abnormal behaviour.

Intelligence

Thinking first about intelligence as a criterion of atypical development, it is important to understand what intelligence is and how it is measured.

Something to do

• Re-read the section on intelligence in Unit 7, pages 337–9.

Taking intelligence quotient (IQ) as a measure, by definition the average child has an IQ of 100. In a normally distributed population, plotting IQ against frequency gives us the bell-shaped curve shown below:

IQ against frequency

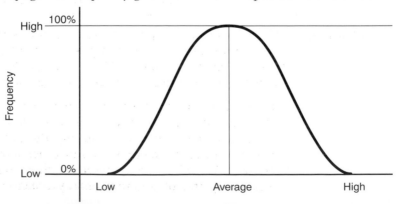

This shows that in a normally distributed population very few people have very low intelligence, most are about average and very few are extremely intelligent. In terms of percentages, we can add to this curve the two vertical lines that show the limits of what is generally considered to be the 'normal' range of intelligence – that is, from an IQ of 70 to an IQ of 130. This covers about 90 per cent of the population, as shown below:

IQ against frequency, showing the 'normal' range of intelligence

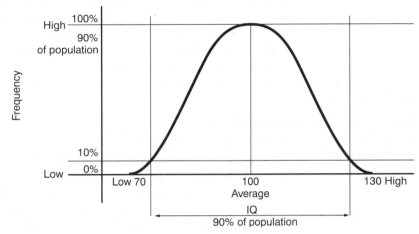

If we assume that the curve is symmetrical and not **skewed**, about 10 per cent of the population is outside the normal range – 5 per cent of whom are below normal intelligence and 5 per cent above the normal range of intelligence. These are the two groups who, in terms of intelligence, are defined as atypical. The two groups can be further subdivided as follows:

Intelligence	IQ	
Above average (5% of population)	>150 150 } 130 }	Genius Gifted
Average (90% of population)	130 } 70 }	Average
Below average (5% of population)	70 } 50 } 50 } 30 } < 30	Moderate learning difficulties Severe learning difficulties Profound learning difficulties

Physical disability Children who are atypical in physical terms may also be divided into two main groups – those with physical disability and those with some form of sensory disability. While sensory disability is still physical, a broad distinction is made between physical and sensory:

- **Physical disability** covers those with large motor control problems such as difficulty with physical co-ordination or physical control (often but not always necessitating the use of a wheelchair), which may be caused by cerebral palsy or other similar conditions.
- **Sensory disability** usually describes those with visual and/or hearing loss or impairment, and sometimes problems with speech and language.

Learning disabilities and associated problems

The third main group of atypical children are those with some mental or learning disability. **Learning disability** can be defined as difficulty with one or more of the basic processes necessary to understand and use language and number. This group includes children who demonstrate emotional and behavioural problems as a result of, or caused by, a specific learning disability or other related mental disability, learned and/or genetic.

There are a number of types of disability; these are given below:

Types of disability/disorder	
ADHD	Short attention span, hyperactive, impulsive behaviour
Aphasia	Problems with speaking and/or comprehension of speech (due to brain damage)
Articulation disorder	Speech problems which may be due to psychological problems
Autism	Literally, 'self orientation'. Absorbed in oneself. Thoughts, feelings, etc., are governed by internal states that do not recognise the reality of the world.
Dysacousia	Difficulty in hearing and/or discomfort with loud noises
Dysagnosia	A general term for any problems with intellectual functioning
Dysarthria	Defective speaking
Dyscalculia	Number problems, particularly with calculations
Dysgraphia	Problems with writing
Dyslexia	Problems with reading and/or spelling and/or writing

The range and complexity of these disabilities is huge, with more being learned about the **aetiology** (cause), diagnosis and treatment all the time. In terms of frequency of occurrence, estimates vary from just a few per cent up to 30 per cent, with three to four times as many boys as girls. Problems associated with learning disability are that some children have multiple difficulties, and that for other children the disorder may not be diagnosed until the child is older, when remedial action may be much more difficult. For the purpose of our discussion, we consider attention-deficit hyperactivity disorder (ADHD), autism and dyslexia.

Attention-deficit hyperactivity disorder (ADHD) Attention-deficit **hyperactivity disorder**, or **ADHD**, is one of a number of what DSM-IV (see page 400) calls **disruptive behaviour disorders**. The behaviour is characterised by poor control and impulsive acting-out behaviour in situations where it would be expected that the person, usually a child, would exercise self control. The title is descriptive of the condition, with a short attention span and hyperactivity. Somewhere between 3 and 5 per cent of primary school children have the syndrome; it is about ten times more common in boys than it is in girls (Barkley, 1990). A key aspect of ADHD is the child's activity, which is not just 'hyper' but frequently lacks direction or purpose – something which even a young active child normally possesses. The lack of attention span, coupled with random hyperactivity, has a powerful negative effect on the child's learning.

In terms of definition, the DSM-IV defines three sub-types:

- predominantly inattentive type;
- predominantly hyperactive/impulsive type; and
- combined type.

Most children are of the combined type, and exhibit a full range of symptoms. Treatment involves teaching parents to handle the child in a very structured manner; and, rather more controversially, drug therapy using Ritalin.

Autism   The term **autism** was first used by Kanner in 1943 to describe what he called 'early infantile autism'. Previously, children with the syndrome had been labelled as schizophrenic because of the similarity of the symptoms. Figures for the frequency of the syndrome vary considerably due to the wide variation in the definition of symptoms, but it is generally considered that between one and two per thousand children suffer from some degree of autism. As with ADHD, more boys than girls are diagnosed as autistic, the ratio being about four to one.

There are generally thought to be four main symptoms present in most cases, despite the range of the autistic spectrum – from very severe to very mild:

- social isolation;
- cognitive problems;
- language problems;
- stereotyped behaviour.

While there is no such thing as 'average autism', social isolation is present in just about every autistic person – baby, child or adult. At the extreme end, the person will withdraw totally from all social contact, refusing any kind of physical contact, eye contact or conversation. At the mild end, the person may engage to a limited degree in some form of contact.

Problems with cognition tend to show as lower mental ability, but not always in traditional ways. Autistic children often do better in finding shape and pattern. (For example, one child known to the author could do jigsaw puzzles with the picture facing down just as quickly as with the picture up. The same child can do complicated word-search puzzles very quickly.) It is thought that the cognitive problems of the autistic person are strictly mental and not related to the other symptoms within the syndrome.

Language problems also range from very severe, with no speech at all, to very mild. The degree to which an autistic child has developed language skills is a reliable indicator of future progress in all aspects of the syndrome.

Most autistic children develop behaviours that they repeat endlessly and usually without any specific purpose. Again, these behaviours can be severe and include physical harm, such as head banging or biting various parts of the body; or mild, such as arranging toys in a certain set order and not actually playing with them.

Dyslexia   **Dyslexia** is a learning disorder where the child is either unable to read – which is rare – or where the child has considerable difficulty with reading fluently. The term is difficult to define accurately, and is usually applied to children who are significantly behind in reading skills and when there is no other evidence of, for example, brain damage or lower mental ability. Most children diagnosed as dyslexic usually develop normally in other learning areas.

Dyslexia occurs in about 5 per cent of the school population, again with the majority being boys.

Explanations – theories and research

Epidemiology

We now need to consider possible explanations for the incidence of atypical development.

Epidemiology is the study of diseases in the context of a population or in an environment. It is usually a multidisciplinary approach involving medical, social, psychological and sometimes demographic data (information about the population as a whole). In terms of research methodology, an **epidemiological approach** is rather like a case study when the researcher investigates all possible causes for a particular condition. In the case of atypical development, the researcher would investigate the relevance of the child's family background – does the atypical condition run in the family? Is the environment in which the child is growing up a part of the cause? Are there other children with the same condition living in the same immediate area? Is the child's learning suffering because of a lack of educational resources? An epidemiological investigation would consider all of these factors, and others that may have relevance, to try to identify the cause or causes for the atypical development. This is the broadest of research methods and can be very effective, but it is costly in terms of time and resources. The data gathered in this way also provide relevant input into any remedial programmes.

Other research methods

Other research methods can be employed to identify illness or disability that is atypical. For example, concern has been expressed about the frequency of cancer in people living near nuclear power plants. In this case, correlation studies are conducted to see if there is a higher incidence of cancer in these localities compared to (correlated to) other communities which are similar in all other respects.

Something to do

- List, with advantages and disadvantages, other research methods that can be used to investigate aspects of atypical development.

Causes of learning difficulties

Children with learning difficulties are frequently within the average range of IQ, one possible cause for their difficulty being due to a lag or delay in development. For example, young children frequently reverse letters such as 'p' and 'q' or 'b' and 'd', but usually quickly develop through this stage; a few children, however, stay at this stage much longer, thus contributing to a learning difficulty. Some research has suggested that the cause may be a neurological problem within the brain, but the specific mechanisms of this are not clear.

In the case of children with low IQs, the causes may be broadly divided into genetic causes and environmental causes (another example of the Nature–Nurture issue). The same is true for children with very high IQs – the causes may be either genetic or environmental.

Abnormality

Definitions of normal and abnormal behaviour

In the above section, we considered 'atypical' mostly in the context of learning. The term 'atypical' is difficult to define precisely, however. As we now consider **abnormality**, we run into even bigger difficulties with definition. At the most basic level, we can say that abnormal is simply that which is not normal – but this immediately raises the question of what then is normal?

Think about it

- Think of all the people you know well and consider as 'normal'.
- How would you define the term 'normal'? Write a definition.

You probably ran into trouble with the above task when it came to deciding what criteria to use. Did you use intelligence – and decide that Einstein was abnormal? Or did you use behaviour and decide that some famous football star was abnormal?

Traditionally, 'abnormal' has been a very difficult word to define and, partly for that reason, other words such as **maladaptive**, **deviant** or 'mentally ill' are being used in its place. Whatever word is used, however, there are still problems with definition, and it is likely that 'abnormal' will remain as the common term. There are a number of ways in which abnormal has been defined, and we consider these below.

Definitions of abnormality

One of the many reasons for the difficulty in defining the word is that it depends on where you are when you attempt the definition. The implication of this is that a given society's values and norms affect the definition, which makes the concept of 'abnormality' relative to the context – usually the society or culture – in which it is used. So 'abnormality' is relative and dependent on a given value system.

Something to investigate

- Go to the reference library, find four books with chapters on abnormal psychology and list and compare the terms used to define abnormality.

While different authors may use different words, for the most part they will be similar. Your list will have perhaps five or six different terms. To make it easier to remember, we have chosen four terms, each beginning with D, to describe abnormal behaviour. As we saw in Unit 2, these are **deviance, dysfunction, distress** and **danger**.

Deviance

To be defined as deviant, behaviour must deviate from an accepted standard. We therefore have to consider what is standard or normal and, as stated above, this depends on a given culture. Every society, however basic or sophisticated, has its own rules or norms of behaviour, either implicit or explicit. These come from that particular society's value system, which in turn will have evolved over years, perhaps centuries. The value system defines what ought and therefore what ought not to take place – behaviour which does not conform to this system is then deviant. For example, if you went out to dinner in an expensive restaurant and were asked to sit on the floor, you would consider this most peculiar – or deviant; but if you were in Seoul or Tokyo, this would be perfectly normal. To take another example, each year the *Gloucestershire Echo* reports that the group who swim in the large open-air pool in Cheltenham on 1st January have to break the ice with a sledgehammer before they can swim. Are these people deviant? They argue that swimming in such cold conditions is extremely invigorating, healthy and good for you.

Dysfunction This is a slightly more straightforward term to define, but is still dependent on the society and its values. The essence of dysfunction has to do with the person's ability to **function** in a normal way in the society of which they are a part. If the person is unable to hold down a job, has difficulty getting up, has 'unusual' eating or sleeping patterns or, in other words, they are unable to carry out normal daily practices, then they are not functioning normally and hence are dysfunctional. In these terms, are the 1st January swimmers dysfunctional? No, because they are able to carry on with the normal everyday business of life.

Distress The question as to whether distress is abnormal is more a question of degree or amount. We all experience distress of one sort or another in varying amounts under various conditions. It is perfectly normal to exhibit distress, perhaps in the form of anxiety or depression, when you experience a distressful incident – someone close to you being killed in a terrible accident, the loss of your job, failing to pass an examination and so on. It is not, however, 'normal' to *stay* in a state of distress longer than is usual for the cause of the distress. Nor is it usual to sink into a much 'deeper' form of anxiety or depression without it being considered abnormal.

Danger Danger can be considered as the most serious of the four Ds. The essence of 'danger', as used here, is behaviour that is or is becoming dangerous to the individual or to others. The danger may simply be the result of carelessness around the home or when out; or it may be deliberate, dangerous behaviour – but this is relatively rare. We should not consider people struggling with severe depression as necessarily dangerous, either to themselves or to others; in fact such people are almost always not dangerous.

Think about it

• The terms listed below are often used to define 'abnormal' or 'abnormality'. They are presented in no particular order. Try to group them together into a systematic order or system.

Self defeating	Personal distress	Dangerous	Faulty interpretation of reality
Socially unacceptable	Dysfunctional	Deviance	Unusual	Distress
Irrational	Statistical criteria	Maladaptive	Mental illness
Unexpected behaviour	Subjective discomfort	Suffering	Unpredictable

Models of abnormality

There is more general agreement when it comes to the question of explaining abnormality than there is in attempting to define it. The various models (or theories or approaches) of abnormality are considered below.

Early history

In most, although not all, of the early explanations, abnormality was thought to be the work of evil spirits, battling within the person's body and influencing their behaviour. Treatment was also spiritual, with the witch-doctor, shaman or medicine man conducting exorcism rites to 'send away' the evil. Later, around the time of classical Greek culture (approximately 500BC to AD500), the 'physicians' and now philosophers began to describe abnormality in more specific terms, using words such as melancholy, mania, hysteria or hallucinations. These terms are still in use today, although not in their original sense.

Something to investigate

- Use a good psychology or reference dictionary (such as *The Penguin Dictionary of Psychology*) and list the terms given above with both their ancient and modern definitions.

The Greek scholar, philosopher and physician Hippocrates (460–377BC) is generally considered to be the father of modern medicine. He made the key distinction that illness – of whatever kind – had natural rather than spiritual causes. He believed that four bodily fluids, called *humours*, when out of balance, caused problems with the brain, which resulted in other 'illnesses'. Galen (AD130–200) distinguished between the purely 'medical', such as a physical head injury, and the 'mental' or 'emotional', such as extreme sadness or problems with a person's love life.

It was at about this point that it was seen that treatment for 'mental' problems needed to be different from treatment for physical problems. As a result, by the middle of the 16th century, people with mental illness were being locked up in asylums (the word comes from the Latin, meaning a sanctuary). Henry VIII gave Bethlehem hospital to the City of London as a gift, to be used for containing the mentally ill. The local pronunciation of Bethlehem was 'Bedlam': the word still used today for noisy, disorganised chaos. By the mid-19th century, things were improving, with Pinel – working in an asylum in Paris – treating patients as human beings in need of more than just minimal care.

Towards the end of the 19th century, the **somatogenic view** became prominent. This believes that abnormality has physical causes. At the same time, the **psychogenic view** was also emerging, arguing that psychological causes are a key factor in abnormal behaviour. Another development at about this time was the use of **hypnotism**, which suggested that a physical problem could have a psychological cause. Breuer, working in Vienna, found that patients, after talking about their problems when under hypnosis, were often cured. This became one of the basic ideas that Freud, also working in Vienna at the same time, incorporated into his work, the result of which was the emergence of the **psychoanalytic approach**.

More recently, advances in our understanding of the brain and the discovery and development of new drugs, particularly **psychotropic drugs**, coupled with a much wider availability of psychotherapy, have developed alongside a reduction in the number of people in mental hospitals and a corresponding increase in treatment within the community.

In the following pages, we outline six main models or ways of viewing abnormality. A seventh, the **sociocultural model**, has emerged most recently with the coming together of sociology and anthropology.

The demonological model

During the Middle Ages (AD500–1300) it was the Church that became the key influence in Western society; the emphasis changed from an emerging science (Hippocrates, Galen, etc.) to a re-emergence of spiritual views, particularly the **demonological** or demon possession – 'the Devil made me do it . . .'. Just about any behaviour that was different was seen as the result of the person's involvement with Satan, or perhaps as a result of God punishing the person (a view not unique to the demonological model). Treatment was exorcism; if that was not successful, frequent beating was employed or the person was even put to death, often by drowning or burning at the stake.

The medical model

There are two interpretations of the term 'medical model'.

- The first has to do with the way mental illness is **classified**. This is discussed in more detail in a later section; for the moment the medical model, in terms of classification, means that there are seen to be close similarities between physical and mental illness, the traditional medical model for physical illness being as follows:

The patient has symptoms. → A diagnosis is reached (based on these symptoms). → The appropriate treatment is given. → The patient gets better.

For physical illness, the medical model of symptom/diagnosis/treatment/healing (usually) works very well, but to apply this model to mental illness is not so successful. In physical terms, the patient may have a temperature of 104°F or may be covered in spots – both *objective* symptoms. It is rather more difficult if the person complains of 'feeling very sad' or 'hearing voices in my head' – very much *subjective* symptoms. Diagnosis of subjective symptoms and therefore treatment of mental illness is difficult.

- The second interpretation when considering the medical model has to do with **cause**. Physically ill people, in this model, are not held to be responsible for their illness, they have just 'caught' it. Using the same (medical) model with mental illness would suggest the same cause – that the person simply 'caught' the 'illness' and is therefore not responsible for the illness, condition or behaviour.

Something to do

- Re-read the section in Unit 7, pages 328–9, on Freud's psychosexual stages of development.

This holds that mental abnormality is the result of unresolved conflicts, usually from childhood. An important point is that symptoms in this theory are not 'accidental'; they are determined by past experiences. Psychodynamic theories are therefore **deterministic.**

Something to do

• Draw up a cross-topic spider diagram using 'determinism' as the key word.

To resolve the conflicts (which have caused the abnormal behaviour), the 'patient' has to be taken back to relive them. The **psychoanalyst** then 'explores' or 'analyses' these past experiences, particularly as they relate to early relationships and traumatic experiences. In this way, 'insight' is gained by the individual into the problem and the cure is effected.

In terms of its evolution, Sigmund Freud (1856–1939) originated **psychoanalysis** while practising medicine in Vienna. Other important theorists such as Carl Jung, Alfred Adler and Erik Erikson initially supported Freud's psychoanalytic theory but went on to develop their own psychoanalytic theories; these played down the emphasis on the sexual, but emphasised other aspects. Jung (1875–1961), who believed we have a collective unconscious which has within it primitive urges, went on to develop what is called **analytic psychology;** while Adler (1870–1937) maintained that we all try to dominate others because we are basically motivated by an **inferiority complex.** His views may have been influenced by the fact that as a child he experienced frequent illnesses, including being crippled by rickets. There is no scientific evidence for this 'inferiority' theory. Adler went on to develop **individual psychology,** which holds that self awareness is important in the development of the personality – an approach that is still used today.

The behavioural model

This is also sometimes known as the **learning theory model.** At a very basic level, it is concerned only with the behaviour of the person and not any (possible) underlying cause. As it is the behaviour that counts, the focus then becomes the learning environment, with the 'patient' acquiring maladaptive behaviour. This model is also deterministic.

The Russian psychologist Ivan Pavlov (1849–1936) is credited with starting the behavioural school when he discovered (by accident) classical conditioning (see Unit 6, page 000). Watson, Thorndike and Skinner are all important figures in the development of behaviourism, which peaked – at least in terms of influence – in the 1950s when it became the common starting point for a great deal of psychological thinking.

The behavioural approach or model in abnormal psychology has two main strands: **classical conditioning** and **operant conditioning.** There is also a third strand, **modelling,** where the individual acquires a behaviour through observation and imitation.

A classic case of behaviour modelling

Bandura's (1963) study with the bobo doll (see also Unit 3, page 111) is a classic example of behaviour modelling. In this study, a large rubber doll, capable of standing erect and rocking on its base, was physically assaulted by an adult. Three groups of children aged between three and six years old watched the aggression either in real life, or on a film or in a cartoon film. A fourth group was the control. The second part of the study was to allow the children to play in their groups, frustrate the play by removing their toys and then measure their aggression. Compared to the control group, the other three groups acted aggressively almost twice as frequently.

Modelling is sometimes described as **social learning** or **observational learning,** and in a sense links the behavioural model to the cognitive model (see below). Modelling has itself developed over time with some theorists (including Bandura) arguing that a **cognitive–behavioural** model was more accurate (see also Unit 6, pages 317–18). In this model, cognitive processes are acquired by behavioural means, while the behaviour follows the person's interpretation, in their own mind, of the learned cognitive processes.

The cognitive model Towards the end of the 1950s, the emphasis within psychology was moving away from pure behaviourism towards an emphasis on cognitive processes, partly because behaviourism was not providing all the answers and partly because of new research and better understanding of the brain. Three cognitive models – the cognitive–behavioural model, the information-processing model and the 'faulty-thinking' model – need to be seen as variations on a theme, rather than three different models.

- The **cognitive–behavioural model** was discussed above in its link with the behavioural model.

- In the **information-processing model,** the abnormality is seen to be caused by faulty processing. (Remember that information processing draws parallels between computer operations and the human brain.) This can include problems with faulty input, faulty storage, faulty retrieval or almost any kind of partial or full breakdown in the processing of information.
- The third strand in the cognitive model is what is known as **'faulty thinking'.** This is not a very precise term, but it refers to problems with making assumptions, faulty perception, oversimplification of complex issues and irrational beliefs and attitudes.

Key people in the formation of the cognitive approach are Bandura with his social learning theory; and Ellis and Beck who, in the early 1960s, were generally considered to be influential in the formation of the cognitive model of abnormality.

The humanistic model

This is sometimes also known as the **humanistic–existential model.** It is essentially concerned with what it is that makes us 'human'. Is it based on our early childhood experiences? Our behaviour? Our thought processes? Or is it something more? A **humanistic** view believes that, while not ignoring behaviour and thought, the essence of 'human-ness' lies in issues such as self awareness, a value system and emotions (joy, sorrow and so on). It is an approach that believes that human beings are naturally friendly and positive in outlook and seek to **self actualise.** Carl Rogers (1902–87) is the name most associated with the humanistic approach; Maslow and Perls being two others.

While 'humanistic' is the name more usually given to this model, 'humanistic–existential' is more accurate, as both of these terms and philosophies combine within the model. Humanism and existentialism evolved at about the same time; both can be traced back to the 1940s. For the **existentialists,** the emphasis came initially from philosophy, with philosophers such as Kierkegaard and Heidegger arguing that human beings must live 'authentic' lives, with the choice to accept the way we exist. If we accept it, then we live healthy, happy lives; if we do not, then our 'existence' is likely to become maladaptive. Psychologists who follow this school – blending existentialism with the humanistic – are theorists such as May, Frankl and Yalom. In a sentence, the existentialist says, 'Take charge of your life'; the humanistic says, 'Your life has value'. According to Rogers, it all starts in early childhood, with the child needing **unconditional positive regard** from others for healthy growth.

This model provides the basis for a wide variety of applications, particularly in terms of therapy (including group therapy) and encounter groups.

Implications for treatment

It is important to realise that while the six views of abnormality may appear as six separate models when considered as theoretical approaches, when considered in a therapeutic setting there is often a blurring of the distinctions between them. This will become clearer when we discuss therapeutic approaches later in the unit. We turn our attention now to the implications of these models for treatment, and related ethical issues.

Something to do

• Redraw the summary chart below and complete the boxes in your own words as you read the following paragraphs.

Implications of models of abnormal psychology			
Models	**Assumptions**	**Implications for treatment**	**Ethical implications**
Medical			
Psychodynamic			
Behavioural			
Cognitive			
Humanistic			

Note that the demonological model is not included. This is because it is no longer considered as valid.

The demonological model
• **Assumptions:** A spiritual force is responsible for the condition.
• **Implications for treatment:** The spiritual force has to be 'driven out' or 'appeased'.
• **Ethical implications:** Ethical considerations were at this stage not codified; religion and superstition were dominant.

The medical model
• **Assumptions:** Abnormal behaviour is a symptom(s) of underlying disorder(s). Treatment focuses on the underlying disorder.
• **Implications for treatment:** Somatic therapies (see pages 420–2). Requires medical expertise to control or cure the biological or chemical problem. Use of ICD (International Classification of Diseases) or DSM classifications of mental disorders (see pages 399–401). Some abnormalities have no identified biological or chemical causes. Treatment (usually) in society, not in institutions.
• **Ethical implications:** The person is not to blame for their abnormality. Drug therapy and electroconvulsive therapy (ECT) can have serious long-term side-effects. Treatment is often not a 'cure' but an alleviation of symptoms. Treatment can be used for 'social control' (for example the use of a pharmacological strait-jacket). ECT and psychosurgery lack rigorous scientific rationale.

The psychodynamic model
• **Assumptions:** Mental disorder has internal/psychological causes, usually related to innate biological drives. A reductionist approach. Deterministic. The individual is not to blame.
• **Implications for treatment:** Long and expensive. Requires re-experiencing past/childhood. Very difficult to predict abnormality.
• **Ethical implications:** Involves re-experiencing past trauma. The theory lacks scientific rigour. Parents are sometimes seen to be the cause of children's problems.

The behavioural model
- **Assumptions:** Abnormal behaviour is acquired (and maintained) through learning principles (stimulus–response and reinforcement). Looks only at overt behaviour. Current work is now considering cognitive behaviour. Deterministic (action determined by experience).
- **Implications for treatment:** The abnormal behaviour is capable of being defined numerically (for example, 'washes hands 20 times per hour'). This produces the baseline for treatment. Cognitive processes are also acquired and maintained by learning principles and can therefore be unlearned and/or more appropriate behaviours learned. Treatment can be tested under laboratory conditions.
- **Ethical implications:** Very directive. The therapist/clinician decides the outcome. Deals only with symptom(s), not cause(s).

The cognitive model
- **Assumptions:** Focuses on human thought. Must understand content and processes of human thought. Rejects medical illness view. Abnormality results from cognitive problems such as false assumptions, illogical thought processes. Human thought is the main contributor to normal *and* abnormal behaviour. Cognitive theories can be tested.
- **Implications for treatment:** Maladaptive thoughts (cognition) may be a consequence of abnormal behaviour, not the cause. Viewed strictly, the model is very narrow – are you a product of only your thoughts? (It is unlikely!)
- **Ethical implications:** Therapist has a powerful influence. Only suitable for some disorders.

The humanistic model
- **Assumptions:** People are free to make choices. 'Self worth' begins in infancy. We need 'unconditional positive regard'. The model disapproves of classification (because all people are unique). Experience is individual.
- **Implications for treatment:** A 'person-centred' approach (not problem-centred). Non-directive. Probably not suitable for serious or extreme cases of abnormality.
- **Ethical implications:** The most ethical of the models, due to its emphasis on the individual.

Cultural and subcultural differences

The essence of this topic is that 'abnormality' – in terms of its definition, classification and diagnosis – is viewed quite differently by different cultures, and is often viewed differently within a given culture. It then follows that treatment will be correspondingly different across cultures. To take perhaps an extreme view of this and to polarise the issue, consider how, for example, west coast America, working-class England and rural China approach the concept of 'depression'. (We might equally have chosen schizophrenia or some other mental disorder.) Starting with west coast America, from where many modern therapies have emerged, how would you describe the culture? Words such as open, brash, physical, 'anything goes', a 'singles' society, trendy, will probably come to mind. Now consider rural China: mostly agricultural, with limited technology, a society based on the extended family, closed and very structured. You would probably put working-class England somewhere between the two. Now consider the question of depression from these three cultural viewpoints. The Californian with depression will probably have it officially diagnosed, recognised and analysed. He or she will see a therapist regularly and possibly want their therapist to 'use' the latest 'theories'. The Chinese farmer may be equally depressed – but already we are using Western ideas, concepts, terminology and diagnosis, so we have a problem right at the start. Even if we can agree with the concept, terminology and diagnosis (which is unlikely), then because of his culture, farmer Hsi will probably choose to 'cover up' his 'depression' and deal with it within his extended family. You would expect the English car worker to be somewhere between these American and Chinese extremes.

Culture-bound behaviours

There are a number of specific conditions within a given society usually caused by its culture, history, lifestyle and pressures. These are sometimes called **culture-bound behaviours**. One of these is **Amok** (or Amuck). We often use the phrase 'he ran amok'. This disorder originated in the Far East, particularly Malaysia and the Philippines, and is characterised by the person – usually a male – moving wildly, using anything that is to hand as a weapon, and attacking anyone and anything quite indiscriminately. Other culture-bound behaviours include Windigo, Koro, Latah and Susto.

Something to investigate

• Research definitions for the culture-bound behaviours mentioned above.

Evidence suggests that subcultural groups, particularly ethnic minority groups, show significant differences in their use of mental health services when compared to the population as a whole. Research in America has shown that factors such as cost, language and cultural belief all hinder ethnic minority groups from using available mental health services, preferring instead to use old-fashioned family or cultural remedies; for example, Hispanic people in the USA often turn to spiritism. On the positive side, where attempts are made specifically to meet the needs of minority groups, then the percentage of people using these services increases to the norm for all users, drop-out rates decrease and satisfaction, as reported by clients, increases (O'Sullivan et al., 1989).

A related issue concerns the way in which personality and intelligence tests are used and interpreted. We need to bear in mind here that these tests are common in Western society, but are not so common in other cultures; and that they are standardised, usually at least, for white middle-class populations. When they are used with subcultural or ethnic minority groups, then the results or scores need to be interpreted with both sensitivity and caution. For example, one question on the Minnesota Multiphasic Personality Inventory (MMPI), a very sophisticated personality inventory, asks:

"True or false: 'Evil spirits possess me at times'."

MMPI

As mentioned above, spiritism is common and considered normal in some minority groups, so a Hispanic person for example may answer 'True', whereas the average Western person is likely to answer 'False' *unless* he or she were suffering from a mental disorder.

Psychiatry and the 'anti-psychiatry' view

We have been talking a lot about the treatment of illness, particularly mental illness, so now may be the place to discuss the function of those who try to 'cure' these illnesses. A psychiatrist practises psychiatry, is trained in medicine, and specialises in the diagnosis and treatment of mental disorders. Traditionally, psychiatry takes the view that a person with serious emotional problems has a medical problem. Also providing treatment is the clinical psychologist – not medically trained, but working in a clinical setting and perhaps specialising in personality or psychotherapy. The emphasis tends to be on the individual as a whole person.

In terms of anti-psychiatry, the name most often quoted in this context is that of Thomas S. Szasz. In his book *The Myth of Mental Illness*, published in 1962, he says:

> *"I submit that the traditional definition of psychiatry, which is still in vogue, places it alongside such things as alchemy and astrology, and commits it to the category of pseudo-science."*
> Thomas S. Szasz, *The Myth of Mental Illness* (1962)

Speaking of his book, he says:

> *"I tried to show how and why the concept of mental illness is erroneous and misleading."*
> Quoted in the preface to Thomas S. Szasz, *The Manufacture of Madness* (1970)

Other thinkers and writers at about the same time published similar views, and so the 'anti-psychiatry' movement was born in the 1960s. While there are many variations on this general theme, the movement has maintained its impetus over the intervening years. Perhaps the essential issue in the debate has to do with the question of what exactly mental illness is. Szasz was not denying the existence of mental illness, he (and others) were concerned with the labels that were attached to people and – at a much deeper level – the social and political reasons why the psychiatric establishment did this.

Szasz argued that mental illness certainly exists, but that it can only be called 'mental illness' if the disease affects the brain or the central nervous system, in which case a better term is 'disease of the brain' or 'neurophysiological disorders'. Other 'illnesses', he then argued, are more to do with 'problems in living' which, according to Szasz, make up the vast majority of what are usually called cases of mental illness. In some circles, this distinction between **organic psychoses** and **functional psychoses** is recognised – organic being the diseases of the brain, functional being problems with living or functioning.

The problem is further complicated when we start to think of the *mind* as being 'ill' or 'sick'. How can something which has no form or physical structure be 'sick'? The answer, according to Szasz, is that these 'problems in living' are labelled as illnesses because the vast majority of members of society are themselves unable to deal with them and are confused and threatened by them. In other words, mental illness is the creation of the society. This viewpoint is expanded in Szasz, *The Manufacture of Madness* (1970).

Think about it

- On page 390, we suggested that a seventh model of abnormality is the **sociocultural model**. What do you think might be the connection between a sociocultural model of abnormality, and the views expressed by Szasz and other writers like him?

(For the answer according to Szasz, see the end of this unit.)

Post-Szasz developments

Szasz, probably more than anyone else, started a shift in thinking in the way that we consider **psychopathology** (see below). He raised issues concerning the importance of sociocultural explanations, the use of language and the way that an institutional setting can influence judgement.

This shift has influenced the revision of the DSM (see page 399) (Pincus et al., 1992). McNamee and Gergen (1992) report that changes in therapeutic approaches are now recognising the fact that different clients have different ways of expressing themselves and that, when coupled with different sociocultural issues, this can significantly affect the interpretation and understanding of the client's 'problem'. It is likely that this shift will continue to influence future thinking.

Think about it

- Do you agree with Szasz that what are labelled 'disorders' can in fact be *sane* responses to an *insane* world?

Psychopathology

'Medical student's illness'

As far as this book is concerned, we should really call this 'psychology student's illness'. It is a strange topic, you may think, but it is in fact an interesting phenomenon and one that is described in many medical textbooks.

What we are talking about is the phenomenon whereby as you are reading the description of an illness, and as the symptoms are described, you become quite certain that the description of the illness fits your own condition right now. In other words, *you* have got the illness that is being described. This phenomenon is quite common and in its own way illustrates the relative closeness of 'normal' and 'abnormal' and the frequently fuzzy line between the two.

By way of reassurance, if the first time that you read about a mental illness corresponds with the first time that you feel that you have the symptoms, the almost certain likelihood is that you do not have the illness. It is only when the symptoms are persistent, troublesome and are perhaps affecting behaviour and thoughts that they might represent a real problem. Most people experience the odd bizarre thought every now and again.

Bear this in mind as we now turn to the classification, description and explanation of a variety of abnormalities and psychological disorders.

The classification of abnormality and psychological disorders

Attempts to classify abnormal behaviour have a long history. The Greek physician Hippocrates (460–377BC) probably recorded the first attempt. As noted above (see page 389), he believed illnesses had natural causes and were not the result of an angry God. Often the brain was the cause, together with an incorrect balance of the four *humours* (fluids that flow around within the body) – yellow and black bile, phlegm and blood. Each of these fluids caused a specific illness – for example, too much black bile caused **melancholia**. Hippocrates went on to describe treatments to cure these imbalances, and so we have the beginnings of a classification system of symptom, diagnosis and treatment. Other Greek physicians followed this lead, notably Galen (AD130–200), who classified emotional problems.

Roman physicians continued along the same lines, as their culture followed on from the Greek. It is interesting to note that in both Greek and Roman medicine, treatment for abnormality usually involved rest, warm baths, music and gentle exercise. More dramatic treatment followed only as a last resort.

Modern systems of classification

These are considered to have begun with the work of Emil Kraepelin (1856–1926), a German researcher who published the first system for classifying abnormal behaviour in 1883. He did this by analysing the records of many patients in mental hospitals and grouping their **symptoms** into **syndromes**. He was then able to identify possible causes and link these with the course of the illness. His use of case records gave him a vast amount of data of actual patients who had been referred, diagnosed and treated. In this way, Kraepelin identified **categories** of illnesses or disorders, and further organised these into a hierarchy. This work formed the basis of the classification system of psychological illnesses which is now used by the World Health Organization and is known as the **International Classification of Diseases (ICD)**. This system has been revised a number of times; it is now in its tenth revision and so is known as ICD-10.

The other main classification system, which is also based on Kraepelin's work, is the system developed in North America; it is known as the **Diagnostic and Statistical Manual of Mental Disorders (DSM)**. This too has been revised a number of times, and is now known as DSM-IV. One of the purposes of the fourth revision was to bring the terminology into line with the ICD-10.

If we think for a moment about the value of a classification system, perhaps the most important element is that different practitioners can use the same language to diagnose a given condition and then communicate with each other without any misunderstanding.

We look briefly at these two systems of classification, and then discuss the important issues of their reliability and validity.

The International Classification of Diseases (ICD-10)

Traditionally, mental illness was divided into two broad areas: **neuroses** and **psychoses**. 'Neurotics build castles in the air, psychotics live in them' used to be the favourite saying of a particular professor as he introduced this topic. If he was feeling somewhat cynical, he would add: 'and psychiatrists collect the rent'. The terms 'neurotic' and 'psychotic' are now considered too broad to be useful, but the professor's colourful pronouncements will help you to remember that **neurotic** means partial loss of reality, while **psychotic** means total loss of reality.

What the ICD-10 does is to ask the person making the diagnosis to identify the client's symptoms from one of 11 groups, and then to refine or focus the diagnosis (within the group) using a more detailed sub-category. This list of categories is given below.

A comparison of ICD-10 and DSM-IV categories of mental disorder (in abbreviated form)

ICD-10	DSM-IV
1. Organic	1. Cognitive disorders
2. Schizophrenia	2. Schizophrenia
3. Psychoactive substance use	3. Substance related
4. Mood/affective	4. Mood
5. Neurotic	5. Anxiety
6. Behavioural/emotional	6. Somatoform
7. Developmental	7. Dissociative
8. Mental retardation	8. Adjustment
9. Adult personality/behaviour	9. Childhood/retardation
10. Behavioural/physiological (psychological)	10. Personality
11. Unspecified other disorder	11. Sexual/gender
	12. Impulse/control
	13. Factitious
	14. Sleep
	15. Eating
	16. Other

Something to do

• Make a list of all the technical terms in this section. Using a psychology dictionary, write out brief, accurate definitions.

The Diagnostic and Statistical Manual of Mental Disorders (DSM-IV)

The approach taken by the classification system DSM-IV, which lists nearly 300 mental disorders, is somewhat different to ICD-10. You will see from the above chart that there are a different number of categories, and that the definitions of the categories do not always correspond. Another major difference is that in DSM-IV, the diagnosis is required to be made over five different axes (axes were first introduced in DSM-III). The principle behind this is to require the diagnosis to be made over a much broader area of functioning, on the basis that most disorders involve aspects of biological and sociological elements as well as of psychological elements. The five axes are as follows:

• **Axis 1:** Clinical disorders.
• **Axis 2:** Personality disorders; lower mental ability.
• **Axis 3:** Medical conditions.
• **Axis 4:** Psychosocial, environmental.
• **Axis 5:** Global functioning.

A diagnosis is normally made by working through the five axes in order. Axis 1 has 16 major subdivisions, each of these with a number of specific disorders. Axis 2 has only two subdivisions: lower mental ability and personality disorders. These tend to be long term and can be overlooked in the presence of Axis 1 disorders. Axes 3, 4 and 5 deal with related problems that may be relevant to the diagnosis: Axis 3 with any general medical condition; Axis 4 with psychosocial or environmental aspects, such as family problems, education, housing, etc.; Axis 5 is a 'global assessment of functioning' (GAF), which is a rating of the person's overall (taking everything into account) level of functioning. The GAF is scored from 0 to 100. A code from 1 to 10 would indicate persistent danger of harming themselves or others, and serious suicidal risk; whereas a code from 90 to 100 indicates no symptoms and effective functioning. A code in the middle, say 50–60, indicates moderate symptoms in social or environmental situations.

Reliability and validity Two major aspects of any test or classification system are reliability and validity. So are ICD-10 and DSM-IV reliable and valid? In the case of DSM-III and IIIR, reliability figures (that is, the consistency of measurement) are given at about 70 per cent. DSM-IV, published in 1994, has major revisions built into it and it is expected to achieve a higher reliability. Greater reliability can only be shown after the test has been in use for some time; it is still too early to put an accurate figure on the reliability of DSM-IV.

With respect to the ICD, reliability is also considered to have improved with each successive version. There is some disagreement with the ICD-10 because of incomplete understanding of the cause or aetiology (sometimes etiology) of mental disorders. This means that the class of mental disorder needs to be derived from descriptions of the symptoms, which those using the ICD-10 do not like, preferring instead a greater emphasis on the cause. One reason for the increased reliability is provision for the use of decision diagrams (Is the person X? If YES, go to Y. If NO, go to Z and so on). Using pre-designed diagrams ensures that nothing is likely to be missed. Another reason is the availability of computer software to assist in the diagnostic process.

In terms of validity – that is, whether you are measuring what you think you are measuring – this is generally considered to be more difficult to assess than reliability. It is further complicated because validity relies in part on reliability. So in the context of the diagnosis of a mental disorder, the question becomes: does the diagnosis accurately (and reliably) reflect the actual disorder?

One aspect of validity is **predictive validity** – that is, whether it helps predict future symptoms. A second aspect is **concurrent validity** – that is, do associated or secondary symptoms feature in the diagnosis? For example, a person with depression will often show concern for their physical health – physical health being the associated symptom. The diagnosis of depression then becomes valid if the associated symptom is present.

Perhaps the major problem with both reliability and validity is that, in this context, they are both being applied to classifying the problems that *people* have – and, of course, every person is different.

However, in the broadest terms, progress is being made and the latest versions of the ICD and the DSM (and other similar systems in other countries) show improvement over earlier versions.

A classic case of abnormality diagnosis

A classic study that is often quoted in the general context of abnormal behaviour and its diagnosis is the 1973 study by Rosenhan: 'On being sane in insane places'. What Rosenhan did was to get eight perfectly normal people with ordinary jobs to turn up at mental hospitals in the USA complaining of 'hearing voices'. The only deception was the person's name, occupation and the presenting symptom. All eight were admitted and diagnosed as having schizophrenia. Once admitted, they stopped 'hearing voices' and were discharged after an average 20 days with 'schizophrenia in remission'. It seems that the only people to be suspicious of these 'patients' were genuine patients.

"Thank you doctor! I used to hear voices, but since that nurse took away my radio—I'm much better!"

In a follow-up study, staff at a teaching hospital were told that there was a likelihood that more 'pseudo-patients' would turn up seeking admission. Out of the next 200 patients, 40 were considered to be 'normal'. They were in fact all genuine patients.

There are a number of criticisms that can be levelled at the original study and the follow-up. Perhaps the main point is that the whole question of diagnosis in respect of mental disorder is, to say the least, difficult.

Something to investigate

• Read the Rosenhan study in the primary source – Rosenhan, D.L., 'On being sane in insane places', *Science*, 179, pp. 250–8 (1973).
  (a) Write a brief critique of the study. Consider its aims, methodology, language used, etc.
  (b) Write a defence of the staff professionals involved in the study.

Description and explanation of disorders

We now turn to the description and explanation of abnormalities and psychological disorders. We then discuss the explanations of the disorders as seen by the various models of abnormality. The explanations include, where relevant, the genetic, neurological and social causes. We do this for a number of main categories of disorder, as follows:

Anxiety disorders
- Phobias
- Obsessive–compulsive disorder
- Acute stress disorder
- Post-traumatic stress disorder

Affective disorders (mood)
- Depression (unipolar)
- Bipolar disorders

Schizophrenia

Eating disorders
- Anorexia nervosa
- Bulimia nervosa

Something to do

- Start another summary chart. Lay it out like the example below, and fill it in as you work through this section.

Disorder	Description	Explanation

Anxiety disorders

ICD-10's equivalent of DSM-IV's 'anxiety disorders' is 'neurotic, stress-related and somatoform disorders'. Under the heading of 'anxiety disorders', DSM-IV lists: panic disorder, agoraphobia, specific phobia, social phobia, obsessive–compulsive disorder and post-traumatic stress disorder. The ICD-10 has a similar list, but has in addition: dissociative disorders, multiple-personality disorder and somatoform and other related disorders. Of all the above, we discuss phobias, obsessive–compulsive disorder and acute stress and post-traumatic stress disorders.

Something to do

- Continue to work on your vocabulary. Ensure that you understand the technical terms that are used.

Anxiety is often distinguished from fear, in that **fear** usually has a specific focus or cause, or perhaps object or event. **Anxiety**, on the other hand, is often focus-less, there is no obvious cause; it is there, it is real, but for no apparent reason. A small amount of anxiety is quite normal and in some respects desirable and can be considered a normal adaptive response. When, however, the fear is irrational and persistent and interferes with normal functioning, it can be defined as a **phobia**.

Phobias The word 'phobia' derives from the Greek word meaning fear or dread. Listed below are some (of very many) phobias.

Name of phobia:	Fear of:
Acrophobia	High places
Agoraphobia	Open spaces
Ailurophobia	Cats
Algophobia	Pain
Anthropophobia	Men
Aquaphobia	Water
Arachnophobia	Spiders
Astraphobia	Storms
Cancerophobia	Cancer
Claustrophobia	Enclosed spaces
Cynophobia	Dogs
Ergasiophobia	Work
Gynophobia	Women
Helminthophobia	Worms
Nycotophobia	Dark
Ophidiophobia	Snakes
Pyrophobia	Fire
Scholionaphobia	School
Siderophobia	Railways
Tachophobia	Speed
Thanatophobia	Death
Xenophobia	Strangers/foreigners

The DSM-IV identifies three broad groups of phobias:

- **Agoraphobia** (fear of open spaces) is probably the most common. The vast majority of those affected are women in early adulthood.
- **Social phobia** is a relative newcomer and is a fear of being in a prominent position in a social setting.
- **Specific phobia** is a fear of a specific object or place or situation.

Explanations of phobic disorders All kinds of explanations and reasons have been given for the development of a phobia: modern-day stress, family or personal problems, learning experiences, cultural or social issues and biological predisposition. As you would expect, the different models of abnormality emphasise or de-emphasise various factors.

<u>Psychodynamic explanations</u>   This model suggests that there is an original source for the fear that is repressed into the unconscious but that then has to be displaced onto some other object or situation – which, of course, appears as irrational. Freud developed this theory from the case of 'Little Hans' (1909).

A classic case of phobia

'Little Hans' is a famous case studied by Freud in 1909. Hans was a five-year-old boy who lived in Vienna and who refused to go out because he was afraid that a horse would bite him. Freud believed that the phobia was caused by the Oedipal struggle which the boy was going through, where on the one hand he felt a strong attachment to his mother, and on the other, intense anxiety that his father would retaliate by castrating him. The theory was that Hans displaced this anxiety onto horses. There was a degree of logic in this as his father wore large black-framed glasses and had a moustache – he looked a little horse-like. Having made the displacement – onto horses – Hans could deal with the anxiety by not going near a horse; but in an era when horses were still the main form of transport, this meant that he could not go out.

<u>Behavioural explanations</u>
- Classical conditioning explanations for anxiety and phobias argue that they are learned through conditioning, first to fear, then to the specific object or situation. The initial fearful event was the unconditioned stimulus, which elicited the unconditioned response of fear. The subsequent phobia (spiders, open spaces) represents the conditioned stimulus, which in the person's mind becomes associated with the initial fear and elicits the conditioned response – the phobia.
- Operant conditioning can also lead to the development of phobic behaviour through (usually) avoidance behaviour. If a person thinks that they are afraid of something, they will go out of their way to avoid it. They therefore are rewarded by not experiencing the anxiety. Whenever they do see or experience the anxiety/fear (the spider, open space), they become anxious.

- Modelling is a third form of behavioural response, particularly with children. If a child observes that its parent is afraid of spiders or open spaces, the child too – through imitation and possibly observation – may develop the same fear.

Evidence suggests that many phobias may be acquired by conditioning means, but it is difficult to prove this.

<u>Cognitive explanations</u>   Cognitive explanations tend to focus on general anxiety disorder rather than specific phobias. The general thrust is that the disorder is caused by irrational or maladaptive assumptions. In other words, the person with the disorder holds to an irrational explanation that influences their understanding and as a result they develop inappropriate emotional reactions. These reactions lead to generalised anxiety or fear. New or stressful experiences – for example starting a new job, or an exam – are likely to be interpreted not just as stressful but as dangerous and threatening. This interpretation of life-events becomes more common and a generalised anxiety disorder develops. Leading proponents of this view are Ellis and Beck.

<u>Biological explanations</u>   Like cognitive explanations, the biological explanations tend to focus on generalised anxiety disorders rather than specific phobias.

In general terms, the biology of the brain allows for increasing levels of neural activity as a normal pattern of response to real fear. In a real fear-provoking situation, this hyperactivity dies down via a feedback mechanism when the fear disappears. In the case of a person with generalised anxiety disorder, the feedback mechanism is thought to be faulty, allowing for long periods of a high level of anxiety (Lloyd et al., 1992). The benzodiazepine groups of drugs (Valium, Librium) have been found to help this situation (Leonard, 1992).

A serious problem with this theory is that the cause of the disorder is not explained; some researchers believe that the biological reaction is a reaction to anxiety and not the cause of it.

Related issues concern the possibility that generalised anxiety disorders may be inherited, or at the very least the person may be predisposed genetically to the disorder. Evidence for this comes from twin studies, where incidence rates move from 4 per cent of the general population to about 15 per cent for twins – the closer the family relationship, the higher the likelihood of the disorder. This is complicated, however, by the fact that family members are likely to share the same environmental circumstances, such as housing, and so an environmental factor may be a contributing factor to the disorder.

Something to do

- Each of the above 'explanations' has limitations. Make a list of them.

Obsessive–compulsive disorders

Moving on from phobias, our next 'anxiety disorder' is obsessive–compulsive disorder. This disorder can be described as serious anxiety manifesting itself in **obsessive** and **compulsive** behaviours. The essential characteristics of an obsession are recurrent and persistent thoughts, ideas and feelings; whilst the key feature of compulsion is behaviour that has become ritualised. Any attempt on the part of the person with the disorder to resist the compulsive behaviour results in an increase in anxiety which is only reduced by going through with the behaviour. The disorder may consist of just obsessions, or just compulsions, either of which we probably all experience in minor non-anxiety-producing ways. For example, we may all have occasional obsessive thoughts that we really might lose control of ourselves and harm someone else; or we may experience a mild compulsion such as checking behaviour – checking several times that you locked the door before going to bed. A combination of the two may result in obsessive–compulsive disorder. In this case, compulsive acts usually follow obsessive thoughts.

Explanations of obsessive–compulsive disorders

Psychodynamic explanations   Freudian theory holds that obsessive–compulsive behaviour results from tension between id impulses, which produce anxiety, and the anxiety-reducing defence mechanisms of the ego – the tension being at the explicit or conscious level, rather than in the unconscious. The id impulse is usually the obsessive thought, while the ego defence attempts to keep the inappropriate thoughts (obsessions) in check by initiating the compulsive behaviour. A classic example might be the man who has repeated (obsessive) thoughts of, say, some forbidden sexual activity, and who counters this by a ritualistic (compulsive) hand-washing routine. Ego-defence mechanisms may take different forms: defence reaction, for example, can mean that the person develops a lifestyle directly opposite to the compulsive behaviour. Freud argued that the stage is set for obsessive–compulsive behaviour in later life, when the child is in the anal stage – about two years old – when the id and ego are in tension due to anger and perhaps shame within the child as it is being toilet-trained.

The cognitive–behavioural explanation   This is an explanation that combines elements of both behavioural and cognitive theories. The theory is quite straightforward. It starts with the assumption that we all, at times, have thoughts that just come into our minds, that are unwanted and unpleasant – thoughts of attacking someone, thoughts of a sexual nature, or thoughts that 'germs' are attacking us. The vast majority of people simply shrug these thoughts off, ignore them, or regard them as meaningless. A very few people, however, either do not or cannot deal with them in this way, believing themselves to be responsible for these awful thoughts; and further believing that the thoughts may lead to the action that the thoughts are about (harming others, etc.). Such people find this possibility so stressful that they then try to get rid of the thoughts by engaging in an activity that will cancel out or neutralise or put right the initial awful thought(s). This activity may consist of behaving very positively towards the person at the centre of the harmful thoughts, excessive hand-washing to remove possible 'germs', and so on. The rest is pure behavioural theory: the person gets relief from the awful thoughts by practising the activity which reduces the stress; this reduces the stress and anxiety and, by doing so, confirms to the person that the thoughts are really awful, or worse; and so the eliminating behaviour needs to be practised even more frequently, resulting in obsessive–compulsive disorder.

The key question in this approach is: if we all experience these thoughts, why do some go on to develop this disorder? There are a number of possible reasons, most suggesting an additional dysfunction. So, for example, a person prone to mild depression, or a person with extreme views of behaviour and morality, is more likely to develop obsessive–compulsive behaviour. More recent research suggests that there may also be a biological predisposition to this disorder – this is discussed below.

<u>Biological explanations</u> There are thought to be two main areas of biological activity that may go some way to explaining obsessive–compulsive behaviour.

- One of these concerns unusually low activity of **serotonin**, the chemical neurotransmitter that carries information between neurons in brain pathways.
- The second concerns the way that the orbital region of the brain functions, in this case with a heightened pattern of activity, which allows unwanted distressing thoughts to 'break through' into the more normal thought patterns (rather like a badly tuned radio with an unwanted station breaking in to the channel being listened to).

To complicate things further, it is possible that these two biological dysfunctions interact with each other, the main result being a biological predisposition to obsessive–compulsive disorder.

The biological explanation of obsessive–compulsive disorder is probably the most satisfactory and holds the most hope for therapy.

Acute stress disorder and post-traumatic stress disorder

We now come to our third type of 'anxiety disorder'. Acute stress disorder and post-traumatic stress disorder occur as a reaction to a psychologically traumatic event. The DSM-IV (1994) defines an abnormality as **acute stress disorder** if the symptoms begin within 28 days of the actual traumatic event and last for 28 days, and as **post-traumatic stress disorder** if the symptoms continue for longer than 28 days. In post-traumatic stress disorder (PTSD), the symptoms may occur shortly after the traumatic event or they may not begin until months or even years afterwards. In both of these disorders, the traumatic event is usually a very real event, such as a major accident, rape or – frequently within the military – warfare or combat. Anyone would find these events traumatic, but only some people develop a disorder. Generalised symptoms of both disorders, described in DSM-IV, include:

- re-experiencing the event, either when awake or in dreams;
- dissociation, or feelings of separation from the real world, often with a reduced level of activity of hobbies or interests; and
- increased levels of arousal: sufferers may 'jump' at the slightest surprise, sleep may be very shallow or disturbed and sufferers may feel guilty that they survived the event – for example an aeroplane crash – while others did not.

Another class of this disorder can occur in those helping at disasters – people in the police force, fire service or other similar agencies. In 1996, members of the police who helped at the 1989 Hillsborough football ground disaster were awarded compensation for the 'mental distress' that they suffered at and following the event.

Explanations of acute stress disorder and post-traumatic stress disorder

In the case of both of these disorders – as opposed, for example, to phobias – there is an obvious cause–effect relationship. You could almost say that it is perfectly normal to experience some after-effects of a trauma, and of course many people do. The point at issue then becomes why it is that only some people develop either of these disorders. Research suggests that figures of about 25 per cent are average, but that there is a wide range depending on the specific stress – lower for accidents, higher for rape (Green, 1994).

None of the usual explanations – psychodynamic, behavioural, etc. – provides very satisfactory reasons for the development of these symptoms, although biological explanations indicate that there may be contributory biological factors.

The likelihood is that there are three factors which may provide an explanation:

- the individual's childhood experiences;
- their personality; and
- the degree of support that the individual received.

In terms of childhood experience, there is very little hard evidence but what evidence there is suggests that children who have suffered a lot tend to **dissociate** themselves from the experience. This pattern is followed in later life and if a major trauma occurs – an accident, disaster or rape, for example – this too will be dissociated psychologically. While dissociation may have worked in childhood, it is not a satisfactory solution in that it does not deal with the trauma effectively, and the person is likely to suffer the disorder. Bremner et al. (1993) suggest that traumatised children are more likely to suffer from acute or post-traumatic stress disorder when adults than others who have had a normal childhood.

Aspects of personality also have a bearing. It seems that some people have a greater tolerance to stress, perhaps to do with attitudes, lifestyle or personal belief (maybe a religion that is fatalistic or a belief in God). Such people have a personality structure that predisposes them not to suffer but to resist, or cope with, a situation that would give rise to stress symptoms in others.

Something to do

- Refer to Unit 7, pages 353–60, on the development of personality. Construct (hypothetically) a personality that is likely to resist stress.

The third possible factor that may explain why some people are better able than others to cope with a major disaster or incident has to do with their personal situation and the kind of support that is available. In some ways this links the first two factors. To take an extreme case, a person who had a happy childhood, is living in a stable relationship within an extended family, enjoys their work, and has wide interests and a large circle of good friends will almost certainly deal with the most awful of experiences rather better than a person who does not have this wide network of support.

The 'bottom line' in this discussion is that it is difficult to be a survivor of a major disaster or incident. All of the issues discussed above may only play a part in the degree to which an individual does, or does not, develop acute or post-traumatic stress disorder.

Affective disorders

It is useful at this point to remember that at a very basic level we can be considered to have three 'parts':

- we are obviously **physical** beings;
- we have **cognitive** ability, as we can think and solve problems; and
- we have emotional feelings and moods – the **affective** part.

Refer back to the chart on page 400 and you will see that both the ICD and the DSM list mood and affective disorders. The term **affective** is often used rather loosely, but the DSM-IV differentiates affective from mood, with **mood** being considered the more severe.

There are two main mood disorders, which tend to be opposites:

- **Depression** is a state in which all seems to be black, despairing, with life simply too much to cope with.
- **Mania**, on the other hand, is exhibited by a high level of energy, almost frenzied in nature, and with a euphoric view of the world.

Most people with mood disorders suffer from depression, usually called **unipolar depression**. Others, with **bipolar disorder**, also known as **manic-depressive disorder**, experience extreme mood swings from depression to mania.

Unipolar depression

As with other disorders discussed above, most of us will at some time in our life experience some degree of depression – mania is not so likely. Most estimates of the frequency with which people suffer from clinical depression suggest a figure of between 5 per cent and 10 per cent of the population. Perhaps more significant is the fact that there has been a steady increase in unipolar depression for many years.

Depression can affect different people in different ways, with the symptoms ranging across a variety of areas. These can include the person's emotional state, a lack of motivation, symptoms that influence the person's cognitive processes, behavioural problems, and general physical problems.

Explanations of depression

<u>The psychodynamic view</u> The starting point for this view occurred when Freud and a student of his, Karl Abraham, observed that the symptoms of depression were similar to the behaviour of someone experiencing grief at the loss of a loved one.

Something to do

- Make parallel lists of symptoms associated with depression and grief.

The essence of the argument is that real or actual loss, such as the death of a spouse or child, which leads to grief is similar to the 'loss' experienced when a person loses their job, for example. In Freudian terms, this is an imagined or symbolic loss. When this is linked with a childhood experience of loss which was never allowed to be expressed – such as the loss, real or imagined, of a significant adult such as a parent, then when older a similar event may lead to the reawakening of the childhood memories and regression to the child-like state may occur. Another dimension is that any unresolved hostility of the child towards the parent re-emerges when the child, now an adult, experiences any kind of loss and the anger is then turned inwards on the self.

There has been considerable debate among psychodynamic theorists as to the precise mechanisms by which this occurs. It is generally accepted, however, that depression is likely to occur when people's relationships have not been good, particularly with respect to parents, and the individual therefore develops either excessive dependence or excessive self reliance. The depression occurs later when problems develop with relationships.

The behavioural view   This view is based mainly on the work of Lewinsohn et al. (1981). They argued that depression begins to occur when a person's lifestyle (behaviour) changes such that they receive many less positive reinforcers. As a result, the person performs less and less positive behaviours, for which they get even less reward, and so they spiral ever downwards into a state of depression. The emphasis here is on social reward. A criticism of this theory is that it is equally likely that the depression may come not as a result of reducing social rewards, but first; and, as a result of the depression, social contact may reduce.

The cognitive view   This view is based on work by theorists such as Beck and Ellis. The key point in this view is the way the person thinks in negative terms. Their thoughts become almost wholly negative in all aspects of their life experiences. Most of the research in this field supports Beck's theories that depressed people have negative thought processes, but is unable to prove that this causes the depression.

The cognitive–behavioural view   In this view, elements of both the cognitive and the behavioural are brought together. Seligman (1975 and 1992), perhaps the key theorist, has developed the **learned-helplessness** model of depression. This theory has two main strands. A person becomes depressed when they believe that they no longer have any control over the reinforcers in their lives; and, second, when they believe that they themselves are responsible for this situation. Subsequent work has established that the person has only to believe that they have no control to become depressed. A further development of the theory suggests that **attribution** (see Unit 3) plays an important part. Does the person attribute the cause to themselves or to other factors, and does the person attribute cause to one or many factors?

The biological view   There are two main strands in this view: the genetic and the biochemical.

The **genetic view** suggests that some people have a predisposition towards depression. This view is supported by studies using families, twins and adopted children:

- In the case of family studies, research has shown that the frequency of depression occurring in the family of someone who is depressed, the **proband**, can be as high as 20 per cent, compared with between 5 per cent and 10 per cent for the population at large.
- In the case of twin studies, frequency of occurrence for identical (monozygotic or MZ) twins where one twin is depressed can be as high as 40 per cent, and 20 per cent for fraternal (dizygotic or DZ) twins.
- In adoption studies, the biological parents had the high incidence rates, the adoptive parents the normal rates.

In the **biochemical view**, the evidence suggests that the neurotransmitters serotonin and norepinephrine may be the cause of depression. There is evidence that abnormal levels of these two neurotransmitters, each of which operates on different types of neurons, affect the manner in which the neurotransmitter either fires or stops firing, thus affecting the transmission of messages in the brain.

As noted above, research into the biological causes of mental disorder appears to be a key area in both understanding the cause and providing possible solutions to these depressive disorders.

Bipolar disorders

To understand bipolar disorder, in a very simplistic manner, imagine a person experiencing all the symptoms of depression, rapidly followed by experiences that are the exact opposite, those of mania, and then reverting to the depressive state, then the manic, and so on. Mania is usually experienced in the same areas as depression: emotion, motivation, cognitive, behaviour and physical.

Just as we all experience depression, we all experience moments of euphoria or extreme 'highs'. The DSM classifies this as mania when extreme euphoric behaviour continues for at least seven days, coupled with at least three other manic symptoms.

As you would expect, there are degrees of severity of the symptoms and the classification of the disorder is defined by the severity and duration of the symptoms. As with depression, bipolar disorders usually begin in adolescence or early adulthood; frequency of occurrence is the same for men and women.

Explanations of bipolar disorders

Explanations of bipolar disorders have been proposed from a variety of theoretical stances, but none has provided satisfactory research evidence. The best evidence is provided by genetic and biochemical studies.

The genetic view   This view suggests that individuals inherit a predisposition to bipolar disorder. Family members of sufferers show a very much higher incidence of the disorder than a normal non-related population. Twin studies report an even higher incidence. Another avenue being studied is the possibility of a specific gene causing the predisposition to the disorder.

Biochemical studies   Biochemical studies have identified the same two neurotransmitters as possible causes for mania as have been linked with depression. In the case of mania, low levels of serotonin and high levels of norepinephrine are thought to be major influences in the cause of the disorder (with opposite levels influencing depressive disorder).

Schizophrenia

On pages 399–400, we made the distinction between neurotic and psychotic disorders. **Schizophrenia** is recognised as a major form of psychosis and this, you will remember, means the loss of contact with reality. Schizophrenia is a serious disorder that is difficult to treat. The word itself is a combination of two Greek words: *schizo*, meaning split, and *phrene*, meaning mind. The term was coined by the Swiss psychiatrist Bleuler in 1911 to replace the term ***dementia praecox***, which means premature dementia, with 'dementia' meaning the loss of intellectual ability to such a degree that it inhibits everyday functioning. The 'split' is between the emotional and the cognitive – so the popular understanding of the term as meaning 'split personality' is quite wrong.

An individual suffering from psychosis may experience **hallucinations** and **delusions**, and may withdraw into their own private world where the real world of people and events have no point of contact.

Schizophrenia is the most common form of psychosis; something like 1 per cent of the population will be diagnosed as schizophrenic. It affects men and women in equal numbers, but is likely to first appear in men in their late teens and in women in their early twenties. It appears in all socioeconomic groups, but is more likely to be present in lower socioeconomic levels. About 2 per cent of single people and 3 per cent of divorced or separated people will suffer from the disorder, compared to the 1 per cent rate for the whole population.

Schizophrenia is an extremely complicated disorder, involving a wide variety of symptoms, behaviours and types. Because of this, some consider that the disorder is not one but many related disorders. However, both the ICD-10 and the DSM-IV describe it as one disorder with a variety of symptoms.

Symptoms of schizophrenia are many and varied and can be roughly grouped into three main patterns:

- The first includes those symptoms which occur to excess or exhibit additional extreme or bizarre forms of behaviour. These are **positive symptoms**.
- Somewhat the opposite and called **negative symptoms** are those symptoms where the person has almost no emotions or feelings – these are 'missing'.
- The third group or pattern concerns **psychomotor** aspects of behaviour, usually involving reduced normal physical activity but with the addition of unusual facial and bodily movements.

Positive symptoms include hallucinations and other forms of disorganised thinking. Hallucinations involve perceptions – such as hearing voices – that have no actual, physical or external origin. Delusions affect thought content: they are beliefs and views that are imaginary, the most common of which are delusions involving persecution.

The DSM-IV identifies three major types of schizophrenia. These are: **paranoid, disorganised** and **catatonic**. Those who do not fit these definitions are classified as **undifferentiated**.

- A person diagnosed as having **paranoid schizophrenia** will have delusions of persecution and grandeur and will probably suffer from hallucinations. These may relate to the delusions or may have no connection.

Other symptoms may be present, such as anxiety, confusion, fear and doubt of identity or gender. This type of schizophrenia is the most common of the three.

- The key to understanding **disorganised** or **hebephrenic schizophrenia** are the words 'silly' or 'disorganised' – in this case, disorganised speech, strange or disorganised behaviour. Other symptoms can include all or some of the following: hearing voices, believing that you are someone else, disorganised delusions of grandeur or persecution, belief that some vital bodily organ is missing or not working, and sustained giggling and nonsensical or silly speech. This type of schizophrenia is considered the most severe.
- **Catatonic schizophrenia** has much more of an effect on motor control, the person remaining in one position for long periods of time – days or even weeks. The position is maintained even when extreme discomfort or circulatory problems are evident. In some instances, this static behaviour alternates with brief interludes of extreme hyperactivity when the person is quite likely to harm themselves or others. They may stay in a position into which they have been put by others – called **waxy flexibility** – and they may also experience **mutism** for periods of time.

It is generally argued that schizophrenia is the most serious of mental disorders. While current classification systems have defined the various types, agreement is by no means general, with some theorists holding the view that the term describes a whole set of conditions or disorders – particularly true when in practice. Classification is complicated because the onset of the disorder is often slow, with different characteristics appearing at different times and in a different order. The disorder often begins in adolescence, with minor symptoms such as losing interest in activities once thought important and periods of withdrawal or lack of interest.

Explanations of schizophrenia

As with other disorders, most major models have offered explanations of the disorder schizophrenia.

The psychodynamic explanation   This explanation suggests that the ego is totally overwhelmed by impulses from the id. This conflict causes the person to regress to the oral stage, which is where the infant has not yet learned that it has a separate identity from the world. As a result, fantasies are confused with realities, which gives rise to hallucinations and delusions. As you would expect, this approach has received considerable criticism – infant behaviour, for example, does not resemble adult schizophrenic behaviour, and the explanation has not been able to predict the onset of the disorder. However, modern explanations seek to link psychodynamic theory with biological views.

The behavioural explanation   In this explanation, the disorder is explained primarily in terms of conditioning; that is, the behaviour the person is exhibiting is reinforced by the attention that they receive as a result of the behaviour. It is also thought that the person acquires the behaviour by observing others. This explanation – as with the psychodynamic – is not considered a very likely explanation, due mainly to the lack of scientific evidence.

The cognitive explanation   In this explanation, the individual's thought (cognitive) processes are delusional – that is, the way the brain processes information is at fault biologically and as a result speech, perception, attention and other cognitive functions or aspects are affected. In this instance, the problem with biological/cognitive aspects is seen as the cause of the schizophrenic condition and not the result. This explanation supports the view that schizophrenia is a disorder with a number of interacting factors.

The genetic explanation   Schizophrenia, like other disorders discussed above, is seen to run in families. In approximate numbers, it occurs in 1 per cent of the general population; in 10–15 per cent of people with one schizophrenic parent; in 35 per cent of people with two schizophrenic parents; in 13 per cent of DZ twins where one is already diagnosed as schizophrenic; and in 45 per cent of MZ twins where one is already diagnosed as schizophrenic (Gottesman, 1991).

You are probably thinking, if this is true why is it that twin studies do not show 100 per cent concordance? The answer is that most evidence now suggests that the genetic cause is only one of a number of causes, but one which predisposes the individual to develop the disorder. Studies with adopted children allow the influence of the environment to be investigated; in these cases it is the genetic connection and not the environment that is seen as the greater cause of the disorder. Other contributory causes may include problems at birth, parenting, environmental or stress-related issues (Gottesman, 1991).

Evidence from a newer technique, called **chromosomal mapping**, which takes DNA from families with schizophrenia and from non-schizophrenic families and compares the two, is finding that a gene (or more likely a cluster of genes) occurs more frequently in families with the disorder (Gurling, 1989).

Biological explanations   There are two main lines of thinking and research in the biological/chemical explanation of schizophrenia:

- abnormalities in brain structure; and
- biochemical abnormalities in the brain.

Advances in technology which allow computer-generated pictures of both brain structure and brain activity – for example, positron emission tomography (PET) and magnetic resonance imaging (MRI) – have been a key factor in advancing knowledge of the brain. This whole area is very technical and beyond the scope of this text; however, evidence so far suggests that certain areas of the brain are enlarged and blood-flow patterns are different in patients with schizophrenic symptoms compared with the population at large.

In terms of biochemical activity in the brain, the focus of research has been (as with other disorders) on the action of neurotransmitters. In the case of schizophrenia, it is the neurotransmitter **dopamine**; hence we have what is called the **dopamine hypothesis**. This has been a long and complicated process over many years, involving slow technical advances, painstaking detective work and a degree of luck. The current state of play suggests not that the person *produces more* dopamine but that they *use more*. This could be because they have more dopamine receptors or because the receptors are more active, or a combination of the two. Further advances in this area of research suggest that while dopamine may be an important factor, it is not necessarily the key factor; other aspects of brain chemistry are influential.

Finally, there are those who have both the above abnormalities and yet show not the slightest symptoms of schizophrenia – so we are back to the view that biological explanations may only predispose the person to the onset of schizophrenia.

Eating disorders

In this category we discuss the two major eating disorders, **anorexia nervosa** and **bulimia nervosa**.

* Anorexia literally means 'loss of appetite'. In fact, the person with the disorder will initially feel just as hungry as anyone who is eating very little. It is not until much later in the course of the disorder that actual loss of appetite occurs.
* In the case of bulimia, the person eats excessive amounts of food and then makes herself vomit or uses laxatives to prevent weight gain.

Since the 1970s, there has been considerable public interest in these disorders, with a number of high-profile women 'telling their story'. The disorders affect females more than males by a ratio of 10:1, with the onset usually occurring in adolescence.

Anorexia nervosa

Both ICD-10 and DSM-IV describe typical symptoms of anorexia. These include a deliberate intention to lose weight to below 85 per cent of normal body weight for the person's age, sex and height; an intense fear of becoming overweight – even when obviously underweight; disturbed thinking about body weight or shape, often involving denial of the obvious; and (in females) **amenorrhea**, which is the absence of at least three consecutive menstrual cycles.

Typically the disorder will begin with the intention simply to 'lose a little weight'. It will often follow a personal difficulty such as a failure in some area or perhaps the separation or divorce of parents. Evidence suggests that the disorder is on the increase. While most recover, something like one in ten anorexics will die as a result of starvation or medical problems caused by starvation. Anorexia predominantly affects females.

The disorder tends to have a downward cycle. Anorexics starve themselves to become thin, which in turn leads to anxiety, depression and often the onset of medical problems. This makes them even more anxious. They then feel that they are losing control over themselves and so determine to regain the control by controlling their eating. Unless effective intervention occurs, hospitalisation follows, with a recovery rate of about 85–95 per cent.

Bulimia nervosa

Bulimia nervosa, the other main eating disorder, is characterised by periods of 'binge' eating, during which the person, again usually a female, consumes vast amounts of food in a relatively short time – usually less than an hour – and then makes herself vomit or uses other measures to avoid weight gain. Bulimia is also known as **binge–purge syndrome**, and sometimes as **dietary chaos syndrome**. The person suffers feelings of loss of control during binges.

DSM-IV classifies the disorder as bulimic when there are recurring binges and recurring purging, both averaging twice a week for three months, and where the person places abnormal emphasis on body weight and shape. The classification is further divided into two groups:

- **purging-type bulimia nervosa**, when the binge is followed by self-induced vomiting and extreme use of laxatives; and
- **non-purging-type bulimia nervosa**, where the binge is followed by extreme dieting or exercising or fasting.

A third variation is **binge-eating disorder**, where the binge is less extreme or less frequent and is not followed by any compensatory action.

Bulimia, as anorexia, occurs in females in 90–95 per cent of cases, with the onset usually in the late teens. The weight of the bulimic person usually stays within the normal range, although fluctuations may occur. The disorder will often last for several years in varying degrees of intensity or frequency of bingeing–purging. Two extremes of bulimia may occur, one where the person becomes underweight and may become anorexic; the other when the person becomes overweight.

Binge-eating will frequently be triggered by tension, or an upsetting event, and an extremely strong need to eat. The person then consumes large quantities of food, usually of a soft texture and sometimes ending with a coloured food as a 'marker'. Vomiting is continued until the marker reappears. Following the binge–purge episode, the person will frequently experience feelings of guilt or depression, or fear of weight gain or of being caught.

As the disorder develops, the purging allows more bingeing which requires more purging and so on. The result is even greater feelings of helplessness. Most recognise that they have the disorder but feel helpless to break the cycle.

Comparison of anorexia nervosa with bulimia nervosa	
Anorexia	**Bulimia**
• Likely to start age 14 to 18	• Likely to start age 15 to 19
• Refusal to maintain an adequate body weight	• Can vary from under- to overweight
• Denial of hunger and disorder	• Perception of binge–purge behaviour as abnormal; intense hunger experienced
• Antisocial behaviour not typical	• Tendency to antisocial behaviour and alcohol abuse
• Amenorrhea (non-menstruation) of three months' duration is common	• Irregular periods common, amenorrhea not common
• Mistrust of others/helpers	• Mistrust of others is not typical
• Tends to be obsessional	• Tends to be dramatic
• Females likely to reject traditional female roles	• Females more likely to accept traditional female roles
• Tendency to pre-disorder – compliance with parents	• Tendency to pre-disorder – conflict with parents

Source: Cromer, *Abnormal Psychology* (Freeman & Co., New York, 2nd edn 1995)

Explanations of eating disorders

Explanations of eating disorders are many and varied; there is very little research evidence to support any one specific model, however. The most promising seems to be a multidimensional approach, which considers a wide range of possible factors that may put the person at risk of developing anorexic or bulimic behaviour.

Psychodynamic explanations   In a theory that involves psychodynamic and cognitive elements (Bruch, 1973 and 1974), it is suggested that the parents' role in training children is influential in that the parents impose their own patterns on the child and as a result the child grows up confused and uncertain between its own awareness of its needs and those expected by its parents. As adolescence approaches, the child seeks to repress developing sexual urges, the poor parent–child (usually mother–daughter) relationship leads to ego deficiencies and possible perceptual and cognitive problems. Often the child is seen as the 'perfect' child. In this context, anorexia is seen as the unconscious effort by the girl to remain the 'child' in the family. Sexual potential, physical maturity and pregnancy are all thus avoided, the mother is rewarded with still having a child, and the daughter continues being dependent on the mother.

Behavioural explanations   These take several forms. Classical conditioning suggests that losing weight becomes habitual – the rewards are admiring glances and positive comments. Operational factors then involve further dieting to 'earn' further rewards.

Social and cultural explanations   These centre on the question: just what is the ideal female form? Since the 1950s, this seems to have been slimmer and ever slimmer. Not unimportant in this context are the frequent warnings from the health professionals that being overweight can damage your health.

Biological explanations   One possible cause of eating disorder is thought to be related to problems in the hypothalamus, resulting in an increase in desire for carbohydrate. The hypothalamus is also thought to provide the mechanism to control body weight, called the **weight set point** (Garner et al., 1985), which when working normally controls the body's **metabolic rate**. This explanation suggests that as dieting takes place the person's weight falls below their weight set point, at which point the brain initiates compensatory actions – the desire to eat, binge, and concern for food. In this state the body seeks to regain the equilibrium, while psychologically the person experiences fear that they are about to lose control. The person may win this conflict and return to normal patterns of eating, or they may not win and so move into typical binge–purge patterns.

Multidimensional explanation   The essential point in this explanation is that rather than just one cause of eating disorders, the likelihood is that the disorders have a number of interlinked causes. It is also thought that there is no set pattern of causes but rather that each person may be predisposed to a certain set or group of causes, different people being influenced by different sets of causes.

Therapeutic approaches

In this section we assess the appropriateness and effectiveness of six different therapies, ending with a discussion of the question of ethical issues involved in therapy.

Therapy and its effectiveness

Before we start discussing the specific therapies, it is worth asking the question: just how effective is therapy? Or, even more difficult in this context: just what does 'effective' mean? Totally cured? Better? Well enough to stop treatment? This raises the question of who decides – the client, the therapist or others? Another important question is that of which is the most effective therapy for a given disorder. A final question concerns the effectiveness of the therapist. Is one therapist more effective with a given set of disorders, and another with a different set? Again, who decides?

There is not space in this text to answer most of these questions fully. However, they are questions that you need to keep in mind as we discuss different therapies below. You also need to be aware that only some of the many and varied types or kinds of therapies are considered here.

Something to do

- Before going on, re-read the section on 'early history' starting on page 389.

As we deal with the six therapies listed in the following chart, we begin each with a description of the model and follow this with a discussion on the appropriateness and effectiveness of the model.

Something to do

- Draw up a summary chart like the one below and complete it as you study this section.

Summary chart for therapeutic approaches				
Theory		**Main theorist**	**Appropriateness**	**Effectiveness**
1. **Somatic**	• Psychosurgery			
	• Chemotherapy			
	• ECT			
2. **Psychodynamic**				
3. **Behavioural**	• Classical			
	• Operant			
4. **Cognitive–Behavioural**				
5. **Humanistic**				
6. **Eclectic**				

Therapies or treatments can be conveniently divided into two groups:

- those that are physical or **somatic** – that is, biological, biochemical or organic; and
- those that are psychological.

Somatic therapies

Soma is the Greek word for body, so **somatic therapies** are those which primarily work in biological or biochemical ways. We consider **psychosurgery**, **chemotherapy** and **electroconvulsive therapy (ECT)**.

Psychosurgery

Psychosurgery can be defined as any surgical procedure carried out on the brain with the intention to relieve severe mental disorder. Its history goes back thousands of years; but in the 1930s, the Portuguese neurologist Moniz is considered to have conducted the first systematic surgical procedure – the prefrontal lobotomy (or leucotomy). It was only used in extreme cases and had very limited success – something of a 'when all else fails' approach. The procedure is rarely used today.

Appropriateness and effectiveness of psychosurgery

Psychosurgery today, as noted above, tends to be used only as a last resort when other less radical interventions have failed. Having said that, it is still used but with very much more limited destruction of brain tissue than in the past, mostly as a result of the increasingly sophisticated technology now available to surgeons. It can therefore be said to have a limited appropriateness and in most modern cases limited effectiveness. Like ECT, it has suffered from a bad press, mostly as a result of the crude and often extreme early procedures.

Chemotherapy

Of the somatic therapies, the use of drugs is the most common, the best understood (still far from perfect, however) and likely to yield the most potential for therapy in the future as more is learned about the chemistry of mental disorder and the effects of drug treatment.

There are many ways or contexts in which to discuss specific drugs. Here we consider three main groups of drugs in terms of the way they act.

<u>Minor drugs</u>   These are usually tranquillisers, depressants or anxiolytic drugs. The term 'minor' implies drugs whose effect is well established and which are often prescribed for outpatients. Drugs in this group include tranquillisers such as Valium and Librium. They work by depressing part of the central nervous system, which in turn reduces heart rate and other physical functions and can reduce feelings of anxiety and tension.

Problems with these drugs are the way that toleration builds up so that increasingly larger amounts are needed; and what is called **rebound anxiety,** which is the way that anxiety returns when the patient stops using the drug.

<u>Major drugs</u>   These are major tranquillisers, or neuroleptics, of the antipsychotic type used with patients with major disorders such as schizophrenia. Most belong to the chemical class of phenothiazines. They act by inhibiting the action of the neurotransmitter dopamine. As a result, they reduce the severity of hallucinations and delusions.

On the negative side, blocking dopamine action can lead to other symptoms. Also, these drugs only suppress the symptoms and do not cure the disorder.

<u>Antidepressant drugs</u>   The main use of **antidepressant drugs,** or stimulants, or antimanics, is in the treatment of anxiety disorders, including obsessive–compulsive behaviours. The media-popularised drug Prozac falls into this category. Antidepressants tend to work by increasing the patient's physical activity, which in turn allows them to function in the world more normally. A sub-type of this group are drugs based on **lithium,** of which there are two main types: lithium carbonate and lithium citrate. They work by limiting the availability of certain neurotransmitters, the effect of which is to reduce the extremes of bi-polar disorders. They can have quite serious side-effects and so their use is monitored closely.

Appropriateness and effectiveness of chemotherapy

Both the appropriateness and the effectiveness of chemotherapy can be argued more convincingly than is the case with either psychosurgery or ECT (see below).

Chemotherapy is probably more appropriate for major disorders than other forms of treatments or therapies, but not so appropriate for the less serious disorders where these other forms of therapy are more likely to be appropriate and less likely to create side-effects.

The effectiveness of drug treatments continues to improve as more is learned about how they work and about the side-effects that they may induce. Because of the scientific nature of this work, newer drugs are more 'focused'. This has helped patients with specific problems and has helped scientists better understand the disorder that they are used on. Chemical therapies can only help by reacting with the body's own chemistry. The essential – and difficult – issue is the matching of the treatment drug to the disorder so that it 'works' but also so that only enough to alleviate the symptom is given, thus not creating any serious side-effects.

Electroconvulsive therapy (ECT)

ECT has an interesting background, involving a physician to the British Royal Family and an Italian psychiatrist visiting an abattoir. The link between these two is that they had both observed that when patients with psychological problems experienced convulsions and coma, they emerged much better than before. In 1785, Dr Oliver – Physician to the Royal Family – accidentally gave a patient an overdose of camphor. The patient experienced convulsions, went into a coma and later recovered and was much better. Other ways of inducing convulsions were tried, including deliberately inducing insulin coma. Much later, in the 1940s, the Italian psychiatrist Ugo Cerletti visited an abattoir and observed how pigs were stunned before slaughter: two electrodes were placed across the head and an electric current administered. ECT had been born! (Cited in Comer, 1995.)

ECT is administered either bilaterally – two electrodes, one on each temple; or unilaterally – the electrodes on one temple only. The patient is given muscle relaxants to minimise the physical effects of convulsions; then a current of about 200 milliamps, at a voltage of between 100 and 200 volts, is applied for a short period of time, usually between half a second to three seconds. ECT increases neurotransmitter activity in all parts of the brain, which include areas that influence or cause depression. It also works with patients with severe delusions. A problem is that the effect of increased neural activity in other parts of the brain is not fully understood. Success rates of about 60 per cent are suggested for patients with severe problems.

Appropriateness and effectiveness of ECT

ECT is usually a last attempt to help a person with severe depression, so it can be said to be appropriate in certain, limited, situations. It also has limited success, and can therefore be said to have a certain degree of effectiveness. Problems with the treatment are that the precise mechanisms of why and how it works are not fully understood. With increasing knowledge of the cause of disorders and of drug treatments, the use of ECT is decreasing.

Psychodynamic therapies

It is helpful to consider why this approach is called psycho*dynamic*. The answer of course is that, in Freudian theory, there is a constant tension – or dynamic – between the three psychic parts or structures: the id, the ego and the superego. The dynamic can be explained by picturing three people holding hands in the form of a triangle. If all three people pull on both hands at the same time and if they all pull with the same amount of energy, the 'structure' will remain in dynamic tension, but also will remain stationary. The moment one of the three either pulls harder or relaxes, the dynamic is changed and the 'structure' moves. (This analogy can also be applied to family therapy – see page 431.)

Freud saw these three psychic forces in conflict all the time, with the behaviour of the person depending on which particular 'force' was 'winning' this three-way tug-of-war. For example, if the id – with its primitive, sensual urges – starts to 'win', the ego begins to erect defences, a result of which is distress. If the super-ego starts to win, then the ego has to deal with extra guilt, the defences go up and distress follows.

Something to do

• Before reading on, review the sections on Freud in Units 2 and 7.

Psychoanalysis

Freud developed the system of therapy called **psycho*analysis***, which is aimed at understanding, by analysis, the three psychic forces and their 'battles' and, in the course of the analysis (the therapy), at supporting the ego. If the ego cannot cope with the onslaught, it defends itself by repressing into the unconscious the demands which caused the conflict. The aim of psychoanalysis is to uncover the repressed demands (externalised by mental disorder) by gaining insight into the cause. Freudian theory holds that the conflict invariably stems from problems in childhood (in one of the psychosexual stages), so the task of the analyst (the therapist) is to take the person (the analysand) back into their childhood to when the initial psychic conflict occurred. This process provides the analysand with insight – why the current problem exists. As they gain insight, their understanding increases and they can then deal with the conflict and resume a normal lifestyle. Freud called the process of getting this repressed psychic energy into the open and getting rid of it **abreaction** or **catharsis**. This leaves us with the all-important question: how does the analyst do this?

The first step in the process occurs when the analyst is being trained and when they themselves undergo analysis. The reason for this is to enable the analyst to understand (and deal with) their own psychic conflicts such that these will not interfere with people they analyse later. The process of analysis can take years, with the therapist using all or some of a number of different techniques. Some of the main techniques used in analysis are hypnosis, free association, word association, dream analysis, transference and, sometimes, countertransference.

<u>Hypnosis</u>   Freud used **hypnosis** as a means of getting into the unconscious, since in a hypnotic state people are more relaxed and less guarded in what they say. It initially appeared to be a valuable therapeutic technique; however, some patients later denied what they had said when under hypnosis, and others found the revelations too distressing when discussing the content later.

<u>Free association</u>   As a result, Freud moved away from using hypnosis, at least regularly, and developed another technique: **free association**. In this technique, the person is asked to talk freely about anything that comes into their mind. The key rule is that nothing is to be censored: if you think it, say it. The theory holds that the repressed thoughts and feelings will want to 'emerge' but the ego will resist this. The analyst will recognise the struggle and will help the individual to gain insight into the situation. This is sometimes helped by the analyst interpreting the comments and perhaps gently guiding the thoughts of the person.

<u>Word association</u>   A similar technique is **word association**. In this case, the analyst will either ask the person to read a list of words and then freely associate, or the analyst may speak a series of words. In either case, it is what the individual associates with the word that provides the clue to the repressed conflict.

<u>Dream analysis</u>   Freud called **dream analysis** the 'royal road to the unconscious'. He argued that when we dream we are dealing not just with actual events, but with unconscious impulses, particularly sexual or aggressive. The symbols in the dream represent taboo topics that cannot be 'allowed' into the conscious. The content of the dream is called the **manifest content**; the hidden or symbolic meaning is the **latent content**. Jones (1953) comments that *The Interpretation of Dreams* was Freud's 'favourite' book; it was written in 1896 but not published until 1903.

<u>Transference (and **countertransference**)</u>   **Transference** occurs when the person 'transfers' feelings that they have towards another – often the parent – onto the analyst. For example, a young person might view the analyst as a father-figure. This of course can work two ways, and so **countertransference** occurs when the analyst transfers his or her feelings onto the analysand. Freud considered this as a natural process which could help in the identification and release of repressed feelings.

Appropriateness and effectiveness of psychoanalysis

Described above is the classical or traditional view of psychoanalysis. It needs to be said that while this form is still used, there are a number of 'variations'. These tend to hold to the importance of the unconscious and the need to gain insight, but they tend to play down the emphasis on the childhood psychosexual stages, emphasising instead issues and conflicts that are current in the person's life – the emphasis shifting from the id to the ego. Another key element in the modern approaches is the change from a slow and very lengthy process to a more contracted and shorter process. Therapies using this general approach are known as **psychoanalytically oriented therapies**.

Whether traditional or modern, psychoanalysis relies on the person or 'client' gaining insight and understanding. Both of these require normal cognitive functioning, which in turn means that people with severe disorders are usually not suitable for this type of therapy. On the other hand, it is considered suitable for people with neuroses.

In terms of effectiveness, it is one of the more difficult therapies to measure. There are problems that involve definition of terms, length of treatment and the possibility of spontaneous recovery (see below). Many terms used in psychoanalysis have complex meanings that are by no means universally understood, let alone capable of scientific definition. The length of treatment, often measured in years, makes effectiveness difficult to measure mainly because of the many other factors that may affect the client over this period of time. One such factor may be **spontaneous recovery**, with the individual regaining their health at some point but without being able to say categorically that it was as a result of the analysis.

Behavioural therapies

Behavioural therapy and **behaviour modification** are usually considered as synonymous terms. The foundational principle in this group of therapies is learning theory. The inappropriate behaviour – the disorder – is learned; therefore it can be 'unlearned' and new and more appropriate behaviours learned in its place.

Something to do

- Review the sections on the behavioural approach and principles of learning in Unit 2, pages 33–4 and Unit 6, pages 311–18.

A major difference between this and other therapies is that behaviourists insist that their methods are established on scientific principles and that the outcome or results can be assessed by measuring the changed behaviour. A result of this is that historical events such as childhood experiences are ignored, since the therapy concentrates on the client's behaviour today – so a client with obsessive–compulsive handwashing behaviour would be asked 'how many times an hour' he washed his hands, not taken back into childhood to gain 'insight' as in psychoanalysis. The goal of this therapy would then be to reduce the frequency of handwashing to a normal, measurable, rate. All behaviour therapy is based on learning principles; the specific techniques used are based on either classical or operant principles. The following table lists the various techniques and indicates the disorders for which they are used.

Disorders matched to behavioural therapies	
Classical techniques	**Disorders**
• Implosion	Fears, phobias, anxieties
• Flooding	Fears, phobias, anxieties
• Aversion	Habits, addictions, self injury
• Systematic desensitisation	Fears, phobias, anxieties
Operant techniques	
• Token economy	Psychotic disorders, conduct disorders
• Assertiveness training	Poor self esteem, social problems, exploitation
• Positive and negative reinforcement	Emotional disturbances, self injury
• Extinction	Disruptive behaviour (children)

Note: Some authors distinguish between behaviour therapy using classical techniques, and behaviour modification using operant techniques.

Classical techniques <u>Implosion and flooding</u>   These are similar techniques used with anxiety-producing disorders. They both expose the client to the feared experience.

- Implosion does this with the therapist getting the client to imagine their worst fears, the anxiety created by this slowly reducing as the patient realises – learns – that no actual harm is coming to them, and so extinction of the symptom occurs.
- Flooding is similar, with the key difference that the client is exposed to the real fearful situation – spiders, open spaces, etc.

<u>Aversion therapy</u>   This is sometimes also called **aversive therapy** or **conditioning**. It pairs the inappropriate behaviour with an aversive or unpleasant stimulus. A client who wishes to stop smoking, for example, will be asked to smoke heavily for a short period, say one hour; he or she is then given a drug that induces violent nausea or vomiting. This process is continued for several days. The client learns to associate a very unpleasant experience with the unwanted behaviour. The treatment is usually supported by **counselling**, often group counselling. A variation of this approach involves the person imagining smoking and then vomiting, rather than it actually happening. This is later replaced with the client imagining pleasant thoughts coupled to resisting or not engaging in the inappropriate behaviour.

<u>Systematic desensitisation</u>   As the name implies, this approach is less dramatic, more systematic and takes longer. The method originated from work conducted by Joseph Wolpe in the 1950s following principles first outlined by Hull in the 1940s. It is argued that relaxation and anxiety cannot co-exist, and so the process starts with the client being encouraged or trained to relax. In this state, the anxiety-producing object or event is slowly introduced. This is done either by imagining it, or by the use of slides or film, or by introducing it for real. The therapist designs a hierarchy, starting with an extremely low level of anxiety-

producing stimulus and then slowly and systematically increasing the level of anxiety. As each stage is successfully coped with, the next stage is introduced. The therapist and client work through the hierarchy until the final stage, when the original fearful event evokes no fear at all.

A variation on this approach is **modelling**. This uses observational learning (Bandura, 1969), where the client will first observe someone else dealing with the fearful object and will then learn to deal with it themselves.

Operant techniques

Operant techniques (sometimes called **instrumental techniques**, although there is a difference) are different from classical techniques in that operational features are the key element. So in operational processes the reward or reinforcer is only given when the person or animal makes an appropriate response. In classical approaches, the reinforcer occurs whether or not the person makes the required response. The other key difference is that classical techniques work on reflex actions (Pavlov's dogs – see Unit 6, pages 312–14), while operant techniques work on voluntary action (Thorndike's cats – see Unit 6, page 315).

Token economy   A **token economy** changes behaviour by providing 'tokens' for the appropriate behaviour. The token is the **secondary reinforcer**, which is later exchanged for the **primary reinforcer**. An example of this is work carried out by this author in a residential school for disturbed children (1973). Classroom behaviour was chaotic, so a token was given to each child for five minutes of uninterrupted work. Tokens could be collected, and either used as 'money' in the school tuck shop or – and this was a favourite – for a set number of tokens the child could choose which television programme to watch for a set period of time in the evening. As the classroom behaviour quite rapidly came under control, the period of time to earn a token was gradually extended.

Assertiveness training   This follows the work of Bandura, who initially worked in **social learning techniques** – **assertiveness training** being one of a number of social skills. The techniques used include observation, role-play, discussion, self monitoring and feedback. This therapy is often used in **group therapy** settings, where members of the group can share both their difficulties and their successes. The training is aimed at making the client more self assured, not more aggressive.

Positive and negative reinforcement   Both positive and negative reinforcing techniques are used in behaviour therapies, some of which are discussed above. In general terms, negative reinforcement or punishment is not as effective as positive reinforcement.

Extinction   This technique quite simply ignores the disturbed behaviour, and usually at the same time rewards more appropriate behaviour.

Something to do

- Observe young children at the checkout counters in a large supermarket. How do parents of small children react if the child screams or throws a tantrum when the parent refuses to buy the child a packet of sweets? (If you are going to do this in anything other than a casual manner, you should ask the branch manager's permission.)

Appropriateness and effectiveness of behavioural therapies

As we have seen, there are a considerable number of quite different behavioural therapies, so the key issue is matching the disorder to the therapy (see the table on page 425). Assuming that the match can be made, the therapy is often quite short in duration. Individual therapies can also be tailored specifically to the disorder. Some of these therapies are also appropriate for use in group therapy.

Because of the nature of the behavioural approach, which is based on specifying and counting, results or the change in behaviour can also be measured. This in turn means that the outcome of the therapy, its effectiveness, can also be measured. Debate will continue, however, as to whether – when a behaviour is cured – the underlying symptom is cured or, as psychodynamic theorists believe, whether it will re-emerge in some other form until it is dealt with at source. The behaviourists' riposte is: 'OK, if it does we deal with it' – and so on.

Cognitive–behavioural therapy

If you briefly recap the previous section on behavioural therapies, you will see that in many of these approaches the client is required to think about or understand certain aspects of their behaviour. For example, in implosion therapy, the client is asked to imagine their fears. Thinking and imagination are cognitive functions, and so it is argued that to separate behavioural and cognitive therapies into two separate approaches is, in practical terms, difficult if not impossible. It is perhaps easier to see the two approaches more in terms of emphasis, with behavioural therapy focusing on specific behaviours and cognitive therapy focusing on cognitive functions. In this context, it is accepted that our cognitive processes (thoughts) have a profound influence on our feelings and behaviours. If we argue that some therapies are **non-directive** – for example psychoanalysis and humanistic approaches – then behavioural and cognitive–behavioural therapies are the opposite – **active** and **directive**, the therapist often directing or telling the client what to do.

Cognitive therapies

Cognitive therapies attempt to change what and how the client thinks. They can be divided into two main groups:

- those that concentrate on cognitive behaviour modification; and
- those that attempt to alter false belief or understanding.

In the first group, the goal of the therapist is to help the client recognise the abnormal behaviour and then to 'modify' it by changing the person's negative self awareness into more positive and constructive understanding. This is achieved by therapist and client setting goals and devising strategies that reduce the negative aspects and encourage the positive. Discussion of the results or effectiveness of these strategies is an important part of the therapeutic process.

In the second group, the emphasis is less on the behavioural components and more on the strictly cognitive – the beliefs, attitudes and thought processes of the client. In this case, the client's problems are due to faulty thinking or understanding in terms of the way we think about ourselves in relation to others in our world. This often involves misinterpretation of the reality of a given circumstance or situation.

Rational emotive therapy   Formulated by Albert Ellis in the 1960s, this is perhaps the most important of the cognitive therapies. Ellis believes that it is the irrational thought patterns of the individual that can cause, or at least allow, the inappropriate behaviour. Two of the most common of irrational beliefs are that you must have the approval of people important to you, and that you must prove yourself to be a competent achiever in all walks of life. In rational emotive therapy, the client is encouraged to explore these irrational beliefs and is frequently challenged by the therapist to justify or explain why these beliefs lead to feelings of worthlessness. Once the client accepts the irrationality of the belief, then more appropriate responses are suggested, the aim being to increase the client's self worth.

Aaron Beck   A second major cognitive therapy is that of Aaron Beck (1987). Similar in many ways to Ellis, Beck also concentrates on inappropriate cognitive responses. He has identified four basic types of cognitive error:

1. Clients falsely interpret some aspects of their world as harmful.
2. Clients assume that because of one negative experience, for example being rejected by a friend, their whole life is therefore worthless.
3. Clients may interpret a negative event much too seriously. You do badly in an exam, so you will never, ever pass an exam.
4. Clients see the world in black and white, or in absolute terms. An illness, perhaps minor, becomes a long-term, life-threatening event.

In therapy, the therapist and client work together to identify the errors of interpretation, often using a third party – the wife or husband of the client – who will know and can reinforce the 'correct' interpretation of events. Other techniques include getting the client to write down their interpretation of events and, with the therapist, discuss why their interpretation may be in error; they then rewrite more appropriate responses. In this process the client's views are evaluated and challenged, any blame may be attributed more accurately, alternative interpretations are suggested, and false assumptions are challenged.

   As with rational emotive therapy, the emphasis is on the 'here-and-now' and the therapist often takes on a directive role, characteristic also of behaviour therapy.

Self-instruction training   A third form of cognitive therapy is that of **self-instruction training**, proposed by Meichenbaum (1974). This approach centres on the way that we all often talk to ourselves when we need to interpret something or consider a given action. In the case of a person with a particular difficulty or problem, Meichenbaum argues that this internal dialogue is at fault, with the person failing accurately, or correctly, to 'self instruct'. The goal of therapy then becomes making the person aware of the errors in their 'self instructions' and providing strategies to correct the faulty process. Other similar approaches are known as **cognitive restructuring**.

Appropriateness and effectiveness of cognitive–behavioural therapy

While this approach is not appropriate for all forms of mental disorder, it is seen as appropriate with clients who have the ability to listen, think and talk. This makes cognitive–behavioural therapy particularly appropriate for anxiety disorders, phobias, sexual dysfunction, depression and stress-related problems.

Cognitive–behavioural therapy is interested in measurable changes in behavioural outcomes, and as such the effectiveness of these therapies can, quite literally, be measured. When compared to psychoanalytic approaches, cognitive–behavioural therapy is seen as particularly effective as the process is much shorter in duration.

Humanistic therapy

The key name in this approach is Carl Rogers (1902–87). Working in America, he introduced what he called **client-centred therapy** in the 1940s; this was later renamed **person-centred therapy**.

The approach is strictly non-directive, with the therapist reflecting back to the client the client's thoughts and expressions, with the aim of the client coming to their own realisation of their needs and aspirations and of becoming **self actualised**. While it seeks to gain 'insight' into the problem, the approach is more **phenomenological** than psychodynamic. The difference is that a phenomenological approach concentrates on the present experience, what is happening in the here-and-now, and not on the interpretation of internal conflict and unconscious processes. The process can only happen if the therapeutic situation or environment is such that the client is perfectly comfortable and therefore willing to talk about him- or herself at a significant level. To achieve this, the therapist needs to demonstrate four particular qualities:

- **Unconditional positive regard:** This is where the therapist expresses unconditional respect for the client as a genuine human being, and provides a positive and safe environment for the client to express themselves.
- **Empathy:** This is where the therapist seeks to enter the client's world by reflecting and seeking to understand the client's experiences and particular feelings.
- **Genuineness:** This is where the therapist is open about their own feelings, and not trying to hide behind the desk and white coat. The therapist is demonstrating or modelling a role. This does not mean that the client or therapist needs to agree with the other's value system.
- **Congruence:** This is where the therapist shows the client that the relationship between thoughts and feelings and behaviour must 'fit' (be congruent).

Of these four, genuineness is considered to be the most important, for without openness between client and therapist, the process of therapy – or the healing relationship – cannot exist.

Rogers' essential belief is that every person has within them the basic tendency or drive to self actualise, which is to achieve one's own potential. This will only occur when the person is in an environment where they feel free and can accept themselves and relate openly and honestly with another human being.

Appropriateness and effectiveness of humanistic therapy

In terms of appropriateness, humanistic therapy is similar to cognitive approaches in that it requires of the client the ability to think about and discuss their own perceptions and feelings. This inevitably makes the approach more appropriate with those who are not experiencing difficulties of a severe nature.

Counselling

We have so far in the discussion consistently used the word 'therapy'. Now is the time to introduce the term **counselling**. The distinction between the two is not always precise, but in general terms 'therapy' tends to be used in a more technical setting and with more severe disorders, while 'counselling' is used in a much broader context. For example, your local school may have a counsellor who would talk to the children about anything from reasons for excessive absence, through bullying to careers advice. Medical doctors' surgeries often make use of a counsellor; and many ministers of the church are trained in pastoral counselling. In many cases, these counsellors will use a humanistic approach, particularly the Rogerian approach. Counselling is appropriate for a wide range of disorders, from moderately severe to much more general problems or difficulties – perhaps even your career choice.

Think about it

- Have you recently had a careers interview or talked with someone about a problem? If so, think about the meeting and try to identify the strategies the 'counsellor' used. Were they Rogerian?

The effectiveness of the humanistic approach is more difficult to assess than its appropriateness. How do you know or measure when someone is fully 'self actualised'? Viewed from another perspective, person-centred therapy is probably the most widely used of all therapies. Smith (1982), in a **meta-analysis**, rated Rogers as the most influential psychotherapist, which can only suggest that person-centred therapy 'works' and can therefore be considered as effective.

The eclectic approach

Reading the above sections on the different types of therapy may lead you to believe that therapy and therapists can be slotted neatly into a nice, tidy, well-defined approach. This is not the case. While there are therapists who practise in one specific manner, it is probably fair to say that many of those who are engaged in therapy take an **eclectic approach**. 'Eclectic' simply means not following one specific approach but rather using a mix of several approaches which the therapist judges will help a specific client with a specific problem. The same therapist may well use a different 'mix' of theoretical approaches or techniques with another client with a different problem.

Is therapy effective?

As already noted, effectiveness is an extremely difficult concept to judge or measure. Hans Eysenck, in 1952, created a storm in the therapeutic world by stating that psychotherapy does not work at all. His review of published studies of a variety of different therapies led him to the conclusion that people with disorders who received no treatment recovered just as frequently as those who had received treatment. He concluded that something like two-thirds of those with neurotic problems will effect a spontaneous recovery (see page 424) within two years. These findings have been criticised for methodological reasons.

Jerome Frank (1973 and 1990) compared the effectiveness or results of a wide variety of therapies, including in his study approaches such as religious ceremonies and even political 'brainwashing'. He concluded that it is the belief of the client that things really can change that is most important in effecting change.

Other related evidence suggests that another important factor is the relationship between therapist and client. Without a genuine empathy, therapy is not effective. With empathy, however, and with a genuine, warm, professional relationship in which the client believes in the process and the skill of the therapist, and the therapist also believes in a positive outcome, then the evidence seems to suggest that the client will improve whatever the therapeutic approach. It is the relationship as much as the approach that influences effectiveness.

Something to investigate

The effectiveness of therapy is complex and involves issues such as:

– the client–therapist relationship;
– matching disorder with approach;
– what defines a cure;
– how the cure is to be evaluated;
– the proportions of cured, not cured, spontaneous recovery; and
– outcome-research studies.

• Research some or all of the above and write a paragraph or two summing up the issues.

Group therapy or individual therapy?

The assumption in all the approaches discussed above is that the therapist-to-client relationship is one-to-one: one therapist helping one client, or 'individual therapy'.

Group therapy, on the other hand, consists of a small group of about eight clients, with one, sometimes two, therapists working with the group. There are a number of ways in which the group can be composed, structured and led.

• Some groups are **open groups** in the sense that the group is ongoing, with members joining and leaving as and when the groups think that they should. Some members may remain in the group for a long time; others may arrive, get the help they need and then leave.
• Other groups are **closed groups**. In this case, the group is formed, agrees to meet for a set number of sessions, usually weekly, and then disbands.

Another aspect of the group approach is that the meetings usually last for longer than individual one-to-one sessions. In terms of leadership, again there are a variety of models. For family therapy, often the group will have male and female co-leaders, with the group itself being sometimes single-sex, sometimes mixed.

A detailed discussion of the considerable strengths and advantages of group therapy is beyond the scope of this text. Starting points for further study in this area are Yalom (1970) and Lieberman et al. (1973).

Ethical issues

The ethical issues involved in the practice of therapy are extremely significant. In a typical situation, the client may be in a very fragile, even deteriorating, psychological state; and in effect asks the therapist to help with their problem. The responsibility placed on the therapist is considerable.

Ethics is concerned with right and wrong, good and bad, and with what is generally acceptable in human behaviour. Ethical issues are discussed in several other units of this book, as they relate to specific situations.

Something to do

• Review the section on ethical issues in Unit 2.

Ethical issues relating to therapy deal with the same general issues, and the ethical guidelines provided by professional organisations such as the British Psychological Society and the American Psychological Association apply. Below we discuss three main ethical issues relating to therapy: informed consent, confidentiality and choice of goals.

Informed consent

The essence of this issue is that the individual needs to be made aware of all aspects of the proposed treatment. Their decision to enter treatment needs to be an informed decision. Information to be given to the client may include specifics on the methodology, likely costs, the probability of success or failure, and confidentiality. The client also needs to be advised that they may terminate therapy at any time. You are probably already thinking about the question of how someone who is seriously clinically depressed is able to make such an informed decision. This, of course, is one of the difficulties with the issue of informed consent.

Confidentiality

Confidentiality is crucial to the client–therapist relationship. Without it, significant progress is unlikely; with it, therapy can proceed smoothly. Confidentiality is not something that can simply be 'switched on'. It usually takes time, with the client often 'testing' the therapist with increasingly significant personal details. As the relationship grows, so does the trust, so does the confidentiality and, it is hoped, so does the effectiveness of the therapy. Inevitably there are limits to the degree of confidentiality that the therapist can promise, and these need to be stated at the start of the therapy. For example, as a result of recent legislation, a therapist must legally disclose to the appropriate authorities instances of child abuse. Similarly, instances of terrorism must be notified. On the positive side, when this author worked in a counselling centre which used single-sex groups, often with the husband in one group and the wife in another, one of the boundaries of confidentiality was that the leaders had the option to discuss confidential matters with the group leader of the spouse's group. This provided a powerful therapeutic tool. In both group and one-to-one therapy, it is also quite normal for the therapist to have a supervisor to discuss issues with; this is another boundary which the client needs to be made aware of at the start of therapy.

Choice of goals   The key aspect of this concerns the possibility that something unpleasant, possibly even harmful, may happen or may be required to happen in the course of the therapy. For example, in a psychodynamic approach it is often considered essential to take the client back to a distressing experience in childhood. This might not harm the client physically, but it may well harm them emotionally. If, however, the therapist has carefully explained the approach and that this recalling and discussing of childhood experiences is necessary, then the therapy may proceed. In other words, working through a painful earlier memory is an essential goal of the therapy. The client is, at the very least, prepared for what might develop or emerge in the course of therapy.

If the client then decides at any point in the therapy that the particular approach is becoming (or is likely to become) too stressful and does not wish to continue the therapy, then the question of **referral** arises. This involves the therapist suggesting another therapy or therapist who uses a different approach. Referral is also considered the only ethical course when a therapist begins to realise that the client's problems are beyond his or her expertise. This can be the case in counselling, where the therapist or counsellor, for example when dealing with, say, marital difficulties, comes to believe that the cause is likely to be linked to specific sexual behaviours which are beyond his or her training and expertise; referral then being the only responsible ethical option.

Something to do

- Review the six therapeutic approaches discussed above. Make a list of any possible harmful consequence that may arise in each approach and which should therefore be discussed in the context of goal-setting at the commencement of therapy. For example:

Therapeutic approach	Area of possible harm
Psychodynamic	Taking the client back to distressing events

Ethical issues are crucial and are becoming more complicated as the whole psychological field advances. For example, an extremely difficult issue, and one that did not exist perhaps ten years ago (or if it did exist, it had not been 'discovered') but which has now emerged, is the question of **false memory**, sometimes called **recovered memory**. This is where a client, in the course of therapy, 'discovers', for example, that they suffered serious abuse as a child. How is such an issue dealt with and what are the associated ethical issues? Both questions have huge implications, which as yet are not clearly defined. This example serves to show that as the science of psychology advances – which invariably means becoming more complex – new guidelines for practising therapy need to be formulated. Also, just as in other fields, moral and ethical issues need further definition. It seems that in society today technology is moving much faster than the development of the moral codes so essential to control the 'nuts and bolts' of progress.

Think about it

- If you were planning on training as a therapist, which of the six models discussed above would you adopt and follow?
- Name your model and give your reasons for choosing this approach.

Revision and practice

● ●

Coursework opportunities

1. Dyslexia is a learning disability which is a failure to learn how to read. It is estimated that between 5 and 15 per cent of children, mostly boys, experience some form of learning difficulty.
   Either: Investigate the degree of correlation between children with dyslexia and *their own* self esteem.
   Or: Carry out some research to see if there are any significant differences between the self esteem of dyslexic children compared to a control group of non-dyslexic children. This will require a sensitive approach, and care with respect to the ethical issues. Remember to seek parent and/or teacher approval before you begin the study.
2. Conduct a study into dream analysis. The traditional method is to keep a diary of daily events *and* a diary of dreams, and then see if there is any kind of correlation.
3. Studies concerning intelligence make interesting coursework.
   Either: Investigate the possibility that IQ can 'improve' with frequent test practice. Give the participant(s) in your study a standard IQ test; then give them practice tests; then retest.
   Or: Devise a study to correlate intelligence with:
   – sporting ability
   – reaction time
   – time of day, etc.
   Or: Test the idea that participants will estimate higher IQs for their father than their mother.

● ●

Examination questions

Question 1 Discuss the use of **two** therapies derived from the behavioural model of abnormality in the treatment of psychological disorders. *(24 marks)*

(AEB, Module Paper 5, January 1997)

Question 1: Unpacked This is a one-part question. 'Discuss' requires you to 'describe and evaluate' by referring to different or contrasting views.

You are to discuss the *use* of *two* therapies, so write about only two (one will limit you to half marks, three or more and the marker will credit you with the best two – but you will have wasted a lot of time and effort).

Your choice needs to be made from *therapies* based on the *behavioural* model:

Behavioural therapies
(see page 425)

{

Classical: Implosion
Flooding
Aversion
Systematic desensitisation

Operant: Token economy
Assertiveness training
Positive reinforcement
Extinction

You need to choose the two that *you* feel comfortable discussing. In cases like this, choose two that are fairly dissimilar. (This type of question can provide a useful guide to revision. In areas such as this, *thoroughly* learn at least two, preferably contrasting, alternatives.)

For the purpose of this essay, we shall take systematic desensitisation and token economy.

As with similar 'discuss'-type questions, you have the choice: either to describe both then evaluate both; or describe and evaluate the first then describe and evaluate the second. Here, the former is probably the better option, with a concluding paragraph comparing and contrasting the two.

Your essay outline will then look something like this:

- **Introduction:** State the two therapies to be discussed with reference to their *use*. Discuss briefly the behaviour therapy/modification issue. (See the note to the chart on page 425). A brief historical background would help.
- **Paragraph 1:** Describe the token economy and the way it is *used*.
- **Paragraph 2:** Describe systematic desensitisation and the way it is *used*.
- **Paragraph 3:** Evaluate token economy. Evaluate systematic desensitisation.
- **Paragraph 4:** Discuss/evaluate similarities/differences/effectiveness.
- **Paragraph 5:** Discuss ethical issues of both.
- **Conclusion** Sum up but do not repeat. You may want to conclude with a 'where the field is going' statement.

Question 2 Describe and evaluate possible contributions of social/psychological factors to **either** any **one** eating disorder **or** any **one** anxiety disorder. *(24 marks)*

(AEB, Module Paper 5, January 1998)

Question 2: Sample answer The following essay was written by a student under simulated exam conditions.

Comments

Good introductory para-
graph, sums up key issues,
accurate use of terms

Helpful transition paragraph

Accurate factual material

Could show the relevance of
these

Useful point, but not followed up

Important point that needs
more explanation

Relevant evidence

Accurate

Relevant discussion

Essay

Anorexia Nervosa is an eating disorder where the individual expresses concern that they are overweight. Often 'concern' becomes obsessive and in many cases the person will become so underweight that normal bodily functioning becomes threatened, a normal lifestyle becomes impossible and in extreme cases death can result. The root meaning of 'anorexic' means loss of appetite, which in most cases does not occur until later in the disorder. Initially the person simply does not eat and will experience normal hunger, it's not until later that normal hunger pains are less evident.

Factors contributing to the disorder can be grouped under social or psychosocial headings.

Social factors that contribute to the disorder are found almost exclusively in western societies – societies where there are no food shortages – and since anorexia occurs mostly in middle and upper-class young people – 95% are young women aged between 13 and 20 years old – lack of money is not part of the cause. What *is* considered as a social cause for anorexia is the prevalent view that the ideal figure for a young woman is slim, often very slim. If social learning theory and social modelling are valid in terms of their influence on people in general and young people in particular then given that the ideal figure as shown in magazines and on TV is very slim, it can be *expected* that young people and young women in particular will seek to imitate the famous.

Psychological factors also contribute to our understanding of anorexia. These can be considered in terms of their psychological orientation, for example the disorder is viewed differently from the psychodynamic and say the behavioural or humanistic viewpoint.

In general psychological terms eating disorders are usually seen as a reflection of emotional problems with parents which go back to the way *children's* feelings about eating are bound up with their parents.

Key psychological factors in anorexia are a false perception of the person's own weight, and a real fear of becoming overweight. For this reason Crisp (1984) has suggested that the disorder is really 'weight phobia'. The individual appears to totally ignore the fact that family and friends all agree that they are seriously underweight.

Causes for anorexia are sometimes thought to be a way of avoiding moving into adulthood particularly in sexual terms as one characteristic in young women is that menstruation ceases.

Another major psychological cause for anorexia has to do with the anorexic's relationship to their family. In most cases of anorexia there are found to be problems within the family. However it's not always possible to be sure which came first, the family problems which led to the anorexic member, or the anorexic behaviour which then caused problems within the family. Social and psychological factors contributing to the onset of anorexia are complex and frequently interlinked. The place of the family and it's dynamics are significant, leading to the use of family therapy as a major form of treatment.

General comments

The essay includes accurate, factual material clearly presented and with only minor omissions. The *evaluation* element is weak and not well presented.

$$Marks: \text{Skill A } \frac{10}{12} \text{ (possibly more)}$$

$$\text{Skill B } \frac{5}{12} = \frac{15}{24}$$

Question 3   Describe and evaluate research into any **two** emotional or behavioural problems in childhood (e.g. attention-deficit hyperactivity disorder; autism; developmental dyslexia).   *(24 marks)*

(AEB, Module Paper 5, January 1997)

Question 4   Describe and evaluate the possible contributions of social/psychological factors to depression.   *(24 marks)*

(AEB, Module Paper 5, Summer 1997)

Question 5   (a) Describe somatic approaches to the treatment of psychological disorders.   *(12 marks)*

(b) Assess these approaches in terms of the ethical issues they raise.   *(12 marks)*

(AEB, Module Paper 5, Summer 1997)

Question 6   (a) Describe some assumptions of the cognitive model of abnormal psychology.   *(12 marks)*

(b) Assess these assumptions in terms of their implications for treatment.   *(12 marks)*

(AEB, Module Paper 5, January 1998)

Question 7   (a) Imagine you are a psychiatrist who is a firm believer in the medical model as an explanation of abnormal behaviour. Write a letter to a psychologist who is doubtful about this model in diagnosing and treating abnormal behaviour.   *(10 marks)*

(b) Now imagine you are the psychologist who has received the letter; write back commenting critically on the points made in the original letter.   *(10 marks)*   *(Total: 20 marks)*

(NEAB, PS04, February 1997)

Question 8   (a) Outline the DSM **and/or** ICD approaches to classifying abnormal behaviour.   *(10 marks)*

(b) Discuss practical **and** ethical implications of using these approaches.   *(15 marks)*

(AEB, Paper 2, Summer 1997)

Question 9   Critically consider the contribution of biological **and** environmental factors to schizophrenia.   *(25 marks)*

(AEB, Paper 2, Summer 1996)

Question 10   (a) Describe the main features of **either** anorexia nervosa **or** bulimia.   *(4 marks)*

(b) Outline **one** psychological explanation for the disorder you have described in (a) above.   *(4 marks)*

(c) Discuss how eating disorders may be treated by psychological intervention. Refer to relevant theory and research in your answer.   *(12 marks)*

(Total: 20 marks)

(NEAB, PSO8, February 1996)

Selected reading list

Gross, R. and McIlveen, R., *Abnormal Psychology* (Hodder and Stoughton, 1996)

Jones, E., *The Life and Work of Sigmund Freud* (vol. 1 of 3) (Basic Books, New York, 1953)

Lieberman, M.A., Yalom, I.D. and Miles, M.B., *Encounter Groups: First Facts* (Basic Books, New York, 1973)

Sachs, O., *The Man Who Mistook His Wife for a Hat* (Picador, 1985)

Szasz, T.S., *The Manufacture of Madness* (Routledge & Kegan Paul, 1970)

Answer to 'Think about it', page 398
Szasz argues that society rather than the individual is the/a main cause of 'abnormality'.

9 Applied psychology: how can we use psychology?

This final unit looks briefly at a number of applications of psychology. Previous units have dealt with theoretical aspects and with how to do research in psychology; we now turn our attention to some of the ways in which psychology is put into practical use in society at large. 'Practical use' is an accurate term because, as you will have discovered, psychology is an extremely practical science in that just about everything we do has a psychological cause or interpretation. It is also a science that, broadly speaking, we can 'use' – as a quick look at the contents of this unit will indicate.

Something to do

- Make a list of possible uses of psychology. Start with the topics covered in this unit.

In this unit, the discussion of a practical application of psychology is followed, where possible, by reference to the appropriate theoretical basis as discussed in the text. The unit covers psychology in the contexts of education; organisations; the workplace; and health. The final section looks at some controversial applications of psychology.

Psychology in education

Psychology in education is a vast field of study, touching on a number of areas that are important in their own right but which come together under this general heading. The subject is also known as **educational psychology**; a professional psychologist working in education is known as an **educational psychologist**. The areas of psychology that most usually fall under this sub-discipline are:

- principles of learning;
- cognitive functioning;
- child development;
- atypical development;
- social development;
- motivation;
- testing; and
- counselling.

Think about it

- Can you add to the above list? Think of your own experience or knowledge.
- For each item on the list, identify the relevant section in this book; there may be several for each topic. Then briefly re-read the sections.

In the context of education, we can make a broad distinction between the use of psychology, and hence psychologists, in two main ways:

- normal situations; and
- abnormal situations.

Under the first of these would be areas such as teacher training and curriculum design; while under the second would come work with children with learning difficulties, school phobia, IQ testing and personal problems that may be linked to the home. This can be shown in schematic form as follows:

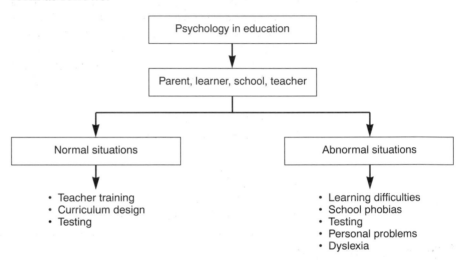

Note, however, that the figure is very simplified: 'parent, learner, school, teacher,' for example, can each involve normal or abnormal situations, and there is no neat division between normal and abnormal.

There is no one single 'application' of psychology in education, but many examples would fall under 'atypical psychology'. This of course can mean many things, so to give a focus to this discussion we take the example of **school phobia**. The term simply means 'fear of school'. A child with this kind of problem will be under the care of an educational psychologist who will try to identify the cause of the problem and then design a treatment programme to get the child back into school. Depending on the particular circumstances, which may include the supposed reasons for the problem, personal and family history, and input from social workers, teachers and perhaps other professionals, the educational psychologist will develop a treatment strategy. This is then put into place and, hopefully, the child will be able, in due course, to return to school.

Something to do

- Choose another area of psychology in education from the list at the start of this section. Jot down some notes on how to apply psychology to this example.

Organisational psychology

The term **organisational psychology** has a wide range of meanings. For example, you can turn it round to mean 'the psychology of organisations'. Other meanings or related terms are 'business psychology', 'organisational dynamics', 'industrial psychology' (an older term) and 'occupational psychology', which is discussed in the next section. With all of these, the key idea is to see what part psychology has to play in the kind of structures and procedures that occur every day in an organisation. 'Organisation', as it is used here, means some form of structure which has a number of parts, all of which belong to the organisation and are controlled by it. So, for example, a multinational company is an organisation, as are the Boy Scouts movement and the local drama club.

What is the psychology that goes on in such an organisation? Just about everything! A multinational organisation is likely to apply psychology in:

- testing procedures;
- personality testing;
- motivation of personnel;
- problem solving;
- advertising;
- ergonomics;
- group dynamics;
- training and re-training; and so on.

Something to investigate

- Expand the above list.
- Contact a large company and ask to interview a manager – probably in the Personnel (or Human Resources) Department – to establish what aspects of psychology they use, and how.

The list of possible uses of psychology in organisations, large and small, is too lengthy to discuss in detail here, so we look at just a few areas. There is, however, a logical way in which to group some of these uses:

- the individual as an **individual**;
- the individual in a **group**;
- the individual and group within the **organisation**.

The individual

Think of yourself for a moment in terms of whatever organisations you may be a part of. You may be at school or college, you may be at work, you may belong to a club or society. Each of these will involve you to some degree in aspects of psychology. For example, you may have faced a personality test and/or an intelligence test when you joined the organisation, or perhaps a vocational test of some kind. You may also at different times feel more or less motivated – what kind of incentives or rewards are in place? Depending on your place or responsibility in the organisation, you may need to exercise information-processing or problem-solving skills. You may also need to learn new skills and exercise your memory. Finally, you may have developed certain attitudes and you may perhaps have adjusted your value system; you may yourself have experienced prejudice and discrimination.

The group   When we turn to consider the way in which the individual functions within a group within the organisation, and the way in which the group influences the individual, a different set of psychological processes comes into play. Group dynamics form an important part of organisational psychology, as just about everyone in an organisation will be a member of at least one group – more usually, several. Related psychological processes include reasons for leaving and joining groups and group processes; this of course can lead to team building and leadership styles, which in turn may involve questions of power, authority and conflict.

Something to do

• Review these topics as they are discussed elsewhere in the text. Note how they apply in a group or organisation.

The organisation   Involved in the psychology of an organisation are areas such as the planning of change, contingency theory, the development of the organisational culture, and what has come to be known as **human resource management**. Also a part of the organisational psychology are questions of health and safety, which will often involve stress.

It would be a mistake to consider organisational psychology strictly in terms of the above three divisions, as there is considerable overlap. The whole field is changing rapidly and at an accelerating rate. In the business and commercial world, which is financially driven, rewards for 'success' are high and 'failure' usually spells the end of an organisation. All of this pressure places high demands on 'psychology' to provide the right answers.

Something to do

• Draw up a chart showing the three broad divisions and their associated psychology, as discussed above. Expand each area as far as you can, and then link *between* the three columns to show interconnected areas.

As an example of the application of psychology in organisations, consider **testing**. This has become an industry in its own right with literally hundreds of tests for the organisational psychologist or, more usually, the 'human resources' manager to use. A quick reference to a book on psychological testing revealed over 50 different tests to measure intelligence alone! To be able to make effective use of these tools, the person giving the test needs to:

• have at least some knowledge of test construction;
• be psychologically aware of what it is that is being measured;
• have knowledge of the kinds of tests available;
• know how to choose the best test to achieve the desired result; and
• have the ability to interpret the result.

All of these require psychological knowledge and application of that psychology to a higher order.

Occupational psychology

There is a certain amount of overlap between organisational psychology and occupational psychology. Organisational issues tend to be of a social nature, while occupational issues tend to deal more with the interface between 'man and machine'.

- Occupational psychology involves testing, but in this case the test(s) would be much more of a vocational type, sometimes theoretical, using pen and paper, other times practical.
- The occupational psychologist is the person involved in the design of training programmes and, with today's rapidly changing technology, in the frequent retraining of employees.
- A key function of occupational psychology is to use psychological principles to ensure the person or operator, whether of a VDU or a heavy industrial machine tool, operates the equipment efficiently and safely. If the operator becomes too tired or bored, they will start to make mistakes and that may lead to an accident. Inefficient working costs money, and so it is the occupational psychologist's job to ensure efficient, safe working.

Ergonomics

How long can an air traffic controller work before becoming tired? Is it better for them to have short periods of work with frequent short breaks, or longer work periods with longer breaks? Or, to take another example, sit in a comfortable position in the driving seat of as many cars as you can, and compare them, not just for comfort, but for accessibility of controls to feet, hands and eyes. This is the subtopic of **ergonomics**, which is applied to everything from space-ship design to kitchen cabinets.

An application of psychological principles to occupational psychology would happen in the case of retraining an older worker whose job has 'disappeared' due to the advance of technology. The employee has been a loyal worker for many years. Is it better to retrain him or her, or to employ a younger person straight from school? If you decide to retrain, what psychological principles are involved? You will need to consider motivation, stress and aptitude. You will then need to assess existing skills, and compare them to new skills. The difference will require a training programme, using learning principles, to be designed and tested. The older worker may need to work in a new position with new, or at least different, co-workers, so you need to consider group dynamics. All of these issues fall under the remit of the occupational psychologist.

Health psychology

We can describe **health psychology** as the way in which psychosocial factors relate to the promotion and maintenance of good health, and also the factors that have to do with cause, prevention and treatment. It involves a wide application of psychological principles and has a long history.

Many ancient tribal groups have ceremonial procedures, the origins of which are lost in time, but the relevance of which has a great deal to do with the relationship *between* body and mind. Modern Western culture, on the other hand, has tended to separate mind and body and to apply the medical model, which focuses on the physical problem and seeks to provide a physical cure; problems of mental illness are usually dealt with separately. It is only relatively recently that the physical and mental aspects of the person have been seen to be linked, and attempts made to deal holistically with problems.

As a consequence of this change in thinking, research is now probing links between biological, psychological and sociocultural factors, giving rise to the **biopsychosocial model,** which says in effect that it is the *interaction* of factors that can give rise to illness. As a consequence, when illness occurs, the medical profession is as likely to ask you about your workload or problems in your family relationships, as it is to take your temperature or to take a blood sample. Biopsychosocial factors in health are outlined schematically below (see also pages 87 and 279).

Biopsychosocial factors in health (based on Weiten, 1994)

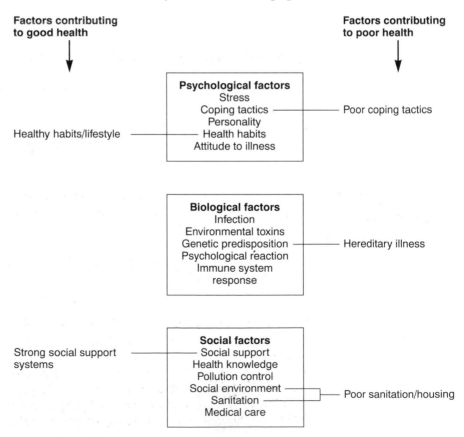

Factors contributing to good health

Factors contributing to poor health

Psychological factors
Stress
Coping tactics —————— Poor coping tactics
Personality
Healthy habits/lifestyle ———— Health habits
Attitude to illness

Biological factors
Infection
Environmental toxins
Genetic predisposition ———— Hereditary illness
Psychological reaction
Immune system
response

Social factors
Strong social support —— Social support
systems
Health knowledge
Pollution control
Social environment ——
Sanitation —————— Poor sanitation/housing
Medical care

As well as dealing with the obvious issues concerning good health, such as examining the relationship between eating habits and heart disease, or the slightly less obvious, such as the relationship between stress and good health, health psychology also seeks answers to questions that deal with the reasons people continue to live a lifestyle that is known to damage health. Why do people often ignore their doctor's advice, and why do they delay seeking medical advice even when they know they probably need treatment? (Are you overdue a visit to your dentist, for example?)

In terms of the way in which psychology is applied to health issues, the question of stress is a key issue.

Something to do

- Re-read the section on stress in Unit 5, starting on page 269.
- Identify and list psychological principles involved in promoting health.
- Copy the chart on page 444 of biopsychosocial factors and see how many ideas you can add to the lists of factors contributing towards good health and towards poor health.

Controversial applications of psychology

This section considers three controversial applications of psychology:

- advertising;
- propaganda and warfare; and
- uses of psychometric testing, in particular personality and intelligence tests.

Applied psychology in advertising

We can usefully start this topic by asking what is advertising, what is its purpose, and where does psychology come into it? The purpose of advertising is to do with:

> *"presenting and praising ... to the ... public ... in order to encourage sales"*
>
> Source: *Collins Dictionary* (1987)

The psychology which deals with this is to do with **persuasion,** so in psychological terms we are looking at, for the most part, **persuasive communication theory.** Someone writes or designs the advertisement in order to sell the product or service to members of the public. The advertisement may be targeted at the public at large, for example in the case of holidays, or at a specific group of people, for example those who play golf or, in the case of the latest toy or game, children.

Something to do

- Think about how advertisements work psychologically.
- Choose several advertisements and analyse them in terms of persuasiveness, colour, symbols, message, humour, etc.

We need to question the place of psychology in this process. Banyard (1996) suggests that there are four main ways in which psychology is involved in advertising:

- developing a need for the service or product;
- presenting the product as the most preferable;
- getting the attention of the target;
- developing buyer loyalty.

The first of these, developing a need for the service or product, argues that the advertisement must convince the person that they *need* this product. An early study in this area was done at a **subliminal level** (literally, below the level of consciousness) and was reported by Brean in 1958. In this study a cinema projector flashed the messages 'Eat popcorn' and 'Drink Coca-Cola' onto the screen as a film was showing. Sales of popcorn and Coca-Cola increased over the period of the study. Later criticism, however, pointed out severe methodological problems with the study. There are obvious ethical concerns with subliminal messages and many countries ban their use.

The second way in which psychology is involved in advertising, that is presenting the product or service as the most preferable, follows on logically from the first, and so the advertisement is designed to make the product seem much preferable to other similar products. Repetition without 'processing' is not effective, however. Processing in the context of advertising a product simply means dealing cognitively with the material in a number of different ways: linking the product with something else is one method; another, relatively recent, tactic is the 'serial' advertisement, in which the same people will be used almost to tell a story – often suggestively.

The third way, getting the attention of the target audience, is to get the customer actually to buy the product. This can involve free handouts, mood creation, linking the advertisement graphics to the packaging graphics, and so on.

The fourth use of psychology in advertising, developing customer loyalty, aims to get the person to go on buying the particular product. This can involve reinforcing messages about the quality of the product and affirming the buyer in their wise choice!

If we accept the above four stages as one possible way to describe 'advertising', we still need to clarify the psychology that is involved. The following chart, 'Advertising psychology', attempts to show this.

Advertising psychology

Advertising process	Psychology involved		Cross reference to text
	What	**How**	
1. Develop a need	(Subliminally –	Now illegal)	
	Persuasion theory Attention and impression formation	Use of colour text, images	
2. Present the product as preferable	Memory processing	Dealing with the message at a variety of levels.	
	Hemisphere studies	Brain hemispheres process different messages: so picture on left, message on right of advertisement.	
	Classical conditioning/ Association	Link product with feeling good.	
	Emotion	Avoid cognitive, apply emotion 'pull'.	
3. Get the customer to buy the product	Imitation effect	We copy others. We know the 'rules' socially.	
		More than just mimicry.	
4. Develop buyer loyalty	Cognitive dissonance	To justify the decision to ourselves.	
	Reinforcement	You really have bought the best.	

Source: Adapted from Banyard (1996)

Something to do

• Re-draw the above chart. Research and expand the 'Psychology involved' column, and complete the cross references by adding unit and page numbers.

Propaganda and warfare

A second controversial use of psychological principles also using persuasion is that of **propaganda**. At its most basic, the term simply means to manipulate belief or opinion. It is a little more complicated than that, however. This is because implied within the term is the idea that information which forms the basis of the propaganda is organised and deliberately intended to persuade or mislead and also to appear as if the misleading information that is being communicated is not propaganda, but the truth. In other words, if the person at whom the propaganda is targeted realises that the communication *is* in fact propaganda, then much of the persuasive power of the message is lost.

One common use of propaganda is by members of religious sects who try to persuade others to join them. What is often happening in this case is a mix of persuasion and propaganda. The individual or sect trying to persuade you to join them may be doing so because they genuinely believe in what they are saying, but they may do so because they have been convinced by the propaganda that has come from their leaders. Persuasion is more to do with pressure, while propaganda is a deliberate attempt to falsify information.

We more readily tend to think of propaganda as being used by governments in warfare, where both armies and the civilian population are led to believe that they are winning even though they may not be. In the Second World War, figures produced at the end of the war showed that the German claims for enemy aircraft shot down were four times too many, while British claims were twice too many. In 1998, the battle of wills between Iraq and the United Nations over the question of arms inspections led the Iraqi leadership to claim a victory over 'British and American aggressors', while the Americans and British claimed 'an Iraqi climbdown'. Both were using propaganda in an attempt to persuade others of the truth of their view.

Propaganda is the not-so-obvious face of warfare that goes on behind the scenes but which nevertheless has a significant impact on outcome. The question that we need to consider is: what part does psychology play in this? It is largely aspects of persuasion that make up the psychology of propaganda and warfare. Persuasion in this context may include, at one extreme, trying to keep up the morale of the civilian population, and, at the other extreme, using sensory deprivation to disorientate the person (prisoner) coupled with what is popularly called **brainwashing**.

Propaganda has been used in one form or another for centuries, but it is only recently that we have made more technical use of our psychological knowledge in this controversial way. An example of the application of a psychological principle to propaganda and warfare is that of information processing. (Remember that it was the Second World War that triggered a huge technological push which in turn provided very sophisticated information-processing systems.) In the 1980s, the Western forces' superior communications network played a major role in the Gulf War, and it was no coincidence that their first targets were Iraqi communication centres. The ability to control the flow of information in propaganda and warfare can be argued to be a very powerful weapon.

Psychometric testing

In this section, we discuss two forms of **psychometric testing**: personality tests and intelligence tests. The term 'psychometric' is fairly clear; it literally means measuring (metric) the mind (psyche). The term is normally used for any test that attempts to measure or define the psychological aspects of a person. Typical uses for personality tests, sometimes called **personality inventories**, are in therapy and in assessment for employment or for promotion in work settings.

The ethics and accuracy of psychometric testing still cause concern in some quarters, but testing is heavily relied upon both in education and in industry and commerce as well as in health, clinical and sports psychology. Intelligence tests are used widely in education and to a lesser degree in the military and in the workplace.

Personality tests

Something to investigate

- Using this book and other resources, find out all you can about personality. Summarise your findings in a spider diagram.

Tests looking at personality are, as stated above, widely applied both in therapeutic settings and in the workplace. Their use in therapy frequently provides an objective starting point for the therapist. There are many such tests; some are extremely complicated, such as the Minnesota Multiphasic Personality Inventory (MMPI), which is probably the most widely used self-report inventory for testing personality. It has 567 questions with true/false/cannot say answers, which are scored on 15 scales. Other tests are less complex, but can have useful features such as the capability to be used in a therapeutic or counselling setting with a couple. In this case, some of the test items or questions will refer to the relationship and the answers given by the test-taker can be used by the therapist or counsellor when discussing issues with the couple.

Personality tests used in the workplace are equally diverse, with perhaps the most common use being for personnel selection, either for employment or for promotion. Tests used in this context have become almost commonplace, and it can be argued that too much reliance is placed on the test result.

The process of test taking can start early in a person's life: many young people aged 14 or 15 take a test to help them and their careers advisor determine a suitable vocation or career. The Morrisby Test is designed for this purpose. Other tests frequently used are the Eysenck Personality Questionnaire (1975), the results from which are scored on four bipolar scales; and Cattell's (1989) 16 PF, which scores results on 16 personality factors.

Intelligence tests

Something to do

- Re-read the section on intelligence in Unit 7, pages 337–9.

Intelligence testing has had a somewhat chequered history since Binet produced the first of many such tests in 1905. The classic problem has been to make the test a fair test for all people. In the past, the main problem was that of cultural bias in terms of language and meaning of the test items. More recent tests have overcome this by using symbols rather than words.

Modern intelligence tests tend to measure intelligence on two main scales (another example of the Nature–Nurture debate):

- **fluid intelligence,** which measures the person's innate reasoning ability and is sometimes called abstract intelligence; and
- **crystallised intelligence,** which is the ability to solve problems based on experience and knowledge and increases with age.

Most Western tests measure both of these, often include items of general knowledge, and test verbal, numerical and spatial skills.

The application of intelligence testing in its various forms is very widespread and is used routinely in educational settings to select children for appropriate classes. It is also used to help identify problems that children may be having with their school work.

The whole process of the design, implementation and interpretation of a test has become very sophisticated, with areas such as reliability and validity receiving a great deal of attention. In general, tests can only be given by trained professionals and, by the same token, the interpretation of the result also needs considerable training and experience. However, on the positive side, recent tests are proving valuable and accurate, and can be very useful when used within their design parameters.

Revision and practice

● ●

Coursework opportunities

1. Investigate the ergonomic design of popular makes of car. You could sit in the driving seat and measure accessibility of controls, view of instruments, etc. Are short/tall people inconvenienced? Does cost or make of the car correlate with design problems?.
2. Investigate stereotyping in television advertisements. Are the sex roles of leading characters sexist in any way? Analyse advertisements for role and sex of characters, types of products, etc.
3. Investigate the place of humour or race in advertising. Play humorous/non-humorous advertisements to participants and test for recall some time later. Do the same for race.
4. Correlate intelligence levels with a number of other factors, such as school/college grades, attendance, hobbies, achievements in sport, etc.
5. Personality testing is difficult, as most professional tests require the user to be trained. However, devise your own test using, say, Eysenck's EPI or Cattell's 16 PF. Try correlating simple results with choice of school/college subjects, hobbies, etc. A variation is to survey people who have already been professionally tested and know their results. Tests such as those given by careers advisers may be used in this case.
6. Investigate biopsychological aspects of health. One way of doing this would be to correlate student absence from school/college with personality type or with some social aspect of their situation.

● ●

Examination questions

Psychology in education

Question 1

(a) 'Rules, Praise, Ignore' is a whole school behaviour modification programme used in primary schools. A series of rules are devised which are stated in positive terms. For example, instead of a rule stating **DO NOT RUN IN CORRIDORS,** the rule says **WE WALK SAFELY IN CORRIDORS.** Teachers then praise children who are walking safely and ignore children who are not walking safely. If a child consistently walks unsafely they are required to spend playtimes in a **TIME OUT** room on their own.

Outline psychological concepts used in the above example of a behaviour modification programme. *(8 marks)*

(b) A number of studies of truants have uncovered certain features in their home lives. Sometimes home conditions are intolerable for the truant, homes may be overcrowded and dirty, and parents may have little interest in their child's welfare. Other studies have identified peer pressure as a cause of truancy.

Behaviour modification programmes are used sometimes in an attempt to reduce truancy.

Discuss ways in which home life, peer pressure and other factors can reduce the effectiveness of behaviour modification programmes. Refer to psychological theory and evidence in your answer. *(12 marks)*
(Total: 20 marks)

(NEAB, PS09, February 1997)

Occupational psychology

Question 1

(a) Discuss the varieties of adjustment that people make to retirement. Make reference to empirical research in your answer. *(10 marks)*

(b) Discuss psychological effects on family and friends that may result from a person retiring from work. Make reference to empirical research in your answer.
(10 marks)
(Total: 20 marks)

(NEAB, PS03, February 1996)

Health psychology

Question 1

Samina is married with children and works in a very demanding job. She works long hours in a busy office and has responsibility for a wide variety of different tasks.

(a) Name and describe **three** possible causes of stress in Samina's life. *(6 marks)*

(b) Discuss what effects these stressors might have upon Samina's health. Make reference to appropriate theory and research in your answer. *(14 marks)*
(Total: 20 marks)

(NEAB, PS08, February 1996)

Selected reading list

Banyard, P., 'Psychology and advertising', *Psychology Review*, 3–1 (1996)
Milner, D., *Success in Advertising and Promotion* (John Murray, 1995)

Glossary

Terms in capitals are those which are most basic, and should be learnt first.

To find the text on the topic related to a particular glossary item, look up the item in the index at the back of the book.

$2\frac{1}{2}$D SKETCH   One of the stages (the third) in Marr's computational theory of vision, concerned with the layout of the object surfaces. Not fully three dimensional.

3D REPRESENTATION   The final (fourth) stage in Marr's computational theory of vision – an information-processing approach that builds on previous stages and involves top-down processing. Full object recognition.

Ablation   removal of tissue, usually surgically.

ABNORMAL BEHAVIOUR   Any behaviour which is considered not normal. A variety of approaches seek to define the term.

Abreaction   A term used in psychoanalysis to describe the removal or release of anxiety. See CATHARSIS.

Absolute refractory period   In neuropsychology, the period of time (up to 2 msec) when a neuron is at rest, or unresponsive, following the transmission of the neural impulse. See 'ALL-OR-NONE' PRINCIPLE.

Accommodate   Psychological or physical adjustment made to prepare for incoming stimuli, e.g. the ciliary muscle of the eye controls accommodation of the lens.

Accommodation   The modifying of an internal and familiar schema to enable it to fit a new experience and to fully adapt.

ACOUSTIC CODING   Material/information dealt with on the basis of its sound. Transformed to enable storage. See ELABORATED CODE/RESTRICTED CODE.

Acoustically   Dealing with sound.

Acquired dyslexia   Problems with reading as a result of brain damage in people who were previously good readers.

Acronym   A word made up from the first letter of a group of words or term or phrase. Can be used to assist memory.

Action potential   The difference in electrical potential between the active and the resting parts of an individual neuron at the time at which it fires. See GRADED POTENTIAL.

ACTIVATED FORGETTING   A form of forgetting. A defence mechanism whereby memories that cause distress are pushed into the unconscious. See REPRESSION.

Activation-synthesis model   A model that suggests dreams reflect biological activity.

Activity theory   This theory suggests that, if older people stay active and involved for as long as possible, they will remain healthier and more satisfied with their lives.

Acute stress disorder   Reaction to a traumatic event where symptoms begin within and last for 28 days of the actual event. See POST TRAUMATIC STRESS DISORDER.

Adaption-level principle   This suggests that our happiness is relative to our previous experience, not some absolute level.

ADOLESCENCE   The period of human development between puberty and adulthood.

ADULTHOOD   The period of human development from adolescence until death. Usually divided into a series of stages.

Adversary problems   Where there is competition from one or more persons, e.g. playing chess. See also NON-ADVERSARY PROBLEM SOLVING.

Aetiology   The study of the causes of diseases.

AFFECTIVE   Emotions and feelings.

Afferent neurons   Neurons that carry messages to the brain. Also called 'sensory neurons'. See also EFFERENT NEURONS.

Affiliate   Generally, coming into a close relationship. (Almost) always with a positive meaning.

AGGRESSION   Behaviour – usually physical but can be verbal – with the intention to harm. A general term for action that is hostile or attacking.

Agoraphobia   Fear of open places. Probably the most common phobia.

ALGORITHM   A procedure that will solve problems by a series of specific rules. See also HEURISTIC.

'All-or-none' principle   In neuropsychology, the principle that a nerve responds to a stimulus. If the stimulus is inadequate the nerve does not respond at all, if it is adequate the nerve responds to maximum capacity. See ABSOLUTE REFRACTORY PERIOD.

Alpha waves (or rhythm)   Brainwaves measured in a person at rest but relaxed, approximately 10 per second.

ALTERNATIVE HYPOTHESIS   The hypothesis that is constructed for use with a non-experimental design, e.g. observation or correlation. See NULL HYPOTHESIS, EXPERIMENTAL HYPOTHESIS.

Altricial   Newborn who are totally dependent on their parents for survival. See also PRECOCIAL.

ALTRUISM   Deliberately placing the welfare of another before yourself.

Amenorrhea   An absence of the menstrual cycle.

AMNESIA   A general term for partial or complete loss of memory.

Amok (or Amuck)   Rushing about in a frenzied manner. A culture-specific syndrome, initially thought to be Malaysian.

Amygdala   Located in the temporal lobe and part of the limbic system. Involved in emotional behaviour and motivation, particularly aggression.

ANAL   Second stage in Freud's psychosexual development. Eighteen months to three years. The child gains sexual pleasure via its anus by the retention or expulsion of faeces.

Anal-expulsive   In Freud's theory of psychosexual development, the idea that the young child can exert influence by the expulsion of faeces. See ANAL-RETENTIVE.

Anal-retentive   In Freud's theory of psychosexual development, the idea that the young child can exert influence by the retention of faeces. See ANAL-EXPULSIVE.

Analysis by synthesis   Neisser's (1976) view that seeks to show the interaction between bottom-up (Gibson) and top-down (Gregory) processing. He started with a bottom-up analysis and then brought to bear a top-down approach that looks for or *analyses* expected features that could be expanded or clarified to make 'better sense' or to *synthesise* the input. If this does not happen, fresh *analysis* takes place leading to fresh *synthesis*.

Analytic psychology   The type of psychoanalysis suggested by Carl Jung.

Animism   The belief that natural objects (e.g. stones, water) are animate living things or possess souls.

Annual monogamy   The relationship, usually sexual, between one male and one female which only lasts for one season.

ANOREXIA NERVOSA   An eating disorder leading to an obsession or fear with weight and being fat. Approximately 95 per cent of cases are young females.

ANTEROGRADE AMNESIA   Memory failure suffered after brain damage, in which the person is unable to learn or remember any information following the injury although memory prior to the injury is not affected.

Anticipatory grief   The feeling that the person is 'ready for death', or has come to terms with impending death.

ANTIDEPRESSANT DRUGS   Groups of drugs used in the treatment of depression. One group causes an increase in the release of seratonin and norepinephrine. Another group, the tricyclics, prevents re-uptake in synapses. Tricyclics have minimal side-effects or dependency.

Anti-psychiatry   Szasz's view that mental illness is to do with 'problems in living'.

Arousal theory   This theory holds that people are motivated to do dangerous things, e.g. mountain climbing, to increase arousal, or are motivated by fear.

ARTICULATORY LOOP   In the working memory model, a component of the short-term memory that is used to remember information for a short time, e.g. a telephone number, or used to hold words that are about to be spoken. Also called the 'inner voice'.

ARTIFICIAL INTELLIGENCE (AI)   An artificial (man-made) system that operates in a human-like manner and can show thinking and/or intelligence. Combines research in computer science and cognitive processes. See STRONG AND WEAK AI and EXPERT SYSTEMS.

Assertiveness training   Technique(s) used to train people who are timid, shy and dependent to be less so.

Assimilation   The process by which a child adapts to a new situation in the light of new experience.

ASSOCIATION   A term used to describe a learned connection between two ideas or events.

Association area   The area of the cortex, usually the frontal and parietal lobes of the brain, where higher mental processes occur, e.g. learning, thought, memory, language.

ATTACHMENT   The way two people wish to be together. For example, a mother/child attachment or bond. Has emotional and dependency elements.

ATTENTION   A term used to describe the processes by which we perceive selectively.

Attention – divided   Where more than one stimuli is attended to.

Attention – focused   See ATTENTION – SELECTIVE.

Attention – selective   Where there are multiple stimuli and one must be selected and attended to. Also called focused attention.

Attention-deficit hyperactivity disorder (ADHD)   A disrupted behaviour disorder characterised by poorly controlled acting-out impulsive behaviour.

The ADHD syndrome is thought to affect 3–5 per cent of children up to the age of 11.

Attenuated   A situation where a signal is turned down as the volume on a radio or TV may be turned down.

Attracted   See ATTRACTION.

Attraction   The characteristic(s) or trait(s) that causes or evokes a desire to be with someone or something.

ATTRIBUTION(S)   The inference(s) that we draw about the *cause* of our own or another's behaviour.

ATTRIBUTION OF CAUSALITY   The way that you attribute someone's behaviour to its cause, either an internal or personal cause, or an external or environmental cause (Heider).

ATTRIBUTION THEORY   The way in which a person attributes certain traits or characteristics to themselves or to another. See FUNDAMENTAL ATTRIBUTION ERROR.

ATYPICAL DEVELOPMENT   Not conforming to expectations. Sometimes used interchangeably with 'abnormal'.

Auditory processing   Information that is processed (e.g. memorised) as a result of hearing it.

AUTISM   Literally, *aut* = self, *ism* = orientation. A condition where the person is unable to relate to another. Usually involves social isolation, cognitive and language problems and stereotyped behaviour.

AUTOBIOGRAPHICAL MEMORY   A person's recall of lifetime events.

Autokinetic effect   An effect where a light which is in fact stationary appears to move.

Automatic processing   See AUTOMATICITY.

Automaticity   Behaviour that has become 'automatised' by performing a process regularly. Requires no formal attention processing.

AUTONOMIC   In classical conditioning, the action of the reflex that is being conditioned.

Autonomic nervous system (ANS)   A major part of the nervous system made up of the sympathetic and parasympathetic systems. Called autonomic because most of the functions it controls are self regulating.

Availability   A determinant of attraction, along with proximity and familiarity.

AVERSION THERAPIES   A therapy which pairs the inappropriate behaviour with an aversive or unpleasant stimulus. Sometimes called aversive therapy or conditioning.

Awareness   Occurs when we are conscious of ourselves and the environment that we are in.

AXON   The part of a neuron that projects from the cell body and ends in a button.

Balance theory   See RECIPROCITY. Also Heider's theory of the attempt to resolve or balance discrepant views or attitudes.

Base-line   In behavioural therapy, the base-line behaviour is the frequency of the behaviour at the start of the treatment.

BEHAVIOUR   Any kind of action, activity, response etc., animal or human, that can be measured.

Behavioural   Objective, observable behaviour.

Behavioural genetics   The study of the effect of genes on behaviour.

BEHAVIOURISM   A psychological approach (or perspective) that argues that scientific psychology should only concern itself with behaviour that can be measured.

Behaviourists   Those who support or practise behavioural theories.

BEHAVIOUR MODIFICATION   Changing the person's behaviour by – usually – using operant conditioning techniques.

BEHAVIOUR THERAPY   Procedures used in a therapeutic setting that are based on classical conditioning techniques.

Binge-eating disorder   An eating disorder characterised by a compulsion to eat large quantities of food at a single sitting. Often followed by self-induced vomiting. See BULIMIA NERVOSA.

Binge–purge syndrome   Popular name for bulimia nervosa. Sometimes known as 'dietary chaos syndrome'.

Biofeedback   The control of physiological functions through deliberate monitoring and relaxation.

Biological determinism   The view that it is the biology of the individual that is the cause of or determines a particular behaviour.

BIOLOGICAL REDUCTIONISM   A point of view that argues that since we are animals we can follow a reductionary route from the complex human animal down the chain to much less complex animals. See PHYSIOLOGICAL REDUCTIONISM.

BIO-PSYCHOLOGY   Sometimes called 'psychobiology'. Broad term for the study of psychological processes from a biological standpoint.

Biopsychosocial model   A view that illness is not just caused by biological factors, but by a combination of biological, psychological and social factors.

BIORHYTHM   An activity or cycle that occurs regularly in a human or animal.

Biosocial   The study of a society, particularly its

behaviour, from combined biological and social perspectives.

Biped Any animal with two feet.

Bipolar depression A mood disorder that swings between the two extremes of mania and depression.

BLIND SPOT The small area on the retina where the optic nerve leaves the eye. It is *blind* because it has no receptors.

BODY LANGUAGE Non-verbal communication (NVC) involving gestures, movements and facial expressions that may be conscious or unconscious.

Body rhythms See BIORHYTHM.

BONDING The process by which the young of a species identifies with its parent.

Bottom-up (Gibson) The process of perception that starts with the sensory input and works 'up' to the brain's cognitive operations. Sometimes called 'data-driven' processing. See TOP-DOWN.

Brain localisation The hypothesis that specific experiences or functions are associated with specific areas of the brain.

Brain plasticity In areas of brain damage, nearby neurons may 'take over' the damaged area by making new *connections* rather than new *cells*.

BRAINSTORMING A group activity used to generate lots of ideas to solve a problem.

Brainwashing Attempting to change a person's beliefs or behaviour using psychological or physical pressure.

BRIGHTNESS CONSTANCY The perception of an object as having the same level of brightness (constancy) in different lighting conditions.

Broca's aphasia (or motor aphasia) Speech *production* problems – not speech *understanding* problems – due to damage to the lower part of the left frontal lobe.

BROCA'S AREA A part of the brain involved with speech, situated in the frontal lobe. First identified by Paul Broca in 1861.

BULIMIA NERVOSA An eating disorder characterised by excessive eating followed by self-induced vomiting. Often associated with depression or guilt. See PURGING-TYPE BULIMIA NERVOSA.

Button The terminal at the end of an axon.

BYSTANDER BEHAVIOUR (or EFFECT) The phenomenon whereby, when help is needed, the more people who are present, the less likely it is that any one of them will help.

Cannibalism The eating of flesh, animal or human, by one of its own kind.

Care giver The person, usually a parent, who provides food, comfort and other basic needs.

CARPENTERED ENVIRONMENT Any physical setting which is made up of straight lines, square corners etc., e.g. a house, and which may affect the perception of people who live there.

CASE STUDY The detailed record of an individual person. It usually includes personal history, test results, clinical notes, etc.

Catatonia A state where muscles are rigid and the person often just stares into space saying nothing. There are various degrees of catatonia. (Adjective = **catatonic**.)

Catatonic schizophrenia A type of schizophrenia affecting motor control. The person remains in one position for long periods of time (days or even weeks). The position is maintained even where extreme discomfort or circulatory problems are evident. The static behaviour sometimes alternates with brief interludes of extreme hyperactivity when the person is likely to harm themselves or others.

Catatonic waxy flexibility A catatonic state where the person's limbs can be moved into any position and will remain there.

Categorical rule In speech production, the rule that limits what is being represented at each level.

Categorical self The way in which a person, usually a child, puts him-/herself into different categories, e.g. male/female, age group, etc.

CATHARSIS In Freudian theory, the release of tension or anxiety by bringing feelings, memories, etc. into consciousness. See ABREACTION.

CAT scan See COMPUTERISED AXIAL TOMOGRAPH.

Causal schema A plan or schema of how certain causes create certain behaviours (Kelley).

Cellular-ageing theory A biological theory of ageing which suggests that the person's DNA breaks down to the point that the body becomes unable to repair itself.

CENTRAL EXECUTIVE The key element in the working memory model that makes decisions.

Central fissure (or fissure of Rolando) The long, narrow gap which separates the motor cortex from the sensory cortex in the forebrain.

CENTRAL NERVOUS SYSTEM The parts of the nervous system (the brain and the spinal cord) that control behaviour and internal bodily processes.

Central-state materialism The view that the mind is a *physical* process that occurs in the central nervous system. Sometimes called the identity view. See MIND–BODY PROBLEM.

Cerebellum   The part of the brain (hindbrain), situated near the top of the spinal cord, that is involved in maintaining muscle co-ordination, particularly high speed (e.g. playing squash), and balance.

CEREBRAL CORTEX   The surface layers of grey matter that cover the brain and which are responsible for higher mental processes e.g. memory, thinking, etc.

CHEMOTHERAPY   The use of chemicals in the treatment of many illnesses, especially cancer.

Chromosomal mapping   The comparison of chromosomes between normal and abnormal conditions.

Chromosome   Part of the cell nucleus which carries the genes. Humans have 46 chromosomes.

Chronobiology   The study of biorhythms, e.g. bird migrations, circadian rhythms, etc.

Chronological   In order of occurrence.

CHUNKING   A term used for a way of grouping items together into chunks as an aid to short-term memory.

Chunks   Groups or units of individual items.

Ciliary muscles   Muscles attached to the lens of the eye. When relaxed the lens is flattened and when contracted the lens is thickened.

CIRCADIAN/CIRCADIAN RHYTHMS   Body rhythms, usually biological, on a 24-hour cycle. See also ULTRADIAN RHYTHMS.

Classical concept   One (of two) types of concept. In a classical concept, all aspects of the concept are shared by all its members. See also PROBABILISTIC CONCEPT.

CLASSICAL CONDITIONING   A form of learning, by association, developed by Pavlov. It involves repeatedly pairing a conditioned stimulus (e.g. sound of a bell) with an unconditioned stimulus (e.g. food) causing a conditioned response (salivation) which was caused previously by the unconditioned stimulus (food).

Clearness   When an image stands out vividly and is the centre of attention.

CLIENT-CENTRED THERAPY   A humanistic form of therapy developed by Carl Rogers, where the 'client' (as opposed to 'patient') is encouraged to solve his or her own problems.

Closed group   In group therapy, a group is formed, agree to meet for a set number of sessions, and then disband. See OPEN GROUP.

Closed-loop feedback   Where feedback from visual or other modes feeds back via a person's information processing to monitor and control behaviour, e.g. the control exerted when riding a bike.

Closed mind   An extension of the authoritarian personality where a person retains old-fashioned ideas, resists change and is strongly authoritarian.

COCKTAIL PARTY EFFECT   A term coined by C. Cherry to describe the perceptual ability to attend selectively to a single message whilst dealing with many.

Coercive compliance   Behaviour that complies to the wishes of others, e.g. conformity and obedience, when some kind of threat or force is implied.

Coevolution behaviour   The way in which behaviours evolve together, with one influencing the other, e.g. animal courtship where communication by the male *coevolved* with the responding female behaviour. Another example is symbiosis.

Coevolved   See COEVOLUTION BEHAVIOUR.

COGNITIVE   Any form of mental activity or behaviour – a very broad term.

Cognitive-behavioural   A model in which cognitive processes are acquired by behavioural means, while the behaviour follows the person's interpretation, in his or her own mind, of the learned cognitive processes. In therapy, the modification of behaviour by cognitive processes.

COGNITIVE BEHAVIOURISM   Similar to social learning theory but with more emphasis on the cognitive processes taking place when learning occurs. In therapy, the influence of cognitive processes on behaviourism.

Cognitive consistency theory   The way in which a person will seek to solve cognitive conflict within themselves by changing their behaviour to be in line with their beliefs.

COGNITIVE DISSONANCE   The state of tension that exists within a person when two thoughts or beliefs (cognitions) are inconsistent. Can also exist when the inconsistency is between a belief and a conflicting behaviour.

Cognitive map   A mental representation, by an animal or human, of the way in which a problem can be solved. A term coined by E.C. Tolman from his work on rats running mazes

Cognitive processing   An information process that is a combination of memory, thinking, problem-solving, etc.

Cognitive restructuring   A form of cognitive therapy which places emphasis on the restructuring or changing of faulty or inappropriate cognitions.

Coital   Sexual intercourse.

Collective behaviour   Behaviour that occurs at the same time or within the context of a social group.

Collectivistic   The way the person is seen more as part of a group rather than as an individual. See also INDIVIDUALISTIC.

COLOUR CONSTANCY   When an object is *perceived* as the same colour even when the lighting conditions change the appearance.

Commisurotomy   The surgical procedure to severe the tissue joining the two hemispheres of the brain. See SPLIT BRAIN.

COMMUNICATION   The transmission of a message, signal, etc. from one location, person or animal to another.

Communication theory   This theory holds that there is a messenger, a message to be sent which is then encoded, a medium over which the message is transmitted, and a receiver who can decode the message.

Companionate love   A form of love based on friendship.

COMPARATIVE PSYCHOLOGY   A branch of psychology that compares the behaviour of animals with humans in an attempt to understand the similarities and differences between them.

Competition   Direct rivalry between two or more humans, animals, groups, etc.

Complex   In Freudian thinking, a group of unconscious wishes.

Complex emotions   Embarrassment, pride, guilt and similar emotions that develop in the child at about 12 months. See also PRIMARY EMOTIONS.

COMPLIANCE   Behaviour that conforms to the wishes of others.

Complimentary   To do with the way we are attracted to others who meet *our* needs.

Compulsive   The type of behaviour that compels a person to act against his or her wishes.

COMPUTATIONAL THEORY   A computer program, or model, developed by D. Marr to simulate the perceptual process. It consists of three stages. The first stage takes the retinal image and converts it into a 'primal sketch'. The second stage takes the initially sorted information and converts it into a '$2\frac{1}{2}$D sketch', while the third stage of the process, full '3D representation', is completed using top-down processing.

COMPUTER ANALOGY   A parallel between the brain and a computer arguing that both process information.

Computer language   The characters that are used to send instructions to a computer.

Computer simulations   Where a computer is programmed to simulate human thought or behaviour.

Computerised axial tomograph (CAT scan)   A procedure for examining the brain whereby the brain is scanned using a narrow X-ray beam and the pattern of absorption is then analysed by a computer system. It provides a 'picture' of the brain.

Concept   A cluster of objects that share some of the same attributes and result in a mental representation.

Concurrent validity   A type of validity using associated or secondary data, where the test scores and criterion scores are established at the same time, e.g. comparing the results of a new IQ test with an older well-validated IQ test.

CONDITIONED RESPONSE   A response resulting from conditioning. See CLASSICAL CONDITIONING.

CONDITIONED STIMULUS   A stimulus that only gives a response after conditioning. See CLASSICAL CONDITIONING.

Conflict   A situation where mutual antagonism exists.

CONFORMITY   The way in which a person can be influenced by the generally held views of a group. Can relate to behaviour or attitude.

CONFOUNDING VARIABLE   An uncontrolled variable in experimental work, the effect of which is not known.

Congruence   In humanistic therapy, a term used when the therapist shows the client that the relationship between thoughts, feelings and behaviour must 'fit' (be *congruent*).

Connectionism   See PARALLEL DISTRIBUTED PROCESSING.

Connectionist theory (or model)   An assumption that cognitive processes operate as a network.

Consciousness   A state of awareness.

Consensus   Everyone reacts in the same way to the cause of a behaviour.

Conservation   A sub-stage within Piaget's Stage of Concrete Operations (7–11 years) where a child understands that an object remains the same although its appearance may change (it is 'conserved').

CONSTANCY   The way that a perceived object is always recognised (e.g. as a door), even though the retinal image may change (e.g. from a rectangle to a trapezium).

Constancy – brightness   See BRIGHTNESS CONSTANCY.

Constancy – colour   See COLOUR CONSTANCY.

Contact hypothesis   Social contact, first discovered by Allport, which holds that the more contact there is between individuals and groups the less prejudice there will be.

Contingency model (or theory)   The expression of a relationship where one circumstance, or event, depends (or is contingent upon) another event.

Continuity   Unbroken, uninterrupted, going on. Gestalt law of organisation: you will 'see' the most obvious continuous arrangement of shape, dots, etc.

Continuous development   The process of development in a steady, regular manner, based on the rate at which new behaviours are learned. See also STAGE THEORY.

Continuous reinforcement   In classical conditioning, *every* time the behaviour occurs it is reinforced.

Controllability   A dimension on Weiner's model of attribution.

CONVERGENCE   In perception, a binocular cue for depth perception. Generally the movement of the eyes to converge on the object.

Co-operation   Working together with a common purpose or task.

Co-operation principle   The principle that both the speaker and the listener must co-operate for successful communication.

CONVERGENT THINKING   A form of thinking where the activity is focused on one solution and involves the bringing together of all relevant data to solve the problem – which usually has only one correct answer. See DIVERGENT THINKING.

Corpus callosum   The band of fibres that connect the two cerebral hemispheres of the brain and transfers information between them.

CORRELATE   If two variables that are systematically related to each other, they co-relate.

Correlation   A statistical procedure that investigates the relationship between two variables.

Correspondent inference theory   In this theory, people infer that the observed behaviour corresponds to the person's general character.

Countertransference   The therapist/analyst's displacement or transference of emotion etc. (back) on the client. *Or* the general emotional involvement of the therapist/analyst. See TRANSFERENCE.

Covariation theory   A theory of attribution in which people act like scientists when trying to make attributions. They analyse behaviour and try to link (*covary*) other factors with it.

Co-vary   A situation where two variables change with respect to each other. See also CORRELATION.

CRITICAL PERIOD   A period of time, that is biologically determined, during which the organism is ready to acquire a specific response. The process of imprinting is an example.

Critical value   Technically the boundary values of the critical region. The value at which a test is either accepted or rejected, usually given in table form in the back of statistics books.

Cross-cultural   The evaluation, study or comparison of different cultures.

Cross-culture theory   A theory which attempts to analyse the behaviour of groups, rather than individuals in a group.

Crowd   A (usually) large temporary gathering of people who share a common interest or purpose.

CRYSTALLISED INTELLIGENCE   Intelligence that can improve with training. The form of intelligence that is measured by the ability to solve novel problems in a creative manner. Sometimes called 'concrete intelligence'. See also FLUID INTELLIGENCE.

Cue   A stimulus that evokes a response.

CUES – BINOCULAR   Visual cue when using *both* eyes.

CUES – MONOCULAR   Visual cue when using only *one* (mono) eye.

Cultural   Pertaining to the beliefs, traditions, attitudes, etc. of a social group.

Cultural determinism   The view that human development is determined by cultural factors.

Cultural norms   The accepted rules or standards any one culture or society has for its members, and which the majority follow.

Culture   Usually the non-genetic passing on of information, traditions, customs, etc. from one generation to the next within a given social group.

Culture-bound behaviours   An abnormal behavioural syndrome which is specific to a particular culture.

Cumulative-deficit hypothesis   An hypothesis proposed by Klineberg to explain why children brought up in poverty-stricken surroundings score below average on IQ tests. The essence of this hypothesis is that the longer the child spends in a deprived environment the lower his or her IQ will be.

Cybernetics   The study of the comparison between man-made and biological control systems.

Data   Facts or information

Data levels   Data from an experimental are usually in one of three forms – interval, nominal or ordinal.

DATA – INTERVAL   Data measured using standard recognised units, i.e. seconds, minutes, etc.

DATA – NOMINAL   Most basic form of data, simply counting categories, e.g. 10 males, 12 females, etc.

DATA – ORDINAL   Data that has order or progression e.g. 1st, 2nd, 3rd, etc.

Decategorisation   An extension of the contact hypothesis where a deliberate attempt is made to reduce the distinctiveness of the group.

Default assignment   An idea developed by McClelland where missing information in memory is filled in on the basis of knowledge of related circumstances or objects.

Defence reaction   A term in psychodynamic theory used to describe unconscious reactions that provide a defence against anxiety.

Defensive attribution   See SELF-SERVING BIAS.

DEINDIVIDUATION   The loss of awareness of one's own individuality (e.g. when in a mob).

Delta waves   Brain waves produced in deep sleep which have large amplitude and slow frequency.

Delusions   Unreal beliefs, false opinions or impressions despite factual evidence to the contrary.

Dementia praecox   Out-of-date term for schizophrenia. Actually means premature dementia.

Demonological   Concerned with spirits or demons. An early model of the cause of abnormality.

Deoxyribonucleic acid (DNA)   The chemical base which 'carries' genetic information.

DEPENDENT VARIABLE   In an experiment, the variable that changes as a result of the manipulation of the independent variable.

DEPRESSION   A mood disorder of despondency and a feeling of inadequacy. There are many variations of depressive disorders.

DEPTH PERCEPTION   The ability to see objects as three-dimensional. Also the distance of objects from the eye.

DESCRIPTIVE STATISTICS   Statistical methods that essentially summarise the data.

Desensitisation   Where a person is repeatedly exposed to something, e.g. violence, they will simply get used to it, it will no longer have an impact, and any suffering as a result is not seen as serious.

Determinism   The philosophy that everything that happens is the consequence of prior conditions, and that nothing happens without a cause.

Deterministic   Not accidental but determined by past experiences. See DETERMINISM.

DEVELOPMENTAL PSYCHOLOGY   Psychology that is concerned with the psychological, physical and social changes that occur with age.

Developmental tasks   Tasks that must be accomplished at certain periods throughout life in order for an individual to develop further and to achieve psychological well-being.

DEVIANCE/DEVIANT   Deviating from an acceptable standard or norm.

Deviation IQ   A measure of intelligence comparing same-age groups rather than the more traditional measure of IQ.

Dialectical   A theory which argues that learning comes from reasoning not from experience.

Dichotic listening tasks   Where two different messages are relayed, one to each ear. See SPLIT-SPAN TASKS.

Diencephalon   A subdivision of the forebrain consisting of the thalamus and the hypothalamus.

Dietary chaos syndrome   See BULIMIA.

Difference   The way in which one or more, e.g. sets of data, are unlike each other.

DIRECTIVE   A form of therapy, e.g. behaviourism, where the client may be *told*, i.e. directed how to proceed, what to do, what not to do, etc.

DISCOURSE ANALYSIS (DA)   The analysis of speech (discourse) units usually larger than a sentence, e.g. in the study of memory 'discourse' is 'analysed' to understand how the person remembers.

Discrimination   Technically the ability to see a difference between two events or stimuli. Socially, the unequal treatment of individuals based on race, sex, etc.

Disengagement theory   A theory which suggests that older people gradually withdraw (disengage) from society.

Disequilibrium   Occurs when a change in an organism or the environment requires revision of the basic structure.

Disorganised   An ability to organise oneself. Confusion, no order. Used in a clinical setting where the behaviour is disorganised, e.g. schizophrenia.

Displacement   The ability to use language across time and space, e.g. when a person speaks of what they did yesterday, or what they plan to do next year.

Dispositional attribution   The case where the attribution of an even or its cause is the result of the internal disposition of the person.

Dispositional characteristics   Circumstances which affect behaviour that are to do with the person's own personality or characteristics (and not, say, the situation).

Disruptive behaviour disorder   Behaviour characterised by poorly controlled acting out; impulsive behaviour in situations where self-control would be expected, e.g. in ADHD.

Dissociate   The way in which children who have suffered trauma 'dissociate' or separate themselves from the experience.

Distortion   An alteration of or to something. A theory of conflict resolution that says that it is easier to act, e.g. hit out, than talk.

Divergent thinking   This form of thinking seeks to draw in all possible relevant, and some not so relevant, ideas that may have a bearing on the problem, so it's quite possible that novel or unique solutions may occur. Can be seen as the opposite of convergent thinking.

Dopamine   A catecholamine that works as a neurotransmitter. It functions in the control of complex motor actions.

Dopamine hypothesis   The hypothesis that an excess of dopamine is thought to cause the symptoms of schizophrenia.

DOUBLE-BLIND   A research procedure where both the participant and the researcher are in the dark concerning the real purpose of the experiment. See also SINGLE-BLIND.

Drive-reduction theory   This theory suggests that whenever there is a physiological need it creates a psychological state that then drives the organism to reduce the need by satisfying it.

DRUG ADDICTION   When a person has a strong craving to continue to use the drug. 'Drug dependency' is now the preferred term.

DRUG DEPENDENCY   See DRUG ADDICTION.

DRUG TOLERANCE   When a drug is taken for a prolonged period of time the body becomes accustomed to the drug so that the drug becomes less effective.

Dual process dependency model   The term in social psychology dealing with social power that includes both coercive compliance and persuasive influence.

Dual-task   An experimental approach to divided attention where participants are told to respond to two or more messages.

Dualism   Any approach that considers the relationship between two parts or states. See MIND-BODY PROBLEM.

Dyadic (also diadic)   Things that have two parts or are paired.

DYSFUNCTION   Not functioning normally in a given society.

DYSLEXIA   A learning disorder usually described as reading difficulties, sometimes including writing and spelling problems.

Early socialisation   See SOCIALISATION. Early socialisation refers to those things which occur first in this process.

ECLECTIC   Selecting and using the best of several systems or theories.

ECOLOGICAL   Deals with the relationship between organisms and their environment.

Ecological approach   An out-of-the-laboratory approach that deals with most areas of cognitive psychology and is based on real situations and real environments and is therefore considered to produce results with 'real' significance or value.

ECOLOGICAL VALIDITY   Relevance to the real (ecological) world.

EDUCATION   The process of teaching and learning.

Educational psychology   A branch of psychology concerned with issues and problems in education.

Efferent neurons   Neurons that carry messages from the brain to muscles, glands, etc. Also called 'motor neurons'. See also AFFERENT NEURONS.

Effort after meaning   A process first described by Bartlett to explain the way that we seek to make sense of, for example, a story we have heard and are trying to recall.

Ego   (Latin for I or self.) The part of the psyche or personality representing cognitive and perceptual processes. The centre around which other psychic events happen. The part of the personality in touch with reality. The ego serves to 'balance the id and superego'.

EGOCENTRIC   Literally, self centred.

Eidetic memory (or eidetic imagery)   The ability to see or remember the image after it has gone. Commonly called 'photographic memory'.

Einstellung   Means 'set' or a readiness in cognitive terms to deal with a particular kind of stimulus such that other forms of stimulus may not register.

Elaborated code   In language theory, the relatively large vocabulary and complex speech constructions of children from higher socio-economic groups. See also RESTRICTED CODE.

Electra complex   Sometimes considered the opposite of the Oedipus complex and therefore applied to girls, by those who assume the Oedipus complex applies to boys only.

Electroconvulsive therapy (ECT)   The use of electric shock for therapeutic purposes/psychiatric disorders. Now mainly used in cases of severe depression where other treatments have failed.

Electroencephalogram (EEG)   The recording of brain waves by placing electrodes or pick-ups on to the scalp and recording the waves (electrical activity) produced when the patient responds in some way.

Electromagnetic energy   The radiation of energy, e.g. light waves.

Emergent norm theory   A view in social psychology that, in a crowd, there is no one *norm* or generally accepted way for the crowd to behave, until it 'emerges'.

EMOTION   Very difficult to define accurately. Generally an umbrella term for those affective parts of human experience such as love, hate, fear, etc.

EMPATHY   In humanistic therapy, a term used when the therapist will seek to understand a client's experiences and feeling to feel at one with them.

EMPIRICISM   An assumption that all knowledge comes from learning and experience. See NURTURE.

EMPIRICISTS   Those who believe that knowledge comes from experience. The method employed by empiricists is the collection and evaluation of data. The current major psychology paradigm.

Encephalisation   As the brain has evolved and grown, the process by which it has taken over more and more of the control of functions of the body.

ENCODE   To change incoming information into a meaningful form, e.g. a sequence of sounds into a word.

ENDOCRINE SYSTEM   The body's system of *ductless* glands that secrete hormones through the bloodstream.

Endogenous   Dealing with those things that originate from *within* the body. See SOMATOGENIC and PSYCHOGENIC.

Endorphins   One of a group of naturally occurring peptides produced by the brain or by the pituitary gland involved in the control of emotional behaviour, e.g. pain, fear.

Engram   A theoretical/suggested biochemical and permanent change to neural material in the brain which represents learned information. (This has never been located.)

Environmental determinism   The view that the environment is the cause of a particular behaviour.

Epidemiological approach   An approach where all possible causes for a condition are investigated.

Epidemiology   The study of diseases. Usually involving psychology, sociology, demographics and medical aspects. An interdisciplinary approach.

EPISODIC MEMORY   Memory for specific events or episodes in the person's experience.

Epistemology   A branch of philosophy that deals with the origins and nature of human knowledge.

Equilibrium   The balance of organised structure. When in balance they aid interaction with the environment.

Equity theory   The essential idea that behaviour in a relationship must be fair to both.

Ergonomics   The way people interface physically with their job or work position to enable efficient and safe working.

EROS   In Freudian theory, the life force or instinct. Greek god of love. See also THANATOS.

ETHICS   That part of philosophy concerned with right and wrong. In practice, a code or guidelines giving guidance on what is and is not acceptable practice.

ETHOLOGY   An interdisciplinary science concerned with the observation of animals in their natural habitat. It uses naturalistic observations. Compare with comparative psychology which normally uses experimental methods.

EVERYDAY MEMORY   An alternative term for 'working memory'.

EVOLUTION   The process by which animal and plant species develop from earlier forms.

Evolutionary stable strategy   Evolutionary behaviour that maximises a species' chance of survival.

Existentialist   One who believes that human beings must live 'authentic' lives, with the choice to accept the way they exist. If they accept it, they live healthy, happy lives; if not, then their 'existence' is likely to become maladaptive. Based on existentialist philosophy.

EXOCRINE SYSTEM   Glands that secrete hormones through a *duct*. See also ENDOCRINE.

EXPERIMENT   A research design in which all variables are controlled except the independent variable which is deliberately changed by the researcher and the dependent variable which may change as a result and which is measured by the researcher. The procedure shows a cause/effect relationship.

EXPERIMENTAL HYPOTHESIS   The hypothesis (H_E) which is to be tested when using the experimental method (other methods use an alternate (H_A) hypothesis).

Expert systems   A form of artificial intelligence based on an extremely large data base or program of knowledge.

External causality   A situation where the cause of an event is due to factors outside the person.

Extinction   In evolution, the disappearance of a whole species. In learning theory, the removal of a stimulus such that the response ceases.

EYE-WITNESS TESTIMONY   The degree to which a person's memory of an event is accurately recalled.

Face-ism   The depiction of the female *body* compared to the male *face* in the media.

False memory   A memory, usually of an event, that is uncovered or 'remembered' in therapy, which did not in fact happen. See RECOVERED MEMORY.

Familiarity   In social psychology, one of a number of reasons why people become attracted to each other.

Faulty thinking   A not-very precise term which refers to problems with making assumptions, faulty perception, over-simplification of complex issues and irrational beliefs and attitudes.

Feature detection   A part of perception that detects or 'sees' a certain distinctive feature in a visual display.

Feature detectors   A specific neuron or group of neurons in the cortex, that detect or 'see' a certain feature arriving via the optic nerve.

Field theory   A development of Gestalt theory. Deals with the total environment of a situation (the 'field') and the forces at play within it, in an attempt to understand behaviour.

FIGURE GROUND   A term used to describe the relationship between a figure and its background. It's a question of which you see as the background and which you see as the figure. See RUBIN'S VASE.

FIXATION   In Freudian theory, becoming fixed or 'stuck' in a given stage of development.

FIXED ACTION PATTERN   In ethology, an innate procedure that occurs at some critical point in the infant's early development. See SPECIES-SPECIFIC, which is the preferred term.

FLASH BULB MEMORIES   A very clear and well-defined memory that occurred in a person's life, usually at a significant time.

FLOODING   A form of therapy usually with phobias where the client is exposed to a massive array of the feared object. See also IMPLOSION.

FLUID INTELLIGENCE   Aspects of intelligence unlikely to change. The ability to solve problems usually based on facts. Sometimes called 'abstract intelligence'. See also CRYSTALLISED INTELLIGENCE.

Foraging   The way in which an animal will search for food when in its natural environment.

FOREBRAIN   The largest major division of the brain. It deals with the higher-order mental functions. It is divided into the diencephalon and the telencephalon.

FORGETTING   The inability to recall previously remembered material.

Fovea   A little depression in the retina of the eye. It is in the middle of the macula lutea (or yellow spot) and is the area of clearest vision.

Frames   General knowledge of objects, places, etc. A subdivision of a *script*, which in turn is a subdivision of a *schema*. Usually in the context of everyday memory.

Free association   Used in a variety of contexts – the person is asked to respond to a stimulus of some kind with the first thought that comes to mind.

Free will   The view that a person's behaviour is under their direct control.

FRONTAL LOBE   The largest of the lobes. Controls small muscles which require precise control. It is positioned in front of the precentral gyrus (the ridge just in front of the central fissure).

FUNCTIONAL FIXATEDNESS   Where objects are seen only as being of use for one function or purpose even though it is possible for them to be used in another context.

Functionalism   A view that analyses behaviour in terms of function (rather than content).

Functional psychoses   'Disease' or problems with living or functioning (an anti-psychiatry view).

FUNDAMENTAL ATTRIBUTION ERROR   The way people attribute the cause of behaviour to internal factors, usually ignoring external factors.

Fusing   Blending or joining together.

Game theory   A decision-making process which takes account of the actions of the other 'player' in the game.

GENDER   The preferred term when discussing differences in role and identity between sexes.

Gender role   See SEX ROLE.

Gender schema   Organised mental structures about males and females, that influence children to process information that they attend to and therefore remember.

General adaption syndrome (GAS)   A three-stage representation of the body's biological reactions to stress – alarm, resistance, exhaustion.

GENERAL PROBLEM SOLVER   A computer program written to simulate the way that humans solve problems.

Generativity versus stagnation   The seventh of Erikson's eight stages of man, resolved through the experience of care.

GENETIC ENGINEERING   The process by which the genetic structure of an animal is altered by the addition or removal of certain genes.

Genetic fingerprinting   The ability to identify an individual from a piece of tissue, e.g. blood, hair, skin, etc.

Genetic transmission   The way in which genes are passed from parents to offspring.

GENITAL The fifth and final stage in Freud's psychosexual development. From puberty into adolescence. The child gains sexual pleasure from sexual feelings towards others.

Genotype In ethology, the genetic, hereditary make-up of a given species. See also PHENOTYPE.

Genuineness In humanistic therapy a term used when the therapist is open about their own feelings.

GESTALT A German word with no English equivalent, but roughly translates as 'form', 'whole' or 'shape'. See GESTALT PSYCHOLOGY.

GESTALT PSYCHOLOGY An approach to psychology founded in the early 19th century in Germany. Psychological phenomena – usually perceptions – can only be understood when viewed as a *whole*. The whole is more than the sum of the parts.

Glial cell (or glia) Special cells that provide a supportive role in the nervous system, e.g. they deal with dead cells.

Goal In social psychology, a 'goal' is a key component in a relationship, perhaps the most important component. It can set the short-term and/or long term direction for the relationship.

Graded potential The process by which the electrical potential required to fire (or inhibit) a neuron builds up by the summation of many smaller impulses, each of which is insufficient on its own to fire the neuron. See ACTION POTENTIAL.

Grey matter The term given to parts of the brain and spinal cord that contains mostly cell bodies. See also WHITE MATTER.

GROUP THERAPY Where a number of people meet together with a therapist. The dynamics within the group can also be therapeutic.

Hallucinations Perceiving objects that are not present in reality. A classic symptom of psychosis. See also DELUSIONS.

HALLUCINOGENICS A group of psychoactive drugs. They produce sensations and perceptions that have no physical cause.

Haploid cells Having only one set of chromosomes (not the usual two sets).

HEALTH PSYCHOLOGY The field of psychology concerned with psychological issues that affect the health of the individual.

Helping behaviour See PROSOCIAL BEHAVIOUR.

HEURISTIC A problem-solving approach that explores a range of *possible* solutions, but does not guarantee a solution. Compare with ALGORITHM which does provide a solution.

Hierarchy The ranking of people, objects, etc. in order from high to low.

HIERARCHY OF NEEDS A hierarchy of needs proposed by Maslow. The 'lowest' are physiological, the 'highest' is self-actualisation.

HINDBRAIN The part of the brain that controls internal body states and co-ordinates motor activity. It also acts as a relay station between the spinal cord and other areas of the brain.

Holistic An approach that considers the whole organism. Implies that a consideration of *parts* of a whole is not adequate.

HOMEOSTASIS The way that the body works to maintain stability by adjusting controlling functions, e.g. when too hot you perspire to lose heat.

Home range The physical territory in which an animal lives and hunts.

Homing The ability to return to the starting place. Used of homing pigeons, salmon, etc.

Homosexual A person whose sexual preference is for a member of his or her own sex.

Homosexuality Sexual contact between two people of the same sex.

HORMONES A general term for a large number of chemicals that carry 'messages' from endocrine and exocrine glands to regulate other parts of the body.

HUMANISTIC An approach which studies human nature, human affairs and knowledge, and the higher-order human activities. (Coined by Maslow.)

Human resource management The control and planning for the effective use of people in an organisation.

HUMANISTIC-EXISTENTIAL MODEL This model is essentially concerned with what it is that makes us human, i.e. early childhood experiences, behaviour, your thought processes or something more. A humanist view does not ignore behaviour and thought but believes that the 'essence' of 'humanness' lies in issues such as self-awareness, a value system and emotions such as joy, sorrow, etc.

Humours Fluids of the body, e.g. the vitreous and aqueous humours of the eye. Also very old-fashioned term for the four bodily fluids suggested to influence temperament.

HYPNOSIS A state of consciousness similar to sleep but not showing normal sleep patterns. The subject has limited attention or behaviour, etc.

Hypothalamus A small, complicated structure at the base of the brain, controlling the autonomic nervous system. Part of the limbic system.

HYPOTHESIS A proposition or assumption that can be tested.

ID   In Freudian theory, one of the three main parts of the psyche or personality. It houses the deepest unconscious desires and responds to biological needs within the body; it demands immediate satisfaction. Concerned with the pleasurable state. See EGO and SUPEREGO.

Identity achievement   The final stage or status of Marcia's model of adolescent development. Follows identity confusion, identity foreclosure, and moratorium.

Identity confusion   The initial status in Marcia's model of adolescent development. See IDENTITY ACHIEVEMENT.

Identity foreclosure   The second status in Marcia's model of adolescent development. See IDENTITY ACHIEVEMENT and IDENTITY CONFUSION.

Identity status   The 'status' or stage of development in Marcia's model of adolescent development. There are four levels or stages. See above entries.

Identity view   See CENTRAL-STATE MATERIALISM.

IDIOGRAPHIC   An approach that regards a person as a unique individual. See NOMOTHETIC.

IMAGERY (VISUAL)   Simply, a picture in your mind.

Immortality   Literally, living for ever. In developmental psychology, an issue which old people have to face as death approaches.

IMMUNE SYSTEM   The body's system to protect itself from infection. White blood cells produced in the bone marrow and thymus gland, 'fight' infectious bodies.

Implosion   A form of therapy where the client is told to *imagine* that they are in the presence of what they fear. See FLOODING.

IMPRINTING   The way in which the newborn develops a bond with its parent. It occurs during the critical period.

In group/out group schema   The first gender schema that a young child forms which allows the child to classify objects and behaviour as suitable to either gender, e.g. dolls for girls, guns for boys.

Inclusive fitness (for survival)   The way an animal will behave so as to ensure the survival of the maximum number of its genes.

Independent behaviour   A condition where behaviours are not dependant on external influence.

INDEPENDENT-MEASURES DESIGN   A research design or situation where two different groups of participants are tested.

INDEPENDENT VARIABLE   In an experiment, the variable that is manipulated so as to observe the effect upon the dependent variable.

INDIVIDUAL DIFFERENCES   An approach to psychology where the emphasis is on the differences between people. Often includes areas such as intelligence, personality and abnormality.

Individualistic   The way the person is viewed as an individual, without the influence of the social culture. Compare with COLLECTIVISTIC.

Individual psychology   The approach to psychology first defined by Adler.

Infanticide   Killing infants or newborn, often to provide food.

INFERENCE   A judgement of view which is based on some form of evidence. A cognitive process.

INFERENTIAL STATISTICS   Generalisations concerning data that use probability to make references about the population from a smaller sample.

Inferiority complex   Having a very low opinion of oneself and one's abilities. Having low self esteem.

Informational processes   In conformity, the process that occurs when the person is anxious to do the right thing in a given social setting.

INFORMATION PROCESSING   Cognitive operations taking place in stages.

Informational social influence   Variation of 'informational processes'.

Infradian   Body rhythms with a cycle of more than 24 hours.

Infundibulum stalk   The 'stalk' which joins the pituitary gland to the forebrain. (Literally means a 'funnel shape'.)

Ingratiation   A form of social power where the more a person likes someone, the more they will comply.

Inherited   The passing on of the parent's characteristics to its offspring.

Inhibition   The reduction in memory effectiveness due to the presence of other information. Sometimes used synonymously for 'interference'.

INNATE   The characteristics, abilities, etc. that are 'in' the animal at birth. Also: inborn, inherited, nativistic, etc.

Innate releasing mechanism   In ethology, the way in which instinctual behaviour is set in motion when the sign stimulus occurs.

Insight   In general terms, the apprehending, usually intuitively, of a solution to a problem, or of a situation not previously understood. In therapy, the comprehension of the client's mental state, not previously understood.

INSOMNIA   Difficulty going to sleep and/or staying asleep for a normal period.

Instinct theory   The way that a given animal in a given situation will act instinctually. Also an early Darwinian theory of motivation (since discredited).

Instrument   A broad term used for a measuring device or method. Also used to describe questionnaires or tests for measuring, for example, personality or intelligence.

Instrumental techniques (or conditioning)   A special form of operant conditioning where the reinforcement is given only when the subject has responded correctly: a correct response is *instrumental* in producing the reinforcement. Operant conditioning is a looser term.

Intellectual   The rational thought processes of the human mind.

INTELLIGENCE   Traditionally difficult to define. The ability to learn from experience, solve problems, reason, achieve goals, etc.

INTELLIGENCE QUOTIENT (IQ)   A measure of intelligence derived from standardised tests of intelligence. IQ the ratio of mental age to chronological age $\times$ 100. By definition the average IQ is 100.

INTENTIONALITY   In language studies, the intention to deliberately communicate a message.

Interactive program   An early form of artificial intelligence where a person interacts with a computer.

INTERFERENCE   See PROACTIVE INTERFERENCE and RETROACTIVE INTERFERENCE. Sometimes used synonymously for inhibition. Interference is the preferred term.

Intergroup action   In crowd behaviour, where a group has a definite *group* identity which sets limits on the way in which the group can be expected to behave and when it confronts another group.

Interjectional   An early theory of the origin of language. The natural exclamation, or production of words or sounds. See also ONOMATOPOETIC and NATURAL RESPONSE THEORY.

Intermittent reinforcement   In learning theory, the use of a reinforcer, but *not* every time the correct response is achieved.

Internal causality   A situation where the cause of an event is due to factors from within the person.

Internalised   Taken into oneself, made something one's own, e.g. acting, believing morally like your parent.

Interneuron   A neuron in the central nervous system that relays message from sensory neurons to other interneurons or to motor neurons.

INTERPERSONAL PERCEPTION   Personal impressions that you make of others, and others make of you.

INTERPERSONAL ATTRACTION   The liking or attraction existing between two people.

Interposition   A powerful depth cue caused by one object partially blocking the view of another.

Intimacy versus isolation   In Erikson's developmental psychology, the first stage or psychosocial crisis in adulthood. The sixth of his eight stages.

INTROSPECTIONISM   An early approach to psychology: the method of looking into oneself to try to understand mental processes.

Invariants   The key idea in Gibson's view of direct perception.

Isolation effect   To highlight something so it will stand out and be more easily seen or remembered. See VON RESTORFF EFFECT.

James-Lange theory   Early theory of emotion suggesting that physical changes in the body *follow* the perception of the emotive event and that we *then* become angry, afraid, etc.

Jigsaw classroom   A study (in America) to reduce existing prejudice by co-operation, requiring children in a class to work together toward a common goal.

Kin selection   An evolutionary, altruistic process when one animal puts the survival of a member of its family above its own survival, to enable more of its genes to survive.

KORSAKOFF'S SYNDROME   Memory loss found in alcoholics: usually affects recent events.

LANGUAGE   At a simple level this term is well known and obvious – the spoken and written words we use to communicate. Usually includes sign language, computer language and animal language, all with different meanings.

Language acquisition device (LAD)   Chomsky argues that children have a LAD that is a biologically based, predetermined mental structure in addition to innate abilities.

Language acquisition support system (LASS)   A social view of language development that recognises the importance of social interaction to the child and its language development.

LATENCY   Fourth stage in Freud's psychosexual development. From six to twelve years. In this stage the child's sexuality is repressed or latent.

Latent   Suppressed or hidden.

Latent content   In Freudian theory, the hidden or symbolic meaning of a dream. See also MANIFEST CONTENT.

Latent learning   Learning that is available to apply to a given situation as required, e.g. the application of a schema or cognitive map.

Latent (sexuality)   In Freud's latency stage of psychosexual development, the idea that the child's sexuality becomes latent or dormant, as its interests focus on friends and other interests.

LATERAL THINKING   A term coined by de Bono (1977), and in some ways an extension of divergent thinking. De Bono was interested in novel or unique approaches to problem solving, but only those that would give the 'right' answer.

LAW OF EFFECT   A basic law of learning that says that a stimulus response (S–R) is strengthened when the response is followed by a reward, and weakened when there is no reward.

LAW OF PRÄGNANZ   In Gestalt thinking, the principle that says that the simplest organisation will emerge or stand out from the rest.

LAW OF PROXIMITY   In Gestalt psychology, a law which states that we see objects that are closer as being grouped together.

Law of similarity   In Gestalt psychology, a law which states that similar shapes will be seen as groups.

Leader   A person who holds a position of influence in a group.

LEADERSHIP   The way in which authority is put into practice in a group setting. Often used as a personality characteristic.

Learned helplessness   A model of depression which has two main strands. A person becomes depressed when they believe that they no longer have any control over the reinforcers in their lives; and second, when they believe that they themselves are responsible for this situation. See ATTRIBUTION.

LEARNING   A wide term generally defined as a relatively permanent change in behaviour due to experience.

Learning difficulty   Specific difficulties in learning skills, e.g. to read, write and do maths.

Learning disability   Used to be known as 'mental handicap'.

LEARNING THEORY   The very general term that seeks to explain the process of learning.

Lesions   A limited area of damage to tissue caused by injury, disease or surgical operation.

LEVELS OF PROCESSING   In memory, levels of (usually) increasing depth, leading to better storage and hence better recall (Craik and Lockhart's model of memory).

Life-change unit (LCU)   The numerical value given to a 'life event' on the SRRS.

Life–dinner principle   An evolutionary view that says the prey will run faster than the predator because the 'life' of the prey is at stake, but only the 'dinner' of the predator.

LIFE EVENTS   Events of major or minor importance in a person's life used in the SRRS to measure and predict stress levels. See SRRS.

LIFE SPAN DEVELOPMENT   A way of viewing human development as occurring throughout life.

Limbic system   Part of the forebrain including the amygdala, hippocampus septum and basal ganglia that work together to regulate emotion, memory and some movements.

LINGUISTIC RELATIVITY HYPOTHESIS   Whorf's view that language develops *before* and therefore *determines* thought. The hypothesis has three degrees of strength.

Lithium   A chemical salt often used in the treatment of psychotic disorders, e.g. bipolar disorder or manic behaviour. The way it works is not known; highly toxic.

Locus of cause   Concerned with the place – or location – of the cause of a certain behaviour. See ATTRIBUTION.

Locus of control   Where the control of what happens is seen as understood to come from. Can be internal or external.

LONG-TERM MEMORY (LTM)   Memory of information previously processed by short-term memory (STM). Generally has unlimited capacity and duration. Organised in various ways, e.g. semantic, episodic, etc.

Looking-glass self   A person's image of themselves formed by an awareness of how others see the person (Cooley). See also SELF PERCEPTION.

Love   Technically difficult to define, but the popular use of the term is usually adequate.

Magnetic resonance imaging (MRI)   A procedure that provides a detailed 'picture' of a 'slice' of body tissue. It involves a strong magnetic field which causes certain molecules in the body to spin. A radio wave is then passed through the body which 'sees' the spinning nucleus, and a computer draws the picture.

Magnetite   A material sensitive to a magnetic field, found in the skull of homing pigeons and believed to aid homing.

Maladaptive   In a clinical sense, behaviour that can cause problems or distress, such that some form of therapy is needed.

Maladjusted   Generally used in social or cultural settings where there are problems with relationship to the environment.

Mania   A certain type of psychotic or compulsive act. Totally preoccupied with a certain activity, e.g. pyromania.

Manic-depressive disorder   A bipolar disorder involving mood swings between manic and depressive states.

Manifest content   In Freudian theory, the obvious or actual part of a dream. See LATENT CONTENT.

MARIJUANA   The hemp plant. The sativa variety is grown to produce hemp and a derivative cannabis, which is used as a psychoactive drug. Other names: hash, hashish.

MATCHING HYPOTHESIS   A theory that suggests people are attracted to other people who have the same degree of attractiveness.

Materialistic   Generally, knowledge achieved by understanding the physical world. In a social context placing emphasis on things rather than personal or emotional.

MATERNAL DEPRIVATION   The effects on a child of being separated from its mother (Bowlby).

Maternal instinct   The instinct, innate concern or desire in the female to provide and care for her young.

MEANS–ENDS ANALYSIS   A problem-solving approach that breaks down the problem into a number of sub-problems, each of which need to be solved in turn. See PROBLEM-SPACE THEORY.

MEDICAL MODEL   A major approach in abnormal and atypical psychology and psychiatry. The model holds that a disorder is produced by a physical or medical cause which, if treated, will produce a cure. See SOMATIC.

Medulla   A general term used for the inner part of something.

Medulla oblongata   The area between the pons and spinal cord which controls initial bodily functions such as blood pressure, heart beat, etc.

Melancholia   Acute depression which often brings on emotional and mental stress.

MEMORY   The retention of information; the mental storage system. A complex term with a very wide usage.

MEMORY TRACE   The mental/neurological 'connections' that form a (relatively) permanent memory.

Mental age (MA)   The age at which a child's measured intelligence is statistically the same as its chronological age. A higher MA equates with higher intelligence. See INTELLIGENCE QUOTIENT.

Meta-analysis   Research or analysis that takes into account *all* previous studies of the topic in question.

Metabolic rate   The rate or speed at which the body changes as a result of gaining energy from breaking down food tissue (input), and losing energy from burning it (output).

Metamemory   'Meta' (usually) meaning 'all about', hence knowing about one's memory.

METHOD OF LOCI   A memory aid that uses locations associated with the material to be remembered.

MIDBRAIN   The smallest of the three major parts of the brain. Situated between the pons and the diencephalon.

Mid-life crisis   A major stage or turning point in Levinson's theory of adult development.

Migration   The movement of large groups of animals due to climate, breeding or food supplies.

Mind–body problem   A philosophical debate that is concerned with the relationship between the mind (mental) and the body (physical).

MMPI   *Minnesota Multiphasic Personality Inventory*. One of the most common and most comprehensive self-report inventories to assess personality. Contains 567 questions, scored on 15 scales.

MNEMONIC   A term used to describe any memory aid.

Mob   Technically the same as the popular use of the term, but with the implication of potential violence.

Modal model   Another name for Atkinson and Shiffrin's stages model of memory.

MODALITY   Any sensory system, e.g. the visual mode (or modality).

Modelling   Imitating the behaviour of someone else. Using someone as a role model. A basic learning process, particularly in socialisation.

MODEL   A simple definition regards a model as a way of viewing reality.

Modularity theory   A theory which assumes the mind has a number of relatively independent 'modules', each dealing with a specific cognitive function.

Monism   An approach which argues that there is only one way to view something.

Monogamy   A mating pattern between one male and one female. See ANNUAL MONOGAMY and PERENNIAL MONOGAMY.

MOOD   An emotional state that may be short term or long term. Mood disorders are extreme examples.

Moral code   A set of rules for defining the behaviour which is considered right or wrong by those who agree with that particular code.

MORALITY   Behaviour that is right or wrong, often in the context of a moral code.

Moratorium   A stage in Marcia's model of identity status during adolescence, which sees the adolescent in a state of ongoing crisis.

MOTIVATION   An internal drive or force that impels the organism into action.

Motive   The reason of cause of a certain course of action.

Motor aphasia   The loss of language ability (aphasia) due to lesions in the cortex which control the motor aspects of speech.

Motor cortex   That part of the cortex that controls the voluntary action of muscles.

Motor neurons   Neurons that carry messages *from* the brain to muscles and glands. Also called 'efferent neurons'.

Multiple requests   A form of social power where a person starts with an easy request, and builds up to what they really want.

Mutism   The inability to produce speech, possibly due to the organs necessary for speaking failing to develop or to severe emotional problems.

Mutualism   See SOCIAL CO-OPERATION.

Myelin sheath   The material that wraps around and insulates the axons of some neurons.

N ach (or n.Ach)   Abbreviation for 'need for achievement', implying high achievement.

Naive scientist   The way that a person (a non-scientist) will intuitively follow the scientific method.

Narcotic   Technically any drug that has both sedative and analgesic properties, that is the opiates.

NATIVISM   An innate, genetic capacity to perceive and understand. See NATURE.

NATURALISTIC OBSERVATION   Non-experimental investigation where data are gathered in a natural (that is, non-laboratory, non-structured) setting.

Natural response theory   An early theory explaining language.

NATURAL SELECTION   Darwin's theory of evolution. Inheritable traits that contribute to a species' survival are 'selected' to be passed on to following generations.

Nature–Nurture debate   One of the classic debates. Are we influenced more by nature (genetics) or nurture (experience)?

Need for achievement   Abbreviation n.Ach. A social motivation to achieve more than the next person.

NEGATIVE REINFORCEMENT   The use of a negative reinforcer.

Negative reinforcer   A stimulus that when removed or reduced *increases* the probability of a given response.

Negative symptoms   Symptoms in schizophrenia where the person has almost no emotions or feelings.

NEONATE   Very young child, newborn.

Neural impulse   The electrical potential that triggers the chemical process causing the release of neurotransmitters.

Neurhypnology   Early term for the treatment of nervous disorders by hypnotism.

Neurhypnotism   Early term for what became 'hypnotism'.

NEURON   Nerve cell; the basic unit of the nervous system. Nerve cells can vary in shape, but all consist of body, axon and dendrites.

NEUROSES   Anxiety-based disorders often due to malfunction in the nervous system. Also called 'neurotic disorder'.

NEUROTIC   Partial loss of reality as displayed by a person who has a neurosis.

Neurotoxin   Literally 'nerve poison'. A substance that destroys neurons.

NEUROTRANSMITTER   The chemical released by the terminal button of one neuron that passes across the synaptic gap to relay information to the receiving neuron.

Neutral response   In classical conditioning, a response that occurs incidentally and not as a result of conditioning.

Neutral stimulus   In classical conditioning, a stimulus that does not normally produce a conditioned response.

Nodes of Ranvier   The small gap in the myelin sheath of a nerve fibre.

NOMOTHETIC   An approach that relates to people in general, or as part of a group. See IDIOGRAPHIC.

Non-adversary problem solving   Problem solving on your own, e.g. solving the nine dot problem. See also ADVERSARY PROBLEMS.

NON-DIRECTIVE   A form of therapy, e.g. humanistic, where issues are discussed, but the client is not told or directed how to solve the problem.

Non-purging type bulimia nervosa   Binge-eating followed by extreme dieting, exercise or fasting, but not forced vomiting.

Non-state theories   These theories hold that a hypnotised person is not in a special state but is simply acting-out a suggested role. See also STATE THEORIES.

NON-VERBAL COMMUNICATION (NVC)   Human or animal communication using signals, gestures, etc. that are not verbal.

Norm   Behaviour that is typical of a given group or society.

NORMAL FORGETTING   The inability to recall/retrieve information from memory (but see AMNESIA).

Normative processes   The need to belong or to be approved of or liked.

Normative social influence   See NORMATIVE PROCESSES.

NULL HYPOTHESIS   The hypothesis that any difference found between the experimental group and the control group occurred by chance and is therefore not significant.

Number–rhyme system   A memory-enhancing system based on use of rhyming numbers.

Number–shape system   A memory-enhancing system based on use of the shape of numbers.

NURTURE   To do with experience and environmental factors. See NATURE–NURTURE DEBATE.

OBEDIENCE   Behaving in accord with rules or orders. See also COMPLIANCE.

Observational learning   Learning that occurs when the learner observes a model. See SOCIAL LEARNING THEORY.

OBSERVE   To look at, watch, make notes, record, etc.

Observed value   Simply the value of the event being measured or observed. *Or* the figure arrived at by calculating the relevant statistic (which is then used to find the critical value).

Obsessive   The mind is filled or totally preoccupied with a specific idea or thought.

Occipital lobe   The lobe situated at the rear of the brain which deals with most visual processing.

OEDIPUS COMPLEX   A complex developed by children, aged three to six years, which is sexual desire for the parent of the opposite sex and jealousy of their same sex parent. In Freud's view the unresolved Oedipus complex is the *major* cause of psychoneuroses.

Onomatopoetic   A word formed to imitate or mimic the sound of the thing named. An early (not very scientific) theory for the acquisition of language.

Ontogeny   The development of an individual. Used for plants and animals, but not humans. See also PHYLOGENY.

Open group   In group therapy, a group which is on-going with members joining and leaving as and when the *group* think that they should. See CLOSED GROUP.

Open-loop feedback   An 'open' as opposed to closed feedback system. Usually, where there is no feedback, consequent errors occur.

OPERANT CONDITIONING   The learning process where the desired response is reinforced only when it occurs. See CLASSICAL CONDITIONING and INSTRUMENTAL CONDITIONING.

Operant techniques   The various techniques or practices where the response to a stimulus requires a reinforcement (compare with classical techniques).

OPTIC CHIASMA   The area in the brain where nerve fibres from the two optic nerves (one from each eye) cross over (*chi* = cross) and then go to different brain hemispheres. It is arranged so that *both* hemispheres get both left and right information from both eyes.

OPTIC FLOW PATTERN   To do with the way we move relative to what we see. The flow of visual information reaching the eyes.

Optic tract   Part of the nerve pathway from the optic chiasma to the lateral geniculate nuclei.

OPTICAL ILLUSION   An illusion involving vision. What you 'see' is not in fact what is real.

OPTIC ARRAY   The pattern of light that reaches the eye. Gibson believes that this provides all the information necessary for perception (a direct theory).

Optimal arousal level   In motivational theory, the in-built inclination to try to reach the 'optimum' relationship between arousal and performance. See YERKES-DODSON LAW.

ORAL   First stage in Freud's psychosexual development. Birth to eighteen months. The child gains sexual pleasure via its mouth.

Organic psychoses   Diseases of the brain. Compare with FUNCTIONAL PSYCHOSES.

ORGANISATIONAL PSYCHOLOGY   A branch of psychology concerned with the application of psychological principles to an organisation.

Orthography   A writing system.

Own-sex schema   A gender schema, formed in young children which contains information about how the child should behave in sex-typed ways.

Pair-bond   The relationship between one male and one female (only used to describe non-human relationships).

PARADIGM   A way of viewing, or an approach to research, or a procedure.

Paradoxical sleep   Occurs while in REM sleep. The paradox is that the body appears calm and at rest, but internally is in a state of arousal. See REM SLEEP.

PARALLEL DISTRIBUTED PROCESSING (PDP)   A theoretical model based on the idea that processing occurs simultaneously in a number of parallel and interconnected paths.

PARAMETRIC   A statistical method based on a sample from a known normal distribution.

PARAMETRIC TEST ASSUMPTIONS   A procedure used in choosing an appropriate statistical test. The data must meet three criteria:
1. The data must be interval.
2. The data must come from a normally distributed population.
3. The variation in the scores from the two sets of data is essentially the same, i.e. homogenity of variance.

PARANOID   A delusional disorder: mental derangement usually with delusions of grandeur, extreme jealousy or persecution. Onset is usually slow.

Paranoid delusions (delusional disorder) False beliefs which are usually of grandeur or persecution. The term is used when there are no other mental disorders.

Paranoid schizophrenia A type of schizophrenia in which delusions of persecution or grandeur occur and possibly also hallucinations which may relate to the delusions or may have no connection.

Parasympathetic nervous system The subdivision of the autonomic nervous system that enables the body to operate under normal non-stressful situations. See SYMPATHETIC NERVOUS SYSTEM.

Parental care The care, nurture, protection, etc. provided by one or both parents.

Parent-offspring conflict The conflict that can occur between parent and offspring, when the offspring will try to manipulate the parent into providing maximum resources for the offspring.

Parietal lobe Situated above the temporal lobe and to the rear of the frontal lobe, involved in visual input and spatial awareness, and also deals with the sense of touch and language.

Participant A person who takes part in an experiment, to provide data (previously 'subject').

PAVLOVIAN CONDITIONING Alternate term for classical conditioning, named after Pavlov.

PEER PRESSURE Pressure to conform exerted by members of the person's peer group.

PEG-WORD SYSTEM A system to aid memory, based on association and using key or 'peg' words.

Penis envy Freud's theory that girls in the phallic stage (three to six years old) develop penis envy as they come to realise that boys have a penis and they haven't.

PERCEPTION Simply, those processes that 'make-sense' of sensory input.

Percepts The result of processing visual information: the outcome of perception.

PERCEPTUAL CONSTANCY The way in which all perceived objects remain constant. See SIZE CONSTANCY, COLOUR CONSTANCY.

Perceptual modes Senses which influence perception, i.e. visual mode, acoustic mode, etc.

PERCEPTUAL ORGANISATION A Gestalt approach to perception, emphasising the holistic approach and including perceptual constancy, depth perception, etc.

Perceptual set A state in which a person's perception is influenced or 'set up' by factors such as motive, emotion, expectation and culture.

Perceptual span The field of view. In normal left to right reading the span is 3 or 4 letters to the left and 15 to the right of the fixation point.

Perennial monogamy A mating pattern where the pair-bond is a permanent relationship lasting for the lifetime of the partners.

Performance deficits An error made when a person is not paying attention, sometimes called absentmindedness, attentional slips or attentional errors.

Peripheralistic A theoretical view of the behaviourists, particularly Watson. It argues that all 'peripheral' aspects of a person, e.g. speech, emotion can be explained by behaviourist principles.

Peripheral nervous system A major division of the nervous system. All those subsystems which are not a part of the central nervous system (i.e. *not* brain or spinal cord).

Peripheral vision Vision using the outside edge of the retina – that which is furthest away from the fovea and therefore rather poor.

PERSONALITY Very broad term, the definition of which depends partly on the theoretical perspective of the writer. Generally, the pattern of behaviour, thought and emotions that characterise a person.

Personality inventory An instrument used to 'measure' personality. See MMPI.

Person-centred therapy Humanistic therapies where the client is seen as the centre of the therapeutic approach. Sometimes called 'client-centred therapy'.

Perspective The ability to see the relationship between certain visible objects which usually provides depth information.

Persuasion To get someone else to believe something.

Persuasive communication theory The way or type of communication by which a person is persuaded to believe something.

Persuasive influence A form of social influence or power.

PERTINENCE MODEL A model of attention proposed by Deutsch and Deutsch where incoming information is filtered in terms of its pertinence or relevance.

PET scan See POSITRON EMISSION TOMOGRAPHY.

PHALLIC Third stage in Freud's psychosexual development. From three to six years. The child gains sexual pleasure via its genitals.

Phenomenological Concerned with the event or phenomenon. The study of a person's perceived world and their experience.

Phenotype In ethology, the physical, observable characteristics of a species. See also GENOTYPE.

Pheromone A chemical produced by a species to communicate messages, e.g. sexual or territorial.

Phi phenomenon   The illusion of movement caused by rapid presentation of stimuli. (Often seen in fair ground lights.)

PHOBIA   An unreasonable fear of something or someone.

Phonemic code   The form of the acoustic information in the primary acoustic store in the working memory model.

Photographic memory   See EIDETIC MEMORY.

Phrenology   The historical – now disproved – practice of attempting to assess a person's personality and intelligence from the shape of the skull.

Phylogeny   The origin and evolution of a *species* of plant or animal, not human. See also ONTOGENY.

Physical culture   Part of the culture of a people. To do with technology, artefacts, etc. See SOCIAL CULTURE, the other main part.

Physiological reductionism   This approach argues that because we are made up from 'components' neurons, chemicals, etc. all behaviour including perception memory and all else can be reduced to a neural level.

Pituitary gland   The key gland in the endocrine system because of the way that it regulates the other glands. Attached to the base of the brain by the infundibulum stalk and has two lobes each of which control different functions.

Polyandry   In ethology, a mating system where one female will mate with more than one male. Most usually occurs when male investment in rearing the young is high.

Polygamy   In ethology, a mating system where a member of one sex mates with several members of the opposite sex.

Polygyny   In ethology, a mating system where one male mates with several females. Most usually occurs when female investment in rearing the young is high.

Pons   Literally, tissue that joins two or more parts together.

Pons varolii   Part of the hindbrain that works with the medulla and diencephalon. Controls bodily rhythms, e.g. heart and also sleep and arousal.

POPULATION   In statistics/research methods, the total number of people about which a conclusion can be drawn, and from which the sample to be tested is selected. See SAMPLE.

POSITIVE REINFORCER   The stimulus or event which serves to 'reinforce' the likely occurrence of the desired behaviour.

Positive symptoms   Symptoms which occur in schizophrenia to excess or exhibit additional extreme or bizarre forms of behaviour.

Positivistic (or positivism)   The philosophy that all knowledge is contained within scientific boundaries and the scientific method.

Positron emission tomography (PET scan)   A procedure that analyses brain activity. Radioactive material is injected and an X-ray beam is passed through the head to identify areas of the brain that are 'working'. Data are passed to a computer that produces a 'picture' of the brain structures. See also CAT SCAN.

Post-traumatic stress disorder (PTSD)   A condition caused by experiencing severe and distressing psychological trauma, e.g. a natural disaster or rape. An anxiety disorder, defined by patient experiencing PTSD for a minimum of one month.

Postsynaptic membrane   The membrane at the surface of the receiving neuron to which the neurotransmitter will attach itself at the receptor site. See also PRESYNAPTIC MEMBRANE.

Power   In social psychology, the amount of control a person or group has over another person or group. It can be exerted in a number of different ways.

Precocial   The state of being born in a stage of development that will need very little parental care in order to survive. See also ALTRICIAL.

Predator   The animal that hunts, catches and eats its prey. Predation describes the activities.

Predictive validity   The manner in which the scores on a test can predict the actual behaviour or performance of the test-taker.

PREJUDICE   An attitude, almost always negative, toward a minority group.

Presynaptic membrane   The membrane at the surface of the axon terminal from which the neurotransmitters flow to the postsynaptic membrane.

Prey   The animal which is being hunted by the predator for food.

PRIMACY EFFECT   The way the material that is presented first is recalled better than material presented later. See also RECENCY EFFECT.

PRIMACY-RECENCY EFFECT   In cognitive psychology, the way in which the first and last items or information are recalled better than items in the middle.

PRIMAL SKETCH   The first stage in Marr's computational theory; it does little more than recognise light, shade and boundaries of the object being viewed.

PRIMARY ACOUSTIC STORE   The store in Baddeley's working memory model that deals with or processes acoustic/auditory information. Also called the 'inner ear'.

Primary emotions   Emotions that develop in the first few months of life, e.g. distress, happiness. See SECONDARY EMOTIONS and COMPLEX EMOTIONS.

Primary motor cortex   The part of the motor cortex that deals with the control of large muscles.

Primary reinforcer   In a token economy, this is the main reinforcer, sometimes achieved via a secondary reinforcer.

Primate   The highest order of mammals.

PRINCIPLE OF CLOSURE   A Gestalt principle of organisation where there is a tendency to see incomplete figures as complete, by joining up lines, etc.

Proactive inhibition   See PROACTIVE INTERFERENCE.

PROACTIVE INTERFERENCE   Difficulty in recall old information owing to 'interference' from new information.

Probabilistic concept   One (of two) types of concepts. In probabilistic only some aspects of the concept are shared by its members. See also CLASSICAL CONCEPT.

PROBABILITY   The likelihood that an event will occur. The probability, p, is normally expressed as a decimal; thus $p = 0.05$ means that the probability that the event will occur in 95 times in every 100, or that 5 times in every hundred the event will occur by *chance*.

Proband   A person with a mental or physical disorder who *first* comes to the attention of an investigator who subsequently investigates that person's family to determine if there is a genetic link to the disorder.

PROBLEM SOLVING   In cognitive psychology, the area concerned with the mental processes involved in the solving of a problem.

Problem–space theory   An approach to problem solving that divides the 'space' between the problem and the solution into a number of parts, or smaller problems, each of which are solved in turn. See MEANS–ENDS ANALYSIS.

PROCEDURAL MEMORY   Memory of procedures that have (usually) become automatic, e.g. riding a bicycle.

Production systems   A model of cognitive processing based on rules for dealing with a given situation.

Productivity   In language, the way in which human animals can combine words in original ways.

Programmed or non-programmed decisions   Two types of decision making. Programmed refers to routine, repetitive decisions; non-programmed refers to unique one-off decisions. Usually relates to decision making in organisations.

Programmed teaching machine   Any machine or equipment used to aid learning. The principle involved is to learn in small steps, each of which require a correct answer before the machine will 'allow' the learner to proceed to the next step.

Promiscuity   In ethology, mating behaviour where both male and female mate several times with different individuals.

Propaganda   To deliberately manipulate or control opinion, usually by telling only part of the truth.

PROSOCIAL BEHAVIOUR   Those behaviours that essentially co-operate with others, e.g. friendship, helping.

Protocol analysis   In cognitive psychology and the study of writing, protocol analysis is the thinking out loud of what is about to be written.

PROXIMITY   In *perception*, a Gestalt law of organisation: objects that are closer together will be seen as belonging together. In *social psychology*, the idea that you are likely to be attracted to someone who lives or works nearby.

Psychedelic   The effect of altered perceptions and/or sensory experience caused by hallucinogenic psychoactive drugs.

Psychoactive drugs   A group of drugs that affect perception and behaviour by altering the person's awareness of the real world.

PSYCHOANALYSIS   The practice of psychoanalytic theory.

PSYCHOANALYST   One who practises psychoanalysis.

Psychoanalytically oriented therapy   Therapy based on the theory and methods of psychoanalysis.

PSYCHOANALYTIC THEORY   The theoretical structure first formulated by Sigmund Freud to explore the unconscious motives and instincts of human behaviour.

PSYCHODYNAMIC   The general term used to describe pyschological theories that stress dynamic elements such as instinctual drives or motivation, e.g. Freud's view of personality. Sometimes a synonym for psychoanalytic.

Psychogenic   The view that psychological causes are the key factor in abnormality. See also SOMATOGENIC.

Psychogenic amnesia   A form of activated forgetting, usually involving personal details, for which there is no obvious reason such as a blow to the head. In Freudian theory, caused by repression.

Psycholinguistic   The scientific field of study concerned with psychological aspects of language, e.g. the acquisition of language and development of reading skills.

Psycholinguistic theory   To do with language and linguistics, e.g. acquisition of language and other language-related behaviours.

PSYCHOLOGICAL METHODS   The various

methods or schools of thought that are used as a basis for the approach to and study of psychology.

Psychological moratorium In Marcia's developmental psychology of adolescence, the third status where the young person is in unresolved crisis and hence has no commitment. See also IDENTITY STATUS.

PSYCHOLOGICAL PERSPECTIVES A way of organising or viewing something, e.g. the behaviourist perspective in psychology.

PSYCHOMETRIC TESTING Literally, the measuring and testing of aspects of psychology, including intelligence, personality, attitudes, etc.

PSYCHOMOTOR Generally, the relationship bet-ween the psyche and body movement. Also aspects of schizophrenic behaviour, usually involving reduced normal physical activity but with the addition of unusual facial and bodily movements.

Psychoneuroimmunology or psychoimmunology The interdisciplinary science of the way that psychology, behaviour, neurology and immunology relate.

Psychopathology The scientific study of mental disorders.

Psychopharmacology The use or study of drugs to investigate their psychological effect.

Psychoses A mental disorder involving the whole personality and where frequently the person is quite out of touch with reality.

PSYCHOSEXUAL DEVELOPMENT Freud's term for the developmental stages from birth to about thirteen years that all children pass through. Each stage sees the child gaining sexual pleasure from a different part of the body. Successful achievement of these stages is required to achieve healthy adulthood.

PSYCHOSOMATIC Generally mind/body connections, usually implying that one affects the other.

Psychosurgery Surgery performed on brain tissue to relieve psychological disorders.

PSYCHOTIC Total loss of reality as displayed by a person diagnosed as having a psychotic disorder.

Psychotropic drugs Drugs which alter a person's mind or moods, i.e. their psychological functioning. Used in therapy. Includes hallucinogens, e.g. LSD, Mescaline.

Punishment A process that uses aversive behaviours to decrease the frequency of the undesirable behaviour. Compare with NEGATIVE REINFORCEMENT.

Purging-type bulimia nervosa Binge-eating followed by self-induced vomiting and/or extreme use of laxatives. See BULIMIA NERVOSA.

QUALITATIVE In the context of stages of development, qualitative has to do with the *kind* of changes taking place during a person's development. See QUANTITATIVE.

QUALITATIVE DATA (or ANALYSIS) Data gathered from non-laboratory, non-experimental procedure(s) that (usually) do not involve numbers. A wide range of alternate approaches to the quantitative method. See QUANTITATIVE DATA.

QUANTITATIVE In the context of stages of development, quantitative has to do with the *amount* of changes taking place during a person's development. See QUALITATIVE.

QUANTITATIVE DATA (or ANALYSIS) Data gathered from laboratory and experimental procedures that (invariably) use numbers. See QUALITATIVE DATA.

RANDOM SAMPLE A sample selected such that each member of the population has an equal probability of being selected.

RAPID EYE MOVEMENT (REM) The rapid eye movements which occur in one stage of sleep. See SLEEP and REM SLEEP.

Rational emotive therapy A form of psychotherapy developed by Ellis. Very directive, confrontational and involves the client in cognitive awareness by challenging illogical, self-defeating attitudes or beliefs.

Rationalist/rationalism A philosophical perspective which argues that truth can be established through reasoning or rational thought.

Reasoning An application of thinking skills in a logical and purposeful way, usually aimed at solving some kind of problem, the emphasis being on the cognitive processes that are going on rather than the logic behind them.

Rebound anxiety A condition where anxiety (or some other condition) re-occurs when drug treatment is stopped.

RECALL The process by which we retrieve information from memory.

RECENCY EFFECT The way in which material presented last is recalled better than material presented earlier. See also PRIMACY EFFECT.

RECIPROCAL ALTRUISM Term used mostly in socio-biology. Triver's term for altruism where a return altruistic is normal and expected. See SYMBIOTIC.

Reciprocity A form of attraction where we like people who like us. See BALANCE THEORY.

Reconstruction in memory The theory that memories of things or events are 'reconstructed' during the recall process.

Recovered memory   Occurs when a client in therapy (usually a child) 'discovers' or 'recovers' a memory previously lost. Sometimes called 'false memory'.

REDUCTIONISM   The view that a complex situation or phenomenon can be broken down – or reduced – to its component parts to gain greater understanding of the whole.

Reductionist   A view that complex phenomena are best understood by breaking them down into their most basic parts.

REFERRAL   A situation where one therapist suggests the client should transfer to another therapist with more experience or specialised knowledge.

REHEARSAL   In memory, repeating the to-be-remembered material many times.

REINFORCEMENT/REINFORCER   Usually used in learning theory, operant conditioning, etc. to mean the event which strengthens the behaviour that it follows. Aids the acquiring, maintenance or extinction of a behaviour.

Relationship dissolution model   A four stage model that a relationship will pass through whilst breaking down. The Intra-psychic, Dyadic, Social and Grave-Dressing phases.

Relative depravation principle   This suggests that our happiness is relative to others.

RELIABILITY   In psychological tests or measurements, is the measure consistent or repeatable. There are a number of ways to test for reliability. See also VALIDITY.

REM   See RAPID EYE MOVEMENT.

REM rebound   The state where a person will return to REM sleep for a longer period of time, if previous REM sleep is disturbed. See REM SLEEP.

REM sleep   The stage of sleep when REM occurs and when dreams will occur. Occurs approximately every 90 minutes in sleep. See also PARADOXICAL SLEEP.

REPEATED-MEASURES DESIGN   A research design or situation where the *same* participants are tested under two conditions.

REPLICATE   To repeat (an experiment) in as much detail as possible to see if the same result is obtained.

REPRESSION   In Freudian theory, the basic defence mechanism that excludes painful, anxiety-producing thoughts, feelings, etc. from consciousness. It operates at an unconscious level.

Reproductive effort   The amount of 'effort', energy, time resources, etc. put into reproduction and rearing of the young by male and female parents.

Reproductive fitness   The ability of 'fitness' of either a male or female member of a species to breed successfully. It may be bigger and stronger or have more territory than its competitor.

Resources   In ethological terms, any resources such as food, shelter, territory, etc.

Resting potential   See ACTION POTENTIAL.

Restricted code   In language theory, the relatively limited vocabulary, constructions, etc. of children from lower socioeconomic groups. See ELABORATED CODE.

Reticular activation system (RAS)   Part of the reticular formation that plays a minor role in dreaming. See RETICULAR FORMATION.

Reticular formation   The network of nerve cells situated within the midbrain, pons and medulla that arouse the cerebral cortex to attend to new situations, e.g. attention, sleep and reflex action.

RETINA   The light-sensitive surface at the back of the eye. It has a layered structure with three main layers – the ganglion cell layer, the bipolar cell layer, and the photoreceptor layer which contains the rods and cones.

Retinal disparity   A binocular cue for depth perception. It occurs because each eye has slightly different retinal images due to their different positions with respect to the object.

RETRIEVAL   In memory, the process of recall or of retrieving the memories.

Retroactive inhibition   See RETROACTIVE INTERFERENCE.

Retroactive interference   Difficulty in recall of new information owing to 'interference' from old information.

RETROGRADE AMNESIA   Loss of memory for events that occurred prior to the incident causing the amnesia. Most likely to be loss of retrieval ability rather than loss of actual memory.

Retrospective   Dealing with that which has passed.

REWARD   In general terms, anything pleasurable given in return for doing something. See REINFORCER.

Ribonucleic acid (RNA)   A group of nucleic acids that are present in all living cells, and that play an essential role in the synthesis of proteins.

Risky-shift effect (sometimes choice-shift)   The change or shift that occurs when a group make a decision, compared to the decision of the individual in the group when faced with the same problem. The group decision can however sometimes move in the direction of being more cautious.

ROLE   A form of behaviour where the person is expected to behave in a certain way. Often involves duties.

ROTE MEMORY   Learning something by repetition – rehearsal – only.

RUBIN'S VASE   An illustration to show the relationship between figure and ground. It is a vase, or is it two faces?

Rule   A formal system, code, or way of doing something.

Saccadic movement   The movement or jump from one fixation point to the next made by the eye when scanning something, e.g. when reading.

Sadistic   Gaining pleasure or sexual gratification from inflicting pain on others.

SAMPLE   Part of the population selected by a set procedure (e.g. random sampling) to take part in a study or research project.

Schedules or reinforcement   Most usually in operant conditioning, occasionally in classical conditioning. The schedule, or order, or plan by which reinforcement is conducted, e.g. simple or continuous (when every correct response is reinforced) or fixed interval (when the reward is made at fixed intervals only).

SCHEMA   A framework of knowledge or experience about a given topic. A cognitive/mental plan.

Schema theory   The theory that the human mind is capable of constructing schemas.

SCHIZOPHRENIA   This is a general name given to a number of psychotic disorders. The individual often has delusions and hallucinations and is divorced from reality. Often involves a 'split' in the mind between feeling and thinking.

Schizophrenia (disorganised or hebephrenic)   The main type of schizophrenia. Key words 'silly' or 'disorganised'. In this case disorganised speech, strange or disorganised behaviour. Other symptoms can include all or some of the following: hearing voices, believing that you are someone else, disorganised delusions of grandeur or persecution, belief that some vital bodily organ is missing or not working, and sustained giggling and nonsensical or silly speech. This is considered to be the most severe type of schizophrenia.

SCIENTIFIC METHOD   The process by which phenomena are investigated using a formal series of steps: observe, hypothesis, test, conclude.

Scripts   A person's knowledge of a scenario or series of events or behaviours, e.g. who does what when entering a restaurant.

Search theory   A theory of forgetting similar to interference, but where the person 'searches' for clues in memory to find the correct answer.

Seasonal mood disorder (or seasonal affective disorder (SAD))   A wide term used to describe a mood disorder that occurs – usually annually – as a result of the change in seasons/weather.

Secondary emotions   Sometimes called 'complex emotions'. Emotions expressing feelings that require moderately complex cognitive understanding, e.g. guilt or embarrassment. See also PRIMARY EMOTIONS.

Secondary reinforcer   In a token economy the reinforcer that may be needed to achieve the primary reinforcer.

Selective reinforcement   Reinforcing only certain selected behaviours to achieve the required outcome behaviour.

SELF ACTUALISATION   The highest level of psychological need/achievement after more basic needs have been met/achieved. To realise one's full potential (Maslow).

Self actualise   See SELF ACTUALISATION.

Self concept   Our thoughts and feelings about ourselves. The answer to the question 'Who am I?'

SELF ESTEEM   The amount one values oneself. Referred to as either high or low self esteem. Can be measured using the Coopersmith inventory.

Self-instruction training   A form of cognitive therapy which centres on the way in which we all talk to ourselves when we need to interpret something or to consider a given action. In the case of a person with particular difficulties it is argued that this internal dialogue is at fault with the person failing to accurately 'self-instruct'.

Self perception   A person's attitudes and beliefs, formed by the person's observations of their own behaviour. See also LOOKING-GLASS SELF.

Self-serving bias (sometimes 'defensive attribution')   A bias in interpreting events that is to the advantage of the person doing the interpreting.

Semantically   The process of giving meaning to something.

SEMANTIC MEMORY   Memory for the meaning of things or events.

Semantic network   An association of concepts that are related directly or indirectly to the main or node concept.

SEMANTIC PROCESSING   The 'deepest' stage of processing in Craik and Lockhart's model of memory which gives meaning to the memory.

SEMANTICS   The study of meaning.

SEMANTICITY   The meaning or way that words can be used as symbols for all kinds of things, from simple objects to complicated philosophies.

SENSATION   The physical information available to the person and registered by one of the body's sensory systems, e.g. eye, ear, etc. The first stage of perception.

SENSITIVE PERIOD   A broad term defining a period of time during which an organism is sensitive to a specific stimulus. See also CRITICAL PERIOD.

Sensory aphasia   A serious problem with the understanding of speech. See also WERNICKE'S AREA.

Sensory cortex   The area of the cortex at the front of the parietal lobes that register and then process bodily sensations.

Sensory input   The sensory input into the sensory memory (sometimes called 'sensory registers').

Sensory memory   The first stage of memory which receives the sensory input.

Sensory neurons   Any individual afferent neuron. The neuron that transmits signals from a sensory receptor, e.g. the eye, to the brain.

Separation anxiety   The anxiety experienced (usually) by a child when separated from its mother or other care giver.

Septum   Generally a dividing or separating membrane. Specifically part of the limbic system dividing the fluid filled lateral ventricles.

Serial monogamy   A form of monogamy where the person has a series (one after the other) of monogamous relationships. See MONOGAMY.

Serial reproduction   A technique used in the study of memory. The participant reads or listens to a story and is then asked to pass it on to another person, and so on.

Serotonin   A chemical found in the central nervous system which acts as a neurotransmitter. Thought to be involved in depression and bipolar disorders.

Sex role   The expression of behaviour and attitudes appropriate to the person's sex.

Sex typing   Old term for 'sex role'.

Sexuality   A person's make-up and behaviour related to his or her sex.

Shadow   A visual cue that can provide depth information. *Also* Jung expresses this as the negative side of one's personality, or one's 'alter ego'.

Shaping   Behaviour achieved by successive reinforcement.

SHORT-TERM MEMORY (STM)   A limited capacity memory store. Can hold 7 ± 2 'bits' of information for perhaps 15–20 seconds without rehearsal.

SIGNIFICANCE   Statistical, e.g. $p < 0.05$ meaning that for the given results the data are 95 per cent certain, *or* that the results could have occurred by chance in less than 5 out of 100 times.

Significant life change   A change to existing life patterns, e.g. promotion at work, birth of a baby.

SIGN LANGUAGE   A physical movement or gesture usually made by the hand(s) which represents a word or idea. Used by people with hearing impairments.

Sign stimulus   In ethology, the species-specific stimulus that triggers the fixed action pattern. See also SPECIES-SPECIFIC.

Similarity   A law in Gestalt psychology where things resembling each other will be seen as belonging together.

SINGLE-BLIND   A research procedure where the participants of a study are kept in the dark as to the purpose of the study. See also DOUBLE-BLIND.

SINGLE CHANNEL   One single input, mode, or channel. Often used in models of attention.

Situational attribution   The case where the attribution of an event or its cause is the result of the situation.

SITUATIONAL FACTORS   Circumstances which effect behaviour that are to do with the situation in which the behaviour occurs.

SIZE CONSTANCY   The way the size of an object is recognised however near or far it is, e.g. a person is still seen as 6 foot tall whether close or far away.

Skewed   The degree to which a normal curve, e.g. a frequency distribution, lacks symmetry.

Skill memory   See PROCEDURAL MEMORY.

SKINNER BOX   Experimental apparatus designed by B.F. Skinner to study operant behaviour. Consists of a box with a lever which, when pressed, opens a chute to provide a food pellet or some other reinforcer.

SLEEP   A state of loss of consciousness which can be defined by certain behavioural and neuropyschological conditions. Usually divided into REM and Non-REM sleep. See REM.

Sleep spindles   A short burst of brain activity normally in stage two sleep.

Sleep stages   A series of different stages, each with its own physiological characteristics that you pass through in normal sleep.

Slow-wave sleep   Sleep in stages three and four. Sleep waves are typically slow, large amplitude, delta waves.

SOCIAL   A very broad term used in any situation which involves two or more – usually humans – although also used in the same sense for other species. Most often used in a combined form (see following entries).

SOCIAL APPROVAL   Recognising approval, etc. gained within a social group or setting.

Social cognition   How people thing about the way they relate socially.

Social comparison theory (Festinger)   The way that

a person will compare themselves with others in order to obtain a positive view of themselves.

Social constructionism (or social constructivism) The idea that knowledge comes from the ideas views, general understanding or mental constructions of the members of a society.

Social control The control that a given society exerts over its members, usually through normal socialising. Often negative or positive social control.

Social co-operation In ethology, where members of a species co-operate in various ways, e.g. in defence, attack or helping. Sometimes called 'mutualism'.

Social culture The social beliefs, values, customs, etc. of a given culture. See also PHYSICAL CULTURE.

Social evolution The view that human society has evolved social behaviours which benefit the whole of that society. Compare with SOCIO- BIOLOGY.

Social exchange theory The idea or model that much of social behaviour is based on the idea that what you do will influence what the other person will do.

Social identity theory The idea that people will look for friends who are much like themselves.

Social influence The way in which a person or group influences the behaviours, attitudes, etc. of another person or group.

Social influence theory A general term for the many different ways in which people influence other people.

Social leaders/relationship oriented leaders Leadership style that focuses on the social and relational aspect of the task and those working on solving it.

Social learning Learning that occurs in a social context and as a result of watching and imitating a role model. Sometimes called 'observational learning'.

Social learning techniques Techniques developed to facilitate social learning.

SOCIAL LEARNING THEORY (SLT) In social behaviour, the way that learning takes place by imitation of role models (Bandura and Walters).

Social motivation Motives acquired by learning (usually imitation), directed at achieving a social goal. (Murray used the term 'needs'.)

Social norms Behaviour or actions that are typical of a given group or society.

Social phobia Fear of being in a prominent position in a social setting.

SOCIAL PSYCHOLOGY Psychology that deals with human behaviour as it relates to individual and group relationships.

Social Readjustment Rating Scale (SRRS) A scale devised by Holmes and Rahe (1967) in an attempt to measure stress objectively.

SOCIAL RELATIONSHIP The associations that we form with others whose presence causes a reaction that we respond to.

Social representation The idea that a given society or culture has a set of generally accepted views or ways of behaving.

Social responsibility The view that 'psychology' exists and operates in the real world and cannot be studied apart from its social setting.

Social trap In a situation of mutual antagonism both parties fall into the 'social trap' because of selfish interests. If both parties considered the other, the outcome would be more favourable for both.

SOCIALISATION A process by which we learn the things we need to know to enable us to fit into the society to which we belong.

Sociobiology The science that emphasises the biological basis for social behaviour. Relies heavily on evolutionary principles to explain social behaviour.

Sociocultural model A model to account for abnormality which emphasises the importance of social-cultural issues.

Soft determinism The idea that determinism can only go so far and that, at root, it is impossible to fully determine cause.

SOMATIC To do with the body as a whole, distinct from the mind (Greek *soma* = body).

SOMATIC NERVOUS SYSTEM Part of the nervous system that deals with voluntary, conscious, sensory and motor functions.

SOMATIC THERAPIES From *soma*, the Greek word for body. So somatic therapies are those which work on the body primarily in biological or biochemical ways.

Somatogenic view An old-fashioned view which believes that abnormality has physical causes. See also PSYCHOGENIC.

Spatial disorientation A situation where you are unable to orient yourself in space relative to a fixed object, datum or event.

SPATIAL METAPHOR The earliest model of the memory: 4th century BC idea that the memory can be represented by a bird cage where the birds represent individual memories.

SPECIES A biological classification usually defined by the ability to inter-breed.

SPECIES-SPECIFIC The typical behaviour common to all members of a particular species under the same circumstances. Sometimes known as 'species-typical'.

Species-specific behaviour   The behaviour exhibited only by members of a given species.

Species-specific stimulus   The stimulus that causes the release of the fixed action pattern.

Species-typical behaviour   See SPECIES-SPECIFIC BEHAVIOUR.

SPECIFIC PHOBIA   Fear of a specific object, place or situation.

SPINAL CORD   The column of neural tissue running through the spinal cord, terminating in the brain stem.

Spinal nerves   31 pairs of nerves join the spinal cord to various parts of the body.

Spinal reflexes   A bodily reflex action, unlearned and not involving the brain.

Spirituality   Generally, a person's beliefs about religion, faith, the soul. In development psychology, sometimes considered important to enable full adjustment to the final stages of life as death approaches.

SPLIT BRAIN   Results from the severing of the corpus callosum (the tissue joining the two hemispheres). Done surgically in cases of severe epilepsy.

Split-span tasks (or procedures)   A procedure whereby separate and different messages are sent to each ear.

Spontaneous generalisations   In PDP memory theory, the idea that you can recall information which has not been specifically learned, provided that other relevant material can be used to provide cues.

Spontaneous recovery   In therapy, when a client is considered to have recovered naturally, without the help of the therapist.

Spoonerism   A speech error that will occur at the stage when the root morpheme (minimal units of meaning) are being worked out, and the switching of these in a clause, e.g. 'you have tasted the whole worm' (wasted the whole term).

Spreading activation   The way that the meaning or connotation of a given concept can 'spread' to other related concepts; the meaning becoming weaker as it moves from the original concept.

SRRS   See SOCIAL READJUSTMENT RATING SCALE

STAGE THEORY   A view that development occurs progressively through a series of stages each defined in some way, e.g. Freud's psychosexual stages. Erikson's eight stages of man. Theories tend to be either biologically based or interactionist.

Stanford Hypnotic Susceptibility Scale   A scale designed to show a person's susceptibility to hypnosis.

STATE THEORIES   Usually thought of in terms of 'states' of awareness or consciousness. Specifically used to describe the state of being hypnotised. See also NON-STATE THEORIES.

STATISTICS   Numerical manipulation of data to provide significant value or meaning.

Status   A term in developmental psychology used by Marcia to describe the state of self-awareness of the young person in terms of crisis or commitment.

STEREOTYPE   Relatively permanent and usually simplistic generalisations about a group of people.

STIMULUS   An event that has an impact which modifies the behaviour of someone or something else.

STIMULUS–RESPONSE (S–R)   The way in which the stimulus and the response are connected.

STORE (MEMORY)   The holding of encoded information in memory over time.

STRATEGIC KNOWLEDGE   In the production of writing, the key knowledge used in planning the writing. Used by 'expert' writers.

STRESS   The effect caused by physical, social or psychological tension or pressure(s), called stressors.

STRESSOR   The actual situation or event that gives rise to stress.

Strong and weak artificial intelligence (AI)   *Strong AI* argues that a suitably programmed computer is capable of limited cognitive processes, i.e. it is capable of 'thinking' and therefore can be said to have intelligence. *Weak AI* argues that, however sophisticated the computer and program, it does not have its own intelligence. See *artificial intelligence*.

STRUCTURALISM   The idea that the purpose of psychology is to analyse consciousness into its basic elements (or structure) and investigate how they are related.

Structure   The structure of the world in which the person is currently a part. The structure will change as the person transitions into the next stage (Levinson).

SUBCULTURE   A culture within a culture, which reflects the elements of the main culture but has its own values, norms and customs.

SUBLIMINAL   Literally, below the level or surface, usually with respect to consciousness.

SUBSTANCE ABUSE   The use of a substance (alcohol, drugs, etc.) in an unauthorised/ unsupervised manner to such an extent that a person's normal functioning or lifestyle is affected, but is not (yet) dependant on the substance.

SUPEREGO   Another unconscious part of the psyche or personality; concerned with morals and ethics. A form of conscience. Concerned with the *ideal* state. See ID and EGO.

Superordinate A classification that places someone or something above others. Usually implies authority.

SURVEY A type of research design which typically uses a questionnaire or interview to gather the data.

SYMBIOTIC A relationship where two members, each of a different species, are mutually dependent on each other. See RECIPROCAL ALTRUISM.

Sympathetic nervous system The division of the autonomous nervous system that arouses the body to deal with stressful situations. See also PARASYMPATHETIC NERVOUS SYSTEM.

SYMPTOMS Observed changes in the body or its functions, usually indicating the onset of disease.

SYNAPSE The junction or space between the axon tip of the neuron sending the message and the dendrite of the receiving neuron.

Synaptic activity The term used to describe the action that takes place in and across the synapse.

Synaptic cleft The small space (20–30 mm) between the transmitting and receiving neurons, across which neurotransmitters flow.

Synaptic vesicles The small areas in the neuron terminal buttons that contain the neurotransmitters.

SYNDROMES A number of features and characteristics that are in some way related. In medicine and clinical psychology, a number of symptoms that occur together and often indicate a certain disease or abnormality.

SYSTEMATIC DESENSITISATION An approach which argues that relaxation and anxiety cannot co-exist. So the process starts with the client being encouraged to relax, and while they are in this state the anxiety-producing object or event is slowly introduced, either by imagination, the use of slides of film, or by introducing it for real. This starts with a low level of anxiety-producing stimulus which is slowly and *systematically* increased by stages until the original fearful event evokes no fear at all.

Tabula rasa Literally, 'blank tablet'. Refers to the early empiricist view that we are born with no innate ideas.

Task-oriented leaders Leadership style that focuses on the task to be achieved.

Telencephalon A major subdivision of the forebrain which includes the cerebral cortex, basal ganglia and limbic system.

Temporal lobe The lobe of the cerebrum positioned below the lateral fissure and in front of the occipital lobe.

TERRITORIALITY The defence or protection of personal space which may be literally the space around the person, or an area or territory in which an animal lives.

TESTING A procedure used for assessment or for measuring. Usually used in a given context, e.g. intelligence test of or personality test.

Texture (or texture gradient) A monocular cue providing depth information. The detail of a surface – or its texture – becomes less clear with distance.

Thalamus A subdivision of the diencephalon in the forebrain. All sensory information – except smell – must pass through it to get to the cerebral cortex.

THANATOS In Freudian theory, the instinct or drive toward death. From the Greek god of death. See also EROS.

The 'great person' theory The view that an individual 'great person' is (or was) responsible for the discovery or establishment of an important theory.

Theology The systematic study of the existence and nature of God.

THERAPY A general and broad term used for various forms of treatment of disorders, e.g. behavioural therapy, chemotherapy.

THINKING Broadly, any deliberate cognitive processing involving ideas, symbols, words, concepts, etc.

THOUGHT A very general term dealing with the cognitive processes of thinking.

Thymus gland A gland located above the heart which produces the hormone thymosin that is involved in the development of the immune system.

Tip-of-the-tongue (TOT) A speech error that occurs when there is a discrepancy between the concept or idea to be expressed and the specific word needed to express it.

TOKEN ECONOMY A form of behaviour therapy where a 'token' (e.g. a plastic counter) is given as a secondary reinforcer) which is later exchanged for the primary reinforcer.

Top-down (Gregory) The process of perception that starts with past experience, knowledge and motivation, and *then* brings in sensory information.

TRACE The hypothesised arrangement of neurons in the brain as a result of stimulation, e.g. the memory of something will form a 'trace'.

TRACE DECAY The slow decay of a memory trace, usually over time.

Trait approach The view that personality consists of a number (usually a large number) of traits, or ways of acting, thinking, feeling etc. that together are unique to the individual. See TYPE APPROACH.

Transference   The displacing or transferring of anger, emotion, etc. felt toward a person (e.g. parent) onto the therapist. See also COUNTER-TRANSFERENCE.

Transitions   In Levinson's developmental view, the person transitions into the next stage of development. A key point of significant change.

Trephine   To bore a small hole in the skull.

Trigram   A three-letter sequence, with no meaning, usually consonant, vowel, consonant, e.g. *puj*, *tiv*, etc. Sometimes called a nonsense syllable.

Trouble theory   When thinking, the 'trouble' is the problem or mismatch between what we expect to happen and what does not happen when it should. See COGNITIVE DISSONANCE.

Type approach   The view that personality can be considered as a number of types of personality which are common to many people. See TRAIT APPROACH.

Ultradian rhythms   Any of the biological rhythms that are shorter than 24 hours. See also CIRCADIAN RHYTHMS.

Unconditional positive regard   A term in humanistic psychology for when a parent gives a child feelings of self worth (Rogers).

Unconditioned response (UR)   A response that occurs as the result of an unconditioned stimulus without any previous conditioning.

UNCONDITIONED STIMULUS (US)   The stimulus that causes an unconditioned response without any previous conditioning.

UNCONSCIOUS   Generally, a mind that lacks awareness. That part of our mind that is at work but of which we are not aware (Freudian).

Undifferentiated   Facts poorly arranged. In psychiatry, a form of schizophrenia that falls outside the three normal areas: paranoid, disorganised and catatonic.

Unipolar depression   Depressive episodes without the manic phase.

VALIDITY   In a testing procedure, the ability to measure what is supposed to be measured. See also RELIABILITY.

Value added   In popular current use in education, the extra value or worth earned or achieved above that which is expected or normal.

Viscera   The internal organs, especially those in the abdominal cavity.

Visceral level   The slang term 'gut feeling' is remarkably accurate, i.e. a non-thinking emotive response.

VISUAL ATTENTION   Using the perceptual visual mode – looking and seeing – to pay attention to something in the visual field of view.

Visual code   Material encoded in a visual form.

VISUAL PERCEPTION   The perception, view, information from the outside world received visually.

Visual processing   Processing of information as a result of seeing.

VISUO-SPATIAL SCRATCH (SKETCH) PAD   Part of the working memory model that deals with visual or spatial information. Uses a visual code. Also called the 'inner eye'.

VON RESTORFF EFFECT   A physically distinctive item will be more obvious in a list of less physically obvious, similar items, e.g. using a highlighter pen.

WAR OF THE GHOSTS   A story used by Bartlett to investigate serial reproduction.

Warfare   The act of waging war.

Waxy flexibility   See CATATONIC WAXY FLEXIBILITY.

Weight set point   The point at which the body's weight is controlled by the action of the hypothalamus.

Wernicke's area   An area of the brain first identified by Wernicke, and concerned with difficulties with language.

White matter   The term given to parts of the brain and spinal cord that contain mostly myelinated fibres. See also GREY MATTER.

Withdrawal symptoms   The symptoms experienced when people stop taking drugs on which they have been dependent.

Word association   Similar to free association but where the stimulus is a word which the person responds to with the first word that comes to mind.

Word superiority effect   The idea that letters which form a word are more easily recognised than a series of letters that do not make a word.

WORKING MEMORY MODEL   A model of short-term memory proposed by Baddeley and Hitch to overcome difficulties with multi-store models. It consists of a central executive which provides the control, a visuo-spatial sketch pad (the inner eye), the primary acoustic store (the inner ear), and the articulatory loop (the inner voice).

Yerkes–Dodson law   The law which states that task difficulty interacts with arousal. For difficult tasks low arousal improves performance; for easy tasks high arousal improves performance.

Zone of proximal development   A term coined by Vygotsky. The imagined zone or space between what a child can do when on their own, and with help from another.

Bibliography

Adelmann, P.K. and Zajonc, R.B., 'Facial efference and the experience of emotion', *Annual Review of Psychology*, 40, 249–80 (1989)

Adorno, T.W. et al., *The Authoritarian Personality* (Harper Collins, New York, 1950)

Ainsworth, M.D.S., 'The development of infant-mother attachment', in B.M. Caldwell and H.N. Riciutti (eds), *Review of Child Development Research* (vol. 3) (University of Chicago Press, Chicago, 1973)

Alden, P., 'Hypnosis – the professional's perspective', *The Psychologist*, 8, 78 (1995)

Allport, D.A., Antonis, B. and Reynolds, P., 'On the division of attention: a disproof of the single channel hypothesis', *Quarterly Journal of Experimental Psychology*, 24, 225–35 (1972)

Allport, G.W., *Personality: A psychological interpretation* (Henry Holt and Company, New York, 1937)

Allport, G.W., *The Nature of Prejudice* (Addison-Wesley, Reading, Massachusetts, 1954)

Allport, G.W. et al., 'On the division of attention: a disproof of the single channel hypothesis', *Quarterly Journal of Experimental Psychology*, 24, 225–35 (1972)

Archer, D., Iritani, B., Kimes, D.D. and Barries, M., 'Faceism: five studies of sex differences in facial prominence', *Journal of Personality and Social Psychology*, 45, 725–35 (1983)

Argyle, M., *The Psychology of Interpersonal Behaviour* (Penguin, 4th edn 1983)

Argyle, M., *The Social Psychology of Work* (Penguin, 2nd edn 1989)

Aronson, E., *The Social Animal* (W.H. Freeman, New York, 1984)

Asch, S.E., 'Effects of group pressure upon the modification and distortion of judgements', in H. Guetzkow (ed.), *Social Psychology* (Holt, Rinehart & Winston, New York, 3rd edn 1951) pp. 174–82

Asch, S.E., 'Opinions and Social Pressure', *Scientific American*, 193, 31–5 (1955)

Atkinson, R.C. and Shiffrin, R.M., 'Human memory: a proposed system and its control processes', in K.W. Spence and J.T. Spence (eds), *The Psychology of Learning and Motivation* (vol. 2) (Academic Press, 1968)

Baddeley, A.D. and Hitch, G., 'Working memory', in G.A. Bower (ed.), *Recent Advances in Learning and Motivation* (vol. 8) (Academic Press, New York, 1974)

Bandura, A. and Walters, R.H., *Social Learning and Personality Development* (Holt, Rinehart and Winston, New York, 1963)

Bandura, A., Ross, D. and Ross, S., 'Vicarious reinforcement and imitative learning', *Journal of Abnormal and Social Psychology*, 67(6), 601–7 (1963)

Bandura, A., *Principles of Behaviour Modification* (Holt, Rinehart and Winston, New York, 1969)

Bandura, A., *Aggression: A Social Learning Analysis* (Prentice Hall, 1973)

Bandura, A., *Social Learning Theory* (Prentice Hall, Englewood Cliffs, New Jersey, 1975)

Bandura, A., 'Self efficacy: toward a unifying theory of behaviour change', *Psychological Review*, 84, 191–215 (1977)

Banyard, P., 'Psychology and advertising', *Psychology Review*, 3(1), 24 (1996)

Barkley, R.A., *Attention-Deficit Disorder: A Handbook for Diagnosis and Treatment* (Guilford Press, New York, 1990)

Baron, R.A., *Human Aggression* (Plenum, New York, 1977)

Bateson, P., 'When to experiment on animals', *New Scientist*, 109, 30–2 (1986)

Bateson, P., 'Do animals feel pain?', *New Scientist*, 134, (1818), 30–3 (1992)

Baumrind, D., 'Current patterns of parental authority', *Developmental Psychology Monographs*, 4, 99–103 (1967 and 1971)

Beck, A.T., 'Cognitive therapy', in J.K. Zeig (ed.), *The Evolution of Psychotherapy* (Brunner/Mazel, New York, 1987)

Ben-Amos, I.K., *Adolescence and Youth in Early Modern England* (Yale University Press, New Haven, 1994)

Berk, L.E., *Child Development* (Allyn and Bacon, Needham Heights, Massachusetts, 4th edn, 1997)

Blakemore, C. and Cooper, G.F., 'Development of the brain depends on the visual environment', *Nature*, 228, 477–8 (1970)

Bloom, F.E. and Larzerson, A., *Brain, Mind and Behaviour* (W.H. Freeman & Co., New York, 2nd edn 1988)

Boden, M., *Artificial Intelligence and Natural Man* (Cambridge University Press, Cambridge, Massachusetts, 2nd edn 1987)

Bower, G.H., Black, J.B. and Turner, J.T., 'Scripts in memory for text', *Cognitive Psychology*, 11, 177–220 (1979)

Brean, H., 'What hidden sell is all about', *Life*, 31 March, 104–14 (1958)

Bremner, J.D. et al., 'Childhood physical abuse and combat-related post-traumatic stress disorder in Vietnam veterans', *American Journal of Psychiatry*, 150(2), 235–9 (1993)

Brislin, R., 'The Ponzo Illusion: additional cues, age, orientation and culture', *Journal of Cross-Culture Psychology*, 5, 139–61 (1974)

Brislin, R., *Understanding Culture's Influence on Behaviour* (Harcourt Brace, Forthworth, Texas, 1993), p. 416

Broca, P., 'Remarques sur le siège de la faculté du langage articulé suivée d'une observation d'aphemie', *Bulletin de la Société Anatomique*, 6, 330–57 (Paris, 1861)

Bronfenbrenner, U., *The Ecology of Human Development: Experiments by Nature and Design* (Harvard University Press, Cambridge, Massachusetts, 1979 and 1989)

Brown, R., *Psycholinguistics: Selected Papers* (Free Press, Macmillan, New York, 1970)

Brown, R., *The First Language: The Early Stages* (Allen and Unwin, 1973)

Bruce, V. and Young, A., 'Understanding face recognition', *British Journal of Psychology*, 77, 305–27 (1986)

Bruch, H., *Eating Disorders: Obesity, Anorexia Nervosa and the Person Within* (Basic Books, New York, 1973)

Bruch, H., 'Anorexia nervosa', *American Handbook of Psychiatry* (Basic Books, New York, 2nd edn 1974)

Bruner, J.S., *Child's Talk: Learning to Use Language* (Oxford University Press, 1983)

Bruner, J.S. and Minturn, A.L., 'Perceptual identification and perceptual organisation', *Journal of General Psychology*, 53, 21–8 (1955)

Burr, V., *An Introduction to Social Constructionism* (Routledge, 1995)

Byrne, D., *The Attraction Paradigm* (Academic Press, New York, 1971)

Byrne, R.W., 'Brute intellect', *The Sciences*, pp. 42–7 (May/June 1991)

Calhoun, J.B., 'Population density and social pathology', *Scientific American*, 206(3), 139–48 (1962)

Campbell, D.T., 'On the conflicts between biological and social evolution and between psychology and moral tradition', *American Psychologist*, 30(12), 1103–26 (1975)

Cannon, W., *Bodily Changes in Pain, Hunger, Fear and Rage* (Appleton Century Crofts, New York, 1919 and 1929)

Cannon, W., *The Wisdom of the Body* (Norton, New York, 1932)

Carmichael, L. et al, 'An experimental study of the effect of language on visually perceived forms', *Journal of Experimental Psychology*, 15, 1–22 (1932)

Case, R., 'Intellectual development from birth to adulthood: a neo-Piagetian interpretation', in Siegher, R. (ed.), *Children's Thinking: What Develops?* (Erlbaum, Hillsdale, New Jersey, 1978)

Cherry, E.C., 'Some experiments on the recognition of speech with one and two ears', *Journal of the Acoustical Society of America*, 25, 975–9 (1953)

Chomsky, N., 'A review of B.F. Skinner's *Verbal Behaviour*', *Language*, 35, 26–129 (1959)

Charlton, J., 'Exposure to television as a cause of violence'. *Interim Findings from a Naturalistic study in St Helena, South Atlantic.* (Cheltenham and Gloucester College of Higher Education, 1998)

Clamp, A. and Russell, J., *Comparative Psychology* (Hodder and Stoughton, 1998)

Collins, A.M. and Loftus, E.F., 'A spreading activation theory of semantic processing', *Psychological Review*, 82, 407–28 (1975)

Comer, R.J., *Abnormal Psychology* (W.H. Freeman and Co., New York, 2nd edn 1995)

Comstock, G.A. and Paik, H., 'The effects of television violence on antisocial behaviour: a meta analysis', *Communication Research*, 21, 269–77 (1994)

Coolican, H., *Research Methods and Statistics in Psychology* (Hodder and Stoughton, 2nd edn 1994)

Coopersmith, S., 'Studies in self-esteem', *Scientific American*, 218, 96–106 (1968)

Coren, S., Ward, L.M. and Enns, J.T., *Sensation and Perception* (Harcourt Brace, New York, 1994)

Craik, F. and Lockhart, R., 'Levels of processing', *Journal of Verbal Learning and Verbal Behaviour*, 11, 671–84 (1972)

Crick, F. and Mitchison, G., 'The function of dream sleep', *Nature*, 304, 111–14 (1983)

Crutchfield, R.S., 'Conformity and character', *American Psychologist*, 10, 191–8 (1954)

Cumming, E. and Henry, W.E., *Growing Old: The Process of Disengagement* (Basic Books, New York, 1961)

Cunningham, J.D. and Antill, J.K., 'Changes in masculinity and femininity across the family life cycle: a re-examination', *Developmental Psychology*, 20, 1135–41 (1984)

Damon, W., *Social and Personality Development: Infancy through Adolescence* (Norton, New York, 1983)

Darley, J.M. and Latané, B., 'Bystander intervention in emergencies: diffusion of responsibility', *Journal of Personality and Social Psychology*, 8, 377–83 (1968)

Darwin, C., *On the Origin of Species by Means of Natural Selection, or the Preservation of Favoured Races in the Struggle for Life* (John Murray, London, 1859)

Darwin, C., *The Expressions of the Emotions in Man and Animals* (John Murray, 1872)

de Bono, E., *The Use of Lateral Thinking* (Penguin, 1967)

Dell, G.S., 'A spreading-activation theory of retrieval in sentence production', *Psychological Review*, 93, 283–321 (1986)

Deutsch, J.A. and Deutsch, D., 'Attention: some theoretical considerations', *Psychological Review*, 70, 80–90 (1963)

Dey, I., *Qualitative Data Analysis. A User-friendly Guide for Social Scientists* (Routledge, 1993)

Dillard, J.F., 'Cognitive science and decision-making research in accounting', *Accounting, Organisations, and Society*, 9, 343–54 (1984)

Dipboye, R.L., Arvery, R.D. and Terpstra, D.E., 'Sex and physical attractiveness of raters and applicants as determinants of resume evaluations', *Journal of Applied Psychology*, 61, 288–94 (1977)

Dollard, J., Doob, L.W., Miller, N.E., Mowrer, O.H. and Sears, R.R., *Frustration and Aggression* (Yale University Press, 1939)

Dom, M. and Avarmaet, E. van, 'The conformity effect: a timeless phenomenon?', *Bulletin of the British Psychological Society*, 34, 383–5 (1981)

Donnerstein, E., Slaby, R.C. and Eron, L.D., 'The mass media and youth aggression', in L.D. Eron, J.H. Gentry and P. Schlegel (eds), *Reasons to Hope: A Psychological Perspective on Violence and Youth* (Washington DC, 1994)

Duck, S., *Relating to Others* (Open University Press, 1988)

Duck, S., *Human Relationships* (Sage, 2nd edn 1992)

Durkin, K., *Developmental Social Psychology: From Infancy to Old Age* (Blackwell, 1995)

Dutton, D. and Aron, A., 'Some evidence for heightened sexual attraction under conditions of high anxiety', *Journal of Personality and Social Psychology*, 30, 510–7 (1974)

Ebbinghaus, H., *Memory* (Teachers College Press, New York, 1885/1913)

Elliott, J., 'The power and pathology of prejudice',

in P.G. Zimbardo and F.L. Ruch, *Psychology and Life* (Scott Foresman, Glenview, Illinois, 1977)

Ellis, A.W. and Young, A.W., *Human Cognitive Neuropsychology* (Lawrence Erlbaum Associates Ltd, 1988)

Emler, N. et al., 'The social context of delinquent behaviour', Journal of Child Psychology and Psychiatry, 28, 99–109 (1987)

Endler, J.A., 'Interactions between predator and prey', in J.R. Krebs and N.B. Davies (eds), *Behavioural Ecology: An Evolutionary Approach* (Blackwell, 1991)

Eysenck, H.J., 'The effects of psychotherapy: an evaluation', *Journal of Consulting Psychology*, 16, 319–24 (1952)

Eysenck, M.W., *A Handbook of Cognitive Psychology* (Lawrence Erlbaum Associates, 1984)

Eysenck, M.W., *Perspectives on Psychology* (Lawrence Erlbaum Associates, 1994)

Eysenck, M.W. and Keane, M.J., *Cognitive Psychology* (Lawrence Erlbaum Associates, 1990)

Fauber, R.L. et al., 'A meditational model of the impact of marital conflict on adolescent adjustment in intact and divorced families: the role of disrupted parenting?, *Child Development*, 61, 1112–23 (1990)

Festinger, L., 'A theory of social comparison processes', *Human Relations*, 7, 117–40 (1954)

Festinger, L., Pepitone, A. and Newcomb, T.M., 'Some consequences of deindividuation in a group', *Journal of Personality and Social Psychology*, 47, 382–9 (1952)

Fiedler, F.E., *A Theory of Leadership Effectiveness* (McGraw-Hill, New York, 1967)

Fiedler, F.E., 'Validation and extension of the contingency model of leadership effectiveness: a review of empirical findings', *Psychological Bulletin*, 76, 128–48 (1971)

Flanagan, C., *Psychology Practicals Made Perfect* (Richard Ball Publishing, Birkenhead, 1993)

Fletcher, W.L. and Hansson, R.O., 'Assessing the social components of retirement anxiety', *Psychology and Ageing*, 6, 76–85 (1991)

Fodor, J.A., *The Modularity of Mind* (MIT Press, Cambridge, Massachusetts, 1983)

Forster, K., 'Levels of processing and the structure of the language processor', in W.E. Cooper and E.C.T. Walker (eds), *Sentence Processing: Psycholinguistic Studies Presented to Merrill Garrett* (Lawrence Erlbaum Associates Ltd, Hillsdale, New York, 1979)

Frank, J.D., *Persuasion and Healing* (Johns Hopkins University Press, Baltimore, USA, 3rd edn 1990)

French, J.R.P. and Raven, B.H., 'The bases of social power', in D. Cartwright (ed.), *Studies in Social Power* (University of Michigan Press, Michigan, 1959)

Freud, S., *The Interpretation of Dreams* (Penguin, Middlesex, 1976). Original work published 1900.

Freud, S., *The Psychopathology of Everyday Life* (Penguin, Middlesex, 1976). Original work published 1901.

Freud, S., *Three Essays on the Theory of Sexuality* (Penguin, Middlesex, 1977). Original work published 1905.

Freud, S., *Analysis of a Phobia in a Five-Year-Old Boy* (Penguin, Middlesex, 1977). Original work published 1909.

Freud, S., *Beyond the Pleasure Principle* (Penguin, Middlesex, 1984). Original work published 1922.

Freud, S., *The Ego and the Id* (Penguin, Middlesex, 1984). Original work published 1923.

Freund, L.S., 'Maternal regulation of children's problem-solving behaviour and its impact on children's performance', *Child Development*, 61, 113–26 (1990)

Friedman, M. and Rosenman, R.F., *Type A behaviour and your heart* (Knopf, New York, 1974)

Fry, W.E., 'Humour, physiology and the ageing process', in L. Nahemo et al. (eds), *Humour and Ageing*, 181–98 (Academic Press, Orlando, 1986)

Fryer, D. and Payne, R., Being unemployed: a review of the literature on the psychological experience of unemployment', in C.L. Cooper and I.T. Robertson (eds) *International Review of Industrial and Organisational Psychology* (Wiley, Chichester, 1986)

Garner, D.M. et al., 'Cognitive therapy for anorexia nervosa', in D.M. Garner and P.E. Garfinkel (eds) *Handbook of Psychotherapy for Anorexia Nervosa and Bulimia* (Guilford, New York, 1985)

Garner, D.M. et al., 'The validity of the distinction between bulimia with and without anorexia nervosa', *American Journal of Psychiatry*, 142, 581–7 (1985)

Garnham, A., *Artificial Intelligence: An Introduction* (Routledge & Kegan Paul, 1988)

Garrett, M.F., 'The organisation of processing structures for language production: applications to aphasic speech', in D. Caplan, A.R. Lecours and A. Smith (eds), *Biological Perspectives on Language* (MIT Press, Cambridge, Massachusetts, 1984)

Gazzaniga, M.S., *Mind Matters: How Mind and Brain Interact to Create our Conscious Lives* (Houghton Mifflin, Boston, 1988)

Gergen, K.J., 'Social psychology as history', *Journal of Personality and Social Psychology*, 26, 309–20 (1973)

Gibson, E.J. and Walk, P.D., 'The visual cliff', *Scientific American*, 202, 64–71 (1960)

Gibson, E.J., *Principles of Perceptual Learning and Development* (Appleton-Century-Crofts, New York, 1969)

Gibson, J.J., *The Senses Considered as Perceptual Systems* (Houghton Mifflin, Boston, 1966)

Gibson, J.J., *The Ecological Approach to Visual Perception* (Houghton Mifflin, Boston, 1979)

Gilligan, C., 'In a different voice: women's conceptions of self and morality', *Harvard Educational Review*, 47, 481–517 (1977)

Gilligan, C., *In a Different Voice: Psychological Theory and Women's Development* (Harvard University Press, Cambridge, 1982)

Gottesman, I.I., *Schizophrenia Genesis* (W.H. Freeman, New York, 1991)

Gould, S.J., *Ever Since Darwin: Reflections in Natural History* (Penguin, 1978)

Gray, J.A., 'On the morality of speciesism', *The Psychologist*, 4(5), 196–8 (1991)

Gray, J.A. and Wedderburn, A.A., 'Grouping strategies with simultaneous stimuli', *Quarterly Journal of Experimental Psychology*, 12, 180–4 (1960)

Gray, J.A. and Wedderburn, A.A. (1966)

Green, Simon, *Principles of Biopsychology* (Erlbaum, Sussex, 1994)

Gregory, R.L., 'Visual illusions', in B.M. Foss (ed.), *New Horizons in Psychology* (vol. 1) (Penguin, 1972)

Gregory, R.L., 'Perceptions as hypotheses', *Philosophical Transactions of the Royal Society of London Series B*, 290, 181–97 (1980)

Gregory, R.L. (ed.), *The Oxford Companion to the Mind* (Oxford University Press, 1987)

Grice, H.P., 'Logic and conversation', in P.J. Cole and J.L. Morgan (eds), *Studies in Syntax*, Vol. III (Seminar Press, New York, 1967)

Grier, J.B., Counter, S.A. and Shearer, W.M., 'Prenatal auditory imprinting in chickens', *Science*, 155, 1692–3 (1967)

Gross, R.D., *Psychology. The Science of Mind and Behaviour* (Hodder and Stoughton, 2nd edn 1992, 3rd edn 1996)

Gross, R. and McIlveen, R., *Abnormal Psychology* (Hodder and Stoughton, 1996)

Gunter, B. and McAleer, J.L., *Children and Television – The One-eyed Monster?* (Routledge, 1990)

Gurling, H.M. et al., 'Recent and future molecular genetic research into schizophrenia', *Schizophrenia Bulletin*, 15(3), 373–82 (1989)

Hampson, S.E., *The Construction of Personality: An Introduction* (Routledge, London, 2nd edn 1988)

Harcourt, A.H., 'Help, co-operation and trust in animals', in R.A. Hinde and J. Groebel (eds), *Co-operation and Pro-social Behaviour* (Cambridge University Press, 1991)

Harlow, H.F., 'Love in infant monkeys', *Scientific American*, 200(6), 64–74 (1959)

Hatfield, E. and Walster, G.W., *A New Look at Love* (Addison-Wesley, Reading, USA, 1981)

Havighurst, R.J., *Human Development and Education* (Longmans, New York, 1953)

Havighurst, R.J., 'Flexibility and the social roles of the retired', *American Journal of Sociology*, 59, 309–11 (1964)

Hayes, J.R. and Flower, L.S., 'Writing research and the writer', *American Psychologist*, 41, 1106–13 (1986)

Hayes, N., *Doing Qualitative Analysis in Psychology* (Psychology Press, 1997)

Heider, E., 'Universals in colour naming and memory', *Journal of Experimental Psychology*, 93, 10–20 (1972)

Heider, F., *The Psychology of Interpersonal Relations* (Wiley, New York, 1958)

Heider, F. and Simmel, M., 'An experimental study of apparent behaviour', *American Journal of Psychology*, 57, 243–59 (1944)

Held, R. and Hein, A., 'Movement-produced stimulation in the development of visually guided behaviour', *Journal of Comparative and Physiological Psychology*, 56, 872–6 (1963)

Herek, G.M. and Glunt, E.K., 'An epidemic of stigma: public reaction to AIDS', *American Psychologist*, 43, 886–91 (1988)

Hetherington, E.M., 'Children and divorce', in R.W. Henderson (ed.), *Parent-Child Interaction: Theory, Research and Prospects* (Academic Press, New York, 1981)

Hetherington, E.M., 'Coping with family transitions: winners, losers and survivors', *Child Development*, 60, 1–14 (1989)

Hetherington, E.M. et al., 'Effects of divorce on parents and children', in M.E. Lamb (ed.), *Non-Traditional Families* (Erlbaum, Hillsdale, New Jersey, 1982)

Hilgard, E.R., *Hypnotic Suggestibility* (Harcourt, Brace, Jovanovitch, New York, 1965)

Hobson, J.A. and McCarley, R.W., 'The brain as a dream state generator: an activation-synthesis hypothesis of the dream process', *American Journal of Psychiatry*, 134, 1335–48 (1977)

Hockett, C.F., 'Animal "language" and human language', *Human Biology*, 31, 32–9 (1959)

Hofling, C.K., Brotzman, E., Dalrymple, S., Graves, N. and Pierce, C.M., 'An experimental study into nurse-physician relationships', *Journal of Nervous and Mental Disease*, 143, 171–80 (1966)

Hogg, M.A. and Vaughan, G.M., *Social Psychology: An Introduction* (Prentice Hall, 1995)

Holmes, T.H. and Rahe, R.H., 'The social readjustment rating scale', *Journal of Psychosomatic Research*, 11, 213–8 (1967)

Hubel, D.H. and Wiesel, T.N., 'Brain mechanisms of vision', *Scientific American*, September, 45–53 (1979)

Hudson, L., *Contrary Imaginations* (Methuen, 1966)

Huesmann, L.R., Eron, L.D., Klein, R., Brice, P. and Fischer, P., 'Mitigating the imitation of aggressive behaviour by changing childhood attitudes about media violence', *Journal of Personality and Social Psychology*, 44, 899–910 (1983)

Huesmann, L.R., Eron, L.D. and Yarmel, P.W., 'Intellectual functioning and aggression', *Journal of Personality and Social Psychology*, 52(1), 232–40 (1987)

Hummert, M.L., 'Multiple stereotypes of elderly and young adults: a comparison of structure and evalu-ations', *Psychology and Ageing*, 5, 182–93 (1990)

Humphreys, G.W., 'On varying the span of visual attention: evidence for two modes of spatial attention', *Quarterly Journal of Experimental Psychology*, 33A, 1–15 (1981)

Hunt, M., *The Story of Psychology* (Doubleday, New York, 1997)

Hurlock, E., *Developmental Psychology* (McGraw-Hill, New York, 1959)

Insko, C.A., Thibaut, J.W., Moehle, D., Wilson, M., Diamond, W.D., Gilmore, R., Soloman, M.R. and Lipsitz, A., 'Social evolution and the emergence of leadership', *Journal of Personality and Social Psychology*, 39, 431–48 (1980)

Izard, C. (ed.), *Measuring Emotions in Infants and Children* (Cambridge University Press, New York, 1982)

Jackson, S., 'Great Britain', in M.E. Lamb (ed.) *The Father's Role: Cross-Cultural Perspectives* (Erlbaum, Hillsdale, 1987)

Jacobs, B.L., 'How hallucinogenic drugs work', *American Scientist*, 75, 386–92 (p. 186) (1987)

James, W., *Principles of Psychology* (Holt, New York, 1890 and 1892)

James, W., in G. Allport (ed.), *Psychology – The Briefer Course* (Harper Torchbooks, New York, 1892)

Jensen, A.R., 'How much can we boost IQ and scholastic achievement?' *Harvard Educational Review*, 39, 1–23 (1969) Johnston, W.A. and Dark, V.J., 'Selective attention', *Annual Review of Psychology*, 37, 43–75 (1986)

Jones, E., *The Life and Work of Sigmund Freud* (vol. 1 of 3) (Basic Books, New York, 1953)

Jones, E.E. and Davis, K.E., 'From acts to dispositions: the attribution process in person perception', in L. Berkovitz (ed.), *Advances in Experimental Social Psychology* (vol. 2) (Academic Press, New York, 1965)

Kahneman, D., *Attention and Effort* (Prentice Hall, Englewood Cliffs, New Jersey, 1973)

Kahneman, D. and Henik, A., 'Perceptual organization and attention', in M. Kubovy and J.R. Pomerants (eds) *Perceptual Organization* (Lawrence Erlbaum Associates, Hillsdale, New Jersey, 1979)

Kaplan, R.M., 'The controversies relating to the use of psychological tests', in B.B. Wolman (ed.) *Handbook of Intelligence: Theories, Measurements and Applications* (Wiley, New York, 1985)

Kaufer, D. et al., 'Composing written sentences', *Research in the Teaching of English*, 20, 121–40 (1986)

Kelley, H.H., *Attributional Theory in Social Psychology* (Nebraska Symposium on Motivation, 15, 1967)

Kelley, H.H., 'The process of causal attribution', *American Psychologist*, 28, 107–28 (1973)

Kellogg, R.T., 'Attention overload and writing performance: effects of rough draft and outline strategies', *Journal of Experimental Psychology: Learning, Memory and Cognition*, 14, 355–65 (1988)

Kellogg, R.T., 'Writing', in M.W. Eysenck (ed.), *The Blackwell Dictionary of Cognitive Psychology* (Blackwell, 1990)

Klineberg, O., 'Negro–white differences in intelligence test performances: a new look at an old problem', *American Psychologist*, 18, 198–203 (1963)

Kobasa, S.C., 'Stressful life events, personality and health: an enquiry into hardiness', *Journal of Personality and Social Psychology*, 37, 1–11 (1979)

Kohlberg, L., 'A cognitive-development analysis of children's sex-role concepts and attitudes', in E.E. Maccoby (ed.), *The Development of Sex Differences* (Stanford University Press, Stanford, California, 1966)

Köhler, W., *The Mentality of Apes* (Harcourt, Brace, Jovanovich, New York, 1925)

Koluchova, J., 'Severe deprivation in twins: a case study', *Journal of Child Psychology and Psychiatry*, 13, 107–14 (1972)

Krebs, J., in G. Ferry (ed.), *The Understanding of Animals* (Blackwell, 1976)

Krebs, J.R. and Davies, N.B., *An Introduction to Behavioural Ecology* (Blackwell Science Ltd, 3rd edn 1993)

LaBerge, D., 'Spatial extent of attention to letters and words', *Journal of Experimental Psychology: Human Perception and Performance*, 9, 371–9 (1983)

Labov, W., 'The logic of non-standard English', in F. Williams (ed.), *Language and Poverty* (Markham, Chicago, 1970)

Latané, B. and Darley, J.M., *The Unresponsive Bystander: Why Doesn't He Help?* (Appleton-Century-Crofts, New York, 1970)

Laupa, M. and Turiel, E., 'Children's concepts of authority and social context', *Journal of Educational Psychology*, 85, 191–7 (1993)

Lazarus, R.S., 'Theory-based stress measurement', *Psychological Inquiry*, 1, 3–13 (1990)

LeBon, G., *The Crowd: A Study of the Popular Mind* (Unwin, 1908)

Ledoux, J., 'Emotion, memory and the brain', *Scientific American*, p. 354 (June, 1994)

Leonard, B.E., 'Effects of pharmacological treatments on neurotransmitter receptors in anxiety disorders', in G.D. Burrows, S.M. Roth and R. Noyes, Jr. (eds), *Handbook of Anxiety* (vol. 5) (Elsevier, 1992)

Levinger, G., 'Toward the analysis of close relationships', *Journal of Experimental Social Psychology*, 16, 510–44 (1980)

Levinson, D.J., *The Seasons of a Man's Life* (Ballentine, New York, 1978)

Levy, J., 'Right brain, left brain: facts and fiction', *Psychology Today*, 19(5) (1985)

Lewinsohn, P.M. et al., 'Behavioural treatment of depression: a social learning approach', in J.F. Clarkin and H.I. Glazer (eds), *Depression: Behavioural and Directive Intervention Strategies* (Academic Press, 1981)

Lewinsohn, P.M. et al., 'Depression-related cognitions: antecedent or consequence?', *Journal of Abnormal Psychology*, 90(3), 213–9 (1981)

Lewis, M. and Brooks-Gunn, J., *Social Cognition and the Acquisition of Self* (Plenum, New York, 1979)

Lewis, M. et al., 'Self-development and self-conscious emotions', *Child Development*. 60, 146–56 (1989)

Lewis, M. and Sullivan, M.W. (eds), *Emotional Development in Atypical Children* (Lawrence Erlbaum Associates, New Jersey, 1996)

Lieberman, M.A., Yalom, I.D. and Miles, M.B., *Encounter Groups: First Facts* (Basic Books, New York, 1973)

Lima, S., Valone, T.J. and Caraco, T., 'Foraging efficiency – predation-risk trade-off in the grey squirrel', *American Behave*, 33, 155–65 (1985)

Lindemann, E., 'Symptomology and management of acute grief', *American Journal of Psychiatry*, 101, 141–8 (1944)

Lippitt, R. and White, R., 'The social climate of children's groups', in R.G. Barker, J. Koumin and H. Wright (eds), *Child Behaviour and Development* (McGraw-Hill, New York, 1943)

Lippman, W., *Public Opinions* (Harcourt and Brace, New York, 1922)

Lloyd, B.B. and Duveen, G., *Gender Identities and Education: The Impact of Starting School* (Harvester, 1992)

Lloyd, G.K., et al., 'GABA agonists as potential anxiolytics', in G.D. Burrows, S.M. Roth and R. Noyes, Jr. (eds), *Handbook of Anxiety* (vol. 5) (Elsevier, 1992)

Logan, G.D., 'Toward an instance theory of automisation', *Psychological Review*, 95, 492–527 (1988)

Lorenz, K.Z., *On Aggression* (Methuen, London, 1966)

Luchins, A.S., 'Primacy recency in impression formation', in C.H. Howland (ed.), *The Order of Presentation in Persuasion* (Yale University Press, New Haven, 1957)

Maccoby, E.E., *Social Development – Psychological Growth and the Parent-Child Relationship* (Harcourt, Brace, Jovanovich, New York, 1980)

Manstead, A.R. and McCulloch, C., 'Sex-role stereotyping in British television advertisements', *British Journal of Social Psychology*, 20, 171–80 (1981)

Marcia, J.E., 'Development and validation of ego identity status', *Journal of Personality and Social Psychology*, 3, 25–31 (1966)

Marcia, J.E., 'Identity in adolescence', in J. Adelson (ed.), *Handbook of Adolescent Psychology* (Wiley, New York, 1980)

Marr, D., *Vision* (W.H. Freeman, San Francisco, 1982)

Marslen-Wilson, W. and Tyler, L.K., 'The temporal structure of spoken language understanding', *Cognition*, 8, 1–71 (1980)

Martin, C.L. and Halverson, C.F. Jr., 'A schematic processing model of sex typing and stereotyping in children', *Child Development*, 52, 1119–34 (1981)

Martin, C.L. and Halverson, C.F. Jr., 'The roles of cognition in sex roles acquisition', in D.B. Carter (ed.), *Current Conceptions of Sex Roles and Sex Typing: Theory and Research*, 123–37 (Praeger, New York, 1987)

Maslow, A.H., *Motivation and Personality* (Harper and Row, New York, 1954)

Maynard-Smith, J., 'Group selection and kin selection', *Nature*, 201, 1145–7 (1964)

McClelland, J.L., 'Retrieving general and specific information from stored knowledge of specifics', *Proceedings of the Third Annual Meeting of the Cognitive Science Society*, 170–2 (1981)

McClelland, J.L. and Rumelhart, D.E., 'An inter-active activation model of context effects in letter perception: part I, an account of basic findings', *Psychological review*, 88, 375–407 (1981)

McClelland, J.L. and Rumelhart, D.E., *Parallel Distributed Processing* (vol. 2) (MIT Press, Cambridge, 1986)

McKay, K., *An Introduction to Psychology* (Macmillan, 1973)

McNamee, S. and Gergen, K.J. (eds), *Therapy as Social construction* (Sage, 1992)

Meichenbaum, D.H., *Cognitive Behaviour Modification* (General Learning, Morristown, New Jersey, 1974)

Merriam, S.B., 'The structures of simple reminiscence', *Gerontologist*, 29, 761–7 (1989)

Milgram, S., 'Some conditions of obedience and disobedience to authority', *Human Relations*, 18, 56–76 (1963)

Milgram, S., *Obedience to Authority* (Harper Row, New York, 1974)

Milner, D., *Success in Advertising and Promotion* (John Murray, 1995)

Mischel, W., 'Sex typing and socialisation', in B.H. Mussen (ed.), *Carmichael's Manual of Child Psychology*, vol. 2 (Wiley, New York, 1970)

Money, J. and Ehrhardt, A.A., *Man and Woman, Boy and Girl* (Johns Hopkins University Press, Baltimore, 1972)

Moody, R., *Life after Life* (Stackpole Books, Harrisburg, Pennsylvania, 1976)

Moray, N., 'Attention in dichotic listening: affective cues and the influence of instructions', *Quarterly Journal of Experimental Psychology*, 11, 56–60 (1959)

Mortimer and Van Doren, *How to Read a Book* (Simon and Schuster, New York, 1972)

Moscovici, S., in R.M. Farr and S. Moscovici (eds), *Social Representation* (Cambridge University Press, 1984)

Munroe, R.H. et al., 'Gender understanding and sex-role preferences in four cultures', *Developmental Psychology*, 20, 673–82 (1984)

Murray, H.A., *Explorations in Personality* (Oxford University Press, New York, 1938)

Murstein, B.I., *Theories of Attraction and Love* (Springer, New York, 1971)

Myers, D.G., *Exploring Psychology* (Worth Publishers Inc., Holland, Michigan, 3rd edn 1996)

Neisser, U., 'Visual search', *Scientific American*, 210, 94–102 (1964)

Neisser, U., *Cognitive Psychology* (Appleton-Century-Crofts, New York, 1967)

Neisser, U., *Cognition and Reality* (W.H. Freeman, San Francisco, 1976)

Nelson, K., 'Structure and strategy in learning to talk', *Monographs of the Society for Research in Child Development*, 38, 149 (1973)

Newcomb, T.M., Koenig, D.E., Flacks, R. and Warwick, D.P., *Persistence and Change: Bennington College and its Students After Twenty-Five Years* (Wiley, New York, 1967)

Newell, A. and Simon, H.A., *Human Problem Solving* (Prentice Hall, Englewood Cliffs, New Jersey, 1972)

Newman, B.M. and Newman, P.R., *Development Through Life. A Psychosocial Approach* (Brooks/Cole, California, 6th edn 1995)

Norman, D.A., 'Memory while shadowing', *Quarterly Journal of Experimental Psychology*, 21, 85–93 (1969)

Norman, D.A., *Memory and Attention* (Wiley, 2nd edn 1976)

Norman, D.A. and Shallice, T., *Attention to Action: Willed and Automatic Control of Behaviour* (CHIP Report 99) (University of California, San Diego, California, 1980)

Northedge, A., *The Good Study Guide* (The Open University, Milton Keynes, 1994)

Nsamenang, A.B., 'Human development in cultural context: a third world perspective', *Cross-Cultural Research and Methodology Series*, vol. 16 (Sage, Newbury Park, California, 1992)

O'Sullivan, M.J. et al., 'Ethnic populations: community mental health services ten years later', *American Journal of Community Psychology*, 17, 17–30 (1989)

Packer, C., 'Reciprocal altruism in *Papio anubis*', *Nature*, 265, 441–3 (1977)

Parkes, C.M., *Bereavement: Studies of Grief in Adult Life* (International Universities, Madison, Connecticut, 2nd edn 1987)

Pascal-Leone, J. 'Compounds, confounds and models in developmental information processing: a reply to Trabasso and Foellinger, *Journal of Experimental Child Psychology*, 26, 18–40 (1978)

Paton D., 'Disaster research: the Scottish dimension', *The Psychologist*, 5, 535–8 (1992)

Perrins, S. and Spencer, C., 'The Asch effect: a child of its time?', *Bulletin of the British Psychological Society*, 32, 405–6 (1980)

Piaget, J., *The Moral Judgement of a Child* (Routledge & Kegan Paul, 1932)

Piaget, J., *The Child's Conception of the World* (Littlefield, Adams, Totowa, New Jersey, 1967)

Piaget, J., *The Language and Thought of the Child*, translated by Gabain, M. (The New American Library, New York, 1974)

Pincus, H.A., Francis, A.J., Davis, W.W. and First, M.B., 'DSM-IV and new diagnostic categories: holding the line on proliferation', *American Journal of Psychiatry*, 149(1) 112–7 (1992)

Pratt, M.W. and Norris, J.E., *The Social Psychology of Ageing* (Blackwell, Oxford, 1994)

Pym software. Available from Haworth, G., 6 Frencham Close, Canterbury CT2 7DS

Reason, J.T., 'Actions not as planned', in G.D. Underwood and R. Stevens (eds), *Aspects of consciousness* (Academic Press, 1979)

Reber, A.S., *Dictionary of Psychology* (Penguin, 2nd edn 1995)

Reicher, G.M., 'Perceptual recognition as a function of meaningfulness of stimulus material', *Journal of Experimental Psychology*, 81, 274–80 (1969)

Reicher, S.D. and Potter, J., 'Psychological theory as intergroup perspective', *Human Relations*, 38, 167–80 (1985)

Ridley, M., *Animal Behaviour* (Blackwell, 2nd edn 1995)

Riley, M., *Animal Behaviour* (Blackwell Scientific Publications, Oxford, 1995)

Rokeach, M. (ed.), *The Open and Closed Mind* (Basic Books, New York, 1960)

Rosenhan, D.L., 'On being sane in insane places', *Science*, 179, 250–8 (1973)

Ross, L., 'The intuitive psychologist and his shortcomings', in L. Berkovitz (ed.), *Advances in Experimental Social Psychology* (vol. 10) (Academic Press, New York, 1977)

Rutter, M., *Maternal Deprivation Reassessed* (Penguin, 2nd edn 1981)

Sachs, O., *The Man Who Mistook His Wife for a Hat* (Picador, 1985)

Sandford, R.N., 'The effects of abstinence from food on imaginal processes', *Journal of Psychology*, 2, 129–36 (1936)

Schaffer, H.R., in H. Tajfel and C. Fraser (eds), *Introducing Social Psychology* (Penguin, 1978)

Scott, W.A. et al., 'Family relationships and children's personality: a cross-cultural, cross-source comparison', *British Journal of Social Psychology*, 30, 1–20 (1991)

Segall, M.H. et al., 'Cultural differences in the perception of geometric illusions', *Science*, 139, 769–71 (1963)

Seligman, M.E.P., *Helplessness* (W.H. Freeman and Co., San Francisco, 1975)

Shaffer, D.R., *Developmental Psychology – Childhood and Adolescence* (Brooks Cole Publishing Co., California, 3rd edn 1993)

Shaffer, L.H., 'Multiple attention in continuing verbal tasks', in P.M.A. Rabbit and S. Dormi (eds), *Attention and Performance* (vol. 5) (Academic Press, 1975)

Shallice, T. and Warrington, E.K., 'Independent functioning of verbal memory stores: a neuropsychological study', *Quarterly Journal of Experimental Psychology*, 22, 261–73 (1970)

Sherif, M., 'A study of some social factors in perception', *Archives of Psychology*, 27, 1–60 (1935)

Sherif, M., *Group Conflict and Co-operation* (Routledge & Kegan Paul, 1966)

Sherman, P.W., 'Nepotism and the evolution of alarm calls', *Science*, 197, 1246–53 (1977)

Sherman, P.W., 'Kinship demography and Belding's ground squirrel nepotism', *Behavioural Ecology and Sociobiology*, 8, 251–9 (1981)

Shiffrin, R.M. and Schneider, W., 'Controlled and automatic human information processing: 11 – perceptual learning, automatic attending and a general theory', *Psychological Review*, 84, 127–90 (1977)

Simmons, R.G., Burgeson, R., Carlton-Ford, S. and Blyth, D.A., 'The impact of cumulative changes in early adolescence', *Child Development*, 58, 1220–34 (1987)

Skinner, B.F., *Verbal Behaviour* (Appleton-Century-Crofts, New York, 1957)

Smith, D., 'Trends in counselling and psychotherapy', *American Psychology*, 37(7), 802–9 (1982)

Solley, and Haigh (1958), quoted in Hayes, N. and Orrell, S., *Psychology: An Introduction* (Longman, Harlow, 1987)

Spanos, N.P. and Coe, W.C., 'A social-psychological approach to hypnosis', in E. Fromm and M.R. Nash (eds), *Contemporary Hypnosis Research* (Guilford, New York, 1992)

Sprafkin, J.N., Liebert, R.M. and Poulos, R.W., 'Effects of pro-social televised example on children's helping', *Journal of Experimental Child Psychology*, 20, 119–26 (1975)

Stack, S., 'The impact of divorce on suicide

1959–1980', *Journal of Marriage and the Family*, 52, 119–28 (1990)

Sternberg, R.J., *The Triangle of Love* (Basic Books, New York, 1988)

Stratton, G.M., 'Some preliminary experiments on vision', *Psychological Review*, 3, 611–7 (1896)

Stroop, J.R., 'Interference in social verbal reactions', *Journal of Experimental Psychology*, 18, 643–61 (1935)

Szasz, T.S., *The Myth of Mental Illness* (Routledge & Kegan Paul, 1962)

Szasz, T.S., *The Manufacture of Madness* (Routledge & Kegan Paul, 1970)

Thibaut, J.W. and Kelley, H.H., *The Social Psychology of Groups* (Wiley, New York, 1959)

Toffler, A., *Future Shock* (Bantam Books, New York, 1970)

Tolman, E.C., *Purposive Behaviour in Animals and Man* (Appleton, New York, 1932)

Treisman, A.M., 'Verbal cues, language and meaning in selective attention', *American Journal of Psychology*, 77, 206–19 (1964)

Treisman, A.M. and Reiley, J.G.A., 'Is selective attention selective perception or selective response: a further test', *Journal of Experimental Psychology*, 79, 27–34 (1969)

Triandis, H.C., *Culture and Social Behaviour* (McGraw Hill, New York, 1994)

Trivers, R.L. 'Parent–offspring conflict', *American Zoology*, 14, 249–64 (1974)

Tryphon, A. and Vonèche, J. (eds), *Piaget–Vygotsky: The Social Genesis of Thought* (Psychology Press, Hove, 1996)

Tulving, E., 'Episodic and semantic memory', in E. Tulving and W. Donaldson (eds), *Organization of Memory* (Academic Press, 1972)

Turnbull, C.M., *The Forest People* (Simon and Schuster, New York, 1961)

Turner, J.C., *Social Influence* (Open University Press, 1991)

Turner, R.H., 'Collective behaviour', in R.E.L. Faris (ed.), *Handbook of Modern Sociology* (Rand-McNally, Chicago, 1974)

Von Senden, M., p. 149 in P. Heath (trans.), *Space and Sight: The Perception of Space and Shape in the Congenitally Blind Before and After Operation* (Free Press, Glencoe, Illinois, 1932, reprinted 1960)

Vyogtsky, L.S., *Thought and Language* (MIT Press, Cambridge, Massachusetts (1962) originally published, 1934)

Walster, E., Aronson, V., Abrahams, D. and Rottman, L., 'Importance of physical attractiveness in dating behaviour', *Journal of Personality and Social Psychology*, 4, 508–16 (1966)

Walster, E., Walster, G.W. and Berscheid, E., *Equity: Theory and Research* (Allyn and Bacon, Boston, 1978)

Ward, C., 'Culture and altered states of consciousness', in W.J. Lonner and R. Malpas (eds), *Psychology and Culture* (Allyn and Bacon, Boston, 1994)

Wernicke, C., *Der Aphasischer Symptomen Komplex; Eine Psychologische Studie auf Anatomischer Basis* (Breslau, 1874)

Weiner, B., *Achievement, Motivation and Attribution Theory* (General Learning Press, Morristown, New Jersey, 1974)

Weiner, B., *An Attributional Theory of Motivation and Emotion* (Springer, New York, 1986)

Weiten, W., *Psychology – Themes and Variations* (Wadsworth, California, 1994)

The Wellcome Trust, 'Psychology Activity Pack'. Available from 210 Euston Road, London NW1 2BE.

Wertheimer, M., 'Investigations of the doctrine of Gestalt', (1923), reprinted in English in W. Ellis (1955)

Wheeler, L.R., 'The intelligence of East Tennessee children', *Journal of Educational Psychology*, 23, 351–70 (1932)

Wheeler, L.R., 'A comparative study of the intelligence of East Tennessee mountain children', *Journal of Educational Psychology*, 33, 321–34 (1942)

Whiting, B.B. and Edwards, C.P., *Children of Different Worlds* (Harvard University Press, Cambridge, Massachusetts, 1988)

Whorf, B.L., 'Science and Linguistics', in J.B. Carroll (ed.), *Language, Thought and Reality: Selected Writings of Benjamin Lee Wharf* (p. 272) (MIT Press, Cambridge, Massachusetts, 1956)

Williams, T.M., *The Impact of Television: A Natural Experiment in Three Communities* (Academic Press, Orlando, Florida, 1986)

Wilson, E.O., *Socio-Biology: A New Synthesis* (Harvard University Press, Cambridge, Massachusetts, 1975)

Yalom, I.D., *The Theory and Practice of Psychotherapy* (Basic Books, 1970)

Zajonc, R.B., 'Attitudinal effects of mere exposure', *Journal of Personality and Social Science*, 9, 1–27 (1968)

Zajonc, R.B., 'On the primacy of effect', *American Psychologist*, 39, 117–23 (1984)

Zillman, D., *Hostility and Aggression* (Lawrence Erlbaum Associates, Hillsdale, New Jersey, 1979)

Zimbardo, P.G., Banks, W.C., Craig, H. and Jaffe, D., 'A pirandellian prison: the mind is a formidable jailer', *New York Times Magazine*, 8 April, 38–60 (1973)

Zimbardo, P.G. and Weber, A.L., *Psychology* (Collins, New York, 1994)

Zimiles, H. and Lee, V.E., 'Adolescent family structure and educational progress', in *Developmental Psychology*, 27, 314–20 (1991)

Index